THE POWERS
OF GOVERNMENT

Volume I

Bernard Schwartz

A Commentary on
THE CONSTITUTION
of
THE UNITED STATES

PART I

THE POWERS
OF GOVERNMENT

THE MACMILLAN COMPANY, NEW YORK
MACMILLAN NEW YORK, LONDON

Second Printing 1963

The Macmillan Company, New York
Collier-Macmillan Canada, Ltd., Galt, Ontario
Division of the Crowell-Collier Publishing Company

Printed in the United States of America

Library of Congress catalog card number: 62-19994

DESIGNED BY CHRISTIAN OHSER

VOLUME I

Federal and State
Powers

FOR
AILEEN
AND
BRIAN

PREFACE

"In the body of our Constitution," stated Chief Justice Warren near the beginning of his 1962 James Madison Lecture, "the Founding Fathers insured that the Government would have the power necessary to govern." Such is, in fact, the conclusion which dominates these two volumes on the Constitution: that of government endowed with all the necessary authority to enable it to fulfill the high purposes set forth in the Preamble. That is what has made it feasible for a basic document, drawn up in an age of knee breeches and lace, to serve the needs of an entirely different day—one whose complexities and problems the Framers could, at best, but dimly foresee. Of course, this has not been possible without important changes of constitutional doctrine. Yet these have, in the main, been responses to the fact that the American society has been in process of drastic transformation since the founding of the Republic. In this sense, it is not so much the organic concepts that have been altered as the community which they have served. The unfolding of the Constitution has mirrored the unfolding of the society itself.

These two volumes themselves are the first part of a comprehensive commentary on the Constitution. They deal with the powers of government. The second part will cover the rights of the individual. Macaulay, in a celebrated passage, derided our organic instrument as "all sail and no anchor." This work, as is made plain at the very beginning, rejects such notion. While this first part treats in detail of the sails (the authority that enables the polity to function), the portion still to be published will discuss the anchor (the guarantees of the individual which serve as basic limitations upon governmental power).

ix

These volumes have been written upon the assumption that the working of the Constitution is more than the private preserve of the legal profession. As such, they have sought to deal with all of the important areas appropriate to a constitutional commentary—while at the same time seeking to avoid the arid pedantry all too often characteristic of a legal treatise. It is, to be sure, true that much of the discussion concerns subjects that can hardly be presented with all the fluency of popular fiction. Yet even such matters need not be obscured in the technical vacuum of legal language. Even they can be presented in readable fashion and in a manner that makes clear their significance to those interested in the operation of what Gladstone once termed "the most wonderful work ever struck off at a given time by the brain and purpose of man." That, at any rate, is the faith upon which these volumes are based.

It would be an act of uncommon ingratitude for the author not to acknowledge his debt to those who have made this work possible. Chief thanks must be paid to Dean Russell D. Niles for his constant encouragement and interest, and his faith in what may at times have seemed an unduly gargantuan project, as well as to my colleagues on the New York University Law Faculty for providing the intellectual environment which stimulates the creation of volumes like these. I also wish to acknowledge the aid received from the Macmillan Company in producing these volumes, especially from A. L. Hart, Jr., Virginia Hyne, and Ruth Murdock.

And, finally, words alone can never adequately express my debt to the dear ones to whom this commentary is dedicated.

BERNARD SCHWARTZ

OCTOBER, 1962

CONTENTS

CHAPTER 7

COMMERCE AND THE STATES   238

CHAPTER 8

JUDICIAL POWER   321

Footnotes, Table of Cases, and Index appear at the end of Volume II.

VOLUME I

Federal and State Powers

I

INTRODUCTION

1
CONSTITUTION "Wᴴᴀᴛ is a constitution?" asked a member of the United States Supreme Court in 1795. "It is the form of government, delineated by the mighty hand of the people, in which certain principles of fundamental laws are established." [1] In this sense, the term *constitution* means the basic law of a country, which contains the guiding principles according to which that country is governed.

A definition so broad would encompass all forms of government, for, even in the most despotic system, certain leading principles prevail—even if they be only those according to which the governors may do and order what they please. Under such an approach, every country may be said to possess a constitution. No doubt the educated Turk of a century ago might thus allude to the constitution of the Sublime Porte, and the same is presumably true of his counterpart in any contemporary totalitarian country.[2]

In the American system, the word "constitution" is used in a much more restricted sense. "A constitution, in the American sense of the word," Justice Miller informs us, "is a written instrument by which the fundamental powers of the government are established, limited, and defined, and by which these powers are distributed among several departments, for their more safe and useful exercise, for the benefit of the body politic." [3]

In this definition, a constitution is seen as an organic instrument, under which governmental powers are both conferred and circumscribed. Such stress upon both grant and limitation of authority is fundamental in Amer-

1

ican theory. "The office and purpose of the constitution is to shape and fix the limits of governmental activity." [4] Plainly, the American Constitution is not, despite Macaulay's famous assertion, meant to be "all sail and no anchor." On the contrary, if there be one thing that stands out in the American concept of constitutionalism, it is the emphasis in it upon restrictions on governmental power. "By an inspection and examination of all the constitutions of our own country, they will be found to be nothing more than so many restrictions and limitations upon the departments of the government and people." [5] In the United States, in the phrase of one court, the primary purpose of a constitution is to place limitations upon government.[6]

But the American Constitution is more than mere brake. Our very system rests upon it as the continuously operating charter of government. Whatever may be one's view with regard to the theoretical bases of sovereign power as between the people and the states in 1787, there is little doubt today that, from a legal point of view, all power flows from the organic document. The Constitution is, in other words, the basic source from which government in the United States must derive its authority. "It is . . . to the departments of government, what a law is to individuals— nay, it is not only a rule of action to the branches of government, but it is that from which their existence flows, and by which the powers (or portions of the right to govern,) which may have been committed to them, are prescribed— It is their commission—nay, it is their creator." [7]

2

CONSTITUTIONAL LAW

The framers of the French Napoleonic Code, it is said, were dominated by the desire to present the law in a complete form, readily accessible to all. Like Jeremy Bentham, they sought to be able to say: "Citizen, what is your condition? Are you a farmer? Then consult the chapter on Agriculture."

The same was clearly not the case with the men who drew up the Federal Constitution. With Lincoln in his First Inaugural Address, they saw that "No organic law can ever be framed with a provision specifically applicable to every question which may occur." No foresight, the Framers knew, can anticipate, nor basic document contain, express provisions for all possible contingencies. "The constitution," says Justice Story, "deals in general language. It did not suit the purposes of the people, in framing this great charter of our liberties, to provide for minute specifications of its powers, or to declare the means by which those powers should be carried into execution." [8]

The Constitution partakes not at all of the prolixity of a political code; [9] from its nature, it deals in generals, not details.[10] Solely its great outlines are marked, its important objects designated; the minute particulars left to be deduced.[11] The organic instrument states, not rules for the passing hour, but principles for an ever-expanding future.[12]

That the Federal Constitution lays down only the framework of the governmental system is obvious if one considers the brevity of the organic document, with its six thousand words more or less.[13] Compared with the succinctness of this basic text, the volume of constitutional-law materials is immense. The Supreme Court has decided well over four thousand cases involving questions of constitutional interpretation, with the result that more than fifty thousand pages of the *United States Supreme Court Reports* are devoted to constitutional-law topics. The suggestion that the Constitution contains in embryo the entirety of this mass of materials confronts the will to believe with a well-nigh impossible test.[14]

The generality of the Constitution means that *constitutional law* is much more than the literal law laid down in the basic document. It is erroneous to assume that the resolution of any constitutional issue involves merely correct application of the canons of legal construction. Even the highest Court, let it be noted, has not avoided this mistake. "When an act of Congress is appropriately challenged in the courts," asserts a 1936 opinion, "as not conforming to the constitutional mandate the judicial branch of the Government has only one duty,—to lay the article of the constitution which is invoked beside the statute which is challenged and to decide whether the latter squares with the former." [15]

Such a picture of constitutional law as only a mechanical process, akin to the construction of a contract or a will, is a distortion of reality. The most important cases in American constitutional law have stemmed from a mere handful of skeleton clauses in the organic instrument. Chief among these have been the grant of Congressional power "To regulate Commerce . . . among the several States" and the prohibition against deprivation "of life, liberty, or property, without due process of law." Such phrases, as Justice Frankfurter has pointed out, "do not carry contemporaneous fixity. By their very nature they imply a process of unfolding content." [16] In clothing these wholesale clauses with meaning, the Supreme Court has been left almost completely at large. Furnished with no guide, beyond the very general language of the text, the high bench has been able to give meaning to such phrases in accordance with its own policy considerations in specific cases—not even, alas, entirely subject to the normal necessity of keeping the corpus of the law internally consistent.

With a basic document such as ours, drawn in so many particulars with purposed vagueness,[17] constitutional law must be more than machinelike exegesis of a fundamental text. It is true that, however the highest Court may interpret the Constitution, it is still the Constitution which is the Law —not the decisions of the Court.[18] In Justice Frankfurter's words: "the

ultimate touchstone of constitutionality is the Constitution itself and not
what we have said about it." [19] Yet, in most cases of consequence, the constitutional language is not so precise as to make its application automatic.
On the contrary, as Chief Justice Hughes once so candidly remarked: "We
are under a Constitution, but the Constitution is what the judges say it is."
The Federal Constitution is not a self-executing document. The *ought* laid
down in 1787 must run the gantlet of judicial interpretation before it attains
the practical status of an *is*. This is, perhaps, true of all legislation; but it is
especially true of a constitution like ours which, by its very nature, is much
less specific and detailed than an ordinary law. Such a constitution must, in
practice, be what the judges say it is.

Looking at the American system from this point of view, it becomes apparent that, with us, *constitutional law* is largely what the judges have said
the Constitution is. It includes all the rules which affect the distribution or
the exercise of governmental authority which have been laid down in decisions interpreting the organic instrument. Of course, the starting point in
all of these cases must be the constitutional text itself. But, as already emphasized, the text constitutes only a minute portion of the law in this field.
The main source of American constitutional law is the case-law—especially
the jurisprudence of the United States Supreme Court.

A commentary upon the Constitution must thus concentrate almost entirely upon court decisions. Its author must arrange them in their order,
explain their meaning, and exhibit their logical connection.[20] His task is, in
the main, similar to that faced by a commentator on any other branch of
the law. He is called upon to deal partly with written law, but mostly with
judge-made law. His position in this respect differs from that of Story and
Kent—the great early commentators on the Constitution. Writing at the
very beginning of American constitutional development, their work involved primarily the explanation of a definite legal document. They could
seek to ascertain the meaning of the Constitution in much the same way as
a lawyer might try to elicit the meaning of any other newly adopted enactment. Today, such an approach alone would be of little value. A commentary on the Constitution based solely upon the text would be comparable in worth to a treatise on the law of real property which relied only upon
the language of the Statute of Westminster II.[21]

3

CONFEDERATION   At its very outset, the Constitution affirms that its
                 primary purpose is "to form a more perfect Union."
To grasp the intent of the Framers in this respect, it is necessary to have an
understanding of the preconstitutional Confederation which they sought to
transform.

"The blessings of society," wrote John Adams in 1776, "depend entirely on the constitutions of government." [22] That being the case, it was only natural that the men of the Revolution should turn to constitution-making, when once the conflict with Britain had reached the stage where independence was the only real alternative to submission. Full separation from the mother country made necessary a new organic structure in the Colonies, thenceforth to be absolved from allegiance to the British Crown. The need was met by the adoption, during the Revolution, of constitutions by the different states, as well as the drafting of an organic instrument for the Union—the Articles of Confederation, which went into effect in 1781.

It has been well said that "Coalitions find it possible to agree, as a rule, only on what *not* to do. This is the reason why their tendency is so often to do nothing at all." [23] The united Colonies could act effectively to end the connection with the mother country, for they could decide unanimously that they did not want to be governed by Britain. When it came to deciding upon the details of a more permanent Union, at the same time, there was not the same accord. On the contrary, the drafting of an organic document brought to the fore the interstate and intersectional differences, which even the needs of war for independence had not fully suppressed. That being the case, it is scarcely surprising that the Articles of Confederation themselves provided for anything but a truly powerful Union, endowed with all the authority needed to render it effective as a nation.

The polity provided for by the Articles was strikingly different from that set up in the Revolutionary state constitutions. They were based upon a strict separation of powers, providing as they did for three fully developed departments. The Articles, on the other hand, concentrated all the governmental authority provided for under it in a unicameral legislative body. Before the Constitution, "Congress was the general, supreme, and controlling council of the nation, the centre of union, the centre of force, and the sun of the political system." [24]

The concentration of all the authority of the Union in the Congress was, however, more than offset by the absence of the requisites of effective national power. The government established in 1781 suffered from two fundamental defects. The first stemmed from the fact that the authority of the nation did not rest on the people, but upon the states. The Congress was composed of delegates chosen and paid by the state legislatures and each state had one vote. The Articles themselves stated that they established a "league of friendship between the states." [25]

The second defect flowed naturally from the first. It was the lack of effective coercive authority in the Union. Since the authority of the Confederation Congress did not extend to individual citizens of the different states, its measures could become operative only through implementation by the states themselves. But there was no compulsive power to compel the states to give effect to Congressional decrees; Congress had no authority to exact obedience, or punish disobedience, to its ordinances. This, said Hamilton in *The Federalist,* was the "great and radical vice, in the construction of the confederation, . . . the principle of LEGISLATION for STATES or GOVERNMENTS, in their CORPORATE or COLLECTIVE CAPACITIES, and as contradistinguished from the INDIVIDUALS of whom they consist." [26]

The result was that, though in theory the acts of the Confederation Congress were laws, in practice they were mere recommendations to the states. Hence, the concurrence of all of the thirteen states was really needed for the effective execution of every Congressional measure of importance.[27] Such a system, strikingly declared John Marshall, "could only be rescued from ignominy and contempt by finding [the states] administered by men exempt from the passions incident to human nature." [28]

The weaknesses of the Articles of Confederation can be explained by the experience of the colonists in their struggle against Parliamentary authority. It rendered them unready to concede to Congress powers which they had strongly refused to Parliament. The pre-Revolutionary experience had instilled in them the belief that governmental powers should be exercised only by their own local assemblies. It is hardly to be wondered at, that so soon after the rupture with Britain, they were not fully ready to concede to the nation what they had denied, at such cost, to the mother country.

Yet, if the Articles of Confederation did less than set up that more perfect Union which Americans were soon to find necessary, their positive part in the constitutional evolution of the United States should not be overlooked. Until the Articles went into effect, the Declaration of Independence was the only written instrument binding the nation together. And if the first central government was not as effective as some would have liked, its mere creation was the vital first step in the molding of the Union.

The Articles of Confederation, with all their weaknesses, did give a legal basis to the *de facto* national government which had existed under the Continental Congress. Their provision for a "perpetual Union," [29] and the operation, however inadequate, of a government of such Union, accustomed Americans to think of themselves as one nation. Deficient though they were, the Articles, in Marshall's characterization, "preserved the idea of union until the good sense of the nation adopted a more efficient system." [30] When the Union proved defective, the question was not, how to do away with it, but how to make it more perfect.

4

MAKING OF
CONSTITUTION

Though recent research has provided a corrective to the extreme attitude of denigration commonly expressed by historians toward the Articles of Confederation,[31] it can scarcely be gainsaid that the polity established by that instrument was inadequate for the needs of the new nation. The Articles provided for a government without power to tax, to raise troops, to regulate commerce, or to execute or enforce its own laws and treaties—a government in which each of the states had power to tax, to make its own money, to impose its own import and export duties, and to conform or not, as it chose, to the measures enacted by the nation, or its requisitions for money or troops.[32] Well might Washington declare, in 1785, that "the confederation appears to me to be little more than a shadow without the substance; and congress a nugatory body, their ordinances being little attended to." [33]

Of particular significance in this respect was the lack under the Articles of Confederation of effective power to regulate commerce. "When victory relieved the Colonies from the pressure for solidarity that war had exerted," we are informed by the Supreme Court, "a drift toward anarchy and commercial warfare between states began." [34] Such a situation naturally gave rise to dissension. Grievances were multiplied in every direction; animosities between states were fostered to so high a degree as to threaten the Union itself.[35] "Agriculture, manufactures and commerce were at their lowest ebb. There was infinite danger to all the States from local interests and jealousies, and from the apparent impossibility of a much longer adherence to that shadow of a government, the Continental Congress." [36]

Even while the Framers sat in 1787, New Jersey passed a law taxing the lighthouse at Sandy Hook, owned by New York but situated on New Jersey land—in retaliation for New York's imposition of entrance and clearance fees for ships bound from or to New Jersey and Connecticut.[37] Similar state laws imposing duties and commercial burdens on other states were widespread. "The oppressed and degraded state of commerce previous to the adoption of the Constitution," affirmed Chief Justice Marshall, "can scarcely be forgotten." [38]

It has become fashionable of late to criticize Charles A. Beard's economic interpretation of the work of the Framers.[39] At the same time, it is surely beyond question that the immediate cause of the Constitution was an economic one. "It may be doubted," Marshall tells us, "whether any of the evils proceeding from the feebleness of the Federal Government contributed more to that great revolution which introduced the present system, than the deep and general conviction that commerce ought to be regulated by Congress." [40] It was to secure freedom of commerce—to break down

the structure of interstate barriers being erected—that the drive which led
to the Convention of 1787 was initiated. The sole purpose for which Virginia inaugurated the movement which ultimately produced the Constitution was "to take into consideration the trade of the United States; to examine the relative situations and trade of the said states; to consider how
far a uniform system in their commercial regulation may be necessary to
their common interest and their permanent harmony," and for that purpose
the Virginia legislature in January, 1786, named commissioners and proposed their meeting with those from other states.[41] The need to federalize
the regulation of commerce may thus be taken as the proximate cause of
our present constitutional existence.[42]

The resolution of the Virginia legislators and the Annapolis Convention
convened pursuant thereto led directly to the calling of the Philadelphia
Convention of 1787, which the Confederation Congress itself resolved
should be appointed "for the sole purpose of revising the Articles of Confederation" and of reporting such alterations as would "render the Federal
Constitution adequate to the exigencies of Government, and the preservation of the Union." [43] The men who met in accordance with such resolve
went far beyond mere amendment of the Articles and produced an entirely
new charter of government and one which was to be ratified, not by Congress, but by the people themselves, in state conventions assembled for the
purpose.

Until recently the attitude of Americans toward the Framers recalled
with singular fidelity that with which, according to Burke, the Englishman
of a century and a half ago should have looked upon the institutions of his
country: "We ought to understand it according to our measure; and to ven-
erate where we are not able to understand." [44] Yet, if to our grandfathers
and our fathers the work of the Founding Fathers was a sacred specimen
of American statesmanship, in our own day the pendulum has swung somewhat the other way. Now we are told that the Constitution was less a
product of farseeing sagacity than a biased attempt by the Framers to safeguard their own economic interests.

Of course, the organic document of 1787 reflects the economic as well
as the political difficulties that confronted the new nation. "Most of our
political evils," wrote Madison in 1786, "may be traced to our commercial
ones." [45] It was not unwonted for men of such opinion to attempt to remedy
such commercial evils in the instrument which they drafted. Yet the fact
that the Constitution has an economic, as well as a political, basis hardly
detracts from the remarkable nature of the Framers' achievement.

Such achievement would scarcely have been possible had not the Philadelphia Convention been composed of as notable an assembly as ever sat
for legislative purposes—"an assembly of demi-gods," Jefferson well termed

them.[46] The fifty-five men who came to Independence Hall had a background of ability and public service which admirably fitted them for the task they were undertaking. Thirty-nine of them had served in the Congress under the Articles; eight had been signers of the Declaration of Independence; eight had helped to draft their state constitutions; seven had served as chief executives of their states.[47] Nor were these men whose productive years were all behind them. Though, as Franklin wrote, this was *"une assemblée des notables,* a convention composed of some of the principal people from the several States," [48] more than half of them were also to become leaders in the new nation which they established: two became Presidents; one, Vice-President; two, Chief Justices; three, Justices of the Supreme Court; and six, state governors. Eighteen were elected to the first Congress under the Constitution.[49]

Of special significance was the fact that nearly two-thirds of the Framers were members of the legal profession, of whom ten had been state judges. Such training and experience in the law was essential if the document which they drafted was to prove to be a practical charter of government, rather than a mere product of academic speculation. Voltaire, in a famous exclamation, demanded the total destruction of all existing law: "Do you want good laws? Burn yours and make new ones!" [50] Men who were themselves practitioners of the law realized better. From their own training, they knew that law was reason codified by experience. An attempt to write the fundamental law of a people on a *tabula rasa* may turn out favorably in Greek myth. In real life, the successful constitution-maker must work upon an existing political and historical mold. "Experience must be our only guide," affirmed one of the Framers. "Reason may mislead us." [51]

Their legal realism enabled the Founders to avoid the cardinal error that is so common in the draftsmen of fundamental laws. The men who write constitutions, all too often, seek to provide expressly for all foreseeable contingencies. The same was happily not the case with the Framers of the Federal Constitution. That document, as we saw in section 2, lays down only the framework of the governmental structure created by it. Only thus, the highest Court has said, "could such instrument be expected to endure through a long lapse of ages, the events of which were locked up in the inscrutable purposes of Providence." [52]

Thomas Hardy, in describing the character of one of the women in his novels, once stated that, "Like the British Constitution, she owes her success in practice to her inconsistencies in principle." There are those who would make the same assertion about the American Constitution. It is true that the Philadelphia Convention could operate effectively because the Framers were able to reconcile the important differences that existed between them. Time and again, opposing viewpoints were harmonized, or recourse had to language that left open the issue. In this sense, the document drafted in 1787 was a bundle of compromises.[53]

At the same time, if we survey the overall result of its work, we must conclude that the Philadelphia Convention was dominated not so much by the spirit of compromise as by that of audacious achievement. Concessions there were, to be sure, to reconcile differences among the Framers. But these were, in the main, on subsidiary matters. In essence, there was only one compromise—the Great or Sherman Compromise which settled the question of representation as between the large and small states.[54] Without it, there might, as a practical matter, well have been no Constitution at all.

The agreement that the states should be represented equally in the upper house, while proportional representation according to population should be the rule in the lower, may have been necessary if all the states, regardless of size, were to be able to adhere to the new Union. From the point of view of the modern constitutional historian, however, the question of legislative representation seems of minor importance.[55] The problem it was designed to meet—that of conflict between the large and small states— has never since been a pressing one in American history.

On all the important constitutional issues before them, the Framers spoke and thought with remarkable unanimity.[56] This was true, first of all, with regard to the crucial decision at the outset of whether there was to be a new constitution at all. The letter of their mandate limited the men of 1787 to revision of the Articles of Confederation. But, with a boldness that was to prove characteristic of all their important decisions, they determined, soon after they began their meetings, to go far beyond mere alteration of the existing organic document. Randolph's resolutions, unanimously adopted as the basis for the initial work of the Convention, wholly ignored the Articles and provided instead for an entirely new charter of government. With the adoption of the Virginia Plan as the foundation for the Framers' work, the die was definitively cast in favor of a new constitution. When, half a month later, the New Jersey Plan was presented, its return to mere revision of the Articles was overwhelmingly rejected. During the two weeks' discussions, the Framers had become accustomed to what might well have appeared to them at the outset as somewhat radical ideas.[57]

5

ORGANIC   The Philadelphia Convention resolved upon an en-
FRAMEWORK   tirely new organic instrument because its members
                 were acutely aware of the essential flaws in the exist-
ing Articles. The Confederation, they knew, could not provide the effective government that the new nation needed. That being the case, it is scarcely surprising that, once they had determined to make a new constitution, the

Framers then devoted their major efforts at correcting the deficiencies of the Articles of Confederation. If one compares the instrument which they wrote with the Articles, he finds that they were amazingly successful in such endeavor.

At almost the very beginning of their deliberations, the Framers resolved to eliminate what have already been termed [58] the two fundamental defects of the government established under the Confederation. Meeting in Committee of the Whole to consider Randolph's resolutions, the Convention committed itself on May 30 to the basic proposition: "that a *national* Government ought to be established consisting of a *supreme* Legislative, Executive and Judiciary." [59] With this step the Framers went to the root of the whole matter before the Convention. Under the Articles, Madison was later to explain, while the central government "operated within the extent of its authority through requisitions on the Confederated States, and rested on the sanction of State Legislatures, the Government to take its place was to operate within the extent of its powers directly and coercively on individuals, and to receive the higher sanction of the people of the States." [60]

The Confederation, we saw in section 3, rested the authority of the nation upon the states, not on the people. And there was no coercive authority provided for its decrees: Congress could only supplicate; it could not enforce.[61] The Constitution rests directly on the people, as its Preamble and mode of ratification specifically indicate. And, more important, the measures of the Federal Government are vested with compulsive effect. They operate directly on individuals and do not require state implementation before they can be rendered effective. The government of the nation was to be one which would "directly operate on individuals" and possess compulsive power over the people of the nation.[62]

The device adopted by the Framers to attain such result was as simple as it was effective. The key constitutional provision in this respect is the Supremacy Clause of Article VI. Under it, not only the Constitution, but all federal laws and treaties are expressly declared to be "the supreme Law of the Land." Nor is the principle of federal supremacy thus enunciated only a hortatory one. On the contrary, under the Supremacy Clause, "the Judges in every State shall be bound" by federal laws and treaties, "any Thing in the Constitution or Laws of any State to the Contrary notwithstanding."

The acts of the Federal Government, in other words, are to be operative as supreme law throughout the Union. They possess such status because they are self-executing, since they prescribe rules that, standing alone, are enforceable in all the courts of the land. This enables the mandates of Washington to prevail without any need for state implementation. The states have no power to impede, burden, or in any manner control the operation of the laws enacted by the government of the nation. This is the basic consequence of the supremacy which the Constitution has declared.[63]

Through the Supremacy Clause, the Framers prevented the Federal Government from becoming subordinate to the states in the manner that had destroyed the effectiveness of the original Confederation. In addition, they provided that the government of the nation was to be a fully developed structure, with separate legislative, executive, and judicial branches. That they would so provide was clear from almost the beginning of their deliberations, for Randolph's resolution, already quoted, contemplated a National Government divided into three distinct departments. "The moment, indeed," wrote Madison in 1835, "a real Constitution was looked for as a substitute for the Confederacy, the distribution of the Government into the usual departments became a matter of course with all who speculated on the prospective changes." [64]

What the Framers provided for, in establishing a tripartite Central Government, whose decrees are directly operative as law on the people of the nation, was the existence throughout the United States of two centers of government, each with its own complete apparatus of lawmaking and law enforcement. Two governments, provided with the complete accoutrements of political power, coexist and issue their mandates, binding directly their respective citizens. Neither is dependent upon the other for the execution of its ordinances. Instead, in Bryce's phrase, there are two governments covering the same ground, yet distinct and separate in their action.[65]

Americans have by now become so accustomed to the federal system established by the Constitution that they tend to forget that its creation in 1787 was a political invention of the highest order. The United States, to be sure, was not the first example of a federated body politic. In prior federations, however, as under the Articles of 1781, the member states had generally agreed to obey the mandates of a common government for certain stipulated purposes, but had retained to themselves the right of ordaining and enforcing the laws of the confederation. The form of federation offered by the Framers was new in history. "I know not," said a member of New York's ratifying convention, "that history furnishes an example of a confederated republic coercing the states composing it by the mild influence of laws operating on the individuals of those states. This, therefore, I suppose to be a new experiment in politics." [66] Well could de Tocqueville assert that the federal frame established at Philadelphia should "be considered a great discovery in modern political science." [67]

To make the federal system work, it was essential that the Central Government be more than a mere paper polity. The nation had to be endowed with the authority needed to make it effective. More specifically, it had to be given the vital substantive powers whose lack had rendered the Confederation sterile. What those powers are was stated in classic language by Chief Justice Marshall: "the great powers to lay and collect taxes; to borrow money; to regulate commerce; to declare and conduct a war; and to raise and support armies and navies. The sword and the purse, all the external relations, and no inconsiderable portion of the industry of the nation." [68] These are precisely the powers vested in the Federal Government by the Constitution, which have enabled it to fulfill the great purposes intended by the Framers.

In this respect, of particular significance is the express grant of the power to tax and the power to regulate commerce. The former freed the nation completely from the financial dependence on the states which had, in the phrase of a 1786 Congressional committee, hazarded the very existence of the Union.[69] The latter enabled the Federal Government to put an end to the economic autarchy of the states. More than that, the Commerce Clause has promoted a system of free trade throughout the Union. "Our system," the Supreme Court has declared, "is that every farmer and every craftsman shall be encouraged to produce by the certainty that he will have free access to every market in the Nation. . . . Such was the vision of the Founders." [70] Upon such vision has been based the commercial success of the nation. "With all doubts," as Justice Frankfurter has said, "as to what history teaches, few seem clearer than the beneficial consequences which have flowed from this conception of the Commerce Clause." [71]

It has already been mentioned that the Framers were virtually unanimous in their decision to base the organic framework which they were creating upon the separation of powers. The administrative ineptitude of the Congress, in whom all the powers granted by the Confederation were vested, made the division of the new government into three autonomous departments, each endowed with the powers appropriate to it, a practical, as well as a philosophical, necessity.

By setting up the Federal Government with distinct executive and judicial branches, completely separate from the legislative department, the Founders were able to ensure that each of the three great powers essential to a true National Government would be effectively exercised. This was particularly true with regard to the establishment of an independent executive department. The composition of such department posed a very real dilemma. On the one hand, there was the pressing need for an executive strong enough to penetrate to the remotest reaches of the Union. At the same time, there was the danger of stirring up the prevalent popular fear of monarchy. Those hostile to the Union they were creating, the men of 1787 well knew, would be all too ready to picture the new executive with a diadem on his brow and the purple flowing in his train.

That the Framers resolved the problem by creation of the Presidency was an act of political boldness of the first magnitude. By rejecting the notion of a plural executive, the unity essential to effective action was provided for. By discarding the idea of election by the legislature, the independence necessary for Presidential power and prestige was established. The state executives, Madison had complained, were little more than ciphers, with all power absorbed into the legislative vortex.[72] The same could scarcely be said of the polity provided for by the able gentlemen who burned midnight candles in Philadelphia the better part of two centuries ago.

Scarcely less significant, from a constitutional point of view, was the provision of an independent judiciary as one of the three coordinate departments. The want of a judiciary power, asserts Hamilton in *The Federalist,* crowned the defects of the Articles of Confederation.[73] National laws must remain ineffective without national courts to expound and define their meaning and operation. Without an independent judicial department, clothed with the authority to ascertain and enforce the powers of the Union, the laws, the treaties, and even the Constitution of the United States would become a dead letter.[74] By setting up a federal judicial branch, the Framers gave to every person having a claim involving a federal question a right to submit his case to a court of the nation.[75] The judicial arm of the nation itself is to have the controlling word in the enforcement of its basic instrument and laws.

The Framers crowned the positive powers of the new government by deriving them, not from the states, but from the people. Next to the determination that there was to be a new Constitution, not a mere revision of the existing Articles, this was perhaps the most daring of all the decisions made at the Philadelphia Convention. For it meant that the Constitution was the act of the people themselves, not that of the states which had joined together to form the Confederation.

Speaking in the Virginia Convention in 1788, Patrick Henry demanded to know: "What right had they to say, *We, the people?* Who authorized them to speak the language of, *We, the people,* instead of, *We, the States?*" [76] In strict law, Henry may have been correct, since the Framers sat under the resolution of the Confederation Congress giving them only limited authority to revise the Articles and then report any such alterations to Congress and the state legislatures, which revisions would become effective only "when agreed to in Congress, and confirmed by the States." [77] But the limits of their original mandate had been completely overturned by the seminal decision to write a new governmental charter. Having acted on that decision, it was not unnatural for the writers of the document to consider themselves more than mere agents of Congress or the states. The draftsmen wrote in the name of the people of the nation and they provided for ratification by the people, in conventions assembled, entirely omitting any reference to Congress in the Ratification Article.

The Framers were well aware of the legal significance of their action in the name of "We the People." During the debate on the method of ratification, Madison stated that "He considered the difference between a system founded on the Legislatures only, and one founded on the people, to be the true difference between a *league* or *treaty,* and a Constitution." [78] From this it follows emphatically that the document drawn up in 1787 is not a mere compact between the states. "This, Mr. President," declared James Wilson in the Pennsylvania Convention, "is not a government founded upon compact. It is founded upon the power of the people." [79]

The Constitution itself is thus inconsistent with the notion of sovereignty in the states. Though the Union, like all federations, is composed of a number of autonomous political entities, the Constitution did not emanate from them as independent commonwealths. The Preamble itself bears witness to the fact that the Constitution was the act, not of the states, but of the nation. The states make up, but they did not make, the Union.

6

WRITTEN   Perhaps the greatest contribution of the Framers was
SUPREME LAW   their translation into reality of the very concept of a
written constitution as the supreme law of the land. The Constitution, reads an oft-cited passage, is "the written instrument agreed upon by the people . . . as the absolute rule of action and decision for all departments and officers of the government . . . and in opposition to which any act or rule of any department or officer of the government, or even of the people themselves, will be altogether void." [80]

It has been said by one court that our constitutional law is merely an American graft on English jurisprudence.[81] Such a view may be correct with regard to other branches of the law. As far as the law of the Constitution is concerned, however, it is wholly inaccurate. The adoption of the Federal Constitution as supreme written law sharply differentiates American constitutional law from that which prevails in Britain.

The distinction between the American and English systems in this respect was pointed out by a member of the Supreme Court at the very outset of our constitutional history. "In England, . . ." said Justice Paterson in 1795, "the authority of the Parliament is transcendent, and has no bounds." [82] There is no written constitution, no fundamental law, to confine the exercise of legislative power. Contrast this with the situation in the United States. "In America the case is widely different: . . . The constitution is certain and fixed; it contains the permanent will of the people, and is the supreme law of the land; it is paramount to the power of the legislature." [83]

The cardinal contribution of the Framers of the American system to the science of government is precisely the notion of a written fundamental law which limits the powers of the people and their political delegates. This idea was not, it is true, novel with them; but they were the first to transform it into actuality. As the highest Court has aptly put it: "It is the peculiar value of a written constitution that it places in unchanging form limitations upon legislative action, and thus gives a permanence and stability to popular government which would otherwise be lacking." [84]

As already emphasized, the system drawn up by the Founders rests upon the Constitution as an instrument framed and adopted by the people themselves. "The people made the Constitution, and the people can unmake it. It is the creature of their will and lives only by their will." [85] The Constitution was ordained and established, not by the states as compacting sovereigns, but emphatically—as the Preamble itself declares—by "We the People of the United States." [86] The organic instrument is "the voice of the people speaking in their sovereign capacity." [87]

Yet, though our system may be said to be a government of the people (since in form and in substance it emanates from them),[88] it is wholly antithetical to the concept of extreme popular sovereignty. A constitution like the American one serves as a basic check upon the popular will at any given time. It is the distinctive function of such written document to classify certain things as legal fundamentals; these fundamentals may not be changed except by the slow and cumbersome process of amendment. The people themselves have decided, in constitutional convention assembled, to limit themselves and future generations in the exercise of the sovereign power which they would otherwise possess. And it is precisely such limitation that enables those subject to governmental authority to appeal from the people drunk to the people sober, in times of excitement and hysteria. The Constitution, in the neat phrase of the Iowa court, is the protector of the people against injury by the people.[89]

The Constitution as "the supreme Law of the Land" prescribes rules of decision that are binding upon courts throughout the country. Its provisions constitute the fundamentally permanent feature in a system that has undergone so many transformations since it was instituted in an age of knee-breeches and three-cornered hats. Amid all the crises of government, social and economic exigencies—even the all-consuming demands of total conflict—the Constitution has stood as the one basic constant in an inherently inconstant world. "Notwithstanding the competition of opposing interests, and the violence of contending parties, it remains firm and immovable, as a mountain amidst the strife of storms, or a rock in the ocean amidst the raging of the waves." [90]

7

JUDICIAL REVIEW In 1796, John Marshall, Esq., then a leader of the Virginia Bar, was retained to plead before the United States Supreme Court in an important case. In the course of his argument, he maintained that "the judicial authority can have no right to question the validity of a law; unless such a jurisdiction is expressly given by the constitution." [91]

Had this assertion with regard to judicial power prevailed, the American system of constitutional law would have developed along lines altogether different from the course actually taken. As is well known, however, the contention of *lawyer* Marshall in this respect was rejected by the highest Court in 1803, when *Chief Justice* Marshall delivered his landmark opinion in *Marbury v. Madison*.[92]

As an act of judicial statesmanship, the opinion in *Marbury v. Madison* stands without a par in our constitutional history. Marshall's logical presentation of authority in the courts to rule on constitutionality established judicial review as a basic principle of the American system.

To be sure, despite Marshall's statement at the Bar, quoted at the beginning of this section, the jurisdiction of the courts in this respect is not expressly provided for in the Constitution. But the mere constitutional silence does not resolve the issue. "For," to quote a member of the highest Court more than a century and a half ago, who was himself one of the draftsmen of the Constitution, "in an instrument well drawn, as in a poem well composed, silence is sometimes most expressive." [93]

Judicial review was not specifically spelled out in the Constitution because it was not deemed necessary. Judicial review as an essential element of the law was part of the legal tradition of the time. Written constitutions had developed as the fruit of the colonial struggle for limited government. As the embodiment of limitations on government, they came to represent the basic protection of minorities and property rights. Such protection could prove effective only because constitutions were recognized to have the status of fundamental law. The notion of such immutable law, derived from nature itself, was the very basis of eighteenth-century jurisprudence and philosophy.

The concept of a constitution as fundamental law led naturally to that of enforcement of its provisions by the courts. Lord Coke had urged judicial authority in this respect in his famous dictum in 1610 "that in many cases the common law will controul Acts of Parliament, and . . . adjudge them to be utterly void." [94] Modern scholars have debated over the exact meaning of these words. To the men of the formative era of American constitutional law, on the other hand, such meaning was clear. The Lord Chief Justice was stating as a rule of positive law that there was a fundamental law which limited government. Had not my Lord Coke concluded that "when an Act of Parliament is against common right and reason . . . , the common law will controul it and adjudge such Act to be void"? [95] Did not this mean that, when the people had reduced the principles of common right and reason to written form in a constitution, the courts were to adjudge any legislative acts contrary to its provisions to be void?

Countless commentators have pointed out the lack of originality in the *Marbury v. Madison* holding that the judges possessed the power to review the constitutionality of laws. To one familiar with the fact that law, like the history of which Maitland speaks, is a seamless web,[96] such revelation with regard to Marshall's contribution states but an inevitable truism. Of course, the law laid down by Marshall was inextricably woven with that expounded by his contemporaries and predecessors. Judicial review, as already stated, was part of the legal spirit of the time. With the appearance during the Revolution of written constitutions, the review power began to be stated in modern terms. Between the Revolution and *Marbury v. Madison,* state courts asserted or exercised the power in at least twenty cases. Marshall himself could affirm, in *Marbury v. Madison,* not that the Constitution establishes judicial review, but only that it "confirms and strengthens the principle." [97] Soon after the Constitution went into effect, assertions of review authority were made by a number of federal judges.

That Marshall's opinion was not radical innovation does not at all detract from its position as the cornerstone of the constitutional edifice erected by the Supreme Court. The great Chief Justice, like Jefferson in writing the Declaration of Independence, may have merely set down in clear form what had already been previously declared. Yet, as Marshall's biographer well says,[98] Thomas Jefferson and John Marshall as private citizens in Charlottesville and Richmond might have written Declarations and Opinions all their lives, and today none but the curious student would know that such men had ever lived. It was the authoritative position that those two great Americans happened to occupy that has given immortality to their enunciations. If Marshall's achievement in *Marbury v. Madison* was not transformation, but only articulation, what has made it momentous is the fact that it was magisterial articulation as positive law by the highest judicial officer of the land.

A page of history, according to the noted statement of Justice Holmes, is worth a volume of logic.[99] When *Marbury v. Madison* came before the Supreme Court in 1803, the page pointed in the direction taken by Marshall's epochal opinion. Yet, despite the Holmes dictum, the logic of the situation was worth at least as much in militating against any holding by the Court other than that actually rendered.

An organic instrument is naught but empty words if it cannot be enforced by the courts. It is judicial review that makes the provisions of a constitution more than mere maxims of political morality. Addressing the court in the *Five Knights' Case* (one of the great State Trials of Stuart England), the Attorney General, arguing for the Crown, asked, "Shall any say, The King cannot do this? No, we may only say, He will not do this." [100] It was precisely to ensure that, in the American system, one would be able to say, "The State *cannot* do this" that the people enacted a written constitution containing basic limitations upon the powers of government. Of what avail would such limitations be, however, if there were no legal machinery to enforce them?

Without such machinery, our system would prove no more effective than that set up under the Articles of Confederation. "Government itself would be useless," as the first United States Attorney General well said, "if a pleasure to obey or transgress with impunity should be substituted in the place of a sanction to its laws. This was a just cause of complaint against the diseased confederation." [101]

To avoid the weaknesses which had rendered the Confederation futile, the Constitution must incorporate, the men of 1787 well knew, "a coercive principle"—the only question, one of the Framers declared, was whether it should be "a coercion of law, or a coercion of arms." [102] The provision of effective "coercion of law" for enforcement of the Constitution has been the uniquely American contribution to the science of government. "Force, which acts upon the physical powers of man, or judicial process, which addresses itself to his moral principles . . . , are the means to which governments can resort in the exercise of their authority. The former is happily unknown to the genius of our constitution." [103] For the ineffectiveness of other constitutions whose violations could be censured only by force, we have substituted the institution of review by the Supreme Court. "The framers of our admirable constitution would have deserved the wreath of immortality which they have acquired, had they done nothing else than to establish this guardian tribunal, to harmonize the jarring elements of our system." [104]

The decision of questions of constitutionality is of the very essence of judicial power under the Constitution. "The judicial Power," reads Article III, "shall extend to all Cases . . . arising under this Constitution," and the Constitution itself, as already emphasized, is expressly declared to be "the supreme Law of the Land." This must mean, in Marshall's phrase, that the courts "must be capable of deciding every judicial question which grows out of the constitution." [105]

How are they to decide such questions? Through exercise of the traditional function of the judge to interpret the law and apply it to the facts of a particular case.

The power to interpret the laws, in the American theory, necessarily involves the power to determine whether they are repugnant to the Constitution. If repugnancy does exist, the judicial duty is to give effect to that which is of paramount obligation. In such a case, the Constitution ought to be preferred to the statute, the intention of the people to that of their agents.[106]

A case arising under the Constitution cannot be properly decided unless the organic instrument itself is given effect as superior, paramount law. "It is emphatically the province and duty of the judicial department," declares *Marbury v. Madison*, "to say what the law is. Those who apply the rule to particular cases, must of necessity expound and interpret that rule. If two laws conflict with each other, the courts must decide on the operation of each. So if a law be in opposition to the constitution; if both the law and the constitution apply to a particular case, so that the court must either decide that case conformably to the law, disregarding the constitution; or conformably to the constitution, disregarding the law; the court must determine which of these conflicting rules governs the case. This is of the very essence of judicial duty." [107]

It is the position of the Constitution as the supreme law of the land that has made judicial review a practical necessity. If such paramount position is to be maintained in practice, the courts must refuse to enforce laws that conflict with constitutional provisions. To hold otherwise would be, in effect, to make a solemn mockery of the restrictions contained in the organic document. "To what purpose are powers limited, and to what purpose is that limitation committed to writing, if these limits may, at any time, be passed by those intended to be restrained?" [108] Such limitations can be preserved in practice in no other way than through the courts; without them, all the reservations of particular rights and privileges amount to nothing.[109]

Nor is it consistent with reality to urge, as is too often done, that the true meaning of the Constitution is to have each branch as the final interpreter of its own constitutional powers. Even the best of men can hardly be trusted to act impartially as arbiters of their own authority. We need not necessarily agree with Lord Acton that great men are almost always bad men; but our constitutional law should clearly be based upon some such assumption. Indeed, the whole organic structure has been erected upon the assumption that the king not only is capable of doing wrong but is more likely to do wrong than other men if he is given the opportunity.

Law alone, the Founders knew, saves a society from being rent by internecine strife or ruled by brute power, however disguised.[110] All governmental acts must be subject to law, as interpreted by its traditional custodians, the judges.

The universal sense of America has come to realize that there can be no Constitution without law administered through the Supreme Court.[111] When, in a real controversy, an appeal is made to law, the issue must be left entirely to the judgment of the highest tribunal. This principle, in the phrase of an English constitutional lawyer, provides the only adequate safeguard which has hitherto been invented against unconstitutional legislation.[112] It is, in truth, the *sine qua non* of the constitutional structure. "So long, therefore, as the Constitution shall endure, this tribunal must exist with it, deciding in the peaceful forms of judicial proceedings the angry and irritating controversies between sovereignties, which in other countries have been determined by the arbitrament of force." [113]

8

RULE OF LAW   On Sunday, November 13, 1608,[114] occurred one of the memorable scenes in Anglo-American legal history. For it was on that day that James I confronted "all the Judges of England and Barons of the Exchequer" with the claim that, since the judges were but his delegates, he could take any case he chose, remove it from the jurisdiction of the courts, and decide it in his royal person. The judges, as James saw it, were "his shadows and ministers . . . and the King may, if he please, sit and judge in Westminster Hall in any Court there and call their Judgments in question." [115]

"To which it was answered by me," states Lord Chief Justice Coke, "in the presence, and with the clear consent of all the Judges . . . , that the King in his own person cannot adjudge any case . . . , but that this ought to be determined and adjudged in some Court of Justice, according to the law and custom of England."

To this, James made the shrewd reply "that he thought the law was founded upon reason, and that he and others had reason as well as the Judges."

Coke then delivered his justly celebrated answer, "that true it was, that God had endowed His Majesty with excellent science, and great endowments of nature; but His Majesty was not learned in the laws of his realm of England, and causes which concern the life, or inheritance, or goods, or fortunes of his subjects, are not to be decided by natural reason but by the artificial reason and judgment of law, which law is an act which requires long study and experience, before that a man can attain to the cognisance of it: that the law was the golden met-wand and measure to try the causes of the subjects." [116]

It is hardly surprising that the king was, in Coke's description, "greatly offended." "This means, said James, that I shall be under the law, which it is treason to affirm." To which, says Coke, "I said, that Bracton saith, *quod Rex non debet esse sub homine, sed sub Deo et lege.*" [117]

Needless to say, the king's anger only increased. According to one on-looker, in fact, "his Majestie fell into that high indignation as the like was never knowne in him, looking and speaking fiercely with bended fist, offering to strike him etc." [118]

James's indignation was well justified. Coke's articulation of the supremacy of law was utterly inconsistent with Stuart pretensions to absolute authority. In the altercation between Coke and the king, indeed, there was personified the basic conflict between power and law which underlies all political history. Nor does it affect the importance of Coke's rejection of James's claim that, with the king's fist raised against him, Coke was led personally to humble himself. That he "fell flatt on all fower" [119] to avoid being sent to the Tower, does not alter the basic boldness of his clear assertion that the law was supreme even over the Crown.

Coke's dramatic statement of the doctrine of the supremacy of law had immense influence, particularly in America. The men who drew up the American system of government were nurtured upon Coke's writings. "Coke's *Institutes,*" wrote John Rutledge before the Revolution, "seem to be almost the foundation of our law." [120] When Coke, after affirming the subordination of prerogative to law, announced, "It is not I, Edward Coke, that speaks it but the records that speak it," [121] men on the western side of the Atlantic took his assertion that he was only declaring, not making, law as the literal truth.

Of course, the doctrine of the supremacy of law was not original with Coke. That doctrine is, on the contrary, as old as political theory itself. "He who bids the law rule," said Aristotle, "bids God and reason rule, but he who bids man rule adds an element of the beast, and passion perverts rulers, even though they be the best of men. Therefore the law is reason free from desire." [122] The sense of this passage was to be repeated, off and on, for over two thousand years—not least of all by Coke's medieval English predecessors, notably Bracton.

Nevertheless, Coke's contribution was a fundamental one. He stated the rule of law in terms of positive law. And it was in those terms that the doctrine was of such import to the Founders of the American Republic. They sought to translate the doctrine into the bulwark of a practical political system. "The historic phrase 'a government of laws and not of men' epitomizes the distinguishing character of our political society. When John Adams put that phrase into the Massachusetts Declaration of Rights he was not indulging in a rhetorical flourish." [123]

The conception of the rule of law dominated the thoughts of the men who founded the United States and wrote its Constitution. Where, asked Thomas Paine, is the king of America? The law itself, was his answer: "let a crown be placed thereon, by which the world may know, that so far as we approve of monarchy, that in America the law is King." [124]

That the supremacy of the law is the central feature of the American polity is now almost axiomatic. More difficult is to determine what is included in that concept. Like so many phrases for which men fight, the rule of law is not capable of precise definition. It is rather an attitude, an expression of certain basic principles, in themselves vague when it is sought to analyze them, but clear enough in their results. There are many facets to free government and it is simpler to recognize it than to define it.[125]

It is far easier to describe the rule of law in negative, rather than positive, terms—to state what it is not, rather than what it is. It is, in the first place, clear that law in the sense in which we are using it here is not synonymous with mere legality. It is not enough to say that the powers of the State must be derived from regularly enacted law, for that is the case in even the most despotic country. The powers of Louis XIV, of the Russian Tsar or Turkish Sultan, of the totalitarian rulers of our own day, all these are derived from duly decreed positive law. In truth, if the Stuart kings had prevailed in their claims to legislate and tax without the consent of Parliament and to suspend and dispense with laws, their power would have been recognized as legal—but the rule of law would have disappeared from the English constitution.[126]

The distinction between law and legality is fundamental to the rule of law. What is done officially is almost always done in reliance upon law. The State in this respect is a veritable King Midas in whose hands everything is transformed into law.[127]

The rule of law requires much more than that governmental authority be exercised in accordance with regularly enacted laws. Manifold are the crimes constantly committed in the name of positive law. Anglo-Americans, who have lived under governments with limited powers for almost three centuries, tend too often to ignore this. Those with personal experience of other systems more rarely make the same error.

Typical in this respect was the experience of Voltaire, only a few years before Blackstone delivered his famous eulogy of English law. In 1717, Voltaire was sent to the Bastille for a poem which he had not written, whose author he did not know, and with whose views he did not agree. When he visited England, it is scarcely surprising that his predominant feeling was one of having left the realm of despotism for a land where, though the laws might sometimes be harsh, men were ruled by law and not by caprice. Here, said Voltaire, the very air that one breathes is free, for there is no place for arbitrary power.[128]

Voltaire's judgment was most acute. The absence of arbitrary power is, without a doubt, the first essential of the rule of law. " 'A government of laws and not of men' was the rejection in positive terms of rule by fiat." [129] In this sense, the rule of law is contrasted with every system of government based on the exercise by persons in authority of wide, arbitrary powers.[130] Law and arbitrary power are, in Burke's phrase, in dreadful enmity.

A. V. Dicey, the great Victorian constitutional lawyer, went even further. In his celebrated exposition of the rule of law, he asserted that that concept excludes the existence of wide discretionary authority on the part of government. Such an approach is, however, inconsistent with reality. "The idea is utopian," the Supreme Court said almost a century and a half ago, "that government can exist without leaving the exercise of discretion somewhere." [131] Few of the regulatory and social service schemes undertaken by the modern State would be feasible if their detailed implementation were not, to some extent, left to administrative discretion.

There is, nevertheless, all the difference in the world between conferring discretionary power and the vesting of absolute discretion in some government official. The latter is incompatible with the rule of law. "Law has reached its finest moments," eloquently declares Justice Douglas, "when it has freed man from the unlimited discretion of some ruler. . . . Where discretion is absolute, man has always suffered." [132] In a system governed by the rule of law, discretion, where conferred, must be confined within clearly defined limits. Discretion, as Lord Mansfield stated it in classic terms in the *Case of John Wilkes,* "means sound discretion guided by law. It must be governed by rule, not by humour: it must not be arbitrary, vague, and fanciful." [133] It is in this sense that the rule of law may be said to be the sworn enemy of caprice—the twin sister of liberty.

A second essential of the rule of law is the subjection of the State itself and its officials to the ordinary law of the land. "At the foundation of our civil liberties," states a frequently cited passage by Justice Brandeis, "lies the principle which denies to government officials an exceptional position before the law and which subjects them to the same rules of conduct that are commands to the citizen." [134] With us, every man, whatever his rank or condition, is subject to the ordinary law and amenable to the jurisdiction of the ordinary courts. From this point of view, the rule of law means equality before the law.[135]

The rule of law rejects the conception of the Dual State,[136] in which the application of law is characterized by its dualist quality. In such a State, law plays a controlling part only in the ordering of the relations between private citizens. Legal concepts are not applicable to the political sphere, which is regulated by arbitrary measures, in which the dominant officials exercise unfettered discretionary prerogatives. Into the areas involving governmental powers, the law penetrates only slightly. A person suspected of hostility to the regime may be arrested by the secret police, held incommunicado indefinitely, tried secretly, and sentenced to hard labor —and this without benefit of counsel or any possibility of appeal. On the other hand, even in such a system, there may be many areas which are governed by well defined legal standards administered by true judges.[137] In a State of this type, it may be said, a system of law and a system of force exist side by side. But it is the latter which dominates and gives its distinctive character both to State and law. In such a State, it is, to use Lenin's phrase, "not the *corpus juris Romani,* but our revolutionary consciousness of justice" [138] that governs.

Such a dualized legal order, in which governmental acts are placed in a privileged position of immunity from control by law, is utterly inconsistent with the rule of law. The notion that the administration of justice must be dualist in character—that different rules are to be applied to State action, that differing consequences are to follow where the acts of government officials are involved—this is foreign to our basic constitutional concept. It wholly repudiates the consequences flowing from these ideas: that the public officer is to be placed upon a higher plane than the individual; that immunity from law must be given to officials *qua* officials. In a government of law, official acts must be subject to as strict legal scrutiny as the acts of ordinary citizens. "No man in this country is so high that he is above the law . . . ," declares the classic expression of the highest Court. "All the officers of the government, from the highest to the lowest, are creatures of the law, and are bound to obey it." [139]

Closely related to what has just been said is a third essential of the rule of law—that there are certain fundamental principles above the State itself, which the State, sovereign power though it be, cannot abrogate. Governmental action is valid only if it does not conflict with these principles. The principles in question are those we usually comprehend by the expression "individual rights of the person." They are what an earlier age called "the natural rights of man" and are the sort of thing guaranteed in American bills of rights. "It must be conceded," the Supreme Court has affirmed, "that there are such rights in every free government beyond the control of the State. A government which recognized no such rights, which held the lives, the liberty, and the property of its citizens subject at all times to the absolute disposition and unlimited control of even the most democratic depository of power, is after all but a despotism. It is true it is a despotism of the many, of the majority, if you choose to call it so, but it is none the less a despotism." [140]

It may be true that men may differ about specific items which must be included in their catalogue of fundamental rights. True it is, also, that with

increasing need for governmental intervention, individual rights have come
to be restricted in favor of what have been conceived to be the overriding
interests of society. But an inviolable minimum of individual self-assertion,
there must still remain. Freedom of the person, of belief, and of expression
of opinion—these, at the least, must remain in a system governed by the
rule of law. There is, therefore, a fundamental truth in Lord Chief Justice
Hewart's comment that the "principle of the Rule of Law is really the
security for what are often called the liberties of the subject." [141]

9

SAME: The rule of law, we have just seen, has three essential
IMPLEMENTATION   elements:

1) The absence of arbitrary power;
2) The subjection of the State and its officers to the ordinary law; and
3) The recognition of basic principles superior to the State itself.

To say thus much is, however, to remain far from the heart of the
constitutional concept. The rule of law, like other organic principles, would
become but "as sounding brass or a tinkling cymbal," if it were asserted
only as a matter of academic theory. For effective law, implementation is
far more important than articulation.

One versed in Anglo-American constitutional history well knows that
there is no single, exclusive answer to the question of the proper implementation of the rule of law. In Britain itself, the constitutional structure
is, in many ways, the very antithesis of that which prevails in the United
States. Yet there is no real doubt that Englishmen are ruled by the law
and by the law alone, at least as much as Americans are.

This is true despite the theoretical omnipotence of the British legislature, under the doctrine of Parliamentary supremacy. Parliament, so runs
the almost proverbial aphorism, can do everything but make a woman a
man, and a man a woman. From a purely legal point of view, indeed, Parliament can do even these things, for its authority is so transcendent and absolute that it cannot be confined within any defined bounds.[142] There is no
written constitution, no division of governmental powers, no judicial review to restrain the exercise of Parliamentary sovereignty.

It is, all the same, erroneous to assume that the doctrine of Parliamentary supremacy in its actual operation presents any real danger to the
rule of law. Of course, it is theoretically possible that this doctrine could be
carried to its logical extreme. As far as the purely legal limits on its powers
are concerned, Parliament *could* (as it once did, in fact) [143] provide for
boiling the Bishop of Rochester's cook to death. Merely to refer to such

illustration is, nevertheless, to state its remoteness from reality today. It assumes an elective despotism [144] of a type that is the complete opposite of the British system in practice.

It is impossible, says de Tocqueville, to think of the English as living under any but a free government.[145] The rule of law has, in truth, so pervaded English life that the lack of the formal legal and institutional props that Americans deem so essential has mattered not one whit. The absence of arbitrary authority, the subjection of government officials to ordinary law, the "liberties of the subject"—these are as much fundamentals of the British system as if they were enshrined in an enforceable organic document. Respect for personal rights and the law lies so deeply in the hearts of Englishmen that it needs no constitution, no law, no court to give effect to it. In England, in de Tocqueville's apt phrase, there is more liberty in the customs than in the laws of the people.[146]

Britain, however, homogeneous island that it is, "bound in with the triumphant sea," is a uniquity, so far as its constitutional institutions are concerned. We in the United States, whose origins and culture have been far more diffuse, have seen the need for more formal legal implementation. With us, the existence of fundamental principles superior to the State itself is assured by the embodiment of such principles in a written constitution, which is enforced by the courts as the supreme law of the land. The absence of arbitrary authority in government is ensured by the division of powers as between nation and states and within the Federal Government itself. In this sense, the rule of law is but a reflection of the political balance of power which permeates the constitutional structure. And, finally, the subjection of the State to the ordinary law is guaranteed by the review power of the courts. "Every act of government may be challenged by an appeal to law, as finally pronounced by this Court." [147]

Implementation by an independent judiciary is vital to the practical effectiveness of the rule of law. "What is a right?" asks Justice Story in an important case. "That which may be enforced in a court of justice." [148] The rights vouchsafed to the individual by the rule of law would be devoid of practical content if they, too, could not be enforced in a court. In the words of a penetrating French constitutional lawyer, "For a country to live under the rule of law, it is absolutely indispensable that it have a high court, with all possible safeguards of independence, impartiality, and competence, before whom can be brought an action to set aside any act challenged as contrary to law." [149]

What has just been said is as true in Britain as it is in the United States. There, also, an independent judiciary can enforce the rights of the citizen and the subjection of public officials to the law. It is this which leads the chronicler of English legal history to state that the rule of law "means that the Courts can see to it that the powers of officials, and official bodies of persons entrusted with government, are not exceeded and are not abused, and that the rights of citizens are determined in accordance with the law." [150] To an Englishman, as to an American, the rule of law means at bottom the right of the courts to restrain any illegal act by whomsoever committed.[151]

To look at the rule of law solely in this way is, nevertheless, to obtain only a partial picture. Americans too often tend to forget this, with their emphasis upon the formal constitutional checks that characterize their system. A written organic document and judicial review—these are certainly significant safeguards; but one wonders whether they alone can preserve the rule of law in a society. It is with constitutions as with religions: the form may survive the substance of the faith.[152]

It was with profound insight that one of the greatest of American judges declared, in a passage that has become deservedly famous: "I often wonder whether we do not rest our hopes too much upon constitutions, upon laws and upon courts. These are false hopes, believe me, these are false hopes. Liberty lies in the hearts of men and women; when it dies there, no constitution, no law, no court can save it; no constitution, no law, no court can even do much to help it. While it lies there it needs no constitution, no law, no court to save it." [153]

Constitutions and courts alone can hardly be relied upon to secure us against all political harm. Civil liberties can at best draw only limited strength from judicial guarantees. The rule of law, as the experience of Britain so clearly shows, has roots far deeper than a formal fundamental document and the decisions of the judges enforcing it.

It is not mere idle speculation to inquire which comes first, judicial enforcement of a written constitution or a free and tolerant society. Must we first maintain a system of free government to assure a free and independent judiciary, or can we rely upon an aggressive, activist judiciary to maintain free government? [154] Americans not infrequently overlook the answer to this question. It is the basic attitude of the society, rather than its formal legal machinery alone, that is the controlling force in the implementation of the rule of law.

That the rule of law can flourish only among a people imbued with a legal spirit and trained to reverence the law is as certain as can be any conclusion of political speculation.[155] "All the instruments in the world," eloquently states Justice Miller in his *Lectures on the Constitution,* "though they were written in letters of gold upon the most imperishable tablets, will be but as ropes of sand if the people themselves have no respect for law or for those who administer it." [156]

The rule of law substitutes litigation for legislation.[157] The lawsuit has become a principal instrument of power in the American system: struggles over power that in Europe call forth regiments of troops, in the United States call forth only regiments of lawyers.[158] None but a law-abiding people will be inclined to regard the decision of a suit as settling basic issues of power. The main reason, says Dicey, why the American system works in this respect "with unequalled success is that the people of the Union are more thoroughly imbued with legal ideas than any other existing nation." [159] Americans have become a people of constitutionalists and even matters that excite the strongest popular feeling are entrusted to the courts. Though they possess neither the sword of the executive nor the purse of the legislature, the judgments of the courts are normally adhered to without question by those who direct the strength and wealth of the society. Indeed, habitual acquiescence by a people in the finality of even possibly mistaken judgments is the underlying indispensable condition for implementation of the rule of law.

One can go further and assert that the rule of law is utterly dependent upon the existence of a free society whose political institutions are endowed with authority only to promote such freedom. This was clearly pointed out by Justice Jackson in an address delivered on the 150th anniversary of the United States Supreme Court: "However well the Court and its bar may discharge their tasks, the destiny of this Court is inseparably linked to the fate of our democratic system of representative government." [160] The rule of law is thus both the effect and the cause of the American system of government. Representative democracy without the rule of law is a contradiction in terms. At the same time, the supremacy of the law, enforced by the courts, can only be effective in a democratic society; it is that kind of society alone that is really willing to submit its conflicts to adjudication and to subordinate power to reason.

NATION and STATES

10
SOVEREIGNTY
AND THE STATES

*T*HE American Revolution, it has been well said, replaced the sway of a king with that of a document.[1] For the sovereign power which the Framers believed to be concentrated in the person of George III, they substituted the limited government provided for in the Constitution. The organic document is both the charter and the yardstick of governmental power.

At the same time, what shall we say about the possessor of sovereignty in the American polity? Juridical writers have generally assumed that sovereign power must reside in some defined person or institution in the body politic.[2] "If a determinate human superior," reads the famous definition of John Austin, "not in a habit of obedience to a like superior, receive habitual obedience from the bulk of a given society, that determinate superior is sovereign in that society." [3] Austin's definition is, to be sure, wholly accurate as a description of the society of which he was himself a member—i.e., that of Britain. English law ascribes to the Parliament all the attributes of sovereignty; [4] it is dependent on no man or institution, accountable to no one, and owes no kind of subjection to any superior jurisdiction.[5]

In the United States, on the contrary, the Austinian concept of sovereignty is entirely out of place. At the base of Austin's approach is a notion of law as command which is itself inconsistent with American institutions. This notion, as one of the draftsmen of the Federal Constitution tells us, "contains the germ of the divine right—a prerogative impiously attempted to be established—of princes, arbitrarily to rule; and of the corresponding obligation—a servitude tyrannically attempted to be imposed—on the people, implicitly to obey." [6] In our own day, the concept of law as command has had within it the seeds of a revived systematic despotism [7] in the modern totalitarian State. The claims of such State assert a moral sanction superior to those of all others. The individual must surrender his personality before its demands; he must fuse his will into its own. It claims, may we not without paradox say, to be right—whether it be right or wrong.[8]

Sovereignty, in the sense given by Austin to that term, is the supreme political power in a polity: "supreme, absolute, uncontrollable power, the *jus summi imperii,* the absolute right to govern." [9] Such a conception, however, is hardly valid in the American Commonwealth. "It is not true," declared John Quincy Adams in an 1831 oration, "that there must reside in all governments an absolute, uncontrollable, irresistible, and despotic power; nor is such power in any manner essential to sovereignty." [10]

Where, then, does sovereignty reside in the American system? The answer is that, in the Austinian sense, there exists in the United States no person or body of persons possessed of legal sovereignty. "To the constitution of the United States," said Justice Wilson in a 1793 case, "the term *sovereign* is totally unknown." [11] Indeed, it is difficult to see how sovereignty, in Austin's meaning, could be vested in any organ of American government, unless our system itself were utterly changed. If the Congress were endowed with legislative sovereignty in the British sense, New York and Massachusetts would be as subject to its authority as is Scotland to that of the Parliament. If, on the other hand, the legislature of a state like Arkansas possessed true sovereign power, the authority of the National Government would be illusory; the United States would sink from a nation into a collection of independent countries, united only by the bond of temporary alliance.[12]

That no organ of the Federal Government is vested with sovereignty in the Austinian sense is clear from the basic principle that it is a government only of limited powers. "This government," affirms the classic Supreme Court statement, "is acknowledged by all to be one of enumerated powers. The principle, that it can exercise only the powers granted to it, . . . is now universally admitted." [13] Sovereignty and such restriction are incompatible. A government that may exercise only the powers granted by a constitution is one of limited, not sovereign, authority.

Shall we not say, then, that the states which make up the Union are the true possessors of sovereignty in the American system? "From the accepted doctrine that the United States is a government of delegated powers, it follows that those not expressly granted, or reasonably to be implied from such as are conferred, are reserved to the states." [14] If that is true, are not the states endowed with sovereign power, except as they have voluntarily surrendered their authority to the nation?

No doctrine involving more pernicious consequences for the American Constitution was ever invented by the wit of man than that the states are vested with the attributes of sovereignty.[15] It is that doctrine that has been responsible, throughout our history, for efforts to set the Constitution at naught. From the Kentucky and Virginia Resolutions of 1798, to the supreme trial of the Union in the Civil War, to the refusals to implement the Equal-Protection Clause in our own day—all of these have rested ultimately upon alleged violations of the rights of the supposedly sovereign states.

In truth, the use of the term sovereignty in connection with the states which make up the American Union is and always has been a misnomer. "The governments of the states," the Supreme Court has said, "are sovereign within their territory save only as they are subject to the prohibitions of the Constitution or as their action in some measure conflicts with powers delegated to the National Government, or with Congressional legislation enacted in the exercise of those powers." [16] But sovereignty with such qualifications is not really sovereignty at all. Nor does it alter the situation to call the states only "quasi sovereign," as the highest Court did in one case.[17] Sovereignty imports the supreme, absolute, uncontrollable power by which any State is governed; a State is called a *sovereign state* when this supreme power resides within itself.[18] But a State which is hemmed in by the limitations binding upon the members of the American Union is not (no matter how the term "sovereign" may be misapplied to it) truly sovereign.

Both history and law militate against the notion that the states in this country have ever actually been endowed with the attributes of sovereignty. Before the Revolution, of course, the states were only colonies, settled under and subjected to the British Crown; [19] they were mere dependencies of Britain. It is, nevertheless, erroneous to assume that the Declaration of Independence transformed them, Minerva-like, into thirteen fully grown sovereigns. "Was then the American revolution effected, . . . was the precious blood of thousands spilt, and the hard-earned substance of millions lavished, not that the people of America should enjoy peace, liberty, and safety; but that the governments of the individual states . . . might enjoy a certain extent of power, and be arrayed with certain dignities and attributes of sovereignty?" [20] On the contrary, when "the external sovereignty of Great Britain in respect of the colonies ceased, it immediately passed to the Union." [21] The union of the colonies indeed preceded the Declaration of Independence, which was itself a joint act.[22] "The truth is," declared a Supreme Court Justice in 1795, "that the states, individually, were not known nor recognised as sovereign, by foreign nations, nor are they now." [23]

Nor was the situation in this respect changed essentially with the ratification in 1781 of the Articles of Confederation. That document was more than a mere treaty between allied sovereigns, who had deputed to a Congress of Ambassadors the duty of deliberating on matters of common concern.[24] Unfortunately, the basic weaknesses of the Confederation have led many to overlook this and to look upon the states prior to the Constitution as sovereign, completely independent, and connected with each other only by alliance.[25] Such a view is erroneous, unless it uses the word "sovereign" in so restricted a sense as to change its meaning.[26] Even under the Confederation, there were limitations upon the power of the states, incompatible with their possession of true sovereignty. "The states," forcefully stated Rufus King during the Framers' Convention, "were not 'sovereigns' in the sense contended for by some. They did not possess the peculiar features of sovereignty. . . . Considering them as political beings, they were dumb, for they could not speak to any foreign sovereign whatever. They were deaf, for they could not hear any propositions from such sovereign." [27]

Whatever may have been the case, however, before the adoption of the Constitution, it is clear that that document is utterly inconsistent with the notion of sovereignty in the states. According to Justice Douglas, the Constitution is a compact between sovereigns.[28] Yet this, as we have just seen, was not even the case with the Articles of Confederation. It is certainly not true of the organic instrument drawn up in 1787. The Preamble itself bears witness to the fact that the Constitution was the act, not of the states, but of the people. "This system," well stated Justice Wilson when he was a member of the Constitutional Convention, "is not a compact. The introduction to the work is not a meaningless flourish; the system itself tells us what it is, an ordinance, an establishment of the people." [29] The Constitution sets up, in Chief Justice Marshall's celebrated language, "emphatically and truly, a government of the people. In form, and in substance, it emanates from them." [30]

The drawing up of the Constitution thus renders any concept of the states as independent sovereignties wholly obsolete. "It was generally agreed," wrote Madison in 1787, "that the objects of the Union could not be secured by any system founded on the principle of a confederation of sovereign states." [31] That this was in fact the view of the men who were themselves the statesmen of the Revolution is shown by *Chisholm v. Georgia*,[32] the first important case to be decided under the Constitution. The question for decision was whether a state could be sued in the Supreme Court by individual citizens of another state.[33] To decide it, the high Court really had to determine the issue of state sovereignty. "One of the parties . . . ," Justice Wilson affirms in his opinion, "is a State, certainly respectable, claiming to

be sovereign. The question to be determined is, whether this state, so respectable, and whose claim soars so high, is amenable to the jurisdiction of
the supreme court of the United States?" [34]

If Georgia was in fact intended to be a sovereign state under the Constitution, it could not be sued. It is inherent in the nature of sovereignty not
to be amenable to the suit of an individual without its consent.[35] In deciding
that Georgia was subject to suit, the *Chisholm* Court was really rejecting
the claim that the state was vested with the traits of sovereignty. "As to the
purposes of the Union . . . ," states Justice Wilson, "Georgia is not a
sovereign state." [36]

Chisholm v. Georgia is completely incompatible with any concept of
the states as independent sovereignties. As a contemporaneous ruling on
the effect of the Constitution in this respect, the *Chisholm* case is of the
greatest importance. It is true that, a century after it was rendered, a majority of the Supreme Court asserted that it had been incorrectly decided.[37]
To the present writer, on the contrary, Justice Harlan was correct in his
opinion that the *Chisholm* decision "was based upon a sound interpretation of the Constitution as that instrument then was." [38]

The real question at issue in *Chisholm,* declared Justice Wilson there
was "one, no less radical than this—'do the People of the United States
form a Nation?' " [39] Justice Iredell, who dissented, in the words of a newspaper account reporting the decision, "considered the States as so many
separate independent sovereignties." [40] The rejection of his view means
that the Constitution is more than a mere alliance or league between sovereign and independent communities.[41] The people themselves have formed
a veritable Union, whose very being rebuts the claim of existence of inconsistent sovereignties. "Here," said Chief Justice Jay in *Chisholm,* "we
see the people acting as sovereigns of the whole country; and in the language
of sovereignty, establishing a constitution by which it was their will, that the
state governments should be bound, and to which the state constitutions
should be made to conform." [42]

Perhaps the real difficulty in this area is, after all, only one of semantics.
As Justice Story points out, "The term 'sovereign' or 'sovereignty' is used in
different senses, which often leads to a confusion of ideas, and sometimes to
very mischievous and unfounded conclusions." [43] To Americans, the states
are at least as much a part of their polity as is the Government in Washington. Local patriotism and sentimental attachment to the particular state
still retain much of their vigor. It is only natural that devotees of the states
should seek to associate them with the almost mystical attributes connected
with the term sovereignty. The states may, in the light of cold fact, be only
provinces, of which the sovereignty has never been real. But they are still
provinces which, with all their limitations, have something of the magic of
Athens and Rome, of Venice and Florence.[44]

True sovereignty and the term used with regard to the American states are two entirely different things. If there does exist sovereignty in the sense of supreme political power in the American system, it exists only in the people as a whole, from whom springs all legitimate authority.[45] "Any one," said Daniel Webster in his argument in an important case, "who should look to any other source of power than the people would be as much out of his mind as Don Quixote, who imagined that he saw things which did not exist. Let us all admit that the people are sovereign." [46]

Yet, though the ultimate source of power is thus the people, it is plain that, since the adoption of the Constitution, they have not been vested with sovereignty, as Austin defined that term. The voice of the people can be heard only when expressed in the times and under the conditions which they themselves have prescribed and pointed out in the Constitution.[47] The truth is, indeed, that, as already emphasized, sovereignty in the Austinian sense does not exist in the American system. The Constitution, to paraphrase Lord Coke's famous language, is such a fellow that he will have no sovereign.

11

NATURE OF THE UNION   Truncated sovereignty (which, at most, the states can pretend to) is not true sovereignty at all, but a mere shadow. Yet, what malignant effect has not this baneful shadow had upon our history! For this *ignis fatuus,* devoid of real legal substance, men have been willing constantly to dispute, to contend—even to die. It was with profound insight that Charles C. Pinckney stated in 1788, "Let us then consider all attempts to weaken this union by maintaining, that each state is separately and individually independent, as a species of political heresy, which can never benefit us, but may bring on us the most serious distresses." [48]

From the claim of sovereignty in the states have flowed most attempts to frustrate the governmental structure created in 1787. Upon it have been based the doctrines of interposition, nullification, and secession, which, at various times in American history, have been urged against exercises of federal authority. The foundation of those doctrines has been the assertion that the Constitution was only a compact among the several states, which left them with sovereignty unimpaired, and free to meet federal coercion by interposing their own authority.[49]

The notion of the states as separate sovereignties contains the seeds of dissolution of the Union. This can be seen from the theoretical justifications advanced by those who have relied on a supposed right of secession. The very first advocate of such right in the Congress, Josiah Quincy in 1811, referred to the bonds binding the states as only "moral obligations" [50]—a conception grounded squarely upon the Constitution as a mere revocable agreement between independent sovereigns. If that is the case, with the states, in Calhoun's phrase, "form[ing] the compact, acting as sovereign and independent communities," [51] the states clearly have the right to withdraw their adhesions. "That a State, as a party to the constitutional compact, has the right to secede,—acting in the same capacity in which it ratified the constitution, cannot, with any show of reason, be denied by any one who regards the constitution as a compact." [52]

A right of secession is hence the necessary consequence of the recognition of sovereignty in the states. But such right and the temporary contractual nature of the Union upon which it depends have both been rejected by the Supreme Court. The landmark case in this respect is *Texas v. White*,[53] decided just after the Civil War. In it, the State of Texas brought an original action to enjoin the payment of certain United States bonds owned by the state before the war and negotiated by the Confederate state government to the defendants. The key issue presented to the high bench was whether Texas was then a state of the Union and, as such, capable of bringing suit. Defendants contended that she was not—that, having seceded and not yet being represented in the Congress, she was still out of the Union. As so presented, the case turned on the question of whether or not Texas had ever left the Union.

According to Chief Justice Chase's opinion for the Supreme Court, that question had to be answered in the negative. As far as the law was concerned, the ordinance of secession by Texas was a nullity. Texas consequently always remained a state within the purview of the Constitution. "When, therefore, Texas became one of the United States, she entered into an indissoluble relation. . . . The act which consummated her admission into the Union was something more than a compact; it was the incorporation of a new member into the political body. And it was final. . . . There was no place for reconsideration, or revocation." [54]

It is all too easy to dismiss *Texas v. White* as only the judicial ratification of the real decision on the validity of secession which had been made at Appomattox Courthouse. To be sure, if the actual outcome of the conflict had been different, the Supreme-Court decision could never have been made. But that is true because the constitutional nature of the Union would have been completely altered by military power. On the other hand, as a purely legal decision, under the Constitution as it is written, *Texas v. White* is clearly sound.

It is "self evident," in Cooley's words, "that the Union could scarcely have had a valuable existence had it been judicially determined that powers of sovereignty were exclusively in the states." [55] The very words of the organic document refute the notion that the states do have a sovereign right to secede at will. The Articles of Confederation themselves declared the

Union's character to be "perpetual." "And," says Chief Justice Chase, "when these Articles were found to be inadequate to the exigencies of the country, the Constitution was ordained 'to form a more perfect Union.' It is difficult to convey the idea of indissoluble unity more clearly than by these words. What can be indissoluble if a perpetual Union, made more perfect, is not?" [56]

The Constitution is thus a bond of national unity—not a mere federal league dissoluble at the pleasure of any party to it.[57] "The Constitution of the United States," said Justice Bradley in 1871, "established a government, and not a league, compact or partnership. . . . The doctrine so long contended for, that the Federal Union was a mere compact of States, and that the States, if they chose, might annul or disregard the acts of the National legislature, or might secede from the Union at their pleasure, and that the General Government had no power to coerce them into submission to the Constitution, should be regarded as definitely and forever overthrown." [58]

From a legal point of view, then, the nature of the Union is definitely settled. The Union instituted by the men of 1787 is complete, perpetual, and indissoluble. "The Constitution," declares *Texas v. White,* "in all its provisions, looks to an indestructible Union, composed of indestructible States." [59]

12
NATIONAL   "In our complex system," reads a passage from one
SUPREMACY   of Chief Justice Marshall's most celebrated opinions,
"presenting the rare and difficult scheme of one general government, whose action extends over the whole, but which possesses only certain enumerated powers, and of numerous state governments, which retain and exercise all powers not delegated to the Union, contests respecting power must arise." [60] The mere existence of two levels of government, operating in the same territorial area, makes such contests all but inevitable. Even if each order of government is wholly unmotivated by a desire to extend its authority, instances will always arise where the action of one may impinge upon the competence of the other. How are such conflicts of competence to be resolved?

The Constitution supplies the answer in the Supremacy Clause of Article VI, which provides: "This Constitution, and the Laws of the United States which shall be made in pursuance thereof; and all Treaties made, or which shall be made, under the Authority of the United States, shall be the supreme Law of the Land; and the Judges in every State shall be bound thereby, any Thing in the Constitution or Laws of any State to the Contrary notwithstanding."

The Supremacy Clause is the veritable keystone of the arch of federal

power. The principle of national supremacy, more than anything else, ensures the effective functioning of the Union. It is that principle which prevents the Federal Government from becoming subordinate to the states in
the manner that had rendered the original Confederation so futile. Without
the Supremacy Clause, the Constitution would be founded upon an in-
version of the fundamental principles of government. The authority of the
whole society would be everywhere subordinate to the authority of the
parts; the polity would be a veritable monster, in which the head was under
the direction of the members.[61]

At the very outset of our constitutional history, the highest tribunal was
called upon to give effect to the Supremacy Clause. In 1796, the Supreme
Court held that the terms of a federal treaty overrode the conflicting provisions of a state statute. "A treaty cannot be the supreme law of the
land . . . ," said Justice Chase, "if any act of a state legislature can stand
in its way." [62] The declared will of the people, expressed in the Supremacy
Clause, requires a state statute to give way to a federal law or treaty, and
fall before them.

The full import of the constitutional provision was developed after John
Marshall became the occupant of the high tribunal's central chair. In terms
so clear that they have never been questioned, the great Chief Justice
construed the Supremacy Clause as the bulwark of national power it has
since remained. In the Marshall interpretation, the Supremacy Clause meant
essentially two things: 1) the states may not interfere in any manner with
the functioning of the Federal Government; and 2) federal action (whether
in the form of a statute, treaty, court decision, or administrative act), if
itself constitutional, must prevail over state action inconsistent therewith.

The first of these two meanings was stated in now-classic terms in
McCulloch v. Maryland.[63] At issue in it was a state tax upon a federal instrumentality. Such taxation, Marshall affirmed, was a clear interference
with the functioning of the Federal Government and, as such, contrary to
the Supremacy Clause. "The states," he declared, "have no power, by taxation or otherwise, to retard, impede, burden, or in any manner control, the
operations of the constitutional laws enacted by congress to carry into
execution the powers vested in the general government. This is, we think,
the unavoidable consequence of that supremacy which the constitution has
declared." [64] Any other approach would prostrate the nation at the foot of
the states; it would, in fact, transfer the supremacy in the American system
to the states.[65]

In *Gibbons v. Ogden*,[66] Marshall articulated the second meaning of the
Supremacy Clause already referred to. The Supreme Court there held certain New York statutes which had granted an exclusive license to use steam
navigation on the waters of the state to be invalid so far as they applied to

vessels licensed under Acts of Congress to engage in coastwise trade. "It has been contended," said Marshall, "that if a law, passed by a state in the exercise of its acknowledged sovereignty, comes into conflict with a law passed by Congress in pursuance of the constitution, they affect the subject, and each other, like equal opposing powers. But the framers of our constitution foresaw this state of things, and provided for it, by declaring the supremacy not only of itself, but of the laws made in pursuance of it. The nullity of any act, inconsistent with the constitution, is produced by the declaration that the constitution is the supreme law. The appropriate application of that part of the clause which confers the same supremacy on laws and treaties, is to such acts of the state legislatures as do not transcend their powers, but, though enacted in the execution of acknowledged state powers, interfere with, or are contrary to the laws of Congress, made in pursuance of the constitution, or some treaty made under the authority of the United States. In every such case, the act of Congress, or the treaty, is supreme; and the law of the state, though enacted in the exercise of powers not controverted, must yield to it." [67]

The outstanding feature of the American federal system, according to an English study of federalism, is the footing of equality upon which the general authority and the regional authorities stand: "The principle of organization upon which the American association is based is that of the division of powers between distinct and co-ordinate governments." [68] Such an approach, however, ignores the effect of decisions like those in *McCulloch v. Maryland* and *Gibbons v. Ogden*. The Supremacy Clause prevents the principle of equality between the two centers of government from being the dominant one in the American federation.

The basic rule under the Constitution is that whatever the Central Government ordains—within the broad and ever-expanding area of its authority—is *supreme law,* enforceable as such and binding no less upon state executives, legislatures, and judiciaries than upon officers of the nation itself. If state action is seen to be incompatible with any legitimate exercise of power by the Federal Government, it loses all claim to validity. And this is true even though the state action in question is taken within a sphere in which the states might otherwise act. Because of the Supremacy Clause, we must, in Webster's phrase, conclude that federal and state powers do not stand upon equal elevation.[69]

13

RESERVED POWERS Nor is it really a valid objection to Marshall's interpretation of the Supremacy Clause that it enables the nation to impinge upon the sphere reserved to the states under the organic document. That sphere itself is, by the Supremacy Clause, limited by the overriding authority of the Federal Government exercised in pursuance of its constitutional powers.

It must, however, be admitted that, after Marshall's death, the Supreme Court receded somewhat from his view in this respect. Read logically, the Supremacy Clause appears to require that federal powers be determined by a fair reading of the grants of authority contained in the Constitution itself, without reference to any powers that might be possessed by the states.[70] In the century following Marshall, on the other hand, the high bench seemed to take its legal bearings more from the Tenth Amendment than from the Supremacy Clause. The powers reserved to the states under that Amendment were held to have the effect of withdrawing various matters from the reach of power otherwise committed to the Federal Government. Thus, the state police power over local manufacturing, according to a leading 1918 case, barred the Congress from enacting a law prohibiting the transportation in commerce of goods made by child labor.[71] Such federal action, in the Court's view, constituted an unwarranted infringement upon the reserved powers of the states.

Under more recent decisions, the Supreme Court has returned to the Marshall view that the powers reserved to the states under the Tenth Amendment cannot be invoked to curtail federal authority. In 1941, indeed, the high tribunal went so far as to state expressly that "The amendment states but a truism that all is retained which has not been surrendered. There is nothing in the history of its adoption to suggest that it was more than declaratory of the relationship between the national and state governments as it had been established by the Constitution before the amendment." [72]

To look upon the Tenth Amendment as a mere "truism" is to deny it any substantive effect in our constitutional law. At first glance, this might seem to contravene the principle that, in construing the Constitution, "every word must have its due force, and appropriate meaning; for it is evident from the whole instrument, that no word was unnecessarily used, or needlessly added." [73] In the case of the Tenth Amendment, nevertheless, the purpose of the draftsmen was not to add a substantive provision to the terms of the basic document. "The Tenth Amendment," the Supreme Court has said, "was intended to confirm the understanding of the people at the time the Constitution was adopted, that powers not granted to the United States were reserved to the States or to the people. *It added nothing to the instrument as originally ratified.*" [74]

The Tenth Amendment, in other words, was added to the Constitution out of an abundance of caution. Its purpose was only to allay fears that the new National Government might seek to exercise powers not granted; [75] its sole design was to exclude any interpretation by which powers beyond those which were granted might be assumed.[76] But it has no substantive effect, either upon the question of what powers are granted to the nation or upon the operation of the Supremacy Clause. It is really an express affirmation of what would, in any event, on any just reasoning, be a necessary rule of interpretation,[77] "leaving the question, whether the particular power which may become the subject of contest, has been delegated to the one government, or prohibited to the other, to depend on a fair construction of the whole instrument."[78]

The Tenth Amendment is consequently not a yardstick for measuring either the extent of federal power or the effect of the Supremacy Clause.[79] This was indicated by James Madison himself (the sponsor of the Amendment) while it was pending in the Congress. "Interference with the power of the States," he affirmed, "was no constitutional criterion of the power of Congress. If the power was not given, Congress could not exercise it; if given, they might exercise it, although it should interfere with the laws, or even the Constitutions of the States."[80] With or without the Tenth Amendment, this is the plain impact of the Supremacy Clause. Argument against federal supremacy, because of alleged interference with the reserved powers of the states is, as Marshall himself strikingly put it, actually "an objection to the constitution itself."[81]

14

INTERPOSITION   The doctrine of state sovereignty is, all the same, a ghost that refuses to remain in repose. It is true that the decision of Appomattox put an end to the extreme assertion of that doctrine in the claim of a right of secession. At the same time, lesser claims grounded upon the alleged sovereignty of the states have been urged throughout American history. Essentially, these have been based upon the theory of interposition, which was first urged by James Madison in 1798. Madison's articulation of that theory was called forth by the enactment by the Congress of the Alien and Sedition Acts. Feeling ran high against those laws in many states as an unwarranted invasion of constitutional rights and the legislatures of Virginia and Kentucky determined to take a positive stand. The result was the Kentucky and Virginia Resolutions of 1798 and 1799, which were drafted by Jefferson and Madison.

The initial statement of the interposition doctrine as such was in the Madison-drafted Virginia Resolutions. According to them, the Constitution is a compact, to which the states are parties; federal powers are limited by "the plain sense and intention" of that compact. And "in case of deliberate, palpable, and dangerous exercise of other powers not granted by the said compact, the states, who are parties thereto, have the right, and are in duty bound, to interpose, for arresting the progress of the evil, and for maintaining, within their respective limits, the authorities, rights, and liberties appertaining to them."[82]

Interposition as thus stated asserts a legitimate authority in a state to suspend within its borders the binding effect of an exercise of federal power. It assumes that, since the Constitution is a compact between sovereigns, each party to such compact has the right to judge for itself what shall constitute an infraction of its provisions. It completely rejects the view that the Federal Government, or any agency thereof, is to decide such questions. As recently explained by a federal court, "Interposition is an amorphous concept based on the proposition that the United States is a compact of states, any one of which may interpose its sovereignty against the enforcement of any decision of the Supreme Court or act of Congress." [83] In essence, the doctrine denies the constitutional obligation of the states to respect those federal acts with which they do not agree.

In actual practice, the interposition doctrine has most frequently been asserted in connection with an alleged right of the states to suspend the enforcement of federal judicial decisions within their borders. "The ultimate right of the [states]," said Madison, "to judge whether the compact has been dangerously violated, must extend to violations by one delegated authority as by another; by the judiciary as well as by the executive or legislature." [84] In accordance with this view, the states have, at different times in American history, attempted to nullify the enforcement of federal decisions which were themselves claimed to be illegal.

From a legal point of view, such attempts to implement the interposition doctrine could only result in failure. Interposition itself rests upon principles clearly inconsistent with the fundamental framework of the Constitution. In an early state case in which the doctrine was asserted, the Pennsylvania court justified its decision by relying on the theory that the Constitution was a mere "league or treaty." "When two nations differ about the meaning of any clause, sentence, or word in a treaty, neither has an exclusive right to decide it"; so, in our system, each state must have "a right to retain its own interpretation" of the Constitution.[85]

Such an approach, contrary as it was to the very existence of the United States as a nation, was bound to be rejected by the Supreme Court. The issue was put directly to the high tribunal in the 1809 case of *United States v. Peters*.[86] That case arose out of a judgment by a federal district judge in a prize case, awarding the value of the prize to a private individual, as against a claim set up by the State of Pennsylvania. The state legislature then passed an act asserting its duty to declare that the jurisdiction entertained by the federal judge "was illegally usurped and exercised, in contradiction to the just rights of Pennsylvania," and that the judgment "ought not to be supported or obeyed." It also directed all state officials to disregard "any process whatever issued out of any federal court."

As the Supreme Court opinion in the *Peters* case recognizes, this Pennsylvania act was plainly based upon an asserted state right of interposition.

Such alleged right was, however, wholly contradicted by the necessary power of the Supreme Court to determine the jurisdiction of the courts of the Union. To permit the states to suspend federal judgments, said Chief Justice Marshall, would be to put at naught both the Supremacy Clause and the Constitution which is dependent upon it: "If the legislatures of the several states may, at will, annul the judgments of the courts of the United States, and destroy the rights acquired under those judgments, the constitution itself becomes a solemn mockery; and the nation is deprived of the means of enforcing its laws by the instrumentality of its own tribunals. So fatal a result must be deprecated by all; and the people of Pennsylvania, not less than the citizens of every other state, must feel a deep interest in resisting principles so destructive to the Union, and in averting consequences so fatal to themselves." [87] The State of Pennsylvania, Marshall concluded, has no constitutional right to resist the legal process of the federal courts.[88]

Interestingly enough, this first decision by the highest Court on the question arose out of an attempt at interposition by a northern state. Indeed, until our own day, most of the important cases on state defiance of federal authority originated in states outside the South. It was this which led a historian of the Supreme Court acutely to note that, "throughout American history, devotion to State-Rights and opposition to the jurisdiction of the Federal Government and the Federal Judiciary, whether in the South or in the North, has been based, not so much on dogmatic, political theories or beliefs, as upon the particular economic, political or social legislation which the decisions of the Court happened to sustain or overthrow. No State and no section of the Union has found any difficulty in adopting or opposing the State-Rights theory, whenever its interest lay that way." [89]

But, if it has thus been interest, more than conviction, that has led different parts of the country at various times to assert the doctrine of interposition, the same has not been true of the judicial reception of that doctrine. Without exception, the Supreme Court has refused to recognize any right in the states to frustrate federal supremacy—and that regardless of the political philosophy of the judges who, for the time being, sat on the high bench. If it was Chief Justice Marshall (stanch nationalist that he was) who rejected the state pretensions in *United States v. Peters,* it was Chief Justice Taney (as firm a believer in states' rights as ever presided over the Supreme Court) who delivered the most stinging judicial rebuke to the interposition notion.

Taney's opinion on the issue was delivered in 1859 in *Ableman v. Booth.*[90] It arose out of the arrest by federal authorities of an abolitionist newspaper editor in Wisconsin for violation of the Fugitive Slave Act. After his conviction in a federal court, defendant secured a writ of habeas corpus from a Wisconsin judge, which was upheld by the highest court of the state, on the ground that the Fugitive Slave Act was unconstitutional. A writ of error was taken to the United States Supreme Court, but the state court directed its clerk to make no return, declaring that its judgment in the matter was final and conclusive. In effect, the Wisconsin judges were asserting a power to nullify action taken by the federal courts. In Chief Justice Taney's characterization, "the supremacy of the State courts over the courts of the United States, in cases arising under the Constitution and laws of the United States, is now for the first time asserted and acted upon in the Supreme Court of a State." [91]

To uphold the state power thus asserted would, said Taney, "subvert the very foundations of this Government." [92] If the states could suspend the operation of federal judicial power, "no one will suppose that a Government which has now lasted nearly seventy years, enforcing its laws by its own tribunals, and preserving the union of the States, could have lasted a single year, or fulfilled the high trusts committed to it." [93] The Constitution itself, in its very terms, refutes the claimed state power; the language of the Supremacy Clause, in this respect, "is too plain to admit of doubt or to need comment." [94]

The supremacy conferred on the Federal Government could not be maintained unless it were clothed with effective judicial power: "the supremacy . . . so carefully provided in the clause of the Constitution above referred to, could not possibly be maintained peacefully, unless it was associated with this paramount judicial authority." [95] In affirming its authority to set federal judicial action at naught, in truth, Wisconsin really "has reversed and annulled the provisions of the Constitution itself, and the act of Congress of 1789,[96] and made the superior and appellate tribunal the inferior and subordinate one." [97]

Ableman v. Booth rejects the notion of a state right of interposition so conclusively that it would appear to make continued assertion of any such right a mere academic matter, at least so far as American constitutional law is concerned. Unfortunately, however, in this area, the law alone, no matter how definitively settled by a uniform course of Supreme-Court jurisprudence, has not been able finally to lay to rest the specter of state sovereignty. On the contrary, in our own day, a century after *Ableman v. Booth,* the interposition doctrine has once again been asserted—this time to frustrate federal attempts to enforce the Equal-Protection Clause.

Shortly after the Supreme Court announced its decisions holding the segregation of Negroes in public schools unconstitutional,[98] so-called resolutions of "interposition" were adopted by the legislatures of several southern states. That passed in Georgia in 1956 is typical of all of them and may be referred to for illustrative purposes. Expressly headed a resolution "to invoke the doctrine of interposition," it asserts that the "decisions and orders of the Supreme Court of the United States relating to separation of the races in the public institutions of a State . . . are null, void and of no force or effect." In view of this, the resolution goes on, "There is declared the firm intention of this State to take all appropriate measures . . . to avoid this illegal encroachment upon the rights of her people." [99]

As a matter of constitutional law, such state assertions of a right of interposition are no more valid than those stricken down so decisively by the Marshall and Taney Courts. In the 1958 case of *Cooper v. Aaron*,[100] the Supreme Court was presented directly with the claim that the Governor and legislature of Arkansas were not bound by the decisions invalidating school segregation. This contention was disposed of in incisive terms. No principle, said the Court, is more firmly established in American public law than that binding the states to interpretations by the highest tribunal of the supreme law of the land. *Marbury v. Madison* [101] "declared the basic principle that the federal judiciary is supreme in the exposition of the law of the Constitution, and that principle has ever since been respected by this Court and the Country as a permanent and indispensable feature of our constitutional system." [102]

The conclusion is consequently clear that interposition is not a *constitutional* doctrine. At best, it is illegal defiance of constitutional authority.[103] If the states can nullify federal action in the manner claimed by advocates of the interposition doctrine, the Constitution itself, declares the *Cooper v. Aaron* opinion (repeating Marshall's language in the *Peters* case), "becomes a solemn mockery." [104]

From a strictly legal point of view, perhaps, *Cooper v. Aaron* may appear to constitute merely the superfluous hammering of additional nails into the coffin of dead constitutional doctrine. It is, nevertheless, essential that the law seize every opportunity to repudiate a doctrine so completely opposed to the fundamentals of the American constitutional system. To be sure, the essential tenet of the interposition doctrine denies the very authority of the Federal Supreme Court to make decisions binding on the states in such cases. "WHEREAS the States," categorically affirms the 1956 Alabama interposition resolution, "being the parties to the constitutional compact, it follows of necessity that there can be no tribunal above their authority to decide, in the last resort, whether the compact made by them be violated." [105]

Thus to deny the authority of the highest Court in constitutional questions concerning the states is, in effect, to deny to our federalism the means of operating effectively. In Justice Frankfurter's words, "Compliance with decisions of this Court, as the constitutional organ of the supreme Law of the Land, has often, throughout our history, depended on active support by state and local authorities. It presupposes such support. To withhold it, and indeed to use political power to try to paralyze the supreme Law, precludes the maintenance of our federal system as we have known and cherished it for one hundred and seventy years." [106]

In section 7, we emphasized that judicial review is an essential element in the enforcement of a written Constitution such as the American one. This is particularly true insofar as the implementation of the federal system is concerned. The legal supremacy of the Federal Constitution is absolutely indispensable to the very existence of the federation. The glory of the Founders of the Republic is to have devised means whereby the organic document became in reality, as well as name, the supreme law of the land, binding upon all the constituent parts of the Union. This end they attained by adherence to the basic principle embodied in the Supremacy Clause and by the creation of appropriate legal machinery for carrying this principle into effect.[107]

The Supremacy Clause, as already underscored, may well be called the central clause of the Constitution. Without it, there would be no real federal system, but only a moral union between the states. Draw out this particular bolt, in other words, and the federal machinery falls to pieces.[108]

In practice, however, the Supremacy Clause can be implemented only through the exercise by the Supreme Court of its power of judicial review. "The jurisdiction claimed for the Federal Judiciary is truly the only defensive armor of the Federal Government, or rather for the Constitution and laws of the United States. Strip it of that armor, and the door is wide open for nullification, anarchy and convulsion." [109] If federalism is to work, an independent judicial tribunal must be its arbiter. "What is essential for federal government," to quote a leading English study, "is that some impartial body, independent of general and regional governments, should decide upon the meaning of the division of powers. . . . No alternative scheme with less inconveniences seems possible, consistently with maintaining the federal principle." [110]

It may seem paradoxical that the ultimate arbiter of American federalism is itself an organ of the National Government. Yet the power of arbitrament must be vested somewhere in the system. And, in the Supreme Court, we have a tribunal peculiarly endowed with the essential requisites of complete impartiality as between the different centers of government. The high Justices are men set apart—the depositories of the law—who by their disciplined training and tradition and withdrawal from the usual temptations of private interest may be expected to be as free from partiality as the lot of man will admit.[111]

The alternative to the Supreme Court as arbiter of federalism is that urged by advocates of interposition—to allow each state to be the judge. That would actually mean the end of the Supremacy Clause and hence of the federal system as we have known it. "Will the case be better, when [fifty] different states are to settle such questions, as they may please, from day to day, or year to year; holding one opinion at one time and another at another? . . . Did any statesmen ever conceive the project of a constitution of government for a nation or state, every one of whose powers and operations should be liable to be suspended at the will of any one, who should doubt their constitutionality?" [112]

It is no answer to this to assert that the states, no less than the nation, may be relied upon to uphold and preserve the Constitution. This is to seek to reconcile all the frictions inherent in federalism by the magic word *confidence*.[113] But this is not at all a question of confidence. As Daniel Webster so well put it in his celebrated Reply to Hayne, "the honorable gentleman says, that the States will only interfere, by their power, to preserve the Constitution. They will not destroy it, they will not impair it; they will only save, they will only preserve, they will only strengthen it! Ah, Sir, this is but the old story." [114]

15

SUPREMACY AND   As indicated in section 12, the Supremacy Clause
STATE TAXATION   bars the states from interfering with the functioning
                    of the Federal Government. This has been clear in
our system ever since the 1819 decision in *McCulloch v. Maryland*,[115]
which held invalid a state tax on the notes issued by banks not chartered by the state legislature, insofar as it was applied to a branch of the Bank of the United States—a government corporation created by the Congress to be used as a depository for federal funds and to print bank notes which would serve as a convenient medium of exchange. The Bank of the United States, said the high Court, is a federal agency and, as such, must be immune from taxation by the states. This is the unavoidable consequence of that national supremacy which the Constitution has declared.

The power to tax, declares perhaps the most celebrated dictum of Chief Justice Marshall, involves the power to destroy.[116] To permit the states to tax federal agencies would place in their hands the power to nullify federal operations: "they may tax all the means employed by the government, to an excess which would defeat all the ends of government." [117] This would substitute federal dependence for the supremacy designed by the Framers. "The question," Marshall states, "is, in truth, a question of supremacy; and if the right of the states to tax the means employed by the general government be conceded, the declaration that the constitution, and the laws made in pursuance thereof, shall be the supreme law of the land, is empty and unmeaning declamation." [118]

Ever since *McCulloch v. Maryland,* it has been settled that federal immunity from state taxation is a necessary concomitant of the Supremacy Clause. "It was," says Justice Miller, "a terse statement of a great truth which was made by Chief Justice Marshall in the great case, in regard to the United States Bank, that the power to tax, where unlimited, involves the power to destroy." [119] Nor is the force of the famous Marshall dictum really impaired by the oft-quoted Holmes gloss that "The power to tax is not the power to destroy while this Court sits." [120] The power to tax is one which is peculiarly insusceptible to quantitative differences of degree. "If the right to impose a tax exists, it is a right which, in its nature, acknowledges no limits." [121] If the power to tax federal functions and instrumentalities exists, it may be exercised to whatever extent the state chooses to carry it.[122] The only alternative consistent with the Supremacy Clause is to deny the power altogether to the states.

The only question that remains is that of whether the incidence of a particular state tax is in fact upon a federal function or instrumentality. If the state tax must be paid directly by a federal agency, it is, of course, invalid. In this sense, an agency of the United States is any authority within the Federal Government (regardless of whether its formal title be that of department, bureau, division, commission, board, or some other name, or where in the tripartite governmental structure it be located) or owned by the Government.[123] In the latter category would fall the government corporation, of the type involved in *McCulloch v. Maryland* itself, whose stock is owned by the United States.

Within this meaning, for the federal tax immunity to apply, the body on which the tax falls must be a part of, or owned by, the Federal Government. It is not enough that it owes its existence to the United States, as is the case, for example, with a private corporation chartered under federal law. Even though such corporation has been chartered by the Congress to carry out specified federal policies, it cannot be deemed a federal instrumentality for purposes of tax immunity. This has been clear since the Supreme Court denied such immunity to the Union Pacific Railroad Company, as against the claim that it had been constituted and organized as the agent of the Federal Government, chartered by the Congress to carry out its power to create national roads and other means of communication between the states.[124] A mere private agent used by the United States is not a federal agency. Such private agent of the Federal Government does not share in its tax immunity, even though it has been created by federal law for the purpose of such agency.[125]

If, however, the railroad in question had been built and operated by a federally owned corporation, there could be no doubt of its immunity from state taxation. If the state tax falls directly upon a federal agency, in the sense in which that term has been defined, it cannot stand. And that regardless of the nature of the functions performed by the particular agency. Thus, where a federal agency is concerned, we cannot distinguish between a so-called proprietary function, such as the operation of a railroad, and the more traditional type of governmental function. As Chief Justice Warren has put it, "our decisions have made it clear that the Federal Government performs no 'proprietary' functions." [126] All lawful activities of the National Government are considered as governmental, for the purposes of tax immunity,[127] even though the particular activity is one that has traditionally been carried on by private business, rather than government. Consequently, a state tax on those manufacturing and selling electric power cannot be applied to the sale of such power from a federally operated hydroelectric plant.[128]

In *Federal Land Bank v. Bismarck Lumber Co.*,[129] the state argued that the lending functions of federally owned and operated banks could not be rendered immune from state taxation. The Supreme Court rejected this argument. According to its opinion, "The argument that the lending functions of the federal land banks are proprietary rather than governmental misconceives the nature of the federal government with respect to every function which it performs. The federal government is one of delegated powers, and from that it necessarily follows that any constitutional exercise of its delegated powers is governmental. . . . It also follows that when Congress constitutionally creates a corporation through which the federal ₁overnment lawfully acts, the activities of such corporation are governmental." [130]

The immunity of federal agencies from state taxation thus turns not at all upon the nature of such agencies or the nature of their activities; all the activities of a federal agency must be considered as governmental and, as such, entitled to the full immunity that attaches to functions performed by the Federal Government.

16

SAME: FEDERAL   The same general principles apply to the state taxa-
PROPERTY   tion of federal property. In *McCulloch v. Maryland*
itself, it is true, Chief Justice Marshall stated expressly that his opinion "does not extend to a tax paid by the real property of the bank, in common with the other real property within the state." [131] It has, nevertheless, since been settled that any property owned by the Federal Government or an agency thereof is, in fact, immune from state taxation. This has been established law since *Van Brocklin v. Tennessee* (1886).[132] The rule as stated there is that, "whether the property of the United States shall be taxed under the laws of a State depends upon the will of its owner, the United States, and no State can tax the property of the

United States without their consent." [133] And, under the case-law, there is no distinction in this respect between property owned directly by the United States and that owned by a federal agency, such as a government corporation.[134] The Marshall dictum quoted at the beginning of this paragraph notwithstanding, both are wholly exempt from state taxes.

Such immunity does not depend at all upon the use to which particular federal property is being put. In a 1943 case, a federal judge asserted that tax immunity did not extend to property held in the name of the Federal Public Housing Authority for use as a low-cost public housing project. Such use, said he, "is not such a governmental function or purpose as to permit its exemption from State, County or Municipal taxation." [135] But this view was stated in dissent, and the majority decision rejecting it was affirmed by the Supreme Court.[136] For the purposes of tax immunity, in other words, all federally owned property must be treated as held for public purposes; it makes no difference whether such property is being used in furtherance of a proprietary or governmental function.

Despite the Marshall dictum to the contrary, the rule of exemption of all federal property is the only one consistent with the Supremacy Clause. "Under the confederation," Webster informs us, "when the national government, not having the power of direct legislation, could not protect its own property by its own laws, it was expressly stipulated, that 'no impositions, duties, or restrictions should be laid by any state on the property of the United States.' Is it supposed, that property of the United States is now subject to the power of the state governments, in a greater degree than under the confederation? . . . The United States have, and must have, property locally existing in all the states; and may the states impose on this property, whether real or personal, such taxes as they please?" [137] If *McCulloch v. Maryland* itself is sound (and its legal principle has never really been questioned in almost a century and a half), the immunity established by it must apply to all federally owned property. The power to destroy can be exercised just as easily by a tax against the real property of a federal agency as it can by the type of tax which Maryland directed against the operation of the Bank of the United States. "If this power of taxation be admitted, what is to be its limit?" [138]

Problems may still arise, however, where federal property is being used by a private citizen. In *United States v. Allegheny County* (1944),[139] the Government entered into a contract with a private company, under which the latter undertook to make and deliver certain weapons. The company lacked some of the necessary machine tools and the Government furnished various lathes and other machinery which were "leased" to the company and installed in its factory in Pennsylvania. The contract provided that the Government would reimburse the company for any taxes which it might have to pay on the machinery. Subsequently, the relevant local assessing authorities revised the company's previously determined assessment for ad valorem taxes by adding thereto the value of the government-owned machinery and assessed an additional tax on that account. The Supreme Court held that such assessment was invalid. The tax in question, said Justice Jackson, was a general property tax; the government property itself was the subject of the tax, just as much as if the machinery had been taxed in form. "We hold that the substance of this procedure is to lay an ad valorem general property tax on property owned by the United States." [140]

With the *Allegheny* decision should be compared the more recent case of *United States v. Detroit*.[141] At issue in it was a Michigan law which provides that, when tax-exempt real property is used by a private party in a business conducted for profit, the private party is subject to taxation to the same extent as though he owned the property. A tax was assessed under this law against a corporation which had leased an industrial plant owned by the United States in Detroit. The plant was leased at a stipulated annual rental for use in the lessee's private manufacturing business. The lease provided that the lessee could deduct from the agreed rental any taxes paid by it on the property.

This time the high Court upheld the challenged state tax. The tax was treated by it as one on a private person for the use of property (which happens to be owned by the Government). In taxing the use of such property, the state is taxing an interest of the private taxpayer, not that of the Federal Government. As the Court saw it, "Any taxes due under the statute are the personal obligations of the private lessee or user. The owner is not liable for their payment nor is the property itself subject to any lien if they remain unpaid." [142]

The *Detroit* opinion states specifically that the *Allegheny* case was not controlling. The reason, says Justice Black, is that the tax there "was simply and forthrightly imposed on the property itself, not on the privilege of using or possessing it." [143] In the Court's view, there is a basic difference between a *property* tax and a *privilege* tax. The state may not, as in *Allegheny,* levy a tax directly on federal property even where such property is in the hands of a private bailee from whom the tax is to be collected; the state may, on the other hand, as in *Detroit,* impose a tax upon a private person for the privilege of using federal property, even though the value of the property serves as the measure of the tax.

The distinction between "property" and "privilege" taxes as a yardstick for judging constitutionality appears purely artificial.[144] If that is true, the practical effect of *Detroit* is to overrule the limitation on state taxing power laid down in *Allegheny*. A state can always frame its tax in the form of a privilege, rather than a property, tax. That being the case, there is really no constitutional limitation on the state taxation of federal property that is being used by a private person—unless the state is inept enough to impose the tax directly on a federal agency or to label the tax in question as an express tax on the property, rather than only on the privilege of its use.[145]

17

SAME: FEDERAL EMPLOYEES   In the just-discussed *Detroit* case, the result was not changed because the state tax involved the imposition of an increased financial burden upon the Federal Government, since the amount of the tax was deductible from the rent paid to the Government. "It is undoubtedly true, as the Government points out," the *Detroit* opinion concedes, "that it will not be able to secure as high rentals if lessees are taxed for using its property. But . . . the imposition of an increased financial burden on the Government does not, by itself, vitiate a state tax." [146]

The high bench's ruling in this respect reaffirms what is now the fundamental principle governing the law of governmental tax immunity. It should, nevertheless, be recognized that, for over a century after *McCulloch v. Maryland,* the trend was all the other way. Chief Justice Marshall's famous opinion was seized upon as the basis of a broad doctrine of tax immunity.[147] The Supreme Court, in the post-*McCulloch v. Maryland* cases, gave an expanded scope to what were deemed to be "instrumentalities of government" for the purposes of immunity. The key assumption upon which such expansion was based was that the economic burden of a tax on any interest derived from the Federal Government imposes a burden on the Government itself so as to involve an undue interference with the functioning of the Government. Hence, a state tax on any interest derived from the Federal Government contravened both the Supremacy Clause and the governmental tax immunity derived from it.

Acting on the assumption just stated, the high Court, in *Dobbins v. Commissioners of Erie County* (1842),[148] held that a state could not tax the salary paid to a federal officer. Such officer, said the Court, is one of the means used by the Federal Government to carry out its powers and his compensation the means by which his services are procured and retained. The state tax was invalid because it constituted an "interference with the constitutional means which have been legislated by the government of the United States to carry into effect its powers." [149] But what of the fact that the salary became the personal property of the officer when once he earned it? Here the Court relied directly upon the supposed financial burden that would result from the tax upon the Government itself. "If it can be taxed by a state as compensation," asked *Dobbins,* "will not congress have to graduate its amount with reference to its reduction by the tax?" [150]

Under *Dobbins,* the immunity from taxation vested in the Federal Government was also accorded to the officials through whom the Government operated. More recently, the high tribunal has moved away from the assumption that the Government is actually burdened if its functionaries, as other citizens, are required to pay for the upkeep of their state governments.[151] The result has been a rejection of the *Dobbins*-created immunity of federal officials from state taxes. Such rejection occurred specifically in the 1939 case of *Graves v. New York ex rel. O'Keefe,*[152] where it was decided that the imposition of a state income tax on the salary of a federal employee was valid. A nondiscriminatory tax, laid on the income of all members of the community, said the Court, casts no unconstitutional burden on the Government whose employees are taxed: "The theory, which once won a qualified approval, that a tax on income is legally or economically a tax on its source, is no longer tenable." [153]

It may well be true that the denial of tax immunity to its employees does impose some financial burden upon the Government. One wonders, all the same, whether the mere possible increase in salary that the Government may have to pay is enough to justify the *Dobbins* holding. The sole purpose of tax immunity in these cases is to prevent undue interference by the states with the functioning of the Federal Government.[154] It is hard to see how a nondiscriminatory tax on the net income of federal employees, in common with that of all other citizens, can really be said to obstruct the performance by the Government of its functions.[155] In Justice Jackson's expression: "However persuasive the argument for governmental immunity, there was little reason in law and none in sound government for holding that officeholders shared the government's immunity from tax." [156] To suggest that it makes inroads upon the Federal Government's immunity by making its employees pay their aliquot share of the cost of maintaining their state governments is to trivialize the whole notion of governmental immunity. To subject public employees to a general income tax is merely to recognize that they are also citizens, and that their particular function in government does not generate an immunity from sharing with their fellow citizens the material burdens of government.[157]

18
SAME:
GOVERNMENT
CONTRACTORS

Dealing with another aspect of governmental immunity, Chief Justice Marshall asked, in an 1824 case: "Can a contractor for supplying a military post with provisions, be restrained from making purchases within any state, or from transporting the provisions to the place at which the troops were stationed? or could he be fined or taxed for doing so? We have not yet heard these questions answered in the affirmative." [158]

The last part of the questions thus posed and answered by Marshall was presented directly to the Supreme Court in *Panhandle Oil Co. v. Knox* (1928).[159] By a bare majority there, the Court answered the question of the government contractor's amenability to state taxation much as Marshall had done. According to it, a state could not impose any tax upon a contractor with the Federal Government, where the result of the tax would be to increase the amount which the Government would have to pay under the contract.[160] Such a tax, said the high bench, was, in substance and legal effect, "to tax the United States—to exact tribute on its transactions and apply the same to the support of the State." [161]

The *Panhandle* decision was, of course, based upon the theory that, in such a case, the burden of the tax was really not on the contractor, but on the Government; hence the tax contravened its immunity. But this theory was basically similar to that which had supported the *Dobbins* holding of immunity of federal employees from state taxation. It is hardly surprising that it, too, has been abandoned by more recent decisions.

The most important of these recent decisions is that rendered in 1941 in *Alabama v. King and Boozer*,[162] which expressly overruled the *Panhandle* case. The Court there sustained a state sales tax imposed on a contractor, in respect of materials which he purchased for the performance of a "cost-plus-fixed-fee" contract with the United States. In this case, it was clear that, since the Government, pursuant to the "cost-plus" contract, had to reimburse the contractor for the amount of the tax, the state tax did increase the amount the United States had to pay under the contract. Yet this did not, in the high bench's view, mean that there was an infringement of the Federal Government's immunity: "So far as such a non-discriminatory state tax upon the contractor enters into the cost of the materials to the Government, that is but a normal incident of the organization within the same territory of two independent taxing sovereignties. The asserted right of the one to be free of taxation by the other does not spell immunity from paying the added costs, attributable to the taxation of those who furnish supplies to the Government and who have been granted no tax immunity." [163]

Alabama v. King and Boozer makes it plain that the Constitution does not prohibit a tax exacted from a government contractor merely because such tax is passed on economically, by the terms of the contract or otherwise, as a part of the cost to the Government.[164] In this respect, *King and Boozer* adopts the analysis urged in 1873 by a member of the highest Court, whose powers of penetrating analysis in this field have more recently been termed second to none.[165] It is one thing, said Justice Bradley then, to accept the full immunity of the Federal Government itself. But that "case differs *toto coelo* from that wherein the government enters into a contract with an individual or corporation to perform services necessary for carrying on the functions of government—as for carrying the mails, or troops, or supplies, or for building ships or works for government use. In those cases the government has no further concern with the contractor than in his contract and its execution. It has no concern with his property or his faculties independent of that. How much he may be taxed by, or what duties he may be obliged to perform towards, his State is of no consequence to the government, so long as his contract and its execution are not interfered with." [166]

Unless a state taxes the government contract itself or interferes directly with its execution, the Federal Government's immunity is not infringed. It is, in other words, the contract alone—not the contractor—that is exempt from state taxation or interference. To give contractors immunity from taxation for their property, profits, or purchases is to set up what amounts to a vast area of private immunities for those who deal with the Government. To reject such private immunities is in no way to infringe upon the tax immunity of the United States. Nor is the state tax rendered invalid because the contractor may be able to shift the burden to the Government. The law on the subject has, in Justice Frankfurter's words, "shifted from that of an argumentative financial burden to the Federal Government to that of freedom from discrimination against transactions with the Government and freedom from direct impositions upon the property and the instrumentalities of the Government." [167]

The test today is not whether the Federal Government may have to bear the cost of a tax which a state imposes on a third person who has business relations with the Government. Even in such a case, the state tax should be valid where the state could clearly impose such a tax upon such a third person but for the fact that the transaction which gave rise to it was not with a private person but with the Government.[168]

The rule that a government contractor is not entitled to tax immunity was adopted by the Supreme Court in *King and Boozer* at the insistence of the United States itself.[169] It was not long, however, before the Government repented its generosity.[170] In an age of ever-mounting government expenditures and consequent attempts to cut down burdens on the federal treasury, by decreasing the costs to the Government on "cost-plus" and similar types of contracts, it is not surprising that federal contracting officers have made efforts to avoid the *King and Boozer* doctrine. They have done so by changing the relevant provisions in the contracts drawn by them so as to assert a direct property interest of the Federal Government in the work and assets of the contractor. Post-*King and Boozer* contracts by the Government have been purposefully drawn so as to vest title to the property that is the subject of the tax in the Government, and thereby seek to withdraw it from the taxing power of the states.[171]

The type of contractual provision referred to can be seen from the 1954 case of *Kern-Limerick, Inc. v. Scurlock.*[172] The Supreme Court there decided that a state sales tax could not validly be applied to a sale by which certain contractors acquired two tractors for use in constructing a naval ammunition depot for the United States under a "cost-plus" contract. The Court justified this holding on the ground that here, unlike *King and Boozer,* the contract purported to make the contractors purchasing agents for the Government, and the purchase order involved in the sale in question provided: "This purchase is made by the Government." This, said the Court, distinguished this case from *King and Boozer,* for here the United States was the purchaser and would have had to pay the tax.

The difficulty with this rationale is that the Government was, in actuality, the real party in interest as much in *King and Boozer* as it was in *Kern-Limerick.* Yet the high Court in *King and Boozer* held that that did not prevent the state from taxing the sale to the contractor. As already pointed out, the form of the particular contract and purchase order in *Kern-Limerick* had been drafted by the relevant contracting officers to avoid the effect of the *King and Boozer* decision and thus to conserve federal funds. That may well be a laudable purpose; but should it be enough to defeat the right of the states to impose nondiscriminatory taxes on private sales within their borders?

Detroit v. Murray Corporation (1958) [173] indicates that, insofar as *Kern-Limerick* is inconsistent with the *King and Boozer* case, it can no longer be considered as controlling. In the *Murray* case, Murray was acting as a subcontractor under a prime contract for the manufacture of airplane parts between two other companies and the United States. Under the relevant contract, Murray received partial payments as it performed its obligations. Title to all parts, materials, and work in process acquired by Murray in performance of the subcontract vested in the United States upon any such partial payment, even though Murray retained possession. The City of Detroit assessed a tax against Murray which in part was based on the value of materials and work in process in its possession to which the United States held legal title under the title-vesting provisions of the subcontract.

The Supreme Court upheld the challenged tax as against the contention that it violated the Federal Government's tax immunity. Though the tax was styled a personal property tax by the state statute, it was actually, in the Court's view, more like a tax on the privilege of using property. "We see no essential difference so far as constitutional tax immunity is concerned between taxing a person for using property he possesses and taxing him for possessing property he uses when in both instances he uses the property for his own private ends." [174] As a levy on a private person possessing property (which happens to belong to the Government under the relevant contract), which he was using in the course of his own business, the state tax was valid: "Lawful possession of property is a valuable right when the possessor can use it for his own personal benefit." [175]

It must be conceded that the *Murray* tax went to the very boundary of permissible state power, for title to the property involved did, under the contract, vest in the United States. But such title does not change the essential nature of the tax as one on a private person using the property for purposes of private profit. The form of the particular contract should not defeat the state's taxing power and vest in a government contractor immunity from taxes which his competitors must pay. Of course, such holding in *Murray* is inconsistent with the *Kern-Limerick* decision—"a case whose relevance is not minimized by the loud silence the Court's present opinions accord it." [176] The *Murray* result is, however, more consonant with the basic thrust of the recent cases on tax immunity which reject the notion that tax exemption should be given to private citizens because of their participation in governmental functions. *Kern-Limerick* allowed the federal contracting officers to draw the line of permissible state taxation by changing a few words in a contract. Under *Murray,* the legitimate powers of the states cannot be defeated by the drawing of such artificial line.[177]

19

SAME: "I am not aware," caustically commented Justice
OTHER PRIVATE Holmes in a 1928 dissent, "that the President, the
IMMUNITIES   Members of Congress, the Judiciary or, to come
               nearer to the case at hand, the Coast Guard or the
officials of the Veterans' Hospital, because they are instrumentalities of government and cannot function naked and unfed, hitherto have been held entitled to have their bills for food and clothing cut down so far as their butchers and tailors have been taxed on their sales; and I had not supposed that the butchers and tailors could omit from their tax returns all receipts from the large class of customers to which I have referred." [178]

At the same time, if we adopt as the test, for purposes of tax immunity, the theory that a tax on income is a tax on its source (with the burden of a tax on any interest derived from the Federal Government being considered to impose an invalid burden on the Government itself), the illustrations supposed by Justice Holmes are not really as farfetched as they may seem at first glance. As already pointed out in our discussion of federal employees and government contractors, that theory was the very one followed by the Supreme Court for many years. Acting under it, the Court built up a whole series of what were, in effect, private tax immunities for those who had dealings with the Federal Government. While the high tribunal did not perhaps go quite so far as the extreme cases posited by Holmes, some of its decisions, it must be admitted, were not too far removed from them.

The starting point for the development of the private immunities referred to was *Weston v. Charleston* (1829).[179] The Court there struck down a local tax on securities issued for loans made to the United States. "The tax on government stock," reads the opinion by Chief Justice Marshall, "is thought by this court to be a tax on the contract, a tax on the power to borrow money on the credit of the United States, and consequently to be repugnant to the constitution." [180]

Since *Weston,* the Supreme Court has consistently held that all obligations of the Federal Government are immune from state taxation. This rule, said Justice Harlan in 1955, was aimed at protecting the borrowing power of the United States from state encroachment.[181] It applies, not only to the direct taxation of federal securities, such as that involved in *Weston,* but also to the indirect taxation of such obligations as, for example, through their inclusion in a tax imposed on all the property of a taxpayer. Thus, a state tax on the capital stock of corporations could not be imposed upon a bank whose capital was invested in United States bonds.[182]

From this holding, it was an easy step to decide that the income from federal securities was also immune from state taxation. As the highest Court put it in a 1927 case, "where the principal is absolutely immune, no valid tax can be laid upon income arising therefrom. To tax this would amount practically to laying a burden on the exempted principal. Accordingly, if the challenged act . . . imposes a direct charge upon interest derived from United States bonds, it is pro tanto void." [183]

From the *Weston* case to this holding, the high bench had to move from the direct immunity of the United States itself to what was really the private immunity of those who happened to be holders of federal bonds. However, for a Court wedded, as we have seen, to the assumption that a tax on income was a tax on its source, the transition was a natural one. But the Supreme Court did not limit its holdings in this respect to the income received from United States obligations. Instead, it extended the concept of tax immunity so as to place under its protective umbrella almost all who had financial dealings with the Federal Government.

Some extreme cases will illustrate how far the high Court went. In *Gillespie v. Oklahoma* (1922),[184] a state tax upon the income of a lessee of Indian lands derived from the sale of oil produced on such lands was held invalid. According to the Court there, the lessee was "an instrumentality of the United States in carrying out duties to the Indians"; [185] a tax upon his "profits is a direct hamper upon the effort of the United States to make the best terms it can for its wards." [186] From this case it was a simple step to exempt all income derived from the leasing of government-owned land.[187] Taken with the contemporaneous rule applicable to government employees and contractors, the Court was in effect applying a wholesale rule of tax immunity for practically all financial interests derived from the Federal Government.[188]

Yet the Supreme Court did not even stop with such a broadside rule of immunity. Thus, in *Macallan Co. v. Massachusetts* (1929),[189] a state franchise tax on a corporation was declared invalid because interest from federal bonds was included in measuring the tax. And, in *Long v. Rockwood* (1928),[190] the Court actually went so far as to hold that a state could not tax the royalties received for the use of a patent granted by the United States. This was, indeed, the *reductio ad absurdum* of the Court's extension of immunity to those who dealt with the Government. Even the illustrations quoted from Justice Holmes at the beginning of this section are really no more extravagant than this decision. As Holmes himself put it, dissenting in *Long*: "Obviously it is not true that patents are instrumentalities of the government. They are used by the patentees for their private advantage alone." [191]

The more recent decisions, already discussed, removing the mantle of tax immunity from federal employees and government contractors, have also had their effect in the areas of private immunity just dealt with. A series of decisions during the 1930's expressly overruled the *Macallan, Long,* and *Gillespie* cases.[192] The most important of these was *Helvering v. Mountain Producers Corporation* (1938),[193] where the highest Court overruled both *Gillespie* and the broader holding that all income derived from the leasing of federal lands was exempt from state taxation. "Where," says Chief Justice Hughes, "it merely appears that one operating under a government contract or lease is subjected to a tax with respect to his profits on the same basis as others who are engaged in similar businesses, there is no sufficient ground for holding that the effect upon the Government is other than indirect and remote." [194]

The basic theme in the present law is thus the repudiation of private tax immunity—to refuse immunity from nondiscriminatory taxation sought by a private person for his property or gains because he is engaged in operations under a government contract or lease or has otherwise derived his interest from the United States.[195] In the words of the high bench itself: "this Court's more recent pronouncements have beaten a fairly large retreat from its formerly prevailing ideas concerning the breadth of so-called inter-governmental immunities from taxation, . . . to restrict the scope of immunity of private persons seeking to clothe themselves with governmental character from . . . state taxation." [196] Private persons can no longer claim immunity for their ordinary business operations (even though in connection with governmental activities) merely because the federal treasury may be remotely affected.[197]

It should, however, be pointed out that one area of private tax im-

munity still remains. This is the immunity from state taxation of obligations of the United States and the interest derived therefrom. There is little
doubt that the holding of *Weston v. Charleston* is still good law.[198] But the
ramifications of *Weston* already dealt with have also been followed in recent cases. Thus, a 1955 decision refuses to permit a state to tax the capital
of a bank insofar as such capital includes United States bonds.[199] Nor,
under the cases as they now stand, can the states validly reach the income
from federal securities.[200]

It is one thing to exempt obligations of the Federal Government from
direct taxation by the states. To permit such taxation is to give the states the
power directly to impede the exercise of the federal authority to borrow
money. The grant of that essential federal power "is incompatible with a
restraining or controlling power, and the declaration of supremacy is a
declaration that no such restraining or controlling power shall be exercised." [201] Yet, even if that be true, it is hard to see why it requires the
vesting in persons who happen to own federal securities of an exemption
from state taxes which all other like persons must pay. A nondiscriminatory
tax imposed on the capital of a corporation which happens to be invested
in federal securities is no more an interference with the Government's borrowing power than a tax upon a government contractor is an impairment
of the federal power to contract. Why should such corporation be vested
with private immunity from a tax which all others must pay?

The lack of justification for such private immunity is even clearer when
the income from federal securities is involved. The only rationale behind
such immunity is the theory that a tax on income is a tax on its source. As
already emphasized, that theory has generally been abandoned by the
Supreme Court. There is no more reason to apply it in the case of income
from federal securities than in the other cases discussed. Here, too, the basic
rule should be that the mere fact that property or income is derived from
the United States is insufficient to support the claim of tax exemption.[202]
"Why should one who enjoys all the advantages of a society purchased at
a heavy expense, and lives in affluence upon an income derived exclusively
from interest on government stock, be exempted from taxation?" [203]

20

SAME:
CONGRESSIONAL
POWER

Sections 15–19 deal with the constitutional power
of the states to impose taxes where the Congress has
made no provision in the matter. Under the Supremacy Clause, as it has been interpreted by the Supreme
Court, at the same time, it is established that the federal legislature has an
overriding authority in this field.

We have already seen that, except in cases involving federal securities, the private immunities, with which those deriving financial interests from the United States had been vested under the earlier case-law, have been done away with by the most recent decisions. Such private immunities can, nevertheless, be revived by the Congress itself, if it chooses to exercise its authority in this area. As it was stated by Justice Frankfurter: "in carrying on effectively the task committed to it, the United States can . . . go beyond the judicial doctrine of implied immunity from taxation. I have no doubt that Congress, by appropriate legislation, could immunize those who deal with the Government from sales and property taxes which States otherwise are free to impose." [204]

To put it another way, the high Court will not imply tax immunity in private citizens who deal with the United States simply because the federal treasury may ultimately be affected. But the possible financial burden does give the Congress the power to accord immunity. Congress not only has the authority to empower the performance of governmental functions; it also has the power to protect and preserve the operations thus validly authorized.[205] To safeguard such operations, tax immunity much wider than that implied from the Constitution alone may be conferred.

The Congressional authority in this respect may be seen from *Carson v. Roane-Anderson Co.,*[206] which denied to a state the power to apply its use tax to private contractors for the Atomic Energy Commission on goods purchased by such contractors for the performance of their contracts with the Commission. The decision was based entirely on a prohibition, contained in the federal law setting up the Atomic Energy Commission, of any state taxes upon AEC "activities," and on the finding that the contracts involved in the case and their performance were Commission "activities" within the meaning of the prohibition. The Congress, said the Court, clearly had the authority to confer such exemption from state taxes upon government contractors: "The power stems from the power to preserve and protect functions validly authorized . . . —the power to make all laws necessary and proper for carrying into execution the powers vested in the Congress." [207]

What is true of the government contractor is true also of others deriving financial interests from the Federal Government. Thus, the Congress has the authority to confer immunity from state taxes upon federal officials and other functionaries,[208] upon the lessees of federal lands,[209] and upon other private persons having financial dealings with the United States. It is consequently clear that what the Supreme Court (in decisions like *King and Boozer*) [210] giveth to the states, the Congress can take away.

But the converse of this is also true: what the high Court denies to the states, the Congress itself can give. It can expressly provide for the subjection to state taxation of federal property or activities. Hence, it can by law provide that the real property of a specified federal agency is to be subject to state or local taxes,[211] or it can provide for payments by particular agencies to state and local governments in lieu of property or other taxes.[212]

It should be emphasized that the question of whether any federal tax immunity should be renounced is solely one for the Congress. Similarly, it is discretionary with the Congress whether to reassert any immunity which may have been waived. Under the older cases, shares of national bank stock could not be taxed by the states.[213] By statute, Congress expressly permitted such taxation and the Supreme Court construed such permission to include state power to tax national bank shares held by a federal corporation.[214] At this, the Congress passed a law specifically exempting shares so held from taxation. To the claim that such statute was invalid, the Supreme Court stated: "When Congress authorized the states to impose such taxation, it did no more than gratuitously grant them political power which they theretofore lacked. Its sovereign power to revoke the grant remained unimpaired, the grant of the privilege being only a declaration of legislative policy changeable at will." [215]

21
SUPREMACY AND STATE POLICE POWER

What is true of state taxation is also basically true of state regulation under the police power. Here, too, the Supremacy Clause operates to bar state action. Under that clause, the Supreme Court has said, federal "dominance is required also to avoid a breakdown of administration through possible conflicts arising from inconsistent requirements. . . . A corollary to this principle is that the activities of the Federal Government are free from regulation by any state. No other adjustment of competing enactments or legal principles is possible." [216]

When the United States acts directly through its own officers or employees, state regulation is clearly barred, and the Supreme Court has consistently so held. The first important case was *Ohio v. Thomas* (1899),[217] in which the Court reversed the conviction of the officer in charge of a federal old soldiers' home for serving oleomargarine there in violation of a law of the state in which the home was located. Such federal officer was "not subject to the jurisdiction of the state in regard to those very matters of administration which are thus approved by federal authority." [218] Similarly, a state may not require that, before the construction of a federal dam may be undertaken within its boundaries, the approval of the state engineer must be obtained as prescribed by the state's laws; [219] nor may it subject fertilizer distributed by the Federal Government to farmers as part of a soil-building program to the provisions of a state inspection law, including the payment of inspection fees; [220] and a state may not regulate the rates to be charged by common carriers for the transportation of federally owned property.[221] To all these attempted exertions of state power, the short answer is that given by Justice Brandeis in 1931: "The United States may perform its functions without conforming to the police regulations of a state." [222]

Though federal agencies themselves thus may not be burdened by state regulations, it would be going too far to state unequivocally that all federal functionaries are completely exempt from state police power while going about their duties. Such officials cannot wholly escape every consequence arising from a fact so pervasive and insistent as is the fact of location in the midst of a civilized community whose orderly existence and continuance are dependent upon adherence to local, as well as national, laws.[223] Federal employees do not secure a general immunity from all state laws while acting in the course of their employment—but only from such laws as interfere with the functioning of the agencies by which they are employed.[224]

The dividing line in this respect may be illustrated by *Johnson v. Maryland*.[225] It arose out of the arrest and conviction by a state of a post-office employee driving a mail truck for not having obtained a state driver's license. The conviction was reversed by the Supreme Court. "It seems to us," states Justice Holmes, "that the immunity of the instruments of the United States from state control in the performance of their duties extends to a requirement that they desist from performance until they satisfy a state officer upon examination that they are competent for a necessary part of them and pay a fee for permission to go on. Such a requirement does not merely touch the Government servants remotely by a general rule of conduct. It lays hold of them in their specific attempt to obey orders and requires qualifications in addition to those that the Government has pronounced sufficient. It is the duty of the Department to employ persons competent for their work and that duty it must be presumed has been performed." [226]

In the course of his *Johnson* opinion, Justice Holmes distinguishes the case of what he terms "general rules that might affect incidentally the mode of carrying out the employment—as, for instance, a statute or ordinance regulating the mode of turning at the corners of streets." [227] In such a case, he concedes, the mail driver would, in the absence of federal law to the contrary, be subject to local law.

The federal employee is consequently subject to local police regulations which affect the performance of his functions only incidentally. The mail driver must, for example, follow local traffic regulations governing speed, traffic signals, and the like.[228] But the state law may not, as in the *Johnson* case, prescribe directly how the federal agency itself is to operate—as by imposing a requirement of fitness on its employees in addition to those demanded by the agency's own statutes and regulations.

Another case illustrating the line here is *Ex parte Willman*.[229] It reversed the conviction of a mail driver who had been convicted because the lights on his truck did not conform to the requirements of a state statute, where his lighting was that prescribed by post office regulations. In this case, as in *Johnson,* the state was attempting to regulate the Post Office Department itself. Where the Postmaster General prescribed the manner in which mail trucks were to be operated, the state could not interfere. On the other hand, had there been no federal rule on the matter, the mail driver might well have been subject to the state requirement. In such a case, adherence by the driver to the state safety regulation would affect performance of his duties only remotely.[230] Thus, in an early case, the driver of a mail stage was held bound by an ordinance prohibiting the driving of a carriage on runners without sleigh bells on the horses.[231]

A different situation arises where the state police power affects, not a federal agency or employee directly, but some private person, such as a government contractor, who may be doing work for the United States. As a general proposition, there is no more reason to grant immunity to such private person here than there is in the tax cases already discussed.[232] This is true even though the state regulation in question may involve an ultimate financial burden on the federal treasury. The tax cases tell us that such burden alone is not enough to justify the creation of private immunities in government contractors and others dealing with the United States.

The leading case upholding state regulation of government contractors is *Penn Dairies v. Milk Control Commission*.[233] The Supreme Court there sustained the refusal of a state regulatory commission to renew the license of a milk dealer who had violated the state's milk control law by selling milk to the United States at prices below the minima fixed by the commission. According to the Court, the minimum price regulation prescribed by the state law could constitutionally be applied to the sale of milk by a dealer to the United States, the sale being consummated within the territorial limits of the state in a place subject to its jurisdiction.[234] Though there is immunity from state regulation of the performance by federal agencies and their employees of their functions, "those who contract to furnish supplies or render services to the government are not such agencies and do not perform governmental functions." [235] The fact that the price which the United States has to pay for milk may be increased is not enough to lead to a different result. Such burdens, said the Court, as in the tax cases, "are to be regarded as the normal incidents of the operation within the same territory of a dual system of government, and . . . no immunity of the national government from such burdens is to be implied from the Constitution." [236]

As explained in another case, the *Penn Dairies* decision rests upon the fact that the state regulation "directly affected persons who were acting for themselves and not for the United States." [237] More difficult is the case where the contractor is clearly acting for a public purpose on behalf of the Federal Government. Such a case was *James Stewart and Co. v. Sadrakula*,[238] where the contractor was constructing a post office in New York City. One of its employees fell from an unplanked tier of steel beams and was killed. A New York statute required steel beams to be planked during construction work, and the trial court found that the proximate cause of the accident was the contractor's failure to plank the beams as required by the statute. The contractor contended, however, that the requirements of such state law could not be binding on one engaged in construction work for the United States. This contention was rejected by the Supreme Court. The state law, said it, must give way only where its enforcement would handicap efforts to carry out the plans of the United States: "May it be said that the continued application of [the New York statute] will interfere with the construction of the building upon this site? This is like other squares in the city. There are, of course, differentiations because of its ownership, but ownership as such has nothing to do with the safety requirements." [239]

The *Stewart* decision turns upon the fact that, to require the contractor to follow the New York safety regulation, while doing his work for the United States, would not interfere with the federal construction.[240] At the most, it would only mean an increase in expense. "It is true," the Court conceded, "that it is possible that the safety requirement of boarding over the steel tiers may slightly increase the cost of construction to the government, but such an increase is not significant in the determination of the applicability of the New York statute." [241] Under the present law, we have repeatedly emphasized, financial burden upon the Federal Government alone does not justify vesting immunity from state laws in private citizens.

What happens, all the same, if the state regulation does directly control the work which the contractor is performing for the United States? May the contractor be required, for example, to submit to the requirements of a local building code, which regulates in detail the manner in which buildings are to be constructed? Here, the answer must be a negative one.[242] To require the contractor to comply with the provisions of such building code is to subject the details of the federal construction to local supervision. In such a case, the local law does directly interfere with the construction of the federal building. The same is true of local zoning laws and laws requiring permits and submission to inspection by builders.[243] The temporary safety requirement at issue in the *Stewart* case does not affect the manner in which the federal building is to be constructed; the building code and zoning law do, on the contrary, tell the builder just how he is to do his building.

The government contractor, then, is not immune from state regulation, except where the state attempts to prescribe the manner in which he is to perform his contract with the United States. In such a case, the state is interfering directly with the performance of the government contract—an interference which clearly contravenes the Supremacy Clause.

It should, however, be noted that, in the field of state regulation, as in that of state taxation, the Congress has an overriding authority to modify the principles just discussed. Thus, the high Court, in its *Stewart* opinion, expressly recognized that Congress could, by appropriate legislation, exempt government contractors from all the requirements of state and local laws.[244] The Constitution, in Chief Justice Stone's phrase, has left Congress free to set aside both local taxation and local regulation of government contractors.[245] At the same time, as in the case of taxation, the Congress can subject federal property and activities to state regulation. As the Court put it, in a case already referred to: "It lies within Congressional power to authorize regulation . . . by the state of federal instrumentalities." [246]

22
SUPREMACY
AND STATE
IMMUNITIES

The starting point of governmental tax immunity, we have seen, was *McCulloch v. Maryland*.[247] Since Chief Justice Marshall's opinion there was based squarely upon the Supremacy Clause, the doctrine of immunity announced applied only to the Federal Government and its agencies. In the cases after Marshall's day, nevertheless, it was held that implicit in the *McCulloch* holding was a broad doctrine of intergovernmental immunity, which protected the states as well as the Government in Washington. As Justice Frankfurter has explained it, "The fear that one government may cripple or obstruct the operations of the other early led to the assumption that there was a reciprocal immunity of the instrumentalities of each from taxation by the other. It was assumed that there was an equivalence in the implications of taxation by a State of the governmental activities of the National Government and the taxation by the National Government of State instrumentalities." [248]

The leading case articulating the tax immunity of the states was *Collector v. Day* (1871).[249] "If the means and instrumentalities employed by that [i.e., the national] government to carry into operation the powers granted to it are, necessarily, and, for the sake of self-preservation, exempt from taxation by the States, why are not those of the States depending upon their reserved powers, for like reasons, equally exempt from Federal taxation?" asked the high Court there. In both cases, the Court declared: "the exemption rests upon necessary implication, and is upheld by the great law of self-preservation." [250] If, to put it another way, state power to tax federal agencies involves the power to destroy them, the same is also true of federal authority to tax state agencies.

In *Collector v. Day* itself, the salary of a state officer was held immune from federal taxation. At a time when the highest Court acted on the assumption that a tax on income was a tax on its source, such holding flowed logically from the view that the states were vested with tax immunity equivalent to that possessed by the Federal Government. And the same holding was reached with regard to federal taxation of state and local bonds and the interest thereon,[251] of sales by private contractors to state and local agencies,[252] and of income derived by the lessees of state-owned lands.[253] In all these cases, the Court erected areas of private tax immunity comparable to those which sheltered those who then had financial dealings with the Federal Government.[254]

With the abandonment already discussed by the Supreme Court, in the cases involving state taxation, of the theory that a tax on income is a tax on its source, it was only natural that *Collector v. Day* and its progeny, too, should be overruled.[255] The only area where doubt may still exist with regard to the possible existence of private immunity from federal taxation is in that of state and local bonds and other securities. There is probably as much ground for denying power in the Federal Government to tax such state securities directly as there was to deny a comparable power in the states vis-à-vis federal securities in *Weston v. Charleston*.[256] The same is not, however, true of a federal tax on the income derived from such bonds. Of course, as we have emphasized, the Congress has the authority to immunize such income from federal taxation.[257] As a matter of constitutional law, all the same, the only justification for immunity is the repudiated notion that a tax on income is a tax on its source. Despite some indications in the case-law to the contrary,[258] logical consistency would require the high bench to uphold the power of the Congress if it ever seeks to subject the income from state and local obligations to the federal income tax.

There is thus no longer any constitutional immunity from federal taxation for private persons who have dealings with the states, even though such taxation may impose a direct financial burden upon the states concerned. A more difficult question is that of the immunity of the states themselves and the agencies through which they operate. Of course, if the reasoning behind *Collector v. Day* were wholly valid, this question would not present any problems. *Collector v. Day* assumed an exact equivalence in immunity as between the states and the Federal Government. Since, as we have already seen, all federal agencies are wholly exempt from state taxes, regardless of the nature of the functions performed by them,[259] if *Collector v. Day* were correct in its assumption of equality as between states and nation in this respect, all state agencies would be similarly exempt from federal taxes.

If one thing has been settled by the more recent decisions, it is that the *Collector v. Day* assumption of equivalence in intergovernmental tax immunities was unwarranted. The immunities of the nation and the states do not stand upon an equal constitutional plane. As Justice Frankfurter expressed it in a 1946 case: "The considerations bearing upon taxation by the States of activities or agencies of the federal government are not correlative with the considerations bearing upon federal taxation of State agencies or activities. The federal government is the government of all the States, and all the States share in the legislative process by which a tax of general applicability is laid. 'The taxation by the State governments of the instruments employed by the general government in the exercise of its powers . . . is a very different thing. Such taxation involves an interference with the powers of a government in which other States and their citizens are equally interested with the State which imposes the taxation.' " [260]

The rule of federal immunity from state taxation is grounded squarely upon the Supremacy Clause, which covers with its protective umbrella all valid federal action. Since that is the case, there is no basis for distinguishing between different federal agencies because of the nature of the functions which they perform. Hence, as we have already seen, federal tax immunity does not depend upon the performance in the given case of a traditionally governmental, rather than proprietary, function.[261] But the same is not true of state immunity. Such immunity is based, not upon a categorical constitutional command like the Supremacy Clause, but upon implications arising from the very nature of our federalism. "In recognizing that implication for the first time," the high bench has said, "the Court was concerned with the continued existence of the states as governmental entities, and their preservation from destruction by the national taxing power. The immunity which it implied was sustained only because it was one deemed necessary to protect the states from destruction by the federal taxation of those governmental functions which they were exercising when the Constitution was adopted and which were essential to their continued existence." [262]

If that is true, state immunity extends only as far as is necessary to preserve the states themselves from destruction. It is consequently dependent on the nature of the function being performed by the state agency, and does not extend to such activities as might be thought not essential for the preservation of state government.[263] Only when a state agency is performing an essential governmental function is there constitutional immunity from federal taxes. If, on the contrary, the function being performed is not one traditionally associated with government, there is no exemption. In the highest Court's phrase, "The true distinction is between the attempted taxation of those operations of the states essential to the execution of its governmental functions, and which the state can only do itself, and those activities which are of a private character." [264]

This distinction has been settled since the 1905 case of *South Carolina v. United States*.[265] In it, the Supreme Court upheld the collection of the federal liquor tax from a state which had established a state-operated monopoly in the sale of liquor: "whenever a state engages in a business which is of a private character, that business is not withdrawn from the taxing power of the nation." [266]

Though the principle stated in the *South Carolina* case was reaffirmed in subsequent decisions,[267] it was again called into question in 1946 in *New York v. United States*.[268] That case arose out of an action by the Federal Government to recover taxes assessed against the State of New York on the sale of mineral waters taken from springs on state-owned land at Saratoga Springs and bottled and sold by a state agency. The federal tax in question is one imposed on all mineral waters sold in this country. New York claimed that it was immune from the tax, but its claim was rejected by the Supreme Court. In a case like this, the nation may tax the state activity upon the same basis as it does private individuals engaged in that activity. When a state enters the market place seeking customers, it divests itself of its immunity *pro tanto,* and takes on the character of a private trader, at least so far as the federal taxing power is concerned. "If Congress . . . ," said Justice Frankfurter, who announced the judgment of the Court, "taxes all vendors of mineral water alike, whether State vendors or private vendors, it simply says, in effect, to a State: 'You may carry out your own notions of social policy in engaging in what is called business, but you must pay your share in having a nation which enables you to pursue your policy.' " [269]

New York v. United States permits the Federal Government to include the states in levying a tax also exacted from private persons engaged in the same business. State immunity is thus restricted to traditional governmental activities. Only a state can own a Statehouse; only a state can carry on its essential governmental functions. Immunity from federal taxation is limited to such functions as we have traditionally known them. When a state takes over an activity men have been accustomed to carry on as a private and, therefore, taxable enterprise, then the activity can be taxed by the nation. In Justice Frankfurter's words, "so long as Congress generally taps a source of revenue by whomsoever earned and not uniquely capable of being earned only by a State, the Constitution of the United States does not forbid it merely because its incidence falls also on a State." [270]

Of course, the *New York* decision confirms the point already made that the basic theme of the law of tax immunity is not equality as between states and nation. The states are immune from federal taxation only with regard to activities deemed essential to their continuance as independent governments. But the Congress can tax all functions deemed nongovernmental—such as the sale of liquor or mineral waters—even though carried on by a state. As Chief Justice Stone put it, concurring in *New York:* "Not the extent to which a particular State engages in the activity, but the nature and extent of the activity by whomsoever performed is the relevant consideration." [271] The Federal Government, at the same time, as has been emphasized, remains wholly immune from state taxation—an immunity which is not at all affected by the nature of the particular function being performed.

What is true of state immunity from federal taxation is also true of state immunity from federal regulation. A federal regulatory law presumably could not operate to curtail the exercise by a state of its essential governmental functions. On the other hand, where a state engages in an activity not uniquely governmental, it can be subjected to any federal law that controls such activity. When a state, for example, operates a railroad, such railroad must comply with the requirements of the Federal Safety Appliance Act.[272] Similarly, such state-owned railroad is subject to the regulatory jurisdiction of the Interstate Commerce Commission [273] and its wages and working conditions are governed by the Federal Railway Labor Act.[274] This is true even though the latter statute conflicts with the state's civil service laws, which had theretofore governed labor conditions on its railroad. The same principle applies whenever a state engages in a nongovernmental activity that is otherwise regulated by federal law.

Here again, the basic legal picture is not one of equality between states and nation. While the states may be regulated in their nongovernmental activities by the Federal Government, all of the latter's agencies are, as we have seen, wholly immune from the state police power, regardless of the nature of the functions performed by them.[275] If this, at first glance, seems unfair, it is nonetheless compelled by the Supremacy Clause. Fairness, it may be said, demands reciprocity in immunities, as between states and nation. It does not, however, follow that such fairness must have a constitutional foundation.[276]

23

GUARANTY OF
REPUBLICAN
GOVERNMENT

Federalism, to function properly, implies obligations, as well as powers, on the part of the Central Government. Article IV, section 4, of the Constitution expressly imposes important obligations to the states upon the Federal Government. Under it, the United States shall guarantee to every state "a Republican Form of Government" and shall protect each of them against invasion and domestic violence.

The purpose of the guaranty of a republican form of government, according to Cooley, "is to protect a Union founded on republican principles, and composed entirely of republican members against aristocratic and monarchical innovations." [277] The Constitution, however, nowhere tells us what the republican principles that are to govern state political institutions are. In a 1793 case, Justice Wilson gave the following as his short definition of a government that is republican: "one constructed on this principle, that the supreme power resides in the body of the people." [278] In actuality, the constitutional provision may be interpreted as requiring a form somewhere between a monarchy or oligarchy, on the one hand, and a pure democracy, on the other.[279] The constitutional guaranty is aimed as much at the latter, as at the former extreme.[280]

The Constitution, in this respect, is plainly based upon the notion that republican institutions are a signal benefit which the nation is to guarantee to the people of each state, and which the latter can demand, as a right, from the Federal Government.[281] But the organic instrument is not clear on the means by which the guaranty is to be made effective in practice. The "United States" is designated as the guarantor, but the Constitution does not specify what branch of the Government is responsible for effectuating the guaranty.

In the great case of *Luther v. Borden* (1849),[282] it was claimed that the right to a republican form of government was one that could be enforced by the federal courts. The case grew out of the so-called Dorr Rebellion in Rhode Island in 1841. That state was then still operating under the royal charter which had been granted in 1663. It provided for a very limited suffrage and, worse still from the point of view of those who considered it completely out of date, it contained no procedure by which amendments might be made. Popular dissatisfaction led to mass meetings in 1841, which resulted in the election of a convention to draft a new constitution. A new constitution was then drawn up providing for universal suffrage. Elections were held under it and Dorr was elected governor. All these acts were completely unauthorized by the existing charter government, which declared martial law and called out the militia to repel the threatened attack. In addition, it appealed to the Federal Government for aid, and the President, expressly recognizing the charter government as the rightful government of the state, took steps to extend the necessary help, declaring that he would use armed force if that should prove necessary. The announcement of the President's determination in this respect caused Dorr's Rebellion soon to die out. *Luther v. Borden,* decided several years later, was left by it as its constitutional legacy.

The actual case arose out of the efforts of the charter government to suppress the Dorr Rebellion. When one of its agents broke into the house of a strong Dorr supporter and arrested him, the latter brought an action of trespass. Defendant justified his action by the plea that he was acting under the authority of the legal government of the state. Plaintiff countered with the contention that the charter government was not republican in form as required by the Constitution. Therefore, he asserted, that government had no valid existence and the acts of its agents were not justified in law. Essentially, he was claiming that the action of the charter government violated his constitutional right to live under a republican government and that such claim was cognizable in a court.

The Supreme Court rejected this claim, denying that it was within judicial competence to apply the constitutional guaranty. On the contrary, the enforcement of such guaranty is solely for the Congress. Under Article IV, section 4, declares the opinion of Chief Justice Taney: "it rests with Congress to decide what government is the established one in a State . . . , as well as its republican character." [283] Moreover the Congressional decision in the matter is not subject to any judicial scrutiny: "its decision is binding on every other department of the government, and could not be questioned in a judicial tribunal." [284]

Likewise, it is up to the Congress "to determine upon the means proper to be adopted to fulfill this guarantee." [285] Under an act of 1795,[286] that body had delegated to the President the responsibility of determining when the Federal Government should interfere to effectuate the constitutional guaranty, and, in this case, as already pointed out, the President had acted to support the charter government. After such action by the President, asked Taney, "is a circuit court of the United States authorized to inquire whether his decision was right? Could the court, while the parties were actually contending in arms for the possession of the government, call witnesses before it and inquire which party represented a majority of the people? . . . If the judicial power extends so far, the guarantee contained in the Constitution of the United States is a guarantee of anarchy, and not of order." [287]

Since *Luther v. Borden* (later referred to by Chief Justice White as "the leading and absolutely controlling case" on the subject),[288] it has been settled that it is not for the federal courts to consider whether the guaranty contained in Article IV, section 4, has been violated. Thus, the high Court has refused to consider whether the provision in a state constitution of machinery for direct participation by the people in legislation by initiative and referendum deprived the state of a republican form of government.[289] Similar results were reached with regard to claimed violations of the constitutional guaranty because of a delegation of legislative power to a state administrative agency,[290] the improper determination of a gubernatorial election contest by a state legislature,[291] or the fact that a state did not permit women to vote.[292] In all these cases, said the Court, the question of enforcement of Article IV, section 4, is solely for the political departments of the Federal Government.

In *Luther v. Borden* itself, it had been argued that an uncontrollable power in the political branches might easily be abused.[293] To this, the Supreme Court answered that the possibility of abuse is no ground for denying the existence of a power. As a general proposition, this is doubtless true, but it hardly answers the question of whether a given power can safely be rendered beyond all judicial review. "All power," says the Taney opinion, "may be abused if placed in unworthy hands. But it would be difficult, we think, to point out any other hands in which this power would be more safe." [294] Yet, is this not only another attempt to reconcile us to the dangers inherent in absolute power by the magic word *confidence?* In truth, as Marshall pointed out in classic terms in *McCulloch v. Maryland,*[295] the question has nothing at all to do with confidence.

What uncontrollable power in the political departments to enforce the guaranty of republican government can mean in practice is shown by the authority assumed by the Congress over the reconstruction of governments in the southern states after the Civil War. It has already been emphasized that the guaranty contained in Article IV, section 4, is in the form of an obligation by the Federal Government to the people of the states: it is the duty of the former to ensure to the latter that they will live under a republican form of government. If, however, enforcement of the guaranty is left in the absolute discretion of the Congress, there is no legal check to restrain that body from converting the obligation imposed upon them into a source of tremendous power. In writing about the constitutional provision in question in *The Federalist,* Madison acutely asked "whether it may not become a pretext for alteration in the State governments without the concurrence of the States themselves." [296] The possibility referred to became an actuality at the end of the Civil War.

In *Texas v. White,*[297] the highest Court construed the Guaranty Clause of Article IV, section 4, as authorizing the Congress to establish and maintain governments in those states which had attempted to secede. But the Congress did not limit itself to ensuring to the people of the southern states the establishment of republican governments responsible to themselves. Instead it assumed complete control over the reconstruction of government in those states. Governments were imposed and retained in power by military force during the entire reconstruction period; these governments the Congress termed republican in form, though they were instituted against the will of most of the citizens of the states concerned.[298]

There may well have been justification for treating the postbellum South as occupied territory to be ruled by military governments established by the occupying power. There was none for perverting the constitutional form and doing utter violence to the Guaranty Clause. At the same time, from the legal point of view alone, it is plain that the decision in *Luther v. Borden* vested uncontrollable authority in the matter in the Congress. The holding of *Luther v. Borden,* the opinion in *Texas v. White* affirms, can be applied "with even more propriety" to the situation after the Civil War: then, too, "the power to carry into effect the clause of guaranty is . . . a legislative power, and resides in Congress." [299]

24

INVASION AND
DOMESTIC
VIOLENCE

In addition to the Guaranty Clause just discussed, Article IV, section 4 provides that the United States "shall protect each of them [i.e., the states] against Invasion; and on Application of the Legislature, or of the Executive (when the Legislature cannot be convened) against domestic Violence."

About the protection against invasion, little need be said. Such protection is, in Madison's phrase, "due, from every society, to the parts composing it." [300] The constitutional provision in this respect is simply a corollary of the power of the nation to defend itself. Of course, it is clear that no court could order the Federal Government to discharge its duty to furnish such protection. But it is inconceivable that the obligation would be violated, while the nation retained any of the physical force needed to fulfill it.[301]

The obligation to guarantee the states against domestic violence is similarly one whose performance has been held not subject to judicial control. In *Luther v. Borden,*[302] Chief Justice Taney stated, with regard to the Domestic-Violence Clause, "It rested with Congress, too, to determine upon the means proper to be adopted to fulfill this guarantee." [303] The Congress, he went on, might have "placed it in the power of a court to decide when a contingency had happened which required the Federal Government to interfere. But Congress thought otherwise." [304] By the act of 1795, mentioned in the prior section, it authorized the President to use armed force "in case of an insurrection in any State." [305] By this law, said Taney, "the power of deciding whether the exigency had arisen upon which the government of the United States is bound to interfere, is given to the President." [306]

It may be apprehended that the uncontrollable power thus vested in the political branches to enforce the Domestic-Violence Clause can be subjected to the same type of abuse that was noted in the prior section in connection with the Republican-Guaranty Clause. The draftsmen of the clause in question sought, nevertheless, to avoid this danger by inserting the requirement that federal intervention be applied for by the state concerned. "Every pretext," declares Justice Story, "for intermeddling with the domestic concerns of any state, under colour of protecting it against domestic violence, is taken away by that part of the provision, which renders an application from the legislature, or executive authority of the state endangered necessary to be made to the general government, before its interference can be at all proper." [307]

The safeguard referred to might well be entirely adequate if the only authority of the Federal Government to deal with domestic violence were that derived from Article IV, section 4. It is clear, however, that the Government in Washington, like the possessor of political power in any other society, has the inherent power of self-preservation, which includes the authority to deal with disorder and violence. In confirmation of this necessary attribute of any effective national government, the Framers expressly provided, in Article I, section 8, that the Congress shall have power "To provide for calling forth the Militia to execute the Laws of the Union, suppress Insurrections and repel Invasions."

Here, too, the Congress has delegated the authority to exercise the power in question to the President. The act of 1795, already referred to, in addition to empowering the President to use force to suppress an insurrection in any state, on application of its legislature or governor, goes on to authorize the President to act as well on his own motion, under the power given in Article I, section 8. Under it, "whenever the laws of the United States shall be opposed, or the execution thereof obstructed, in any state, by combinations too powerful to be suppressed by the ordinary course of judicial proceedings," the President may call forth the militia to suppress such combinations and cause the laws to be obeyed.[308]

As a matter of practical reality, the provision of the 1795 statute just quoted, taken together with the clause of Article I, section 8, upon which it is based, vest in the Federal Government the power to deal with domestic violence, though there has been no request for assistance from the state concerned, and even, it should be noted, over the strong opposition of the latter's officials. Those engaged in acts of violence within a state do not normally proceed according to the niceties of theoretical federalism. Their actions are threats against law and order generally—without regard to the nuances between federal and state competence. Any such threats, if he considers them serious enough, can be deemed by the President to justify resort to armed force, on his own motion, under the act of 1795.

The breadth of the federal power in this respect is well shown by *In re Debs*,[309] which arose out of the use of troops to cope with domestic violence by President Cleveland in 1894. A strike against the Pullman Company, accompanied by violence on both sides, had caused an almost complete shutdown of railroads operating out of Chicago. The United States Attorney in that city had obtained an injunction against Eugene Debs and other leaders of the union, ordering them not to interfere with the mails or to obstruct interstate commerce. The injunction had no effect and violence in the area began to reach alarming proportions. At this, the federal marshal informed Washington that this was an emergency with which he was unable to contend. The President then ordered federal troops into Chicago to restore order and railroad operations.

In the *Debs* case itself, the Supreme Court upheld contempt convictions of the union leaders for their disobedience of the injunction. In the course of the opinion, however, the power of the President to act was considered and sustained in strong language: "The entire strength of the nation may be used to enforce in any part of the land the full and free exercise of all national powers and the security of all rights entrusted by the Constitution to its care. The strong arm of the national Government may be put forth to brush away all obstructions to the freedom of interstate commerce or the transportation of the mails. If the emergency arises, the army of the Nation, and all its militia, are at the service of the Nation to compel obedience to its laws." [310]

The federal power to act against domestic violence was thus upheld, even though there had been no request from the state for assistance.[311] Since the broad holding of the *Debs* case, in fact, the limitation contained in the Domestic-Violence Clause has been of little, if any, practical importance. When the Federal Government finds it necessary or proper to use armed force to quell domestic violence, it can rely on its power to suppress insurrection, remove obstructions to its laws, protect its property, prevent interference with the mail, or protect interstate commerce from interruption by labor disputes or otherwise.[312] These will furnish adequate legal warrant for its action, without any need to rely on the Domestic-Violence Clause.

Recent illustrations of this were the use of troops by President Eisenhower in 1957 in Little Rock, Arkansas, and by President Kennedy in 1962 in Oxford, Mississippi, to secure enforcement of federal court orders providing for desegregation in local educational facilities. Such orders had originally been frustrated by the action of the governors of the states concerned, who had used state officers to bar the Negro students. The relevant federal courts then issued injunctions against the state officials, but their enforcement was also prevented, in the case of Little Rock, by mob violence which the local police could not control,[313] and, in the case of Oxford, by direct action by the governor and other state officials, aided by mob violence. Eisenhower and Kennedy, acting under the modern derivative of the Act of 1795,[314] then dispatched federal troops to the scene, and, under their protection, admission of the Negro students to the school and university concerned was effected. In his order directing the use of troops, President Eisenhower declared that such action was necessary because of the willful obstruction of enforcement of the federal court orders: "such willful obstruction of justice hinders the execution of the laws of that State and of the United States, and makes it impracticable to enforce such laws by the ordinary course of judicial proceedings." [315] A like statement is contained in Mr. Kennedy's similar order.[316]

Though the propriety of the Presidential dispatch of troops to Little Rock and Oxford may have been a subject of some contemporary controversy, from a legal point of view, the *Debs* decision makes it plain that such action was well within the Presidential authority.[317] This is true even though the federal intervention was bitterly opposed by the governors of the states concerned. Since the Presidents' orders, while clearly aimed at mob violence, were not issued under the Domestic-Violence Clause, their ability to act was not dependent upon any request for assistance from the relevant state officials.

25

EXPANSION OF THE UNION   One of the great virtues of the Constitution has been its provision for territorial expansion of the Union. This has enabled a federation originally limited to the Atlantic seaboard to grow to continental extent and, in recent years, to spread even beyond the North American mainland.

To be sure, territorial expansion is anything but new in the history of nations. Much of man's record, in truth, is nothing more than an account of the physical ebbs and flows of empire. What is novel about the American experience in this respect is the basic rejection of the notion of conquest as determining the status of newly acquired territory. From the very beginning of the Republic, the fundamental principle was that no area that should, by conquest, cession, or purchase, come within the control of the United States should permanently be held in a territorial status.[318] On the contrary, the Constitution contemplates that territory acquired by this country should in due time be formed and organized into states and, as such, admitted into full and equal partnership in the Union. The Constitution, in Chief Justice Taney's words, "has been held to authorize the acquisition of territory, not fit for admission at the time, but to be admitted as soon as its population and situation would entitle it to admission. It is acquired to become a State, and not to be held as a colony and governed by Congress with absolute authority." [319]

Article IV, section 3, provides that "New States may be admitted by the Congress into this Union." As just pointed out, the contemplation of the Framers was that newly acquired territory would be formed into states as soon as practicable. It is, at the same time, settled that the question of when a particular territory should be admitted as a state is one solely for the political departments.[320] The Congressional judgment in this respect is not subject to any judicial control.[321] The Constitution does not provide how the admission of a new state is to be effected. The customary procedure has been for the Congress to admit new states by joint resolution. As such, admission has been subject to the President's veto power, which has, to that extent, made him a participant in the admission process.

The only limitation contained upon the Congressional power of admission is the provision of Article IV, section 3, prohibiting the formation of a new state within the jurisdiction of an existing state or by the junction of two or more states or parts of states "without the Consent of the Legislatures of the States concerned as well as of the Congress." This limitation, it should be noted, is one that can be violated by the political branches without legal remedy, since, as noted above, their decision with regard to admission is conclusive on the courts. During the Civil War, after Virginia had seceded, the State of West Virginia was formed from that portion of Virginia territory which remained loyal to the Union. The consent of Virginia to the cession was given by what was actually a rump legislature from the area concerned convened especially for the purpose. In effect, in consenting to the admission of the new state in these circumstances, the political departments practically decided that, when a state sought to secede, any part of it, however small, which remained loyal, might maintain a government for the whole state, and that this government might give consent to the erection of a new state within the limits of the old.[322]

The Constitution itself does not expressly prescribe the terms upon which new states are to be admitted. It is, nevertheless, basic that equality is the dominant theme of the American Union. When once admitted, therefore, a new state stands upon an equal footing with all existing states.[323] "Equality of constitutional right and power is the condition of all the States of the Union, old and new." [324]

Despite this basic rule of equality, the Congress has not infrequently sought to impose preadmission restrictions upon new states, as conditions precedent to Congressional consent to admission. These have ranged from the requirement exacted of Ohio that it pass a law, irrevocable without the consent of Congress, not to tax for five years all public lands sold by the United States, to the requirement imposed on Nevada that her Constitution should harmonize with the Declaration of Independence and that the right to vote should not be denied persons because of their color, to that subjecting Utah to a perpetual prohibition of polygamy.

Such restrictions, which place a new state under political restrictions other than those imposed upon all the states by the Federal Constitution, patently contravene the basic rule of state equality and are unenforceable after the state has been admitted. As the highest Court put it, with regard to certain limitations placed upon Illinois: "Whatever the limitations upon her powers as a government while in a territorial condition . . . , it ceased to have any operative force, except as voluntarily adopted by her after she became a State of the Union. On her admission, she at once became entitled to and possessed of all the rights of dominion and sovereignty which belonged to the original States. She was admitted and could be admitted only on the same footing with them." [325]

A striking case always cited to illustrate the invalidity of preadmission conditions is *Coyle v. Smith*.[326] Oklahoma had been admitted as a state only upon the condition inserted in the admission statute that the state capital should be located at Guthrie for at least seven years. Notwithstanding this condition, the state legislature (after only four years) passed a law providing for the immediate removal of the capital to Oklahoma City. This law was found valid by the Supreme Court, which held the state not bound by the Congressional restriction. The power of Congress in this respect, declares the opinion, "is to admit 'new States into *this* Union.' 'This Union' was and is a union of States, equal in power, dignity and authority." [327] A state is not on an equal footing with the others if she cannot determine the proper location of her seat of government.

It should, however, be pointed out that the "equal footing" concept has, in the 1950 phrase of the high bench, long been held to refer only to political rights and to sovereignty; it does not include proprietary interests of states and nation.[328] Thus, preadmission requirements which do not affect equality of political power, but only reflect diversity in economic ownership as between states and nation will be upheld. In the Supreme Court's words, "The requirement of equal footing was designed not to wipe out those diversities but to create parity as respects political standing and sovereignty." [329]

The leading case on restrictions involving proprietary interests is *Stearns v. Minnesota*.[330] At issue there was an agreement imposed on the state which limited its right to tax lands given to it by the United States at the time of its admission, which were subsequently to be granted to a railroad. In upholding this agreement, the high tribunal emphasized the difference between preadmission agreements in reference to political rights and obligations and those solely in reference to property: "a mere agreement in reference to property involves no question of equality of status, but only of the power of a State to deal with the Nation . . . in reference to such property." [331]

The "equal footing" theory has nonetheless been held applicable to the property rights of new states to the soil under their navigable waters. In an early case, *Pollard v. Hagan*,[332] it was held that the original states had reserved to them the ownership of the soil under their navigable waters; under the doctrine of equality, the title to such soil passed to a new state upon admission, regardless of the provisions of any preadmission requirement.

In the more recent case of *United States v. Texas*,[333] the converse of the *Pollard* decision was applied. In 1943, the Supreme Court had refused to extend *Pollard* to the three-mile belt along the coasts, holding that the original states had not owned the soil beneath such belt.[334] In the *Texas* case, it was conceded that, since Texas had been an independent nation before admission, it had owned its coastal belt. But, said the Court (in effect, showing that the "equal footing" theory can be a two-edged sword for the states), Texas surrendered its dominion over its coastal belt when it entered the Union on terms of equality with the existing states. The "equal footing" concept, declares Justice Douglas, "prevents extension of the sovereignty of a State into a domain of political and sovereign power . . . from which the other States have been excluded, just as it prevents a contraction of sovereignty . . . which would produce inequality among the States." [335]

26

COOPERATIVE FEDERALISM: BETWEEN STATES AND NATION

Through much of American history, the emphasis has been upon the competitive nature of our federalism. Such emphasis has perhaps been inevitable in a system based upon a sharp division of authority between states and nation. This has led to constant litigation on the question of where the line between state and federal power is to be drawn in particular fields. Not unnaturally, the attention of constitutional lawyers has been focused almost entirely upon the rivalry between the two centers of government in seeking to have the boundary placed so as to involve the least possible curtailment of their own authority.

Reflection will demonstrate, however, that cooperation must be at least as prominent a feature as competition in any successful federation. To be sure, some friction will always occur from the operation of two governments within the same territorial area. Such inevitable friction should not, all the same, obscure the fact that the wheels of government have continued to turn and to do so to the mutual benefit of both centers. Comity, rather than conflict, has been the day-to-day working principle of our Union.

From a legal point of view, cooperation between states and nation may give rise to certain problems. The type of problem referred to is illustrated by *Ponzi v. Fessenden*.[336] At issue there was the power of the Attorney General of the United States to authorize the transfer of a federal prisoner to a state court to be put on trial upon indictments there pending against him. The prisoner urged that there was no express authority permitting such transfer; hence, no such power existed. The Supreme Court rejected this argument, finding the necessary power in the basic need for cooperation between state and federal authorities. "We live," declared Chief Justice Taft, "in the jurisdiction of two sovereignties, each having its own system of courts to declare and enforce its laws in common territory. It would be impossible for such courts to fulfill their respective functions without embarrassing conflict unless rules were adopted by them to avoid it. The people for whose benefit these two systems are maintained are deeply interested that each system shall be effective and unhindered in its vindication of its laws. The situation requires, therefore, not only definite rules fixing the powers of the courts in cases of jurisdiction over the same persons and things in actual litigation, but also a spirit of reciprocal comity and mutual assistance to promote due and orderly procedure." [337]

The spirit of cooperation referred to by Taft makes it possible for either government to permit its agents to act on behalf of the other. In actual fact, indeed, the Federal Government has frequently availed itself of the services of state officers and agencies in carrying out its own governmental powers.[338] This has been done from the very founding of the Republic. The first Congress, in 1789, authorized state justices of the peace to issue warrants for the arrest of offenders against federal laws and to admit such offenders to bail.[339] The Fugitive Slave Act of 1793, the Naturalization Act of 1795, and the Alien Enemy Act of 1798—all of these made use of state courts to enforce their provisions.[340] More recently, state officials have been employed by the Federal Government in the exercise of its power of eminent domain, and in the enforcement of the national selective service and prohibition laws.[341]

For the nation thus to entrust state officials with the enforcement of federal laws would appear to raise no constitutional question. As the high Court summarily put it, in the 1918 *Selective Draft Law Cases:* "We are of opinion that the contention that the act is void as a delegation of Federal power to State officials because of some of its administrative features is too wanting in merit to require further notice." [342]

A more difficult matter is that of the obligation of the states to lend their officials to the execution of federal statutes. Of course, if the states consent to such execution, there is no legal problem. But, in the absence of state consent, can the National Government, in effect, impose upon state officials any duty to enforce federal laws?

Under the earlier cases, the existence of any such authority in the nation was denied. In the words of Chief Justice Taney in 1861: "we think it clear that the Federal government, under the Constitution, has no power to impose on a state officer, as such, any duty whatever, and compel him to perform it." [343]

Such a view ignores the effect of the Supremacy Clause upon the problem under discussion. The fact that state officers derive their existence and functions from state laws is no reason for them to be free from federal laws. On the contrary, they are subject also to the laws of the United States, and are just as much bound to recognize these as operative within their state as they are to recognize the state's own laws.[344] The more recent cases repudiate the assumption that federal laws can in this respect be considered by the states as though they were laws emanating from a foreign sovereign. Such laws, under the Supremacy Clause, are the supreme law of the land. If valid, they must be obeyed by state officials regardless of the means of execution they provide.[345] Under the Constitution, it is for the Congress to choose the machinery which it considers necessary and proper for carrying into execution the powers granted to it.

That this is, in fact, the present view of the Supreme Court is shown by *Testa v. Katt*.[346] It arose out of a provision of the Emergency Price Control Act of 1942, under which a person who had been charged more than the ceiling prices prescribed under the Act could bring suit for treble damages in "any court of competent jurisdiction"—federal, state, or territorial. In *Testa* itself, suit was brought in a state court in Rhode Island, but the highest court of that state held that the federal statute in question was a "penal statute" which the state courts could not be required to enforce. The Supreme Court reversed. The state court's decision, said Justice Black, "flies in the face of the fact that the States of the Union constitute a nation" [347] and disregards the purpose and effect of the Supremacy Clause. State officers and agencies "do not bear the same relation to the United States that they do to foreign countries." [348] Under the Supremacy Clause, the states are bound by the provisions of federal laws, even though they may be contrary to local laws and policies: "the obligations of states to enforce these federal laws is not lessened by reason of the form in which they are cast or the remedy which they provide." [349]

Testa v. Katt shows that even the concept of cooperative federalism is dominated by the Supremacy Clause. The Federal Government may avail itself of the services of state officers to carry out its laws. In the normal case, to be sure, the states will voluntarily consent to lend their aid to the nation. Yet, even if they choose not to cooperate, that does not end the matter. The Supremacy Clause enables the Government in Washington to compel the states to use their officials to execute federal laws. Thus, co-operative federalism has behind it the ultimate sanction of federal coercion —contradiction in terms though that may be.

27

SAME: BETWEEN THE STATES   The fundamental principle governing the relations between states and nation, we have seen at length, is that articulated in the Supremacy Clause: federal laws validly enacted prevail over all other legislation, throughout the length and breadth of the Republic. The relations that exist between the states have an entirely different basis. The dominant theme here is not the Supremacy Clause, but the basic equality of the component parts of the Union. From a legal point of view, unless otherwise provided by the Constitution, the states stand toward one another as independent, equivalent political entities. The laws of a state, unlike those of the nation, can have no overriding effect outside the boundaries of the state concerned. In the words of a Supreme Court Justice over a century ago, "no State . . . can enact laws to operate beyond its own dominions." [350]

Even more so than is the case between states and nation, cooperation must be the guiding principle in the relations between the states. Where those concerned are equals, with none possessing an overriding power such as that derived by the Federal Government from the Supremacy Clause, comity alone can prevent the discordances that might otherwise char-acterize interstate relations. It is true that, to some extent, the Constitution itself imposes a legal duty upon the states to cooperate. Thus, under the Full-Faith-and-Credit Clause, each state must give effect within its bound-aries "to the public Acts, Records, and judicial Proceedings of every other State." Similarly, under what is usually termed the Comity Clause,[351] no state is permitted to discriminate against citizens of other states in favor of its own. But these are essentially the only constitutional provisions that impose legal compulsion upon the states in their relationships with one another. Aside from them, interstate relations can be governed only by comity—not coercion.

That this is true is strikingly shown by the 1861 case of *Kentucky v. Dennison*.[352] Under Article IV, section 2, "A person charged in any State with Treason, Felony, or other Crime, who shall flee from Justice, and be found in another State, shall on Demand of the executive Authority of the State from which he fled, be delivered up, to be removed to the State having Jurisdiction of the Crime." In 1793, the Congress passed a law imposing upon the governors the duty to deliver up fugitives from other states.[353] In the *Dennison* case, the Governor of Ohio refused a request from the Governor of Kentucky to surrender a fugitive from justice in the latter state. Kentucky then brought an action in the Supreme Court for a writ of mandamus to compel Ohio to turn over the fugitive. The high bench held that the writ could not issue. Neither the Constitution nor the Act of 1793 provided any means to compel the performance of a governor's duty of extradition. In effect, then, the duty of extradition is a mere moral duty which cannot be enforced by the federal courts.

Another question would be presented if the federal statute on the matter were interpreted as compelling the state governors to surrender fugitives. Though the *Dennison* opinion itself denies the power of the National Government to impose any such duty on state officials,[354] under the more recent cases, as we saw in the prior section, such federal law would be valid. The Act of 1793 itself, however, was construed in *Dennison* as not indicating an intent on the part of its draftsmen to exercise such a coercive power. The performance of the duty of extradition is "left to depend on the fidelity of the state executive." [355] Rendition of fugitives is consequently entirely a question of interstate cooperation—"a matter of comity, which the several sovereignties have extended to one another for their mutual benefit." [356]

The Constitution itself clearly contemplates cooperative action among the states in the Compact Clause of Article I, section 10. Under it, "No State shall, without the Consent of Congress . . . enter into any Agreement or Compact with another State." Subject to the requirement of Congressional consent, the states can enter into any agreement among themselves. Indeed, under *Virginia v. Tennessee*,[357] the need for Congressional consent itself does not exist in the case of all interstate agreements. According to the Court: "There are many matters upon which different States may agree that can in no respect concern the United States." [358] Such matters include the minor adjustment of boundaries,[359] construction of a bridge or railroad,[360] and other matters which can have no impact on the balance between state and federal power. The prohibition of interstate compacts without Congressional consent, said the Court, "is directed to the formation of any combination tending to the increase of political power in the States, which may encroach upon or interfere with the just supremacy of the United States." [361]

The compact technique itself has its roots deep in colonial history. It is part and parcel of the long and familiar story of colonial boundary disputes, which were usually resolved by negotiation.[362] "Adjustment by compact . . . of existing rights," the Supreme Court informs us, "had been practiced in the Colonies, was practiced by the States before the adoption of the Constitution." [363] During the first century or so of our existence as an independent nation, the experience under the Compact Clause duplicated that before 1789. Boundary disputes constituted the stuff of almost all interstate agreements until almost our own day.

During the present century, however, the compact technique has expanded to meet the growing need for interaction in the affairs of the several states. As the high bench has put it, "The growing interdependence of regional interests, calling for regional adjustments, has brought extensive use of compacts." [364] The interstate compact has been used to an increasing extent as an instrument for state cooperation in carrying out joint programs to deal with common problems. The most noted such use of the compact clause was the execution in 1921 between New York and New Jersey of a compact creating the Port of New York Authority (an interstate administrative agency) to develop and operate harbor and transportation facilities in the bistate area comprising the Greater New York metropolitan area. More recently, in 1953, the same two states set up a commission to regulate employment practices along the New York waterfront. In recent years, compacts between different states have covered the conservation of natural gas and other resources, civil defense, regulation of fishing, mutual sharing of waterpower, flood and pollution control, production of tobacco, and many other matters.[365]

A compact between states, duly entered into and ratified by the Congress,[366] has all the binding effect of a valid federal law. In this respect, it is not entirely accurate to say, as is often done, that a compact has the same legal effect as a treaty between sovereign powers.[367] If a treaty is violated, there is no legal sanction to compel compliance with its terms.[368] The same is not true of a compact between states of the American Union. In *West Virginia v. Sims*,[369] West Virginia had entered into a compact with seven other states to control pollution in the Ohio River basin. After the Congress had consented to the compact, the highest court of the state held that it violated the state constitution and was consequently not binding on the state. The Supreme Court reversed, declaring that a state cannot unilaterally decide that a compact violates its constitution and use that as a basis for withdrawal: "If the compact system is to have vitality and integrity, she may not raise an issue of *ultra vires*, decide it, and release herself from an interstate obligation." [370]

The sanction that is lacking in international law to enforce the principle *pacta sunt servanda* thus exists insofar as the adaptation of the treaty-making power to interstate relations in the American Union is concerned. "A State," declares the high Court in the *Sims* case, "cannot be its own ultimate judge in a controversy with a sister State." [371] But this is the basic principle which governs all interstate relations which give rise to justiciable controversies. Such relations will, as already pointed out, normally proceed upon a cooperative basis, comity being the only feasible guiding principle between equal political entities. Disputes arising from such relations may be resolved in particular matters by a legislative means [372]—the interstate compact. Where that is not feasible, the dispute may in appropriate cases be brought before the Supreme Court as a controversy between states. The high tribunal's jurisdiction in such cases will be discussed at a later point.[373] Suffice it to say here that, in deciding cases between states, the Supreme Court's function is analogous to that of an international tribunal [374]—with the added element of a legal sanction behind the Court's decisions, i.e., the essential that is so sorely lacking in international law itself.[375]

3

THE CONGRESS

28
NATURE OF
LEGISLATIVE
POWER *I*N CONSIDERING the nature of legislative power, it is natural that we should recur to the Parliament in Britain, for it is from that body that Americans derive their very conception of legislative authority.[1] It is from the Parliament, too, that the Framers took their model of the representative assembly in which such authority was to be vested. In doing so, however, we must be careful not to measure the extent of legislative power in the United States by that possessed by the British Parliament, nor to assume without reflection that whatever the latter can do may also be done by the Congress.

The British Parliament is endowed with sovereign power to an extent unknown under the American Constitution. "The power and jurisdiction of Parliament, says Sir Edward Coke, is so transcendent and absolute, that it cannot be confined, either for causes or persons, within any bounds. . . . True it is that what the Parliament doth, no power on earth can undo." [2] Commenting upon this classical passage from Blackstone, a member of the Supreme Court declared in 1795, that from it: "it is evident, that, in England, the authority of the parliament runs without limits, and rises above control. . . . it is omnipotent in the scale of political existence." [3] From a legal point of view, parliamentary supremacy is the dominant characteristic of the British polity. DeLolme has summed up the matter in an aphorism which has become almost proverbial: "It is a fundamental principle with English lawyers, that Parliament can do everything but make a woman a man, and a man a woman." [4]

In the American system, as already emphasized, the situation is an entirely different one.[5] The Congress possesses nothing like the supreme status enjoyed by its counterpart in Britain. Like all other organs of government in the United States, the legislature is vested only with the powers granted to it by the Constitution. Legislative power with us is derivative, not original, power. The legislative department itself is wholly a creature of the written organic document. In the words of the Supreme-Court Justice already quoted, "The constitution is the work or will of the people themselves, in their original, sovereign, and unlimited capacity. Law is the work or will of the legislature in their derivative and subordinate capacity. The one is the work of the Creator, and the other of the creature. The constitution fixes limits to the exercise of legislative authority, and prescribes the orbit within which it must move." [6]

Yet, though the American legislature is thus clearly not sovereign in the British sense, its position in the governmental structure should not be minimized. Many of the men who drew up the Constitution, indeed, tended to go to the other extreme and, influenced no doubt by the direct example of the Parliament, to overmagnify the extent of legislative power. "The legislative department," wrote Madison, "is everywhere extending the sphere of its activity, and drawing all power into its impetuous vortex." [7] In the same paper, he referred to the "superiority in our governments" of the legislative department.[8] Such a view, we have just stressed, is erroneous, insofar as it is based upon the notion that the extent of legislative power with us is comparable to that which prevails in Britain. But it does show clearly that the Framers did consider legislative power to rank first among the departments of government which they were creating.

The importance which the Founders attached to legislative power may also be seen from the structure of the Constitution itself. The very first Article, which provides for the Congress and its powers, constitutes over half of the original organic document. All of the important substantive powers vested in the Federal Government are contained in Article I.[9] In form, they are delegations of authority to the national legislature. More important, the Constitution expressly bestows upon the Congress *all* of the legislative power conferred by it. The first words of Article I provide that "All legislative Powers herein granted shall be vested in a Congress of the United States, which shall consist of a Senate and House of Representatives."

What is the nature and extent of the legislative power thus vested in the Congress?

The basic principle that governs all authority exercised by the National

Government is, we shall see more fully in the next section, that limiting federal powers to those enumerated in the Constitution. At the same time, as will be noted, the grants in Article I include, not only the powers specifically enumerated, but also all those which can reasonably be implied. Insofar as the legislative power vested in the Congress is concerned, this means that the whole is greater than the mere sum of its parts: legislative power comprehends more than only the express powers specifically listed in Article I, section 8.

This becomes clear if we consider the different functions embraced in the concept of legislative power. To be sure, as the term itself implies, the primary province of a body vested with legislative authority is to legislate —i.e., to enact laws. It would, nevertheless, be erroneous to conceive of the functions of a legislative assembly solely in terms of law making. "The political philosopher of these days of self-government," wrote Woodrow Wilson in 1884, in criticizing the extent to which the work of the Congress was then devoted almost exclusively to legislation, "has . . . something more than a doubt with which to gainsay the usefulness of a sovereign representative body which confines itself to legislation to the exclusion of all other functions. . . . Quite as important as legislation is vigilant oversight of administration; and even more important than legislation is the instruction and guidance in political affairs which the people might receive from a body which kept all national concerns suffused in a broad daylight of discussion. There is no similar legislature in existence which is so shut up to the business of lawmaking as is our Congress." [10]

There is a great deal of truth in this criticism of a representative assembly whose time is spent solely in passing laws. Important though the law making function itself may be, a legislative body is hardly worthy of the title of Congress or Parliament if it merely grinds out legislation as a sausage maker grinds out sausages.

Under contemporary conditions, the legislature in Washington is the one great forum of expression that can be reached by the individual citizen. His Congressman is the one national official who is in contact with, and responsible to, a relatively small local area. It is through its representative in the federal assembly alone that the locality is normally able to make its views heard on the national level.

But the legislative body is more than a "committee of grievances" where those represented can ventilate their opinions and complaints. It is even more important as a molder than as a receptacle of public opinion. Its job in this respect is to enlighten and educate by ensuring adequate discussion of the important issues before the country. The debate in the legislature should clarify those issues and enable the nation intelligently to support or oppose the position finally taken in the two Houses.

As consequential as its position as the forum of the nation is the legislature's role as overseer of the administration. It is almost a truism that the critical point of present-day governmental developments is the consistent growth of executive authority. The type of activity which contemporary public opinion requires government to engage in can, as a practical matter, be carried on only by the executive branch. For its officers to operate effectively in the administration of the vast regulatory and social-service schemes undertaken by government, they must be vested with large areas of discretionary authority. The delegation of powers to the executive in a particular field does not, however, relieve the legislature of responsibility over that field. On the contrary, the consistent transfer of authority to the administration only increases the difficulty, from the point of view of the effective working of representative government.

If the basic premises of our representative system are to be preserved, the legislature must not surrender control as it has delegated power. Unless the exercise of the authority delegated to him is closely supervised by the elected representatives of the people, the administrator may, in practice, be placed in a position of all but complete irresponsibility. This is what makes supervision of administration so important an aspect of the work of the legislature. Since the Revolution of 1688, it has been a part of the Anglo-American tradition that the legislative assembly control the policies and acts of the executive.[11] That tradition is as valid in the United States as it is in that country from which American political and legal institutions are derived.

But the legislative functions just discussed (those of lawmaking, molding of public opinion, and supervision of administration) could hardly be performed properly if the legislature did not also exercise an informing function.[12] One can go further and say that none of the constitutionally recognized functions of the Congress could be discharged satisfactorily without the authority to secure, by compulsory process if necessary, the facts on which informed legislative decisions can be made.[13] Hence legislative power presupposes the possession of adequate investigatory authority.

The authority to enact laws is thus but a part of what is comprehended in the grant to the Congress of legislative power. Comparable in consequence to the lawmaking function itself are the legislative responsibility to supervise the executive, its duty to serve as a national forum for the expression, formulation, and molding of public opinion, and its position as grand inquest of the nation. In addition, there are other functions expressly delegated to the Congress under the Constitution. These include its constituent function, i.e., its role in proposing amendments to the organic document, its electoral function, if no candidate for the Presidency or Vice-Presidency obtains a majority in the electoral college, and its judicial function of impeachment. Finally there is the important function, which may be termed membership, i.e., the power over internal matters, especially the judging of the qualifications and conduct of the delegates to the legislative assembly.

An understanding of the multifold functions embraced in the concept of legislative power is essential to an adequate comprehension of the constitutional role of the Congress. In Woodrow Wilson's oft-quoted words: "As the House of Commons is the central object of examination in every study of the English Constitution, so should Congress be in every study of our own. Anyone who is unfamiliar with what Congress actually does and how it does it, with all its duties and all its occupations, with all its devices of management and resources of power, is very far from a knowledge of the constitutional system under which we live; and to every one who knows these things that knowledge is near." [14]

29
ENUMERATED AND All federal constitutions are based upon a distinc-
IMPLIED POWERS tion between enumerated and reserved powers. To
the American, it is most natural for the Central
Government to be limited to those powers enumerated in the organic instrument, with all other authority reserved to the constituent parts which make up the Union. That such is not, however, the only workable method upon which powers may be parceled out in a federation is shown by the experience of our northern neighbor. Under the Canadian Constitution: "a general power was given to the new Parliament of Canada to make laws for the peace, order, and good government of Canada without restriction to specific subjects, and excepting only the subjects specifically and exclusively assigned to the Provincial Legislatures." [15] In other words, the Federal Government in Canada possesses all legislative authority not expressly granted to the Provinces. The latter have no "powers of legislation either inherent in them or dating from a time anterior to the Federation Act. . . . Whatever is not thereby given to the provincial legislatures rests with the [federal] parliament." [16]

The distribution of powers under the Constitution of the United States is, of course, based upon an entirely different theory. With us, the nation possesses only the powers granted to it under the Constitution. The Federal Government is a government of enumerated powers, limited to the authority delegated to it, while the constituent states are governments of residual powers, retaining all of the authority not accorded to the Government in Washington. "This government," declares the classic statement of Chief Justice Marshall, "is acknowledged by all, to be one of enumerated powers. The principle, that it can exercise only the powers granted to it, would seem too apparent, to have required to be enforced by all those arguments, which its enlightened friends, while it was depending before the people, found it necessary to urge; that principle is now universally admitted." [17]

If the Federal Government is limited to the powers enumerated in the Constitution, how can the legislative power vested in the Congress by Article I be said to encompass the functions discussed in the prior section, most of which are not even mentioned in Article I?

Such a result flows from the doctrine of implied powers, which has become a basic part of American constitutional law. That doctrine is grounded squarely upon the last clause of Article I, section 8. The prior seventeen clauses of that section enumerate the specific powers conferred upon the Congress. Clause 18 then authorizes the national legislature "To make all Laws which shall be necessary and proper for carrying into Execution the foregoing Powers, and all other Powers vested by this Constitution in the Government of the United States, or in any Department or Officer thereof."

The legal operation of the Necessary-and-Proper Clause was settled definitively by *McCulloch v. Maryland*.[18] Chief Justice Marshall's landmark opinion there resolved the controversy that raged in the early days of the Republic between those who favored a strict and those who supported a broad construction of the clause. The strict view, urged by Jefferson, emphasized the word *necessary* in the clause: it endowed the National Government only with those powers indispensably necessary for the exercise of its enumerated powers. The broader view, advocated by Hamilton, maintained that to take the word in its rigorous sense would be to deprive the clause of any practical effect. As Webster put it in his *McCulloch* argument (itself largely a reiteration of the Hamiltonian view): "if Congress could use no means but such as were absolutely indispensable to the existence of a granted power, the government would hardly exist; at least, it would be wholly inadequate to the purposes of its formation." [19]

McCulloch v. Maryland itself arose out of the incorporation by the Congress of the second Bank of the United States in 1816, which was employed as a depository for federal funds and which was authorized to print bank notes to serve as a medium of exchange. Nowhere in the Constitution, to be sure, is the Federal Government given the express authority to establish such a national bank. "Among the enumerated powers," concedes Marshall, "we do not find that of establishing a bank or creating a corporation. But there is no phrase in the instrument which . . . excludes incidental or implied powers; and which requires that everything granted shall be expressly and minutely described." [20]

Looking to the express language of the Constitution, the great Chief

Justice found delegated there the powers to impose and collect taxes; to borrow money; to regulate commerce; to declare and conduct a war; and to raise and support armies and navies: "The sword and the purse, all the external relations, and no inconsiderable portion of the industry of the nation, are entrusted to its government." [21] If the establishment of a national bank would aid the Government in its exercise of these granted powers, the authority to set one up would be implied. "We admit, as all must admit," declared Marshall in the key portion of his opinion, "that the powers of the government are limited, and that its limits are not to be transcended. But we think the sound construction of the constitution must allow to the national legislature that discretion, with respect to the means by which the powers it confers are to be carried into execution, which will enable that body to perform the high duties assigned to it, in the manner most beneficial to the people. Let the end be legitimate, let it be within the scope of the constitution, and all means which are appropriate, which are plainly adapted to that end, which are not prohibited, but consist with the letter and spirit of the constitution, are constitutional." [22]

McCulloch v. Maryland conclusively put to rest the view that the Necessary-and-Proper Clause extended only to laws which were indispensably necessary. "It would be incorrect," stated Marshall even before his *McCulloch* opinion, "and would produce endless difficulties if the opinion should be maintained that no law was authorized which was not indispensably necessary to give effect to a specified power." [23] On the contrary, the constitutional clause, as the passage quoted in the prior paragraph makes clear, embraces "all [legislative] means which are appropriate" to carry out "the legitimate ends" of the Constitution, unless forbidden by "the letter and spirit of the constitution." [24]

As so construed, the Necessary-and-Proper Clause (aptly termed "the sweeping clause" at the time of the adoption of the Constitution) [25] has been the fount and origin of vast federal authority. Indeed, practically every power of the National Government has been expanded in some degree by the clause.[26] Thus, to take some important illustrative cases, the authority of the Congress under the clause has been held to include the power to enact laws to carry out treaties; [27] to utilize all appropriate means for collecting the revenue, including the distraint of property; [28] to acquire property by the power of eminent domain; [29] to make treasury notes legal tender; [30] to create corporations; [31] to exclude and deport aliens; [32] and to fix and determine maritime law.[33]

It is under the Necessary-and-Proper Clause that the Congress has enacted the Federal Criminal Code. As the Supreme Court has explained, "Although the constitution contains no grant, general or specific, to Congress of the power to provide for the punishment of crimes, except piracies and felonies on the high seas, offences against the law of nations, and counterfeiting of securities and current coin of the United States, no one doubts the power of Congress to provide for the punishment of all crimes and offences against the United States." [34] The Congressional power in this respect—to create, define, and punish crimes and offenses whenever deemed necessary to effectuate the objects of the Federal Government—stems entirely from the Necessary-and-Proper Clause.[35]

It is under that clause, too, that the Congress has made necessary and proper provision for the exercise of "The judicial Power" conferred by Article III. The Constitution, in the high bench's words, "delineated only the great outlines of the judicial power . . . , leaving the details to Congress, in whom was vested, by express delegation, the power to pass all laws necessary and proper for carrying into execution all powers except their own. The distribution and appropriate exercise of the judicial power must therefore be made by laws passed by Congress." [36]

The extent to which the Necessary-and-Proper Clause can be used to build upon a skeleton constitutional foundation is well shown by the postal power. The grant in Article I, section 8, gives to the Congress only the bare authority "To establish Post Offices and post Roads." Yet, as it was expressed in 1866 by a federal court, this provision is construed to include the power to set up the Post Office Department, with its offices throughout the country; to define the duties and compensation of postal employees; to cause the mails to be carried to all parts of the world; and to punish crimes relating to the postal service, including all obstructions to the mail.[37] In addition, the Federal Government may take all measures appropriate to ensure the safe and speedy transit of the mail and the prompt delivery thereof. The latter power was one of the grounds relied on in the already-discussed *Debs* case [38] to justify a Presidential order directing troops to restore order during a railroad strike. Presumably the same reasoning would justify federal intervention against any disorder which interfered with the transmission of the mails.

More recently, the postal power has been employed as a potent regulatory device. Under many modern statutes, the use of the mails is denied to persons violating the prescriptions of the statute or the relevant administrative agency. Such laws have been upheld on the theory that "when Congress lays down a valid regulation pertinent to the mails, it may withdraw the privilege of that use from those who disobey." [39] Hence, one of the most effective sanctions available to the Congress, upon which much of contemporary federal regulation rests, has its legal basis in the Postal-Power Clause, so briefly expressed in the Constitution itself, when that clause is read together with the Necessary-and-Proper Clause.

Several recent cases well illustrate the way in which the Necessary-

and-Proper Clause can be used to uphold Congressional powers not expressly enumerated. In *Perez v. Brownell,*[40] the issue was the constitutionality of a federal law providing that an American national shall lose his nationality by voting in a foreign political election. The high Court held that the power to deal with foreign relations should reasonably be deemed to include a power to deal with the participation of American citizens in foreign elections. The decision depended directly on the Necessary-and-Proper Clause. "The question," states Justice Frankfurter, "must finally be faced whether, given the power to attach some sort of consequence to voting in a foreign political election, Congress, acting under the Necessary and Proper Clause, Art. I, § 8, cl. 18, could attach loss of nationality to it. Is the means, withdrawal of citizenship, reasonably calculated to effect the end that is within the power of Congress to achieve, the avoidance of embarrassment in the conduct of our foreign relations attributable to voting by American citizens in foreign political elections?" [41]

Adams v. Maryland [42] is another case which turns upon the constitutional clause under discussion. It involved the validity of a statute declaring that no testimony given by a witness in any Congressional inquiry shall be used as evidence in any criminal proceeding against him in any court, state as well as federal. In finding the statute constitutional, the Supreme Court relied on the clear Congressional authority to summon witnesses to testify before either House or before their committees: "Article I of the Constitution permits Congress to pass laws 'necessary and proper' to carry into effect its power to get testimony. § 8. We are unable to say that the means Congress has here adopted is not 'appropriate' and 'plainly adapted to that end.' " [43]

What makes *Adams v. Maryland* particularly interesting is that the power to compel testimony is itself an implied power, based, not upon express enumeration, but upon the delegation to the Congress of legislative power, construed together with the Necessary-and-Proper Clause.[44] Thus, in *Adams,* the Necessary-and-Proper Clause was used to sustain an implied power deemed appropriate to carry into effect what was itself a power implied from the broad grant of legislative power in the first section of Article I.

If the doctrine of implied powers, as it has been applied by the Supreme Court, illustrates anything, it is the judicial tendency to construe the Constitution so as to give the National Government sufficient power to enable it to meet the problems with which it has been confronted. Chief Justice Marshall himself set the theme when, in *McCulloch v. Maryland,* he pronounced the basic truth that "we must never forget that it is a *constitution* that we are expounding" [45]—an instrument "framed for ages to come, and . . . designed to approach immortality as nearly as human institutions can approach it." [46] Such a document ought not to be read with the same rigid spirit that may be appropriate for the construction of a deed or a will. Not the crabbed pedantry of a Baron Parke, but the statesmanlike vision of a John Marshall, is what is needed to make constitutional rules more than mere fetters of the past upon the needs of the present. Constitutional construction is bound to be inadequate if it makes a fortress out of the dictionary.[47]

In the civil law, it may well be proper to construe grants of authority strictly against the grantor. The same is not, however, true in the case of an instrument of government, drawn up by the people and designed to create a nation endowed with powers adequate to effectuate the ends for which it was conceived. "In construing a constitution of government, framed by the *people* for their own benefit and protection, for the preservation of their rights, and property, and liberty; where the delegated powers are not, and cannot be used for the benefit of their rulers, who are but their temporary servants and agents; but are intended solely for the benefit of the people, no such presumption of an intention to use the words in the most restricted sense necessarily arises." [48]

Where the powers of the National Government are concerned, the doctrine of strict construction has no constitutional basis. In Marshall's query, "It has been said that these powers ought to be construed strictly. But why ought they to be so construed? Is there one sentence in the Constitution which gives countenance to this rule?" [49] Narrow, literal construction would, in truth, often cripple the nation and render it unequal to the objects for which it is declared to be instituted.[50] It could, in Marshall's salient phrase, "explain away the constitution of our country, and leave it a magnificent structure indeed, to look at, but totally unfit for use." [51]

This is manifest if we look only at the letter of the powers enumerated in Article I, section 8. To restrict federal power to them, taken literally, would be to read the National Government out of practical existence. "They have never been construed literally," the Supreme Court has affirmed, "and the government could not exist if they were. Thus the power to carry on war is conferred by the power to 'declare war.' The whole system of the transportation of the mails is built upon the power to establish post-offices and post roads. The power to regulate commerce has also been extended far beyond the letter of the grant." [52] The powers enumerated in Article I have proved adequate for the building of a nation only because they have been read together with the Necessary-and-Proper Clause. That clause, and the doctrine of implied powers derived from it, have been the true cement of the national edifice built on the blueprint laid down in 1787.

30

MEMBERSHIP The Constitution itself provides for the organization of the Congress into a Senate and a House of Representatives. It then goes on to prescribe the qualifications for the members of each House. No person may be a Representative who has not attained to the age of twenty-five years, and been seven years a citizen of the United States, and who is not, when elected, an inhabitant of the state in which he is chosen. Members of the Senate must be at least thirty years of age, citizens for at least nine years, and inhabitants of the states for which they are chosen.

These are the only qualifications for members of the national legislature contained in the organic document. May further qualifications be added? As far as the states are concerned, the answer is clear. No state may add to the qualifications prescribed in the Constitution for Senators and Congressmen.[53] Thus, a state law cannot require a candidate for Congress to file an affidavit that he is not a subversive person who seeks the forcible overthrow of the Government.[54] Similarly, a state law prohibiting a judge from running for any other office during his term cannot operate to prohibit the election of a Senator or Congressman who ran while still a judge.[55]

Especially noteworthy in this respect is a 1958 decision holding invalid a state law that required every candidate for the House of Representatives to be a resident of the Congressional district in which he sought election. Such requirement, declared the Maryland court, was an attempt by the state to impose an additional qualification to that portion of Article I, section 2, which provides only that a Representative shall "be an inhabitant in that State in which he shall be chosen." The decision was based squarely "on the ground that a state cannot, in any manner, impose additional qualifications to those named in the Federal Constitution upon a candidate for Representative." [56] What makes the decision particularly striking is the fact that, in actual practice, the residence requirement for Congressmen *has* become stricter than that prescribed in Article I, section 2. By custom and usage, it has become the well-nigh universally accepted (though unwritten) rule that members of the House must be residents of the district which they are elected to represent. An attempt by a state to conform the written law to the actual practice, however, runs counter to the settled principle that the states cannot prescribe qualifications for members of Congress, or establish disabilities.

A more difficult question is that of the power of the Congress itself to add to the qualifications of its members. From the point of view of the letter of the law, the answer, here too, is not difficult. The qualifications of the persons who may be chosen for the Congress, as Hamilton stated in

The Federalist, "are defined and fixed in the constitution; and are unalterable by the legislature." [57] What little case-law there is on the subject appears to bear out Hamilton's view.[58]

On the other hand, Article I, section 5, provides expressly that "Each
House shall be the Judge of the Elections, Returns, and Qualifications of its
own Members." Under this provision, the two Houses are vested with the
sole authority to determine whether the constitutional qualifications for
membership have been met in particular cases.[59] Since this means that the
legislative determination of the qualifications of members is vested with
finality, it may happen that, though neither House may formally impose
qualifications in addition to those specified in the Constitution, or waive
those that are mentioned, each may, in practice, do either of these things.[60]
Thus, in 1900, the House excluded a duly elected Representative from
Utah on the ground that he was a polygamist. Other individuals have also
been refused seats by the House concerned, though they had been duly
elected and possessed all the constitutional qualifications for membership.[61]

Article I also contains certain disqualifications. By the sixth section of
that Article, "no Person holding any Office under the United States, shall
be a Member of either House during his Continuance in Office." This
provision bars the appointment of members of Congress to positions in the
executive [62] and judicial branches, unless they resign their seats.[63] It has,
nevertheless, become settled by legislative practice that visitors to academies,
directors and trustees of public institutions, and members of temporary
commissions who receive no compensation as such, are not "officers"
within the meaning of the constitutional inhibition.[64] Similarly, Senators
and Congressmen may be appointed to represent this country on temporary
diplomatic assignments without doing violence to the constitutional bar.[65]

Article I, section 6, also disqualifies a Senator or Representative,
"during the Time for which he was elected," from being appointed "to any
civil Office under the Authority of the United States, which shall have
been created, or the Emoluments whereof shall have been encreased during
such time." Most recently, this clause was a subject of discussion when
Senator Hugo Black was appointed to the Supreme Court despite the fact
that a statute had just improved the financial position of Justices retiring at
seventy and Black's Senate term had not yet expired. An action was
brought in the Supreme Court to bar the new Justice from sitting, but the
Court declined to pass on the validity of the appointment.[66] In view of this
decision, it is difficult to see what legal remedies exist, even if the constitutional prohibition were to be violated.[67]

The two Houses, in addition to their power to determine the rights of
newly elected members to their seats, also possess continuing authority over
members. Under Article I, section 5: "Each House may . . . punish its

Members for disorderly Behaviour, and, with the Concurrence of two thirds, expel a Member." The power delegated by this provision has been interpreted most broadly.[68]

According to the highest Court: "The right to expel extends to all cases where the offence is such as in the judgment of the Senate is inconsistent with the trust and duty of a member." [69] The offense involved need not constitute an indictable crime. The Supreme Court has cited with approval the action of the Senate in 1797 in expelling a member for attempting to seduce an American agent among the Indians from his duty and for negotiating for services in behalf of the British government among the Indians. This, says the Court, "was not a statutable offense, nor was it committed in his official character, nor was it committed during the session of Congress, nor at the seat of government." [70]

In other words, the question at issue in an expulsion proceeding is not as to guilt of a criminal character, but only as to unfitness for participation in the proceedings of the Congress.[71] The determination of such question is solely for the House concerned; its decision and the grounds upon which it was based are not subject to any judicial scrutiny.[72]

31

ELECTIONS   The Constitution, we have seen, prescribes the qualifications of those who may be elected to the Congress. The same is not, however, the case with regard to the qualifications of the electors themselves. Article I, section 2, provides that "the Electors in each State shall have the Qualifications requisite for Electors of the most numerous Branch of the State Legislature." [73]

Under this provision, the qualifications of those who may vote for members of the national legislature are fixed by state law. The power of the states in this particular, the highest Court has said, is supreme—at least until Congress acts in the matter.[74] This statement is, of course, true only if it takes account of certain constitutional limitations upon state power in this respect. These include both the specific restrictions contained in the Fifteenth and Nineteenth amendments [75] and the general limitations laid upon state power in the organic document. Thus, a law disenfranchising specific individuals would run afoul of the organic prohibitions against bills of attainder.[76] Similarly, an arbitrary exclusion from the franchise would contravene due process.[77] Yet these limitations apart, the states do possess complete power over the suffrage. "Beyond doubt," the Supreme Court has expressly affirmed, "the [Fifteenth] Amendment does not take away from the state governments in a general sense the power over suffrage which has belonged to those governments from the beginning." [78]

The states have a similar general authority over the manner in which elections for the Congress are held. According to Article I, section 4: "The Times, Places and Manner of holding Elections for Senators and Representatives, shall be prescribed in each State by the Legislature thereof." The highest Court has construed the power given to the states by this language most broadly. "It cannot be doubted," to quote an important case, "that these comprehensive words embrace authority to provide a complete code for congressional elections." [79]

State power over Congressional elections is, nevertheless, clearly subject to the overriding authority of the Federal Congress. It should, in the first place, be stressed that, though the states do have the general power over the suffrage already noted, the right to vote for Senators and Representatives is derived, not from state, but from federal law. "The right to vote for members of the Congress of the United States," the Supreme Court has declared, "is not derived merely from the Constitution and laws of the state in which they are chosen, but has its foundation in the Constitution of the United States." [80] Hence, the right emanates from the Constitution itself, though the conditions upon which the right may be exercised may be determined by state law.

Since a federal right is involved, it is one that can be protected by appropriate federal legislation. In Justice Douglas's words, "Congress has ample power to legislate in this field and to protect the election of its members from fraud and corruption." [81] Federal law may validly make it a criminal offense to fail to count ballots lawfully cast at a Congressional election [82] or to stuff the ballot box with fraudulent ballots.[83] "We regard it as equally unquestionable," the high bench has affirmed, "that the right to have one's vote counted is as open to protection by Congress as the right to put a ballot in a box." [84]

But the Congressional power in this respect is not limited to protection of the physical right to cast an effective ballot. The national legislature is vested with a paramount authority over all aspects of the Congressional electoral process. Article I, section 4, after giving each state the power, discussed above, to prescribe the times, places, and manner of holding Congressional elections, goes on to provide, "but the Congress may at any time by Law make or alter such Regulations, except as to the Places of chusing Senators."

"The phrase 'such regulations,'" states Chief Justice Hughes, in explaining this provision, "plainly refers to regulations of the same general character that the legislature of the State is authorized to prescribe with respect to congressional elections. In exercising this power, the Congress may supplement these state regulations or may substitute its own. . . . It 'has a general supervisory power over the whole subject.'" [85]

The power over Congressional elections is thus lodged primarily in the states, and ultimately in the nation. The Framers submitted the regulation of such elections, in the first instance, to the relevant state authorities. But they reserved to the national authority a right to interpose, whenever it deems such action necessary.[86]

The Congress first exercised its authority over the Congressional electoral process in 1842 by an enactment requiring the election of Representatives by districts. In 1870 and 1872, Congress for the first time passed comprehensive statutes dealing with elections. Under them, federal offenses were made of false registration, bribery, voting without legal right, false returns, interfering with officers of election, and neglect of duty by such officers. In addition, provision was made for the appointment of federal officers to supervise elections directly.

The statutes just referred to were part of the Reconstruction legislation of the postbellum era and were almost entirely repealed in 1894. All that was left standing on the federal statute book were provisions protecting the rights of individuals to vote. Such provisions make no attempt to regulate affirmatively the manner in which Congressional elections may be conducted.

Despite their repeal, the Reconstruction election laws remain of great significance, for they illustrate dramatically the extent of Congressional power over the election of Senators and Representatives. Under them, the Congress not only prescribed detailed regulations governing such elections; it also provided for federally appointed officials to supervise them.

The Congressional assertion of such power was upheld in *Ex parte Siebold* (1880).[87] Petitioners there were state-appointed election judges who were convicted of interfering with and resisting federal supervisors of elections and deputy marshals appointed to oversee a Congressional election under the act of 1870. Petitioners claimed that the federal law in question was unconstitutional. The Court rejected this claim. Under Article I, section 4, said Justice Bradley, "the power of Congress over the subject is paramount. It may be exercised as and when Congress sees fit to exercise it. When exercised, the action of Congress, so far as it extends and conflicts with the regulations of the State, necessarily supersedes them." [88]

The *Siebold* case indicates that, if it chooses to exercise it, the national legislature may assert plenary authority over the election of its members. Under the Constitution, in the Court's words, "Congress may, if it sees fit, assume the entire control and regulation of the election of Representatives. This would necessarily involve the appointment of the places for holding the polls, the times of voting, and the officers for holding the election; it would require the regulation of the duties to be performed, the custody of the ballots, the mode of ascertaining the result, and every other matter relating to the subject." [89]

The power of the Congress over elections extends not only to general elections themselves, but also to the primaries at which Congressional candidates are chosen. *Newberry v. United States* (1921) [90] cast doubt on Congressional authority in this respect, for it held that the Federal Corrupt Practices Act could not limit the expenditures made to secure a primary nomination to the Senate. Elections within the meaning of Article I, section 4, according to a bare majority of the Court, meant only the "final choice of an officer by the duly qualified electors," not the nomination of such officer in a primary.[91] This decision is, however, no longer followed by the Supreme Court. In *United States v. Classic* (1941),[92] the right of the Congress to regulate primary elections for the nomination of its members was squarely recognized. "We think," said Justice Stone, "that the authority of Congress, given by § 4, includes the authority to regulate primary elections, when, as in this case, they are a step in the exercise by the people of their choice of representatives in Congress." [93] The Congress consequently has the same complete authority to regulate Congressional primaries that it possesses with regard to Congressional elections.

The power of the national legislature is also plenary over election disputes. Under Article I, section 5: "Each House shall be the Judge of the Elections, Returns . . . of its own Members." This provision makes each House the sole judge of election disputes and its determinations in such disputes are conclusive. "In other words, the power of the respective Houses of Congress with respect to the . . . election of its members is supreme." [94] In this respect, it is interesting to note that the situation in this country is basically similar to that which prevailed in Britain prior to 1868. In that year, Parliament enacted a law under which disputed elections were decided by the courts. The present British system appears superior to that which prevails on this side of the Atlantic. Though, according to the Supreme Court, the House and Senate, in judging elections, act as judicial tribunals,[95] too frequently this has been purely a matter of legal theory. In practice, contests over seats in the Congress all too often tend to be decided in favor of the candidates of the dominant party.

32

APPORTIONMENT   Closely related to the election of members of the national legislature is that of the apportionment of Congressional seats themselves. This is, of course, a subject that can arise only with regard to the House of Representatives, for the Constitution expressly apportions seats in the Senate on the basis of two to each state.

Representation in the lower House is based upon population. Under the controlling organic provision,[96] "Representatives shall be apportioned among the several States according to their respective numbers,[97] counting the whole number of persons in each State, excluding Indians not taxed." [98] Article I, section 2, provides for an "Enumeration" to be made within three years after the first meeting of the Congress and every ten years thereafter. Though "the power to apportion representatives after this enumeration is made is nowhere found among the express powers given to Congress, . . . it has always been acted upon as irresistibly flowing from the duty positively enjoined by the Constitution." [99] One can, in fact, go further and assert that the basic document imposes a positive mandate upon the Congress to reapportion Representatives among the states after the decennial census is taken.

It is nevertheless settled that there is no legal machinery available to compel the Congress to perform its constitutional duty of reapportionment. "Congress," Justice Frankfurter informs us, "has at times been heedless of this command and not apportioned according to the requirements of the census. It never occurred to anyone that this Court could . . . compel Congress to perform its mandatory duty to apportion." [100] The lack of any judicial remedy was strikingly apparent in the experience after the 1920 census, when the Congress was unable to reach agreement on any reapportionment plan. It was not until nine years later, in 1929, that a new apportionment law was enacted. It fixes the membership of the House at 435.[101] This number is to be distributed among the states in accordance with the population figures declared in each succeeding census, under an apportionment formula fixed in the law.

Fixing the membership of the House of Representatives and apportioning it among the states is actually only the first stage of the apportioning process. Unless Representatives are to be elected from the states at large, the seats allotted to each state must be apportioned among election districts within the state. Under the Constitution, this stage of the apportionment process is a state responsibility. What happens, however, in the event a state fails to apportion its Representatives in accordance with the population distribution revealed in the latest census returns?

Under the high bench's jurisprudence prior to 1962, there appeared to be no legal remedy in such a case.[102] The decision in *Baker v. Carr* [103] drastically changes such result. In that case, a state apportionment law was attacked on the ground that it created legislative districts which had become glaringly unequal in population. This, it was claimed, was unconstitutional because it deprived the voters in the most populous districts of the equal protection of the laws. The Supreme Court held that the federal courts had jurisdiction to entertain such case and that the complaint stated a justiciable controversy. It is true that the law at issue in *Baker v. Carr* was only one that involved districting for the state legislature and, as such, the decision is not, strictly speaking, determinative in the matter of Congressional apportionments. Yet, as will be seen in our more detailed discussion of the case,[104] the *Baker* decision lays down a broad rule of justiciability for challenges to state apportionments on equal-protection grounds. As such, it should apply to state apportionments of Congressional seats, as well as of seats in the state legislatures. One must therefore conclude today that the remedy for state unfairness in districting (at least where it is so extreme as to contravene the Equal-Protection Clause) is in the courts, as well as in the legislature itself.

It is, at the same time, plain that the manner in which the states internally apportion the Representatives allotted to them is also subject to the control of the Congress itself. The Congress, under the clause in Article I, section 4, empowering it to make or alter regulations by the states prescribing the times, places, and manner of holding Congressional elections,[105] has "ample powers" to remedy unfairness in districting.[106] In 1842, the Congress provided for the election of Representatives by districts. In 1862, it required that the districts be of contiguous territory. In a law of 1872, as reinforced by a 1911 statute, Congress added the requirement of substantial equality of inhabitants.[107] But the act of 1929, which now governs the districting for the election of Representatives, has no requirements "as to the compactness, contiguity and equality in population of districts." [108] In *Wood v. Broom*,[109] the highest Court held that this omission was intentional and repealed the requirements of the previous statutes in this respect.

At the present time, there are no federal requirements which the states must follow in their internal apportionment of the House seats assigned to them.[110] On the other hand, under the cases, the Congress does have the undoubted authority to compel "fair representation" by the states in the lower House.[111] It could itself redistrict a state which refused to reapportion in conformity to the latest census or intervene to correct specific inequalities in a state's districting plan. The Congress could, in other words, do whatever it deemed necessary to implement the constitutional intention to have representation in the popular House based upon state election systems designed to give approximately equal weight to each vote cast.[112] That Congress may have been in default in exacting from the states obedience to the constitutional mandate [113] does not at all bear upon the question of whether or not the national legislature possesses authority to compel such obedience.

33

PRIVILEGES   Much of British Parliamentary history is an account
                  of the legislative struggle to assert certain basic
privileges for its members. In the Supreme Court's words, "The privilege of
legislators to be free from arrest or civil process for what they do or say in

legislative proceedings has taproots in the Parliamentary struggles of the Sixteenth and Seventeenth Centuries." [114] As Parliament achieved increasing independence from the Crown, it was able to establish the freedom from arrest and the freedom of speech of its members. The same privileges were expressly included among the peculiar rights enjoyed by members of the Congress under the Federal Constitution. Article I, section 6, provides: "The Senators and Representatives shall . . . in all Cases, except Treason, Felony and Breach of the Peace, be privileged from Arrest during their Attendance at the Session of their respective Houses, and in going to and returning from the same; and for any Speech or Debate in either House, they shall not be questioned in any other Place." In this sentence, the privileges of Parliament already referred to are made privileges of the Congress. [115]

The immunity from arrest is at present of no practical significance. As it has been construed by the courts, it is settled, in the first place, that the privilege has no application to criminal offenses. The Framers, in excepting "Treason, Felony, and Breach of the Peace" from the privilege were, in effect, agreeing with the contemporary remark of Lord Mansfield that "The laws of this country allow no place or employment as a sanctuary for crime." [116] The constitutional exception, the highest Court has held, must be understood "as excluding from the . . . privilege all arrests and prosecutions from criminal offenses; in other words, as confining the privilege alone to arrests in civil cases." [117] Since arrest of the person is now almost never authorized except for crimes, it follows that the freedom from arrest given to members of the Congress is today of little more than theoretical consequence. [118]

The same is not the case with regard to the privilege of freedom of speech. If anything, indeed, this privilege, which has been termed the essential attribute of every free legislature, [119] is even more important at the present time than it was when the Constitution was adopted. This is true because of the broad interpretation that the courts have given to the immunity conferred by the privilege in question. The language of Article I, section 6, restricts the privilege to "any Speech or Debate in either House." Taken literally, this would appear to immunize only statements made on the floor of the Congress. But the immunity of legislators has not been confined by the courts to acts performed on the floor of the chamber concerned. "It would," the Supreme Court has asserted, "be a narrow view of the constitutional provision to limit it to words spoken in debate. The reason of the rule is as forcible in its application to written reports presented . . . by committees, to resolutions offered, . . . and to the act of voting. . . . In short, to things generally done in a session of the House by one of its members in relation to the business before it." [120]

In the leading case of *Kilbourn v. Thompson* (1881),[121] members of the House of Representatives were held not liable to an action for false imprisonment because of their initiation of legislative proceedings under which plaintiff had been improperly arrested. More recently, a suit brought against legislators for an alleged violation of plaintiff's civil rights was dismissed for failure to state a cause of action.[122] The violation asserted was the alleged action of a legislative committee in summoning plaintiff, not for a legislative purpose, but to prevent him from exercising his constitutional rights. Such action was taken by the committee concerned in its official capacity and was, as such, within the immunity protected by the Constitution.

Nor did it make any difference that the plaintiff in the case just discussed alleged that the action which injured him was not in pursuance of any valid legislative purpose. "The claim of an unworthy purpose does not destroy the privilege." [123] One can go further and state that the privilege in question is an absolute one, which shields the legislator from liability for damages done by his acts and statements, made or done in his official capacity, even though they are knowingly wrong or false and motivated by personal malice on his part.[124] As the high Court has put it, "The privilege would be of little value if they could be subjected to the cost and inconvenience and distractions of a trial upon a conclusion of the pleader, or to the hazard of a judgment against them based upon a jury's speculation as to motives." [125]

It has already been pointed out that the privilege for statements made by legislators is not restricted to debates upon the floor. It extends to work performed on committees. If a member be out of the chamber, sitting in a committee, executing the commission of the House concerned, he is still within the immunity.[126] And, since the working of legislative committees depends, in large part, upon information received from witnesses, the privilege has been extended to such witnesses. Witnesses appearing before Congressional committees are entitled to at least the same immunity as witnesses in the courts.[127] This is true even though Congressional committees are not uncommonly composed of persons who do not have the judges' impartial concern with ensuring that proceedings are properly conducted in accordance with the rules of evidence. All too frequently, in legislative hearings, characters are compromised by evidence that would never see the light of day in a courtroom. The possibility of injury to individuals is, nevertheless, outweighed by the public interest in ensuring that those who appear before the legislature will tender information or advice freely and without fear.

The privilege under discussion does not extend to the outside publication of defamatory matter uttered in Congressional proceedings. The member of Congress or witness who circulates a libel through the mails or over the radio or television is not protected, though he would be wholly immune if the same statement had been made only in the precincts of the House or the committee room. Thus, a Senator who sends copies of a defamatory speech delivered by him on the floor of the Senate to his constituents is not immune from a libel suit.[128] Similarly, in the celebrated affair of Alger Hiss, it was necessary for Whittaker Chambers to repeat his accusation that Hiss was a Communist on a television program, in response to Hiss's challenge to do so in a place other than a Congressional hearing, before Hiss could sue him for libel. While the accusation in question was confined to testimony before a legislative committee, it could not be made the basis of any legal action.

Closer to the borderline is a recent state case, which arose out of a statement made by the chairman of a Senate committee at a press conference held at the close of an executive session, purporting to summarize what had occurred at the session. Plaintiff, alleging that he was defamed by the statement,[129] sued a newspaper which printed it. The court held that the Congressional privilege covered such a statement, which summarized for the press the testimony given at a secret committee hearing.[130] This would, however, seem to be extending the privilege too far. The reason for the privilege—to render legislators immune from deterrents to the uninhibited discharge of their legislative duty [131]—is fully served by an immunity localized to the precincts of the Congress and the committee room. To extend the privilege to a statement like that made in this case is to give an unscrupulous legislator [132] a veritable invitation to irresponsibility.[133]

34

PROCEDURE Perhaps the basic privilege of any legislative assembly is that of regulating its own internal procedure. According to Article I, section 5: "Each House may determine the Rules of its Proceedings." "No person," asserts Justice Story, "can doubt the propriety of the provision authorizing each house to determine the rules of its own proceedings. If the power did not exist, it would be utterly impracticable to transact the business of the nation, either at all, or at least with decency, deliberation, and order. The humblest assembly of men is understood to possess this power; and it would be absurd to deprive the councils of the nation of a like authority." [134]

It is true that the Constitution itself prescribes certain rules of legislative organization and procedure. Thus, Article I, section 4, as amended,[135] provides that the Congress must assemble at least once every year, at noon, on the third of January.[136] In addition, Article I provides that the Vice-President is to be President of the Senate, that a majority is to constitute a quorum of each House, and that each House is to keep and publish a journal of its proceedings.

These constitutional provisions must, of course, be followed by the national legislature.[137] As such they do restrict the privilege of the Congress over its own internal functioning. It should, however, be noted that there are only a mere handful of such provisions in the Constitution. The existence of a few such sections in the fundamental law does not really derogate essentially from the overall power of the Congress over its proceedings—though it does limit it in some minor details.

The basic authority of the Congress to determine its own rules was construed broadly in *United States v. Ballin* (1892).[138] At issue in it was a rule adopted by the House of Representatives which provided that members present in the chamber, but not voting, would be counted in determining the presence of a quorum. This rule was upheld as a valid exercise of the power of the House to govern its own proceedings. According to Justice Brewer, who delivered the *Ballin* opinion, the only limitations upon the Congressional power in this respect are those contained in the constitutional provisions already referred to. "But within these limitations all matters of method are open to the determination of the House. . . . The power to make rules is not one which once exercised is exhausted. It is a continuous power, always subject to be exercised by the House, and within the limitations suggested, absolute and beyond the challenge of any other body or tribunal." [139]

It is thus clear that the rules adopted by each House for its own governance are not subject to judicial control. On the other hand, where a Congressional rule is applied in such a way as to affect private rights, it may well become the subject of justiciable controversy. In *United States v. Smith* (1932),[140] for example, the high bench held that the rules of the Senate did not empower that body to reconsider its confirmation of a person nominated by the President to be a member of the Federal Power Commission. In so doing, the Court rejected the interpretation of the relevant rule adopted by the Senate itself. It is not for the Court, Justice Brandeis conceded, to say that the rule made by the Senate is not proper. But the interpretation of the rule in a case like this is a different matter: "As the construction to be given to the rules affects persons other than the Senate, the question presented is of necessity a judicial one." [141] In such a case, the Court is not concluded by the Senate's own construction.

As already mentioned, the Constitution requires each House to "keep a Journal of its Proceedings, and from time to time publish the same." [142] The implementation of this provision is entirely up to the Congress itself. As the Supreme Court expressed it, "It is clear that, in respect to the particular mode in which, or with what fullness, shall be kept the proceedings of either house . . . ; these and like matters were left to the discretion of the respective houses of Congress." [143]

What is the effect of entries in the legislative journals upon the enactment of laws? The question has arisen when the validity of federal statutes has been challenged on the ground that they were not enacted by the Congress in accordance with the requirements of the Constitution or the rules of the two Houses themselves. In the already-discussed *Ballin* case, the Court held that the journal of either House would be accepted as conclusive proof of the facts stated therein with regard to the existence of a quorum or the vote on any particular matter. The journal, said Justice Brewer, "must be assumed to speak the truth." [144]

Field v. Clark (1892) [145] goes even further in attributing conclusiveness to Congressional proceedings. Under it, an enrolled bill, which has been signed by the Speaker of the House and the President of the Senate and has been approved and signed by the President and deposited in the Department of State, is unimpeachable. Such a statute may not be challenged by resort to the journals, committee reports, or other printed documents, in an effort to show that the bill as actually passed contained a section omitted in the enrolled act. Such an act, on its face, carries the solemn assurance of the legislative and executive branches that it was duly passed by the Congress. In the Court's words, "The respect due co-equal and independent departments requires the judicial department to act upon that assurance, and to accept, as having passed Congress, all bills authenticated in the matter stated: leaving the courts to determine, when the question properly arises, whether the act so authenticated, is in conformity with the Constitution." [146]

The 1949 case of *Christoffel v. United States* [147] has been said to cast doubt upon both the *Ballin* and *Field* decisions. In *Christoffel,* a witness in a Congressional committee hearing who was tried for perjury was permitted to show by oral testimony that a quorum of the committee had not been present when he made his allegedly perjurious statements.[148] According to the dissenting opinion, the Court was, in effect, putting "out a doctrine by which every Congressional Act . . . can be overturned on oral testimony of interested parties." [149] It may be questioned, however, whether *Christoffel* really stands for so extreme a result. It is one thing to permit a criminal defendant to prove by all means available to him that the tribunal before which his alleged offense was committed was not competent for lack of a quorum. It is quite another when a federal statute, duly solemnized and authenticated, is attacked by oral testimony tending to show it was not properly enacted. In the latter case, the basic rule of *Field v. Clark* must still govern—i.e., an enrolled act is conclusive proof that it was passed in accordance with the requirements of the Constitution and the rules of the Congress.

If the enrolled bill indicates upon its face that it was not properly enacted, that is, of course, an entirely different matter. In one case, a federal court was confronted with a revenue statute which showed on the face of the enrolled act that it had not originated in the House of Representatives, as required by the Constitution.[150] In such a case, it was decided, the statute never became a valid law: "When the Congress, through its proper officials, certifies that it has gone through the forms of lawmaking in violation of an express constitutional mandate, is the result a law at all? Of course it is not." [151] Interestingly enough, the court rejected the Government's argument that, so far as the enrolled act showed that it had originated in the Senate, it was mistaken and that this was evident from the journals of Congress. The rule of *Field v. Clark* prevents a court from going behind an enrolled act, even when, to do so, might save its constitutionality.

35

ADMINISTRATIVE   As emphasized at the outset of this chapter,[152] the
SUPERVISION   grant to the Congress of legislative power includes
                    more than the mere authority to enact laws. Among
the most consequential of Congressional tasks today is that of exercising effective control over administration.

The legal basis of legislative control is to be found in the fact that all exercises of authority by the federal administration must find their source in a Congressional act. Our law, as will be seen,[153] rejects the notion of inherent or autonomous lawmaking power in the executive. Thus, the officers and agencies of the executive branch owe their authority and, indeed, their very existence to delegations of power by the Congress.

It follows from this that the administration, in the exercise of its delegated powers, acts as the agent of the legislature. But, if that is true, the latter must possess the authority to exercise continuous supervision over administrative activities. It is a fundamental principle of the law of agency that a principal retains continuing control over his agent. It is the primary duty of an agent continually to account to his principal, and a corollary responsibility of the principal to exercise continuing supervision over his agent.[154] In the American system, the administration, as the agent of the Congress, owes the same duty to its principal, and the latter has the responsibility to ensure that such duty is performed.

That the relationship of principal and agent is, in actual fact, that which does exist between the Congress and executive departments and agencies is shown by *Kendall v. United States* (1838).[155] That case arose out of a sum of money owed by the United States under certain contracts for the transportation of the mail. The Postmaster General, acting on the instructions of the President, refused to make payment. Congress then passed a law directing that the sum be paid. The Postmaster General, nevertheless, still declined payment, and a mandamus action was brought to compel compliance. The Postmaster General claimed that executive officers are under the exclusive control and direction of the President. The Supreme Court rejected this view, holding that it is erroneous to assume that the departments and agencies in the executive branch act solely as the agents of the President. To be sure, the high bench conceded, the Constitution vests the executive power in the President. "But," it went on, "it by no means follows, that every officer in every branch of that department is under the exclusive direction of the President . . . . it would be an alarming doctrine, that Congress cannot impose upon any executive officer any duty they may think proper, which is not repugnant to any rights secured and protected by the Constitution." [156]

Nor is the situation in this respect altered by the grant to the President of the authority to "take Care that the Laws be faithfully executed." [157] The Faithful-Execution Clause does not make executive officers subject to the sole direction of the President with regard to their duty to execute statutes. "This is a doctrine," declares the *Kendall* opinion, "that cannot receive the sanction of this court. It would be vesting in the President a dispensing power, which has no countenance for its support, in any part of the Constitution; and is asserting a principle, which, if carried out in its results, to all cases falling within it, would be clothing the President with a power entirely to control the legislation of Congress, and paralyze the administration of justice." [158]

The *Kendall* case clearly establishes the constitutional position of the Congress vis-à-vis the administration. Executive officers are responsible for the performance of their functions, not only to the Chief Executive, who is the hierarchical head of their department, but also to the legislature, from whence their very being is derived. The authority of such officers finds its source in Congressional delegations, and, like all agents, their exercise of the delegated authority is subject to the scrutiny and supervision of their principal.

What constitutional tools are available to the Congress to enable it to perform its role as overseer of administration?

Most important, of course, is the basic legislative power granted by Article I, for it permits the Congress to control the sources of administrative authority themselves. If the grant of authority is not exercised by the agent in accordance with the desires of the principal, it can at any time be revoked or modified by the latter. By its legislative power, the Congress can create, alter, or abolish any departments or agencies and the powers vested in them.[159]

Equally important as a practical matter is the control of the Congress over expenditures. The power over the purse is the constitutional birthright of the legislature.[160] Through the power to appropriate, Congress can control the nature and extent of administrative activity. Appropriations are made upon a yearly basis, and this enables well-nigh constant supervision to be maintained.

Finally, there is the power of the Congress to investigate, which will be discussed more fully in the next chapter. Investigatory authority is a whip, which enables the Congress to examine into corners suspected to be dirty.[161] More than that, threat of its exercise can act as a spur, impelling action in accordance with legislative desires. In recent years, in truth, the power to expose has become in many ways the most effective deterrent against action disapproved of by members of the legislature.

It cannot be denied that Congressional control over delegations of authority and appropriations, as well as the power to investigate, are substantial instruments to implement the responsibility of the legislature to supervise administration. At the same time, few familiar with the actual working of government would dispute the conclusion that they have hardly proved effective save in sporadic instances. Observers of the Congressional process must still echo the words of Woodrow Wilson that "it is quite evident that the means which Congress has of controlling the departments and of exercising the searching oversight at which it aims are limited and defective." [162] The vast range of modern administrative authority and the innumerable instances in which such authority is constantly being exercised tend to make continuing control by an unwieldly nonexpert body like the Congress more a matter of form than of substance most of the time. Here, as in other areas of our constitutional law, much is to be explained by the maxim attributed to Napoleon that "The tools belong to the man who can use them." The organic document may vest vast authority in the hands of the Congress, but only Congress itself can prevent such powers from slipping through its fingers.[163]

36

IMPEACHMENT   In British history, the most effective weapon available to the Parliament in its struggles to control the executive was the impeachment power. Before the development of the modern system of Parliamentary government, indeed, impeachment was the major means available to the Commons to call to account executive officials appointed by and responsible to the Crown. Now that the British executive is directly responsible to the Parliament, there is no longer need to employ the cumbrous instrument of impeachment.[164] From a device used roughly once a year during the constitutional struggles of the seventeenth century, impeachment has declined to the status of a weapon of purely antiquarian interest in the Parliamentary arsenal.[165]

In the United States, impeachment has never been widely used as a means of legislative control over the executive. According to Justice Miller, this has been due to the limited tenure of federal policy-making officials: "As most of the officers of the Government have a term fixed to the enjoyment of their offices, it has usually been thought wiser to let the limitation effect the removal, than to engage in this costly and unsatisfactory process of impeachment." [166] In actual practice, the power of impeachment has been resorted to only twelve times since the founding of the Republic. And nine of those cases involved federal judges, whose life tenure makes the reasoning of Justice Miller inapplicable.[167]

The constitutional provisions on impeachment, though brief, raise interesting legal problems. Article II, section 4, provides: "The President, Vice President and all civil Officers of the United States, shall be removed from Office on Impeachment for, and Conviction of, Treason, Bribery, or other high Crimes and Misdemeanors."

In the first place, there is the question of who may be impeached. Under English precedents, all citizens are subject to impeachment. But the constitutional provision just quoted clearly limits impeachment to federal "civil officers." A member of Congress is not an officer of the United States within the constitutional meaning of the term.[168] The Senate so held in 1799, when impeachment proceedings were brought against a Senator, and its decision to that effect has never been questioned. In addition, military and naval officers are not civil officers, within Article II, section 4. There are no cases, since no attempt has ever been made to impeach a member of the armed forces.

Resignation does not give a federal officer immunity from impeachment for acts committed while in office. In the very first impeachment proceeding, that already referred to in 1799, counsel for the defendant conceded this. "I shall certainly never contend," he declared, "that an officer may first commit an offense and afterwards avoid punishment by resigning his office." [169] The point was squarely settled in 1876 when the Senate held that the resignation of the officer concerned, in anticipation of the impeachment proceeding, did not deprive it of jurisdiction to try him. Such holding is consistent with the relevant provision of the organic document. Under Article I, section 3, the judgment in an impeachment proceeding may entail, not only removal from office, but also disqualification to hold federal office thereafter.[170] Where an offense warranting impeachment has been committed, it may be in the public interest to have such future disqualification imposed, even though the offender has relinquished his office.

The most important legal question raised by the constitutional provisions concerning impeachment is that of what offenses are impeachable. Article II, section 4, it will be recalled, provides for impeachment for "Treason, Bribery, or other high Crimes and Misdemeanors." Treason and bribery are, of course, offenses which are clearly defined in the law. "High

Crimes and Misdemeanors" are quite another matter. On its face, the organic language seems limited to criminal offenses. It has, nevertheless, been urged that this is too narrow an approach. The Constitution, it is said, permits impeachment for any misconduct in office, even though no indictable offense has been committed.

The extreme assertion of the view just stated was made by the managers of the impeachment proceeding against Justice Samuel Chase in 1805. As they put it: "removal by impeachment was nothing more than a declaration by Congress to this effect: you hold dangerous opinions. . . . We want your offices for the purpose of giving them to men who will fill them better." [171] Under this approach, in effect, impeachment would become a device for the removal of any officers whose actions were sufficiently unpopular with the Congress. Chase's acquittal, however, went far toward putting so broad an assertion of legislative power in this respect to rest for over half a century.

The impeachment of President Johnson in 1867 was grounded upon an attempted revival of the theory upon which the action against Justice Chase had been based. The articles of impeachment against Johnson charged, not any indictable offense, but his failure to carry out certain laws and his public utterances, especially those attacking the Congress. This, in the argument of the managers of the proceeding, was enough. An impeachable offense, they urged, "may consist of a violation of the Constitution, of law, of an official oath, or of duty, by an act committed or omitted, or, without violating a positive law, by the abuse of discretionary powers from improper motives or for an improper purpose." [172]

Johnson's acquittal represents the definitive rejection of this view, at least so far as the impeachment of executive officers is concerned. Former Justice Curtis, in his argument in Johnson's defense, stated what may be taken as the prevailing law: "when the Constitution speaks of 'treason, bribery, and other high crimes and misdemeanors,' it refers to, and includes only, high criminal offenses against the United States, made so by some law of the United States existing when the acts complained of were done." [173]

It should, at the same time, be pointed out that, during the present century, a broader view of impeachable offenses has come to prevail in cases involving federal judges. In 1912 and 1936, members of the federal bench were removed from office by impeachment, even though the acts which they had committed were conceded not to be indictable. In both cases, it was held, the judges had acted so as to cast doubts on their integrity, though their acts had not constituted crimes.[174] These cases, Justice Burton informs us, establish that a federal judge can be impeached and removed "because of his abuse of judicial authority . . . , although his offenses were not indictable." [175]

The broader interpretation of "high Crimes and Misdemeanors," where judges are concerned, is explainable by the tenure given members of the federal bench. Since Article III provides that judges are to hold office during "good behaviour," there is no means, other than impeachment, to remove a judge who has proved himself unfit to remain on the bench. To put it another way, impeachment is the only method indicated by the Constitution for determining whether a judge's behavior has been "good" within the meaning of Article III.[176] Hence a high crime or misdemeanor for which a federal judge may be impeached includes misconduct which need not constitute an indictable offense. As Chief Justice Taft put it in a 1913 address: "By the liberal interpretation of the term 'high misdemeanor' which the Senate has given, there is now no difficulty in securing the removal of a judge that for any reason shows him unfit." [177]

37

LEGISLATIVE
VERSUS
JUDICIAL POWER

"Mr. Chief Justice," declared Benjamin R. Curtis, himself a former Supreme Court Justice, in his address for the defense at the impeachment of Andrew Johnson, "I am here to speak to the Senate of the United States sitting in its judicial capacity as a court of impeachment, presided over by the Chief Justice of the United States, for the trial of the President of the United States." [178]

Impeachment itself is clearly a function which is judicial in nature. In trying impeachment cases, the Senate has accorded to defendants the basic rights they would have in a law court, including counsel, compulsory process for obtaining witnesses, and confrontation of witnesses against them.[179]

Though impeachment is thus a judicial function, it is one which is expressly delegated to the legislature, rather than the courts, by the Constitution.[180] The reason is, of course, largely historical. The power to impeach was developed and exercised by the Parliament, not the bench, in Britain. The Framers found it natural to vest the same power in the national assembly which they were creating.

In this connection, it must be borne in mind that, at the time the fundamental document was drawn up, the distinction between legislative and judicial power was far more blurred than it has since become. The Parliament itself, from whence the Founders drew their conceptions of legislative power, had been both a legislative assembly and a court. Lord Coke, in his treatment of the jurisdiction of the English courts, deals first with "The High and most Honourable Court of Parliament." [181] "They were not only called so," the Supreme Court informs us, "but the assembled Parliament exercised the highest functions of a court of judicature, representing in this respect the judicial authority of the King in his Court of Parliament." [182]

During the early part of our history as an independent nation, the sovereign power of the Parliament, both in regard to legislative and judicial power, was of great influence upon American legislatures. Taking Parliament as their example, legislatures in this country, from the Revolution to the Civil War, constantly asserted authority that we would now deem judicial in character. The extent of such assertions has been well stated by Chief Justice Vanderbilt: "We find state legislatures by special act annulling or reversing judgments, granting new trials after final judgment in the courts, giving the right to appeal after the time to do so had expired, probating wills after their rejection by the courts, dictating details of the administration of particular estates, validating specified marriages that were invalid under the general law, suspending the statute of limitations for individual litigants, designating the particular cases to be heard at the next term, empowering the sale of the estates of decedents, infants or incompetents in situations not permitted under the general law, foreclosing mortgages and awarding dower to particular widows." [183]

One of the most striking exercises of judicial power by early American legislatures was the granting of divorces. In upholding the constitutionality of legislative divorces, the Supreme Court followed the broad view of legislative power in this respect that prevailed in the first part of our history. The legislature, said Justice Field, "has acted upon everything within the range of civil government. . . . Every subject of interest to the community has come under its direction. It has not merely prescribed rules for future conduct, but has legalized past acts, corrected defects in proceedings, and determined the *status,* conditions, and relations of parties." [184]

More recently, we have come to see that so broad a view of legislative power is inconsistent with the separation of powers upon which the American constitutional structure is based. "It is believed to be one of the chief merits of the American system of written constitutional law," the highest tribunal has stated, "that all the powers intrusted to government, whether State or national, are divided into the three grand departments, the executive, the legislative, and the judicial." [185] The doctrine of the separation of powers itself, though not expressly provided for in the Constitution, is implicit in it, as a conclusion logically following from this division of the three departments. In the Supreme Court's words, "It may be stated then, as a general rule inherent in the American constitutional system, that, unless otherwise expressly provided or incidental to the powers conferred, the legislature cannot exercise either executive or judicial power; the executive cannot exercise either legislative or judicial power; the judiciary cannot exercise either executive or legislative power." [186]

What this means specifically in terms of the exercise by the legislature of judicial functions was spelled out in classic language by Justice Miller: "The

Constitution declares that the judicial power of the United States shall be vested in one Supreme Court, and in such inferior courts as the Congress may from time to time ordain. If what we have said of the division of the powers of the government among the three departments be sound, this is equivalent to a declaration that no judicial power is vested in the Congress or either branch of it, save in the cases specifically enumerated." [187]

Under the influence of this reasoning, the courts now show no hesitancy in striking down legislative exercises of judicial power not expressly authorized by the organic instrument. For example, declaratory acts [188] seeking to interpret earlier legislation and to give such interpretation retroactive effect are generally condemned.[189] The legislature cannot set aside a construction of the law already applied by the courts in actual cases.[190] As the high bench once put it, "To declare what the law is, or has been, is a judicial power; to declare what the law shall be, is legislative. One of the fundamental principles of all our governments is, that the legislative power shall be separated from the judicial." [191] Similarly, the legislature cannot interfere directly in litigation. Thus, it cannot annul, set aside, vacate, reverse, modify, or impair the judgment of a competent court.[192] It cannot compel the courts to grant new trials, order the discharge of offenders, or direct what particular steps shall be taken in a particular judicial proceeding.[193]

More difficult are the cases involving so-called curative statutes [194] which impair judgments or render them ineffective, as by validating action which a court had held void. Though the decisions involving such statutes may appear hopelessly in conflict,[195] in actuality they turn upon the principle laid down in 1856 in *Pennsylvania v. Wheeling & Belmont Bridge Co.*[196] Some four years prior to that decision, the Supreme Court had found that two bridges over the Ohio River were obstructions to navigation and had ordered them abated as nuisances.[197] The Congress then enacted a statute declaring that the bridges were lawful structures. The Court held that this curative act was valid, even though it prevented the enforcement of the order to abate the bridges as nuisances. The opinion drew a distinction between private and public rights, insofar as the effect of the curative law was concerned. The Court conceded that, "if the remedy in this case had been an action at law, and a judgment rendered in favor of plaintiff for damages, the right to these would have passed beyond the reach of the power of Congress." [198] The decree at issue, however, enjoined interference with the free navigation of the river. Such interference, said the Court, "constituted an obstruction of a public right secured by Acts of Congress." [199]

The distinction thus drawn by the Supreme Court is that followed in most of the cases: Where a public right is involved, a curative statute is valid, even though it may impair or render ineffective a judgment concerning such right.[200] Where a private right is at issue, on the other hand, a curative statute is void, insofar as it affects a judgment adjudicating such right.[201] "The line of demarcation seems to be that private rights of parties, which have become vested by the judgment of the court, cannot be taken away by subsequent legislation but may be thereafter enforced by the court regardless of such legislation. This rule, however, does not apply to a suit brought for the enforcement of a public right." [202]

The distinction upon which the curative-act cases turn is not inconsistent with the reasoning already discussed which bars the legislature from exercising judicial functions. A public right, in the sense in which that term was used in the *Wheeling Bridge* case, is one which depends entirely upon the will of the legislature. In such a case, the existence of a court judgment affirming the existence of the right under the statute book as it then stands does not affect the power of the legislature over such right. Where the legislature has the power to pass a statute modifying or abrogating such public right in the absence of a judgment, the entry of a judgment does not convert the exercise of a legislative function into the exercise of a judicial function.[203]

38
LEGISLATIVE VERSUS EXECUTIVE POWER

What is true of judicial functions is also basically true of executive functions. The legislature itself may not exercise functions which are executive in nature, unless clearly authorized to do so by the Constitution. Thus, the legislature itself may not appoint a committee of its members as its executive agent to carry out a law.[204] In the phrase of a state judge: "the Legislature cannot become an administrative body, or through its members or committees, perform the work of the executive." [205] A statute cannot empower the legislature to designate certain of its members to serve on an administrative board.[206] Nor can the legislature give the chairmen of its appropriations committees the power to share with the chief executive his authority to determine how appropriations are actually spent.[207] While the legislature has full control over appropriations, it cannot administer the money after it has been appropriated.[208]

The power to appoint government officers has been involved in a number of cases. The power of appointment is plainly executive in character. "Legislative power," the Supreme Court has said, "as distinguished from executive power, is the authority to make laws, but not to enforce them or appoint the agents charged with the duty of such enforcement. The latter are executive functions." [209] The Constitution does, nevertheless, expressly permit the legislature to participate in the appointment process by requiring that all appointments by the President must be made "by and with the Advice and Consent of the Senate." Such express provision apart, however, it is settled that the legislature cannot itself play a direct part in the executive function of appointing government officers. The legislature cannot itself appoint such officers,[210] nor can it designate a panel of candidates, from among whom the specific executive appointee must be chosen.[211] And, where "purely executive officers" [212] are concerned, legislative consent cannot be imposed as a condition to removal from office; with regard to such officers, the power to remove is a necessary corollary of the executive authority to appoint.[213]

The leading case on the legislative exercise of executive functions—*Springer v. Philippine Islands* [214]—is closer to the borderline. At issue in it was the power to vote government-owned stock in certain corporations. The relevant statute vested such power in a board, a majority of whose members were specified members of the legislature. In holding such law invalid, the high Court examined the power to vote stock, decided that it was clearly not legislative or judicial in nature, and hence concluded that it must be executive: "It is clear that they are not legislative in character and still more clear that they are not judicial. The fact that they do not fall within the authority of either of these two constitutes logical ground for concluding that they do fall within that of the remaining one of the three among which the powers of government are divided." [215]

The Court's approach in the *Springer* decision reminds one of that followed in the familiar parlor game: "It is not animal. It is not vegetable. Therefore, it must be mineral." One wonders whether it is the way to deal with a difficult case of separation of powers. When the power at issue is a doubtful one, which does not manifestly belong to one of the three branches, it should, in Justice Holmes's phrase, "fall into the indiscriminate residue of matters within legislative control." [216] Such an approach, recognizing that there are equivocal powers which need not be arbitrarily fitted into a procrustean trichotomy, holds that it is for the legislature to determine which branch shall exercise such powers.[217]

4

CONGRESSIONAL INVESTIGATORY POWER

39
CONSTITUTIONAL
BASIS

FEW aspects of Congressional authority have received more public attention in recent years than the power of investigation. At times, in truth, it has seemed as if the chief role of the Congress has become that of what William Pitt the Elder once called the "Grand Inquest of the Nation." Since World War II at least, the Congressman *qua* inquisitor has all too often seemed to place the Congressman *qua* legislator in the shade.

It can hardly be denied at this late date that the power of inquiry is an essential auxiliary to the legislative function. The proper performance of that function presupposes the existence of an informed judgment on the part of the members of the legislative assembly. "An informed Congress," Harry S. Truman has declared, "is a wise Congress; an uninformed Congress surely will forfeit a large portion of the respect and confidence of the people." [1] It is by use of investigatory power that the Congress obtains the information needed to enable it adequately to exercise its functions. It is, indeed, not too much to say that, under contemporary conditions, investigating committees have become, in large part, the eyes and ears of the legislative department. "Without the power to investigate . . . ," as Chief Justice Warren has put it, "Congress could be seriously handicapped in its efforts to exercise its constitutional function wisely and effectively." [2]

Yet, important though the legislative investigatory power clearly be, it is one which is nowhere authorized in the Constitution. In the words of the Supreme Court in a leading case: "there is no provision expressly investing either house with power to make investigations and exact testimony, to the end that it may exercise its legislative function advisedly and effectively. So the question arises whether this power is so far incidental to the legislative function as to be implied." [3]

From the founding of the Republic, the Congress has proceeded upon the assumption that it possessed investigatory authority as a necessary incident of the powers expressly delegated to it. The power was first asserted in 1792, when the House of Representatives appointed a select committee to inquire into the disaster that befell General St. Clair and his army in their expedition against the Indians. From the St. Clair probe to our own day, the investigatory power has been exercised with ever-increasing frequency. "The power of inquiry," the Supreme Court informs us, "has been employed by Congress throughout our history, over the whole range of the national interests concerning which Congress might legislate or decide upon due investigation not to legislate." [4]

Though the Congress has thus, from the beginning, acted on the supposition that its power to investigate was a "necessary and proper" implied power,[5] it was not until *McGrain v. Daugherty* [6] in 1927 that the constitutional basis of Congressional investigatory authority was specifically spelled out by the Supreme Court. The *McGrain* case arose out of a Senatorial investigation of the executive departments implicated in the Teapot Dome scandals. The investigating committee had issued a subpoena to the brother of the Attorney General. When he refused to obey, the Senate directed that he be brought before its bar. Before that could be done, the recalcitrant witness secured a writ of habeas corpus from a federal district court on the ground that the Senate, in making the investigation, had exceeded its powers.

In reversing, the Supreme Court delivered an opinion broadly sustaining the Congressional power of inquiry: "We are of opinion that the power of inquiry—with process to enforce it—is an essential and appropriate auxiliary to the legislative function. . . . A legislative body cannot legislate wisely or effectively in the absence of information respecting the conditions which the legislation is intended to affect or change; and where the legislative body does not itself possess the requisite information—which not infrequently is true—recourse must be had to others who do possess it. . . . Thus there is ample warrant for thinking, as we do, that the constitutional provisions which commit the legislative function to the two houses are intended to include this attribute to the end that the function may be effectively exercised." [7]

McGrain v. Daugherty definitely sustains the power of either House of the legislature, in the high Court's words, "through its own process, to compel a private individual to appear before it or one of its committees and give testimony needed to enable it efficiently to exercise a legislative function belonging to it under the Constitution." [8] To say thus much, however, does not answer the question of how the power to investigate can be made effective in practice nor that of what limitations, if any, the power may be subject to under the Constitution. To these questions—those of sanctions and restrictions—we must now turn.

40

SANCTIONS   "Experience," said Justice Van Devanter in the *McGrain* opinion, "has taught that mere requests for . . . information often are unavailing, and also that information which is volunteered is not always accurate or complete; so some means of compulsion are essential to obtain what is needed." [9] Investigatory authority shorn of the sanction of compulsory process is but a truncated power.

The basic sanction behind the Congressional power of inquiry is the contempt power. Either House may treat the failure of an individual to comply with its process as a contempt and may itself commit him or otherwise punish him for such flouting of its authority. The Congressional contempt power was first judicially confirmed in the 1821 case of *Anderson v. Dunn*.[10] The question there [11] was whether the House of Representatives had power to attach and punish a person other than a member for contempt of its authority—in fact, an attempt to bribe one of its members. The Supreme Court answered the question in the affirmative, regarding the contempt power as an essential implied power. As explained in a later case, in *Anderson v. Dunn,* it was "explicitly decided that from the power to legislate given by the Constitution to Congress there was to be implied the right of Congress to preserve itself; that is, to deal by way of contempt with direct obstructions to its legislative duties." [12]

Since *Anderson v. Dunn,* it has been settled that either House of the Congress has the power to commit for contempt any person who obstructs its investigatory authority by ignoring its process or refusing to answer its inquiries.[13] It is, at the same time, important to bear in mind that Congressional contempt power is limited by its object—i.e., to prevent interferences with the legitimate functions of the two Houses. No act is punishable as a contempt of the Congress, the Supreme Court has said, "unless it is of a nature to obstruct the performance of the duties of the Legislature." [14] In *Marshall v. Gordon,*[15] an individual had written to the chairman of a House subcommittee an ill-tempered letter attacking the subcommittee and its actions. The House then committed him for contempt, asserting that the letter was "defamatory and insulting and tends to bring the House into public contempt and ridicule." The Supreme Court held that the House could not thus punish the writing of the letter because such act was not of a character to affect the legislative process: "the contempt relied upon was not intrinsic to the right of the House to preserve the means of discharging its duties, but was extrinsic to the discharge of such duties." [16] The power to punish for contempt may not be extended to defamatory attacks which present no immediate obstruction to legislative processes.[17]

In *Jurney v. MacCracken*,[18] it was argued that the just-discussed limitation upon the contempt power bars the punishment of a witness who, having been subpoenaed to appear before the Senate with certain papers, destroyed them before his appearance. It was asserted that, since the contempt power in this case could not remove any obstruction to the legislative process,[19] it could not be used to punish the witness. The high bench rejected this contention. The power to punish for a past contempt, said Justice Brandeis, is an appropriate means for "vindication of the established and essential privilege of requiring the production of evidence." [20] In other words, assertion of the contempt power has the twofold purpose of inducing the contumacious individual to cease his obstruction of the legislative process and to punish his contumacy. The punishment may be imposed even if it cannot result in removing the obstruction.[21]

Perhaps the most significant practical limitation upon the Congressional contempt power is that laid down in the very beginning in *Anderson v. Dunn*.[22] According to the opinion there, imprisonment for contempt of either House must terminate with the adjournment of the chamber concerned.[23] This limitation, it was soon recognized, gravely impaired the effectiveness of the contempt sanction: "imprisonment limited to the duration of the session," the Supreme Court tells us, "was not considered sufficiently drastic a punishment for contumacious witnesses." [24]

In 1857, the Congress dealt with the problem by a law making it a misdemeanor for any person summoned by the authority of either House to refuse to answer or to produce papers. Thus a criminal sanction was added to make the power to compel testimony more effective. The act of 1857 was upheld as constitutional in *In re Chapman*.[25] A law to compel witnesses to disclose evidence was an act "necessary and proper" for carrying into execution the Congressional investigatory power.

The high Court in the *Chapman* case emphasized that the purpose of the 1857 statute was merely to supplement the power of contempt by providing for additional punishment. Enactment of the statute does not affect the contempt power itself, which continues unimpaired in the two Houses. Punishment of a recalcitrant witness through contempt proceedings is not precluded merely because punishment may be inflicted for the same act as a statutory offense.[26] In recent years, nevertheless, the Congress has practically abandoned its practice of utilizing the coercive sanction of contempt proceedings at the bar of the relevant House. Instead it has invoked the aid of the courts in protecting itself against contumacious conduct.[27] It has become customary to refer "contempt of Congress" cases to the Department of Justice for criminal prosecution under the modern version of the 1857 statute.[28]

41
JUDICIAL REVIEW

"That the Commons are, in the words of Lord Coke, the general inquisitors of the realm, I fully admit . . . ," stated an English judge in an important case. "I would be content to state that they may inquire into everything which it concerns the public weal for them to know; and they themselves, I think, are entrusted with the determination of what falls within that category." [29]

It is settled in English law that a commitment by the House of Commons is not examinable by any court.[30] The exclusion of *lex parliamenti* [31] from the *lex terrae,* or law of the land, has precluded judicial review of exercises of the legislative contempt power.[32] From the seventeenth century, the bench in Britain has upheld the Parliamentary claim that no court had jurisdiction to consider such matters.[33]

In the 1881 case of *Kilbourn v. Thompson,*[34] it was contended that the contempt power of the House of Representatives was comparable in this respect to that possessed by the House of Commons. The Supreme Court refused to follow this view. According to it: "the powers and privileges of the House of Commons of England, on the subject of punishment for contempts, rests on principles which have no application to other legislative bodies, and certainly can have none to the House of Representatives of the United States." [35]

American courts have never followed the English precedents on the nonreviewability of legislative exercises of the contempt power. On the contrary, with us, as Chief Justice Warren states: "Unlike the English practice, from the very outset the use of the contempt power by the legislature was deemed subject to judicial review." [36]

The very first case to reach the highest Court, *Anderson v. Dunn,*[37] illustrates the attitude of American judges on the matter. In that case, it will be recalled, the House of Representatives had asserted its contempt power over a person who had attempted to bribe a member. The House had ordered its sergeant-at-arms to arrest the person concerned and convey him to the bar of the House, where he had been formally reprimanded by the Speaker. He then brought an action of trespass for assault and battery and false imprisonment against the sergeant-at-arms. The latter pleaded the order of the House in justification. Under the English decisions, this would have ended the case. The Supreme Court, however, found it necessary fully to review the legality of the action taken by the House before it sustained defendant's plea.

Anderson v. Dunn established the review power of the American courts in legislative-contempt cases. It is true that there have been few cases requiring such review. Indeed, it was not until sixty years after *Anderson v. Dunn* that another case dealing with Congressional investigatory authority arose. The case referred to—*Kilbourn v. Thompson* [38]—will be discussed more fully at a later point.[39] It settled beyond all question the authority of the courts to review legislative exercises of the contempt power, for it held that both the investigation of the House of Representatives involved in the case and a commitment for contempt for refusing to testify in such investigation were invalid. "We cannot give our assent," the *Kilbourn* opinion declares, "to the principle that, by the mere act of asserting a person to be guilty of a contempt, they [40] thereby establish their right to fine and imprison him, beyond the power of any court or any other tribunal whatever to inquire into the grounds on which the order was made." [41]

The basic principle of American constitutional law, applicable here as in other areas, is that which denies the existence of unreviewable governmental authority. All acts of power must be subjected to an appeal to law, as ultimately pronounced by the highest tribunal of the land. Absolute unreviewable authority is utterly inconsistent with the genius of the American system. This is as true of Congressional exercises of investigatory power as it is of other governmental acts. In the words of the *Kilbourn* opinion, "The House of Representatives . . . is not the final judge of its own power and privileges in cases in which the rights and liberties of the subject are concerned, but the legality of its action may be examined and determined by this court." [42]

In cases involving direct Congressional exercises of the contempt power, judicial review may be obtained in one of two ways: 1) as in *Anderson v. Dunn*,[43] the individual committed can later sue the officials involved for false imprisonment; [44] or 2) he can, while committed, petition for a writ of habeas corpus.[45] In either case, the court concerned must review the legality both of the investigation involved in the case and of the facts constituting the alleged contempt before it can decide. If the particular exercise of Congressional investigatory authority was itself invalid, it is obvious that a contempt could not have been perpetrated.

As already pointed out,[46] punishment for "contempt of Congress" is, at the present time, usually imposed under the statute making it a misdemeanor to refuse to answer or produce papers in response to the process of either House, rather than by the direct exercise of the contempt power by the Congress itself. In a criminal prosecution of a recalcitrant witness, there can be no doubt of the power of the court to review the validity of the given exercise of legislative investigatory power. Unless the court upholds the legality of the particular investigation and the manner in which it was carried on, it must find that no offense has been committed.

To say that the courts can review exercises of Congressional investigatory authority does not, however, tell us upon what basis the judicial review power itself should be employed. We must now examine more specifically the scope of legislative investigatory power and the limitations, if any, imposed upon it by the courts.

42

SCOPE OF INVESTIGATORY POWER

The Commons, says Lord Coke in a passage already referred to, are "the general inquisitors of the realm." It would be difficult, in the words of an English judge commenting on the statement, "to define any limits by which their inquiries can be bounded." [47]

American courts have rejected the notion that legislators are "the general inquisitors of the realm." In the United States, the fundamental principle governing the scope of the Congressional power of inquiry is that laid down in *Kilbourn v. Thompson*.[48] According to the high Court there, investigatory authority could properly be employed only "in aid of the legislative function." [49] The power of inquiry is an auxiliary power which may be utilized solely to aid the Congress in the exercise of the legislative powers delegated to it. Investigation may be availed of by the legislature, according to *McGrain v. Daugherty,* only to secure "testimony needed to enable it efficiently to exercise a legislative function belonging to it under the Constitution." [50]

It is, on the other hand, important to bear in mind that a power as significant as that of inquiry is not one that is niggardly to be construed. Even with the limitation just referred to, Congressional investigatory authority is most broad.[51] It may be employed over the whole range of the national interests concerning which the Congress may legislate or decide, upon due investigation, not to legislate; it may similarly be utilized in determining what to appropriate from the national purse, or whether to appropriate. As the high bench expressed it in 1959, "The scope of the power of inquiry, in short, is as penetrating and far-reaching as the potential power to enact and appropriate under the Constitution." [52]

Congressional investigatory authority is consequently as broad as the legislative power delegated by Article I. It encompasses both the sword and the purse and may be utilized in any area in which Congressional power itself may be exerted.

Nor, it should be noted, is it necessary for a particular inquiry to be valid to show that it will result in the enactment of specific laws. In *McGrain v. Daugherty*,[53] the highest Court held that investigation by the Senate into corruption in the handling of federal oil leases was proper, even though the resolution directing the investigation did not in terms avow that it was intended to be in aid of legislation. In such a case, said the Court, it would be presumed that the object of the inquiry was to aid the Senate in its legislative functions. A legitimate legislative purpose, in other words, had to be assumed whenever "the subject was one on which legislation could be had and would be materially aided by the information which the investigation was calculated to elicit." [54]

Congressional power of inquiry is thus not limited to securing information directly bearing on some proposed measure, the enactment of which is presently being calculated. As one judge has put it: "If the subject under scrutiny may have any possible relevancy and materiality, no matter how remote, to some possible legislation, it is within the power of the Congress to investigate the matter." [55] This language may go too far, but it is clear that the power of inquiry is coextensive with the power of legislation and is not limited to the scope or the content of contemplated legislation. Potentiality, not actuality, of legislation is the measure of the investigatory power.[56]

At the same time, from *Kilbourn v. Thompson* down to our own day, the cases rebound in denials that the scope of Congressional investigatory authority is unlimited. In the 1957 phrase of Chief Justice Warren, "broad as is this power of inquiry, it is not unlimited." [57]

What are the limitations referred to? In the opinion just quoted from, the Chief Justice indicated these in the following language: "There is no general authority to expose the private affairs of individuals without justification in terms of the functions of the Congress. . . . Nor is the Congress a law enforcement or trial agency. These are functions of the executive and judicial departments of government. No inquiry is an end in itself; it must be related to, and in furtherance of, a legitimate task of the Congress." [58]

To determine more precisely what these limitations mean, it is necessary to discuss the cases that have arisen. This will be done in the following sections, first, with regard to investigations of government officials, and then with regard to inquiries into the affairs of private individuals.

43

PUBLIC
OFFICERS

Lecturing in Philadelphia in 1791, Justice Wilson, himself one of the leading draftsmen of the Constitution, declared "The house of representatives . . . form the grand inquest of the state. They will inquire diligently into grievances, arising both from men and things." [59]

The concept of the Congress as a "grand inquest" is peculiarly appropriate to investigations by either House into the workings of the executive branch. In such inquiries, the legislative authority is at its maximum, for the Congress is patently acting in pursuance of a legitimate legislative function—i.e., that of supervision of administration. When the House of Representatives, in its very first investigation, called upon the Father of his Country himself to produce the records relating to the expedition of General St. Clair, President Washington's Cabinet unanimously determined: "First, that the House was an inquest and therefore might institute inquiries. Second, that they might call for papers generally." [60]

Where a Congressional investigation is one into the operation of a government agency, the scope of inquiry cannot be restricted. Any aspect of such operation is a legitimate subject for scrutiny. Only thus can the Congressional responsibility to oversee administration be effectively vindicated. The Supreme Court itself has expressly "recognized the danger to effective and honest conduct of the Government if the legislature's power to probe corruption in the executive branch were unduly hampered." [61]

To a claim by a government official that a particular probe into his conduct is beyond the scope of permissible inquiry, the Congress may well say, as did the Massachusetts House of Representatives in 1722, that it is "not only their Privilege but Duty to demand of any Officer in the pay and service of this Government an account of his management while in the Public Imploy." [62]

In *McGrain v. Daugherty*,[63] where the investigation was one into the misconduct of the Attorney General and other executive officials in the handling of federal oil leases, it was claimed that what the Senate was really doing was to determine the guilt of the Attorney General. As it was put by the lower court, which upheld such claim, "What it has done is to put him on trial before it. In so doing it is exercising the judicial function. This it has no power to do." [64]

The Supreme Court, in reversing, specifically stated that the lower court's ruling on this point was wrong. It sufficiently appears, said Justice Van Devanter, that the object of the investigation was to obtain information for legislative purposes. The subject investigated was the administration of the Department of Justice—plainly one on which legislative action could be had. "This becomes manifest," the *McGrain* opinion went on, "when it is reflected that the functions of the Department of Justice, the powers and duties of the Attorney General, and the duties of his assistants are all subject to regulation by congressional legislation, and that the department is maintained and its activities are carried on under such appropriations as in the judgment of Congress are needed from year to year." [65]

Where, in other words, a Congressional investigation inquires into the conduct of federal officers, such officers cannot protest on the ground that they are being subjected to a nonjudicial trial. That the investigation may disclose crime or wrongdoing on the part of such officers is not a valid objection.[66] Exposure of wrongdoing is an essential tool to enable the Congress to perform its role as supervisor of the executive branch. Such role, as Chief Justice Warren has put it, "comprehends probes into departments of the Federal Government to expose corruption, inefficiency or waste." [67]

In *Watkins v. United States*,[68] as will be seen more fully in section 45, the high Court declared that Congressional investigatory authority did not include the power "to expose for the sake of exposure." [69] It should, nevertheless, be emphasized that this limitation has no application to inquiries into the operation of the executive. In such inquiries, there is not the same danger of exposure for exposure's sake that may exist in a case like *Watkins,* which concerned only the investigation of a private individual.

The opinion of the Court in *Watkins,* indeed, contains a clear recognition of the distinction in this respect between investigation of private persons and inquiry into the executive branch. "The public," categorically declares Chief Justice Warren, "is, of course, entitled to be informed concerning the workings of its government." [70] And he goes on to state expressly: "We are not concerned with the power of the Congress to inquire into and publicize corruption, maladministration or inefficiency in agencies of the Government. That was the only kind of activity described by Woodrow Wilson in *Congressional Government* when he wrote: 'The informing function of Congress should be preferred even to its legislative function.' . . . From the earliest times in its history, the Congress has assiduously performed an 'informing function' of this nature." [71]

Watkins itself thus plainly implies a preferred position for Congressional investigations into the workings of federal agencies. The legislative power, says the opinion there, "encompasses inquiries concerning the administration of existing laws as well as proposed or possibly needed statutes." [72] Where such inquiries are at issue, the Congress may rightly assert as once did William Pitt the Elder: "We are called the Grand Inquest of the Nation, and as such it is our duty to inquire into every Step of publick management, either Abroad or at Home, in order to see that nothing has been done amiss." [73]

44

PRIVATE   What happens, however, if it is, not "publick man-
INDIVIDUALS   agement," but private affairs that are being inquired
                         into by the legislature? The right to be informed of
the workings of government, the Supreme Court has declared, "cannot be
inflated into a general power to expose where the predominant result can
only be an invasion of the private rights of individuals." [74]

The leading case on the lack of authority in the Congress to inquire
generally into private affairs is *Kilbourn v. Thompson*.[75] The question at
issue there was whether the House of Representatives had exceeded its
power in directing a particular investigation. The inquiry related to a private
real estate pool or partnership in the District of Columbia. A certain company had had an interest in the pool, but had become bankrupt, and its
property was in course of administration in a federal court. The United
States was one of its creditors. The trustee in the bankruptcy proceeding had
effected a settlement of the bankrupt's interest in the pool. Some of the
creditors, including the United States, were dissatisfied with the settlement.
In these circumstances, the House resolution directed its committee "to
inquire into the matter and history of said real estate pool and the character of said settlement, with the amount of property involved in which
Jay Cooke and Company were interested, and the amount paid or to be
paid in said settlement, with power to send for persons and papers and
report to the House."

The Supreme Court held that such an investigation was beyond the
legislative power. Justice Miller pointed out that the resolution authorizing
the inquiry contained no suggestion of contemplated legislation; that the
matter was one in respect to which no valid legislation could be enacted;
and that the United States and other creditors were free to press their
claims in the bankruptcy proceeding. For these reasons, the Court concluded, "we are of opinion that the House of Representatives not only
exceeded the limit of its own authority, but assumed a power which could
only be properly exercised by another branch of the government, because
it was in its nature clearly judicial." [76]

Kilbourn v. Thompson rests on the proposition that, in conducting an
inquiry into the private affairs of a citizen, the House was exercising power
judicial in nature.[77] What was the investigating committee authorized to do?
asks Justice Miller. "To inquire into the nature and history of the real
estate pool. How indefinite!" [78] Was the pool "charged with any crime or
offense? If so, the courts alone can punish the members of it." [79] To probe
generally into the business of a stranger is beyond the authority of the
legislative committee, where such business is not directly subject to federal
control. "Can the rights of the pool, or of its members, and the rights of

the debtor, and of the creditor of the debtor, be determined by a report of the committee or by an Act of Congress? If they cannot, what authority has the House to enter upon this investigation into the private affairs of individuals who hold no office under the government." [80]

As explained in a later case, *Kilbourn v. Thompson* stands for the holding that "neither House of Congress possesses a 'general power of making inquiry into the private affairs of the citizen'; that the power actually possessed is limited to inquiries relating to matters of which the particular house 'has jurisdiction' and in respect of which it rightfully may take other action." [81]

Kilbourn v. Thompson prevents the Congress from assuming the role of general inquisitors, with authority to pry into everyman's innermost affairs—to run the eye up and down all individual accounts, sniff into every corner, peep behind curtains and under beds, and examine every cupboard, no matter how personal. The *Kilbourn* decision has been criticized; but it does mark a limit beyond which investigatory power may not go. Who is to say from what Congressional autos-da-fé the mere judicial drawing of the line has preserved us?

It should not, at the same time, be thought from the above that *Kilbourn* imposes an absolute bar to legislative probes into the business of ordinary citizens. What is beyond Congressional power, under the Supreme Court decision, is probing into purely private affairs. Where, on the other hand, a private individual is engaged in dealings with the Government or its officials, his affairs should not be immune from inquiry.

Sinclair v. United States [82] well illustrates the Congressional authority in such cases. Like the *McGrain* case already discussed,[83] it also arose out of the Teapot Dome scandals involving corruption in the handling of federal oil leases in the 1920's. Appellant was the president of a large oil company who had procured a lease of extensive oil lands from the Secretary of the Navy and the Secretary of the Interior. He was called as a witness before the Senate committee set up to investigate leases upon federal oil reserves. Upon his refusal to answer certain questions, he was indicted and convicted under the law, already discussed,[84] making it a misdemeanor to refuse to testify before a Congressional committee. In upholding the conviction, the Supreme Court decided that the Senate was clearly authorized to conduct an investigation touching the rights and equities of the United States as owner of the oil lands in question. "The committee's authority to investigate," it declared, "extended to matters affecting the interest of the United States as owner as well as to those having relation to the legislative function." [85] That being the case, it could inquire into the leases made by the Government as owner with a private individual. The latter's dealings with the Government were not purely private affairs, within the rule of

Kilbourn v. Thompson: "While appellant caused the Mammoth Oil Company to be organized and owned all its shares, the transaction purporting to lease to it the lands within the reserve cannot be said to be merely or principally the personal or private affair of appellant. It was a matter of concern to the United States." [86]

The business of a private individual is also within the Congressional investigatory power where it is subject to federal regulation. In such a case, the business concerned is one over which the relevant administrative agency possesses all-pervasive investigatory authority.[87] It could hardly be contended that such broad powers of inquiry are possessed by an agency which is only a delegate of the Congress and not by the Congress itself from whence the delegate derived its authority.

The result is similar where the Congress exercises its investigatory power in order to determine whether or not a given field of economic activity should be brought under government regulation. An outstanding illustration of such a case is the so-called Wall Street investigation of 1933, in which the Congress sought and obtained information about banking and stock-exchange practices that led to a series of regulatory statutes, which sought to curb the abuses found to be prevalent in the investment business.

It should, however, be emphasized that where the basis for exertion of the investigatory power against a private citizen is his dealings with the Government, the actual existence of such dealings by him is essential before the Congressional power can be exercised. In *Kilbourn v. Thompson* itself, it will be recalled, the United States was a creditor of the company which had invested in the real estate pool which was being investigated. According to the Supreme Court, all the same, this did not make the private business of the pool a direct concern of the Government: "Upon the allegation that the United States is a creditor of a man who has an interest in some other man's business, the affairs of the latter [cannot] be subjected to the unlimited scrutiny or investigation of a congressional committee." [88] The link between the person being investigated and the Government must be more direct to make the inquiry into his business more than an incursion into purely private affairs.

45

EXPOSURE FOR   Between *Kilbourn v. Thompson* and our own day,
EXPOSURE'S SAKE   there was little occasion for the courts to apply the
                    rule against Congressional probing into purely private
affairs. Aside from the Teapot Dome cases already discussed,[89] which plainly did not transgress the *Kilbourn* limitation, there were few challenges to legislative inquiries in the courts.

This has all changed in recent years. As Chief Justice Warren has pointed out: "In the decade following World War II, there appeared a new kind of congressional inquiry unknown in prior periods of American history. Principally this was the result of the various investigations into the threat of subversion of the United States Government, but other subjects of congressional interest also contributed to the changed scene. This new phase of legislative inquiry involved a broad-scale intrusion into the lives and affairs of private citizens." [90]

It can hardly be denied that not all of the recent investigations into the problem of subversion have been conducted with the restraint which characterized most prior probes. On the contrary, the country has become accustomed to the "free-wheeling" Congressional committee, whose powers have been exercised, not so much for legitimate legislative purposes, as for the personal aggrandizement of the investigators themselves. In the work of such a committee, we have had, if not exposure for the sake of exposure, all too often at least exposure designed to propel and maintain the Senators and Congressmen concerned in the nation's headlines.

Congressional inquisitions such as those referred to have given rise to widespread expressions of legitimate anxiety. In Justice Frankfurter's words: "we would have to be that 'blind' Court, against which Mr. Chief Justice Taft admonished in a famous passage, . . . that does not see what '[a]ll others can see and understand' not to know that there is widespread concern, both in and out of Congress, over some aspects of the exercise of the congressional power of investigation." [91] This concern led directly to the Supreme Court's sharp rebuff to the Congressional power of inquiry in the 1957 case of *Watkins v. United States.*[92]

In *Watkins,* for the first time in almost a century,[93] the high bench found that an exercise of Congressional investigatory authority exceeded the permissible limits upon legislative power. Perhaps the most striking portion of the *Watkins* opinion was the statement already referred to: "We have no doubt that there is no congressional power to expose for the sake of exposure." [94]

It has been shown in section 43 that this language has no application to legislative inquiries into the conduct of government officials. *Watkins* itself did not involve such an investigation. It concerned an investigation by the Un-American Activities Committee of the House of Representatives of a private individual, who had no dealings with the United States. In such a case, what is the practical effect of the Court's prohibition of "exposure for exposure's sake"?

One may strongly sympathize with the high tribunal's feeling of revulsion toward inquisitions such as those conducted by the House Committee on Un-American Activities and the late Senator McCarthy as well as with the effort in *Watkins* to impose a judicial check upon Congressional excesses. The difficulty arises when we attempt to apply the exposure-for-exposure's-sake limitation in an actual case. Such application must involve inquiry into Congressional motives of a type for which the judicial process is wholly unsuited. "According to an early English judge, 'The devil himself knoweth not the mind of man,' and a modern . . . court is not much better equipped to lay bare unexposed mental processes." [95] If a Congressional probe is one that appears to serve a proper legislative purpose, shall a court hold that it is vitiated solely because the underlying motive of the investigators is to expose for the sake of exposure?

That the solution to the problem of Congressional excesses in this area is not to be found in the judicial testing of the motives of committee members is shown by *Barenblatt v. United States* (1959).[96] It arose out of petitioner's refusal to answer certain questions put to him by the House Committee on Un-American Activities in the course of an inquiry into Communist activities. This was the Committee whose action had been condemned in *Watkins* and, not unnaturally, petitioner in *Barenblatt* urged that here, too, the investigation at issue should be deemed invalid because the true objective of the Committee was purely "exposure." A minority of the Supreme Court agreed with this contention. The majority, however, rejected it, in terms that indicate that the *Watkins* prohibition against "exposure for exposure's sake" itself is to be taken largely as *obiter*.

Under the majority approach in the *Barenblatt* case, the only question for the Court to answer is whether the particular investigation was related to a valid legislative purpose. In *Barenblatt,* such relationship was said to be clearly established: "That Congress has wide power to legislate in the field of Communist activity in this Country, and to conduct appropriate investigations in aid thereof, is hardly debatable." [97]

That being the case, it is irrelevant that petitioner claims that the true objective of the committee was "exposure" rather than the furtherance of a legislative purpose. "So long," states the *Barenblatt* opinion, "as Congress acts in pursuance of its constitutional power, the Judiciary lacks authority to intervene on the basis of the motives which spurred the exercise of that power." [98] If a Congressional investigation, in other words, is related to a valid legislative purpose, it cannot be invalidated because the Court feels that its real purpose is the exposure of those being investigated.

Under *Barenblatt,* the courts may not go behind the ostensible objective of an investigatory committee to determine that the true motive of the Congressmen was only "exposure." It may be objected that such an approach will leave the citizen helpless before abuses of Congressional investigatory power. One wonders, nevertheless, whether such an objection can validly be addressed to the courts in our system. As the high tribunal put it in a 1951 case: "Legislative committees have been charged with losing sight of their duty of disinterestedness. In times of political passion, dishonest or vindictive motives are readily attributed to legislative conduct and as readily believed. Courts are not the place for such controversies." [99]

Nor should it be forgotten that *Kilbourn v. Thompson* still remains as a fundamental check against roving commissions of inquiry that have no relationship to legitimate legislative objectives. Under *Kilbourn,* the Congress still may not pry into purely private affairs. As a practical matter, indeed, the *Kilbourn* rule enables the courts to restrain many legislative probes, whose only purpose is the exposure of private individuals, without requiring the judges to set themselves up as censors of Congressional motives.

46

ENABLING   A Congressional committee, like all other agencies
RESOLUTIONS   of American government, possesses only delegated
                 powers. The source of its authority is the enabling
resolution passed by the chamber setting up such committee. As is true of all power in our system, that of a Congressional committee can rise no higher than its source. A committee of either House is wholly a creature of the resolution establishing it and can only act in accordance with the provisions of that instrument. The enabling resolution is, in other words, the controlling charter of the committee's powers.[100] Any investigatory authority exercised beyond the scope authorized by such charter is *ultra vires* and void.

The principle just stated was the basis for the 1953 decision in *United States v. Rumely.*[101] The House of Representatives had adopted a resolution establishing a select committee to investigate "lobbying activities." Respondent was the secretary of an organization which, among other activities, engaged in the sale of books and other literature of a political nature. He refused to disclose to the House select committee the names of those who made bulk purchases of these books for further distribution. He was convicted of "contempt of Congress," but the Supreme Court reversed. The House, according to the Court, had meant to authorize its select committee only to investigate lobbying in its "commonly accepted sense," that is, "representations made directly to the Congress, its members, or its committees." [102] That being the case, the committee had acted beyond its authority in investigating the selling of books by respondent's organization.

A more difficult matter is that of the validity of a particular enabling resolution itself. In recent years, that question has arisen with regard to the charter of the House Committee on Un-American Activities. Under the resolution setting it up, that Committee is authorized to investigate "un-American" activities and propaganda in this country that attack "the principle of the form of government as guaranteed by our Constitution."

In the already-discussed *Watkins* case,[103] the high Court cast doubt upon the validity of a resolution containing such a broad investigatory mandate. "It would be difficult," declared the opinion of Chief Justice Warren, "to imagine a less explicit authorizing resolution. Who can define the meaning of 'un-American'? What is that single, solitary 'principle of the form of government as guaranteed by our Constitution'?" [104]

The scope of inquiry that a Congressional committee is authorized to pursue must be defined with unambiguous clarity; the relevant enabling resolution must spell out the committee's jurisdiction and purpose with sufficient particularity.[105] In Justice Frankfurter's words: "The actual scope of the inquiry that the Committee was authorized to conduct . . . must be shown to have been luminous." [106] Implicit in the portion of the Court's opinion in the *Watkins* case quoted in the preceding paragraph is the view that the enabling resolution of the House Committee on Un-American Activities was too vague to be valid.

The difficulty with this view is that it loses sight of the practical realities of the legislative process. The exigencies of the Congressional calendar make it impossible for the mandates of committees to be laid down in other than broad terms. There is certainly as much justification for broad standards here as there is in the delegation of powers to administrative agencies.[107] The *Watkins* approach might invalidate the charters of most Congressional committees, since the common practice is for such committees to be given power "in exceedingly broad terms." [108] In addition, it is hard to see, under the *Watkins* language, how a body like the Un-American Activities Committee could be given a valid charter. Its area of investigation must, of necessity, be defined through terms such as "un-American." If such a term cannot be defined with mathematical precision, it does nonetheless, in its broad contours, cover sufficiently a field which comes within the legitimate concern of the Congress.

In *Barenblatt v. United States,*[109] dealt with in the prior section, petitioner relied on *Watkins* as holding that the resolution authorizing the Un-American Activities Committee was invalid because of its vagueness in delineating the Committee's jurisdiction. The majority of the Court rejected this argument. "We cannot agree with this contention," declared Justice Harlan, "which in its furthest reach would mean that the House Un-American Activities Committee under its existing authority has no right to compel testimony in any circumstances." [110] The holding here is more consistent with legislative reality than the broad *Watkins* language. Whatever one may think of the manner in which the role of the Un-American Activities Committee has at times been exercised, that does not bear upon the Congressional power to constitute such a committee.

47
FIRST AMENDMENT AND OTHER CONSTITUTIONAL LIMITATIONS

Speaking of Congressional investigatory power in the already-discussed *Barenblatt* case,[111] Justice Harlan was careful to say that it must be exercised "subject to the limitations placed by the Constitution on governmental action." [112] Put in this way, of course, the statement is more or less a truism: All governmental authority in our system must be exercised subject to constitutional limitations. Investigatory power, too, being derived from the Constitution, can rise no higher than its source.[113]

More difficult than stating the rule of subjection of legislative investigatory authority to constitutional guarantees and restraints is that of determining its practical impact in particular cases. To be sure, where the Congressional power of inquiry is confronted by a specific organic prohibition, it is the former that must give way. Thus, it is clear that limitations on the power to investigate are found in the specific individual guarantees of the Bill of Rights, such as the Fifth Amendment's privilege against self-incrimination.[114] When the matter first reached the Supreme Court, the Government itself did not challenge the right of a witness before a Congressional committee to invoke the Fifth Amendment privilege.[115] Though there are no express cases, the same result would doubtless be reached where a legislative probe infringed upon rights such as those guaranteed by the Fourth Amendment.[116]

The question in this respect that has given the most concern in recent years is that of the extent to which Congressional investigatory authority is limited by the First Amendment. Legislative inquiries since World War II have not, like earlier investigations, been concerned only with the actions of those being investigated. Instead, they have probed into beliefs, expressions, and associations. This has been a well-nigh inevitable consequence of attempts to investigate subversion, such as those which have become prominent in recent years. At the same time, such legislative inquiries have directly raised the question of the relationship of Congressional investigatory authority to the First Amendment. When the investigative process tends to impinge upon such highly sensitive areas as freedom of speech or press, freedom of political association, and freedom of communication of ideas, it is bound to present difficult problems for the judicial process in a country where the First Amendment constitutes a basic article of political faith.

As a starting point, it is clear, as Chief Justice Warren has said, that a

Congressional investigation "is subject to the command that Congress make no law abridging freedom of speech or press or assembly. While it is true that . . . an investigation is not a law, nevertheless an investigation is part of lawmaking. . . . The First Amendment may be invoked against infringement of the protected freedoms by law or by lawmaking." [117]

To say that legislative probes are subject to the First Amendment is, nevertheless, only the beginning, not the end, of inquiry in the matter. Despite the unqualified nature of its language, it is settled that the First Amendment does not bar all legislative restrictions of the rights guaranteed by it.[118] If this is the case, it must follow that the Amendment also does not bar all legislative inquiries into the areas covered by it.

The argument against investigations into matters covered by the First Amendment was succinctly stated in a federal case: "Congress is prohibited from legislating upon matters of thought, speech, or opinion; ergo a statute empowering a Congressional committee to investigate such matters is unconstitutional." [119] According to the court which thus stated the argument: "The mere statement of this syllogism is sufficient to refute it." [120] Congressional restriction of First-Amendment rights is justified if there is a "clear and present danger" that the exercise of such rights in the particular circumstances will bring about substantive evils that the Congress has a right to prevent.[121] The Congress *can* legislate upon matters protected by the First Amendment if the "clear and present danger" test is satisfied. If this is true of legislation, it must also be true of investigation. The Constitution does not bar Congressional inquiry into First-Amendment freedoms which can themselves be restricted by legislation.

This is not, to be sure, to assert an unlimited power in the Congress to probe into matters of speech, association, and belief. That no such wholesale authority exists is shown by *Rumely v. United States.*[122] It arose out of an investigation by a House committee into the sale of books and other literature of a political nature by an organization called the Committee for Constitutional Government. The House committee concerned acted under a resolution authorizing it to investigate "all activities intended to influence, encourage, promote, or retard legislation," which it construed as giving it the power to inquire into activities "to influence legislation indirectly by influencing public opinion." [123] Such an investigation, it was held, was beyond the power of the House. The Congress cannot legislate concerning attempts to influence public opinion by speech, where there "is no suggestion that the publication or distribution of these books and documents constitutes any public danger, clear or otherwise, present or otherwise." [124] The power of investigation is similarly limited. "Since Congress could not," in Justice Douglas' words, "by law require of respondent what the House demanded, it may not take the first step in an inquiry ending in fine or imprisonment." [125]

A case like *Rumely* indicates that "In the political realm, as in the academic, thought and action are presumptively immune from inquisition by political authority." [126] But this does not prevent the Congress from inquiring into First Amendment rights whose exercise in the particular circumstances may be restricted by legislation under the "clear and present danger" test. This is shown clearly by the cases involving attacks on First Amendment grounds upon Congressional investigations into Communist activity. A number of lower-court decisions categorically uphold the legislative power to make such inquiries.[127] It is true that there is language in the already-discussed *Watkins* opinion [128] implying that any Congressional inquiry infringing upon First Amendment rights would be invalid.[129] Such language was, however, not necessary for the Court's decision, and the more recent *Barenblatt* case [130] indicates that it is to be given only the effect as *obiter* enunciated by Chief Justice Marshall in a famous statement—i.e., general language which goes beyond the actual case ought not to control the judgment in a subsequent suit.[131]

In *Barenblatt* itself, as our previous discussion of it indicated, what was at issue was a Congressional investigation into un-American activities. The particular hearing was one on Communist infiltration into the field of education. Petitioner, a college teacher, was asked about Communist activities and affiliations while he had been a graduate student. He urged that such inquiries transgressed the First Amendment. The Court rejected his contention. In its view: "Where First Amendment rights are asserted to bar governmental interrogation resolution of the issue always involves a balancing by the courts of the competing private and public interests at stake in the particular circumstances shown." [132] In a case like this, what the Court termed "the close nexus between the Communist Party and violent overthrow of government" [133] was found to justify this Congressional inquiry into an area covered by the First Amendment.

Subversive activities coming within the "clear and present danger" test are thus not to be treated as purely private affairs rendered immune from legislative scrutiny by the rule of *Kilbourn v. Thompson*.[134] On the contrary: "That Congress has wide power to legislate in the field of Communist activity in this Country, and to conduct appropriate investigations in aid thereof, is hardly debatable." [135] The power of the existing machinery of government to inquire into potential threats to itself must in the last analysis rest on the right of self-preservation—the ultimate value of any society.

Nor was the legislative authority in a case like *Barenblatt* defeated because its investigation was one into the field of education. In *Sweezy v. New Hampshire*,[136] decided the same day as the *Watkins* case, the high Court implied that education was completely immunized from legislative inquiry. *Sweezy* itself, it should be noted, involved questioning about affiliations with the Progressive Party and the advocacy of socialism by a professor in a university lecture. Certainly such interrogation does not appear justified. The Progressive Party was a legal political party [137] and, without more shown, an individual should be as free from inquiry into his affiliations with it as he is from compulsory inquiry into his membership in the Democratic or Republican parties. And the same is true of the probe into whether a professor taught socialist doctrine.

But this is not to say that all legislative inquiry into the field of education is precluded. In *Barenblatt,* the Court repudiated such broad implication: "We think that investigatory power in this domain is not to be denied Congress solely because the field of education is involved. Nothing in the prevailing opinions in *Sweezy* . . . stands for a contrary view." [138]

The *Barenblatt* clarification in this respect seems most salutary. The university with us is not a closed, monastic community. The claims of academic freedom hardly justify the wholesale prohibition of inquiries into Communist activity in the field of education. *Barenblatt* holds specifically that the Constitution is no bar against action by the Congress "inquiring into the extent to which the Communist Party has succeeded in infiltrating into our universities, or elsewhere, persons and groups committed to furthering the objective of overthrow." [139]

What has been said in this section has been based upon the assumption that investigation, like legislation, in the area of First Amendment rights can be justified only if it meets the requirements of the "clear and present danger" test.[140] According to one case, however, such a restriction is not justified in the case of investigatory power. In its view: "it would be sheer folly as a matter of governmental policy for an existing government to refrain from inquiry into potential threats to its existence or security until danger was clear and present. . . . How, except upon inquiry, would the Congress know whether the danger is clear and present?" [141]

Reflection will, it is believed, demonstrate that such a view tilts the balance unduly against the rights guaranteed by the First Amendment. Of course, government may deal at any time with threats to its security expressed in acts. Where speech, association, and other First Amendment rights are involved, on the other hand, the power of investigation should be no more far-reaching than that of legislation. In our system, authority over a subject matter involving speech, press, assembly, and the like must not go beyond the power to do that which is essential to be done in protection against a public danger.[142] Civil liberties may not be abridged by investigatory authority merely in order to determine whether they should be abridged.[143]

48

PERTINENCY AND
PROCEDURE
PROBLEMS

In *McGrain v. Daugherty*,[144] the Supreme Court articulated two basic grounds upon which witnesses could refuse to comply with Congressional investigative demands: "a witness rightfully may refuse to answer where the bounds of the power are exceeded or the questions are not pertinent to the matter under inquiry." [145] The question of the proper bounds of legislative investigatory authority has been dealt with in prior sections. That of pertinency must now be gone into.

That a witness has the right to refuse to answer a question on the ground of pertinency was the true basis of the high Court's decision in *Watkins v. United States*,[146] which has been referred to above at several points. Petitioner in *Watkins* had been questioned by a subcommittee of the House Committee on Un-American Activities, which was conducting an investigation into alleged Communist infiltration in labor unions. He was asked to identify some thirty persons, but refused to tell whether he knew them to have been members of the Communist Party. According to the Court, such questions were not clearly shown to be relevant to the subcommittee's inquiry. This conclusion was based upon the fact that many of the persons about whom petitioner was asked had no connection with any unions. "When almost a quarter of the persons on the list are not labor people," said the Court, "the inference becomes strong that the subject before the Subcommittee was not defined in terms of Communism in labor." [147]

This holding by the *Watkins* Court constitutes a needed check upon Congressional investigations. Under *Watkins,* for a witness to be convicted of "contempt of Congress," it must have been shown to him that the questions he refused to answer were clearly pertinent to an authorized inquiry of the investigating committee. As the Court put it: "knowledge of the subject to which the interrogation is deemed pertinent . . . must be available with the same degree of explicitness and clarity that the Due Process Clause requires in the expression of any element of a criminal offense." [148]

The *Watkins* test of pertinency was the basis for the more recent decision in *Scull v. Virginia*.[149] Defendant there was convicted of contempt in a Virginia court for refusing to obey a court order to answer certain questions put to him by an investigating committee of the Virginia legislature. The committee in question had been set up after the Supreme Court's decision invalidating segregation in public schools [150] and appeared to be aimed at organizations and individuals attempting to secure integration in Virginia schools. The resolution setting up the committee specified that it could inquire into three general subjects: (1) the tax status of racial organizations and of contributions to them; (2) the effect of integration or its threat on the public schools of Virginia and on the general welfare of the state; and (3) the violation of the laws against champerty, barratry, and maintenance of the unauthorized practice of law. Defendant was asked thirty-one specific questions, but it was not shown how any of them was pertinent to these subjects. In reversing defendant's conviction, the Supreme Court ruled that this violated the *Watkins* pertinency test. Defendant, said the Court, did not in these circumstances, "have an opportunity of understanding the basis for the questions or any justification on the part of the Committee for seeking the information he refused to give." [151]

One familiar with the workings of legislative committees and their all-too-common tendency to stray beyond the bounds of their authorizing resolutions cannot but agree with the *Watkins-Scull* approach. A reading of the questions asked in *Scull* is bound to make one wonder how most of them had any relationship at all to the subjects the committee was authorized to investigate.[152] Under *Watkins,* investigative power must at least be canalized within the bounds of pertinency—a limitation that imposes a needed check upon legislators who not infrequently interpret their investigative mandates as roving commissions to inquire into anything which appears suited to propel themselves into the headlines.[153]

Apart from pertinency, there may be certain other defenses which can be raised by a witness before a Congressional committee. Thus, he can claim that the committee concerned was improperly constituted for lack of a quorum. In *Christoffel v. United States* (1949),[154] the highest Court ruled that a witness could not be prosecuted for perjury committed before a House committee, unless it affirmatively appeared that a quorum of the committee was actually in the hearing room at the time the allegedly false testimony was given. The following year, on the other hand, in *United States v. Bryan,*[155] which arose out of a prosecution for failure to produce records pursuant to a House committee subpoena, the Court held that the Government was not required to prove that a quorum of the committee was still present when the default occurred.

Though *Bryan* does not directly overrule *Christoffel,* it is plainly inconsistent with that decision. Of the two decisions, it is *Bryan* that, in the opinion of the present writer, is the more sound. Congressional custom has established that committee members may engage in temporary absences, unless there is objection, without disabling those remaining from continuing to function as a committee. Under *Christoffel,* this Congressional custom is rejected. Under it, even if there is no objection whatever at the time, a Congressman may step out of a committee room only at the risk of nullifying the whole proceeding.[156]

Aside from a matter such as lack of quorum, procedural questions have been left by the courts almost entirely to the relevant legislative committees themselves. The provision of Article I, section 5, already discussed,[157] under which "Each House may determine the Rules of its Proceedings," is thus construed to apply to proceedings in committee as well as those on the floor of the chamber itself. Though there are no specific cases on the point, it has generally been assumed that legislative hearings are not subject to the procedural requirements that govern judicial-type proceedings in our law. This assumption is one upon which Congressional committees themselves have consistently proceeded. Hence, witnesses before such committees have not had any legal right to such elementary safeguards as the right to be accompanied by counsel or that to be heard only in public proceedings.

Though, as just stated, it has been supposed that the law on the subject is fixed in favor of judicial nonintervention in procedural matters, one may express a "modest doubt" as to whether the general supposition in this respect is soundly based. It is one thing for the courts to grant the legislature all but plenary autonomy where only its internal procedure is involved. It is quite another to adopt a complete hands-off policy where the basic rights of a private individual have been violated. How can a court uphold a conviction for "contempt of Congress" if the procedure before the committee concerned did not itself conform to the rudimentary requirements of fair play?

From this point of view, a Congressional committee should no more be able to deny fundamental adjective rights to an individual before it than can a court or an administrative agency. This appears particularly true of the practice of questioning unwilling witnesses in secret sessions. The right to a public hearing has been the essential characteristic of our system ever since it freed itself from the practice of Star Chamber of interrogating in secret for hours on end.[158] "Secret inquisitions," Justice Black has well said, "are dangerous things justly feared by free men everywhere." [159] During an executive session of a Congressional committee, the witness is alone, all but at the mercy of his inquisitors: torture, though formally abolished, all too often returns under new guises, nonphysical but nonetheless cruel. It is surely an anachronism for American law to retain this sad inheritance from the era of Stuart tyranny, so inconsistent with respect for the human personality.[160]

At the other extreme from the secret Congressional hearing is that which is carried on in the full glare of modern communications media. In one federal case, it was argued that a committee hearing was so lacking in decorum because of the presence of microphones, television cameras, and photographers that the committee concerned was not "a competent tribunal" for purposes of a perjury prosecution. The court rejected this contention, though it did articulate a doubt as to whether such procedure was not "better calculated to achieve publicity for the investigators than to promote their investigations." [161]

One wonders whether such a decision upholding Congressional inquisition under klieg lights does not overlook the realities of such procedure. When the rights of an individual are so drastically affected, it is essential that a legislative proceeding be conducted with proper decorum. In the atmosphere of the Roman circus that inevitably prevails in a hearing held in the glare of television lights and press bulbs, the bedazzled witness finds it difficult to retain his wits. He can be coerced, tricked, or confused to an extent that makes it hard for him to state his case as he would in the dignity and decorum customarily associated with judicial procedure. Excessive publicity at a hearing may violate the fundamentals of fair play as much as does the Star Chamber proceeding.

The problem of procedure is intensified when viewed from the standpoint of the witness who appears before a Congressional committee. He must decide at the time the questions are asked whether or not he should answer. As the Supreme Court has put it: "the witness acts at his peril. . . . An erroneous determination on his part, even if made in the utmost good faith, does not exculpate him if the court should later rule" that the investigation itself and the questions asked were proper.[162]

The witness before a Congressional committee who feels that his rights are being violated may consequently be presented with a veritable Hobson's choice. He is free to assert his rights only in the sense that those who do not conform to investigatory demands which may be determined to be lawful are free by their choice to accept the legal consequences of their acts.[163] He can assert his right to refuse to answer only at the risk of a criminal sentence, which will be imposed if it turns out that the committee was acting properly.

49
JUDICIAL INTERFERENCE WITH CONGRESSIONAL PROCEEDINGS

As just emphasized, it is only when he is prosecuted for "contempt of Congress" that a witness can secure a court decision on the legality of a particular legislative investigation and of the questions propounded to him. Even though a given committee's action may be considered illegal, it is settled that the courts will not intervene directly, by injunction or otherwise, to prevent such action from being carried out.

In the first case in which the matter came up, *Hearst v. Black* (1936),[164] a publisher sought to enjoin a special Senate Committee from copying and using telegraphic messages in the possession of the telegraph companies sent by him to his employees in the conduct of his business. The court held that, even assuming for the purposes of the case that the committee's action was without authority of law, it could not be enjoined. In its words, "If a court could say to the Congress that it could use or could not use information in its possession, the independence of the Legislature would be destroyed and the constitutional separation of the powers of government invaded." [165]

The holding of *Hearst v. Black*—that legislative investigatory power, whether rightfully or wrongfully exercised, is not a proper subject for direct judicial interference by injunction and similar remedies—has been consistently followed in subsequent cases. Thus, the courts have refused to quash Congressional subpoenas directing witnesses to appear and testify [166] or to enjoin the chairman of a Senate committee from forcing individuals to produce documents in their possession.[167] It is, we have already seen, "entirely proper for a Court to consider the validity of the legislative act when and if its effect was in fact to injure the plaintiffs, as, for example, by prosecution for contempt. But the legislature cannot be compelled to submit to the prior approval and censorship of the judiciary before it may ask questions or inspect documents through its investigating subcommittees." [168]

A related problem may arise after the investigatory stage of Congressional work when a committee is ready to publish its report or other documents. Here, the lack of judicial authority to interfere is even clearer. In a case before a three-judge district court, it was decided that a federal court did not have jurisdiction to enjoin a Senate committee from printing and distributing a report which defamed plaintiff. According to the opinion there, judicial power does not include the authority in the courts to "censor congressional language they think libelous. We have no more authority to prevent Congress, or a committee or public officer acting at the express direction of Congress, from publishing a document than to prevent them from publishing the Congressional Record." [169]

50
EXECUTIVE
PRIVILEGE

A question that has generated increasing interest in recent years is that of so-called executive privilege. Ever since the founding of the Republic, the President has claimed a power to refuse to comply with a Congressional demand for documents when he deems that production of such papers would be contrary to the public interest. From Washington's refusal in 1796 to submit certain correspondence to the House of Representatives relating to the negotiation of a treaty to similar denials in our own day, the claim of executive privilege vis-à-vis the Congress has been asserted.

Not surprisingly perhaps, there has been a plethora of Attorney General *ipse dixit*s which have invariably supported the claims of the executive to withhold information. Thus, in a memorandum to the President of May 17, 1954, the Attorney General asserted categorically that "our Presidents have established . . . that they and members of their Cabinets and other heads of executive departments have an undoubted privilege and discretion to keep confidential, in the public interest, papers and information which require secrecy." Moreover, he went on, "the President and the heads of departments have an uncontrolled discretion to withhold the information and papers in the public interest."

It has consistently been claimed by proponents of executive privilege that the law is settled in their favor. The Attorney General's memorandum just quoted flatly affirms that "Courts have uniformly held that the President and the heads of departments have an uncontrolled discretion to withhold the information and papers in the public interest."

This assertion is, in the words of one commentator "remarkable and inexact." [170] It is all the more remarkable in that there is no judicial decision dealing expressly with the power of the executive to deny documents to the Congress. Certainly, there is no authority in decisions of the Supreme Court for the withholding of information from the legislature. The cases usually cited as sustaining executive claims in this connection are *Boske v. Comingore* [171] and *United States ex rel. Touhy v. Ragen.* [172]

But those cases held only that the head of an executive department can lawfully centralize in himself the authority to determine whether documents of the department may be released for use of persons outside the department. The decisions in both cases were confined to this narrow issue. This is shown clearly by the Court's conclusion in the *Boske* opinion, where it says: "In our opinion the Secretary, under the regulations as to the custody, use and preservation of the records, papers and property appertaining to the business of his Department, may take from a subordinate, such as a collector, all discretion as to permitting the records in his custody to be used for any other purpose than the collection of the revenue, and reserve for his own determination all matters of that character." [173]

As Justice Frankfurter emphasized, in concurring in the *Touhy* case: "There is not a hint in the *Boske* opinion that the Government can shut off an appropriate judicial demand for such papers." [174]

In fact, as the learned Justice pointed out, the question of the immunity of the Attorney General from the duty to disclose information in his department's possession was not before the Court: "Specifically, the decision and opinion in this case cannot afford a basis for a future suggestion that the Attorney General can forbid every subordinate who is capable of being served by process from producing relevant documents and later contest a requirement upon him to produce on the ground that procedurally he cannot be reached. In joining the Court's opinion I assume the contrary—that the Attorney General can be reached by legal process." [175]

The *Boske* and *Touhy* cases are hence not relevant to the question of executive withholding of information, and certainly not to the Congressional right to information. The Supreme Court held only that a department head can forbid his subordinates from disclosing information. But to assume from this that the department head himself is able conclusively to determine whether information should be withheld from Congress is to jump to a conclusion which the Supreme Court tells us expressly [176] it was not called upon to reach. As Justice Frankfurter pithily expresses it: "To hold now that the Attorney General is empowered to forbid his subordinates, though within a court's jurisdiction, to produce documents and to hold later that the Attorney General himself cannot in any event be procedurally reached would be to apply a fox-hunting theory of justice that ought to make Bentham's skeleton rattle." [177]

In actuality, there are no federal cases in which the legality of an executive refusal to furnish information to the Congress was squarely at issue. What decisions there are involve executive privilege in courtroom proceedings, i.e., cases where the executive refuses to furnish documents whose production is demanded for use in litigation in the courts. Though some of these decisions go the other way, the great mass of them repudiates the concept of unlimited privilege in the executive in such cases.[178]

The only judicial authority directly in point on the power of the legislature to obtain information from the executive is a Massachusetts opinion which arose out of a clear executive attempt to pull down in the legislature's face the curtain of privilege. In 1951, the Massachusetts Development and Industrial Commission, an agency within the executive department, ordered a study made of business conditions. When this study was completed and a report made, the State Senate ordered the chairman of the commission to produce the report. He refused, asserting that "the legislature may not attempt to interfere with action taken by the executive department." He was backed up in his refusal by a formal vote of the commission directing that the report be turned over to a private advisory group. Thus, there was squarely presented to a court the direct question of whether the executive may refuse to turn over to the legislature an internal communication on the ground of executive privilege.

The claimed privilege was rejected by the Massachusetts court, which upheld the power of the State Senate to enforce its demand for the report, by contempt proceedings if need be. According to the court: "If the legislative department were to be shut off in the manner proposed from access to the papers and records of executive and administrative departments, boards, and commissions, it could not properly perform its legislative functions." [179]

It needs little iteration to note the extreme relevancy of this Massachusetts opinion. Here we have the only case in which the pretensions of the executive to a power to withhold documents from the legislature on the ground of privilege were squarely presented to a court. And the court expressly repudiated the assumption of such a power in the executive to frustrate a legislative inquiry.

It is hardly surprising that, in a field where there is no judicial authority other than the state opinion just discussed,[180] the law is anything but settled. In the absence of clear judicial authority, it is natural that conflicts between the Congress and the executive on the point have occurred throughout our history. More than that, it should not be forgotten that, in political, as in natural, science, nature abhors a vacuum. If the Congress is derelict in asserting any of its prerogatives, executive pretensions are bound to rush in to fill the power vacuum. While executive officials other than the President are subject to the Congressional contempt power,[181] it is most improbable that the legislative authority in this respect would ever be pushed to the extreme of imposing a jail sentence upon an executive officer. Consequently, the exact status of executive privilege vis-à-vis the Congress appears likely to remain a dark continent of our constitutional law, to be dealt with, in specific instances, more by political, than by legal, considerations.

5

TAXATION and OTHER FISCAL POWERS

51
GENERAL
WELFARE *A*T the very outset, the Constitution, in its Preamble, tells us that among the objects comprehended by it is the promotion of "the general Welfare." A mere league of states can possess neither the means nor the power to accomplish this great object. Only in the "more perfect Union" contemplated by the Framers can the common welfare truly be furthered. One who studies the operation of the Articles of Confederation cannot but contrast the comparative ease and expedition, the noiseless uniformity, with which the interest of the whole is now furthered through the instrumentality of the Federal Government. "Thus we see, that the national government, suitably organized, has more efficient means, and more extensive jurisdiction to promote the general welfare, than can belong to any single state of the confederacy." [1]

The Preamble of the Constitution, according to the Supreme Court, is not of itself the source of any substantive power conferred upon the Federal Government. Although, therefore, one of the declared objects of the Framers was to "promote the general Welfare," no power can be exerted to that end by the United States unless, apart from the Preamble, it be found in some delegation of power in the constitutional text, or in some power properly implied therefrom.[2]

149

The object of furthering the general welfare is not, however, limited to the Preamble of the organic document. The term "general welfare" is also used in the body of the Constitution, in the clause vesting the National Government with perhaps its broadest authority. Under Article I, section 8: "The Congress shall have Power To lay and collect Taxes, Duties, Imposts and Excises, to pay the Debts and provide for the common Defence and general Welfare of the United States."

What is included in the power to provide for the general welfare?

Is the General-Welfare Clause a distinctive source of power, or a mere modification of the power of taxation?

Some have argued that the clause in question is an independent grant of authority—not only a qualification of the taxing power. The constitutional phraseology, it is said, was intended as a comprehensive delegation of authority to the Congress to take any action which might promote the general welfare of the country. This extreme position has not been followed. As it was expressed by Justice Story over a century ago, to accept such a view would be to create, "a general authority in congress to pass all laws, which they may deem for the common defence or general welfare. Under such circumstances, the constitution would practically create an unlimited national government. The enumerated powers would tend to embarrassment and confusion; since they would only give rise to doubts, as to the true extent of the general power, or of the enumerated powers." [3]

The view of the General-Welfare Clause that has prevailed is that stated by Thomas Jefferson: "the laying of taxes is the *power,* and the general welfare the *purpose* for which the power is to be exercised. . . . [The Congress] are not *to do anything they please* to provide for the general welfare, but only to *lay taxes* for that purpose." [4] The General-Welfare Clause is, put otherwise, not an independent grant of power, but a qualification of the taxing power. "Not being a distinct clause by itself, it would seem probable that these words are a limitation upon the purpose for which taxes may be laid and collected." [5]

What then is the constitutional power thus to tax in order to provide for the general welfare? In the *Federalist,* there is a sharp disagreement between Madison and Hamilton on this question. Madison contended that the power should be regarded as merely incidental to the remaining powers of the Congress; in his view, the power to tax must be confined to the enumerated legislative fields committed to the Congress.[6] Hamilton, on the other hand, adopted the literal, broad meaning of the constitutional language. He maintained that the General-Welfare Clause confers a power separate and distinct from those later enumerated and is not restricted in meaning by the grant of them.[7] In the Hamiltonian interpretation, the taxing power is not limited by the direct grants of legislative power found in the Constitution.

From the founding of the Republic, the Congress has followed the Hamiltonian view. In *United States v. Butler* (1936),[8] the Supreme Court, too, gave the express imprimatur of its authority to Hamilton's position. According to the *Butler* opinion, under Madison's approach, the "general welfare" phrase is "mere tautology." [9] Hamilton's interpretation, giving a separate and distinct meaning to the phrase, is more consistent with the correct canons of constitutional construction. As *Butler* put it, "While, therefore, the power to tax is not unlimited, its confines are set in the clause which confers it, and not in those of section 8 which bestow and define the legislative powers of the Congress. It results that the power of Congress to authorize expenditure of public moneys for public purposes is not limited by the direct grants of legislative power found in the Constitution." [10]

To put it another way, the Congress is vested with a substantive power to tax which is limited only by the requirement that it shall be exercised to provide for the general welfare of the United States.[11] Consequently, though, as we have seen, the General-Welfare Clause is not an independent source of authority, but only a qualification of the taxing power, it still, under the *Butler*-Hamilton approach, confers tremendous powers upon the Government in Washington. If the Congress may impose taxes to promote the general welfare, it means, because of the broadness of the term used, that its taxing authority is practically unlimited. This, in fact, as we shall see, is the present posture of the law on the subject.

52

EXTENT OF   "That the taxing power," declares a typical opinion
TAXING POWER   of Chief Justice Marshall, "is of vital importance; that it is essential to the existence of government; are truths which it cannot be necessary to re-affirm." [12] To vest in the nation the powers of taxation which they deemed essential for its survival was a primary purpose which motivated the men of 1787. In the Confederation set up in 1781, they had witnessed at first hand a government shorn of such powers. Such a government, they well knew, presented only a spectacle of political futility. The lack of the power to levy taxes under the Articles of Confederation, indeed, had, in Hamilton's phrase in *The Federalist,* "chiefly contributed to reduce us to a situation, that affords ample cause of mortification to ourselves, and of triumph to our enemies." [13]

The Framers, then, were convinced that, if there was to be a real, effective National Government, it must be vested with a power of taxation coextensive with its powers, wants, and duties.[14] Such power, they felt, was as necessary to the existence and prosperity of a nation as the air he breathes is to the natural man.[15] It was this feeling which led them to confer upon the Congress the general power of taxation contained in the first clause of

Article I, section 8. If a nation is to succeed, its powers must be proportionate to its objects. Revenue is the essential engine by which the means of answering national needs must be procured.[16] The power of procuring it must necessarily be granted in terms equal to the necessities of the nation. "The power to tax," the Supreme Court has declared, "is the one great power upon which the whole national fabric is based."[17] The Government in Washington must, in other words, be endowed with an unqualified power of taxation for all national purposes.[18]

The language of the first clause of Article I, section 8, appears broad enough to vest just such a taxing power in the nation. It may be true that the constitutional delegation is not, in terms, unqualified, since the general authority conferred must be exercised to accomplish the purposes stated in the relevant clause. What, however, are these purposes? As stated, they are "to pay the Debts and provide for the common Defence and general Welfare of the United States."

When looked at from the point of view of the Framers and the end of a strong National Government which dominated their efforts. these purposes are not really limitations at all. What can be broader, in truth, than a power to impose any taxes that will further defense and the general welfare? In substance, the constitutional provision authorizes the imposition of any tax deemed in the public interest.

The phrase in the clause under discussion permitting taxes "to pay the Debts . . . of the United States" is, as a practical matter, of little legal significance. Even if the phrase were not expressly included, there could be no doubt of the existence of authority to impose taxes for such a purpose. The power to pay the debts was made express because of the concern of most of the Framers that the new Government live up to the financial commitments already incurred by the nation.

In several cases, the question of what constitutes debts of the United States for whose discharge taxes may be levied has been considered. As it was expressed in the most recent decision of the Supreme Court on the point: "The power of Congress to provide for the payment of debts . . . is not restricted to payment of those obligations which are legally binding on the Government. It extends to . . . claims which are merely moral or honorary."[19] Hence, it has been held proper to appropriate tax revenues to pay producers of sugar a bounty promised them under a federal statute which was unconstitutional.[20] The reliance of the producers upon the statute constituted a sufficient basis for a moral obligation which the Congress might recognize and discharge.

Other cases go even further. According to *Cincinnati Soap Co. v. United States*,[21] the moral obligation of the United States to protect, defend, and provide for the general welfare of the inhabitants of the Philippine Islands [22] constituted a "debt," as that term was used in the taxing clause of the Constitution. With the term construed so broadly, the Congressional power, in effect, extends as far as the legislature chooses to make it go. "The determination of Congress," the *Cincinnati Soap* opinion affirmed, "to recognize the moral obligation of the nation to make an appropriation as a requirement of justice and honor, is obviously a matter of policy and discretion not open to judicial review." [23]

If anything, the power of the Congress to tax to "provide for the common Defence and general Welfare" is construed even more broadly. The terms themselves, in fact, are, under modern conditions, so wide that they seem to cover almost any exercise of the taxing power by the legislative department. This is particularly true of the phrase "general welfare." If the elected representatives of the people vote to tax for an end which to them seems meet and appropriate, who is to say that the imposition does not in some way further the general welfare?

The highest tribunal itself has stated that, whether a given tax serves any of the purposes stated in the first clause of Article I, section 8, is a practical question addressed to the lawmaking department. It requires a very extreme case to warrant the courts in setting aside the conclusion of the Congress in that regard.[24] More specifically, it is settled that it is for the national legislature, not the courts, to draw the line of general welfare in a particular case, i.e., to determine whether a given exercise of the power to tax will promote the general welfare. In Justice Cardozo's language, in the leading case of *Helvering v. Davis:* [25] "The line must still be drawn between one welfare and another, between particular and general. Where this shall be placed cannot be known through a formula in advance of the event. There is a middle ground or certainly a penumbra in which discretion is at large. The discretion, however, is not confided to the courts. The discretion belongs to Congress. . . ." [26]

53

PURPOSE OF
TAXATION:
PRESERVATION

What has just been said plainly indicates the broad scope of the taxing power vested in the Congress. That such power "is exhaustive and embraces every conceivable power of taxation," the Supreme Court has affirmed, "has never been questioned." [27] Moreover, the Court has said, it "reaches every subject, and may be exercised at discretion." [28] In Marshall's classic language in *McCulloch v. Maryland:* [29] "The power of taxing the people and their property is essential to the very existence of government, and may be exercised on the objects to which it is applicable to the utmost extent to which the government may choose to carry it." [30]

To say thus much is not, at the same time, to answer the question raised by Justice Story over a century ago—that of "whether the government has a right to lay taxes for any other purpose, than to raise revenue, however much that purpose may be for the common defence, or general welfare." [31]

Of course, a tax is primarily a means of securing revenue. From the beginning of American history, nevertheless, it has been recognized that a tax may be much more than just that. The power to tax, reads Marshall's celebrated statement, involves the power to destroy.[32] But it may also involve other results. As the highest Court expressed it more than three quarters of a century after the Marshall dictum: "It is not only the power to destroy, but it is also the power to keep alive." [33] In addition, the power to tax may involve the power to regulate. The taxing power can serve as the basis for governmental regulation, with the imposition of taxes serving as the sanction behind the particular regulatory scheme.

May the taxing power be used to destroy, to "keep alive," or to regulate? In all of these cases, the power is exerted primarily to promote desired economic objectives. May the main motive behind a tax be the attainment of such objectives, rather than the raising of revenue?

If the constitutional language be all that is considered, the answer should be a clear affirmative. Article I, section 8, vests in the Congress the authority to impose any taxes to promote the general welfare. There is here no restriction to employment of the taxing power for revenue purposes only. In addition, as we saw in the last section, it is basically for the Congress to determine whether a given tax will further the general welfare. If the people's representatives exercise their power in this connection, shall a court hold the tax invalid simply because the relevant statute was actuated by a motive other than the raising of revenue?

The Supreme Court, despite the breadth of the relevant organic language, has not always answered this question in the negative. On the contrary, until our own day, the question of the underlying purpose behind a taxing statute was of basic importance in determining the validity of such law—at least insofar as taxes imposed to destroy or regulate were concerned.

Relatively easy to deal with has been the use of the taxing power for purposes of preservation—or, as the Supreme Court put it, in the passage already quoted, "to keep alive." The very first instances in which the Congress employed its taxing power to attain desired economic objectives involved protective tariff laws which sought to preserve American industry from foreign competition. The second statute enacted by the first Congress itself was a tariff law which recited that it was necessary for "the encouragement and protection of manufactures." [34]

Though the constitutionality of the protective tariff was debated by many during the first part of our history, that did not deter the Congress from continuing to pass protective tariff laws. In Chief Justice Taft's words, "The enactment of a number of customs revenue laws drawn with a motive of maintaining a system of protection since the revenue law of 1789 are matters of history." [35] It was not until 1928 that the Supreme Court had to rule squarely on the constitutionality of the protective tariff. At that time, the Court had no difficulty in upholding such use of the taxing power.[36] The fact that the Congress was motivated by a protective purpose, as well as the securing of revenue, could not be deemed to render the law at issue invalid. Where Congress uses its taxing power for purposes of preservation, in other words, the fact that revenue is obtained is enough to uphold its exercise of power. In such a case, whether the true Congressional motive is "to keep alive," rather than revenue, is not for a court to determine.

54

SAME: DESTRUCTION AND REGULATION   That a tax might be used to suppress an activity deemed harmful by the Congress was seen at an early time. In the first important case involving such a tax, *Veazie Bank v. Fenno* (1869),[37] the Congress had imposed a tax of 10 per cent on any state bank notes thereafter circulated as currency. The purpose behind the tax was concededly to drive all state bank notes out of circulation.[38] Since the purpose of the Congress was thus destruction, rather than revenue, it was claimed that this was not a valid exercise of the taxing power. This contention was rejected by the Supreme Court. According to it, the fact that the law indicated a purpose on the part of the Congress to destroy the subject of the tax did not render it invalid.

Veazie Bank does not, however, necessarily stand for the proposition that the Congress has the unrestricted authority to utilize its taxing power for purposes of extermination whenever it so chooses. The Court was careful to emphasize that the purpose sought by the Congress—the elimination of state bank notes—could be accomplished directly through a law based upon the Congressional power to provide for a national currency. "Congress," its opinion said, "may restrain, by suitable enactments, the circulation as money of any notes not issued under its own authority. Without this power, indeed, its attempts to secure a sound and uniform currency for the country must be futile." [39] Since the Congress could directly suppress state bank notes under its power to control the currency, it could utilize its taxing power to accomplish the same purpose.

Under *Veazie Bank v. Fenno,* the taxing power may be employed to effectuate a purpose that could be attained by the use of some other Congressional power. In such a case, it makes no difference that the motive behind the tax law was destruction, rather than revenue. What happens, nevertheless, when the power to tax is used to destroy an activity which Congress does not have the authority to suppress directly?

In *Bailey v. Drexel Furniture Co.* (1922),[40] usually known as the *Child Labor Tax Case,* it was held that, in such a case, the tax statute is vitiated by its underlying purpose. A prior decision [41] had invalidated a federal law barring from interstate commerce products made by child labor, on the ground that the national commerce power did not extend so far. The Congress then enacted a law imposing a 10 per cent tax upon the profits of all persons employing children. The purpose of the law was, of course, to achieve precisely the result aimed at by the statute previously held unconstitutional, i.e., to eliminate child labor. This motive, said the Supreme Court, rendered the exercise of the taxing power invalid. In reality, what the Congress was seeking to accomplish was to suppress an activity which, under the prior decision referred to, could be controlled only by the states. According to the Court: "here the so-called tax is a penalty to coerce people of a state to act as Congress wishes them to act in respect of a matter completely the business of the state government under the federal Constitution." [42]

Under the *Veazie Bank* and *Child Labor Tax* cases, whether a tax statute seeks to destroy is unimportant where the Congress possesses power both to tax and to destroy. But the underlying purpose is crucial where the Congress has only the power to tax, but no general authority to suppress.

What is true of suppression is also true of regulation. A tax may be employed as a powerful regulatory instrument, with the taxing power used as the sanction to enforce regulatory prescriptions laid down by the Congress. Under the *Veazie Bank* approach, there is, of course, no problem if the particular regulatory scheme is one which the Congres may impose directly under its power to regulate commerce or some other granted power. Where Congress possesses authority both to tax and to regulate, it may use either power to accomplish the regulatory end. The difficulty arises when the taxing power is utilized for regulatory purposes in an area where the Congress has no direct regulatory power. In such a case, if the *Child Labor Tax* approach be followed, the tax itself must be invalidated because of its improper underlying purpose.

The *Child Labor Tax* approach was applied to regulation by taxation in *United States v. Butler.*[43] At issue in it was the Agricultural Adjustment Act of 1933. That law, one of the most important regulatory measures of the early New Deal, was based entirely upon the taxing power. It sought to eliminate overproduction of farm products by furnishing the farmer with sufficient inducement for curtailing his production. Under the Act, a processing tax was levied upon different agricultural commodities, and the proceeds from this tax were used to compensate farmers who agreed beforehand to raise less or none of such commodities. It is obvious that the prime purpose of this exercise of the power to tax was the regulation of agricultural production, rather than the securing of revenue. It was for this reason that the law in question was held unconstitutional in *Butler* by the Supreme Court, for, at that time, as we shall see in the next chapter,[44] the Congress could not, under the prevailing decisions, directly regulate agricultural production.

The Agricultural Adjustment Act, said the high bench, attempted to regulate local production under the guise of an exercise of the taxing power: "If the act before us is a proper exercise of the federal taxing power, evidently the regulation of all industry throughout the United States may be accomplished by similar exercises of the same power. It would be possible to exact money from one branch of an industry and pay it to another branch in every field of activity which lies within the province of the states. The mere threat of such a procedure might well induce the surrender of rights and the compliance with federal regulation as the price of continuance in business." [45] In the opinion of the majority of the Court, the taxing power could not be used to accomplish regulation of agricultural production, which (under the highest Court's decisions at that time) was beyond the scope of the Congressional commerce power.

Under both the *Child Labor Tax Case* and *United States v. Butler,* otherwise valid exercises of the taxing power were condemned because of what the Supreme Court found to be their underlying purposes. As Justice Stone put it, in dissenting in *Butler,* the pivot on which the decision was made to turn was the holding "that a levy unquestionably within the taxing power of Congress may be treated as invalid because it is a step in a plan to regulate agricultural production and is thus a forbidden infringement of state power." [46] In other words, the tax was declared void, not because it did not come within the specifically granted power to tax for the general welfare, but because it was actuated by an improper motive. "The present levy," said the Stone dissent, "is held invalid, not for any want of power in Congress to lay such a tax to defray public expenditures, including those for the general welfare, but because the use to which its proceeds are put is disapproved." [47]

Few things are more dangerous than for a court to invalidate legislative acts on the ground of improper underlying purpose. It hardly becomes the judges to assume the characters of censors of Congressional motives.

The *Butler* approach may, indeed, render all but ineffective the federal power under the General-Welfare Clause. In Justice Stone's apt words in his *Butler* dissent: "The limitation now sanctioned must lead to absurd consequences. The government may give seeds to farmers, but may not condition the gift upon their being planted in places where they are most needed or even planted at all. The government may give money to the unemployed, but may not ask that those who get it shall give labor in return, or even use it to support their families. It may give money to sufferers from earthquake, fire, tornado, pestilence, or flood, but may not impose conditions, health precautions, designed to prevent the spread of disease, or induce the movement of population to safer or more sanitary areas. All that, because it is purchased regulation infringing state powers, must be left for the states, who are unable or unwilling to supply the necessary relief." [48]

Even before the *Child Labor Tax* and *Butler* cases, there were several Supreme Court decisions that went the other way, on the ground that it was not the judicial function to probe into the motives that induced an otherwise valid exercise of Congressional power. Thus, in *McCray v. United States*,[49] decided at the beginning of the present century, the Court upheld a tax of 10 cents per pound on oleomargarine colored to look like butter, while the tax on uncolored margarine was only ¼ cent per pound. It was argued that the real purpose of the tax was to control the manufacture of margarine [50]—a matter beyond the Congressional commerce power (as it was then construed).[51] The Court categorically rejected this claim, flatly denying "that the judiciary may restrain the exercise of lawful power on the assumption that a wrongful purpose or motive has caused the power to be exerted." [52]

Since *Butler,* the high tribunal has repudiated the limitation imposed by that decision upon the taxing power, returning in this respect to the approach followed in *McCray v. United States*. The Agricultural Adjustment Act of 1938, which actually differed only in details from that held invalid in the *Butler* case, was sustained in 1939. The motive of the Congress in exerting its power, said the Supreme Court then, is irrelevant to the validity of its legislation.[53] In other post-*Butler* decisions, too, the high bench has refused to invalidate taxes merely because their primary purpose was claimed to be regulation, not revenue. A tax, in the Court's present view, is not any the less a tax because it has a regulatory effect; [54] a tax does not cease to be valid merely because it regulates, discourages, or even definitely deters the activities taxed.[55] This is true even though the revenue obtained from such tax is negligible or the revenue purpose of the relevant statute is clearly secondary.[56]

Even more important is the specific rejection of the approach which bars utilization of the taxing power to accomplish regulatory ends beyond the direct authority of the Congress. Declared the high Court in 1950, in upholding a heavy federal tax imposed on dealers in marihuana: "Nor does a tax statute necessarily fall because it touches on activities which Congress might not otherwise regulate." [57] An exercise of taxing power, the Court went on, will be sustained, though the taxes were "imposed with the collateral intent of effecting ulterior ends which, considered apart, were beyond the constitutional power of the lawmakers to realize by legislation directly addressed to their accomplishment." [58]

What the view thus expressed by the highest Court means in terms of present-day Congressional use of the taxing power for regulation or suppression is well shown by the 1953 case of *United States v. Kahriger.*[59] At issue in it was the constitutionality of the so-called gambler's occupational tax law, enacted by the Congress in 1951. That law, which Justice Frankfurter has characterized as "a spurious use of the taxing power as a means of facilitating prosecution of federal offenses," [60] levied a tax of fifty dollars per year upon persons engaged in the business of accepting wagers, and required such persons to register with the Federal Collector of Internal Revenue their names, addresses, and places of business. Though ostensibly a revenue measure, the primary purpose of the wagering tax law was clearly to aid in the suppression of gambling. To quote from Justice Frankfurter's dissent in the *Kahriger* case: "The context of the circumstances which brought forth this enactment—sensationally exploited disclosures regarding gambling in big cities and small, the relation of this gambling to corrupt politics, the impatient public response to these disclosures, the feeling of ineptitude or paralysis on the part of local law-enforcing agencies—emphatically supports what was revealed on the floor of Congress, namely that what was formally a means of revenue for the Federal Government was essentially an effort to check if not to stamp out professional gambling." [61]

The law under discussion was intended to place the professional gambler on the horns of a legal dilemma. If he were not to register and pay the tax required by the law, he would commit a federal offense for which he could be punished criminally. On the other hand, if he were to come forward to register and, in effect, confess that he was engaged in the business of gambling, he would lay himself open to prosecution by local law-enforcement authorities, for there are antigambling laws on most state statute books. The act at issue, in the words of one member of the Supreme Court, "creates a squeezing device contrived to put a man in federal prison if he refuses to confess himself into a state prison as a violator of state gambling laws." [62]

Although the object of the wagering tax law was thus the suppression of professional gambling rather than the securing of revenue, it was held by the high Court that this did not render it unconstitutional. "A federal excise tax does not cease to be valid," states its opinion, "merely because it discourages or deters the activities taxed. Nor is the tax invalid merely because the revenue obtained is negligible. . . . The instant tax has a regulatory effect. But regardless of its regulatory effect, the wagering tax produces revenue." [63] Or, to put it another way, the Court will not go behind what is formally a revenue measure to determine whether the raising of revenue is, in actuality, its primary purpose. The fact that the taxing power is used as an instrument of regulation or suppression does not, in the present view of the Supreme Court, affect the validity of its exercise. "It is axiomatic," said the *Kahriger* opinion, "that the power of Congress to tax is extensive and falls with crushing effect on businesses deemed unessential or inimical to the public welfare. . . . As is well known, the constitutional restraints on taxing are few." [64]

Under a decision like that in the *Kahriger* case, just discussed, the Congress is provided with a ready means, in its power to tax, of asserting authority over matters that were formerly deemed to be within the competence of the states. We can take the regulation of professional gambling, at issue in *Kahriger,* as a good example. According to the *Kahriger* dissent, such regulation falls within the reserved powers of the states, at least where purely local gambling is involved. Even under the expanded concept of the national commerce power which, we shall see,[65] now dominates the jurisprudence of the Supreme Court, it may be questioned whether such local gambling can be considered to have any effect upon interstate commerce so as to be subject to federal regulatory authority. Yet, by framing its regulatory law in the form of a nominal taxing measure, the Congress is, under the *Kahriger* decision, enabled to make what might otherwise be an inadmissible intrusion into a domain of legislation reserved for the states. According to the *Kahriger* dissent, indeed, the Court's decision there gravely affects the balance of powers within the federal system: "To allow what otherwise is excluded from congressional authority to be brought within it by casting legislation in the form of a revenue measure could . . . offer an easy way for the legislative imagination to control 'any one of the great number of subjects of public interest, jurisdiction of which the States have never parted with. . . .' " [66]

55

SAME: Another important limitation upon the purposes for
PUBLIC VERSUS   which the taxing power might be used was laid down
PRIVATE PURPOSES   in 1875 in *Loan Association v. Topeka.*[67] In it, the
                    taxing power had been employed by a city to make a
substantial grant to a bridge manufacturing company, in order to induce the company to locate its factory in the city. Such utilization of the taxing power was held invalid by the Supreme Court, on the ground that it was induced by an improper purpose. According to the opinion of Justice Miller: "there can be no lawful tax which is not laid for a public purpose." [68]

In the instant case, said the high bench, the power to tax had been employed, not for a public, but for a private purpose—the granting of assistance to a mere private business. Nor, in the Court's judgment, was the private nature of the purpose changed by the fact that the town might have benefited from the location of the bridge factory there. The same, declared Justice Miller, can be said of any other business, which may equally promote the public good and be equally deserving of public aid. "No line," said he, "can be drawn in favor of the manufacturer which would not open the coffers to the importunities of two thirds of the business men of the city or town." [69]

The *Loan Association* holding rests upon the view which had been previously expressed by Cooley that, "taxation having for its only legitimate object the raising of money for public purposes and the proper needs of government, the exaction of moneys from the citizens for other purposes is not a proper exercise of this power, and must therefore be unauthorized." [70] In this theory, if imposed for other than a public purpose, the exaction is not a tax at all, but a mere attempt to take property without due process. In Justice Miller's words, "To lay, with one hand, the power of the government on the property of the citizen, and with the other to bestow it upon favored individuals to aid private enterprises and build up private fortunes, is none the less a robbery because it is done under the forms of law and is called taxation." [71]

Looked at in this way, it is clear that, though the *Loan Association* case involved only the taxing power of states and their subdivisions, its principle is as applicable to the taxing power of the Congress. The limitation laid down was intended as a basic restriction upon all exercises of taxing power in this country. As it was put in a lecture by Justice Miller (himself the author of the *Loan Association* opinion): "No State Government, nor that of the United States, nor any other authority professing a regard for the rights of the people, is at liberty to take money out of their pockets for any other than a public purpose." [72]

To one who has read the prior section, it will not be surprising that the recent reluctance of the Supreme Court to invalidate taxes on the ground of improper purpose should have had drastic impact upon the present validity of the *Loan Association* doctrine. If anything, in fact, in the light of present-day notions of the proper scope of judicial power, it is even harder to justify that doctrine than the result in a case like *United States v. Butler*.[73] At least *Butler* rested upon a link (however slight it might seem to some) between the taxing power and a power denied to the Congress under the then-prevailing Supreme-Court decisions. But the *Loan Association* holding did not rest upon even such tenuous basis. In the words of the dissenting Justice there, what the Court was really doing was to nullify a tax "on the vague ground that they think it opposed to a general latent spirit supposed to pervade or underlie the Constitution, where neither the terms nor the implications of the instrument disclose any such restriction." [74]

To permit the courts to strike down a tax because it was not imposed for a public purpose is to give them a ready means of negating governmental programs of which they happen to disapprove. Government exists to provide for the welfare of its people.[75] If a given tax is deemed by the legislature to accomplish that end, is that alone not a sufficient indication that a public purpose is involved?

It should not be forgotten that we have been living in an era in which the concept of public purpose itself has consistently been expanding. What might have been viewed in an earlier day as an improvident or even dangerous expenditure of public funds may today be judged an indispensable use of the public purse.[76] Decisions in the past invalidating taxes and disbursements which would be considered by most observers today to promote valid governmental ends [77] should caution us of the perils involved in setting up the judiciary as censors of the public purposes motivating particular tax laws.

It is true that the *Loan Association* doctrine has never been expressly overruled by the Supreme Court. On the other hand, except for one case decided only a few years after *Loan Association* itself,[78] all of the high-bench decisions have upheld taxes as against the claim that they were not levied for public purposes. Thus, the Court has sustained taxes levied to maintain a city coal and fuel yard,[79] to support an extensive program of state ownership (including a state bank, warehouses and grain elevators, and homebuilding projects),[80] to build a railway tunnel,[81] and to provide free books for children attending private as well as public schools.[82]

The fact that payments are made to private individuals does not, despite the contrary implication in the *Loan Association* case, require a decision that only a private purpose is involved. This is clear under *Carmichael v. Southern Coal & Coke Co.*,[83] where the high Court upheld an unemployment compensation law, rejecting the argument that, because payments were made only to private individuals, a public purpose could not be served. "When public evils," said Justice Stone, "ensue from individual misfortunes or needs, the legislature may strike at the evil at its source. If the purpose is legitimate because public, it will not be defeated because the execution of it involves payments to individuals." [84]

Since the *Loan Association* decision is still referred to as good law, particularly in the state cases,[85] it may appear foolhardy to assert that its limitation is no longer of any real practical effect. At the same time, the Supreme-Court decisions just referred to, as well as cases like *United States v. Kahriger*,[86] discussed in the prior section, indicate that such is, in fact, the present situation. It is true that, in its most recent pronouncement on the subject, in a case upholding transportation of parochial school children as a valid public purpose, the high tribunal did point to the judicial power to strike down taxes under the *Loan Association* doctrine. But, it was careful to emphasize: "this far reaching authority must be exercised with the most extreme caution. . . . Otherwise, a state's power to legislate for the public welfare might be seriously curtailed, a power which is a primary reason for the existence of states." [87]

To put it another way, under the high bench's present view, even if the *Loan Association* doctrine is formally followed, it has all but lost its practical effect as a limitation upon the taxing power. As the Court put it, in the already-mentioned *Carmichael* case, for a tax statute to be declared invalid, "it would require a plain case of departure from every public purpose which could reasonably be conceived." [88] Under such an approach, it is hard to conceive of a taxing statute which could not run the public-purpose gantlet. Indeed, under the present Supreme-Court jurisprudence, the test is really that stated some years ago by a state court: "If there be the least possibility that [the tax] will be promotive in any degree of the public welfare, it becomes a question of policy . . . , and the determination of the legislature is conclusive." [89]

56

SPENDING POWER "That the governmental power of the purse is a great one," said Justice Stone in his *Butler* dissent, "is not now for the first time announced. Every student of the history of government and economics is aware of its magnitude and of its existence in every civilized government." [90] The power of the purse, in its broadest sense, is comprehended in the grant to the Congress of the taxing authority. The power to tax thus includes the power to spend.

That the spending power is wholly within the control of the Congress is clear from the provision in Article I, section 9, that "No Money shall be drawn from the Treasury, but in Consequence of Appropriations made by Law." This means simply that no money may be paid out of the federal treasury unless it has been appropriated by an act of Congress. The constitutional clause in question is a restriction upon the disbursing authority of the executive and does not in any way limit the power of the Congress to appropriate.[91]

More difficult is the question of whether there are any other constitutional limitations upon the Congressional spending power. As a starting point, it is settled that the power to spend is at least as broad as the power to tax. Funds in the treasury, the highest Court has said, "can never accomplish the objects for which they were collected, unless the power to appropriate is as broad as the power to tax. The necessary implication from the terms of the grant is that public funds may be appropriated 'to provide for the general welfare of the United States.' " [92]

Can the disbursement of federal funds be attacked on the ground that it is motivated by an invalid purpose? The answer must depend upon that already given in sections 53–55, in our discussion of whether a tax can be nullified because of its underlying purpose. Under a case like *United States v. Butler*,[93] an expenditure by the Congress to attain an end which could not be directly attained by that body is invalid. *Butler* itself, it should be noted, involved both the taxing and the spending power and the Court held specifically that the spending scheme authorized by the Congress was unconstitutional, because its purpose was to regulate agricultural production —an end prohibited to the Congress under the then-prevailing interpretation of the commerce power.[94] We have already discussed *Butler's* invalidation of the taxes imposed to attain such end. As the opinion there asked, "Is a statute less objectionable which authorizes expenditure of federal moneys to induce action in a field in which the United States has no power to intermeddle?" [95]

The more recent rejection by the high bench of the *Butler* limitation on exercises of the taxing power has meant a similar rejection with regard to the Congressional power to spend. If the Supreme Court will not look behind an otherwise valid tax law to see that it was not motivated by an improper regulatory or other purpose, the same should be true where the spending of revenue secured by taxes is concerned. As the Court put it, in a leading case upholding expenditure of public moneys: "No presumption can be indulged in that they will be misapplied or wasted. Even if they were collected in the hope or expectation that some other or collateral good would be furthered as an incident, that without more would not make the act invalid." [96] Funds disbursed to promote what the Congress deems to be the general welfare cannot be condemned because the money is being spent to induce action in an area which Congress may not be able to control directly.

This means that the power of the purse can be utilized for whatever purpose the Congress chooses, including the attainment of regulatory objectives. Such objectives can be secured through the imposition of conditions which must be complied with before particular funds may be disbursed. The result has been the widespread use of federal bounties or grants to attain specific desired ends. To secure such ends, the grants are made conditional, i.e., the payments are made on terms which will ensure use by the selected recipients in a manner prescribed by the Congress.

The conditional grant-in-aid has, in fact, become an established part of the federal system. A large proportion of state revenues has come to be derived from federal grants of this type. That such grants are valid was strongly urged by Justice Stone in his dissent in the *Butler* case: "Expenditures would fail of their purpose and thus lose their constitutional sanction if the terms of payment were not such that by their influence on the action of the recipients the permitted end would be attained. The power of Congress to spend is inseparable from persuasion to action over which Congress has no legislative control." [97]

The Stone view in this respect was adopted by the Supreme Court in its decisions upholding the Social Security Act of 1935, a federal statute which made extensive use of the conditional grant-in-aid device. Under that law, the Federal Government made grants to the states for old-age assistance, administration of state unemployment compensation laws, aid to dependent children, maternal and child welfare, public health, and assistance to the blind. Compliance with federally prescribed conditions was, however, imposed upon the states in return, for state legislation and machinery and methods of administration had to conform to standards prescribed by the federal statute and the Social Security Board, the agency set up to administer it. An old-age insurance fund was established. The money paid into the fund was to be derived from income taxes on employees and excise taxes on their employers. For unemployment compensation, a federal tax was levied upon employers alone. Employers in states which enacted satisfactory unemployment compensation laws were to receive credit up to 90 per cent of the federal tax. Since the federal tax was to be collected whether or not any such state law existed, pressure was put, at least indirectly, upon each state to enact unemployment compensation legislation meeting the standards laid down in the federal statute.[98]

The Social Security Act was sustained in a series of cases as against the contention that it amounted to an unconstitutional attempt by the Federal Government to coerce and control the states in the manner in which they dealt with the problem of unemployment. "Even though it be assumed," declared Justice Stone in one of the cases referred to, "that the exercise of a sovereign power by a state, in other respects valid, may be rendered invalid because of the coercive effect of a federal statute enacted in the exercise of a power granted to the national govrnment, such coercion is lacking here. . . . The United States and the State of Alabama are not alien governments. They coexist within the same territory. Unemployment within it is their common concern. Together the two statutes now before us embody a cooperative legislative effort by state and national governments, for carrying out a public purpose common to both, which neither could fully achieve without the cooperation of the other." [99]

The language of Justice Cardozo was even stronger in its assertion of the validity of the federal scheme. "Who then is coerced," he asked, "through the operation of this statute? Not the taxpayer. He pays in fulfilment of the mandate of the local legislature. Not the state. Even now she does not offer a suggestion that in passing the unemployment law she was affected by duress. . . . For all that appears she is satisfied with her choice, and would be sorely disappointed if it were now to be annulled. . . . Every rebate from a tax when conditioned upon conduct is in some measure a temptation. But to hold that motive or temptation is equivalent to coercion is to plunge the law in endless difficulties." [100]

In each of the Social Security Act cases, it was a private citizen who complained that the statute contemplated use of the federal purse to "purchase compliance" with regulations that invaded state sovereignty. In such a case, the high Court could rightly emphasize that the state involved was a willing partner in the federal plan. This should not, nevertheless, lead to the conclusion that it is only where the states are cooperative that the conditional grant-in-aid device may be validly used. On the contrary, in *Oklahoma v. Civil Service Commission*,[101] the power of the Congress to impose conditions upon grants-in-aid even over the objection of a state was squarely settled. The state there protested against enforcement of a provision in a federal statute, under which its right to receive federal highway funds would depend upon its removal from office of a member of the State Highway Commission who was found to have taken an active part in politics. The federal law in question, without any doubt, sought to use the power of the purse to accomplish the desired end of a politically neutral government service. In the highest Court's words, "The end sought by Congress through the Hatch Act is better public service by requiring those who administer funds for national needs to abstain from active political partisanship." [102]

The Supreme Court has held that the Congress can directly regulate the political activities of federal employees.[103] Regulation of state officials in this respect is, at the same time, a matter wholly within the power of the states themselves. But the Congress can utilize its spending power to accomplish such regulation, even though the regulation itself is not directly within Congressional authority. This, at any rate, was the decision in *Oklahoma v. Civil Service Commission*. According to the opinion there, even though the action of the Congress does have effect upon matters within the reserved powers of the states, such effect does not make the federal act invalid. "While the United States is not concerned and has no power to regulate local political activities as such of state officials," said the Court, "it does have power to fix the terms upon which its money allotments to states shall be disbursed." [104]

It has been argued that the policy of federal grants tends to break down state initiative and to paralyze local policies. In actual practice, however, its true effect has, in many instances, been exactly the opposite. This, at any rate, has been the view of the Supreme Court. "States and local governments," said Justice Cardozo, speaking for the Court in its opinion upholding the old-age assistance provisions of the Social Security Act, "are often lacking in the resources that are necessary to finance an adequate program of security for the aged. . . . Apart from the failure of resources, state and local governments are at times reluctant to increase so heavily the burden of taxation to be borne by their residents for fear of placing themselves in a position of economic disadvantage as compared with neighbors or competitors." [105] It was only because of federal aid that many of the states were able to initiate necessary measures such as old-age relief. Even so conservative a study as that of the first Hoover Commission had to conclude that "The cooperative system based on grants-in-aid has provided needed standards of public services throughout the country in many fields—services that many States would be unable to supply. It has provided for some redistribution of resources from States that have superior means to those who lack them." [106]

A word should also be said about the relative rarity of cases involving challenges to exercises of the spending power. In *Butler* and the Social Security Act cases, the statutes joined together both the spending programs involved and the tax arrangements for financing them. The suits were brought by individuals who were resisting collection of the taxes imposed. The high Court, in such a case, could rule on the validity of the spending program, on the ground that the tax and spending provisions were interwoven as parts of a single scheme.[107]

Such joinder of a spending program with the tax arrangements for financing it is rather unusual. In the typical case, a spending program is provided for in an appropriation act which stands alone. It is financed by funds drawn generally from the federal treasury, not from the earmarked proceeds of a specific tax. Consequently, it is normally quite impossible to obtain a court test of Congressional exercises of the power to spend.

Under *Massachusetts v. Mellon,*[108] to be discussed more fully at a later point,[109] an individual taxpayer does not have standing to question the legality of federal expenditures. In addition, the Supreme Court held there that a state could not challenge a federal spending program on the ground that it invaded its reserved powers. The result of *Massachusetts v. Mellon* is to insulate practically all Congressional exercises of the spending power from judicial review. If neither the states nor individual taxpayers (the only parties who could possibly object to spending statutes) are permitted to raise the constitutional issue, it is difficult to see how such issue can ever be raised. In a practical sense, then, unless a statute providing for a spending program contains the specific tax provisions under which funds earmarked for the program will be obtained,[110] or unless the Congress should expressly make judicial review available,[111] such statute is rendered immune from constitutional attack.

57

DIRECT TAXES   The Constitution divides the taxes which the Congress may impose into two principle classes: a) capi-
tation and other direct taxes [112] and b) duties, imposts, and excises.[113] Together, the Supreme Court has said, these two classes include every form
of tax appropriate to sovereignty.[114] As the Court put it in 1895, "although
there have been from time to time intimations that there might be some
tax which was not a direct tax nor included under the words 'duties, imposts and excises,' such a tax for more than one hundred years of national
existence has as yet remained undiscovered, notwithstanding the stress of
particular circumstances has invited thorough investigation into sources of
revenue." [115]

It is important to determine whether a given tax belongs to the one or
the other of these classes because their levy is subject to different constitutional rules. Under Article I, section 9: "No Capitation, or other direct,
Tax shall be laid, unless in Proportion to the Census or Enumeration herein
before directed to be taken." This means that direct taxes must be apportioned among the states on the basis of their respective populations.
With regard to indirect taxes, as we shall see in the next section, the only
requirement is that of uniformity.

In the soon-to-be-discussed *Pollock* case, Chief Justice Fuller categorically asserted that "it is apparent . . . that the distinction between
direct and indirect taxation was well understood by the framers of the
Constitution and those who adopted it." [116] Against this confident dictum
should be set the following from Madison's notes on the Constitutional
Convention: "Mr. King asked what was the precise meaning of *direct* taxation? No one answered." [117]

The Supreme Court was first called upon to give an answer to Mr.
King's question at an early date. In the 1796 case of *Hylton v. United
States*,[118] it was argued that a fixed yearly tax on all carriages used for the
conveyance of persons was a direct tax and hence invalid, because not apportioned among the states according to population. The Court unanimously
held that the tax at issue was not a direct tax within the meaning of Article
I, section 9. According to the opinions rendered, since the Direct-Tax Clause
constitutes an exception to the general taxing power of the Congress, it
should be strictly construed. No tax should be considered "direct" unless it
could be conveniently apportioned. "As all direct taxes must be apportioned," said Justice Iredell, "it is evident, that the constitution contemplated none as direct, but such as could be apportioned. If this cannot be
apportioned, it is, therefore, not a direct tax in the sense of the constitution.
That this tax cannot be apportioned, is evident." [119]

Justice Paterson, himself one of the Framers, stated that the constitutional provision on direct taxes had been intended to allay the fears of the southern states lest their slaves and lands be subjected to special taxes not equally apportioned among the northern states.[120] From this, it was a natural step to the view, expressed by all the Justices, that "the direct taxes contemplated by the constitution, are only two, to wit, a capitation, or poll tax, simply, without regard to property, profession or any other circumstance; and a tax on land." [121]

The view thus stated in the *Hylton* case was uniformly followed for a century. After the Civil War, it was applied to several of the taxes which had been imposed to meet the needs of that conflict,[122] including the general tax on incomes to which the Congress had resorted in 1864, for the first time in our history. The income tax referred to was sustained in *Springer v. United States* (1881),[123] where the high bench ruled unanimously that an income tax was not a direct tax. The Court's conclusion there categorically reaffirmed that expressed in *Hylton*. In the words of the *Springer* opinion, *"direct taxes,* within the meaning of the Constitution, are only capitation taxes . . . and taxes on real estate." [124] The two taxes mentioned exhausted the class of direct taxes referred to in Article I, section 9.

When the Congress, in 1894, enacted a new income-tax law,[125] it had every reason, under the uniform jurisprudence of a century, to feel confident of its constitutional authority in the matter. In *Pollock v. Farmers' Loan & Trust Co.* (1895),[126] however, a divided Court repudiated the *Hylton-Springer* view. The effect of the *Pollock* decision was strikingly stated by a dissenting Justice:

"And now, after a hundred years . . . and after repeated adjudications of this court, this interpretation is overthrown, and the Congress is declared not to have a power of taxation which may at some time, as it has in the past, prove necessary to the very existence of the government." [127]

In the *Pollock* case, the Supreme Court held squarely that an income tax was a direct tax within the meaning of Article I, section 9. This was true whether the income being taxed was derived from real estate, from municipal bonds,[128] or from personal property, such as stocks and bonds.[129]

From a legal point of view, the *Pollock* decision must be considered erroneous. In deciding as it did, the Court rejected both the consistent case-law of a century and the uniform practice of the political branches, including that of the men who drew up the Constitution themselves. To be sure, constitutional questions need not necessarily be considered as finally settled unless they are settled rightly. But this hardly justified the Court in nullifying a great national power, unquestioned for so many years, where the constitutional language does not compel such result. Where a distinction "so uncertain and vague" [130] as that between direct and indirect taxes is involved, surely the views of judges who themselves had participated and witnessed the drafting of the Constitution are more relevant than the personal predilections of their successors a century later.

The *Pollock* decision can be explained less in purely legal terms than in terms of the personal antipathies of the Justices who made up the majority of the highest Court. Counsel opposing the statute at issue depicted the income tax as "a doctrine worthy of a Jacobin Club"—the "new doctrine of this army of 60,000,000—this triumphant and tyrannical majority—who want to punish men who are rich and confiscate their property." [131]

Such attack upon the income tax (though, technically speaking, irrelevant to the case) found a receptive ear in the *Pollock* majority. "The present assault upon capital," declares Justice Field, "is but the beginning. It will be but the stepping-stone to others, larger and more sweeping, till our political contests will become a war of the poor against the rich; a war constantly growing in intensity and bitterness." [132] If the Court were to sanction the income-tax law, "it will mark the hour when the sure decadence of our present government will commence." [133] And this, it should be noted, was said about a law that levied a tax of 2 per cent on incomes above $4,000!

While the bases of the *Pollock* decision may thus be questioned, its contemporary legal effect was all too clear. In effect, the high Court's ruling removed from the Congress its power to impose a workable income tax. "When, therefore," declared Justice Harlan, in dissent, "this court adjudges, as it does now adjudge, that Congress cannot impose a duty or tax upon personal property, or upon income arising either from real estate or from personal property . . . , except by apportioning the sum to be so raised among the states according to population, it practically decides that, without an amendment of the Constitution . . . such property and incomes can never be made to contribute to the support of the national government." [134]

The *Pollock* decision provoked a veritable storm of contemporary criticism, which was not assuaged by decisions upholding inheritance taxes,[135] taxes on sales at exchanges or boards of trade,[136] and levies on the net income of corporations as excises.[137] The result was the adoption, in 1913, of the Sixteenth Amendment, under which "The Congress shall have power to lay and collect taxes on incomes, from whatever source derived, without regard to any census or enumeration."

According to the Supreme Court, the purpose of the Sixteenth Amendment was to correct the basic error of the *Pollock* decision by restoring income taxes to the category of indirect taxes. The Amendment, said the Court in the first case construing its provisions, "forbids the application to [income] taxes of the rule applied in the Pollock Case by which alone such taxes were removed from the great class of excises, duties, and imposts . . . and were placed under the other or direct class." [138] The Sixteenth Amendment thus transformed the income tax, which *Pollock* had held to be direct, into an excise, and hence an indirect tax not subject to the requirement of apportionment. As the high Court put it, "The Sixteenth Amendment conferred no new power of taxation but simply prohibited the previous complete and plenary power of income taxation possessed by Congress from the beginning from being taken out of the category of indirect taxation to which it inherently belonged." [139]

The Sixteenth Amendment goes far in the direction of bringing us back to the view articulated in the pre-*Pollock* cases,[140] under which only capitation taxes and taxes on real estate come within the class of direct taxes. The *Pollock* case, however, in addition to its ruling on the income tax, held also that taxes on personal property fell within the category of direct taxes. This holding of the *Pollock* Court is not affected by the Sixteenth Amendment and is still good law. At the present time, therefore, we may define a direct tax as one imposed upon persons themselves or upon the property owned by them.[141] The class of direct taxes today includes capitation taxes and all taxes on property, real or personal. But a tax on the income from property must, since the Sixteenth Amendment, clearly be considered an indirect tax.

58

INDIRECT TAXES As just pointed out, under the Sixteenth Amendment, an income tax is placed in the category of indirect taxes. As such, it is not subject to the requirement of apportionment among the states according to the census imposed upon direct taxes by Article I, section 9. As an indirect tax, nevertheless, it is subject to another constitutional requirement—that of uniformity. Under Article I, section 8, "all Duties, Imposts and Excises shall be uniform throughout the United States." [142]

The rule of uniformity for indirect taxes is one that is easy to obey.[143] "According to the settled doctrine," Justice Cardozo has said, "the uniformity exacted is geographical, not intrinsic." [144] This means only that the same principles must be used to define the existence, the amount, and the enforceability of the liability for the tax throughout the entire territorial area of the United States.[145] In the words of the highest Court in a leading case: "The uniformity here prescribed has reference to the various localities in which the tax is intended to operate. 'It shall be uniform throughout the United States.' Is the tax on tobacco void, because in many of the States no tobacco is raised or manufactured? Is the tax on distilled spirits void because a few States pay three-fourths of the revenue arising from it? The tax is uniform when it operates with the same force and effect in every place where the subject of it is found." [146]

Under the above approach, the requirement of uniformity is not violated because the levy of a tax is not intrinsically equal and uniform in its operation upon individuals. This was definitely settled by *Knowlton v. Moore,*[147] where the constitutionality of a federal inheritance-tax statute was at issue. The law in question provided for progressive taxation, i.e., it provided for a tax rate progressing according to the amount of the particular legacy. It was claimed that such progressive taxation contravened the uniformity requirement, since its operation was not equal and uniform in its operation upon individuals. In rejecting this claim, the Supreme Court made it clear that, as already pointed out, "the words 'uniform throughout the United States' do not relate to the inherent character of the tax as respects its operation on individuals, but simply requires that whatever plan or method Congress adopts for laying the tax in question, the same plan and the same method must be made operative throughout the United States; that is to say, that wherever a subject is taxed anywhere, the same must be taxed everywhere throughout the United States, and at the same rate." [148] To put it another way, the words "uniform throughout the United States" have "reference purely to a geographical unity and as synonymous with the expression 'to operate generally throughout the United States.' " [149]

The Uniformity Clause affords no protection against tax classifications based on any other than a territorial factor.[150] It places no obstacle in the way of legislative classification for the purpose of taxation, once the requirement of geographical uniformity is met.

59
TAXES ON   Under Article I, section 9, "No Tax or Duty shall be
EXPORTS   laid on Articles exported from any State." [151] In
              earlier cases, it was assumed that the prohibition applied, not only to goods exported to foreign countries, but also to goods carried from one state to another.[152] It is, however, now generally agreed that the term "exports" is limited to goods exported to foreign countries.[153] Hence, the provision under discussion does not bar taxes on goods whose destination is another state or a territory of the United States.[154]

The constitutional prohibition is violated by any tax levied directly on goods exported or on the right to export them. Hence, federal stamp taxes imposed upon foreign bills of lading,[155] upon policies insuring cargoes during their export voyage,[156] or upon charter parties exclusively for the carriage of goods from the United States to foreign countries [157] have been held void as, in effect, taxes upon exports themselves. Nor did the fact that the amounts involved were very small make any difference. The constitutional mandate, said the highest tribunal in the leading case, was imperative: "The question is never one of amount, but one of power." [158]

Where the tax is not laid on the articles themselves while in the course of exportation, the Supreme Court has indicated that the test of its validity is whether it so directly and closely bears on the process of exporting as to be in substance a tax on the exportation.[159] Where the tax at issue has only a remote and indirect effect upon exports, it is not barred. Consequently, a general tax, laid on all property alike, and not levied on goods in course of exportation, nor because of their intended exportation, is not within the constitutional prohibition.[160] Thus, a manufacturing tax on all filled cheese is valid, though it is levied on cheese manufactured for export as well as upon other filled cheese.[161] Articles intended for export are not relieved from the ordinary burdens of taxation which rest upon all property similarly situated. In the Supreme Court's phrase, "The exemption attaches to the export, and not to the article before its exportation." [162]

Upon like grounds, the high bench has sustained a tax on the income of a corporation engaged in the export business. The tax in question was imposed under a general income-tax law, taxing, not income from the export trade as such, but net income from all sources. In the Court's view, if articles manufactured and intended for export are subject to general taxes up to the time they are actually put in course of exportation, the net income from the exportation when completed must be subject to similar taxation. In such a case, too, said the Court, "At most, exportation is affected only indirectly and remotely." [163]

60

FISCAL POWERS Apart from taxation, the fiscal powers of the Congress rest upon two brief constitutional provisions in Article I, section 8. According to them: "the Congress shall have Power . . . To borrow Money on the credit of the United States" and "To coin Money, regulate the Value thereof, and of foreign Coin." In addition, the Congress is given the authority to protect the foregoing powers by acting "To provide for the Punishment of counterfeiting the Securities and current Coin of the United States."

These provisions vest in the Congress extremely wide powers. "The breadth and comprehensiveness of the words of the Constitution," the highest tribunal has asserted, "are nowhere more strikingly exhibited than in regard to the powers over the subjects of revenue, finance, and currency." [164] In actual fact, indeed, the Constitution has been construed to vest in the Federal Government all of the fiscal powers generally understood to belong to sovereignty.[165] This results, both from the express provisions already referred to, and the aggregate of the powers granted to the Congress, including the implied powers derived from the Necessary-and-Proper Clause.[166]

At the very beginning, in *McCulloch v. Maryland*,[167] it was held that the fiscal powers of the Congress included the authority to charter banks and to vest in them the right to issue circulating notes. It was upon this holding that Congress relied in creating the national banking system, and the Supreme Court upheld its action in this respect by direct reliance upon the *McCulloch v. Maryland* principle.[168] More recently, the same result has been reached with regard to the establishment of the Federal Reserve System,[169] the Federal Land Bank system,[170] and the federal system for the insurance of bank deposits.[171] Nor will the high Court undertake to assess the relative importance of the public and private functions of a banking institution which the Congress has seen fit to create. Thus, it sustained the law setting up the Federal Farm Loan Banks to provide mortgage funds against the contention that the right of the Secretary of the Treasury, which he had not exercised, to use these banks as depositories of federal funds, was merely a pretext for chartering the banks for private purposes.[172]

More important, however, even than the bare holding of *McCulloch v. Maryland* in the fiscal field was the expansive nature of the approach followed in Chief Justice Marshall's landmark opinion there. The Marshall approach, read together with the fiscal provisions of the Constitution, have resulted in the possession by the National Government of practically unlimited authority over every phase of the subject of currency.

During the Constitutional Convention itself, debate arose over a provision in the original organic draft authorizing the Congress to "emit bills on the credit of the United States." The Framers' strong distrust of paper money led them to strike out the power to "emit bills." Despite this deletion, all the same, the Federal Government has issued bills of credit and other paper obligations from the founding of the Republic. Its authority to do so has never really been questioned. There was, on the other hand, serious controversy for many years over the power of the Federal Government to make its bills legal tender.

The matter came before the Supreme Court in connection with the "greenbacks" issued by the Congress as currency during the Civil War. Under the relevant statute, such Treasury notes were expressly made legal tender at face value in the payment of debts between private individuals. In the 1871 *Legal Tender Cases*,[173] the high bench finally put to rest the controversy over the Federal Government's power in the matter. According to the Court, the nation's fiscal powers, viewed in the light of the *McCulloch v. Maryland* approach, included the authority to issue paper money vested with the quality of legal tender. It is for the Congress to determine what is money. The grant of the power to coin money, made in terms so liberal and unrestrained, must include the authority to declare Treasury notes a legal tender, where such declaration is appropriate and adapted to carrying into execution the admitted powers of the Government.[174] As the Court put it in a later case upholding the issuance of legal tender notes in peacetime: "we are irresistibly impelled to the conclusion that the impressing upon the treasury notes of the United States the quality of being a legal tender in payment of private debts is an appropriate means, conducive and plainly adapted to the execution of the undoubted powers of congress, consistent with the letter and spirit of the constitution, and therefore within the meaning of that instrument, 'necessary and proper for carrying into execution the powers vested by this constitution in the government of the United States.' " [175]

The authority of the Congress over the currency expressly includes the power to "regulate the Value thereof." [176] The power so conferred is far broader than the authority only to fix the face value of coins and paper money. It comprehends as well the power of the Congress to determine the amount of the monetary metal that is to constitute the monetary unit and standard of value. This, in turn, includes the power of devaluing the monetary unit by reducing its gold content.

The Congressional power in this respect was definitively settled in 1935 in *Norman v. Baltimore & O.R. Co.*[177] It arose out of Congressional and executive action reducing the gold content of the dollar. Under the devaluation program adopted, gold payments by the Treasury were suspended and all persons were required to deliver to the Treasury all gold and gold certificates owned by them, in exchange for other currency. In addition, a Joint Resolution abrogated so-called "gold clauses" (which purported to give obligees a right to require payment of obligations to them only in gold) in all private contracts and government bonds. Under the Resolution, all such contracts and bonds must be "discharged upon payment, dollar for dollar, in any coin or currency which at the time of payment is legal tender."

In the *Norman* case, the holder of a railroad bond bearing an interest coupon payable in gold, of face value of $22.50, which had been issued before the gold content of the dollar had been lowered, brought suit for payment in gold or for $38.10, the equivalent of gold in devalued dollars. The Supreme Court denied his claim, holding that he was required to accept the face value of his interest coupon in the devalued dollars. It is, said the Court, for the Congress to determine what constitutes valid money and to fix its value. The Congressional power in this respect cannot be frustrated by private contracts such as the gold clauses. According to the Court, "Contracts, however express, cannot fetter the constitutional authority of the Congress." [178] The Congress clearly has the power to devalue the dollar.

To make such devaluation effective, and to secure a uniform currency, it may invalidate private contracts that interfere with realization of the purposes of devaluation. The abrogation of the gold clauses might reasonably be deemed by the Congress to be an appropriate means of carrying out its devaluation policy. "Can we say," asks the *Norman* opinion, "that this determination is so destitute of basis that the interdiction of the gold clauses must be deemed to be without any reasonable relation to the monetary policy adopted by the Congress?" [179]

A more difficult question was presented in *Perry v. United States*,[180] where the gold clauses in the Government's own bonds were at issue. To decide whether such gold clauses could be abrogated by the Joint Resolution already referred to, the high Court had to determine the relationship between the fiscal power of the Congress and its borrowing power.

As emphasized above, the Congress possesses the widest authority over the monetary system, including that of fixing the monetary unit and its value and determining what is to constitute legal tender. Such authority, we have just seen, cannot be frustrated by gold clause provisions in private contracts. On the other hand, the Congress is also vested with the power to "borrow Money on the credit of the United States." The borrowing power is at least as broad as the power to tax and spend, i.e., it may be exercised for any purpose which the Congress determines will promote the "general welfare." The power to borrow includes the power to issue, in return for the money borrowed, obligations of the United States in the appropriate form, such as government bonds.[181] Such bonds are, without any doubt, definite and binding contractual obligations. "The binding quality of the promise of the United States," the Supreme Court has said, "is of the essence of the credit which is so pledged." [182]

In the *Perry* case, plaintiff sued as owner of a Liberty Loan bond, issued in 1918, which provided that the principal and interest would be paid "in United States gold coin of the present standard of value." The Supreme Court held that the Joint Resolution already mentioned, insofar as it abrogated such gold clauses in government, as well as private contracts, went too far. When the United States borrows money, it creates a binding obligation to pay the debt as stipulated and cannot thereafter vary its agreement. The power to coin money and regulate the value thereof may not be so exercised as to impair the terms of the obligations which the Government has issued. As the *Perry* opinion expressed it, "Having this power to authorize the issue of definite obligations for the payment of money borrowed, the Congress has not been vested with authority to alter or destroy these obligations." [183]

Justice Stone, in a separate opinion, strongly urged that the *Perry* majority was wrong in this holding. In his view, it was unwarranted "to

suggest that the exercise of the sovereign power to borrow money on credit
. . . may nevertheless preclude or impede the exercise of another sovereign
power, to regulate the value of money." [184] Surely, he declared, the obligation of the gold clause should not be deemed superior to the power to
regulate the currency.

The writer would be inclined to support the Stone view in the matter,
but it should be pointed out that the question has been rendered academic,
both by the *Perry* decision itself and subsequent developments. In *Perry*,
the high bench, as already noted, ruled that the Congress could not abrogate
gold clauses in government bonds previously issued. Yet the Court went on
to hold that a creditor of the United States could not show any actual
damage when he was paid the face value of his bond in currency vested
with the quality of legal tender. Since the Congress had proscribed the
private ownership of gold and its export, there was no real damage. Gold
might still be bought and sold in the world markets; but plaintiff had no
right to resort to such markets.[185] In Justice Stone's words: "it is declared
that there is no damage because Congress, by the exercise of its power to
regulate the currency, has made it impossible for the plaintiffs to enjoy
the benefits of gold payments promised by the Government." [186]

Thus, in *Perry,* the gold clauses in government bonds were vindicated
as a matter of abstract theory, but rendered unenforceable as a practical
matter by the Court's holding that no damages could be proved where they
were violated. In addition, the right of action itself in such a case depends
upon the consent of the United States to be sued. The *Perry* problem may
consequently concededly "be transferred wholly to the realm of speculation by the exercise of the undoubted power of the government to withdraw
the privilege of suit on its gold clause obligations." [187] Since the *Perry*
decision, the Congress has, in fact, exercised its power in this respect by
passing a law withdrawing consent to sue the United States on gold clauses
in cases where more than the face value of the obligations involved is
sought.[188]

6

THE COMMERCE POWER

61
GENERAL
CONSIDERATIONS *T*HE want of a national power to regulate commerce was, without any doubt, one of the principal defects of the Articles of Confederation.[1] The oppressed and degraded state of commerce prior to the Constitution was, in truth, perhaps the primary cause that led to the Convention of 1787.[2] "It may," in Chief Justice Marshall's words, "be doubted whether any of the evils proceeding from the feebleness of the federal government contributed more to that great revolution which introduced the present system, than the deep and general conviction that commerce ought to be regulated by Congress." [3]

The need to federalize regulation of commerce was basic in the thinking of the men of 1787. No other federal power was so universally assumed to be necessary. In fact, the necessity of centralized regulation of commerce was so obvious and so fully recognized that the Commerce Clause was little illuminated by debate among the Framers.[4] The clause itself was reported in the first draft of the Constitution substantially as it now stands and was adopted with little (if, indeed, there was any) opposition.[5]

The language of the Commerce Clause is deceptively simple. The Congress, it reads, shall have power "To regulate Commerce with foreign Nations, and among the several States, and with the Indian Tribes."

"You would scarcely imagine," says Justice Miller, "and I am sure you do not know, unless you have given some consideration to the subject, how very important is that little sentence in the Constitution." [6] The Commerce Clause is the fount and origin of vast power; [7] it is in the Supreme Court's phrase, "one of the most prolific sources of national power." [8] One may go further and assert that it is the direct source of the most important powers which the Federal Government exercises in time of peace. Certainly, the authority of the Congress to enact regulatory laws stems almost entirely from the Commerce Clause.

The full importance of the affirmative grant of power contained in the Commerce Clause did not appear for many years after the adoption of the Constitution. "For nearly a century . . . ," the high bench informs us, "decisions of this Court under the Commerce Clause dealt rarely with questions of what Congress might do in the exercise of its granted power under the Clause." [9] In a society dominated by the laissez-faire conception of government, the Congressional authority over commerce remained largely in repose. Of the fourteen hundred or so cases which the Supreme Court decided under the Commerce Clause before 1900, the overwhelming proportion involved state legislation which was claimed unconstitutionally to curtail commerce.[10] For a century, then, there was, in Justice Jackson's phrase, "little occasion for the affirmative exercise of the commerce power, and the influence of the Clause on American life and law was a negative one, resulting almost wholly from its operation as a restraint upon the powers of the states." [11]

But if the federal sovereign was a legislator who slumbered and slept during the first hundred years of our history, it has more than made up for it by its subsequent spate of activity. "It was not until 1887," the Supreme Court has said, "with the enactment of the Interstate Commerce Act that the interstate commerce power began to exert positive influence in American law and life." [12] Since that pioneer regulatory law based upon the commerce power, the Congress has more and more been exercising legislative authority under the Commerce Clause. This has been particularly true of the period since Franklin D. Roosevelt's first election to the Presidency. In the three decades since that time, the federal statute book has become filled with a whole host of regulatory laws enacted under the commerce power. In our own day, regulation from Washington based on the Commerce Clause has become a commonplace of the American system; it is now almost trite to point out how the operations of the National Government have come to guard and control us from the cradle to the grave.

62

GIBBONS V.   "At the beginning," we are told by the highest Court,
OGDEN   "Chief Justice Marshall described the federal commerce power with a breadth never yet exceeded." [13]
Marshall's overriding concern that the Constitution must be construed so as to make an effective National Government possible led him to emphasize

the embracing and penetrating nature [14] of the Commerce Clause. At least as much as any man, the great Chief Justice knew the mischief that had been caused by the lack of a national commerce power under the Confederation. The grant made by the Constitution must, he strongly felt, "be as extensive as the mischief." [15] "To construe the power so as to impair its efficacy," he asserted, "would tend to defeat an object, in the attainment of which the American people took, and justly took, that strong interest which arose from a full conviction of its necessity." [16]

Marshall's opportunity to give effect to his expansive views on the commerce power came in the great 1824 case of *Gibbons v. Ogden* [17]—the first case in which the Commerce Clause was considered by the Supreme Court. It arose out of the invention of the steamboat by Robert Fulton. The New York legislature granted to the inventor and Robert Livingston the exclusive right to navigate the waters of that state by steam-propelled vessels. Ogden had secured a license from Fulton and Livingston to operate steamboats between New York and New Jersey. Gibbons started to operate his own steamboat line between the same two states in defiance of the New York–granted monopoly, though his boats were enrolled and licensed to engage in the coasting trade under an act of Congress. Ogden secured an injunction in a New York court to restrain Gibbons from operating within New York waters in violation of the state-granted monopoly.

By availing ourselves of the perspective of a century and a half of hindsight, we may assert today that the issue presented to Marshall and his colleagues in *Gibbons v. Ogden* was basically a simple one. Though Gibbons was operating his steamboats in violation of the New York monopoly, he was acting pursuant to a federal license permitting his vessels to engage in the coasting trade. Under these circumstances, the monopoly law of New York came into collision with the federal licensing law and deprived Gibbons of the right to which that law entitled him. "In every such case," as *Gibbons v. Ogden* declared, "the act of Congress . . . is supreme; and the law of the state, though enacted in the exercise of powers not controverted, must yield to it." [18]

If *Gibbons v. Ogden* stood only for the elementary proposition that a state law incompatible with an act of Congress must fall, the opinion there would hardly justify the characterization of Marshall's biographer as "that opinion which has done more to knit the American people into an indivisible Nation than any other one force in our history, excepting only war." [19] *Gibbons v. Ogden* stands as a constitutional landmark because both counsel and Court did not confine themselves to the narrow issue of conflict between state and federal law. Instead, the occasion was seized for a full-scale discussion of the scope of the commerce power.

The Commerce Clause, as already seen, vests in the Congress the power

"To regulate Commerce." The noun *commerce* determines the subjects to which Congressional power extends. The verb *regulate* determines the type of authority that the Congress can exert. Both the noun and the verb were defined most broadly in *Gibbons v. Ogden.*

Counsel for Ogden had argued that "The correct definition of commerce is, the transportation and sale of commodities." [20] The transportation of passengers, he contended, was not included in the term, which was limited to "the exchange of one thing for another; the interchange of commodities; trade or traffic." [21] Daniel Webster, who led the argument for Gibbons, denied that the Commerce Clause was thus limited. "Nothing," urged Webster, "was more complex than commerce; and in such an age as this, no words embraced a wider field than commercial regulation. Almost all the business and intercourse of life may be connected, incidentally, more or less, with commercial regulations." [22]

Chief Justice Marshall, in his opinion, adopted the wide definition of commerce urged by Webster. In his view, commerce could not be restricted "to traffic, to buying and selling, or the interchange of commodities." [23] Commerce, instead, covered all intercourse—a conception extensive enough to include within its scope all business dealings. "Commerce," said Marshall, "undoubtedly, is traffic, but it is something more; it is intercourse. It describes the commercial intercourse between nations, and parts of nations, in all its branches." [24] Very clearly, navigation (the precise subject at issue in the *Gibbons* case) was comprehended in the Marshall definition. "All America," Marshall declared, "understands, and has uniformly understood, the word 'commerce' to comprehend navigation." [25]

It is customary to think of the Supreme Court of Marshall's time solely in terms of its Chief, who, more than any one man, forged the legal bonds of an enduring Union. In *Gibbons v. Ogden,* nevertheless, it is important to note that Marshall's opinion does not stand alone in its emphasis on the wide scope of the Commerce Clause. Even Justice Johnson, the first Jeffersonian appointed to the Court and, as such, inclined toward a less sanguine view of the scope of federal authority than his Chief, concurred in construing commerce most broadly in a separate opinion delivered by him: "Commerce, in its simplest signification, means an exchange of goods; but in the advancement of society, labor, transportation, intelligence, care, and various mediums of exchange become commodities, and enter into commerce; . . . the nation which could not legislate over these subjects, would not possess power to regulate commerce." [26]

Having given such a broad construction to the noun *commerce,* the Marshall Court proceeded to take an equally liberal view of the meaning of the verb *regulate.* "What is this power?" asked Marshall in his *Gibbons v. Ogden* opinion. "It is the power to regulate; that is, to prescribe the rule by which commerce is to be governed. This power, like all others vested in congress is complete in itself, may be exercised to its utmost extent, and acknowledges no limitations, other than are prescribed in the constitution. . . . If, as has always been understood, the sovereignty of congress, though limited to specified objects, is plenary as to those objects, the power over commerce with foreign nations, and among the several states, is vested in congress as absolutely as it would be in a single government." [27] Or, as it was more succinctly stated in Justice Johnson's concurring opinion: "The power of a sovereign state over commerce . . . amounts to nothing more than a power to limit and restrain it at pleasure." [28]

It has been maintained that Marshall's opinion in *Gibbons v. Ogden* was less broad and forthright in its assertion of federal power than it might have been.[29] This may well be true if we regard the Commerce Clause only in the light of recent cases, under which the federal authority has been expanded even beyond that urged by Marshall. If we look, however, at the views generally held in 1824, we can appreciate the very real contribution to national power made by *Gibbons v. Ogden*. The radical departure made by Marshall can be clearly seen if we contrast his opinion with the restricted scope which President Monroe had just given to commerce in his veto of the Cumberland Road Act in 1822. According to Monroe: "Commerce between independent Powers or communities is universally regulated by duties and imposts. . . . The goods and vessels employed in the trade are the only subjects of regulation. It can act on none other. A power, then, to impose such duties and imposts in regard to foreign nations and to prevent any on the trade between the States, was the only power granted." [30]

Marshall's opinion in *Gibbons v. Ogden* ruthlessly brushes aside this narrow theory. Commerce, in the broad sweep given to it by the great Chief Justice, comprehends every species of commercial intercourse: "It describes the commercial intercourse between nations and parts of nations, in all its branches, and is regulated by prescribing rules for carrying on that intercourse." [31] Similarly, Marshall rejected the notion that the power to *regulate* was limited to the authority to impose duties and imposts. The power to regulate, said he, is the plenary power to control, i.e., to prescribe the rule by which the subject of regulation is to be governed. Once commerce was concerned, in Marshall's view, the Congress could lay down whatever limits and restraints it chose. The power to regulate commerce includes both the power to prescribe limits to its freedom and the power to determine what shall remain unrestrained.[32]

So penetrating and pervasive, indeed, was the commerce power, in the Marshall conception, that he was led to warn expressly that effective restraints on its exercise must proceed from political rather than from judicial processes.[33] As he put it, "The wisdom and the discretion of Congress, their identity with the people, and the influence which their constituents possess at election, are, in this . . . the sole restraints on which they have relied, to secure them from its abuse." [34]

63

INTERSTATE   The Commerce Clause speaks of "Commerce with
VERSUS   foreign Nations, and among the several States, and
LOCAL COMMERCE   with the Indian Tribes." In *Gibbons v. Ogden,* Marshall dealt with the meaning of commerce "among the several States." "The word 'among,'" said he, "means intermingled with. A thing which is among others, is intermingled with them. Commerce among the states cannot stop at the external boundary line of each state, but may be introduced into the interior." [35]

But Marshall did not go so far as to claim for the Congress a power over all commerce carried on in the interior of a state. "It is not," he conceded, "intended to say that these words comprehend that commerce which is completely internal, which is carried on between man and man in a state, or between different parts of the same state, and which does not extend to or affect other states. Such a power would be inconvenient, and is certainly unnecessary." [36]

It is erroneous to suppose from this that Marshall assumed a rigid line of demarcation between the commerce over which the Congress had been given authority and the "internal" commerce of the states, with physical movement across state lines deemed the simple test.[37] Marshall's concept was more flexible. As he saw it, the word "among" in the Commerce Clause "may very properly be restricted to that commerce which concerns more states than one." [38]

Marshall, in Justice Frankfurter's phrase, thus had an organic conception of commerce.[39] The test, in his conception, was not mere movement across state lines, but whether the particular commerce affected more than one state. "The genius and character of the whole government," he said, "seem to be, that its action is to be applied to all the external concerns of the nation, and to those internal concerns which affect the states generally; but not to those which are completely within a particular state, which do not affect other states, and with which it is not necessary to interfere, for the purpose of executing some of the general powers of the government." [40] Only the "completely internal commerce of a state," [41] under the Marshall notion, could be considered as excluded from the reach of the Commerce Clause.

The recognition by Marshall of "completely internal" commerce of a state was seized upon after his day as the basis for a rigid dichotomy between interstate and intrastate commerce—with the latter beyond the scope of Congressional regulatory power. Under the post-Marshall approach, the criterion became the physical crossing of state lines. Only commerce which moved across state boundaries was subject to federal regulation. Commercial activity within the confines of a state remained subject alone to its authority. "All commercial action within the limits of a State," said a member of the highest Court a little over a decade after Marshall's death, "and which does not extend to any other State or foreign country, is exclusively under State regulation. Congress have no more power to control this than a State has to regulate [interstate] commerce." [42]

Hence, the Congressional power came to turn upon whether particular commerce actually moved across state lines. Until its boundaries were crossed, the state concerned never surrendered its power over trade and commerce, but might still exercise it free from control on the part of the nation. As it was put by Marshall's successor, Chief Justice Taney: "Every State, therefore, may regulate its own internal traffic, according to its own judgment and upon its own views of the interest and well-being of its citizens." [43]

Taney and his colleagues, in accepting a rigid geographical dichotomy between interstate and local commerce, wholly missed Marshall's realization of the organic relationship of commercial transactions. They assumed that what is actually an interrelated process of commerce constitutes for constitutional purposes disparate transactions confined within two sharply separated and distinct areas of power.[44]

To Marshall, the reach of the Commerce Clause extended to all commerce which concerned more states than one.[45] In the post-Marshall Court, this concept of "effect upon commerce" gave way to emphasis upon transportation across state lines. While commerce remained within the confines of a state, it mattered not that it had impacts which radiated beyond the state's borders. "Nor can it be properly concluded," stated the Supreme Court in 1852, "that, because the products of domestic enterprise in agriculture or manufactures, or in the arts, may ultimately become the subjects of [interstate] commerce, that the control of the means or the encouragements by which enterprise is fostered and protected, is legitimately within the import of the phrase '[interstate] commerce,' or fairly implied in any investiture of the power to regulate such commerce." [46]

64

SAME: PRODUCTIVE   The effect of the post-Marshall approach just dis-
    INDUSTRIES   cussed upon the federal commerce power became
                  clear with the 1888 decision in *Kidd v. Pearson*.[47] It
dealt with the constitutionality of a state statute which prohibited the manufacture of intoxicating liquors, even though they were made for sale outside the state. Such law was upheld on the ground that it involved the regulation,

not of commerce, but of manufacturing. "No distinction," declared the highest Court, "is more popular to the common mind, or more clearly expressed in economic and political literature, than that between manufactures and commerce. Manufacture is transformation—the fashioning of raw materials into a change of form for use. The functions of commerce are different. The buying and selling and the transportation incidental thereto constitute commerce." [48]

The power to regulate commerce, according to *Kidd v. Pearson,* does not include any authority over manufacturing, even though the products made are intended to be the subject of commercial transactions in the future. To hold otherwise, the Court asserted, would be to vest in the Congress control over all productive industries. "The result," it said, "would be that congress would be invested, to the exclusion of the states, with the power to regulate, not only manufacture, but also agriculture, horticulture, stock-raising, domestic fisheries, mining,—in short, every branch of human industry. For is there one of them that does not contemplate, more or less clearly, an interstate or foreign market?" [49]

In *Kidd v. Pearson,* the power at issue was that of a state. What was said there about Congressional authority was thus technically only *obiter.* But it soon became the basis of decision in *United States v. E.C. Knight Co.* (1895),[50] more popularly styled the *Sugar Trust Case.* That case arose out of the first important prosecution brought by the Government under the Sherman Anti-Trust Act. The defendant was a company which had obtained a virtual monopoly over the manufacture of refined sugar in this country. The complaint charged that defendant had violated the Sherman Act by its acquisition of the stock of its principal competitors, several sugar refining companies in Pennsylvania. The Supreme Court held, however, that such acquisition could not be reached by the federal commerce power. The monopolistic acts alleged related only to manufacturing, which under *Kidd v. Pearson* were not within the scope of the Commerce Clause.

Nor did it make any difference, under the high Court's approach, that the product in question was being manufactured to be sold across state lines. In the Court's words, "The fact that an article is manufactured for export to another state does not of itself make it an article of interstate commerce." [51] Monopoly of manufacture alone could not be prosecuted under a law based on the commerce power. "It does not follow," the *Knight* opinion concluded, "that an attempt to monopolize, or the actual monopoly of, the manufacture was an attempt . . . to monopolize commerce, even though in order to dispose of the product, the instrumentality of commerce was necessarily invoked." [52]

According to Justice Harlan, who dissented, the effect of the *Knight* decision was to defeat the main object for which the Sherman Act was passed.[53] It was not, indeed, until the *Knight* restriction was substantially watered down that the Anti-Trust Law itself could effectively be employed as a weapon against practices in restraint of trade.[54] "The Knight decision," said the Supreme Court a half century after *Knight,* "made the statute a dead letter . . . and had its full force remained unmodified, the Act today would be a weak instrument, as would also the power of Congress, to reach evils in all the vast operations of our gigantic national industrial system antecedent to interstate sale and transportation of manufactured products." [55]

The *Knight* decision, like that in *Kidd v. Pearson* upon which it was based, was a logical consequence of the post-Marshall approach to commerce. Once the Marshall conception of commerce as an organic whole gave way to the crossing of state lines as the criterion of Congressional power, the *Kidd-Knight* view followed naturally. The result was the artificial and mechanical separation of "manufacturing" from "commerce," without regard to their economic continuity or the effects of the former upon the latter.[56] Manufacture itself was treated as a "purely local" activity and hence beyond the compass of the Commerce Clause.

What was true of manufacturing was also true of all other forms of "production." "Commerce," stated the high Court in *Knight,* "succeeds to manufacture, and is not a part of it." [57] The same can be said of agriculture, mining, and every other means by which goods are produced. In *Oliver Iron Co. v. Lord* (1923),[58] the Court expressly applied the *Kidd-Knight* approach to the mining of iron ore. "Mining," said the Court, "is not interstate commerce, but like manufacturing, is a local business, subject to local regulation and taxation." [59]

Later cases applied the same reasoning to agriculture,[60] oil production,[61] generation of electric power,[62] and other productive industries.[63] All of these activities were held beyond the reach of the Congressional commerce power, although they, together with manufacturing, constituted the heart of the economic life of the country. The basic consideration in all of these cases was that articulated in the *Knight* opinion: "Slight reflection will show that if the national power extends to all contracts and combinations in manufacture, agriculture, mining, and other productive industries, whose ultimate result may affect external commerce, comparatively little of business operations and affairs would be left for state control." [64]

65

SAME: NEW DEAL   But the converse of the just-quoted assertion was
CASES   also true. If the commerce power did not extend to
                   manufacture, agriculture, mining, and other productive industries, comparatively little of business operations and affairs in this country would really be subject to federal control.

What this restricted conception of the commerce that the Congress could reach meant in practice is shown dramatically by the fate in the high bench of much of the legislation passed by the Congress in seeking to deal with the great economic crisis of the early 1930's. The effect of the decisions discussed in the prior section may be seen clearly in *Carter v. Carter Coal Co.* (1936),[65] where the Supreme Court had before it a federal law regulating the bituminous coal industry by price-fixing, proscription of unfair trade practices, and prescription of labor conditions. In declaring this law, and particularly its labor provisions, invalid, the majority of the Court relied directly upon the narrowed notion of commerce already referred to.

The *Carter* opinion rests upon the proposition that mere manufacturing or mining does not constitute commerce: "The local character of mining, of manufacturing and of crop growing is a fact, and remains a fact, whatever may be done with the products." [66] The effect of the labor provisions of the challenged law, said the Court, primarily falls upon production, not upon commerce. Commerce was said to be a thing apart from the relation of employer and employee, which in all producing occupations was purely local in character. And, in the high Court's view, it made no difference that labor practices in the gigantic coal industry clearly had an effect upon interstate commerce. To the Court, this effect was not "direct" enough; [67] the direct effect was upon production and, then, the production itself affected commerce.

The reasoning of the *Carter* case had been previously applied by the highest tribunal to nullify the two most important antidepression measures of the New Deal—the National Industrial Recovery Act and the Agricultural Adjustment Act. The NIRA was held beyond the reach of Congressional power as applied to small wholesale poultry dealers in Brooklyn. The business done by them was purely local in character, even though the poultry handled by them came from outside the state. And, under the *Carter* approach, it did not make any difference that there was some effect upon interstate commerce by the business being regulated.[68] Similarly, in holding the AAA unconstitutional, the Court relied upon the proposition that agriculture, like manufacturing or mining, is not commerce and hence is immune from federal control.[69] In both cases, the restricted post-Marshall meaning of the term "commerce" had been used to deny to the Congress authority over most vital aspects of the national economy.

The restrictive interpretation of the commerce power in these New Deal decisions was catastrophic in its consequences upon effective governmental regulation. Elimination of manufacturing, mining, agriculture, and other productive industries from the reach of the Commerce Clause rendered the Congress powerless to deal with problems in those fields, however pressing they might become. And so, as Justice Jackson stated, in characterizing the effect of the *Carter* decision: "a national government that has power, through the Federal Trade Commission, to prohibit the giving of prizes with penny candy shipped by the manufacturer from one state to another, was powerless to deal with the causes of critical stoppages in the gigantic bituminous coal industry." [70]

It is true that the Supreme-Court decisions in the cases discussed did not affect the authority of the states to control production within their own boundaries. But state power must necessarily end at the state limits and is hardly competent to cope with modern economic activity which so often extends over more than one state. In addition, regulation limited to that exerted by the states must, of necessity, vary from state to state. State control cannot in most cases have the uniform character necessary for efficacious economic regulation.

If a national industry like bituminous coal production is effectively to be regulated, it must be by regulation that is national in character. As a federal judge has expressed it, "To say that the production of products distributed on a national scale can be effectively controlled by the states is both constitutionally and economically absurd. To deny power in such a field to the national government is tantamount to saying there shall be no legislation concerning them." [71] Under the cases we have discussed, nevertheless, national regulation was precluded. In effect, then, the result of the restricted conception of the Commerce Clause taken by the high Court after Marshall's day was to prevent effectual economic regulation in this country.

Almost needless to say, the recession from the Marshall conception fitted in perfectly with the laissez-faire theory of governmental function that dominated political and economic thinking for a century after the death of the great Chief Justice. To bar federal intervention, as the Supreme Court did in these cases, was all but to exclude the possibility of any effective regulation in them. This was, of course, exactly what was demanded by the advocates of laissez faire; for, to them, the economic system could function properly only if it was permitted to operate free from governmental interference.

The Constitution, states Justice Holmes in a celebrated passage, "is not intended to embody a particular economic theory, whether of paternalism and the organic relation of the citizen to the state or of laissez faire." [72] At the same time, it was most difficult for judges not to assume that the organic document was intended to embody the dominant economic beliefs of their own day. The Constitution may not enact Mr. Herbert Spencer's *Social Statics*.[73] But the Supreme Court's narrow notion of commerce was a necessary complement to the translation of Spencerian economics into the keystone of the American polity.

66

SAME: Commentators on the law often err in assuming that
"CURRENT OF   legal developments unfold in a strictly consistent
COMMERCE"   fashion, with one Supreme-Court decision leading
                 inexorably to its logical successor in the high tribu-
nal's jurisprudence. Perhaps the tendency referred to is due more to a
desire to simplify than to mere error, for only by presenting its work in
terms of a logically unfolding pattern can the mass of Supreme-Court decisions be rendered meaningful.

At the same time, it should be recognized that a picture of the law de-
veloping in terms of a completely consistent evolution is bound to be somewhat distorted. Of course, if we analyze the case-law of a tribunal like the
highest bench on any subject, we will find a basic stream of jurisprudence.
Within it, however, we will note inconsistent currents, at variance with, and
even at cross-purposes to, the underlying drift of the stream.

As already noted, the Supreme Court after Marshall interpreted the
Commerce Clause in a much more restricted manner than the great Chief
Justice had done. In the prior section, we saw how the Court's narrow conception of commerce culminated in the New Deal cases like *Carter v.
Carter Coal Co.,* under which the post-Marshall approach was carried to
its logical extreme. Conveniently simple though it is, nevertheless, to treat
the cases after Marshall's day as complete repudiations of his expansive
view of commerce, it is not entirely accurate. This is true because, contemporary with the post-Marshall decisions discussed in the two prior sections, were cases whose decisions were entirely consistent with the broad
Marshall conception. It was these cases, indeed, which laid the basis for
the rejection in our own day of the restricted view of commerce discussed
in the two prior sections and an expansion of the commerce power along
the lines laid down in *Gibbons v. Ogden.*

As already emphasized, the Marshall conception of commerce was an
organic one. It was plainly that notion of commerce as an organic whole
which served as the foundation for the 1905 decision in *Swift & Co. v.
United States.*[74] Defendants there were stockyard firms in Chicago and other
cities who had been charged with violating the Sherman Anti-Trust Act by
conspiring to monopolize the sale and distribution of fresh meat in the nation's stockyards. Defendants urged that the buying and selling of livestock
in a stockyard was not commerce among the states. The Supreme Court rejected this contention, holding that the local activities involved were part
and parcel of an integrated commercial whole. As Justice Holmes put it in
the key passage of his opinion: "commerce among the States is not a technical legal conception, but a practical one, drawn from the course of busi-

ness. When cattle are sent for sale from a place in one State, with the expectation that they will end their transit, after purchase, in another, and when in effect they do so, with only the interruption necessary to find a purchaser at the stockyards, and when this is a typical, constantly recurring course, the current thus existing is a current of commerce among the States, and the purchase of the cattle is a part and incident of such commerce." [75]

The *Swift* reasoning was applied in *Stafford v. Wallace* [76] to uphold the Packers and Stockyards Act, under which the business of commission men and livestock dealers in the nation's stockyards was subjected to federal supervision. There, too, the highest Court emphasized that the sales at the stockyards were not merely local transactions: "The stockyards and the sales are necessary factors in the middle of this current of commerce." [77] A similar approach was used to sustain the Grain Futures Act, regulating transactions on grain exchanges.[78] In the Court's view, the sales on a particular grain exchange [79] were just as indispensable to the continuity of the flow of wheat from the West to the distributing points of the East as were the sales in a stockyard to the flow of livestock toward the slaughter and packing houses of the East. In both cases, the sales were part of a great interstate movement or current of commerce. As such they could not be treated as purely local incidents, beyond the reach of the commerce power.

Chief Justice Taft has characterized the *Swift* decision as a milestone in the interpretation of the Commerce Clause, which "drew again the dividing line between interstate and intrastate commerce where the Constitution intended it to be." [80] Implicit in Taft's language is the assumption that the "current of commerce" doctrine enunciated in *Swift* was a return to the Marshall conception of commerce. With commerce treated as an organic whole, the local incidents of a great interstate movement, which taken alone are intrastate, cannot be permitted to characterize the movement as such. The total movement must be viewed as an entity, and every phase of it considered as subject to the commerce power. Hence, we are told by Justice Frankfurter, "while the now familiar conception of the 'stream of commerce' was not in terms expressed by Marshall, the phases of commerce embraced by that doctrine were plainly covered by his philosophy." [81]

67
SAME:
SHREVEPORT
DOCTRINE

The same can be said of the doctrine laid down in the 1914 *Shreveport Rate Case*.[82] It is true that, in Justice Frankfurter's words, "One must be on his guard against recreating history by hindsight and attributing to the language of an early legal doctrine the implications which the evolution of experience has put into it." [83] All the same, it does seem clear that Marshall's conception of commerce was broad enough to draw within the radius of federal power even transactions in and of themselves wholly transpiring within a single state, where such transactions affected interstate commerce.

The *Shreveport* doctrine rests precisely upon this notion of commerce. It arose out of the regulation of railroads by the Interstate Commerce Commission. Manifestly, the federal regulation of carriers engaged in interstate transportation falls within the commerce power.[84] The authority of the Congress over such carriers is not, however, limited only to such portion of their activities as constitutes interstate commerce as such. The effective control of the interstate transportation may require regulation of a carrier's other activities which are closely related thereto or even inextricably interwoven therewith.[85] Thus, the power of the Congress to promote safety in the interstate operation of railroads would be frustrated if not made applicable to trains used in intrastate traffic.

The basic question in such a case was stated by the Supreme Court half a century ago: "Is there such a close or direct relation between the two classes of traffic, when moving over the same railroad, as to make it certain that the safety of the interstate traffic and of those who are employed in its movement will be promoted in a real or substantial sense by applying the requirements of these acts to vehicles used in moving the traffic which is intrastate as well as to those used in moving that which is interstate?" [86] The Court answered this query in the affirmative, in upholding the authority of the Congress to protect interstate rail transportation by requiring the equipment used in intrastate traffic to be provided with the same safety devices as those required in interstate transportation.[87]

The *Shreveport Rate Case* itself went one step further, for it sustained an order of the Interstate Commerce Commission fixing intrastate railroad rates alone. The Commission's action was called forth by the fact that Shreveport, Louisiana, competed with Dallas and Houston, Texas, for the trade of the intervening territory. The interstate rates from Shreveport to the intervening Texas cities were much higher than the intrastate rates from Dallas and Houston to the same cities. The result was that the interstate traffic from Shreveport was placed at a severe competitive disadvantage. To correct such discrimination against interstate commerce, the I.C.C. ordered that the intrastate rates from Dallas and Houston should be equalized with the interstate rates from Shreveport. The railroads concerned contended that the fixing of such local rates was beyond the Congressional power.

This contention was rejected by the high Court in a notable opinion by Justice Hughes. The Congress, said he, can prevent discriminations against interstate commerce. It is immaterial, so far as the protecting power of Congress is concerned, that the discrimination in a particular case arises from intrastate rates as compared with interstate rates. The Congress, in the exercise of its paramount authority, may prevent the instrumentalities of intrastate intercourse from being used to the injury of interstate commerce. In the words of the Hughes opinion, "Wherever the interstate and intrastate transactions of carriers are so related that the government of the one involves the control of the other, it is Congress, and not the State, that is entitled to prescribe the final and dominant rule, for otherwise Congress would be denied the exercise of its constitutional authority, and the State, and not the Nation, would be supreme within the national field." [88]

Under the *Shreveport* doctrine, the reach of the commerce power includes the regulation of any intrastate transactions that have become so interwoven with interstate commerce that their regulation may be deemed necessary or proper for the effective control of interstate commerce. Nor is *Shreveport* limited in scope to particular intrastate transactions. Under it, the Federal Government can act against an entire pattern of intrastate trade where that is necessary for the effective regulation of interstate commerce. Thus, the Interstate Commerce Commission may be vested with the authority to remove the general discrimination against interstate commerce that exists when a state maintains its general intrastate rate structure at too low a level. In such a situation, the federal agency may regulate the intrastate rates to compel the local commerce as a whole to pay its own way and prevent the state from thrusting the burden of its support on interstate commerce.[89]

68

EFFECT UPON COMMERCE: DIRECT VERSUS INDIRECT EFFECT   The doctrines of "current of commerce" and the *Shreveport Rate Case* could have opened the door directly to an overruling of the restricted view of "commerce" which, as already seen, prevailed in the Supreme Court after Chief Justice Marshall's death. Under both *Shreveport* and the "current of commerce" concept, the Congress could reach, not only commerce which actually crossed state boundaries, but also all transactions which were intimately related to interstate commerce. The test thus became "effect upon commerce," rather than the physical movement across state lines.

Under this approach, the Congress could regulate, not only where particular commerce moved between states, but also whenever commercial activities affected interstate commerce. "Commerce among the states," declared Justice Story, paraphrasing the opinion in *Gibbons v. Ogden,* "means commerce, which concerns more states than one." [90] *Shreveport* and the "current of commerce" cases opened the way to a complete return to this broad concept of commerce. Under it, productive industries and other activities, which, taken alone, might be considered local, might be brought

within the reach of the Commerce Clause because of their effect upon interstate commerce.

The Supreme Court did not, however, go so far as to repudiate the main
line of the post-Marshall jurisprudence, despite the wide implications of the
Shreveport and "current of commerce" cases. At the time those cases were
decided, and for a generation thereafter, the high bench followed the view
that local activities could not be regulated by the Congress merely because
they had *some* effect upon interstate commerce. As Chief Justice Hughes
put it in a leading case: "In determining how far the federal government
may go in controlling intrastate transactions upon the ground that they 'affect' interstate commerce, there is a necessary and well-established distinction between direct and indirect effects." [91] For Congressional power to extend to intrastate activities, their effect upon commerce had to be *direct*.[92]

The distinction between "direct" and "indirect" effects of intrastate
transactions upon interstate commerce was treated by the high Court "as a
fundamental one, essential to the maintenance of our constitutional system." [93] At the same time, it must be recognized that it was responsible for
some of the most controversial and sharply criticized decisions in Supreme-
Court history.

In *Adair v. United States* (1908),[94] for example, the Court invalidated
a federal law outlawing so-called "yellow dog" contracts (i.e., agreements
by employees not to join labor organizations) as conditions of employment
on interstate railroads. Such a law, it was held, could not be justified as a
regulation of commerce. Even if it could be argued that there was a connection between union membership and the carrying on of interstate commerce, it could, in the Court's view, hardly be said to be a direct one. The
same reasoning was used in a later case to render unconstitutional the Railroad Retirement Act of 1934, under which a compulsory retirement and
pension system was set up for all interstate railroads.[95]

The distinction between direct and indirect effect upon commerce was
the basis, too, for the decisions discussed in section 65 on the validity of
much of the New Deal legislation. Thus, the National Industrial Recovery
Act was held invalid as applied to wholesale poultry dealers in Brooklyn.
The federal regulation at issue sought to control the hours and wages of
those employed by such dealers, on the theory that, since the poultry
handled by them came from outside the state, their activities affected interstate commerce. To the Court, nevertheless, if there was any effect, it was,
at most, indirect. "The persons employed in slaughtering and selling in local
trade," declared the opinion of Chief Justice Hughes, "are not employed in
interstate commerce. Their hours and wages have no direct relation to interstate commerce." [96]

The Hughes opinion, it is interesting to note, conceded that it was most difficult to draw a precise line between direct and indirect effects. The distinction itself, on the other hand, was categorically declared to be both clear in principle and essential to the maintenance of our system. "Otherwise . . . ," asserted the Chief Justice, "there would be virtually no limit to the federal power, and for all practical purposes we should have a completely centralized government." [97]

The already-discussed decision in *Carter v. Carter Coal Co.*[98] also turns upon the direct-indirect distinction. The Supreme Court there held unconstitutional a federal statute regulating prices, trade practices, and labor conditions in the bituminous coal industry. As pointed out in section 65, *Carter* rests upon the proposition that mining does not constitute commerce; hence, its regulation is not within the radius of federal power. But, the Government had argued, the coal industry could be reached by the Congress because of its plain effect upon interstate commerce.

Of course, the high Court could not deny that production or mining, intended for interstate transportation, had some effect upon interstate commerce. Was such effect, however, "direct" enough to justify federal regulation? The answer was a flat negative.

According to the *Carter* opinion: "The word 'direct' implies that the activity or condition invoked or blamed shall operate proximately—not mediately, remotely, or collaterally—to produce the effect. It connotes the absence of an efficient intervening agency or condition." [99] In the *Carter* case, stated the Court, there was no such "direct" effect. The evils at which the federal statute was aimed, it said, "are all local evils over which the federal government has no legislative control." [100] The "direct" effect was upon the local process of production, not upon commerce. The federal regulatory power did not attach until direct effect upon commerce itself occurred, i.e., until interstate commercial intercourse began. Vast though they might be, the objects of regulation here were still purely local—as the Court characterized them, "local controversies and evils affecting local work undertaken to accomplish that local result. Such effect as they may have upon commerce, however extensive it may be, is secondary and indirect. An increase in the greatness of the effect adds to its importance. It does not alter its character." [101]

69

SAME: CRITIQUE   In dissenting in the *Carter* case, Justice Cardozo as-
OF CARTER   serted that the Court had vainly sought to reduce a
                great principle of constitutional law to comprehensive
statement in an adjective. The Commerce Clause, as he saw it, must be interpreted with far more suppleness of adaptation and flexibility of meaning. In the Cardozo view, "The power is as broad as the need that evokes it." [102]

The Cardozo approach drew special pertinence from the grim economic background behind the New Deal measures such as that at issue in *Carter*. Giant industries prostrate, crises in production and consumption throughout the country, the economy in a state of virtual collapse—if ever there was a need for exertion of federal power, it was that which existed after the collapse of 1929. If federal power was not to be as broad as that need, it meant that the nation was helpless in the face of economic disaster.

Under the *Carter* opinion, all this was irrelevant. If there was no "direct" effect upon commerce, in the sense discussed in the prior section, there was no federal power—and that regardless of the size of the industry regulated or the magnitude of the problems involved in such regulation. "The distinction between a direct and an indirect effect," asserted the *Carter* Court, "turns, not upon the magnitude of either the cause or the effect, but entirely upon the manner in which the effect has been brought about. If the production by one man of a single ton of coal intended for interstate sale and shipment, and actually so sold and shipped, affects interstate commerce indirectly, the effect does not become direct by multiplying the tonnage, or increasing the number of men employed, or adding to the expense or complexities of the business, or by all combined." [103]

This aspect of *Carter* was the veritable *reductio ad absurdum* of the direct-indirect distinction. Under it, the matter of degree had no bearing upon the question of federal power: [104] there was no difference between the mining of one ton of coal and ten million tons of coal, so far as the effect on commerce was concerned. Production was purely local. Even though there was a production crisis throughout the country, it could not be dealt with on a national level.[105]

The direct-indirect distinction and its application in *Carter* demonstrated plainly how our constitutional law had come to exemplify the old Simeon proverb that "the gloss, not the text, is the thing." [106] The Commerce Clause itself gave to the nation the power to regulate commerce among the states. Such commerce, said the Supreme Court at the very beginning, is that which concerns more than one state.[107] Any local transaction that affects interstate commerce would appear to be included in this definition. But the Court later came to construe it as including only such activities as *directly* affected commerce, as that term was applied in a case like *Carter*. By the time of the *Carter* decision, the gloss had come to lie so thick that it all but obscured the national power to govern commerce whose provision had been the main motivating factor behind the organic document itself.

The decisions culminating in *Carter* presented a disturbing paradox. As industry became more and more interstate in character, the power of the Congress to regulate was given a narrower and narrower interpretation. The coal industry after 1929, whose regulation was at issue in *Carter,* was one for which national intervention had become a categorical imperative of survival. The market and the states had found the problems of the industry beyond their competence. The choice was between federal action and chaos.[108] A system of constitutional law that required the latter could hardly endure. As the high Court expressed it in 1948, *Carter* and similar decisions, "embracing the same artificially drawn lines, produced a series of consequences for the exercise of national power over industry conducted on a national scale which the evolving nature of our industrialism foredoomed to reversal." [109]

70

SAME: JONES &
LAUGHLIN CASE

Eleven months after the *Carter* decision, the Supreme Court decided the great case of *National Labor Relations Board v. Jones & Laughlin Steel Corp.*[110] In it, the constitutionality of the National Labor Relations Act of 1935 was at issue. Often referred to as the Magna Carta of the American labor movement, the 1935 statute was a comprehensive enactment regulating labor relations throughout the economy. It guaranteed the right of employees to organize collectively in unions and made it an unfair labor practice prohibited by law for employers to interfere with such right or to refuse to bargain collectively with the representatives chosen by their employees.

The Labor Act was intended to apply to economic activities throughout the nation—to those engaged in production and manufacture, as well as to those engaged in interstate commerce, strictly speaking. But this, of course, brought the statute directly into conflict with the line of cases already discussed, holding that production was not commerce and, as such, was beyond the reach of federal power. Nor under decisions like those in *Adair* [111] and *Carter,*[112] could labor relations in productive industries be said to have a *direct* enough effect upon commerce to draw them within the radius of Congressional authority.

In the *Jones & Laughlin* case, the company concerned was engaged only in the business of manufacturing iron and steel. Under the narrow interpretation which had been given to the Commerce Clause only the year before in the *Carter Coal* case, such manufacturing was not commerce and hence not subject to Congressional control. And, under the *Carter* approach, we have seen, it made no difference that the company being regulated was an industrial giant whose operations clearly had an effect upon interstate commerce. Such effect could not, in the *Carter* view, give the Congress authority over purely local production.

It is hardly surprising that the lower court in *Jones & Laughlin* held that the Labor Act lay beyond the range of federal power. Indeed, considering the Supreme Court's resolute language in *Carter,* it is somewhat surprising that it should have even permitted argument on the point. Yet, not only was extensive argument allowed, but the Court itself, in its decision, completely abandoned its previous restrictive approach to the meaning of commerce and returned to the broad sweep which John Marshall had given to the term more than a century earlier.

The company regulated in the *Jones & Laughlin* case relied directly upon the decisions holding that manufacturing in itself was not commerce, arguing that because of them the industrial relations and activities in its manufacturing department were not subject to federal regulation. Chief Justice Hughes, in a masterful opinion for the majority of the Court stated, however, that the fact that the employees here concerned were engaged in production was not determinative: "The close and intimate effect which brings the subject within the reach of federal power may be due to activities in relation to productive industry although the industry when separately viewed is local." [113]

In the *Jones & Laughlin* case, there is no doubt that the production regulated affected interstate commerce. But here the Court declared that, in view of the company's far-flung activities, it would be at variance with reality to say that such effect was only indirect. As the Chief Justice put it: "When industries organize themselves on a national scale, making their relation to interstate commerce the dominant factor in their activities, how can it be maintained that their industrial labor relations constitute a forbidden field into which Congress may not enter when it is necessary to protect interstate commerce from the paralyzing consequences of industrial war?" [114]

The *Jones & Laughlin* rationale rests upon a repudiation of the limited connotation of commerce upon which decisions like that in the *Carter Coal* case had been based. *Carter* had declared that production was not commerce; *Jones & Laughlin* held production to be subject to Congressional regulation under the commerce power. *Carter* had found immaterial the evils which had induced the Congress to act and their effect upon interstate commerce, declaring that, extensive though such effect might be, it was only secondary and indirect; *Jones & Laughlin* was fully cognizant of the catastrophic effect which industrial strife could have upon interstate commerce, and asserted categorically that such effect could not be dismissed as only indirect. "In view of respondent's far-flung activities," declared the Hughes opinion, "it is idle to say that the effect would be indirect or remote. It is obvious that it would be immediate and might be catastrophic. We are asked to shut our eyes to the plainest facts of our national life and to deal with the question of direct and indirect effects in an intellectual vacuum." [115]

71

SAME: PRODUCTIVE The *Jones & Laughlin* decision marks a definite break
INDUSTRIES TODAY with the restricted view that productive industries
are beyond the scope of the Commerce Clause. In
Jones & Laughlin, the Supreme Court held squarely that manufacturing as
such was not automatically excluded from the range of federal power.
Precedents like *Carter,* on which the ink was still hardly dry, had held the
other way. These precedents were not followed. "These cases," laconically
states the *Jones & Laughlin* opinion, "are not controlling here." [116] Instead
the high Court restored to the commerce power the broad sweep it had
had in Marshall's day. Factories, mines, and mills, whose activities had
been deemed "local" and hence immune from federal regulation, were,
under the *Jones & Laughlin* rationale, held to affect interstate commerce
directly enough to justify Congressional control.

Jones & Laughlin itself removed the immunity from the commerce
power which manufacture had come to enjoy. But the Supreme Court soon
extended the *Jones & Laughlin* approach to other productive industries. In
Sunshine Anthracite Coal Co. v. Adkins,[117] the Court upheld a 1937 Congressional act regulating the bituminous coal industry, similar in many
ways to that which had been annulled in the *Carter* case. The opinion delivered by Justice Douglas indicates plainly that the high bench was no
longer of the view that coal mining must be considered immune from the
commerce power. "The regulatory provisions," reads the opinion, "are
clearly within the power of Congress under the commerce clause." [118] The
Congressional authority permits it to undertake economic stabilization of a
productive industry like mining, which constitutes such an important seg-
ment of the economy. "Congress under the commerce clause," states Justice
Douglas, "is not impotent to deal with what it considers to be dire consequences of laissez-faire." [119]

In *Mulford v. Smith,*[120] the high tribunal held valid the Agricultural
Adjustment Act of 1938, whose basic features were not unlike those of the
law of the same name which had been condemned in *United States v.
Butler.*[121] The *Butler* decision had been based upon the proposition that
agricultural production, as such, was not commerce and hence not subject
to the direct regulatory power of the Congress. The *Mulford* case rests
upon a rejection of this reasoning. It is true that the *Mulford* opinion did
not expressly overrule *Butler* on the point under discussion and hold
squarely that agriculture came within the definition of commerce. This
omission led a lower federal court as late as 1954 to assert that "agriculture is not commerce . . . nor does agriculture affect such commerce in a
constitutional sense." [122] Hence, concluded the court, "Federal regulation
of agriculture invades the reserved rights of the states." [123] The Supreme

Court itself quickly laid to rest this ghost of the *Butler* case, declaring categorically, in reversing the lower-court decision referred to, that the regulation of agriculture was within the federal commerce power.[124]

It is thus clear that, under the view that has prevailed in the highest Court since the *Jones & Laughlin* case, productive industries such as manufacture and agriculture are no longer removed from the reach of the commerce power. No longer must production be treated as a purely "local" activity, immune from Congressional control regardless of the impact which it may have upon the commerce of the country. Instead, we have come back to the Marshall conception of commerce as an organic whole, with the Commerce Clause embracing all commerce which concerns more than one state. Under such conception, the federal power is not limited to commerce which actually moves across state lines. It includes all activities which affect interstate commerce, though such activities, taken alone, might be considered "local." The whole point about the post-*Jones & Laughlin* approach is that they can no longer be considered alone. If they have an effect upon interstate commerce, they concern more than one state and come within the radius of the Commerce Clause.

This is true whether or not such effect be considered "direct" or only "indirect," as those terms had been applied in cases like those discussed in section 68. As the high Court put it in an important 1942 opinion: "even if appellee's activity be local and though it may not be regarded as commerce, it may still, whatever its nature, be reached by Congress if it exerts a substantial economic effect on interstate commerce and this irrespective of whether such effect is what might at some earlier time have been defined as 'direct' or 'indirect.' "[125]

The question of federal power today cannot be decided simply by finding the activity in question to be "production," nor can consideration of its effect upon commerce be foreclosed by calling such effect merely "indirect."[126] Whether the subject of regulation is "production" is no longer material for purposes of determining the existence of Congressional power. In the words of the *Jones & Laughlin* opinion: "It is thus apparent that the fact that the employees here concerned were engaged in production is not determinative. The question remains as to the effect upon interstate commerce."[127]

The question referred to remains the only pertinent question in a Commerce-Clause case: Does the subject of regulation affect interstate commerce? An affirmative answer compels the conclusion that it is within the scope of federal power. Mines and mills, factories and farms—all engaged in production, rather than commerce in the literal sense—are brought within the sweep of the Commerce Clause, provided only that they exert some economic effect upon interstate commerce.

72

SAME: The prior two sections have shown how the Supreme
QUANTITATIVE   Court has come back to the view that the test of
ASPECT   federal power under the Commerce Clause is solely
                the existence of effect upon commerce by the subject
of regulation. The question that naturally arises next is that of the quantitative substantiality of the effect that may be required.

In the *Jones & Laughlin* case, we saw, it was held that the iron and steel company's manufacturing activities were subject to Congressional control because they had a clear effect upon interstate commerce; nor, in the high Court's view there, could such effect be dismissed as merely indirect. The company regulated in *Jones & Laughlin* was an industrial giant [128] whose activities, without any doubt, had a substantial impact upon interstate commerce. As the Court put it in a passage already quoted, the effect on commerce of the stoppage of its operations "might be catastrophic." [129] But the high tribunal has not hesitated to employ the *Jones & Laughlin* reasoning in cases involving much smaller companies as well, where no such serious effect could be present.

On the same day that it decided the *Jones & Laughlin* case, the Supreme Court applied its holding to a company manufacturing clothing in Richmond, Virginia.[130] It was "a typical small manufacturing concern which produces less than one-half of one per cent of the men's clothing produced in the United States and employs 800 of the 150,000 workmen engaged therein." [131] The interruption of such a business would hardly have more than a slight effect upon commerce. "The business of the Company," asserted a dissenting Justice, "is so small that to close its factory would have no material effect upon the volume of interstate commerce in clothing." [132] Despite this, the Court ruled that the principles stated in *Jones & Laughlin* justified federal regulation here. Plainly, under this decision, the business involved did not have to be one whose interruption would be "catastrophic" for it to be reached under the Commerce Clause.[133]

How substantial, then, does the effect upon commerce have to be for the federal power to attach? In *National Labor Relations Board v. Fainblatt*,[134] the high bench stated expressly that the operation of the Commerce Clause does not depend on any particular volume of commerce affected. The company concerned in *Fainblatt* was a very small clothing manufacturer, with a factory in New Jersey employing from 60 to 200 employees. According to the Court, the smallness of the volume of commerce affected in the particular case is without significance. "Commerce," said the *Fainblatt* opinion, "may be affected in the same manner and to the same extent in proportion to its volume, whether it be great or small." [135]

Under the *Fainblatt* decision, any activity can be regulated by the Congress—provided merely that it have *some* effect upon interstate commerce. The quantitative aspect of such effect becomes irrelevant under such an approach. As the *Fainblatt* dissent put it, "If the plant presently employed only one woman who stitched one skirt during each week . . . , Congressional power would extend to the enterprise, according to the logic of the Court's opinion." [136] The requirement, in other words, is only that the activity regulated affect interstate commerce—not that it must affect a relatively large proportion of such commerce. The reach of the Commerce Clause cannot be determined on a percentage basis.[137]

Some of the cases do, it is true, state a *de minimis* limitation, i.e., that the amount of commerce affected must not be so trifling that the maxim *de minimis* [138] would apply.[139] Under the actual decisions, however (particularly those to be discussed in the next two sections),[140] this restriction is really of no practical importance. The commerce power turns, not upon volume, but effect. "It extends," in the phrase of a 1941 case, "to those activities intrastate which so affect interstate commerce or the exercise of the power of Congress over it as to make regulation of them appropriate means to the attainment of a legitimate end, the exercise of the granted power of Congress to regulate interstate commerce." [141] The test thus is solely whether the activity regulated affects interstate commerce; if it does it is subject to the commerce power regardless of the actual extent of such effect.

73

SAME: "Almost anything," caustically declared the dissent-
WRIGHTWOOD AND ing opinion in the *Jones & Laughlin* case, "—mar-
FILBURN CASES   riage, birth, death—may in some fashion affect com-
                merce." [142] Under contemporary conditions, the eco-
nomic system has become so interconnected in its parts that there are few, if any, even purely local business activities which may not have at least some repercussions upon commerce which extends beyond state lines.

It can hardly be denied that the present view, discussed in the prior section, of what constitutes consequential effect upon commerce tends to obliterate the distinction between what is national and what is local, insofar as the scope of the Commerce Clause is concerned. In Justice Cardozo's apt words: "Motion at the outer rim is communicated perceptibly, though minutely, to recording instruments at the center. A society such as ours is an elastic medium which transmits all tremors throughout its territory." [143] In a complex, modern society, there is such interdependence of its members that the activities of most of them are necessary to the activities of most others.[144] Activities local in their immediacy may become interstate and even national because of their distant repercussions.[145]

If centripetal forces are thus elevated, to the exclusion of the forces that oppose and counteract them, there is practically no economic activity in this country that is completely immune from Congressional control. If effect upon commerce is the test, irrespective of degree, the radius of the Commerce Clause becomes as broad as the economic life of the nation.

The extent to which the Congress can regulate local activities under the present interpretation of the effect-upon-commerce test is well shown by two 1942 decisions. *United States v. Wrightwood Dairy Company* [146] upheld the constitutionality of federal regulation of the price of milk produced and sold entirely within the State of Illinois. The Supreme Court justified such regulation on the ground that the intrastate milk being regulated was sold in competition with milk transported from outside the state. According to the opinion: "the marketing of a local product in competition with that of a like commodity moving interstate may so interfere with interstate commerce or its regulation as to afford a basis for Congressional regulation of the intrastate activity." [147] The power to regulate milk moving interstate into Illinois includes authority to make like regulations for local milk, because of the latter's competitive effect upon the former.

The *Wrightwood Dairy* decision carries to its logical extreme the *Shreveport* doctrine discussed in section 67. Under *Shreveport,* we saw, transactions wholly within a state could be drawn within the reach of the commerce power where their regulation was necessary for effective Congressional control of interstate commerce. Under *Wrightwood,* the fact that a purely local activity competes with interstate commerce is enough to warrant the exertion of federal authority over it. The competitive effect alone furnishes the occasion for the use of the commerce power. "It is," states *Wrightwood,* "the effect upon the interstate commerce or its regulation, regardless of the particular form which the competition may take, which is the test of federal power." [148]

Yet, if what has just been said is true, one may wonder what form of intrastate economic activity may not be reached by the Congress under the *Wrightwood* reasoning. In the interrelated economy of the modern world, the merchant within the gates is engaged in a constant contest with the stranger from afar. Almost all local commerce competes to some extent with commerce from beyond the state and, according to *Wrightwood,* all such commerce is in consequence within the scope of the Commerce Clause.

The second 1942 decision to be discussed—*Wickard v. Filburn* [149]— sustained, if anything, an even deeper penetration by the Congress into local activities. The Agricultural Adjustment Act of 1938 extends the federal regulation of agricultural production to produce not intended in any part for commerce but wholly for consumption on the producer's farm.

Under the Act, wheat consumed on the farm and never reaching any conventional market could lead to penalties if grown on acreage in excess of that allowed to the producer concerned. As it was put in a comment by Justice Douglas: "Wheat that was eaten by chicken or pigs or consumed by the farmer at his table was treated the same as wheat sent into the vast stream of commerce reaching the nation's grain markets." [150]

In *Wickard v. Filburn* itself, the appellee was, under the 1938 Act, subject to a penalty for producing wheat in excess of the quota allotted to him by the Department of Agriculture. He claimed that his crop was not within the reach of federal regulatory power because it was intended to be consumed on his farm. The Supreme Court conceded that, even under the expanded scope of the Commerce Clause since the *Jones & Laughlin* case: "there is no decision of this Court that such activities may be regulated where no part of the product is intended for interstate commerce or intermingled with the subjects thereof." [151] In the instant case, nevertheless, the Court did hold that the home-consumed agricultural product which never saw the light of commerce could be regulated by the Congress.

The *Wickard v. Filburn* holding was based upon the assertion that a home-consumed product like wheat has an effect upon the price and market conditions for wheat. "This may arise," said the Court, "because being in marketable condition such wheat overhangs the market and if induced by rising prices tends to flow into the market and check price increases. But if we assume that it is never marketed, it supplies a need of the man who grew it which would otherwise be reflected by purchases in the open market. Home-grown wheat in this sense competes with wheat in commerce." [152] This, of course, brings *Wickard v. Filburn* directly within the principle of the *Wrightwood* case, already discussed in this section.

Thus, even the local product which is consumed by the producer himself is said to have an effect upon commerce sufficient to call forth the operation of the Commerce Clause. According to the *Wickard v. Filburn* opinion, "Congress may properly have considered that wheat consumed on the farm where grown if wholly outside the scheme of regulation would have a substantial effect in defeating and obstructing its purpose to stimulate trade therein at increased prices." [153]

Nor, under the principle discussed in section 72, does the fact that the excess wheat involved in the case (some 239 bushels) can scarcely be said to have had any quantitatively substantial effect on the market make any difference. In the high Court's phrase, "That appellee's own contribution to the demand for wheat may be trivial by itself is not enough to remove him from the scope of federal regulation." [154]

74

With the decision just discussed in *Wickard v. Fil-burn,* a climax is reached in the broadening of the definition of commerce which started with the *Jones & Laughlin* case. Indeed, under *Wickard v. Filburn,* federal authority may be exerted over purely local transactions, though they themselves are not even commercial in character.[155] Even so, under the high tribunal's reasoning, they may have sufficient effect upon commerce to furnish the occasion for the exercise of Congressional power.

But, following this approach, it is difficult to see what phase of economic activity within the states may not be subjected to federal authority. If it is the existence of effect upon interstate commerce, no matter how trivial or indirect that is now the test, the commerce power may be utilized to reach practically every aspect of the economic system. By a "house-that-Jack-built" chain of causation, there may be brought within the sweep of the Commerce Clause every stage of economic activity—even the ultimate *causa causarum*—which results in the production of goods for commerce.[156]

The scope of the commerce power under this reasoning is well shown by the cases on the applicability of the Fair Labor Standards Act of 1938, a law which provides for the fixing of minimum wages and maximum hours by a federal agency.[157] The prescribed wages have to be paid to employees "engaged in commerce or in the production of goods for commerce." In *Kirschbaum v. Walling,*[158] this provision was held to include employees engaged in the maintenance and operation of a building in which goods for interstate commerce were produced. Such employees, said the Supreme Court, are necessary for the production of goods for commerce. "Without light and heat and power," its opinion asserts, "the tenants could not engage, as they do, in the production of goods for interstate commerce. The maintenance of a safe, habitable building is indispensable to that activity." [159] As such, the activities of the maintenance employees affect commerce and can therefore be regulated by the Congress.

In other cases, the Supreme Court has held the Fair Labor Standards Act applicable to employees of a window-cleaning company, the greater part of whose work was done on the windows of people engaged in interstate commerce; [160] employees putting in stand-by time in the auxiliary fire-fighting service of an employer engaged in interstate commerce; [161] members of a rotary drilling crew, employed within a state by an independent contractor in partially drilling oil wells, some of whose product "ultimately found its way into interstate commerce"; [162] and employees of a local newspaper with a limited circulation.[163]

The last cited case is of particular interest. The newspaper involved in it had a circulation ranging from 9,000 to 11,000 copies. Of these, only about ½ of 1 per cent circulated out-of-state, amounting to a mere 45 copies. The lower court had applied the maxim *de minimis* [164] to exclude the newspaper from the operation of the Fair Labor Standards Act. The Supreme Court reversed, emphasizing once again that the test of the commerce power is not based upon volume of business. Justice Murphy, who dissented, asserted: "In my opinion, a company that produces 99½% of its products for local commerce is essentially and realistically a local business." [165] Under the present scope of the Commerce Clause, nevertheless, such a company is within the reach of Congressional authority if its activities have any effect upon interstate commerce. Here, such effect would be present even if there were no out-of-state circulation. Using the *Wright-wood-Wickard v. Filburn* reasoning of the prior section, the local newspaper can be said to compete with out-of-state papers. Such competitive effect is enough for the federal power to attach—slight though such effect may be in the actual case.

Cases like those just discussed led Justice Roberts, in his Holmes lectures on the Constitution, to characterize the Fair Labor Standards Act as one whose effect "was to place the whole matter of wages and hours of persons employed throughout the United States with slight exceptions, under a single federal regulatory scheme and in this way completely to supersede state exercise of the police power in this field." [166] That such can be the effect of a federal statute today shows strikingly how far the highest Court has gone in rejecting the narrowed conception of commerce that prevailed before the *Jones & Laughlin* case.

Under the Supreme Court's present expanded view, the commerce power alone can support federal regulation of almost all local action, since it is conceivable that such activity, however remotely, "affects" commerce.[167] To critics of the recent jurisprudence in this field, the Court has all but obliterated the distinction between what is national and what is local, that had heretofore been of such cardinal consequence. As a dissenting Justice put it, "It is but to repeat, in another form, the old story of the pebble thrown into the pool, and the theoretically infinite extent of the resulting waves, albeit too tiny to be seen or felt by the exercise of one's senses." [168]

It should, at the same time, be noted that the high bench, in its Commerce-Clause decisions since *Jones & Laughlin,* has basically come back to the sweeping conception of commerce originally enunciated by Chief Justice Marshall. In Marshall's embracing view, questions of the commerce power were not to be decided by reference to any formula which would give controlling force to nomenclature such as "production" and "indirect." [169] The only test was whether or not the commerce at issue concerned more than one state or, to use the modern terminology, whether or not the particular activity affected interstate commerce.

If there is effect upon interstate commerce, the activity does concern more than the state in which it is carried on. It is true that, in some of the cases considered, the individual effect involved may appear petty. It should, however, be remembered that particular activities are not conducted in their own peculiar vacuums. The given individual's contribution to commerce may be trivial by itself, but, taken together with that of many others similarly situated, is usually anything but trivial. Congress should be able to consider the total effect of "his contribution taken together with that of many others similarly situated." [170]

With inexorable logic, the cases have progressed from *Jones & Laughlin* to *Wickard v. Filburn* and the Fair Labor Standards Act decisions—sweeping within the radius of the Commerce Clause ever more of the country's economic life. In truth, at the present time, so far as the authority of the Congress is concerned, we have become one national economic unit, whose outstanding characteristic is the interdependence of its members. Such interdependence enables the commerce power to penetrate ever more deeply into local activities. Federal penetrations must be upheld, provided only that there is effect—however trifling in the individual case—beyond the locality concerned.

Under the post-*Jones & Laughlin* jurisprudence, in fact, may we not go so far as to say that the commerce power extends to all economic activities whose regulation is deemed necessary and proper by the Congress? The Commerce Clause has, in other words, become as broad as the economic needs of the nation.[171] The commerce power is an affirmative power wholly commensurate with the national needs.[172]

75
NEW INSTRUMENTALITIES OF COMMERCE

An outstanding characteristic of the commerce power is its plastic character. This has enabled it to serve as the basis for governmental regulation of an economy whose dominant feature has been the geometric pace of its unfolding.

The adaptable nature of the Commerce Clause was perceived as early as *Gibbons v. Ogden*,[173] when Marshall recognized that, "in the process of things," the instruments of commerce will change.[174] In *Gibbons v. Ogden* itself, the Supreme Court dealt with an instrument of commerce wholly unknown when the organic document was drawn up, namely, the steamboat. Yet, it was clear that the Commerce Clause applied as much to such vessels as "if they were wafted on their voyage by the winds, instead of being propelled by the agency of fire." [175]

The classic statement of the nonstatic quality of the commerce power is that of Chief Justice Waite in *Pensacola Telegraph Co. v. Western Union*

Co. (1878).[176] The powers granted by the Commerce Clause, declares the statement referred to, "are not confined to the instrumentalities of commerce . . . known or in use when the Constitution was adopted, but they keep pace with the progress of the country, and adapt themselves to the new developments of times and circumstances. They extend from the horse with its rider to the stage-coach, from the sailing-vessel to the steamboat, from the coach and the steamboat to the railroad, and from the railroad to the telegraph, as these new agencies are successively brought into use to meet the demands of increasing population and wealth. They were intended for the government of the business to which they relate, at all times and under all circumstances." [177]

The *Pensacola* decision itself has been described by Justice Frankfurter as an adaptation of abstract doctrine to the changing national economy.[178] At issue in it was the authority of the Congress to regulate telegraph companies. The high Court recognized, of course, that communication by wire was a form of commerce utterly unknown to the Framers. At the same time, it could hardly be disputed that the telegraph had, since its invention, become one of the necessities of commerce. In the phrase of the *Pensacola* opinion, "The electric telegraph marks an epoch in the progress of time." [179] The Commerce Clause is construed so as to keep pace with such progress. As new instrumentalities of commerce are devised, they fall within the scope of Congressional authority. This was as true of the telegraph in the *Pensacola* case as it was of the steamboat in *Gibbons v. Ogden.* "In sanctioning the power which Congress exercised by the Act of 1866," Justice Frankfurter informs us, "[Waite] is loyal to the framers, for he recognized, in the language of one of his colleagues, that the Constitution 'was made for an undefined and expanding future.' " [180]

As the stagecoach gave way to the railroad and telegraph, so in our own day, the railroad has given way to the motor vehicle and airplane and the telegraph to the telephone and radio-television. As these new instrumentalities of commerce have made their appearance, the Congressional power has attached. Comprehensive federal regulatory laws have been enacted with regard to each of them. As far as motor vehicles and airplanes have been concerned, there has been no question, since their invention, that they have been at least as much subject to the commerce power as the railroads have been.[181] Regulation of interstate communication by telephone has likewise presented no problem, since it involves basically the same type of transmission by wire as does the telegraph.[182] Indeed, the Supreme Court has gone so far as to state that, "Interstate communication of a business nature, whatever the means of such communication, is interstate commerce regulable by Congress." [183]

Such a broad approach made it easy for the high tribunal to deal with the newer means of communication by wireless, when federal regulation of them was at issue. In its essentials, said the Court when the question arose, radio does not differ from the sending of telegraph or telephone messages: "In each, transmission is effected by means of energy manifestations produced at the point of reception in one state which are generated and controlled at the sending point in another. Whether the transmission is effected by the aid of wires, or through a perhaps less well-understood medium, 'the ether,' is immaterial, in the light of those practical considerations which have dictated the conclusion that the transmission of information interstate is a form of 'intercourse,' which is commerce." [184]

The Commerce Clause consequently comprehends all forms of economic activity—"commercial intercourse . . . , in all its branches," [185] to use Marshall's expression. It is immaterial that the particular instrumentality is one that was not even within the comprehension of the men who drafted the Constitution. Because of this, the commerce power has proved adequate to the needs of the Industrial Revolution, from the age of steam to that of the atom. The mind can, in truth, scarcely conceive of a mode of economic activity which will not be covered by the Commerce Clause. Whatever the economic needs of the moment, the clause can be construed so as to vest in the nation authority sufficient to deal with them. A charter which saw the light of day in a leisurely age of knee breeches and three-cornered hats may consequently prove equal to the exigencies of twentieth century government.

76

INSURANCE   A field where the effect of economic changes upon the operation of the Commerce Clause is clearly shown is that of the regulation of insurance. In 1869, in *Paul v. Virginia*,[186] it had been decided that insurance was not commerce and was, as such, subject only to state regulation. Contracts of insurance, said the Supreme Court there, "are not articles of commerce in any proper meaning of the word." [187] They are purely local transactions. A state law regulating insurance companies was sustained because "Issuing a policy of insurance is not a transaction of commerce." [188]

When *Paul v. Virginia* was decided, the insurance business was still in its virtual infancy. In the three-quarters of a century that followed, it had grown to such an extent that the Supreme Court could characterize it in 1944 as a business which "holds a commanding position in the trade and commerce of our Nation. Built upon the sale of contracts of indemnity, it has become one of the largest and most important branches of commerce." [189] It involves a continuous stream of intercourse among the states composed of collections of premiums, payments of policy obligations, and the countless documents and communications essential to the negotiation and execution of policy contracts. "Insurance," said the 1944 opinion referred to, "touches the home, the family, and the occupation or the business of almost every person in the United States." [190]

The insurance business had thus developed into an interstate commercial enterprise of gigantic proportions. Under *Paul v. Virginia,* all the same, its constitutional status remained that of a purely local activity subject only to state control. This anomalous situation was removed in 1944 by *United States v. South-Eastern Underwriters Association.*[191] In it, the highest Court overruled *Paul v. Virginia* and held that insurance was commerce. Hence, an association of underwriters could be prosecuted under the Sherman Act for a conspiracy to fix rates and to monopolize trade and commerce. A commercial enterprise like insurance, which conducts its activities across state lines, cannot be held beyond the regulatory power of the Congress.

Even the dissenting Justices in the *South-Eastern Underwriters* case did not deny that insurance had *in fact* become commerce, as that term had been interpreted. They urged, nevertheless, that *in contemplation of law* insurance had acquired an established doctrinal status not based on present-day facts, which the Court should not now disturb. Relying upon *Paul v. Virginia,* the states had established an elaborate structure of regulation and taxation of the insurance business. This state system, the dissenters claimed, would be needlessly upset by the majority decision, with no Congressional policy or scheme of regulation to take its place. The only result of overturning *Paul v. Virginia,* in their view, would be the loosing of a flood of litigation and legislation, in order to establish a new boundary between state and national power in the insurance field.

The dire consequences foreseen by the dissenters did not, however, ensue. This was true because the Congress, within less than a year after the *South-Eastern Underwriters* decision, enacted a law expressly authorizing state regulation and taxation of insurance, whether interstate or local. This 1945 law, the Supreme Court has ruled, relinquished federal jurisdiction over insurance to the states. In the Court's words, "Obviously Congress' purpose was broadly to give support to the existing and future state systems for regulating and taxing the business of insurance." [192] In effect, the law in question returned the situation to what it was before the *South-Eastern* case, at least so far as basic regulatory authority over insurance was concerned.

But the *South-Eastern* ruling that insurance is commerce subject to Congressional power still remains good law. The Congress may, whenever it chooses, itself assume the regulatory authority yielded to the states by the 1945 statute. Indeed, even under that statute, certain aspects of the insurance business are even now subject to federal regulation. Thus, variable annuity policies sold across state lines have been held subject to regulation by the Securities and Exchange Commission [193] and advertising materials mailed into other states by a health insurance company have been held subject to regulation by the Federal Trade Commission, at least to the extent that such advertising matter is unregulated by the laws of the state into which it is sent.[194] These holdings were based upon the high Court's interpretation of the terms of the 1945 statute and other relevant laws.

To put it another way, the Supreme Court, in *South-Eastern Underwriters,* removed the supposed constitutional basis for exemption of insurance from the Commerce Clause. It is, at the same time, wholly up to the Congress to determine whether and to what extent its commerce power over insurance will be exercised.

77
PROFESSIONAL SPORTS

Under the present jurisprudence of the Supreme Court, any commercial enterprise which conducts its activities across state boundaries is subject to Congressional authority. The commerce power, states the opinion in the *South-Eastern Underwriters* case, "is the power to legislate concerning transactions which, reaching across state boundaries, affect the people of more states than one." [195] The Commerce Clause clearly embraces every phase of commercial and business activity and intercourse [196] where state lines are actually crossed.

An important case which seems inconsistent with what has just been said is *Federal Base Ball Club v. National League* (1922) [197]—a case that has attracted much attention, since it concerned something which public opinion considers more important than mere legal matters, namely, a question vital to the continued existence of our great national spectator pastime. In it, the Supreme Court ruled that professional baseball was not commerce. Consequently, an antitrust action attacking alleged monopolistic practices on the part of organized baseball could not be brought. According to Justice Holmes, the fact that major league baseball involves the constant crossing of state lines was irrelevant. As he put it, "the transport is a mere incident, not the essential thing." [198]

This reasoning was, of course, inconsistent with the expanded conception of commerce adopted by the high bench in its decisions since the *Jones & Laughlin* case, and especially with the *South-Eastern Underwriters* decision discussed in the prior section. However, when, in the 1953 case of *Toolson v. New York Yankees,*[199] an attempt was made to have the *Federal Base Ball* case overruled, the Court refused to do so. Instead, the prior determination was expressly reaffirmed in its holding that professional baseball was not within the scope of the antitrust laws.

Despite the high Court's specific disclaimer in *Toolson,* the reasoning in its brief *per curiam* opinion there appears inconsistent with that of the *Federal Base Ball* opinion. In both cases, baseball was ruled exempt from the antitrust laws. In *Federal Base Ball,* this ruling was based upon constitutional grounds. Baseball, said Justice Holmes there, was not commerce. Hence, the clear implication was, it was beyond the reach of Congressional power. In *Toolson,* though, as pointed out, the same result of exemption was reached, there was a significant change in approach. The authority of *Federal Base Ball* is confirmed, states the *Toolson* opinion, "so far as that decision determines that Congress had no intention of including the business of baseball within the scope of the federal antitrust laws." [200] The intimation is that *Federal Base Ball* is not being followed in its constitutional implications.

The Court in *Toolson* confirmed this suggestion when it declared: "We think that if there are evils in this field which now warrant application to it of the antitrust laws it should be by legislation." [201] A statement like this would hardly be warranted, if the highest Court were still of the opinion that organized baseball was not commerce and, as such, beyond the radius of Congressional authority.

That there is in fact no constitutional impediment to assertion of the commerce power over professional sports is shown by *United States v. International Boxing Club.*[202] In it, the high bench sustained a civil antitrust action against defendants engaged in the business of promoting professional championship boxing contests. Such contests were promoted on a multistate basis, coupled with the sale of rights to televise, broadcast, and film the contests for interstate transmission. Defendants argued that *Federal Base Ball* and *Toolson* immunized businesses built around the live presentation of local athletic exhibitions. The Court rejected this contention, holding that defendants' business constituted commerce within the meaning of the antitrust laws.

Radovich v. National Football League [203] applied the *International Boxing Club* decision to professional football. The volume of interstate business involved in organized professional football, said the Court, places it, too, within the provisions of the Sherman Act. That a substantial amount of radio and television transmission is an integral part of defendants' business is alone sufficient to meet the requirements of the Commerce Clause.

To be sure, the decisions in the cases just discussed may strike the observer as peculiar applications of the doctrine of *stare decisis.* That doctrine hardly requires the Supreme Court to make untenable distinctions between baseball and other professional sports or to issue a discriminatory fiat in favor of baseball.[204] Yet that appears to be exactly what the Court has done in these cases. "I have yet to hear of any consideration" that led to the *Toolson* holding, affirms a dissenter in *Radovich,* "that is not equally applicable to football." [205] Indeed, if anything, the interstate aspects of baseball and the extent of its exploitation through mass media are far greater than is true of boxing or football.

Justice Frankfurter, dissenting in one of the cases just discussed, caustically declared: "It can hardly be that this Court gave a preferred position to baseball because it is the great American sport." [206] One wonders, all the same, whether this was not the unarticulated basis of the *Toolson* decision. At issue in it was the so-called "reserve clause" in baseball contracts,[207] which most observers have felt to be necessary to the continuance of organized baseball, despite its theoretical antitrust deficiencies. The high Court may have refused to upset baseball's established arrangements because of the belief that the organized sport could not survive in its present form if the "reserve clause" was stricken down.

From a constitutional point of view, at any rate, it is clear that the limitation on the commerce power embodied in the *Federal Base Ball* decision is no longer followed. *Federal Base Ball* had implied an exemption from the Commerce Clause for all businesses involving the live presentation of local exhibitions. The *International Boxing* and *Radovich* cases tell us that this is no longer true as a general proposition. Under *Toolson,* the immunization of baseball from the antitrust laws continues. This is the case even though the high bench has stated specifically that, "were we considering the question of baseball for the first time upon a clean slate we would have no doubts." [208] But *Toolson,* as already indicated, does not rest on constitutional grounds. It turns, not upon lack of Congressional power, but upon failure to exercise such power over baseball.

When we consider the other decisions involving professional sports, we must, in truth, conclude that *Toolson* is more or less *sui generis* and hence without value as a precedent outside its particular fact pattern. May we not go even further and treat the decision as what biologists call a "sport"—a genetic oddity that defies explanation, but does not signify mutation? [209]

78

IS A COMMERCIAL At first glance, an affirmative answer to this question
ELEMENT appears obvious. Since the authority conferred by the
NECESSARY? Commerce Clause is that to regulate *commerce,* one
may not unnaturally conclude that for an activity to be brought within the Congressional power there would have to be involved at some point a commercial element—i.e., one of trade or exchange of goods or services made or rendered for profit.[210] The Supreme Court has,

nevertheless, held in a number of cases that a commercial element may not actually be necessary for the commerce power to become operative.

The starting point here, as in so much of Commerce-Clause jurisprudence, is the opinion in *Gibbons v. Ogden.*[211] In it, as we saw near the outset of this chapter, Chief Justice Marshall rejected the contention that "commerce" was limited to traffic in commodities. Instead, said he, commerce is something much broader: it is *intercourse.*

It can hardly be claimed that Marshall, wide though his concept of commerce was, intended to say that all intercourse, whether carried on for purposes of gain or not, was commerce. His definition clearly was limited to commercial or business intercourse carried on for financial profit.[212] In more recent cases, however, the high Court has tended to modify this limitation. While retaining the Marshall identification between "commerce" and "intercourse," the Court has removed the requirement that interstate intercourse must be of a commercial character for the Commerce Clause to apply. If there are any activities carried on across state lines, i.e., if any interstate intercourse occurs—the commerce power is operative, even though the activities in question lack a commercial element.

It is, in the first place, settled that all forms of interstate transportation come within the Commerce Clause, regardless of whether or not those being transported have any purposes of trade or business.[213] This result is clear if a carrier for hire is involved, whatever may be the purpose for which the persons or commodities involved are carried.[214] In such cases, the transportation itself is being carried on for purposes of financial gain.

In *Covington Bridge Co. v. Kentucky,*[215] the question was whether a company which operated a bridge between two states was engaged in interstate commerce. The Supreme Court held that it was, saying that "commerce" was " 'intercourse,' and the thousands of people who daily pass and repass over this bridge may be as truly said to be engaged in commerce as if they were shipping cargoes of merchandise from New York to Liverpool." [216] This reasoning would not, it is true, apply to those who used the bridge for noncommercial purposes. Yet, even here, the commercial element was not wholly lacking, since the bridge itself was maintained and operated for purposes of pecuniary gain.

From this case, it is a short step to extension of the Commerce Clause to all forms of interstate transit, whether or not engaged in for purposes of profit. This step was taken in *United States v. Simpson,*[217] where a federal law prohibiting the transportation of liquor in interstate commerce [218] was applied to the carrying across a state line of five quarts of whisky by their owner in his own automobile and for his personal consumption. "That the liquor was intended for the personal use of the person transporting it is not material," [219] said the Court, so long as there was transportation across state lines. In other words, the emphasis has shifted from commercial intercourse to any transportation between states, whether or not for business purposes. This was stressed by Justice Clarke, who dissented in *Simpson.* As he saw it, "The grant of power to Congress is over Commerce,—not over isolated movements of small amounts of private property, by private persons for their personal use." [220]

The *Simpson* holding is really based upon the proposition that the Commerce Clause covers every species of interstate movement, whether for profit or not. Once state lines are crossed, federal power attaches, regardless of the presence or absence of any commercial element.

The cases which show most clearly that such is in fact the prevailing rule of law are those arising under the Mann Act. That statute, commonly known as the White Slave Traffic Act, makes it a crime to transport or cause to be transported in interstate commerce any female for the purpose of prostitution, debauchery, or any other immoral purpose. Of course, no one could seriously contest the application of this law to commercialized vice across state lines, where the transportation of the women concerned is for purposes of gain. Such commercial traffic in women is patently within the Commerce Clause.[221]

In *Caminetti v. United States,*[222] on the other hand, the Mann Act was held applicable to a case where defendant was charged with transporting a woman across a state line for purposes of personal debauchery. Defendant there had paid for the travel of a woman from California to Nevada, with the intent that she should become his mistress in the latter state. Despite the fact that no commercial motive was present, the high Court ruled that the mere fact of interstate transportation for an immoral purpose was enough to bring the case within the Congressional prohibition. The Congress can keep the channels of commerce free from immoral use, even though there is no mercenary element involved.

It may, nevertheless, be contended that, in *Caminetti,* a commercial element was present comparable to that in the already-discussed *Covington Bridge* case,[223] since, though defendant did not have any business motive, the transportation was by a carrier engaged for profit in interstate commerce. In other cases, however, the Supreme Court has held the Mann Act applicable even though there was no transportation for hire involved. "The prohibition," the Supreme Court has stated, "is not in terms confined to transportation by common carrier, nor need such a limitation be implied in order to sustain the constitutionality of the enactment." [224]

In *Cleveland v. United States,*[225] the Court went so far as to apply the Mann Act to the interstate transportation of a plural wife by a member of a Mormon sect which practiced polygamy. The Act, reads the opinion there, "while primarily aimed at the use of interstate commerce for the purposes of commercialized sex, is not restricted to that end." [226] The power of Congress over what crosses state lines is plenary. It may be used to defeat what are deemed to be immoral practices, even in a case like this, where even the remotest commercial element is lacking.

The Mann Act decisions demonstrate plainly that noncommercial intercourse may (anomalous though it may seem) be treated as commerce for constitutional purposes. As long as there is interstate movement of goods or persons or the activity in question contemplates or necessarily involves such movement, the Congressional power attaches, regardless of whether any commercial element is involved.

If there is movement across state lines, the movement itself, the instrumentalities by which it is effected, the transactions which gave rise to it, and those engaged in both the movement and the transactions are subject to the commerce power. The *why* and the *how* of such movement are immaterial, so far as the question of federal authority is concerned. "Not only, then," said the Supreme Court in 1944, "may transactions be commerce though non-commercial; they may be commerce though illegal [227] and sporadic, and though they do not utilize common carriers or concern the flow of anything more tangible than electrons and information." [228]

Yet, even stated so broadly, what has just been said does not exhaust the reach of the commerce power over noncommercial activities. Even where such activities do not involve any movement across state lines, they may be subject to Congressional authority under the present broad approach to the "effect upon commerce" test discussed in prior sections.[229] Under it, any activity which can be said to affect interstate commerce comes within the radius of the Commerce Clause. And, given the breadth of the recent decisions on the subject, if there is the requisite effect, it should make no difference whether the given activity is commercial in character or not.

That such is, in truth, the law today is made clear by the already-referred-to decision in *Wickard v. Filburn*.[230] In that case, it will be recalled, the high bench upheld the exertion of federal regulatory power over the production of wheat, even though the particular wheat was produced and consumed entirely on the farm of the individual concerned. Home-grown wheat, the Supreme Court reasoned, competes with wheat in commerce. As such, it may be said to have an effect upon commerce. This is, of course, all that is needed for the commerce power to attach. Hence, even though the activity involved "may not be regarded as commerce, it may still, whatever its nature, be reached by Congress" [231] under the "effect upon commerce" test.

Wickard v. Filburn indicates plainly that the application of the "effect upon commerce" test does not at all turn upon the presence or absence of a commercial element in the activity over which Congressional authority is asserted. *Wickard v. Filburn* may be said to go even further. In it, there was, not only no "commercial intercourse," but no "intercourse" at all, in the sense in which that term is commonly used. Consequently, it may be asserted that any activity which has an effect upon interstate commerce is subject to the commerce power, whatever may be its character and even though it involves no crossing of state lines at all.

The question posed in the title of this section must thus be answered in the negative. Whenever there is movement across state lines (regardless of its nature) or effect upon commerce (in the broad sense in which that term is now used), the commerce power may be employed. The scope of the Commerce Clause (paradoxical though it may at first glance appear) is not at all limited to *commerce*.

79
NAVIGABLE WATERWAYS

The commerce power includes the power to regulate navigable waterways. "All America," declared Marshall in *Gibbons v. Ogden,* "understands, and has uniformly understood, the word 'commerce' to comprehend navigation." [232] A river is a highway for travel between states—at least, it could be such, if it were navigable.[233] Hence, the Congressional authority under the Commerce Clause extends to the navigable streams of the nation. "Commerce," in the 1866 words of the Supreme Court, "includes navigation. The power to regulate commerce comprehends the control, for that purpose and to the extent necessary, of all the navigable waters of the United States." [234]

The Congressional authority in this respect extends to the regulation of every aspect of the waterway concerned and navigation over it. The high Court has, in fact, gone so far as to assert that, for the purposes of the Commerce Clause, all navigable waters "are the public property of the nation" [235] and, as such, subject to any legislation the Congress may deem requisite. Federal control includes the authority to regulate all vessels plying over such waters, even though they may be engaged only in intrastate commerce.[236] The power comprises the regulation of the registry, enrollment, and license of vessels; the method of recording bills of sale and mortgages thereon; the rights and duties of seamen; and any other aspects of ship operation which the Congress chooses to regulate.[237]

But the federal power over navigable waters is not limited to the instrumentalities of navigation employed on them. It may be used to effect such control over any activities on such waters as may be appropriate to protect or promote their use for purposes of commerce. Thus, the power over navigation extends to persons furnishing wharfs, docks, warehouses, and other terminal facilities to those using waterways.[238] Likewise, Congressional authority includes the power to keep navigable waters open and free from any obstruction; to remove such obstructions when they exist; and to provide, by such sanctions as may be deemed proper, against the occurrence of the evil and for the punishment of offenders.[239] Hence, the Congress could pass a law vesting in the Secretary of War the power to determine whether any bridge over a navigable waterway is an unreasonable obstruction to navigation and to order the removal of such obstruction.[240]

The paramount authority of the Congress over obstructions to navigation is well shown by the *Wheeling & Belmont Bridge* cases decided over a century ago. The first of those cases arose out of an action for an injunction against a bridge over the Ohio River on the ground that it obstructed navigation and should, therefore, be abated as a nuisance. The Supreme Court granted the injunction.[241] An act of Congress was then enacted declaring the bridge to be a lawful structure and authorizing it to be maintained at its existing site and elevation. In the second case, the Court held that this act, in effect, superseded its prior decision. According to it, "The regulation of commerce includes intercourse and navigation, and, of course, the power to determine what shall or shall not be deemed in judgment of law an obstruction of navigation; and that power . . . has been exercised consistent with the continuance of the bridge." [242]

In other words, it is for the Congress to determine what constitutes an obstruction to navigation. When that body, acting in exercise of its power to regulate navigation, deems that a particular structure promotes, rather than impedes, navigation, its judgment must prevail. In such a case, though the structure may, to a judge, seem to be an obstruction in fact, he can no longer treat it as such in the contemplation of law.[243] In short, it is Congress and not the highest Court which is authorized by the Constitution to regulate commerce.[244]

80

SAME: If a waterway is navigable, it is subject to the com-
NAVIGABILITY merce power even if it is wholly located within a
        single state. This has been settled ever since the 1871
case of *The Daniel Ball*.[245] At issue in it was the question of whether a federal law requiring a license for steamboats transporting merchandise or passengers "upon the bays, lakes, rivers or other navigable waters of the United States" could be applied to a vessel which navigated the Grand River, a stream located entirely in Michigan. The Supreme Court answered this question in the affirmative, stating that the fact that the stream at issue was navigable brought it within the range of Congressional authority, regardless of whether or not it crossed state lines. A navigable stream forms

by itself, or by uniting with other waters, a continued highway over which commerce is or may be carried on with other states or foreign countries. As such, it can be reached by the Congress, even though entirely intrastate.

Navigability is thus the sole requirement to exertion of the commerce power over a stream or other waterway. Nor, it should be noted, does it make any difference whether a particular waterway is natural or man-made. "The regulation of commerce," declared an 1893 case, "implies as much control, as much far-reaching power, over an artificial as over a natural highway." [246] This principle has been relied upon to justify treatment of the Erie Canal, constructed by and lying entirely within the State of New York, as a navigable water of the United States. The fact that such canal was rendered navigable by artificial means and that it was wholly within the limits of a particular state, the Supreme Court has said, creates no distinction in principle.[247] The criterion is navigability, not the nature or location of the waterway concerned.

When, however, is a waterway navigable, so as to bring it within the purview of the Commerce Clause?

Until our own day, the test of navigability was that originally articulated by Justice Field in *The Daniel Ball*.[248] According to him there, "Those rivers must be regarded as navigable in law which are navigable in fact. And they are navigable in fact when they are used, or are susceptible of being used, in their ordinary condition, as highways for commerce, over which trade and travel are or may be conducted in the customary modes of trade and travel by water." [249] To put it another way, whether a stream was navigable depended upon whether it could actually be used for purposes of commerce.

More recently, the highest Court has modified this test of "navigability in fact." In *United States v. Appalachian Power Co.* (1940),[250] the lower courts had found as a fact that the New River in Virginia was not navigable. Upon that finding, they had ruled that it was not subject to the commerce power and the Federal Government consequently possessed no authority to prohibit defendant company from constructing and putting into operation a hydroelectric dam in the river. The Supreme Court reversed, declaring that the test of navigability was not whether the river was navigable in fact in its existing condition. As the high Court saw it, "To appraise the evidence of navigability on the natural condition only of the waterway is erroneous. Its availability for navigation must also be considered." [251] Navigability must be determined, not merely in terms of actual navigability in fact, but also in the light of the effect of reasonable improvements. Under the *Appalachian* opinion, "A waterway otherwise suitable for navigation, is not barred from that classification merely because artificial aids must make the highway suitable for use before commercial navigation may be undertaken." [252]

In the *Appalachian* case, the test of navigability in actual fact has given way to one of navigability in fact or potential. For the commerce power to attach, it is not necessary that the stream concerned be actually navigable. It is enough that it may be rendered navigable. Congressional authority is not to be frustrated because of the necessity for improvements to make a waterway available for traffic.

Thus, as Justice Douglas has explained it,[253] a stream may not actually be navigable at present; yet, if it can be made so, it is in the federal domain. Since the New River could be made navigable by improvements which might be made, though not then navigable in fact, it could be considered navigable in law.

Justice Roberts, who dissented in the *Appalachian* case, asserted that the decision subjected well-nigh every stream in the country to federal control. In his words, "If this test be adopted, then every creek in every state of the Union which has enough water, when conserved by dams and locks or channeled by wing dams and sluices, to float a boat drawing two feet of water, may be pronounced navigable because, by the expenditure of some enormous sum, such a project would be possible of execution. . . . If this criterion be the correct one, it is not seen how any stream can be found not to be navigable." [254]

One wonders, nevertheless, whether this extreme result is compelled by the *Appalachian* decision. Justice Reed, who delivered the opinion there, was most careful to stress that, for improvability to make a stream navigable in law, the improvements needed to make it navigable must be *reasonable* ones. The question of reasonableness itself must be determined in the light of both physical and financial factors. "There must," said the Reed opinion, "be a balance between cost and need at a time when the improvement would be useful." [255] Justice Reed cited as an example of the proper approach a case where the improvements necessary to make a river navigable were found to be financially impracticable because of the many millions of dollars that would be required. He approved the conclusion reached in it that navigability did not follow because of the "susceptibility of being so improved by high engineering skill and the expenditures of vast sums of money." [256]

Of course, if enough money is spent, any stream can be made navigable —just as an artificial canal can be built anywhere if cost is no consideration. *Appalachian* does not, however, sweep within the commerce power every waterway—even the most difficult and forbidding mountain torrent. The limitation of "reasonableness," suitably applied, prevents this extreme result. *Appalachian* may substitute capability for actuality as the test of navigability. But it is only *reasonable* capability that the Supreme Court intended to include in its new criterion.

81

SAME: FLOOD CONTROL AND PUBLIC POWER

Exertion of the commerce power over a navigable stream is justified by its actuality or potential as a highway for commerce. A river may, at the same time, be much more than a highway. It may also be a vital source of hydroelectric power. In addition, it may often be a source of danger to the surrounding countryside; flood control may consequently become a subject of proper governmental concern.

In the *Appalachian* case, the highest Court declared that the power over navigable waters was not limited to control for navigation. Instead, it said, federal authority is as broad as the needs of commerce: "Flood protection, watershed development, recovery of the cost of improvements through utilization of power are likewise parts of commerce control." [257]

The extent to which the Congressional power for purposes of flood control and watershed development may be carried is shown by *Oklahoma v. Atkinson Co.*[258] In it, the high bench rejected an Oklahoma challenge to the construction of a federal dam and reservoir upon one of its rivers. The dam at issue was part of a comprehensive scheme for controlling floods in the Mississippi River through reservoir control of its tributaries, of which the river in Oklahoma was one. Oklahoma's case was based upon the fact that the river involved was not navigable. The Supreme Court, in refusing to enjoin the federal project, ruled that this was immaterial in such a case.

In the first place, said the Court, it is settled that the power over navigable waterways includes the authority to foster and protect navigation. Part of the benefits of flood control is protection of navigation. It is, for example, common knowledge that Mississippi floods have paralyzed commerce in the affected areas and have impaired navigation itself. Flood control therefore becomes an essential part of the power to preserve and promote commerce on navigable streams.

In the case under discussion, the high Court went even further. Said the opinion of Justice Douglas: "the power of flood control extends to the tributaries of natural streams. For just as control over the non-navigable parts of a river may be essential or desirable in the interests of the navigable portions, so may the key to flood control on a navigable stream be found in whole or in part in flood control on its tributaries." [259] If flood control of the Mississippi is to be successful, control of its tributaries becomes necessary. Hence, a project to control floods on the Mississippi justifies federal action on a nonnavigable tributary in Oklahoma hundreds of miles away.

In the *Oklahoma* case, the state also attacked the federal dam on the ground that, though labeled a flood-control project, it was primarily intended as a source for the generation of hydroelectric power. The Supreme Court held, however, that the fact that the dam was a multiple-purpose project did not militate against its legality. A project such as this could have a power phase as well as a flood-control phase. The power development may, indeed, promote the ends of flood control in serving as a paying partner to carry some of the costs involved. As the Court put it: "the fact that ends other than flood control will also be served, or that flood control may be relatively of lesser importance does not invalidate the exercise of the authority conferred on Congress." [260]

Hydroelectric power is a natural by-product of a flood-control scheme or any other governmental project to control the flow of a waterway. As a consequence of its authority over navigation, the Congress possesses the right to utilize such power for any purposes it deems necessary—including the right to sell it to help pay the costs of flood control or some other project (as was true in the *Oklahoma* case) or for any other purpose. The right of the Congress in this respect was affirmed half a century ago in *United States v. Chandler-Dunbar Co.*[261] The high Court there held that the Congress could, under a project for controlling and directing the flow of a river, authorize the lease or sale of such excess waterpower as resulted from the conservation of the flow. "If the primary purpose is legitimate," affirmed the Court, "we can see no sound objection to leasing any excess of power over the needs of the government." [262]

That public power is a natural and proper by-product of the commerce power is shown by the vast federal power projects that have been constructed in recent years. Attacks upon the legality of such projects have uniformly been rebuffed by the federal courts. In *Arizona v. California,*[263] a state challenged the law authorizing the construction of Boulder Dam, asserting that the recital in the act that its purpose was the improvement of navigation "is a mere subterfuge and false pretense." The real purpose of the dam, it was claimed, was the production and sale of power. The Supreme Court answered that it could not inquire into the motives behind the challenged law: "As the river is navigable and the means which the act provides are not unrelated to the control of navigation . . . , the erection and maintenance of such dam and reservoir are clearly within the powers conferred upon Congress." [264] The fact that the dam may serve other purposes than navigation does not invalidate the exercise of the authority conferred.

The same reasoning has been used to sustain the public power aspects of the development program of the Tennessee Valley Authority. The dams constructed on the Tennessee River did both improve navigability and aid flood control. Hence they could clearly be built under the commerce power. As the Supreme Court put it, "The power of falling water was an inevitable incident of the construction of the dam. That water power came into the exclusive control of the federal government." [265]

82

POWER TO   As pointed out in section 62, the noun *commerce* in
REGULATE   the Commerce Clause determines the subjects to
                  which Congressional power extends, while the verb
regulate determines the type of authority that the Congress can exert. In
sections 63–81, we dealt with the scope of the "commerce" which the
Congress may reach under the constitutional provision. We turn now to the
range of the term "regulate" in the Commerce Clause.

In our discussion of *Gibbons v. Ogden,*[266] we saw that both the noun
and the verb were defined most broadly there. If anything, in fact, the conception of the power to *regulate* articulated by the Marshall Court was even
broader than its wholesale conception of commerce. "What is this power?"
asked Marshall in an already-quoted portion of the *Gibbons v. Ogden* opinion. "It is the power to regulate; that is, to prescribe the rule by which
commerce is to be governed." [267]

Once commerce was concerned, in the Marshall view, the Congress
could lay down whatever limits and restraints it chose. The power to regulate commerce includes both the power to prescribe limits to its freedom and
the power to determine what shall remain unrestrained. "The power of a
sovereign state over commerce . . . ," declared a member of the Marshall
Court, "amounts to nothing more than a power to limit it and restrain
it at pleasure." [268] To Marshall and his associates, the authority vested
in the Congress was the complete power to control commerce.

83

SAME: REGULATION Does the power to regulate include the power to
    VERSUS   prohibit?
PROHIBITION   The answer to this question is clear under the
                  Marshall conception of regulation. The power to
prescribe the rule by which commerce is to be governed certainly appears
to comprehend the authority to determine whether or not particular articles
should be barred from interstate commerce. The power to limit and restrain commerce at pleasure should embrace within its bounds a power to
exclude persons and commodities from commerce when that is deemed
necessary.

It was not until almost a century after *Gibbons v. Ogden* that the Supreme Court was squarely confronted with the question of whether or not
a power of prohibition is included in the power to regulate commerce. In
Champion v. Ames (1903)—usually known as the *Lottery Case* [269]—the
Court was presented with an attack upon the constitutionality of an act of
Congress prohibiting any person from causing lottery tickets to be carried
from one state to another. The law was upheld in a forceful opinion by

Justice Harlan, who categorically rejected the view that the power to regulate could not be understood to give the power to exclude. "If lottery
traffic, *carried on through interstate commerce,* is a matter of which Congress may take cognizance and over which its power may be exerted," asks
Harlan's opinion, "can it be possible that it must tolerate the traffic, and
simply regulate the manner in which it may be carried on? Or may not
Congress, for the protection of the people of all the States, and under the
power to regulate interstate commerce, devise such means, within the scope
of the Constitution, and not prohibited by it, as will drive that traffic out
of commerce among the States?" [270]

While the *Lottery Case* holds that regulation may appropriately assume
the form of prohibition, it is far from recognizing a general plenary power
in the Congress to close the channels of interstate commerce, whenever it
chooses, to any person, article, or commodity, of whatever kind or nature.
The *Lottery Case* turns upon the noxious nature of the articles involved
and Justice Harlan was most careful to limit his opinion to such commodities. What clause of the Constitution, he inquired, "can be cited which,
in any degree, countenances the suggestion that one may, of right, carry or
cause to be carried from one State to another that which will harm the
public morals?" [271]

The commerce power may be exerted to prevent the pollution of commerce by articles confessedly injurious to the public morals. As the *Lottery
Case* expressed it, "As a State may, for the purpose of guarding the morals
of its own people, forbid all sales of lottery tickets within its limits, so
Congress, for the purpose of guarding the people of the United States
against the 'widespread pestilence of lotteries' and to protect the commerce
which concerns all the States, may prohibit the carrying of lottery tickets
from one State to another." [272]

Even though the high Court in the *Lottery Case* limited its decision to
traffic in articles like lottery tickets which no one can be entitled to pursue
as of right, the case is still a landmark one. It renders explicit what had
been implicit since *Gibbons v. Ogden*—that the authority to control includes the authority to suppress. The power to regulate must, since the
Lottery decision, clearly be understood as embracing the power to destroy.

Since the *Lottery Case,* the Supreme Court has repeatedly applied its
holding to federal laws closing the channels of commerce to commodities
which are themselves dangerous or harmful or which may have an adverse
effect upon the public. In Justice Stone's words in an important case: "Congress is free to exclude from interstate commerce articles whose use in the
states for which they are destined it may reasonably conceive to be injurious to the public health, morals, or welfare." [273]

The anticipated evil or harm may proceed from something inherent in the subject of commerce itself. This is the case with diseased livestock,[274] adulterated and misbranded articles under the Pure Food and Drugs Act,[275] intoxicating liquors,[276] diseased plants,[277] and obscene literature.[278]

Or the evil may lie in the purpose of the transportation involoved. Such is the case with lottery tickets,[279] women transported for immoral purposes,[280] stolen motor vehicles,[281] and kidnaped persons.[282]

Under such cases, adverse effect upon the public alone may justify Congressional exertion of its prohibitory authority over commerce. Prevention of harm to the public becomes a proper end of the commerce power, even though the harm involved does not affect the safety or efficiency of commerce itself. The commerce power includes authority to bar the shipment in commerce of articles, not only with a view of rendering interstate transportation more efficient and safe, but also of preventing a social, economic, or moral result disapproved of by the Congress.[283]

Carried thus far, the commerce power becomes, in effect, a national police power, which may be exerted for the protection of public health, safety, morals, or welfare, whenever the Congress deems necessary. "Congress," said the Supreme Court in a 1925 case, "can certainly regulate interstate commerce to the extent of forbidding and punishing the use of such commerce as an agency to promote immorality, dishonesty, or the spread of any evil or harm to the people of other states from the state of origin. In doing this, it is merely exercising the police power, for the benefit of the public, within the field of interstate commerce." [284] The Congress may, in other words, exert its prohibitory authority to reach any commerce it may reasonably deem injurious to public health, safety, morals, or welfare.

84

SAME: CHILD   Until our own day, however, the Supreme Court did
LABOR CASE   not permit the commerce power to be pushed quite as
      far as just stated. Instead, in its 1918 decision in *Hammer v. Dagenhart*—more popularly known as the *Child Labor Case* [285] —the high bench interposed a fundamental barrier to the full exertion of Congressional prohibitory authority.

The *Child Labor Case* involved the constitutionality of a federal statute which prohibited the transportation in interstate commerce of goods made in factories that employed children under a specified age. This law clearly purported to be limited to the express confines of the commerce power. since, on its face, it merely imposed a bar upon interstate transportation. Yet there is no doubt that, though it did not in its terms attempt to regulate local production, the real purpose of the Congress in enacting the statute was to suppress child labor in productive industries. Denied its interstate market, child labor could not continue upon any widespread scale.

To the majority of the highest Court, the Congressional purpose rendered the law at issue invalid. The federal legislature was seeking primarily to regulate the manner in which manufacturing was carried on. Such manufacturing, we have seen, was not, under the restricted conception of the Supreme Court prior to the *Jones & Laughlin* case,[286] commerce which could be reached by Congressional authority. "In our view," reads the *Child Labor Case* opinion, "the necessary effect of this act is, by means of a prohibition against the movement in interstate commerce of ordinary commercial commodities, to regulate the hours of labor of children in factories and mines within the States, a purely state authority." [287] The Congress could not, even by a statute whose terms were specifically limited to the regulation of interstate commerce, use its commerce power to exert regulatory authority over matters like manufacturing which were not, within the high Court's then-prevailing notion, commerce.

But what of the decisions discussed in the prior section upholding the power of the Congress to close the channels of commerce to specified commodities? According to the *Child Labor Case* majority, those decisions did not require a different result here: "In each of these instances the use of interstate transportation was necessary to the accomplishment of harmful results." [288] The articles involved in the prior cases were said to be harmful in and of themselves; their transportation alone resulted in the evil which the Congress could prohibit. In the instant case, on the other hand, said the Court, "The goods shipped are of themselves harmless." [289] Nor was any evil accomplished by their interstate transportation, since the evils involved in the child labor itself had all occurred before they were sent into commerce. In the Court's words, "When offered for shipment, and before transportation begins, the labor of their production is over." [290]

This attempt to distinguish the cases treated in the prior section is not very convincing. Some of the earlier decisions, too, concerned articles which were of themselves harmless.[291] Congressional prohibitions with regard to them were, nonetheless, justified because of the evils involved in the purposes for which they were being transported. If the Congress may prevent evils which will be produced after the interstate journey ends, even though the goods being transported are harmless, why may it not act against evils before such journey begins, if such evils could not continue but for access to the channels of interstate commerce? Why should the Congress have to afford the facilities of commerce to businesses based upon a practice so universally condemned as evil as that of premature and excessive child labor? [292]

The *Child Labor Case* actually turns, not upon the intrinsic nature of the articles excluded from commerce, but upon the motives which induced the enactment of the prohibitory law. The prohibitions sustained in the decisions dealt with in the prior section all excluded persons and commodities over which "the scope of governmental authority . . . is such that the authority to prohibit is as to them but the exertion of the power to regulate." [293] In the *Child Labor Case,* on the contrary, as already pointed out, the Congress was seeking to prohibit what it could not directly regulate. The commerce power was employed to accomplish, by a prohibition, what could not be achieved by direct regulation, under the high Court's then-prevailing concept of commerce. What was ostensibly only a regulation of interstate transportation was condemned because its underlying motive was beyond the direct powers of the Congress.

Inquiry into Congressional motives such as that which underlay the decision in the *Child Labor Case* is subject to the same basic objections as those discussed in the prior chapter in connection with judicial scrutiny of the motives behind exercises of the taxing power.[294] In the *Child Labor Case,* the act at issue prohibited interstate transportation—on the face of it, plainly a regulation of commerce. If it be said, the motive is not really to regulate transportation, what has that to do with the power? When an act involves an exercise of power concededly given to the Congress, shall it be held invalid only on some collateral ground? [295]

To hold that constitutionality turns, not upon power, but upon the motives of the legislature is to make the Constitution depend upon subjective tests, utterly vague in their application. The Congress could never pass a law without inquisition into the motives of every member; nay, even then, they would be reexaminable by the courts. "No government on earth could rest for a moment on such a foundation. It would be a constitution of sand heaped up and dissolved by the flux and reflux of every tide of opinion." [296]

Inquiry into motives had a particularly distressing result in the *Child Labor Case.* "If there is any matter," asserted Justice Holmes in his dissent there, "upon which civilized countries have agreed . . . it is the evil of premature and excessive child labor." [297] Yet the practical result of the Supreme Court's decision was to render effective regulation of child labor all but impossible. In a country like the United States, if a practice like child labor is to be dealt with effectually, it must be by national regulation. By rigidly excluding the Federal Government from exercising regulatory authority, the *Child Labor Case* virtually decreed that child labor should be left only to whatever controls were afforded by the workings of an unrestrained system of laissez faire. The United States alone, among nations, was precluded from taking effective action against an evil so widely censured by civilized opinion.

85

SAME: Under the Marshall conception of the Commerce
DARBY CASE   Clause, the power of the Congress was a plenary one
—complete in itself and one which acknowledged no limitations save those prescribed in the Constitution.[298] And, as a leading member of the Marshall Court put it, "the motive of the grant of the power is not even alluded to in the constitution." [299] It is clear then that, to Marshall and his colleagues, the power to regulate commerce was one which might be exercised for any reason. The sole question for the Court was whether what was at issue was actually a regulation of commerce. If it was, it was valid under the plenary Congressional power regardless of the motives which had called forth the exercise of such power.

The *Child Labor* decision was based upon an entirely different approach. Under it, the fact that regulation of commerce was involved did not necessarily conclude the case. The Court had to determine also whether the end for which the Congress had exerted its commerce power was one toward which Congressional authority could lawfully be directed.

To one who has read the prior chapter,[300] as well as the discussion in this one of the recent Supreme-Court decisions, starting with the *Jones & Laughlin* case,[301] it should hardly be necessary to point out how inconsistent the *Child Labor Case* is with the whole thrust of the more recent jurisprudence of the high tribunal. In the first place, even if we accept the basic approach of the *Child Labor* decision, *Jones & Laughlin* and the cases following it would require a different result. Under them, as we have seen,[302] the commerce power today extends to manufacturing and other productive industries. That being the case, the Congress could regulate directly what it sought to achieve by the prohibition at issue in the *Child Labor Case*. Where the Congress can accomplish its purpose by direct regulation, it can, even under the *Child Labor* decision, attain such end by exclusion of particular persons or commodities from the channels of commerce. In such a case, in the words of the *Child Labor* opinion itself, "the authority to prohibit is as to them but the exertion of the power to regulate." [303]

Even more important is the fact that an inquiry into Congressional motives such as that made in the *Child Labor Case* is wholly incompatible with the present reluctance of the Supreme Court, discussed in the last chapter,[304] to invalidate laws on the ground of improper purpose. It is scarcely surprising, therefore, that the Court has repudiated the *Child Labor Case* approach in a more recent decision. Such repudiation came in the 1941 case of *United States v. Darby*.[305]

At issue in *Darby* was the constitutionality of the Fair Labor Standards Act of 1938, already discussed in another connection.[306] That statute provides for the fixing of minimum wages and maximum hours by a federal agency. It goes on to prohibit the shipment in interstate commerce of goods manufactured by employees whose wages are less than the prescribed minimum or whose hours of work are more than the prescribed maximum. As such, this law was not unlike that involved in the *Child Labor Case,* which had prohibited the transportation in interstate commerce of goods produced by child labor.

The Fair Labor Standards Act was attacked in *Darby* on the ground that, while the prohibition was nominally a regulation of commerce, its motive was really regulation of wages and hours of persons engaged in manufacture. The high Court candidly recognized that such was in fact the case: "The motive and purpose of the present regulation is plainly to make effective the Congressional conception of public policy that interstate commerce should not be made the instrument of competition in the distribution of goods produced under substandard labor conditions, which competition is injurious to the commerce and to the states from and to which the commerce flows." [307] In this sense, to be sure, the effect of the challenged law was plainly a regulation of the wages and hours of those engaged in what had formerly been held to be only local manufacturing.

But the whole point about the *Darby* decision is that, under it, the end toward which a Congressional exercise of regulatory power over commerce is directed is irrelevant. According to the opinion of Justice Stone for a unanimous Court: "The motive and purpose of a regulation of interstate commerce are matters for the legislative judgment upon the exercise of which the Constitution places no restriction and over which the courts are given no control." [308]

Of course, this reasoning was contrary to the *Child Labor Case* thesis that the motive of the prohibition or its effect to control in some measure the production within the states of the article excluded from commerce could operate to deprive the Congressional regulation of its constitutional validity. The Court in *Darby,* however, expressly disowned the *Child Labor Case* approach. "The reasoning and conclusion of the Court's opinion there," declares *Darby,* "cannot be reconciled with the conclusion which we have reached, that the power of Congress under the Commerce Clause is plenary to exclude any article from interstate commerce subject only to the specific prohibitions of the Constitution." [309] The *Child Labor Case,* the *Darby* opinion concluded, "should be and now is overruled." [310]

The overruling of the *Child Labor Case* returns the highest Court to Marshall's view of the power to regulate under the Commerce Clause as a complete one. In the *Darby* opinion, the Court relied directly upon Marshall's definition of the power to regulate commerce as the power "to prescribe the rule by which commerce is governed." [311] Under *Darby,* once again, the sole question is whether a challenged law does prescribe a

governing rule for commerce. If it does, it is valid, regardless of the ends
which may have induced its enactment. "Whatever their motive and purpose," states *Darby,* "regulations of commerce which do not infringe some
constitutional prohibition are within the plenary power conferred on Congress by the Commerce Clause." [312]

The *Darby* decision marks the culmination in the development of the
Commerce Clause as the source of a national police power, which had begun with the *Lottery Case.*[313] The *Child Labor* decision constituted a significant rebuff to such development. Under *Darby,* whatever limitation it imposed has been removed. According to the *Darby* opinion: "It is no objection to the assertion of the power to regulate interstate commerce that its
exercise is attended by the same incidents which attend the exercise of the
police power of the states." [314]

Under *Darby,* the Congress can utilize its commerce power to suppress
any commerce contrary to its broad conception of public interest. Its prohibitory authority may be called forth to attain any social, economic, or
moral result which it deems desirable. Nor will the end sought be questioned
judicially. If a challenged law does involve a regulation (including prohibition) of commerce, the motive or purpose behind it is irrelevant. The national police power (as this aspect of the commerce power may be termed)
is the plenary power to secure any social, economic, or moral ends, so far
as they may be obtained by the suppression of commerce.

86

SAME: Regulation, in the sense in which that term is nor-
PROMOTION AND   mally used, involves the laying down of controlling
OPERATION   norms. As the California court informs us, "To 'regu-
                 late' . . . ,—a word derived from the Latin word
'rego', signifying to guide or direct, through the noun 'regula', a rule,—
is to prescribe a rule for acting, to direct the mode in which a transaction
should be conducted." [315] As applied to the Commerce Clause, it is, in the
Gibbons v. Ogden definition, the power to prescribe the rule by which commerce is to be governed.[316] It is the authority to direct, to control, to lay
down restraints and limitations.

On its face, then, the power to regulate, even in the broad Marshall
conception, is essentially negative in aspect. It implies, not the establishment of a new thing, but the arranging in proper order and controlling that
which already exists.[317] It appears to be only the power to check—not the
power to create.

Despite the negative connotations thus contained in the term *regulate,*
the Supreme Court has, for over a century, taken a broader view of the
power vested in the Congress under the Commerce Clause. The develop-

ment in this respect parallels that discussed in the prior chapter with regard to the taxing power. We have just seen how the commerce power, like the authority to tax,[318] may be used for purposes of destruction. In addition, we saw in section 53, the taxing power may be employed for purposes of preservation. Under the uniform jurisprudence of the highest tribunal, the same is true of the commerce power. It, too, may be utilized, not only to regulate in the restricted sense referred to in the previous paragraph, but also to foster, protect, and promote.

As early as *The Daniel Ball,*[319] the Supreme Court asserted thus broad a concept of the power to regulate under the Commerce Clause. "That power," stated Justice Field there, "authorizes all appropriate legislation for the protection or advancement of either interstate or foreign commerce." [320] The same approach has been followed in many later cases. To assert that the Congress is vested only with the negative power of prescribing restraints upon existing commerce, said the Court in an important 1924 case, "is too narrow a view of the Commerce Clause. To regulate in the sense intended is to foster, protect and control the commerce . . . , and to promote its growth and insure its safety." [321]

What this wide view of the power to regulate means in practice is that the Congress can take such positive measures to foster and promote commerce as it deems necessary. This aspect of the commerce power was relied upon at an early date with the construction of the Cumberland or National Road across the Alleghenies. If the commerce power comprehends the power to further commerce, it authorizes the Congress to provide facilities for commerce. Hence, the United States may, under the Commerce Clause,[322] itself construct and operate national highways, bridges, and other instrumentalities for carrying on commerce. Or it may authorize others to construct and operate them. "The power to construct, or to authorize individuals or corporations to construct, national highways and bridges from state to state," said the Supreme Court in 1888, "is essential to the complete control and regulation of interstate commerce. Without authority in Congress to establish and maintain such highways and bridges, it would be without authority to regulate one of the most important adjuncts of commerce." [323]

Like the commerce power generally,[324] the positive authority to promote commerce applies to newly developed instrumentalities as well as to those known to the Framers. The statement just quoted was made in a case involving railroads, and the Court held that the commerce power justified the creation of a vast system of interstate railroads, either by the Congress directly [325] or by companies acting under Congressional authorization.

What is true of railroads is true as well of all other facilities and instrumentalities of commerce. Consequently, the Supreme Court had no difficulty in upholding the power of the Congress to provide for the construction and operation of the Panama Canal.[326] The same result would follow with regard to other instrumentalities, such as airplanes, telegraphs, and radio-television. If Congress may build and operate roads, railroads, and canals under the Commerce Clause, it may certainly exert similar positive authority with regard to any other means by which commerce or communication [327] is carried on.

The positive power of the Congress in this respect is not, however, limited to the direct provision of facilities and instrumentalities of commerce. It can, as already noted, authorize others to provide them. Those chosen as agents for this purpose can be private individuals or corporations already chartered under state law. Or, if it so chooses, the Congress can create its own corporate instruments to do the job. Under principles discussed at a prior point,[328] the Congress can, without a doubt, set up a government corporation to carry out its positive powers over commerce. But it can also charter a private corporation for the same purpose.

Under decisions of the highest Court, the Congress has been held to have authority to create a private corporation to construct and operate a railroad [329] or an interstate bridge.[330] The Congress, declares the opinion in the case last cited, "may create corporations as appropriate means of executing the powers of government, as, for instance, . . . a railroad corporation for the purpose of promoting commerce among the states." [331] If this is the case with a private railroad or bridge corporation, it should likewise be so whenever an instrumentality of commerce is concerned. The Congress should be able generally to charter corporations to provide facilities or instrumentalities for commerce.

More difficult, at first glance, is the question of whether the Congressional authority in this respect should extend to the chartering of any corporation engaged in, or whose business has an effect upon, commerce. Yet, if the Congress may charter a private corporation to provide a facility or instrumentality of commerce, such as a bridge or a railroad, in order to foster and promote commerce, it is hard to see why the same reasoning should not apply to corporations set up to engage in commerce. It is true that the Congress has never sought to push its commerce power to such an extent. At the same time, this does not mean that the power does not exist. Since commerce clearly includes the buying and selling of commodities, the Congressional power should extend to the chartering of private companies to engage in the business of buying and selling, or any other aspect of commerce.

As we have already seen, however, the commerce power today is not limited to the carrying on of commerce in the strict sense (i.e., buying and selling). Under the high Court's present construction of the "effect upon commerce" test, any activity which has an effect upon commerce (including productive activities such as manufacture, mining, and agriculture) may be reached by the Congress. But, if that be true, according to our previous reasoning, the United States should also have the power to charter private corporations to engage in such activities.

Under the Supreme Court's wholesale interpretation of the "effect upon commerce" test, this would vest in the Congress a general authority to supersede all state corporation laws with a uniform statute of its own. By the "house-that-Jack-built" type of reasoning already referred to,[332] the Congress could sweep within its powers of incorporation companies engaged in practically every form of economic activity. This, at least, is the logical consequence of the positive aspects of the commerce power.

87
FOREIGN
COMMERCE
COMPARED

The same clause which confers upon the Congress the power to regulate interstate commerce also vests in it authority over foreign commerce. The prior portions of this chapter have been concerned almost exclusively with the power over interstate commerce. A word must now be said about Congressional authority over foreign commerce, with emphasis upon its extent as compared with the power over interstate commerce.

From almost the beginning of the Republic, it has been asserted that the power over foreign commerce is greater than that over domestic commerce. The Embargo Acts of 1807 and 1808, which cut off all commerce with Europe, were based directly upon such premise. Though its legality was never passed upon by the Supreme Court, the embargo was upheld as a valid exercise of the commerce power [333] in a noted lower court decision, which was generally considered as settling the question of constitutionality in the affirmative.[334] By *Gibbons v. Ogden,* indeed, the high Court could refer to "The universally acknowledged power of the Government to impose embargoes." [335] Yet, according to Justice Story (who had himself argued in favor of the embargo in the case referred to), "I have ever considered the Embargo a measure which went to the utmost limits of constructive power under the Constitution; it stands on the extreme verge of the Constitution." [336] Presumably, a similar prohibitory law, which applied only to commerce among the states, would have passed the bounds of legality.

The view that the Congressional power over foreign commerce is more extensive than its authority over interstate commerce has been stated at various times by members of the highest Court. The dissenting Justices in the *Lottery Case* [337] relied strongly upon an alleged difference in the scope of the two powers. As they put it: "the power to regulate commerce with foreign nations and the power to regulate interstate commerce, are to be taken *diverso intuitu,* for the latter was intended to secure equality and freedom in commercial intercourse as between the States, not to permit the creation of impediments to such intercourse; while the former clothed Congress with that power over international commerce, pertaining to a sovereign nation in its intercourse with foreign nations, and subject, generally speaking, to no implied or reserved power in the States. The laws which would be necessary and proper in the one case, would not be necessary or proper in the other." [338]

The power over foreign commerce, in this view, derives additional support from constitutional sources other than the Commerce Clause. The United States, like any other nation, possesses plenary authority over foreign relations. Its power over foreign commerce would flow from such authority, even if there were no Commerce Clause. In the words of a leading case, "As a member of the family of nations, the right and power of the United States in that field are equal to the right and power of the other members of the international family. Otherwise, the United States is not completely sovereign." [339] The United States is vested with the complete control over foreign intercourse that exists in any independent nation.

In accordance with what has just been said, the Congress has, throughout our history, assumed a complete power in itself to exclude persons and commodities from foreign commerce. No exercise of such power has ever been ruled invalid by the highest Court. On the contrary, the Court has expressly affirmed the "plenary power" [340] of the Congress in this respect and "the authority of Congress to absolutely prohibit foreign importations." [341] Said Chief Justice White, in a case in which a Congressional ban on the importation of prize-fight films was attacked: "In view of the complete power of Congress over foreign commerce and its authority to prohibit the introduction of foreign articles recognized and enforced by many previous decisions of this court, the contentions are so devoid of merit as to cause them to be frivolous." [342]

What this means in practice is that the power over foreign commerce has never been subject to the restrictions which the Supreme Court imposed upon the power over interstate commerce in the period between Chief Justice Marshall's death and the *Jones & Laughlin* case.[343] But it also follows that the distinction between foreign and domestic commerce in this respect has itself ceased to have substantial practical significance since *Jones & Laughlin* and the decisions rendered since that case. They have countenanced so drastic an expansion of the domestic commerce power that it, too, has become plenary, both as to the subjects which may be regulated and the power to regulate. With the pre-*Jones & Laughlin* limitations on the commerce power removed, the Congressional authority over domestic commerce has become comparable to that exerted from the beginning over foreign commerce.

"The power to regulate commerce among the several States," declared

Chief Justice Taney over a century ago, "is granted to Congress in the same clause, and by the same words, as the power to regulate commerce with foreign nations, and is co-extensive with it." [344] It has not, all the same, been until our own day that this has really become an accurate statement. Today, it is established doctrine that the power to regulate commerce, whether with foreign nations or among the several states, comprises the power to foster, promote, restrain, or prohibit such commerce at all times for the welfare of the public, provided only that other specific restrictions upon Congressional power (such as the Due-Process Clause) are not transgressed.[345]

88

OUTER LIMITS   The prior sections of this chapter have revealed an almost inexorable recent unfolding of the Commerce Clause.[346] The consistent theme of the post-*Jones & Laughlin* cases [347] is that of constant expansion of Congressional power. After more than a century, the Supreme Court has returned to the sweeping view of John Marshall and has, indeed, in some respects even gone beyond. At the beginning, said the Court in *Wickard v. Filburn,* "Marshall described the federal commerce power with a breadth never yet exceeded." [348] And yet, in the very case in which this statement was made, as our previous discussion of it shows,[349] the high Court itself construed the commerce power more broadly than the great Chief Justice had done.

A question which naturally arises, to one familiar with the Commerce-Clause decisions of recent decades, is that of what constitutional limitations, if any, there still remain upon the commerce power. It must be admitted that a categorical answer to this question is anything but easy. To attempt to draw the outer limits of this plenary power is to essay what the highest Court has expressly refrained from undertaking.[350]

Clearly, under the decisions since *Jones & Laughlin,* activities local in nature may be regulated whenever they can fairly be said to affect commerce.[351] In such a case, regulation of such activities is an appropriate means to the end of regulating interstate commerce itself. This means that practically every aspect of economic activity which has interstate ramifications may be reached by the Congress.

Under the cases discussed, the Congress may regulate the processes of production and distribution in all industries whose products cross state lines [352] or even where they may have only a competitive effect upon such products. The results of such an approach are, of course, far-reaching. It delivers to federal commercial control the fruits of California and the South, the wheat of the West and its meats, the cotton of the South, the shoes and woolens of New England, the coals of West Virginia—and these at the very inception of their manufacture or growth, while the fruits are still unpicked, cotton and wheat ungathered, cattle still "on the hoof," wool unshorn, and coal yet unmined.[353]

To put it another way, since American business can and does ignore state boundaries, the same is now true of federal regulatory power.[354]

Writing in 1935, just before the expansion of the Commerce Clause signalized by the *Jones & Laughlin* decision, Chief Justice Hughes declared, in a prophetic passage: "If the commerce clause were construed to reach all enterprises and transactions which could be said to have an indirect effect upon interstate commerce, the federal authority would embrace practically all the activities of the people, and the authority of the state over its domestic concerns would exist only by sufferance of the federal government." [355]

Have we, in fact, arrived at the position thus prophesied by Chief Justice Hughes? If we have, there are no real constitutional restraints of consequence which remain upon the commerce power.

A number of lower court decisions during the 1950's have continued to assert that there are still limits beyond which the commerce power cannot be pushed. In one case, for example, it was ruled that the installation of burial vaults at a cemetery was not commerce; consequently practices in restraint of trade in connection with such installation did not come within the prohibition of the Sherman Anti-Trust Act. This was true, even though some of the materials used in the manufacture of the vaults were imported from outside the state. The owning and managing of a cemetery, states the court, is intrastate business. At most, the practices involved were said to have only an "incidental, indirect, and remote" effect upon commerce. "They are, therefore, also beyond the purview of Federal authority over interstate commerce." [356]

One may sympathize with the reluctance of this court to sweep within the Commerce Clause literally every activity from the cradle to the grave. Certainly, if any activity is wholly local, it appears to be that connected with burial of the dead. At the same time, under the recent cases already discussed in this chapter, one may wonder whether even such activities cannot be reached by the commerce power. Almost anything—from birth to death—the dissenters in the *Jones & Laughlin* case acutely pointed out, may in some fashion affect commerce.[357] But, if that is true, under *Jones & Laughlin* and later cases, all such matters fall within the compass of the Commerce Clause. If, in *Wickard v. Filburn,* a noncommercial transaction such as the growing of wheat for home consumption was found to have sufficient effect on commerce to bring it within the reach of Congressional authority,[358] it is hard to see why the same is not true of a commercial activity like the installation of burial vaults, particularly where interstate materials were used in their manufacture. It is one thing to hold that the Congress did not intend the Sherman Act to apply to such commerce. To go further and assert that the Congress is constitutionally barred from reaching such commerce appears contrary to the implications of all the recent jurisprudence on the Commerce Clause.

In the *Kahriger* case, discussed in the prior chapter,[359] the highest Court upheld a tax whose purpose was the regulation of intrastate gambling. Justice Frankfurter, who dissented there, was of the view that the Congress could not directly regulate local gambling under the commerce power. A case in which such direct regulation of gambling was squarely at issue is *United States v. Five Gambling Devices*.[360] It arose out of three prosecutions for engaging in the business of dealing in gambling devices without registering with the Attorney General and reporting sales and deliveries as required by an act of Congress. The indictments did not allege that the devices involved in the unreported sales had ever moved in interstate commerce. Both the lower courts and the Supreme Court held that the Congress had not intended the statute to apply to such wholly intrastate matters and that the indictments must consequently be dismissed. The lower courts, however, went further and declared that, if the law did undertake to regulate such purely intrastate transactions, it went beyond the constitutional power of the Congress.[361]

Though the majority of the Supreme Court limited itself to the holding already referred to on Congressional intent, four Justices, dissenting, did go into the constitutional question. According to them, the lower courts were wrong in finding that the Congress had exceeded its constitutional power. Here, said Justice Clark, who delivered the dissenting opinion, the registration and filing requirements with regard to intrastate transactions were an appropriate means for enforcing the ban on interstate transportation of gambling devices. "I think," he declared, "it may accurately be said that every sale of slot machines affects the exercise of the power of Congress over commerce, in view of the elusive nature of the object whose interstate shipment is being controlled." [362]

Yet, even Justice Clark does not go so far as to imply that a local activity like intrastate gambling is now wholly within the commerce power. What he said in support of Congressional authority was limited to the challenged statute's registration and filing requirements. "If Congress by § 3 had sought to *regulate* local activity," the Clark opinion acknowledged, "its power would no doubt be less clear." [363]

It is difficult to see the validity of this attempted distinction between regulation and the requirement of information. In either case, Congressional authority is exerted in aid of the conceded power to ban interstate transportation. In either case, too, Congressional power finds its constitutional justification in the need to reach intrastate acts in order to make its regulation of commerce effective.

Under the basic approach to the Commerce Clause that has prevailed since the *Jones & Laughlin* case, the intimation in the lower court decisions dealt with in this section that certain transactions are beyond the reach of Congressional authority appears unwarranted. The high Court's recent application of the "effect upon commerce" test, as already emphasized, appears sweeping enough to cover practically every aspect of economic activity in the country.

This does not, to be sure, mean that all local activities should necessarily be subjected to regulation from Washington. There may be values in local regulation which are not found in a centralized system. But the question of whether they should be preserved has become more a matter of policy for the Congress, than of law for the courts. From a constitutional point of view, the scope of the commerce power is now practically synonymous with gainful activity. The Commerce Clause embraces within its reach all activities affecting the wealth of the nation. The Congress can, if it chooses, entirely displace the states to the full extent of this far-reaching notion.[364]

7

COMMERCE and THE STATES

A MEMBER of the highest Court once characterized the Commerce Clause as, so to speak, a two-
edged sword, cutting both ways.[1] One edge is the
positive affirmation of Congressional authority. The other, not nearly so
smooth or keen, cuts down state power by negative implication. Hence, in
the words of another Justice: "The Commerce Clause has a negative as
well as a positive aspect. The Clause not only serves to augment federal
authority. By its own force it also cuts down the power of the constituent
State in its exercise of what would normally be a part of its residual police
power." [2]

The negative aspect is not apparent from a literal reading of the dozen
or so words that make up the Commerce Clause. They simply grant the
affirmative commerce power to the Congress; they do not in terms prohibit
the states from acting. As the Supreme Court has put it, "While the Constitution vests in Congress the power to regulate commerce among the
states, it does not say what the states may or may not do in the absence of
congressional action." [3]

At the same time, it must be emphasized that an instrument like our
organic document is more than only the sum total of the words expressed
in it. The Constitution, Justice Miller has said, must be construed in the
light of the doctrine universally applied to all written instruments—that
what is implied is as much a part of the instrument as what is expressed.[4]

As far as the Commerce Clause is concerned, its negative aspect is a necessary implication of the very purpose of the Constitution. When victory relieved the Colonies of the pressure for solidarity that war had exerted, a drift toward anarchy and commercial warfare among the states began.[5] Such a state of affairs necessarily gave rise to serious dissensions. Real or imaginary grievances were multiplied in every direction; state animosities and prejudices were fostered to so high a degree as to threaten at once the peace and safety of the Union.[6]

This unhappy situation, so destructive to the harmony of the states and fatal to their commercial interests, was the immediate cause that led to the Constitution.[7] It was to secure freedom of commerce—to break down the structure of interstate barriers the states were building—that the movement which led to the Convention of 1787 was initiated. Thus, the generating source of the Constitution lay in the rising volume of restraints upon commerce before which the Confederation had been impotent. These were the proximate causes of our national existence down to this very day.[8]

Though the Commerce Clause, as already stated, does not specifically forbid the states to act, its whole purpose was to rescue commerce from the perpetual jarring and hostility resulting from the conflicting regulations of the different states.[9] The clause would accomplish nothing if the states could continue to act as they had been doing.[10] By negative implication, then, the Commerce Clause stripped the states of ability to advance their own commercial interests at the expense of the nation. It sought to put an end to the economic autarchy of the states.[11]

If there were no Commerce Clause, each state could shut out the products of other states or admit them only on conditions. But this is precisely the sort of Balkanization of the economy that the Constitution sought to end. It is not for the states, in pursuit of their local interests, to decide what products from without may cross their boundaries or to admit products on condition that they satisfy local economic policy.[12] The states may shelter their people from menaces to their health and safety and from fraud, even when those menaces emanate from interstate commerce;[13] but they lack power to retard, burden, or constrict the flow of such commerce for their economic advantage.[14] The Constitution, in the apt words of Justice Cardozo, "was framed upon the theory that the peoples of the several states must sink or swim together, and that in the long run prosperity and salvation are in union and not division."[15]

It is consequently clear that the Commerce Clause, in and of itself, affords protection from state legislation inimical to national commerce.[16] The basic principle is that our economic unit is the nation; and its corollary is that the states are not separable economic units, which may place themselves in positions of economic isolation.[17] The Constitution was intended to promote a system of free trade among the states, and to do so by denying to the states the power to impede the free flow of commerce from state to state. And there are few lessons more clearly taught by history than the beneficial consequences of such promotion of free trade between the states. Certainly, the material success that has come to the inhabitants of the states that make up our federal free-trade unit has been the most impressive in the history of commerce.[18]

From the splintered Confederation of the 1780's, cut asunder by commercial warfare between the states, has grown the United States of today. No constitutional provision has played a larger part in that growth than the Commerce Clause. "Our system," said the Supreme Court in a 1949 case, "fostered by the Commerce Clause, is that every farmer and every craftsman shall be encouraged to produce by the certainty that he will have free access to every market in the Nation, that no home embargoes will withhold his exports, and no foreign state will by customs, duties or regulations exclude them. Likewise, every consumer may look to the free competition from every producing area in the Nation to protect him from exploitation by any. Such was the vision of the Founders." [19]

We must now inquire whether it has been given reality by the decisions of the highest Court.

90
EXCLUSIVE VERSUS CONCURRENT POWER

We have just seen that the Commerce Clause, by necessary negative inference, limits the authority of the states. By its very inferential character, the limitation is lacking in precise definition of its scope. The clause, we have said, is a two-edged blade. But the question really posed is the swath of the negatively cutting edge.[20]

To put it more specifically, did the Commerce Clause, of its own force, take from the states any and all authority over interstate and foreign commerce, so that state laws on the subject automatically dropped lifeless from their statute books, for want of the sustaining power that had been wholly relinquished to the Congress? [21] Or was the effect of the clause less sweeping, so that there still remained in the states a portion at least of their residual powers over commerce?

To attempt an answer, we must perforce once again begin with John Marshall. Soon after the great Chief Justice's death, his view on the subject was stated by Justice Story. According to the latter, *Gibbons v. Ogden* [22] rejected the notion that the Congressional power was not exclusive, but only concurrent with that of the states. Marshall, said Story, held that the power given to Congress was full and exclusive: "Full power to regulate a particular subject implies the whole power, and leaves no residuum; and a grant of the whole to one, is incompatible with the grant to another of a part." [23]

In actuality, despite the Story statement to the contrary, the Marshall view of the commerce power was not that of unequivocal federal exclusiveness. It is true that, in *Gibbons v. Ogden* itself, in referring to the argument that the commerce power was an indivisible whole, vested exclusively in the Congress, the opinion states: "There is great force in the argument and the court is not satisfied that it has been refuted." [24] But this is only passing a qualified judgment on a point not relevant to the decision in the case.[25] More significant was Marshall's express recognition that the states did, in fact, possess powers which might be exercised over commerce. As *Gibbons v. Ogden* acknowledged, "Inspection laws, quarantine laws, health laws of every description, as well as laws for regulating the internal commerce of a state, and those which respect turnpike-roads, ferries, etc., are component parts of this mass" [26]—i.e., of state legislation which may, in Marshall's words, have a considerable influence on commerce.

That Marshall was not, in spite of the Story opinion already referred to, an extreme exponent of the view of federal exclusiveness is shown clearly by his opinion in *Willson v. Black Bird Creek Marsh Co.*[27] In that case, a state law had authorized the construction of a dam across a small navigable creek, for the purpose of draining surrounding marshland. It was claimed that this law was repugnant to the commerce power. Marshall rejected this contention, emphasizing in his opinion the benefits to be derived from draining the marsh, in enhancing land values and improving health. "Measures calculated to produce these objects," he said, "provided they do not come into collision with the powers of the general government, are undoubtedly within those which are reserved to the states." [28]

The *Willson* opinion indicates that the Marshall interpretation of the negative aspect of the Commerce Clause was not as far from that of his successor, Chief Justice Taney, as is generally believed. "It appears to me to be very clear," declared Taney in a famous opinion, "that the mere grant of power to the general government cannot, upon any just principles of construction, be construed to be an absolute prohibition to the exercise of any power over the same subject by the States." [29] Yet the *Willson* case indicates that Marshall also shared this view, as far as the commerce power was concerned. Both Marshall and Taney, then, refused to follow the notion of complete exclusiveness of federal power, under which the Commerce Clause, of its own force, removed from the states any and all power over interstate and foreign commerce.

Where Marshall and Taney really differed was in their conception of just how much power over commerce remained in the states. Taney followed his rejection of the complete exclusiveness theory to the opposite extreme and asserted in the states a concurrent power over commerce, limited only by the Supremacy Clause of the Constitution. In his view, the states might make any regulations of commerce within their territory, subject only to the power of the Congress to displace any state law by conflicting federal legislation.[30] In the absence of such Congressional legislation, the states could act over commerce as freely as they chose.

In *Gibbons v. Ogden,* Marshall had squarely rejected this concurrent-power theory, under which the states possess, concurrently with the legislature of the Union, the full power to regulate commerce.[31] The Marshall concept of the commerce power was hence actually somewhere between the antagonistic poles of extreme exclusiveness and concurrent power. The Taney notion of coextensive concurrent power in the states was, of course, utterly incompatible with his predecessor's overriding concern for federalization of commerce. If state powers continued unabated, at least where the Congress was silent, the basic evils the Commerce Clause had been designed to cure might likewise have remained untouched. At the same time, Marshall recognized that the doctrine of a completely exclusive commerce power could not be rigorously applied without completely changing the political character of the states. Virginian that he was, he realized that the effective regulation of local problems should belong to the states. And so, as Justice Frankfurter puts it, while he evolved from the Commerce Clause implied restrictions upon state power, he also felt his way toward another doctrine, the resources of which would be available to meet the diverse local conditions of a sprawling society.[32]

In *Gibbons v. Ogden* itself, Daniel Webster had presented to the highest Court a theory, which, like the Marshall approach just discussed, is somewhere in between the notions of complete exclusiveness and concurrent power. In his argument, Webster contended, "that the power of Congress to regulate commerce was complete and entire, and to a certain extent necessarily exclusive." [33] What he meant by this was well pointed out, during a later stage of the argument: "This proposition was, not that all the commercial powers are exclusive, but that those powers being separated, there are some which are exclusive in their nature." [34]

Webster's conception was based upon acute perception. To those who urged that the commerce power had to be either entirely exclusive or concurrent, he posed the query: "is not the subject susceptible of division, and may not some portions of it be exclusively vested in Congress?" [35] In other words, some, but not all, areas of commercial regulation are absolutely foreclosed to the states by the Commerce Clause.[36] Here was a doctrine of what might be termed "selective exclusiveness," with the Supreme Court determining, in specific cases, the areas in which the Congress possessed exclusive authority over commerce. Its great advantage was that of flexibility. Since it neither permitted nor foreclosed state power in every instance in advance, it might serve as a supple instrument to meet the as yet unrevealed needs of the future.

Why Marshall did not expressly adopt Webster's doctrine of "selective exclusiveness," instead of his own less straightforward approach, must, of course, remain an inquiry of pure theoretical speculation. Perhaps, as Justice Frankfurter surmises,[37] he feared the very flexibility of the Webster formula, realizing that it might be adapted for use by hands bent on upholding state authority. More likely, he may have felt that it would reveal too obviously the large discretionary powers of the judges in applying the Commerce Clause, and thus still further arouse popular concern as to judicial authority. What is clear, at any rate, is that, for whatever reasons may have motivated him, Marshall did not embrace the Webster theory in his *Gibbons v. Ogden* opinion. But that did not mean the demise of that theory. On the contrary, after a quarter century of fruitless efforts by members of the high bench to arrive at some other satisfactory solution,[38] the Webster analysis itself became Supreme-Court doctrine in the 1851 case of *Cooley v. Board of Port Wardens.*[39]

91

COOLEY CASE   If *Gibbons v. Ogden* remains the polestar for decision and discussion on the affirmative aspect of the Commerce Clause, the same can be said of *Cooley v. Board of Port Wardens,*[40] so far as its negative aspect is concerned. One can go further, indeed, and assert that these two landmark decisions alone furnish the essential principles for resolving almost all cases in which the regulation of commerce is at issue. The prior chapter, dealing with the affirmative power of the Congress, was, in many ways, in the nature of a gloss upon *Gibbons v. Ogden.* A similar statement could well be made about the discussion in this chapter of state power to regulate commerce and the decision in *Cooley v. Board of Port Wardens.*

The *Cooley* case itself arose out of a Pennsylvania law requiring vessels using the port of Philadelphia to engage local pilots or pay a fine, amounting to half the pilotage fee, to go to the use of the Society for the Relief of Distressed and Decayed Pilots. Since there was no federal statute on the subject,[41] the question for the Supreme Court was that of the extent of state regulatory power over commerce where the Congress was silent on the matter.

It was contended that the pilotage law was repugnant to the Constitution, because the Commerce Clause had vested the authority to enact such a commercial regulation exclusively in the Congress. In rejecting this contention, the highest Court finally settled the exclusive-concurrent imbroglio [42] in favor of the middle approach which had been advocated by Webster. To the question whether the power of Congress was exclusive, Justice Curtis, who delivered the *Cooley* opinion, took the great step forward of answering, "Yes and No"—or, to put it more accurately, "Sometimes Yes and sometimes No." Such rejection of the either-or approach (to whose delusive attractions judges are all too often prone) is the beginning of wisdom in dealing with the negative implications of the Commerce Clause. It is surely the only workable answer to give to questions that embrace such a variety and diversity of issues that no single answer at either extreme can possibly be suitable for all.[43]

In holding that the Congress possessed exclusive power over commerce only in some situations, Justice Curtis was, as has been stated, more or less adopting Webster's "selective exclusiveness" doctrine. Yet, to recognize that whether the Congressional power is exclusive must vary with the circumstances of particular cases is really not the end, but only the beginning, of the inquiry. Granted that it is a significant first step to say "Sometimes Yes and sometimes No" to the question of Congressional exclusiveness, such an answer really leads only to the next inquiry: "When and why, Yes? When and why, No?" [44]

With regard to that query, too, Webster had pointed the way to an answer. The words of the Commerce Clause, said he, in his *Gibbons v. Ogden* argument, "must have a reasonable construction, and the power should be considered as exclusively vested in Congress, so far, and so far only, as the nature of the power requires." [45] This was the basic approach followed in *Cooley* as well. If the states are excluded from power over commerce, Justice Curtis states: "it must be because the nature of the power, thus granted to Congress, requires that a similar authority should not exist in the States." [46] If that is true, the states must be excluded only to the extent that the nature of the national power requires.[47]

Thus far in his *Cooley* opinion, Justice Curtis had simply followed the analysis articulated by Webster in his *Gibbons v. Ogden* argument. At this point, however, Curtis was able to make a key original contribution of his own. When, he asked, following the approach of the previous paragraph, does the nature of the commerce power require that it be considered as exclusively vested in the Congress? With keen insight, he answered that this depends, not upon the abstract "nature" of the commerce power itself, but upon the nature of the "subjects" over which such power is exercised. In his words, "when the nature of a power like this is spoken of, when it is said that the nature of the power requires that it should be exercised exclusively by Congress, it must be intended to refer to the subjects of that power, and to say they are of such a nature as to require exclusive legislation by Congress." [48]

Having thus transferred the focus of inquiry from the commerce power in the abstract to the subjects of regulation in the concrete, Justice Curtis was then able to examine such subjects pragmatically. If we look at the subjects of commercial regulation, he said, we find that they are exceedingly various and quite unlike in their operation. Some imperatively demand a single uniform rule, operating equally on commerce throughout the United States; others as imperatively demand that diversity which alone can meet local necessities.[49]

Such heterogeneity in the subjects of regulation makes a flat rule of complete exclusiveness or concurrence inappropriate. "Either absolutely to affirm, or deny," said Curtis, "that the nature of this power requires exclusive legislation by Congress, is to lose sight of the nature of the subjects of this power, and to assert concerning all of them, what is really applicable but to a part." [50] Whether the states may regulate depends upon whether it is imperative that the subjects of the regulation be governed by a uniform national system. As the *Cooley* opinion put it, "Whatever subjects of this power are in their nature national, or admit only of one uniform system, or plan of regulation, may justly be said to be of such a nature as to require exclusive legislation by Congress." [51]

On the other hand, where national uniformity of regulation is not necessary, the subject concerned may be reached by state law. That such is the case with a law for the regulation of pilots like that at issue in *Cooley,* Justice Curtis affirms, is plain: "the nature of this subject is such, that until Congress should find it necessary to exert its power, it should be left to the legislation of the States; that it is local and not national; that it is likely to be the best provided for, not by one system, or plan of regulations, but by as many as the legislative discretion of the several States should deem applicable to the local peculiarities of the ports within their limits." [52]

Almost two decades after the *Cooley* decision, Justice Miller, speaking for the Supreme Court, stated, "Perhaps no more satisfactory solution has ever been given of this vexed question than the one furnished by the court in that case." [53] A century later, much the same comment can be made. This is true despite attempts by the high bench since *Cooley* to formulate other tests. Such tests have proved unsatisfactory and the Court has basically continued to follow the *Cooley* approach in cases involving the validity of state regulations of commerce.

The *Cooley* doctrine itself was well summarized by Justice Miller in his *Lectures on the Constitution:* "It may be thus stated: That the power to regulate commerce is one which includes many subjects various and quite unlike in their nature; that whenever subjects of this power are in their nature national, or require one uniform system or plan of regulation, they may be justly held to belong to that class over which Congress has the exclusive power of legislation; but that local and limited matters, not national in their character, which are most likely to be wisely provided for by such diverse rules as the localities and the authorities of the different States may deem applicable, may be regulated by the legislatures of those States in the absence of any act of Congress upon the same subject. Of course when Congress does legislate, as it has a right to do, that excludes the legislation of the States and renders it void so far as it may interfere or conflict with the statutes of the United States." [54]

It should be noted that, with regard to the last sentence just quoted, there has been universal agreement from the beginning. The principle stated in that sentence represents the minimum possible exclusion of state action under the Commerce Clause—if that clause is to have any exclusionary effect, as we have seen it must. No one has ever disputed that, when the Congress has legislated to regulate a matter falling within its commerce power, its regulation nullifies any inconsistent local one.[55] This all accept. The problem arises, as already stated, when the Congress has been silent—i.e., when there is no federal statute applicable to the particular subject of regulation.

Under the *Cooley* test, it has been emphasized, the extreme notion that the Congressional power over commerce must be wholly exclusive is rejected. The scope of the Commerce Clause's implied prohibition against state action is not correlative with the scope of the affirmative commerce power given to Congress.[56] *Cooley,* on the contrary, recognizes that the states still retain authority over commerce in appropriate cases.

The *Cooley* test makes the validity of a state regulation depend upon a balancing of the national and local interests involved. "More accurately," the highest Court informs us, "the question is whether the State interest is outweighed by a national interest in the unhampered operation of interstate commerce." [57] An affirmative answer must be given only when a case falls within an area of commerce thought to demand a uniform national rule. But, in the absence of conflicting legislation by the Congress, there is a residuum of power in the states to make laws governing matters of local concern which nevertheless affect, or even regulate, interstate commerce.[58]

In marking out the areas of permissible state regulation, *Cooley* makes the primary test, not the mechanical one of whether the particular activity regulated is part of interstate commerce, but, rather whether, in each case, the competing demands of the state and national interests involved can be accommodated.[59] State regulations are to be upheld where it appears that the matter involved is one which may appropriately be regulated in the interest of the safety, health, and well-being of local communities. *Cooley* recognizes that there are matters of local concern which may properly be subject to state regulation—matters which, because of their local character and the practical difficulties involved, may in fact never really be adequately dealt with by the Congress.[60]

92

PROPRIETY OF   Before the application of the *Cooley* test to par-
JUDICIAL REVIEW   ticular areas of regulation can be discussed, a preliminary point must be disposed of. That is the
question of the very propriety of judicial review in this field. Does the Supreme Court possess the authority to nullify state legislation on the ground
of its repugnancy to the Commerce Clause?

To one who has read thus far in this volume, such a question may well
seem entirely academic. Of course, he will say, the Court has such power
and he will point to the fact that, from John Marshall's day, the high tribunal has exercised the authority to enforce the policy behind the Commerce Clause. It is true that the power to nullify state action in these cases
was challenged by Chief Justice Taney.[61] But the *Cooley* case itself represented a rejection of the Taney view,[62] and, for the better part of a century
thereafter, not a single member of the Supreme Court cast any doubt upon
the principle that the drawing of a line between permissible and illegal state
regulation of commerce was a judicial function.

In our own day, however, the question of the propriety of judicial review in Commerce-Clause cases has been raised again by several members
of the high bench, notably by Justice Black. The Commerce Clause, stated
that judge in 1946, "means that Congress can regulate commerce and that
the courts cannot. . . . I think that whether state legislation imposes an
'undue burden' on interstate commerce raises pure questions of policy,
which the Constitution intended should be resolved by the Congress." [63] In
the Black view, judicial condemnation of a state law on the ground of
repugnancy to the Commerce Clause is itself a regulation of commerce and
such regulation was given to the Congress, not the courts.[64]

The Black position is really based upon the proposition that a judicial
tribunal is not qualified to make the economic judgments upon which cases
involving alleged state transgressions of the Commerce Clause must be
based.[65] Congress alone, Justice Black has stated, can not only consider
whether particular state legislation "is consistent with the best interests of
our national economy, but can also, on the basis of full exploration of the
many aspects of a complicated problem, devise a national policy fair alike to
the States and our Union." [66]

As a practical matter, one may doubt whether the Congress could actually deal effectively with the myriad problems of state impediments to
national trade. Even if we assume that an assembly so reflective of sectional
interests could acquire the broad view and impartiality necessary to resolve these matters, it is hard to see where it would find the time, when it is
now swamped by the pressures of its normal legislative tasks. And where

is the legislative department to acquire the machinery and the personnel to operate it, which are required to deal speedily and effectively with cases of improper state action as they arise?

It is only the judicial process that is able actively to deal with these cases so as to give immediate practical effect to the policy behind the Commerce Clause. Justice Douglas [67] aptly pointed this out in a 1955 lecture. Speaking of state barriers to commerce, he says: "Congress, of course, could have removed those barriers and probably would have done so. But the judiciary has moved with speed. As a result of the case by case approach, there has been no great lag between the creation of the forbidden barrier or burden and its removal by the judiciary." [68]

No one can claim that the Supreme Court has been a perfect instrument for the implementation of the Commerce Clause, or even that it has been as effective in all cases as it might have been. On the whole, nonetheless, the performance of the judiciary in the field has produced a record far more commendable than might be expected from a legislative assembly. Free trade has, in fact, flourished under the fostering impact of the high Court's Commerce-Clause decisions. That tribunal has been at its best when it has pierced the veil of ostensible regulation in the interest of public health or safety and brought to light a scheme of state discrimination against interstate commerce.[69] Certainly, it has been the American experience that the fulfillment of a policy like that of the Commerce Clause must depend primarily upon the courts. In Justice Douglas' phrase, "Constitutions can say that commerce must be free; but over the years the courts will be largely the ones who will implement these provisions." [70]

The Supreme Court remains the indispensable instrument for implementation of the negative aspect of the Commerce Clause. As that tribunal itself expressed it, in a leading case specifically rejecting Justice Black's view: "in such cases, where Congress has not acted, this Court, and not the state legislature, is under the commerce clause the final arbiter of the competing demands of state and national interests." [71] If the Congress does not act, either the Supreme Court or the state legislatures must be given the final word. There can surely be little doubt as to which can be more relied upon to protect the national interest.

Perhaps the best answer to those who assert the impropriety of judicial power was given some years ago by Justice Holmes, when he said: "I do not think the United States would come to an end if we lost our power to declare an Act of Congress void. I do think the Union would be imperilled if we could not make that declaration as to the laws of the several states. For one in my place sees how often a local policy prevails with those who are not trained to national views and how often action is taken that embodies what the Commerce Clause was meant to end." [72]

93

COOLEY TEST   As emphasized in section 91, the *Cooley* decision
REFINED   remains the polestar in cases on state power over
               commerce, where the Congress has made no pro-
vision in the matter. The *Cooley* opinion itself is not, however, free of certain ambiguities which must be resolved before we can turn, in the following
sections, to the way in which the *Cooley* test is applied in specific cases.

In a key portion of his *Cooley* opinion, Justice Curtis referred to the
fact that the commerce power embraces many "subjects quite unlike in
their nature; some imperatively demanding a single uniform rule, . . . and
some . . . imperatively demanding that diversity which alone can meet the
local necessities." [73] Such a formula may work well enough for the clear-cut
cases at either end of the scale. Yet most cases are not resolved by such
approach, for they involve subjects which do not *imperatively demand*
either uniformity or diversity of regulatory rules. On the contrary, they will
admit of either. [74]

Shall we then rephrase the Curtis language to speak of subjects which
"admit of" uniformity and subjects which "admit of" diversity? The difficulty with such an approach is that most subjects of regulation can fall in
both categories, since, in most instances, they will *admit of* either uniformity or diversity. Then, too, the answer to specific cases, under such an
approach, will depend almost entirely upon the side of the spectrum from
which one starts. If we say that the power is exclusive over subjects which
admit of uniformity but concurrent over those that do not, we favor the
exclusive group. If we say that state authority is concurrent over subjects
which admit of diversity, we widen the scope of state power. [75]

The apparent dilemma here can be resolved if we concentrate upon
the reasons behind the negative aspect of the Commerce Clause. As emphasized at the outset of this chapter, these sprang from the disastrous ex-
periences under the Confederation when the states vied in discriminatory
measures against each other. To end these evils, the Constitution established an immunity for commerce to the extent that the national interest
might demand. [76] This should mean that the states are excluded from regulating commerce solely so far as the national interest may require. [77] That is
true only where the subjects of regulation are of such a nature as to *demand*
that, if regulated at all, their regulation should be prescribed by a single
authority. [78]

The *Cooley* doctrine of "selective exclusiveness" rests upon the proposition just stated that Congressional power over commerce must be exclusive
just so far as the national interest requires. Such is the case whenever the
subject of regulation *demands* one uniform system of regulation throughout
the country. To that extent, we may still follow Justice Curtis in his state-

ment with regard to subjects which "imperatively demand" a uniform rule. But the same is not true of his statement about subjects which "imperatively demand" local diversity. We need not restrict the states' power to act only with regard to such subjects. On the contrary, bearing in mind the purpose of the Commerce Clause itself, if national uniformity in regulation is not required, there is no compelling reason why the states should not be allowed to act. In matters "admitting of" diversity of treatment according to local conditions, the states should be able to impose their own rules.[79]

Despite the ambiguity in the Curtis opinion, *Cooley* thus makes Congressional authority exclusive only as to those phases of commerce which *demand* uniform regulation. Apart from them, the states may be said to enjoy a "concurrent" power of regulation, subject solely to the overriding authority of the Congress.

Attention must also be paid to an even more important respect in which the *Cooley* opinion stands in need of some refinement. In *Cooley,* it will be recalled, Justice Curtis shifted the focus of inquiry from the theoretical nature of the commerce power to the pragmatic nature of the subjects over which it is exercised. This, we saw, was a substantial step forward, for it enabled the Supreme Court to replace the unvarying rule of complete exclusiveness or concurrence with one which could be adapted to the requirements of specific subjects of regulation.

In saying that the existence of state power is to be determined by the nature of the subject over which it is exerted, however, Justice Curtis failed to take into account the nature of the regulation itself.[80] The particular regulation at issue is an essential factor—often, indeed, at least as determinative as the subject involved standing alone.

This can be seen from consideration of the subject of regulation in *Cooley* itself. The subject regulated there was navigation by water in the port of Philadelphia, or, to put it more specifically, pilotage in such port. *Cooley* sustained a requirement to engage a local pilot or pay a fine. Let us assume, at the same time, that the regulation were a prohibition against using any pilot or one which required only vessels in interstate commerce to take on pilots. Laws imposing such requirements would hardly be upheld by any court.[81] Though the subject of regulation in such cases would remain the same, the dissimilarity in the regulatory rules involved would make for a difference in result.

This can be seen even more clearly in the cases to be discussed on railroad regulation.[82] We shall see that the states may apply to interstate trains laws requiring headlights of a specified minimum capacity on locomotives [83] or caboose cars on freight trains; [84] but they may not restrict the length of interstate freight trains [85] or limit the speed of such trains so drastically as to impair efficient operation.[86] In each of these cases, the subject of regulation was the same, i.e., train safety. But the regulatory requirements themselves differed substantially, and this in turn led to the variations in result noted.

To determine whether a state regulation is valid under the *Cooley* test, it is consequently not enough to consider only the nature of the subject of regulation. The nature of the regulation at issue must also be regarded. What is meant here can be put more precisely. The nature of the subject contemplated in the *Cooley* formula is its nature after the state regulation has been applied to it. Its nature is its situation or its characteristics after the regulatory law has impinged upon it.[87]

The question one must ask in applying the *Cooley* test is thus not: Is the subject of regulation alone one which demands national uniformity? The existence of state power cannot really be determined adequately unless we take into account the nature of the particular regulation as well. The question then becomes: Is the given regulation of the subject involved of such a nature that, if regulated at all, it should be by a single national authority? If it is, only the Congress may regulate and the states are barred from acting, even in the absence of a federal law on the subject. If, on the other hand, the particular regulation, as it impinges on the subject concerned, is not of such a nature as to demand nationally uniform regulatory prescriptions, state regulatory power may be exerted.

94

RAILROAD
REGULATION:
RATES

The *Cooley* test has been applied most frequently to determine the validity of state regulations of transportation by land. The first important cases in this area arose out of state laws regulating railroads. In *Munn v. Illinois* (1877) [88]—one of the true landmarks of American constitutional law [89]—the substantive authority of the states to regulate railroads was sustained. State power was expressly held to include the authority to prescribe railroad rates.[90] But this did not settle the question of whether state rate control was valid for transportation within the states which constitute a part of interstate commerce.[91]

That question was directly presented to the high Court in the 1886 case of *Wabash, St. Louis & Pacific Railway v. Illinois.*[92] The issue there was the validity of a state statute which sought to regulate railroad rates for transportation whose origin or destination was beyond the boundaries of the state. To decide that issue, the Court relied squarely on the *Cooley* test. It is one thing, said Justice Miller, for a state to fix the rates for carriage entirely within its borders. It is quite another for it to regulate fares and charges within its limits for a transportation which constitutes a part of commerce among the states.

As far as interstate rates are concerned, if there is to be regulation at all, there is a manifest need for uniformity. If one state may fix interstate rates, all other states may do so, and they need not prescribe the same rates. Unless all the states were to reach identical conclusions with regard to what rates were proper, a uniform standard of rates would be impossible, as the standard would fluctuate and vary, dependent upon the divergent conclusions reached by the various states. In the words of the *Wabash* opinion: "if each one of the states through whose territories these goods are transported can fix its own rules for prices, for modes of transit, for times and modes of delivery, and all the other incidents of transportation to which the word 'regulation' can be applied, it is readily seen that the embarrassments upon interstate transportation, as an element of interstate commerce, might be too oppressive to be submitted to." [93]

Interstate railroad rates, if regulated at all, must be regulated by one national body, to ensure that they are uniform from state to state. As the *Wabash* opinion stated, "That this species of regulation is one which must be, if established at all, of a general and national character, and cannot be safely and wisely remitted to local rules and local regulations, we think is clear." [94] Rate regulation must be uniform and the states have no power over interstate rates, even in the absence of any federal legislation on the subject.

As a practical matter, the *Wabash* decision laid the issue of effective railroad rate regulation directly up to the Congress. Since some three-fourths of the country's railroad tonnage was interstate in character, Congress was behooved to act under its commerce power if railroad rates were really to be regulated. *Wabash* did, indeed, result directly in the passage within a few months of the Interstate Commerce Act of 1887—the first great regulatory law enacted under the federal commerce power. Under that statute, interstate rail rates are now regulated by the Interstate Commerce Commission, though the states still retain their authority over purely intrastate rates.[95]

95

SAME: SAFETY   As far as interstate railroad rates are concerned, we have just seen that the *Cooley* test bars all state regulation. If such rates are to be regulated at all, it must be by a uniform system prescribed from Washington.

The same is not, however, true of regulations governing railroad safety. With regard to them, determination of whether the *Cooley* test precludes state action depends upon the particular safety requirement imposed. The key question, as stated in section 93, is whether the given regulation of the subject involved (i.e., rail safety) is of such a nature that it demands national uniformity. The answer will vary in accordance with the actual manner in which the particular regulation impinges upon interstate commerce by rail. What this means in practice may be seen from the decided cases.

The Supreme Court has started with the proposition that railroad safety is not, as a general matter, a subject that demands national uniformity in regulation. On the contrary, like the regulation of pilotage at issue in *Cooley* itself, it is a subject whose needs may normally be best provided for by divergent regulatory schemes adapted to local peculiarities. One nationally prescribed set of rules will not ordinarily deal as well with local differences in geography, population, and the like—all of which should be taken into account in imposing safety requirements—as will separate systems by the different states concerned.

The leading case upholding state power to prescribe safety regulations is the 1888 decision in *Smith v. Alabama*,[96] where a law requiring locomotive engineers, including those operating interstate trains, to be examined and licensed by a state agency was sustained. The Supreme Court relied directly upon the proposition just stated that safety requirements should be geared to meet specific local conditions. In its words, "The width of the gauge, the character of the grades, the mode of crossing streams by culverts and bridges, the kind of cuts and tunnels, the mode of crossing other highways, the placing of watchmen and signals at points of special danger, the rate of speed at stations and through villages, towns, and cities, are all matters naturally and peculiarly within the provisions of that law from the authority of which these modern highways of commerce derive their existence. The rules prescribed for their construction and for their management and operation, designed to protect persons and property, otherwise endangered by their use, are strictly within the limits of the local law." [97]

The holding of the *Smith* case has been applied to validate state statutes applicable to interstate trains which prohibited the use of stoves to heat passenger cars,[98] required locomotive headlights of a specified minimum capacity,[99] and ordered the elimination of dangerous grade crossings,[100] as well as so-called "full crew" laws, under which trains in the state had to be operated by at least a specified number of employees.[101] All of these laws were upheld as valid safety regulations enacted by the states concerned in order to meet local safety requirements. Persons traveling on interstate trains are as much entitled, while within a state, to the benefit of laws adapted to such requirements as those who travel on domestic trains.[102] As Justice Jackson put it, in a more recent case sustaining a state requirement of caboose cars on freight trains: "It finds its origin in the local climatic conditions and in the hazards created by particular local physical structures, and it has rather obvious relation to the health and safety of local workmen." [103]

What is true of such safety requirements is also true of regulations governing the speed at which trains may be operated. It is, the Supreme Court has said, "within the undoubted province of the state legislature to make regulations with regard to the speed of railroad trains." [104] What is a safe speed depends preeminently upon local physical conditions and state prescriptions adapted to such conditions must be complied with by trains passing through the state.[105]

Similarly, the states may regulate the manner in which interstate trains may approach bridges, tunnels, deep cuts, sharp curves, and dangerous crossings.[106] Such regulation may include the precautions that must be taken, the signals which shall be given, and the control of the train which shall be required.[107] Here, too, the necessary safety regulations will depend upon the particular local circumstances. That being the case, one uniform rule, prescribed from Washington, is clearly not demanded; the states concerned can provide the needed diversity in regulation which can best meet the local necessities. As a general proposition, then, until the Congress sees fit to exert its power, rail safety regulation may be left to the legislation of the states.

At the same time, as stated at the beginning of this section, whether a given safety regulation may validly be imposed upon interstate trains may depend upon the manner in which it impinges upon interstate railroading. The general state power over railroad safety may have to give way where the effect of the particular regulation is such as to impose too great a burden upon interstate commerce, if its details are left to the discretion of each state through which such commerce passes.

We have seen that there is a general authority in the states to regulate the speed of interstate trains. State authority in this respect has been held to include the power to require such trains to slow down at crossings.[108] On the other hand, in the 1917 decision in *Seaboard Air Line R. Co. v. Blackwell,*[109] such a requirement was ruled invalid when applied to an interstate line which crossed 124 highways at grade in 123 miles. None of these crossings presented conditions making them dangerous, yet, at each of them, interstate trains would be required by the state law to slow down practically to a full stop, consuming not less than three minutes at each crossing. Compliance with the law at issue would more than double the running time of interstate trains using the line.

As explained by Chief Justice Stone in a later case, in *Seaboard:* "it was held that the interference with interstate rail transportation resulting from a state statute requiring as a safety measure that trains come almost to a stop at grade crossings, outweigh the local interest in safety, when it appeared that compliance increased the scheduled running time more than six hours in a distance of one hundred and twenty-three miles." [110] The states may, we saw, as a general proposition, regulate the approach to grade crossings. In *Seaboard,* however, to require compliance with the slackening of speed prescribed would be practically destructive of the operation of the interstate railroad.[111] The particular regulation, in other words, impinged upon the interstate commerce involved to such an extent as to constitute an undue burden upon such commerce. Where, on the contrary, the crossings regulated are not so numerous and the state regulation at issue not so severe, the burden to interstate commerce will not be heavy enough to make the general state power over safety give way.[112]

96

SAME: SOUTHERN   The line between valid and invalid state safety regu-
PACIFIC CO. V.   lations, as they are applied to interstate railroads, is
ARIZONA   perhaps even better illustrated by the 1945 case of
Southern Pacific Co. v. Arizona.[113] In it, the high bench was confronted with an Arizona train-limit law which made it unlawful to operate within the state a railroad train of more than fourteen passenger or seventy freight cars in length. The law in question was justified as a safety measure to reduce the number of accidents attributed by the state to the operation of trains of too great length. The Supreme Court indicated doubt that the claim of increased safety was substantiated by the evidence.[114] Yet, even considering the statute as a safety measure, the Court ruled that it could not be upheld. The power of the state to prescribe safety regulations, reads the opinion of Chief Justice Stone, cannot "outweigh the national interest in keeping interstate commerce free from interferences which seriously impede it and subject it to local regulation which does not have a uniform effect on the interstate train journey which it interrupts." [115]

What the high Court meant by this statement can be seen from examination of the actual manner in which the Arizona train-limit law impinged upon interstate train operation. That statute, said the Chief Justice in his opinion, "imposes a serious burden on the interstate commerce conducted by appellant. It materially impedes the movement of appellant's interstate trains through that state and interposes a substantial obstruction to the national policy proclaimed by Congress, to promote adequate, economical and efficient railway transportation service." [116]

Under the reasoning of the *Southern Pacific* opinion, the Arizona law fell within the area in which state action was precluded under the *Cooley* test. The regulation of interstate train lengths, if any be necessary, must be prescribed by a single body having nationwide authority. The states cannot provide uniform control, such as is essential to a national transportation system. "If one state may regulate train lengths," the *Southern Pacific* opinion asserted, "so may all the others, and they need not prescribe the same maximum limitation. The practical effect of such regulation is to control train operations beyond the boundaries of the state exacting it because of the necessity of breaking up and reassembling long trains at the nearest terminal points before entering and after leaving the regulating state." [117]

If this was true of the train-limit law, why was it not also true of the "full crew" laws which, as pointed out in the prior section,[118] have been uniformly upheld? According to the *Southern Pacific* opinion, the difference in result here depends upon the substantial difference in impact, as between the train-limit law and a full-crew law. The latter did, it is true, place an additional financial burden on the railroads affected. But it did not really seriously impede their interstate operation. It had no effects outside the state beyond those of picking up and setting down a few extra employees at the state's boundaries.[119]

As contrasted with this minimal burden [120] imposed by the full-crew laws, train-limit laws involved a most serious impairment of railroad efficiency. Under them, the makeup of the trains themselves might be subject to disturbance at every state line. According to the *Southern Pacific* opinion, "Compliance with a state statute limiting train lengths requires interstate trains of a length lawful in other states to be broken up and reconstituted as they enter each state according as it may impose varying limitations upon train lengths. The alternative is for the carrier to conform to the lowest train limit restriction of any of the states through which its trains pass, whose laws thus control the carriers' operations both within and without the regulating state." [121]

In a case like *Southern Pacific Co. v. Arizona,* no regulation at all is preferable to the confusion and difficulty with which interstate railroading could be burdened under a patchwork of state legislation. To permit Arizona to enforce her law, while train lengths are unregulated or are regulated by varying standards in other states, results inevitably in impairment of efficient railroad operation. To require interstate railroads to conform to "a crazy-quilt of State laws" [122] with regard to train makeup would be to countenance the very sort of thing that the Commerce Clause was intended to put an end to.

Southern Pacific indicates how the *Cooley* test may be used to invalidate a particular safety regulation—though, as emphasized in the prior section, the subject of safety regulation is, as a general proposition, one within state competence. The test in each case is a practical one, in which the actual effect upon interstate or national interests is weighed against the local interest involved.[123]

The Supreme Court, in these cases, is dealing not with absolutes but with questions of degree. The states plainly have great leeway in providing safety regulations for all trains—interstate as well as local. But the burden which a law like the Arizona train-limit statute places on the interstate movement of trains passes the permissible limits even for safety regulations.[124]

97

SAME: SERVICE   Among the most important types of railroad regulations are those governing train service. Such regulations, like those concerning safety, should be adapted to meet local conditions. Hence, the starting point with regard to them has been the possession by the states of a general power to require adequate service for their citizens from railroads, including those operating in interstate commerce. The basic proposition, as enunciated in 1915 by the highest Court, is that it "is competent for the states to require adequate local facilities, even to the stoppage of interstate trains or the rearrangement of their schedule." [125]

In accordance with this approach, the Supreme Court has upheld state laws requiring trains to stop at specified classes of stations for taking on and discharging passengers, where their effect was to provide adequate service for the areas involved, even though this meant the stoppage of trains carrying interstate passengers.[126] The leading case of this type is *Lake Shore & M.S.R. Co. v. Ohio,*[127] where the challenged law required three trains daily, if so many were run, to stop at each city containing over three thousand inhabitants.

State authority in this respect is, however, based solely upon the power to provide for the reasonable convenience of its inhabitants who may desire to use railroad facilities. Implicit in this is the limitation of state power to the imposition of requirements which do, in fact, provide adequate service. Where communities are already adequately provided with local service, for the state to require railroads to furnish additional services imposes an undue burden upon interstate commerce.[128] As the Supreme Court has put it, with adequate local "facilities existing—that is, the local conditions being adequately met—the obligation of the railroad is performed, and the stoppage of interstate trains becomes an improper and illegal interference with interstate commerce." [129] Where a small city had four other through interstate trains, a requirement by the state that two night interstate trains stop there was an unreasonable burden on interstate commerce.[130]

State power in this respect is also limited by the fact that it may only demand *reasonably* adequate service. To require that interstate trains stop at every inhabited place, no matter how small,[131] is plainly to impose an unreasonable burden upon such trains. The same is true of a law that requires every passenger train, regardless of its interstate nature, to stop at every county seat through which it may pass, without regard to its size or the fact that it may already be adequately served.[132] In the high bench's words, "If such passenger trains may be compelled to stop at county seats, it is difficult to see why the legislature may not compel them to stop at every station,—a requirement which would be practically destructive of through travel." [133]

In the same manner, a state may not compel an interstate train to turn aside from its direct route to accommodate a small town on a branch line.[134] Here, too, an undue burden is imposed upon the proper operation of through service.

In these service cases, as in those involving safety regulations, the high Court must balance the local interest in adequate service against the national interest in the unimpaired operation of interstate trains. Since service needs vary from locality to locality, the starting point, under the *Cooley* test, is that this is not an area from which the states are automatically barred. They can, on the contrary, make regulations for reasonably adequate service, though such regulations impinge upon interstate operations. But they cannot go further. Once adequate local service is furnished, the obligation of the railroad is at an end. Nor can the states impose unreasonable burdens, like the requirement that *every* train stop at *every* county seat, which make it unduly difficult to operate a proper through service.[135]

98

MOTOR VEHICLE
REGULATION:
SAFETY

The general power of the states to prescribe safety regulations for those using its highways—whether they be engaged in interstate or purely local travel— is settled. Safety regulations governing motor vehicles should be adapted to local conditions at least as much as those governing the railroads. "There is," the Supreme Court has stated, "need of local supervision of operation of motor vehicles to prevent collisions, to safeguard pedestrians, and the like." [136] There is no doubt, for example, that interstate vehicles must obey local traffic signals, speed limits, and other general safety regulations.[137] Similarly, a state law fixing maximum hours for continuous driving on its highways has been held validly applicable to interstate as well as local vehicles. Unquestionably, said the Supreme Court, reasonable regulation of periods of continuous driving is an appropriate safety measure.[138] Likewise, a state statute which prohibited the operation of any motor vehicle carrying any other vehicle over the head of the driver of such carrier vehicle was sustained, where evidence showed that such operation was dangerous on the curves and grades of the state's highways.[139]

Such regulations of the manner in which motor vehicles may be operated present no real difficulties. The states have not, however, limited themselves to the prescription of safety rules of this type. In the already-discussed case of *Southern Pacific Co. v. Arizona*,[140] the high tribunal felt it necessary to distinguish its earlier decision in *South Carolina Highway Department v.*

Barnwell Bros.[141] In that case, the state law in question was a South Carolina statute which prohibited the use on the highways of the state of motor trucks and "semi-trailer" motor trucks whose width exceeded ninety inches, and whose weight, including load, exceeded twenty thousand pounds. This law was upheld by the Court in the *Barnwell Bros.* case, despite the fact that it appears to be the counterpart, in the field of motor vehicle regulation, of the Arizona train-limit law declared invalid in the *Southern Pacific* case.

How has the Court explained this seeming inconsistency? According to the *Southern Pacific* opinion, the difference between the two cases stems from the difference in the type of transportation involved: "There are few subjects of state regulation affecting interstate commerce which are so peculiarly of local concern as is the use of the state's highways. Unlike the railroads local highways are built, owned and maintained by the state or its municipal subdivisions. The state is responsible for their safe and economical administration." [142]

In the field of motor vehicle regulation, in other words, an added element is present which tips the scale in favor of state regulatory power, namely, that motor vehicles use highways furnished and maintained by the state. The law at issue in the *Barnwell Bros.* case, which regulated the width and weight of vehicles in the state, had a direct relation to the cost of maintenance of the highways provided by the state and was, therefore, upheld.

Since interstate motor vehicles use roads provided by the state, they are subject both to state regulations which promote safety and those which seek highway conservation.[143] The state is not limited to prescriptions as to the manner in which vehicles may be operated; it may also prevent the wear and hazards due to excessive size of vehicles and weight of load.[144] In *Barnwell Bros.*, the challenged law was aimed at both safety and highway conservation. The latter element justified the exertion of state power, despite the fact, already noted, that what was said in the Arizona train-limit case might otherwise be fully applicable here.

The *Barnwell Bros.* reasoning permits the states to go much further in regulating motor vehicles than they can as far as the railroads are concerned. Each state may, under the highest Court's approach, enforce its own rules with regard to the maximum loads of vehicles using its roads, as well as the maximum dimensions of the vehicles themselves.[145] And it makes no difference that adjoining states may prescribe their own diverse loads and dimensions, which may differ greatly from those of the state at issue.[146] The fact that the highways are furnished and maintained by the state itself is held to justify its regulation, even though the practical result may be a substantial burden upon the operation of an interstate trucking business.

The basic rule in this respect was stated by the highest Court in a 1949 decision sustaining a New York traffic regulation forbidding the operation of any advertising vehicle in the streets, even though it was enforced against trucks delivering goods from New Jersey. As the Court's opinion expressed it: "Where traffic control and the use of highways are involved and where there is no conflicting federal regulation, great leeway is allowed local authorities, even though the local regulation materially interferes with interstate commerce." [147]

99

SAME: LICENSING   The Supreme Court has not, however, stopped at upholding state regulations of the type just dealt with, which are adopted to promote safety upon state highways and to ensure their conservation. It has gone further and held that, if the state may regulate by such laws, it may also regulate by means of licensing schemes.

State power in this respect was upheld in 1915 in *Hendrick v. Maryland*.[148] The state law involved in it prescribed a comprehensive scheme for licensing motor vehicles and their drivers. Under it, all vehicles had to be registered with a state agency before they could be used in the state. The high Court held that such law could validly be applied to automobiles coming into the state. The right to use a state's highways even for interstate transportation may be limited to vehicles registered under state law and the right to operate such vehicles may be restricted to drivers licensed by the state.[149]

What is true of individual vehicles is also true of carriers using the highways of a state. The state may require all motor carriers using its highways to obtain licenses from the relevant state agency, and this requirement may validly be applied to interstate as well as intrastate carriers. In *Fry Roofing Co. v. Wood*,[150] the Supreme Court ruled that Arkansas could require a person engaged exclusively in the interstate transportation of goods by motor vehicle to obtain a state license. A mere requirement for a license, said the Court, does not impose any undue burden on interstate commerce.[151]

Nor, it should be noted, is this state power to license confined to persons and carriers using the highways. In *California v. Thompson* [152] the high bench sustained a state law requiring every transportation agent (i.e., one who negotiates for the transportation of passengers in motor vehicles over the highways of the state) to obtain a license. A decision a decade and a half earlier had declared such a law invalid,[153] but the Court stated that the cases which uphold the power of the states closely to regulate their highways justified this regulation of transportation agents, and the earlier decision was accordingly overruled.

100

SAME: In the already-discussed case of *Hendrick v. Mary-*
LICENSE FEES   *land,*[154] the Court stated that the power of the states
to license motor vehicles is based upon the danger
to the public resulting from motor traffic, as well as the fact that such
traffic is abnormally destructive to highways. But, if the latter is true, the
power to license should include the power to tax—at least to an extent
necessary to defray the cost of operating the highways. As the *Hendrick*
opinion put it: "there can be no serious doubt that where a state at its own
expense furnishes special facilities for the use of those engaged in commerce, interstate as well as domestic, it may exact compensation therefor." [155]

Consequently, a state may impose reasonable fees upon interstate motor
carriers for the use of its highways. "Consistently with the commerce
clause," the Supreme Court has said: "a State may impose upon vehicles
used exclusively for interstate transportation a fair and reasonable tax as
compensation for the privilege of using its highways for that purpose." [156]
The amount of the charges and the method of collection are primarily for
determination by the state itself.[157] They can be imposed as flat license fees
per vehicle,[158] or based upon the value of vehicles used in the state,[159] their
horsepower,[160] their carrying capacity,[161] or their mileage.[162]

Such state fees must be upheld if they bear some reasonable relation to
the cost of maintaining and policing the highways. On the other hand, since
the basis upon which the power of the state is upheld is its need to defray the
cost of operating its roads, the fee involved should be levied only as compensation for use of the highways or to defray the expense of regulating
motor traffic.[163] Hence, the Supreme Court has invalidated fees deemed excessive or not related to the extent of use of the highways.[164] The rule has
been stated that "It must appear on the face of the statute or be demon-
strable that the tax as laid is measured by or has some fair relationship to
the use of the highways for which the charge is made." [165] Indeed, the high
bench has even gone so far as to assert that the mere fact that the tax falls
upon one who uses the highway is not enough to give it presumptive
validity.[166]

More recent cases, however, shift the burden from the state to the individual. Unless he can affirmatively show that the fee imposed bears no
reasonable relationship to compensation for use of the highways, the state
law must be sustained. "The burden of proof in this respect," declared the
Supreme Court in a 1950 case, "is on a carrier who challenges a state
law." [167]

Nor is the burden in this respect met only by demonstrating that the fee
imposed is a very large one. In *Bode v. Barrett,*[168] an Illinois tax, imposed

for the use of the public highways and measured by the gross weight of the vehicles involved, was sustained, although the amount of the tax was as high as $1,580 per truck. Merely showing the extent of the financial burden, said the high Court, is not to show that the tax bears no reasonable relation to highway use.

Under a case like this, one may wonder whether the individual concerned can really ever meet the burden of proving that a state license fee is excessive. In theory, the rule remains that such a fee must be justified as a means of securing compensation for road use. In practice, all the same, this requirement is anything but a close accounting responsibility. The states are free to exercise judgment of the loosest sort in fixing a *quid pro quo*.[169]

101

SAME:
LIMITATIONS
The cases involving motor-vehicle regulation turn upon the fact emphasized in section 98 that such vehicles use facilities furnished and maintained by the state. It is this which gives the state much more extensive authority over motorcars passing interstate over its highways than over interstate railroads and justifies the laws discussed in the last three sections.

Despite the high bench's attempt to distinguish these motor-vehicle regulation decisions from the already-discussed Arizona train-limit case,[170] one is nevertheless left with an uneasy feeling that those decisions permit the states to carry on the very restrictive practices that the Commerce Clause was intended to preclude. What the Supreme Court has, in effect, said in a case like *South Carolina Highway Department v. Barnwell Bros.*[171] is that the *Cooley* test [172] should not be the determining factor in the motor-vehicle field because of the part the states play in providing road facilities. Certainly the furnishing of highways by the state is a fact which differentiates road regulation from train regulation of the type at issue in *Southern Pacific Co. v. Arizona.*[173] At the same time, one cannot help but feel that separate regulation in each state may result in the same impediment to commerce by a "crazy quilt" of state laws as that which the Court pointed to with alarm as the inevitable consequence of the Arizona train-limit law. In a country dominated by the free-trade concept of the Commerce Clause, it is anomalous that interstate commerce by motor may be required to obtain permits and pay toll every time it crosses a new state line.

Separate state regulation of motor vehicles, outside the traditional field of safety prescriptions governing operation, should be scrutinized with a jealous judicial eye. For the power to regulate also involves the power to destroy—particularly where it involves an inevitable regulatory patchwork, varying substantially from state to state. Interstate commerce by motor may be faced with a rampart of economic barriers, which constitute a constant clog upon that mobility of commerce which the Constitution was designed to foster.

The Supreme Court has not perhaps been as zealous in the motor-vehicle cases in furthering the policy behind the Commerce Clause as one would hope. But the Court has, nevertheless, been careful to lay down certain limitations upon the exercise of state power in this field. In the first place, under the cases, state power to license truckers cannot be used as a device to protect those already in the field from interstate competition. In *Buck v. Kuykendall*,[174] the high Court held that a state could not use its authority to license interstate carriers to deny access to its market by out-of-state carriers on the ground that the community was already adequately served. Such regulation was, in effect, being used to effect a ban on interstate competition.

Under *Fry Roofing Co. v. Wood*,[175] we saw that the states may require registration of interstate vehicles and exact reasonable fees for their use of local highways.[176] The Court there, however, stated that its decision was based upon the denial by the relevant state licensing agency of any discretion to refuse registration to anyone engaged in interstate carriage. In such a case, the state was plainly not going to use its licensing power to exclude out-of-staters from its roads. In other words, while a state may require the interstate trucker to obtain a permit and pay a fee before using its highways, it must grant such permit to any bona fide interstate carrier whose application is filed with the specified fee. The licensing power may not be employed to exclude the out-of-state trucker from the state's roads.

More recently the high tribunal has gone even further in holding that interstate commerce cannot be barred from a state's highways. In the 1954 case of *Castle v. Hayes Freight Lines*,[177] the Court held that, where an interstate carrier held a certificate of convenience and necessity from the Interstate Commerce Commission, a state could not suspend the carrier's state permit to use the state's highways, even though such suspension was imposed as a punishment for repeated violations of the state law regulating the weight of loads of freight that might be carried on the state's highways. This decision supplies a needed limitation on the cases, already dealt with, which allow interstate commerce traveling on roads to be regulated directly by the states. Under the *Castle* decision, even violators of state regulatory laws cannot be excluded from state highways, if they are engaged in interstate commerce. Even in such a case, state regulatory authority may not be employed to keep interstate commerce off its roads.

It should, at the same time, be emphasized that the *Castle* case does not in any way affect the states' powers to enact regulatory laws of the type discussed in sections 98–100. Nor does it affect the liability of carriers who violate such laws under the conventional sanctions of the criminal law.

Though the interstate carrier may not be driven from the state's highways, the threat of fine or imprisonment will normally be enough to compel him to comply with state regulations.

102

SAME: BIBB CASE   Even more important than the limitations just discussed is the question of whether the Supreme Court has really been correct in its basic holding that the *Cooley* test [178] should not be the determining factor in the motor-vehicle cases because such vehicles use facilities provided by the states themselves. Even if that is true, one may, as already intimated, still wonder whether it is enough to justify so great an extension of state regulatory power, as compared with that which may be exerted over the railroads. If *Cooley* is the proper test in cases involving state regulation of railroads, it should also be such in the motor-vehicle cases, which present essentially the same economic and legal problems.

That the high tribunal itself may be tending toward the view just stated is indicated by its 1959 decision in *Bibb v. Navajo Freight Lines.*[179] The Court there was asked to hold that an Illinois statute requiring the use of a contour type of rear fender mudguard on all trucks operated on the highways of that state conflicted with the Commerce Clause. The district court had concluded that the statute unduly and unreasonably burdened and obstructed interstate commerce, because it made the conventional or straight mudflap, which was legal in at least forty-five states, illegal in Illinois, and because the statute, taken together with a rule of the Arkansas Commerce Commission requiring straight mudflaps, rendered the use of the same motor vehicle equipment in both states impossible. The Supreme Court affirmed, holding unanimously that the challenged statute violated the Commerce Clause.

The Court emphasized the findings below that installation of the contour mudguards imposed a substantial financial burden on truckers [180] and that such mudguard possessed no advantages in terms of safety over the conventional straight flap permitted in almost all states. But this was not the real basis of its decision. The vice of the challenged statute was to be found in the burden it imposed on the movement of interstate commerce. Such burden, said the Court, arose from the prescription by one state of standards for interstate commerce which conflicted with the standards of another state, "making it necessary, say, for an interstate carrier to shift its cargo to differently designed vehicles once another state line was reached." [181] This was clearly true under the rule of the Arkansas commission already mentioned which required straight mudflaps. To permit Illinois to enforce her law, while mudguards remained unregulated or were regulated by varying standards in other states, must inevitably result in an impairment of uniformity of interstate transportation, because truckers were subjected to regulation which was not uniform in its application. Hence the Court's holding that the statute in question resulted in a "rather massive . . . burden on interstate commerce." [182]

Looked at in this way, of course, *Bibb* represents only a simple application of the *Cooley* test. Here, too, the subject of regulation required a uniform system, or plan, of regulation; it was not best provided for by as many systems of regulation as the legislative discretion of the several states should deem applicable.[183] The *Bibb* opinion relied in large part upon *Southern Pacific Co. v. Arizona,*[184] where, as we saw, the state train-limit law was invalidated on grounds exactly like those stated in *Bibb* itself.

And what of cases like *South Carolina Highway Department v. Barnwell Bros.,*[185] which make a clear distinction between regulation of trucks and railroads in this respect? The Court in *Bibb* all but ignores the *Barnwell Bros.* case, saying that the language in it contrary to its decision cannot be read in isolation from such later decisions as *Southern Pacific.* But, as pointed out in section 98, the *Southern Pacific* opinion expressly disclaimed any intent to overrule *Barnwell Bros.;* it rested upon the distinction between highways and railroads which justified more extensive control by the states over the former.

Bibb, on the contrary, rests upon application of the same approach to state regulation of interstate trucks as to state regulation of interstate railroads. As the *Bibb* opinion puts it: "The various exercises by the states of their police power stand . . . on an equal footing." [186] If that is true, it may well indicate that the Supreme Court will henceforth regard state obstructions to motor commerce with the same jealous eye that it turns to state clogs upon railroad mobility.

103

NAVIGATION   The *Cooley* test has been the determining factor in the cases concerned with state prescriptions governing navigable waters and their use. From Chief Justice Marshall's decision in *Willson v. Black Bird Creek Marsh Co.,*[187] it has been recognized that the states can authorize the erection of bridges, dams, piers and wharves, and harbor improvements, as well as the operation of ferries across such waters.[188] These are all local matters, as to which what is demanded is not national uniformity of regulation, but differing rules adapted to varying local conditions.[189]

The same has been true of state regulation of vessels using state waters.[190] In *Kelly v. Washington,*[191] the high bench had before it a state statute which regulated motor-driven tugs not regulated by federal law, this regulation providing for inspection of the hull and machinery of such vessels in order to ensure safety and seaworthiness. In determining whether such a state regulatory law was valid, the high Court relied entirely upon the *Cooley* test. Is the inspection of these tugs to ensure safety and seaworthiness, it asked: "a subject which necessarily and in all aspects requires uniformity of regulation and as to which the State cannot act at all, although Congress has not acted? We hold that it is not." [192] Consequently, the Court concluded, the state could enact a regulatory statute like that at issue.[193]

As was true of the railroad cases, however, the mere fact that the subject of regulation—i.e., navigation—is one that is, generally speaking, within state power under the *Cooley* test does not mean that all state regulations must be sustained. Where the particular regulation impinges upon interstate commerce to such an extent as to make local control undesirable, it will have to give way.[194] In such a case, as in the Arizona train-limit case,[195] if there is to be regulation at all, it must be of a nationally uniform character.

Huron Cement Co. v. Detroit [196] is a 1960 case close to the line between valid and invalid state action. It arose out of the application of certain provisions of a municipal smoke abatement code to ships operated in interstate commerce. The ships in question were equipped with boiler stacks which emitted smoke which in density and duration exceeded the maximum standards allowable under the relevant municipal code. Structural alterations would be required in order to ensure compliance.

The Supreme Court upheld the application of the municipal regulation to the interstate ships, in the absence of conflicting federal prescriptions. Such state regulation, said the Court, "which does not discriminate against interstate commerce or operate to disrupt its required uniformity, may constitutionally stand." [197] In the instant case, the appellant had argued that, in fact, this case was comparable to *Southern Pacific Co. v. Arizona,*[198] since other local governments might impose differing requirements as to air pollution. But, stated the Court, it has pointed to none; the record contained nothing to suggest the existence of any such competing or conflicting local regulations.[199]

The implication is that for the *Southern Pacific* holding to apply, it must be shown that there are actually conflicting state regulations in existence. One wonders whether this is not to misread both *Southern Pacific* and the *Cooley* test upon which it was based. In *Southern Pacific* itself, there was no showing that states other than Arizona had imposed varying train-limit requirements.[200] Yet that did not deter the high Court from ruling that the Arizona law was invalid. It was the possibility, not the actuality, of a "crazy quilt" of train-limit requirements that made a uniform regulatory system essential. The variety of requirements for equipment which the states may prescribe in order to meet their air pollution needs underlines that the same considerations should apply in a case like *Huron Cement Co. v. Detroit.*[201]

104

RACIAL   The *Cooley* test [202] has been used to invalidate state
DISCRIMINATION IN   laws which provide for the segregation of white and
TRANSPORTATION   colored passengers transported by interstate carriers.
                     The leading case is *Morgan v. Virginia,*[203] where the challenged state law required all motor carriers, both interstate and intrastate, to separate their white and colored passengers in their buses traveling in the state. Such state segregation law was held to be an unconstitutional burden on interstate commerce. Motor transportation among the states may not be subjected to the burden of different local rules governing seating of the races every time it passes through a new locality. In the words of the *Morgan* opinion, "It seems clear to us that seating arrangements for the different races in interstate motor travel require a single, uniform rule to promote and protect national travel. Consequently, we hold the Virginia statute in controversy invalid." [204]

In the 1878 case of *Hall v. DeCuir,*[205] the Supreme Court had held that the same rule applied to a Louisiana law forbidding steamboats on the Mississippi to segregate passengers according to race. More recently, however, in its 1948 decision in *Bob-Lo Excursion Co. v. Michigan,*[206] the Court ruled that the Commerce Clause did not prevent Michigan from prohibiting racial discrimination by excursion vessels operating between one of its ports and an island in Canadian territory. The opinion sought to distinguish *Hall v. DeCuir,* but its effort in this respect is not very convincing. Hence we must assume that, under the present law, a state statute requiring segregation is invalid as applied to interstate commerce, while one requiring equality of accommodations for white and Negro passengers will be upheld.

Nor is the difference in result just noted as inconsistent as it may at first glance appear. A state law requiring equal accommodations for all persons, regardless of their race, does not burden commerce within the meaning of *Morgan v. Virginia.* There is no danger of obstruction and confusion from diverse state regulations if such a law is sustained. If a sister state undertook to provide a different local rule (i.e., one barring Negroes or requiring segregation), such rule would plainly be invalid under the *Morgan* decision. If that is the case, a law prohibiting discrimination merely reaffirms the *Morgan* holding and does not interfere with the uniformity essential for movement in commerce. The only constitutional uniformity, indeed, is uniformity in the pattern of such a law.[207]

105

QUARANTINE LAWS In *Gibbons v. Ogden*, Chief Justice Marshall referred
to "that immense mass of legislation which embraces
everything within the territory of a state not surrendered to the general
government." [208] According to him: "Inspection laws, quarantine laws,
health laws of every description . . . are component parts of this mass." [209]

In accordance with Marshall's view in this respect, it has been uniformly
held that the states possess the power to enact reasonable quarantine laws,
applicable as well to interstate as to local commerce. "Quarantine regulations," the high Court has affirmed, "are essential measures of protection
which the states are free to adopt when they do not come into conflict with
Federal action." [210] The Commerce Clause has not rendered the states
impotent to protect the health of their inhabitants. That they may, on the
contrary, take steps to prevent the introduction or spread of disease, although interstate commerce is affected, is beyond question.[211]

A quarantine law, by its very nature, involves an exclusion of commerce. It may either prohibit the introduction of some article from outside
the state or subject the importer or transporter to such liability as to
amount to a practical ban. Such prohibition is justified by the need to protect the health of the state's residents against contagious diseases, to prevent
the infection of its livestock, or to prevent the introduction and spread of
plant diseases. Such need lies at the very foundation of social existence;
it is for the protection of life itself and must necessarily take precedence
over mere property in commerce. As it was put in 1847 by a member of the
high bench, "The exigencies of the social compact require that such laws
be executed before and above all others." [212]

The first cases dealing directly with quarantine laws involved regulations
designed to exclude diseased cattle and other livestock. In the very first
case of this type, the highest Court declared that a state may exclude
"property dangerous to the property of citizens of the State; for example,
animals having contagious or infectious diseases." [213] For the purpose of
self-protection, it may establish reasonable quarantine laws.[214] In accordance with this holding, the Supreme Court has sustained a state regulation
prohibiting the importation of all cattle from an adjoining state where
anthrax was prevalent for a stated period.[215] Other state laws restricting or
excluding the importing of animals to prevent the spread of disease have
similarly been ruled valid.[216] In a more recent case of this kind, a New
York statute forbidding the bringing in of cattle unless certified to be free of
a certain infectious disease by a proper sanitary official of the state of origin
was at issue. Such statute, said the Court, was appropriate for the prevention of further spread of the disease and to safeguard public health.[217]

The power to quarantine is not, at the same time, limited to regulations aimed at diseased animals. In the words of Chief Justice Taft in an important case, "it is well settled that a state, in the exercise of its police power, may establish quarantines against human beings, or animals, or plants, the coming in of which may expose the inhabitants, or the stock, or the trees, plants, or growing crops, to disease, injury, or destruction thereby." [218] In the case in which this statement was made, a state law which quarantined infected trees and plants was ruled invalid, but solely on the ground that it conflicted with a federal statute. In the absence of a federal law on the subject, the state statute, said the high Court, would clearly be constitutional.

State quarantines may, as the Taft passage in the prior paragraph points out, be imposed against persons, as well as against animals and plants. It has never been doubted that, where Congress has not acted, state authority may be exercised to exclude persons infected with contagious diseases or who may have been exposed to such diseases.[219] But the Supreme Court has gone much further and asserted in the states a general inherent power to exclude undesirables. "We think," declared the 1837 opinion in *City of New York v. Miln,*[220] "it is as competent and as necessary for a state to provide precautionary measures against the moral pestilence of paupers, vagabonds, and possibly convicts; as it is to guard against the physical pestilence, which may arise from unsound and infectious articles imported." Such state power, said Justice Grier a decade later, "has its foundation in the sacred law of self-defence, which no power granted to Congress can restrain or annul." [221]

Though state power in this respect was assumed in numerous cases up to the turn of the century,[222] it may nevertheless be asserted at the present time that quarantine authority against persons may not be exerted as broadly as these cases indicate. The basis for this assertion is the 1941 decision in *Edwards v. California.*[223] At issue in it was a law making it a misdemeanor to bring or assist in bringing into the state a nonresident knowing him to be "an indigent person." Such law, the Supreme Court held, imposed an unconstitutional burden on interstate commerce. The state had relied upon the language in the *Miln* case quoted above. The Court in *Edwards,* however, stated that it did not consider itself bound by the language referred to. *Miln* was decided over a century ago. "Whatever may have been the notion then prevailing, we do not think that it will now be seriously contended that because a person is without employment and without funds he constitutes a 'moral pestilence.' " [224] The quarantine power, in other words, is limited to persons and articles which pose a threat to public health and safety. That a state considers persons without economic resources undesirable is not enough for it to bar their movement across its lines. A law excluding persons who will not expose the state's inhabitants to disease or some comparable physical injury is not really a quarantine law and cannot be justified under the power to quarantine commerce.

What has just been said should apply as well whenever a quarantine law does not have the protection of public health as its true purpose. The prevention of disease, the Supreme Court has said, is the essence of a quarantine law. Where state power has been exerted "beyond what is necessary for any proper quarantine," the law at issue must fall.[225]

The case usually cited to illustrate the point just made is *Railroad Co. v. Husen.*[226] At issue in it was a Missouri law which forbade the importation into the state for eight months of the year of any Texas, Mexican, or Indian cattle. Such law, which imposed a flat prohibition without regard to whether the cattle barred were diseased or not or whether they came from a part of the country where they had been exposed to contagion, was found by the high Court not to be a quarantine provision at all. In effect, said the Court, Missouri was saying to all persons and transportation companies: "You shall not bring into the State any of the specified cattle during the specified months, no matter whether they are free from disease or not, no matter whether they may do an injury to the inhabitants of the state or not." [227]

106

INSPECTION LAWS   The power to quarantine must necessarily include the power to inspect, since it is only through inspection that a quarantine can be made effective. In *Gibbons v. Ogden,* as pointed out at the beginning of the prior section, Chief Justice Marshall expressly recognized the authority of the states to enact inspection laws. The cases in the succeeding century and a half have consistently held that the Commerce Clause is not violated by state inspection laws applicable to articles coming from outside the state.[228] As it was put by Justice Hughes in an important opinion: "State inspection laws . . . are valid when reasonable in their requirements and not in conflict with Federal rules, although they may affect interstate commerce." [229]

There are various kinds of state inspection laws. They may, first of all, serve as adjuncts to quarantine statutes. Thus, inspection may be made a condition precedent to the right to introduce an article into a state otherwise barred under a rigid quarantine provision. In *Reid v. Colorado,*[230] the Supreme Court upheld a law prohibiting the importation of cattle into the state from states south of the 36th parallel during seven months of the year unless they were inspected and found free of disease by the state veterinary board. In the execution of its quarantine power, the state may enact laws for the inspection of animals coming from other states with the purpose of excluding those which are diseased and admitting those which are healthy.

The inspection power need not, however, be limited to articles which are diseased and, as such, themselves subject to exclusion under quarantine laws. Inspection may be required to protect the people of the state from fraudulent practices and to ensure that articles brought into the state comply with minimum standards laid down by the competent state authorities. Such inspection requirement, too, will be valid so far as it is a reasonable means of protecting the health, safety, morals, and welfare of the state and its inhabitants. Laws providing for the inspection and grading of flour, the inspection and regulation of weights and measures, the weighing of coal on public scales, and the like, are all competent exercises of state power in this respect.[231]

A leading case is *Savage v. Jones,*[232] where the Supreme Court sustained an Indiana statute which prohibited the sale of concentrated feeding stuffs prior to inspection and analysis for the purpose of ascertaining whether certain minimum standards were met.[233] The purpose of the statute, said the Court, "is to prevent fraud and imposition in the sale of food for domestic animals, a matter of great importance to the people of the State." [234] Such a law, which sought to promote fair dealing in the articles covered, could validly be applied to goods imported into the state.[235]

The inspection power may be exerted over articles intended to be shipped outside the state as well as over those imported from other states.[236] The state may charge an inspection fee to defray the costs involved in making the inspection, and inspection statutes do commonly provide for the payment of fees. Imposition of such fees will be upheld unless it is shown that the given fee is so unreasonable and disproportionate to the cost of the services rendered as to attack the good faith of the statute as an inspection law.[237]

Unless enacted as an adjunct to a valid quarantine law, state inspection power may not be exercised against persons. In an 1883 case, a state law provided for the inspection of persons arriving in its port to ascertain who among them were "habitual criminals or pauper lunatics, idiots, or imbeciles, . . . or orphan persons without means or capacity to support themselves and subject to become a public charge." Such law, the Supreme Court held, "goes far beyond any correct view of the purpose of an inspection law. . . . It may safely be said that these are matters incapable of being satisfactorily ascertained by inspection." [238]

107

PROHIBITORY LAWS Under its quarantine power, we have seen, a state may exclude commerce which may introduce or spread contagion or some comparable injury within its borders. Does state authority extend to the prohibition of other articles of commerce from being brought and sold within its territory?

The basic rule with regard to state prohibitory power outside the quarantine field was laid down in 1888 and 1890 in two cases involving the application of state prohibition laws to liquors brought from beyond the state. In *Bowman v. Chicago and Northwestern Railway Co.*,[239] the highest Court ruled that, so long as the Congress remains silent on the matter, a state may not prohibit the entrance of liquors from another state, even as part of its general law prohibiting all traffic in intoxicants. This decision was soon followed by that in *Leisy v. Hardin*,[240] holding that a state may not forbid the first sale of liquor still in the original package shipped in from a sister state. The Court distinguished the quarantine cases on the ground that, in them, state power was exerted to prevent the spread of disease, pestilence, and death. Articles which are infected are not entitled to the protection of the Commerce Clause. The same is not true of liquor which the Court treated as a "legitimate subject of trade and commerce." [241]

If, for the purposes of the Commerce Clause, liquor is treated as a legitimate article of commerce, whose importation and sale cannot be prohibited by a state, the same should be true of other articles of commerce as well, provided only that the articles themselves are not deleterious in the sense that they may properly be made the subjects of quarantine laws. The immunity conferred on liquors by the cases discussed has been expressly held to cover cigarettes [242] and unadulterated oleomargarine.[243] These, too, were recognized as lawful articles of commerce which could not be wholly excluded from importation into a state or prevented from being sold while in their original packages.

The rule that, outside the quarantine field, the states have no power to prohibit the importation or sale of products from a sister state did, however, receive an important qualification in *Plumley v. Massachusetts*.[244] In that case, the Supreme Court held that a state law forbidding the sale of oleomargarine colored to look like butter could validly be applied to margarine brought in from another state while it was still in its original package. The basic justification for the decision was the fact that the statute at issue sought to suppress false pretenses and promote fair dealing in the sale of an article of food. All it did was to compel the sale of oleomargarine for what it really was by preventing its sale for what it was not.[245]

Under the *Plumley* decision, the Commerce Clause does not require recognition of a right to practice a deception upon the public. The Constitution, declared the *Plumley* opinion, does not leave a state "powerless to prevent the sale of articles manufactured in or brought from another state, and subjects of traffic and commerce, if their sale may cheat the people into purchasing something they do not intend to buy and which is wholly different from what its condition and appearance import." [246] It was said to partake of the nature of fraud to sell margarine colored to look like butter and the Commerce Clause does not protect fraud.

It may perhaps appear unwarranted to assume that a state has greater power to prevent fraud than to prevent the evils flowing from liquor consumption. At the same time, *Leisy v. Hardin,* as compared with *Plumley v. Massachusetts,* does indicate that such is at present the prevailing doctrine. The states may not exclude legitimate articles of commerce—at least those which are what they appear to be, unless they are of such a nature as to come within the quarantine power. But they may exercise their prohibitory power to protect their citizens against fraud, just as they can do so to shield them against contagion.

It is, at the same time, basic that, just as a quarantine law must have the protection of public health as its purpose, so must the authority recognized by the *Plumley* case be limited to the suppression of practices which do, in fact, constitute fraud or deception upon the public. In *Collins v. New Hampshire,*[247] the state law involved prohibited the sale of oleomargarine unless it was colored pink. Such law, said the high Court, was not aimed at the prevention of deception in the sale of margarine. In actual effect, indeed, the purpose of the law was to suppress the sale of a wholesome article of food in its natural state. As the Court put it, "To color the substance as provided for in the statute naturally excites a prejudice and strengthens a repugnance up to the point of a positive and absolute refusal to purchase the article at any price." [248] The permission to sell, accompanied by the imposition of a condition which would effectually prevent any sale, amounted to a virtual prohibition against unadulterated oleomargarine.

Analysis of the statute at issue in *Collins v. New Hampshire* indicates that its true purpose was, not to guard the public from deceptive practices, but to protect the local dairy industry from competition. Such purpose cannot justify exertion by the state of prohibitory power over interstate commerce. The leading case so holding is *Baldwin v. Seelig.*[249] At issue in it was application of the New York law fixing minimum prices for milk sold in the state to a dealer who had bought milk in Vermont for resale in New York. Because the dealer paid less to the Vermont producers than was required under the New York law, New York refused to grant him a license to sell the milk within its borders. This, the Supreme Court held, it could not do consistently with the Commerce Clause.

In the *Baldwin* case, New York was, in effect, prohibiting sales of the Vermont milk to protect its locally produced milk against competition from out-of-state milk. One state cannot so promote its own economic welfare by establishing barriers against competition with the products of other states. "If New York," states *Baldwin,* "in order to promote the economic welfare of her farmers, may guard them against competition with the cheaper prices of Vermont, the door has been opened to rivalries and reprisals that were meant to be averted by subjecting commerce between the states to the power of the nation." [250] The states may exercise prohibitory authority against outside products to curb fraud or exterminate disease. What they may not do is to exercise such power to neutralize the economic consequences of free trade among the states.

108

EMBARGO MEASURES What has been said in sections 105–107 on state power to prohibit importation and sale of articles of commerce applies, generally speaking, as well to state embargo measures forbidding the shipment of such articles outside the state. Thus, a state may exercise its quarantine power to bar shipment beyond its borders of articles which present a health hazard. An illustrative case involved a law prohibiting the transportation in the state of large dead animals (not slaughtered for food). Under the law, the bodies of such animals had to be disposed of within twenty-four hours. The Supreme Court upheld such law as applied to an individual seeking to transport a dead horse to another state. "It seems plain enough," said the Court, "that the challenged statute is a sanitary and health measure." [251]

A comparable case is *Sligh v. Kirkwood*,[252] which concerned a Florida law making it unlawful to ship out of the state any citrus fruits which were immature or otherwise unfit for consumption. Such law was sustained as a legitimate exercise of state authority. Since the fruits involved were unfit for consumption, they could be made the subjects of a quarantine-type measure forbidding their export as deleterious to the public health. But the Court went further and implied that Florida could bar the shipment beyond its borders of immature fruit to preserve the reputation of Florida fruit: "We may take judicial notice of the fact that the raising of citrus fruits is one of the great industries of the state of Florida. It was competent for the legislature to find that it was essential for the success of that industry that its reputation be preserved in other states wherein such fruits find their most extensive market." [253] Florida may, in other words, keep green oranges at home in order to maintain the good name of Florida oranges.

So far as the Supreme Court's reasoning in this respect implies that the state may use its embargo power to protect purely local economic interests, it is contrary to *Baldwin v. Seelig,* dealt with at the end of the last section. Yet the *Sligh v. Kirkwood* approach may be justified if the Florida law be treated as one directed against deceptive practices, of the type discussed in the prior section. To sell citrus fruits which are not ripe is to commit a fraud upon the public. The states can proceed against fraud through the embargo power just as they can through the authority to prohibit importation and sale.

It is not, however, accurate to assume that the embargo power of the states is limited to the prevention of fraud and contagion. In *Geer v.*

Connecticut,[254] the challenged law forbade the shipment out of the state of game killed within the state. Such law was sustained on the ground that the state itself has a peculiar property right in its wildlife. Game within a state is not, until reduced to possession, private property, but belongs to the state itself. Such game is a natural resource which is held by the state in trust for its people. "The common ownership," the *Geer* opinion declares, "imports the right to keep the property, if the sovereign so chooses, always within its jurisdiction." [255] The Commerce Clause does not prevent the state from prohibiting the export of such resources "which belongs in common to all the people of the state, which can only become the subject of ownership in a qualified way, and which can never be the object of commerce except with the consent of the state." [256]

The principle of *Geer v. Connecticut* has been applied in cases involving the conservation of other natural resources. In *Hudson County Water Co. v. McCarter*,[257] New Jersey, reciting the need of preserving the fresh water of the state for the health and welfare of its citizens, had enacted a prohibition against transporting any water out of its streams or lakes into any other state for use therein. The high Court upheld such enactment, Justice Holmes stating simply that the case was covered in this respect by *Geer v. Connecticut*.

Justice Holmes was of the same opinion in *Pennsylvania v. West Virginia*,[258] which involved a law forbidding the transport of natural gas beyond the borders of the state until the reasonable requirements of the people of the state were satisfied. In this case, nevertheless, Justice Holmes spoke in dissent. The majority of the Court held that the *Geer* principle did not apply to an embargo on natural gas. Natural gas, said the majority, unlike game, is a wholly privately owned resource: "Gas, when reduced to possession, is a commodity; it belongs to the owner of the land." [259]

From a strictly logical point of view, the Supreme Court's attempt to remove natural gas from the *Geer v. Connecticut* principle is not very satisfactory. Game and water, too, when reduced to possession, become objects of individual property. Far more pertinent is the effect which embargoes on resources like gas can have. If West Virginia can embargo the export of gas, the same may be done by other states with regard to their resources. As the Court puts it, "Pennsylvania might keep its coal, the Northwest its timber, the mining states their minerals. And why may not the products of the field be brought within the principle?" [260] *Geer v. Connecticut* and the *Hudson County* case should be restricted to their facts. Otherwise, the danger referred to might become a reality. Embargo would be met with embargo and commerce among the states might all but dry up.

109

DISCRIMINATORY
LAWS

The discussion in the prior sections has dealt with the possession by the states of authority over commerce where the state laws involved have operated equally on both interstate and local commerce. As we have seen, the states do possess substantial regulatory power, at least where the Congress has been silent on the subject, where the statutes at issue subject the stranger from afar to no greater burden than the dweller within the gates.[261] The picture is completely changed when state power is employed to discriminate against interstate commerce.

If one bears in mind the primary purpose of the Commerce Clause, it must, at the least, absolutely prohibit the states from using their regulatory authority to eliminate competition from out of state or to discriminate against such competition. "The commerce clause," the high bench has affirmed, "by its own force, prohibits discrimination against interstate commerce, whatever its form or method, and the decisions of this Court have recognized that there is scope for its like operation when state legislation nominally of local concern is in point of fact aimed at interstate commerce, or by its necessary operation is a means of gaining a local benefit by throwing the attendant burdens on those without the state." [262] The Commerce Clause unqualifiedly bars the states from obtaining for those within an advantage at the expense of those without.

The principle just stated is simple to apply when a state law patently discriminates against interstate commerce. Thus, as we have seen, the states may impose license requirements upon certain persons engaged in interstate commerce, as, for example, interstate motor carriers.[263] On the other hand, when the state requires a license and fee only from nonresidents or from those bringing in articles from outside the state, it is obviously discriminating against interstate commerce and its action contravenes the Commerce Clause. In important early cases, the high Court condemned state laws requiring nonresident merchants to obtain licenses to sell out-of-state products [264] or sewing machines.[265] More recently, it reached the same result with regard to a Florida statute which required the inspection of all cement imported into the state and the payment of a substantial fee therefor,[266] when domestic cement was rendered immune from such inspection and its attendant fee. According to the Court, this was a "transparent discrimination in the imposition of heavy inspection fees as between imported and domestic cement" which could not be sustained.[267]

Cases involving such manifest discriminations against interstate commerce are, as has been indicated, not difficult to deal with. But the states are normally not so artless as to avow such obviously unseemly uses of authority. When a state employs its regulatory power for an improper purpose (such as discrimination against interstate commerce), it is not so naïve as to admit it. Instead, it disguises the true motives of its action and seeks to put forth some legal pretext (e.g., that its action is based upon the need for highway safety or to protect its inhabitants against infected meat). The Supreme Court must then unmask the ruse—not always a simple matter.

The leading case concerning a state law of the kind just referred to is *Minnesota v. Barber*.[268] The statute at issue there prohibited the sale in the state of any meat unless the animal from which it was taken had been inspected within twenty-four hours before slaughter by an inspector within the state. Such law, the high Court held, was void as discriminatory against interstate commerce. Its necessary effect was to exclude from the state's market all meat—though entirely sound, healthy, and fit for human food —taken from animals slaughtered in other states and to restrict the slaughtering of animals whose meat was to be sold in the state to those engaged in that business in the state. The effect, in other words, was all but to prohibit sales in the state of meat not slaughtered within its limits. As *Minnesota v. Barber* characterizes it, "If this legislation does not make such discrimination against the products and business of other states in favor of the products and business of Minnesota as interferes with and burdens commerce among the several states, it would be difficult to enact legislation that would have that result." [269]

In *Minnesota v. Barber,* the state had ostensibly exercised its inspection power to protect the health of its citizens. Its underlying purpose, however, was to give an economic advantage to its own slaughterers, at the expense of those in other states.

Dean Milk Co. v. Madison [270] is another case where the Supreme Court found that a similar economic motive underlay a local inspection requirement. The decision there invalidated a Madison, Wisconsin, ordinance which made it unlawful to sell milk within the city unless it was pasteurized and bottled within five miles from the center of town. This excluded milk from plaintiff's pasteurization plants in Illinois, some sixty-five and eighty-five miles away. According to the Court, such ordinance discriminated against interstate commerce as effectively as the law condemned in *Minnesota v. Barber*. This regulation, said Justice Clark, "in practical effect excludes from distribution in Madison wholesome milk produced and pasteurized in Illinois." [271] In such circumstances, the ordinance was not valid simply because it professed to be a health measure.

In the *Dean Milk* case, the city was erecting an economic barrier protecting a local industry against competition from without the state. To permit it to do this, where the regulation was not essential for local health, declared the *Dean Milk* opinion, "would invite a multiplication of preferential trade areas destructive of the very purpose of the Commerce Clause." [272]

The *Dean Milk* principle applies whenever a state seeks to favor home industry against out-of-state competition. Hence, as we saw in *Buck v. Kuykendall*,[273] a state may not use its authority to license motor carriers to deny a license to an interstate trucker on the ground that its market was already adequately served. In such case, the state was employing its licensing power to effect a ban on out-of-state competition.

A case in which the Supreme Court divided sharply with regard to possible discrimination against interstate commerce is *Hood & Sons v. DuMond*.[274] New York there had refused a license to a Massachusetts milk distributor to open an additional receiving plant in eastern New York from which milk would be shipped to the Boston market. New York had acted on the ground that the further diversion of milk to Massachusetts would deprive the local market of a needed supply; this, in turn, "would tend to a destructive competition in a market already adequately served."

The high Court, by a bare majority, held that New York could not thus, to protect its local market, shut its doors to one who would buy its products for shipment to another state. To protect health and safety is one thing; to prevent competition, even though destructive, is quite another. For a state to retard, burden, or constrict the flow of interstate commerce for its own economic advantage is for it to do violence to the Commerce Clause. Under it, the states are not separable economic units which can protect their own inhabitants from outside competition. As explained by Justice Clark in a later case: "The vice in the regulation invalidated by Hood was . . . that it denied facilities to a company in interstate commerce on the articulated ground that such facilities would divert milk supplies needed by local consumers; in other words, the regulation discriminated against interstate commerce." [275]

110

CONGRESSIONAL   Thus far in this chapter, we have been dealing with
CONSENT   cases involving the validity of state regulatory au-
                     thority where there has been no federal law on the
subject. Where the Congress is silent, we have seen, the existence of state power depends primarily on the application of the test laid down in *Cooley v. Board of Port Wardens*.[276] On the other hand, when the Congress does speak with regard to a particular subject of regulation, the legal situation becomes an entirely different one.

In the first place, there is the question of Congressional consent to state action which would otherwise be invalid under the Commerce Clause. This question was first asked in the *Cooley* case itself. Justice Curtis there denied that Congressional consent could validate a state law which infringed upon the Commerce Clause. As he put it, "If the Constitution excluded the States from making any law regulating commerce, certainly Congress cannot regrant, or in any manner reconvey to the States that power." [277]

From a strictly logical point of view, the *Cooley* answer to the question of Congressional consent appears unassailable. Under *Cooley,* as the prior discussion of it has shown, the national commerce power is, in effect, divided into two parts, one of which is exclusive of any similar state power, and the other of which is not. Where national power is exclusive, the Commerce Clause is *pro tanto* a prohibition against state action. How can the Congress permit the states to exercise powers that the Constitution itself denies to them?

Despite the apparent persuasiveness of the *Cooley* reasoning in this respect, later cases have settled that the Congress can authorize state action that would otherwise be held invalid under the Commerce Clause. Congressional power in this respect was first employed to permit state laws prohibiting the sale of liquor. Under *Leisy v. Hardin,*[278] we saw, the states may not prohibit the sale in the original package of liquor shipped in from another state. In its opinion there, the Supreme Court declared that the states may not exclude such articles from commerce "in the absence of Congressional permission." [279]

The clear implication in the statement just quoted was that the state prohibition law ruled invalid in *Leisy* might be legitimized by Congressional assent. The Congress took advantage of the dictum to this effect by enacting the Wilson Act several months after the *Leisy* decision. That law permitted state prohibition laws to apply to sales of imported liquors still in their original packages "to the same extent as though such . . . liquors had been produced in such state." The Wilson Act was quickly upheld in *In re Rahrer,*[280] the high Court stating that there was no reason why the Congress could not permit imported articles to fall at once within local jurisdiction.

The Congress then went further and passed the Webb-Kenyon Act of 1913 which prohibited the importation of liquor into any state if intended to be received, possessed, sold, or used in violation of its laws. This law, too, was ruled to be within Congressional power. To the Supreme Court, if the Wilson Act was valid, so was the later statute, since "it was enacted simply to extend that which was done by the Wilson Act; that is to say, its purpose was to prevent the immunity characteristic of interstate commerce from being used to permit the receipt of liquor through such commerce in states contrary to their laws, and thus in effect afford a means by subterfuge and indirection to set such laws at naught." [281] The Congress could establish a regulation making it impossible for one state to violate the prohibition of the laws of another through the channels of interstate commerce.

The decisions sustaining the Wilson and Webb-Kenyon Acts gave to state regulatory power a scope previously denied to it on the basis of the Commerce Clause. And the same has been true of Congressional legislation patterned upon those statutes enacted to give effect to state laws which prohibited the sale or use of convict-made goods. Such laws were also upheld, on the theory that the Congress could, as in the liquor cases, act to aid the enforcement of state prohibitory laws.[282]

But what of the logical objection raised in the *Cooley* case [283] against the power of the Congress to permit the states to exercise powers forbidden them by the Constitution? As it was asked in 1947 by Justice Rutledge: "If the commerce clause itself forbids state action 'by its own force,' how is it that Congress by expressly consenting can give that action validity?" [284]

The Supreme Court was squarely confronted with this question in *Prudential Insurance Co. v. Benjamin*.[285] In the 1944 case of *United States v. South-Eastern Underwriters Association*,[286] the Court had held that insurance was commerce subject to federal regulatory power. Less than a year later, the Congress enacted a statute expressly subjecting the business of insurance to state regulatory laws. In the *Prudential Insurance* case, this law was challenged on the ground that the Congress could not validly impose any regulation forbidden by the Commerce Clause. In this view, the limits of state power to regulate commerce in the absence of affirmative action by Congress could not be extended by permissive Congressional legislation.

According to the *Prudential Insurance* opinion, such a view must be rejected as contrary to the great weight of decided authority. In the Court's words, "Whenever Congress' judgment has been uttered affirmatively to contradict the Court's previously expressed view that specific action taken by the states in Congress' silence was forbidden by the commerce clause, this body has accommodated its previous judgment to Congress' expressed approval." [287] For the Court to do otherwise than give effect to such approval "would produce intolerable consequences for restricting Congress' power." [288]

It must be admitted that *Prudential Insurance* does not really answer the logical objection to allowing the Congress to legitimize an otherwise unconstitutional exertion of state power over commerce. At the same time, it is clear, under *Prudential* and the other cases discussed in this section, that Congressional consent can impart validity to a state law regulating commerce. "There is no longer any question," the high bench has said, "that Congress can redefine the areas of local and national predomi-

nance . . . , despite theoretical inconsistency with the rationale of the
Commerce Clause . . . as a limitation in its own right. The words of the
Clause—a grant of power—admit of no other result." [289]

The sentence last quoted may furnish a way out of the logical dilemma
posed by the apparent overriding of the Constitution involved in Congressional legitimization of state laws which would otherwise contravene the
Commerce Clause. That clause itself, it must not be forgotten, is primarily
an affirmative grant to the Congress of the power to regulate interstate
commerce. The power to regulate, following Marshall's famous definition,[290]
is the power to prescribe the rule by which commerce is to be governed.
Such power should include the authority to prescribe that commerce shall
be governed by relevant state regulations. Thus, the dilemma is only apparent, not real.[291]

Looked at as an affirmative grant of power, the Commerce Clause gives
to the Congress authority to consent to state laws governing commerce.
"Congress," the Supreme Court has said, "has undoubted power to redefine
the distribution of power over interstate commerce. It may . . . permit
the states to regulate the commerce in a manner which would otherwise not
be permissible." [292] The negative aspect of the Commerce Clause is not an
absolute prohibition of state power over commerce that is national in character, but only a qualified one.[293] The *Cooley* rule prohibits the states from
regulating, where national uniformity is required—but only until the Congress sees fit to lift such prohibition.

111

CONGRESSIONAL   The overriding power of the Congress over com-
CONFLICT   merce is not, however, limited to the cases dis-
                  cussed in the prior section involving Congressional
consent to otherwise invalid state action. The Congress may not only ex-
pand, it may also contract the area of permissible state action. It may, in
Chief Justice Stone's words, "exclude state regulation even of matters of
peculiarly local concern which nevertheless affect interstate commerce." [294]

If the Congress does act so as to exclude state regulation in a particular
area, its intent in this respect must be given effect. A valid Congressional
provision in the matter is the supreme law of the land and any state law incompatible with such Congressional act must necessarily fall. The difficult
question is, of course, to determine whether there is any incompatibility
in a given case. This is not so much a question of constitutional law as it is
one of statutory interpretation, since the answer in any case depends upon
the intent of the Congress in enacting a law operating in the same field as a
state regulation.

As is true of legislation in general, Congressional intent on the compatibility between its laws and state statutes must be determined by the courts and ultimately by the highest bench. The Supreme Court's decisions in this area, while not strictly on points of constitutional law, are nevertheless of cardinal consequence to the practical working of our federalism. In an era of ever-expanding federal authority, when the Court denies few, if any, powers over commerce to the Congress, the extent to which it interprets Congressional authority as compatible with similar power in the states will be vital in determining what authority the states may still legitimately exercise.

The cases involving Congressional action in an area where state regulation also exists fall into three categories: 1) where there is a conflict between the federal and state legislation; 2) where the Congress has acted so as to take over the entire field of regulation; and 3) where the federal and state laws are found to be compatible. Of course, we are dealing in this section with cases which, under the *Cooley* test,[295] would fall within the scope of state power in the absence of any federal law on the subject. If, on the contrary, the subject is such that national uniformity of regulation is required, the states are, under *Cooley,* precluded from exercising any regulatory authority over such subject—and that regardless of whether there is any federal regulatory law on the subject.

The easiest situation to deal with is that of direct conflict between the provisions of federal and state laws regulating commerce. In such a situation, the principle of national supremacy must be invoked, and the state statute must give way. Thus, a state law is unenforceable which penalizes a railroad for refusal to accept freight for interstate shipment where to accept it would involve a violation of the Interstate Commerce Act.[296] Similarly, a state statute which authorized railroads to accept advertising in payment of interstate transportation was found to conflict with the prohibition by the Congress of the acceptance of anything but money in payment for transportation.[297]

The basic principle in such cases of direct conflict is that articulated in 1859: "When, therefore, an act of the legislature of a state prescribes a regulation of the subject repugnant to and inconsistent with the regulation of Congress, the state law must give way; and this, without regard to the source of power whence the state legislature derived its enactment." [298] This, the highest Court has said, results as well from the nature of the government as from the words of the Constitution.[299]

Even if there is no direct and positive conflict between the provisions of federal and state regulatory laws on a particular subject, the latter may still have to fall. Such is the case when the Congress has acted with an intent to take over the field of regulation. When Congress does act to appropriate the entire field, it leaves no room for any supplementary state action. In such a case, Congress has spoken so as to silence the states—has acted so as to bar any state regulation at all in the given field. "When Congress has taken the particular subject-matter in hand," the highest Court has affirmed, "coincidence is as ineffective as opposition, and a state law is not to be declared a help because it attempts to go farther than Congress has seen fit to go." [300]

Whether the Congress has, in a particular law, legislated so as to take over an entire field of regulation is a question to be determined from all the facts and circumstances. As the Supreme Court has put it: "the fate of State legislation in these cases has not been determined by . . . generalities but by the weight of the circumstances and the practical and experienced judgment." [301] In the absence of any mechanical test, the high Court must determine Congressional intent by accommodating the competing demands of the state and national interests involved.[302]

If there is one thing to be noted in the recent decisions on the subject under discussion, it is an overreadiness on the part of the Supreme Court to find that the Congress has acted to take over a regulatory field, with the result that all state regulation in that field is precluded.[303] One may wonder whether the judicial tendency in this respect is justified. Unless Congress expressly manifests an intent to occupy an entire field of regulation, the Court should be most reluctant to sweep the boards of state power. It should not be overlooked that a judicial decision invalidating state authority can have only a negative effect. The high Court can take away power from the states, but is unable to ensure its exercise by the Federal Government.[304] The result may well be a gap in governmental authority—a "no man's land" of regulation—which had previously been filled by state law. Laissez faire, in effect, is introduced outside the provisions of the federal statute concerned.

It is one thing for a state statute to be stricken down as incompatible with an act of Congress where there is direct and positive repugnance, so that the two laws cannot be reconciled or consistently stand together. It is quite another for the Supreme Court to nullify state action, where the state could otherwise clearly regulate, by resort to a metaphor—"occupied the field." [305]

The starting point in these cases should be, not judicial suspicion, but respect for an allowable area of state law, in a field where, under the *Cooley* test,[306] national uniformity of regulation is not demanded. The high bench should not lightly infer that the Congress, by the mere passage of a statute, has impaired the traditional authority of the states.[307] "Since Congress can," said Justice Frankfurter in a 1947 dissent, "if it chooses, entirely displace the States to the full extent of the far-reaching Commerce Clause, Congress needs no help from generous judicial implications to achieve the super-

session of State authority. To construe federal legislation so as not needlessly to forbid preexisting State authority is to respect our federal system.
Any indulgence in construction should be in favor of the States, because
Congress can speak with drastic clarity whenever it chooses to assure full
federal authority, completely displacing the States." [308]

112

TAXATION OF
FOREIGN
COMMERCE:
BROWN V.
MARYLAND

The prior portions of this chapter have dealt with
the power of the states to regulate interstate and
foreign commerce. The Commerce Clause, we saw,
has a negative aspect which precludes state regulation—at least in those areas where national uniformity is deemed essential. But state power over
commerce is not limited to regulation. At least as important in the arsenal
of state authority is the taxing power.

If there were no Constitution, the states would, of course, possess the
same taxing power over interstate and foreign commerce as over commerce carried on wholly within their borders. Such was, in fact, the situation under the Articles of Confederation, and its inadequacies led directly
to the drawing up of the present organic instrument. The Constitution was
intended to make of us one undivided economic aggregation, and not a
collection of parasitic states preying upon each other's commerce.[309] The
taxing power which the states had previously exercised over interstate and
foreign commerce was drastically restricted by the document drawn up
in 1787.

In dealing with the taxing power of the states, we must distinguish between interstate commerce, on the one hand, and foreign commerce, on
the other. Insofar as the former is concerned, as we shall see,[310] the Constitution left a permissive area of taxation to the states. But, in dealing
with foreign commerce, the basic document left no such leeway. Both the
Commerce Clause and the Import-Export Clause withdraw from the states
their taxing power over foreign trade.[311]

The Import-Export Clause, to which reference has just been made, provides that "No state shall, without the consent of Congress, lay any Imposts or Duties on Imports or Exports, except what may be absolutely
necessary for executing its inspection Laws." This language completely bars
the states from exercising taxing authority over foreign commerce, except
to the limited extent mentioned in connection with inspection laws.[312] In
Justice Frankfurter's words, "It rigorously confined the States to what
might be 'absolutely necessary,' the only constitutional permission in terms
so drastically limited, and beyond this permission of what is 'absolutely

necessary' state action was barred except by consent of Congress as expressive of the national interest." [313]

The seminal decision on state taxation of foreign commerce is *Brown v. Maryland* (1827).[314] At issue in it was a state law requiring "all importers of foreign articles or commodities" to take out a license, for which they had to pay fifty dollars, before they could sell such goods. Such a statute furnished the Supreme Court with a ready opportunity for curbing state taxation discriminating against interstate and foreign commerce, for the license fee exacted from wholesalers of imported goods was required of them alone. But Chief Justice Marshall, who delivered the landmark opinion, chose to wrest from the case more far-reaching constitutional doctrine.[315] He dealt with the case as if the tax were a nondiscriminatory measure imposed on all wholesaling of goods, of whatever origin. Even such a general tax, as applied to the sale of imports, he held, conflicted with the Constitution.

The state had argued that its tax was a mere occupational tax, not a forbidden tax on imports. Marshall, however, rejected this contention. As he saw it, "No goods would be imported if none could be sold. No object of any description can be accomplished by laying a duty on importation, which may not be accomplished with equal certainty by laying a duty on the importer." [316] The tax on the importer was consequently treated like a tax on the imports themselves. As such, it contravened both the Import-Export Clause and the Commerce Clause.

As thus stated, the rule of *Brown v. Maryland* is comparatively simple: The Constitution absolutely prohibits the states from levying a tax upon imports. And a tax on the business of importing falls within the bar in question. Since the object of importation in *Brown* had been sale, the importer was entitled to realize that aim without being subject to state taxation.[317]

Brown v. Maryland precludes the states from subjecting imports to even a general nondiscriminatory tax. This raises the further question of how long imported goods retain their immunity from state taxation. This question, too, was discussed by Marshall in *Brown v. Maryland*. As he put it there: "there must be a point of time when the prohibition ceases, and the power of the state to tax commences." [318] This point of time occurs when the goods no longer retain their status as imports.

In words grown familiar with judicial repetition, yet fully deserving of quotation here, the great Chief Justice, in his *Brown* opinion, stated the guide for determining when imported goods cease to be imports, so that state taxing power can begin to be exerted over them: "It is sufficient for the present to say, generally, that when the importer has so acted upon the thing imported, that it has become incorporated and mixed up with the mass of property in the country, it has, perhaps, lost its distinctive character as an import, and has become subject to the taxing power of the State; but while remaining the property of the importer, in his warehouse, in the original form or package in which it was imported, a tax upon it is too plainly a duty on imports to escape the prohibition in the constitution." [319]

Under *Brown v. Maryland,* imports are immune from state taxation just so long as they keep their status as imports. When they have become part of the general mass of property within the state, state taxes are no longer barred. Only while in the hands of the importer in its original form or package does the foreign good remain an import and hence free from state levies.

113

SAME: PURPOSE   The original-package doctrine laid down in *Brown*
OF IMPORTATION   *v. Maryland* has served as the basic formula to de-
                   termine when state taxing power may be exerted
over goods imported from foreign countries. For almost a century and a half since Marshall's memorable opinion, the highest tribunal has held that a state may not tax imports from abroad while retained by the importer in their original package or form prior to their sale.[320]

Marshall's successor, Roger B. Taney, had been the counsel for the state in *Brown v. Maryland,* and had, as such, argued against the view which the Supreme Court followed. Twenty years later, sitting at the head of the highest bench, Taney acknowledged that "further and mature reflection" had convinced him of the correctness of the principles laid down by his predecessor.[321] "Indeed," said Chief Justice Taney, "goods imported, while they remain in the hands of the importer, in the form and shape in which they were brought into the country, can in no just sense be regarded as a part of that mass of property in the State usually taxed for the support of the State government." [322] It was Taney, in truth, who took Marshall's more or less tentative suggestion as to the proper rule on the subject and stated it as binding positive law.

The consistency with which the high tribunal has repeated and applied the formulas of Marshall and Taney in this respect has been notable. In the 1945 words of Chief Justice Stone, "from that day to this, this Court has held, without a dissenting voice, that things imported are imports entitled to the immunity conferred by the Constitution; that that immunity survives their arrival in this country, and continues until they are sold, [or] removed from the original package." [323]

The statement just quoted was made in *Hooven & Allison Co. v.*

Evatt.[324] At issue in it was a state tax assessed on bales of hemp and other fibers imported by a rope manufacturer and stored in its warehouse in their original packages pending their use in manufacturing. The Supreme Court ruled that such imports, held in the factory for processing, were entitled to the protection of the original-package doctrine. "We do not perceive," reads the opinion, "upon what grounds it can be thought that imports for manufacture lose their character as imports any sooner or more readily than imports for sale." [325]

In *Brown v. Maryland,* Marshall had rejected the claim that to grant immunity there would mean that an "importer may bring in goods, as plate, for his own use, and thus retain much valuable property exempt from taxation." [326] In *Hooven & Allison,* on the other hand, the high Court held that the question of immunity was not affected by the purpose of the particular importation. The importer who brought in goods for use in his own manufacturing processes was given the same exemption from state taxation as one who imported for the purpose of sale. Under *Hooven & Allison,* goods imported for *use* share the same immunity as goods imported for *sale.*

A 1959 case, however, indicates that the *Hooven & Allison* holding in this respect is no longer accepted Supreme-Court doctrine. *Youngstown Sheet and Tube Co. v. Bowers* [327] involved a manufacturer of iron and steel, which imported iron ores for use in its plant. Such imported ores were kept apart in storage facilities in the form and shape in which they were brought into the country, until they were actually used in manufacturing. The state in which the plant concerned was located assessed a tax based on the value of the iron ores while they were in storage. The manufacturer contended that the ores had not lost their character as imports and were therefore immune from state taxation.

The Supreme Court rejected this contention, holding that the manufacturer had "so acted upon the materials which they have imported for use in their manufacturing operations as to cause them to lose their distinctive character as 'imports' within the meaning of that term as used in the Import-Export Clause." [328] Though the Court, in its *Youngstown* opinion, expressly disclaimed the intent to overrule *Hooven & Allison Co. v. Evatt,* its decision appears directly contrary to the holding in that case. The holding and approach in *Youngstown,* indeed, are basically similar to those urged by the principal dissenting opinion in *Hooven & Allison* itself.[329]

Youngstown really rejects the *Hooven & Allison* view that the purpose of the particular importation is irrelevant in determining whether goods imported are immune from state taxation. What the high Court did in *Youngstown* was to draw a clear distinction between goods imported for "sale" and goods imported for "use." Only the former are to be protected by the original-package doctrine. The latter are not to share the same immunity. When they are retained by the importer for the purpose for which they were imported, their tax exemption is at an end, even though they are still in their original package or form.

The *Youngstown* holding in this respect appears preferable to that rendered in the *Hooven & Allison* case. The constitutional ban against state taxation of imports, the *Youngstown* opinion informs us, was intended to prevent " '[t]he great importing States [from laying] a tax on the non-importing States,' to which the imported property is or might ultimately be destined, which would not only discriminate against them but also 'would necessarily produce countervailing measures on the part of those States whose situation was less favourable to importation.' " [330] But it hardly requires discrimination in favor of goods imported from other countries. Under *Youngstown,* the Constitution does not require that foreign products purchased for use of the importer be given what amounts to a tax subsidy at the expense of the particular state affected.[331] In such a case, the foreign products should, in *Youngstown's* words, be "subject to taxation just like domestic property that was kept at the same place in the same way for the same use. We cannot impute to the Framers of the Constitution a purpose to make such a discrimination in favor of materials imported from other countries as would result if we approved the views pressed upon us by the manufacturers." [332]

114

INTERSTATE COMMERCE AND THE ORIGINAL-PACKAGE DOCTRINE

The original-package doctrine, we have seen in the prior two sections, bars a state from taxing imports from abroad while in the hands of the importer in their original package. Does the same limitation apply to the taxation of goods brought in from other states?

In *Brown v. Maryland* itself, Marshall had indicated his view that the proper answer was affirmative, stating, at the end of his opinion there, "we suppose the principles laid down in this case, apply equally to importations from a sister State." [333] It was not, however, until the 1869 case of *Woodruff v. Parham,*[334] that the highest Court was called upon to determine directly whether the original-package doctrine did prevent the states from taxing "imports" from sister states. The tax at issue in *Woodruff* was imposed by a municipality upon goods sold at auction. It was claimed that such tax could not validly be levied upon such goods as were brought in by the auctioneer from other states and sold by him in the original and unbroken packages. This claim was rejected by the Supreme Court.

According to Justice Miller, who delivered the *Woodruff v. Parham* opinion, *Brown v. Maryland* and the original-package doctrine laid down therein (despite Marshall's "casual remark" [335] to the contrary) apply only to imports from foreign countries—not to articles introduced from one state into another. The word "import," said he, cannot be understood as having reference to other than foreign commerce. No intention existed in the Framers to prohibit the right of one state to tax articles brought into it from another. To hold otherwise, Justice Miller asserts, would lead to the grossest injustice: "The merchant in a town in Massachusetts, who deals only in wholesale, if he purchase his goods in New York, is exempt from taxation. If his neighbor purchase in Boston, he must pay all the tax which Massachusetts levies with equal justice on the property of all the citizens." [336]

Woodruff v. Parham was reaffirmed a decade and a half later in *Brown v. Houston,*[337] where the highest Court held coal from Pennsylvania subject to a general property tax in Louisiana, while still on the flatboats which brought it down the Mississippi to New Orleans. Such coal, having come to the state of destination, could be taxed by such state on the same basis as other property located therein, though still in the "original package" in which it had been "imported." [338]

The distinction between the immunity from state taxation of imports from abroad in original packages and that of articles coming from interstate commerce in original packages has continued basic in our constitutional law. Imports from foreign countries remain exempt from state taxes while in their original packages. Goods brought in from sister states may be taxed upon a nondiscriminatory basis even though, like the coal in *Brown v. Houston,* they are still in the form or package in which they were transported from their state of origin.[339]

In this respect, there is an important difference between the power of the states to tax and their police power over commerce. Under *Leisy v. Hardin,*[340] we saw that a state may not prohibit the first sale in the original package of an article brought in from another state. The original package thus provides protection against police regulations. But the same is not true of a state taxing measure. Goods from sister states are subject to taxation upon arrival at their destination upon the same basis as domestic goods. The distinction in this respect between the police measure, on the one hand, and the taxing measure, on the other, was well pointed out by Chief Justice Taft: "The one plainly interferes with or destroys the commerce, the other merely puts the merchandise on an equality with all other merchandise in the State and constitutes no real hindrance to introducing the merchandise into the State for sale upon the basis of equal competition." [341] In the tax cases, the original package furnishes no immunity.

115

TAXATION OF   We have just seen that the original-package doctrine
INTERSTATE   does not protect articles coming from interstate
COMMERCE: commerce from state taxation. Yet this does not
GENERAL   mean that interstate commerce may be treated by
CONSIDERATIONS   the states upon the same basis as their purely domestic
                    commerce for purposes of taxation. On the contrary,
it is clear that the Commerce Clause, of its own force, furnishes some pro-
tection from state taxation to interstate commerce.

The Commerce Clause, as emphasized at the outset of this chapter, is
both a grant of authority to the Federal Government and a limitation upon
state power. "These principles of limitation on State power," the Supreme
Court has declared, "apply to all State policy no matter what State interest
gives rise to its legislation. A burden on interstate commerce is none the
lighter and no less objectionable because it is imposed by a State under
the taxing power rather than under manifestations of police power in the
conventional sense." [342] The Commerce Clause, of its own force, places
restrictions upon state power to tax, as well as to regulate, interstate commerce.[343]

That the Commerce Clause does limit state power to tax interstate
commerce is a constitutional truism, reaffirmed in a course of adjudication
unbroken since the founding of the Republic. More difficult is it to determine the exact extent to which state taxing power is limited. For it is
settled today, despite some earlier authority to the contrary, that not all
state taxes which fall upon interstate commerce are invalid. As Justice
Rutledge has stated, "The commerce clause was not designed or intended
to outlaw all state taxes bearing 'directly' on interstate commerce. Its
design was only to exclude those having the effects to block or impede it
which called it and the Constitution itself into being." [344] What state taxes
can be said to produce such effects?

The answer to this question in specific cases must not lose sight of the
overriding need to promote the policy which called forth the Commerce
Clause, if not the Constitution itself. With Justice Jackson: "I make no
concealment of and offer no apology for my philosophy that the federal
interstate commerce power should be strongly supported and that the im-
pingement of the states upon that commerce which moves among them
should be restricted to narrow limits." [345]

This philosophy must be the guiding principle in cases involving the
power of the states to tax commerce. Of course, interstate commerce, like
local commerce, benefits from local government and should share with
local commerce the burdens and costs of it. Interstate commerce should
pay its way and should not secure competitive advantage from tax im-

munity denied to local commerce. On the other hand, if we hold an interstate industry subject to the unlimited taxing power of each state in which it does business, we open the door to the destruction of interstate commerce by local efforts to secure revenue. It may be, as the high Court has stated, that the question is "whether the state has given anything for which it can ask return." [346] But that test, too, can be pushed too far—even, indeed, to its *reductio ad absurdum,* as Justice Jackson once showed. In a very real sense, he said, "every State and Territory in the Union has conferred very real benefits upon every inhabitant of the Union. Some States have seen to it that our food is properly produced and inspected; others have fostered and protected the industry upon which we are utterly dependent for the ordinary conveniences of life and for life itself. All of them have yielded up men to provide government at home and to repel the enemy abroad. I am the very real debtor, but am frank enough to say I hope not a potential taxpayer, of all." [347]

If the Commerce Clause means anything, it means that interstate commerce may not be taxed to the full limit by every state through which it passes. Physical power alone cannot be the criterion in a country governed by a Constitution such as ours; might cannot always make right in the field of taxation.[348] Even if interstate commerce should be required to pay its own way, that does not mean that it should be required to do more. If interstate commerce were subject to the full taxing power of each state through which it moved, the interstate trader would be at a tremendous disadvantage compared with local industries. For this to be avoided, the tax situation must be equalized as between interstate and local commerce. The basic goal should be to prevent an interstate transaction from being saddled with an aggregate tax burden higher than it would bear if it had taken place in the same volume and over the same distance within a single one of the pertinent states.[349]

The goal, in other words, should be to place interstate and local commerce, so far as possible, upon a plane of tax equality. Under this approach, any tax which, if applied generally by the states or their subdivisions, would bear more heavily upon interstate commerce than upon like intrastate commerce should be held invalid. On the other hand, any tax which would not bear more heavily upon interstate commerce than upon like intrastate commerce should be sustained.[350]

It is recognized that the decisions of the Supreme Court in this field have, as often as not, been inconsistent with the general principle just stated. Thus, the Court has often condemned all taxes which were said to be imposed "directly" upon interstate commerce, regardless of whether they did, in fact, charge such commerce with a heavier aggregate burden than like local commerce. At the same time, it must be stated candidly

that the high-tribunal decisions on state taxation of commerce have themselves been anything but logically consistent. The Supreme Court itself
has conceded this. In a 1959 case, it animadverted on the "need for clear-
ing up the tangled underbush of past cases" in this field, asserting that
"the decisions have been 'not always clear . . . consistent or reconcil-
able.' " [351]

The California court put the matter even more bluntly in 1914 when,
after referring to different Supreme Court decisions and the opinions delivered therein, it declared: "We are constrained to admit our inability to
harmonize this language and these decisions, though we make haste to add
that undoubtedly the failure must come from our own deficient powers of
perception and ratiocination, and for this deficiency it is no consolation to
us to note that our Brethren of the Supreme Court of Montana are similarly afflicted." [352]

116

GOODS IN
INTERSTATE
TRANSIT

If the Commerce Clause means anything in the tax
field, it must mean that articles may not be taxed by
the states while they are in actual interstate transit.
For, if they could be so taxed by each state through
which they passed, interstate commerce would plainly be subjected to the
selfsame evils which the Constitution was designed to remedy. The burdens
which states, particularly those possessed of safe and commodious harbors,
imposed by way of imposts upon the transit of merchandise through those
ports to their destination for consumption in other states, were the cause,
as much as any one class of grievances, of the very formation of the organic document.[353]

That the states may not tax property in transit in interstate commerce
was settled in 1873 by the *State Freight Tax Case*.[354] At issue in it was a
state statute which required every company transporting freight within the
state to pay a specified tax on each ton of freight carried. The Supreme
Court held the tax in question invalid so far as it applied to freight other
than that taken up and delivered within the state. The state may not, consistently with the Commerce Clause, impose "a tax upon freight taken up
within the state and carried out of it, or taken up outside the state and delivered within it," [355] or in transit through the state, from one sister state
to another. In the words of the Court: "if one state can directly tax persons
or property passing through it, or tax them indirectly by levying a tax
upon their transportation, every other may, and thus commercial intercourse between states remote from each other may be destroyed." [356]

Justice Miller, referring to the principles laid down in the *State Freight
Tax Case,* has declared that they lie at the foundation of the present

Federal Constitution.[357] Those principles, which bar a state from taxing goods that are moving within it in interstate or foreign commerce, have remained basic limitations upon state taxing power. Goods moving in interstate transit may not be shackled by restrictions imposed by any state in order to place on others the burden of supporting its own government, as was done in the days of the Confederation.[358]

The *State Freight Tax* rule naturally gives rise to the question of when particular goods are in interstate transit so as to render them immune from state taxation. The leading case here is *Coe v. Errol*.[359] In it, logs were held taxable in their state of origin while they were piled on the banks of a stream waiting for the spring floods to float them to another state. According to the Court: "such goods do not cease to be part of the general mass of property in the state, subject, as such, to its jurisdiction, and to taxation in the usual way, until they have been shipped, or entered with a common carrier for transportation to another state, or have been started upon such transportation in a continuous route or journey." [360] Immunity from state taxation, in other words, arises only when interstate transit actually begins. It is not enough for the goods concerned to be intended for exportation. They must have been actually launched on their way to another state or committed to a carrier for transportation to such state.

Related to the question answered in *Coe v. Errol* of when interstate transit begins for purposes of tax immunity is that of when such transit ends. The answer here is given by *Woodruff v. Parham* and *Brown v. Houston* already discussed in section 114. When goods shipped in interstate commerce arrive at their destination, their immunity from state taxation terminates. This is true, as we saw, even though such goods are still in their original form or packages [361] or are still contained on the vehicles or vessels in which they were transported.[362] The fact that further interstate shipment is contemplated or actually occurs does not alter this result.[363]

Thus, goods within the state are taxable if their interstate journey has not yet commenced or has ended. They are immune from taxation only while their interstate journey is actually in progress. What happens where there has been a temporary interruption in the interstate transit?

The effect of such interruption depends upon its occasion or purpose.[364] In the already-discussed case of *Coe v. Errol*,[365] the Supreme Court expressed approval of the holding of the state court [366] that logs being floated down a river on a journey between two points in Maine were not taxable in New Hampshire "although detained for a time within the state by low water or other causes of delay." [367] In such a case, where the delay is due to natural causes, the goods are deemed still "in the course of commercial transportation" and hence still entitled to the protection of the Commerce Clause.[368]

The same is true where delay or interruption in interstate transit is due to the necessities of the journey. In *Kelley v. Rhoades*,[369] Wyoming sought to subject to its property tax a flock of sheep being driven through the state from Utah to Nebraska. The journey through Wyoming took six to eight weeks and the sheep were maintained on the way by grazing. Here, too, the high bench held that the sheep were in interstate transit, so as to render them exempt from state taxation. The time consumed was a necessary incident of such a journey. Nor could Wyoming tax on the ground that the transit was interrupted by the grazing on its land. The local facility enjoyed was directly ancillary to the interstate transit.

On the other hand, where the interruption of the interstate movement was designed for the profit and convenience of the owners of the goods concerned and was not a necessary incident to the method of transportation adopted, such interruption has been held sufficient to remove the goods from the channels of interstate commerce and to subject them to the taxing power of the state. An oft-cited case to illustrate state tax authority when such an interruption occurs is *Minnesota v. Blasius*.[370] In it, a tax had been assessed on cattle owned by a livestock dealer at the St. Paul stockyards. The cattle in question had been bought by the dealer upon their arrival at the stockyards from other states and were quickly sold by him to purchasers for reshipment to points outside the state. The dealer contended that the cattle were not subject to the state tax on the ground that they were still in the course of interstate commerce and transit. The Court ruled, however, that the interruption in transit here was sufficient to permit state taxing power to attach. The interruption was not caused by the necessities of the journey. Its purpose was to enable the goods to be dealt with for personal profit, not to facilitate their safe and convenient transit.

117

DRUMMER CASES   In section 114, we saw that the original-package
doctrine does not protect goods imported from sister states. Goods introduced into one state from another enjoy no immunity from taxes levied upon other property, when once their interstate journey has terminated.

On the other hand, those who introduce such goods into a state may still be vested with tax immunity in certain circumstances. The leading case is *Robbins v. Shelby County Taxing District* (1887),[371] which held invalid a license tax to the extent that it sought to tax the occupation of soliciting orders for the purchase of goods to be shipped into the taxing state.[372] The tax in *Robbins* was a flat license fee imposed on all those selling goods by sample in the locality involved. Defendant there was a "drummer" who solicited orders by sample for an out-of-state company, which subsequently delivered the goods ordered to the purchasers in the state. In striking down the tax upon such drummer, the Supreme Court declared that it is not competent for a state to levy a tax upon the inhabitants of other states for selling or seeking to sell their goods in such state before they are introduced therein. According to the *Robbins* opinion: "The negotiation of sales of goods which are in another state, for the purpose of introducing them into the state in which the negotiation is made, is interstate commerce." [373] A tax imposed upon such negotiation is an invalid tax upon interstate commerce itself.

In the most recent of the cases following the *Robbins* decision, the high Court, in explaining its position, stated that "the drummer is a figure representative of a by-gone day. But his modern prototype persists under more euphonious appellations. So endure the basic reasons which brought about his protection from the kind of local favoritism the facts of this case typify." [374]

In actuality, the immune position of the drummer is somewhat of an anachronism in our law. This can be seen if we examine, by way of comparison, the cases involving state taxation of peddlers. The itinerant peddler is certainly, at least as much as the drummer, a figure representative of a bygone day in America and he, too, persists in modern prototype. But the peddler sells from a stock of goods carried for the purpose, unlike the drummer who solicits sales (with or without the exhibition of samples), with the goods sold thereafter to be transported.

The factual distinction just referred to has been the basis for a difference in constitutional treatment as between the drummer and the peddler. *Robbins v. Shelby County Taxing District,* we saw, renders the drummer who solicits for an out-of-state seller immune from local license taxes. The itinerant peddler, by contrast, is vested with no such immunity, though his stock of goods may have been brought in from outside the state.[375] Peddlers are treated only as persons engaged in purely local sales. Even though they bring in their stocks from outside the state, interstate transit is deemed to have ceased for tax purposes. The Supreme Court has consistently sustained state taxation upon itinerant hawkers and peddlers on the ground that the local sale and delivery of goods is an essentially intrastate process whether a retailer operates from a fixed location or from a wagon.[376]

In their effect upon interstate commerce, it may be urged, the tax upon the drummer and that upon the peddler are really essentially alike. In either case, the flat license fee bears no relation to business done or profits earned in the locality. And their cumulative burden, laid in succession upon the itinerant vendor as he passes from town to town, will obviously place such vendor at a disadvantage as compared with the local merchant. "A day here, a day there, five days now and five days a year or several months later, with a flat license tax annually imposed lacking any proportion to the number or length of visits or the volume of the business or return, can only mean" [377] an undue burden on the itinerant seller.

Despite the fact that their positions are thus, in many ways basically similar, the high Court has turned a deaf ear to the claims of itinerant peddlers that they be treated like drummers for purposes of tax immunity.[378] Indeed, at one point, in 1940, the Court implied that the drummer himself might no longer be vested with immunity.[379] In the 1946 case of *Nippert v. Richmond*,[380] however, the Court expressly refused to overrule *Robbins v. Shelby County Taxing District* and the drummer cases following that decision. Instead it struck down a municipal ordinance imposing upon persons soliciting orders for goods an annual license tax of $50 and ½ of 1 per cent of gross earnings in excess of $1,000. More recently, the same result has been reached with regard to a $500 tax laid upon the privilege of soliciting business for out-of-state laundries.[381]

Under the drummer cases, a tax imposed upon the solicitation of interstate business is an invalid tax upon interstate commerce itself. Solicitation itself may not be regarded as a purely local incident which may be carved out from interstate business for tax purposes. On the contrary, as the high Court has put it with regard to door-to-door solicitation of interstate business, "Interstate commerce itself knocks on the local door." [382]

118

SALES TAXES In the drummer cases, just discussed, the Supreme Court, strictly speaking, dealt only with the validity of flat-license taxes imposed on persons soliciting orders for the purchase of goods to be shipped from outside the state. Yet they have always been understood as applying, not merely to such license taxes, but to sales taxes [383] as well. The negotiation of sales prior to interstate transit, said the Court in an already-quoted portion of its *Robbins v. Shelby County Taxing District* opinion, is interstate commerce which "cannot be taxed at all" by the states.[384] From this language developed the established doctrine that no state might tax an interstate sale. As Chief Justice Taft stated, in a case involving the sale of oil to be delivered from another state: "Such transactions are interstate commerce in its essence and any state tax upon it is a regulation of it and a burden upon it." [385]

The tax immunity of interstate sales was, it should be emphasized, limited to sales negotiated prior to interstate transportation of the goods into the purchaser's state for delivery. Under the cases discussed in section 114, taxes may be imposed upon the sale of goods after interstate transportation into the taxing state, whether sold in the original package or not. The opinion in *Robbins v. Shelby County Taxing District* characterized a tax on such a sale as a "very different thing" from one on a sale negotiated prior to interstate transportation.[386]

When the *Robbins* case was decided, the common tax affecting interstate sales was the fixed license fee, of the type at issue in *Robbins,* imposed upon the business of soliciting orders for subsequent delivery. More recently, the general sales tax has been widely adopted as a basic means of obtaining state and local revenue. As already indicated, it was commonly assumed that the *Robbins* doctrine would bar the imposition of such taxes as well upon interstate sales.

During the economic crisis of the 1930's, the immunity thus accorded interstate sales from local taxation began to have serious consequences upon state ability to secure sufficient tax revenue. The great depression led most states to rely heavily on the sales tax to fill their depleted coffers and to attempt to impose such taxes upon interstate as well as local sales.

In its 1940 decision in *McGoldrick v. Berwind-White Coal Mining Co.,* [387] the Supreme Court for the first time sustained a local sales tax imposed upon an interstate sale. The tax in question was laid under the New York City general sales tax law on sales of coal made in New York under a contract calling for shipment of the coal from Pennsylvania to the purchaser in New York. The coal company, relying upon the prior cases already referred to, had urged that a distinction is to be taken between a tax laid on sales made, without previous contract, after the merchandise has crossed the state boundary, and sales, the contracts for which, when made, contemplate or require the transportation of merchandise interstate to the taxing state. According to the Court, however: "we think this distinction is without the support of reason or authority." [388]

Under the *Berwind-White* decision, the state of the buyer may levy a sales tax upon an interstate sale, at least where the sales contract is entered into in such state. That such a break with preexisting jurisprudence was in large part called forth by the need of the states, in a period of economic crisis, to tap all possible sources of revenue, can scarcely be gainsaid. But the decision can also be supported by practical considerations. The basic goal of the Commerce Clause in the tax field, we have seen, is to vest interstate commerce with tax equality, as compared with local commerce. Such goal is plainly violated where, as in the drummer cases,[389] the mere solicitation of interstate business is subjected to a flat license fee in each locality. The same is not true of a tax on an interstate sale by the state of the buyer. Under such a tax, the out-of-state seller can compete upon an equal basis with the local merchant. If his sales are few, the tax will be small; if many, it will be large. The burden is the same on all sales in the state, interstate or local.

To render the interstate sale exempt from all sales taxes would, on the contrary, confer on the extrastate merchant a distinct competitive advantage over his local rival. Such inequality between competing merchants is hardly required by the Constitution. Indeed, to demand such discrimination in the name of the Commerce Clause is to pervert the very purpose of the organic provision.[390]

The sales tax imposed on the interstate sale results in no discrimination only if cumulative taxation upon the interstate transaction is avoided. In dissenting, in the *Berwind-White* case, Chief Justice Hughes asserted that a tax like that sustained there opened the door to multiple taxation. As he stated it, "If New York can tax the delivery, Pennsylvania can tax the shipment and New Jersey the transshipment. And the latter States, respectively, would be as much entitled to tax the gross receipts from the sales as would New York." [391]

The *Berwind-White* decision does not, despite the Hughes animadversion on the matter, really contain within itself the seeds of a system of multiple taxation that would be destructive of interstate commerce. Under *Berwind-White,* the state of the buyer is permitted to tax interstate sales made in the state. This holding does not mean that other states may also tax such sales. Giving the state of the purchaser the right to tax hardly requires that equal right be given to every state which the interstate transaction touches. In *Berwind-White* itself, New Jersey, the state of transshipment, would be barred from taxing under the rule, discussed in section 116, vesting goods in interstate transit with immunity from state taxation. Nor is taxation by the state of the seller necessarily included within the *Berwind-White* rationale. The New York City sales tax in *Berwind-White* was sustained because it made for tax equality as between interstate and local sales. But such equality does not result, except fortuitously, when the sales tax is imposed by the state of the seller. Unless both states happen to have the same sales tax rates, there is bound to be discrimination against either interstate or local commerce.

In *Freeman v. Hewit,*[392] the Supreme Court held that the state of the seller could not impose a sales tax upon an interstate sale. According to the opinion there: "such a tax by the seller State alone must be judged burdensome in the context of the circumstances in which the tax takes effect." [393]

The Court's reasoning in *Freeman v. Hewit* is, it is true, not entirely satisfactory, since it essentially condemned the tax as one on the interstate sale itself—which can, of course, be said with equal justification about the tax by the buyer's state upheld in *Berwind-White.* Yet the result is sound as a practical matter. The evil of sales taxes in interstate sales lies in the possibility that the state at the beginning and the state at the end of the transaction might each levy a tax, while intrastate sales would be subject to but one assessment. This result is avoided if only one of the states concerned is permitted to tax. For the reasons indicated above, the goal of equality for interstate commerce is best realized in this field where the state of the buyer, rather than that of the seller, lays the tax.

As already indicated, the *Berwind-White* decision permits the state of the buyer to impose a sales tax upon an interstate sale, at least where the contract of sale is entered into in such state. An important limitation upon the *Berwind-White* holding was, however, laid down in *McLeod v. Dilworth Co.*[394] In that case, the highest Court ruled that a sales tax could not validly be imposed by Arkansas on sales to its residents, where orders for such sales were accepted in and the goods shipped from Tennessee, with title passing there upon delivery to the carrier. The seller had neither property nor place of business in Arkansas; it used traveling salesman to solicit orders in that state, which were then sent for approval to its home office in Tennessee. In striking down the Arkansas sales tax, the Court distinguished the *Berwind-White* case on the ground that there the seller had an office in New York and the sales were consummated there; here the seller had no office except in Tennessee and the sales were made there.

Under the *McLeod* decision, a sales tax may not be imposed by the state of the buyer where the seller sends only drummers into the state and the sale is not consummated there. A sales tax, in other words, may not be laid by the state of the buyer unless the sale is made there by a seller who maintains an office or possesses some other property there. This may well, as the dissenters in *McLeod* asserted,[395] mark a retreat from *Berwind-White*. As a practical matter, nevertheless, the impact of *McLeod* is negligible. This is true because, as we shall see in the next section, the state concerned can accomplish the same result by substituting a use tax for the sales tax stricken down in *McLeod*.

119

USE TAXES   The facts in *General Trading Co. v. State Tax Commission*[396] were basically similar to those involved in the just-discussed case of *McLeod v. Dilworth Co.* The seller in the *General Trading* case shipped goods from its Minnesota headquarters ordered by purchasers in Iowa from salesmen sent into the latter state. It maintained no office or other property in Iowa and the orders taken there were always subject to acceptance in Minnesota. In *McLeod,* we saw that, in such circumstances, the state of the buyer may not impose a sales tax. In the *General Trading* case, on the other hand, such state was permitted to collect a use tax on the similar fact pattern presented.

The use tax was a direct result of efforts by the states to overcome the rule, generally followed prior to the *Berwind-White* case,[397] prohibiting

the states from taxing interstate sales. The use tax is an attempt by the
states to avoid competitive advantages otherwise enjoyed by sister states
without sales taxes. As the high Court has explained it: "The use tax, not
in itself a relatively significant revenue producer, usually appears as a
support to the sales tax in two respects. One is protection of the state's
revenues by taking away from inhabitants the advantages of resort to un-
taxed out-of-state purchases. The other is protection of local merchants
against out-of-state competition from those who may be enabled by lower
tax burdens to offer lower prices." [398] The use tax accomplishes the purposes referred to by being levied on the privilege of using in the state
products brought in from other states. The tax rate is normally that imposed by the state's sales tax, with a credit allowed for any sales tax already paid in another state.

The state power to impose use taxes on products brought in from other
states was sustained in *Henneford v. Silas Mason Co.*[399] According to it,
the states may tax the privilege of use of property within their borders,
even though such property was acquired through interstate commerce. As
we have already seen,[400]goods in interstate commerce may be subjected
to a nondiscriminatory property tax, when once they have arrived at their
destination. "For like reasons," said the *Henneford* opinion, "they may be
subjected, when once they are at rest, to a nondiscriminatory tax upon use
or enjoyment." [401]

The high Court in *Henneford* was strongly influenced by the fact that
the tax statute at issue had an offset provision, of the type already referred
to, under which there was deducted from the use tax any sale or use tax
which had previously been paid in another state on the property in
question. This offset provision, the Court emphasized, eliminates the possibility of multiple taxation. "Equality," it declared, "is the theme that runs
through all the sections of the statute." [402]

It is true, in the highest Court's phrase, that, under a tax like that in
Henneford, the stranger from afar is subject to no greater burdens than
the dweller within the gates.[403] One may, all the same, wonder whether the
Henneford holding is wholly consistent with the philosophy behind the
Commerce Clause. What the Supreme Court is saying, in a decision like
Henneford, is that the Commerce Clause does not prevent a state from
using its tax power to secure equality of competitive conditions as between
its merchants and those in other states. That may well be true where the
state power is exerted over its own local markets. Hence, as we saw in the
prior section, the states may, in certain circumstances, tax interstate sales—
but only where the sales are consummated in the states concerned. On
the other hand, to allow the states to create equality as between their own
commerce and interstate commerce not carried on in local markets is to

permit them to impose what really amount to protective tariffs against the products of other states.

The Supreme Court itself has conceded that: "In this respect, the use tax has the same effect as a protective tariff becoming due not on purchase of the goods but at the moment of bringing them into the taxing states." [404] It may be advantageous for the state to be able to say to interstate commerce: You may come into my borders, but your products must be subject to the same tax burdens as local products. There is no doubt that a sovereign country could make such a statement and levy protective tariffs to carry it into effect. One would have thought, however, that the whole point about the Commerce Clause is that it bars the states from laying such tariffs upon commerce from sister states.

120

SAME: COLLECTION The effectiveness of the use tax depends upon the scheme by which it is collected. Such taxes are all but impossible to collect from the countless thousands of individuals who may make purchases across state lines. To overcome these difficulties, the states have attempted to make the out-of-state sellers collect use taxes for them. Such attempts have generally been upheld by the Supreme Court. Thus, the Court has sustained state power to compel an out-of-state mail-order company to collect a use tax on shipments to customers in the state, where the company also operated retail stores in the state concerned.[405] In the *General Trading* case [406] discussed in the prior section, the high bench went further and enforced the same obligation on an extrastate company which had no property in the taxing state and did no business there other than the solicitation of orders by traveling salesmen. "To make the distributor the tax collector for the State," said the Court, "is a familiar and sanctioned device." [407]

In *Miller Bros. Co. v. Maryland*,[408] decided more recently, the high tribunal rendered a decision which seemed to restrict state power in this respect. The state there sought to enforce its statute requiring vendors to collect use taxes against an out-of-state merchandising corporation which sold directly to customers at its out-of-state store. The Supreme Court refused to permit the state to enforce the duty to collect the tax by seizure of a truck used in the state by the company in question. In such a case, where the purchasers traveled from the taxing state to the state of the seller, the burden of collecting the tax could not be shifted to the extrastate merchant.

If *Miller Bros.* were the last word on the subject, it would be necessary to determine the extent to which it modifies earlier decisions like that in the *General Trading* case. However, in the 1960 case of *Scripto, Inc. v. Car-*

son,[409] the Supreme Court indicated that *Miller Bros.* itself is now of little practical effect, at least beyond its immediate fact pattern. *Scripto* arose out of an attempt by Florida to make an out-of-state seller responsible for the collection of a use tax on certain pens sold and shipped by the seller from its place of business in Georgia to purchasers in Florida. The seller had no office or property in Florida and orders in the state were solicited for it by part-time salesmen who were Florida residents. The Court upheld the power of Florida to collect the use tax from the seller as against the contention that *Miller Bros.* required a different result. In effect, the Court in *Scripto* limits *Miller Bros.* to the case of a merchant who makes no effort to sell his product outside his own out-of-state store. But any effort by the seller to solicit business or otherwise exploit the consumer market in the state of the purchaser is enough of a nexus between the seller and such state to enable it to require the seller to serve as its tax collector.

What has been said about use taxes in general in the prior section may be repeated with equal propriety in discussing the state's power to collect such taxes. To be sure, as Justice Douglas has stated: "Unless the States can collect a sales or use tax upon goods being purchased out-of-state, there is a fertile opportunity for the citizen who wants state benefits without paying taxes to buy out-of-state." [410] Yet is it not exactly this opportunity to deal freely beyond his borders that is given to the citizen by the Commerce Clause?

It really adds nothing for the high Court to reiterate in *Scripto* that requiring the seller to collect the use tax is a familiar and sanctioned device.[411] This hardly explains why the remote seller is required to collect and pay over the tax on a sale not made in the taxing state. The sale itself, under *McLeod v. Dilworth Co.,*[412] may clearly not be taxed by such state. "So," as a dissenting Justice pointed out, "we are holding that a state has power to make a tax collector of one whom it has no power to tax." [413] If the extrastate seller does not have sufficient connection with the buyer's state in a case like *Scripto* to make him liable for a sales tax there, how has he enough to make him a collector of a use tax? [414]

121

NET INCOME TAXES — The income tax is today one of the primary sources of governmental revenue. To what extent may such tax be imposed upon those engaged in interstate commerce?

The answer is clear where the taxpayer is a resident of the taxing state or a corporation domiciled therein. The leading case is *United States Glue Co. v. Oak Creek,*[415] where the Supreme Court held that a state could, in levying its general income tax upon the gains and profits of a domestic corporation, include within the computation the net income derived from transactions in interstate commerce. The high bench distinguished such a charge by way of net income derived from profits from interstate commerce from a gross receipts tax. The difference between the two, said the Court, is the difference between a direct and immediate burden upon the business concerned and a charge that is only indirect and incidental. In its words, "A tax upon gross receipts affects each transaction in proportion to its magnitude and irrespective of whether it is profitable or otherwise. Conceivably it may be sufficient to make the difference between profit and loss, or to so diminish the profit as to impede or discourage the conduct of the commerce. A tax upon the net profits has not the same deterrent effect, since it does not arise at all unless a gain is shown over and above expenses and losses, and the tax cannot be heavy unless the profits are large. Such a tax, when imposed upon net incomes from whatever source arising, is but a method of distributing the cost of government." [416]

In the *United States Glue* case, the state did not actually seek to tax all of the net income of the company concerned, but only that proportion of its income derived from business transacted within the state. The taxable amount was determined by an apportionment formula prescribed in the state law. It is, however, settled that, where the taxpayer is a resident of the taxing state or a domestic corporation, as was the case in *United States Glue,* the state is not limited to the taxation only of that portion of the net income which is earned in the state. Where a resident or domestic corporation is concerned, the state may tax the entire net income wherever earned. The privilege of domicile itself in such a case affords a basis for imposing the burden of sharing the cost of government. Neither the privilege nor the burden is affected by the source from which the income of the resident is derived.[417]

Where the taxpayer is not a resident individual or domestic corporation, a different situation is presented. In such a case, too, of course, a tax upon net income is valid where such income is derived from business which is purely local in character. The difficulty arises where the nonresident or foreign corporation is engaged in the state in business which is interstate in character.

The *United States Glue* principle should apply to such a case as well, at least so far as income derived from activities in the taxing state is concerned, even though the business done in such state is both intrastate and interstate in nature. In such a case, the state tax on net income will be held valid, provided only that it is allocated to income arising from activities within the state. It is consequently necessary for the taxing state to determine what portion of the total income of the taxpayer was derived from activities within its borders and is therefore subject to its taxing

power. To accomplish that purpose, most states have adopted apportionment statutes applicable to situations where the taxpayer is doing business
both within and without the state.[418]

The judicial approach to such apportionment statutes will be dealt
with in section 127. Suffice it to say here that the state may reach the net
income of nonresidents and foreign corporations derived from interstate
commerce to the extent that such income is *fairly* related to activities
within the state.[419] Thus, the entire net income of a corporation, generated
by interstate as well as intrastate activities, may be fairly apportioned
among the states for tax purposes by formulas utilizing in-state aspects of
interstate affairs.[420]

Where the nonresident taxpayer is engaged in both interstate and intrastate business in the taxing state, what has just been said presents no problem. The fact that some intrastate business (no matter how small) is done
is held sufficient justification for the tax, even though most of the income
taxed comes from interstate business. Where the taxpayer is engaged only
in interstate commerce in the state concerned, the law has, until recently,
not been settled. The Supreme Court has held that a franchise or other
privilege tax measured by net income could not be imposed upon a concern doing a wholly interstate business.[421] On the other hand, it was not
clear whether the same result would be reached in the case of an allocated
tax imposed directly "on" the net income of a wholly interstate business.

The 1959 decision of the high Court in *Northwestern States Portland
Cement Co. v. Minnesota* [422] has, however, now definitely settled the question of state taxing power in such a case in the affirmative. It upheld the
constitutionality of a state net income tax law levying taxes on that portion of a foreign corporation's net income earned from and fairly apportioned to business activities within the taxing state even when those activities are exclusively in furtherance of interstate commerce. The tax at issue was levied by Minnesota upon the income earned in that state by an
Iowa corporation engaged in the manufacture and sale of cement, locally
in Iowa and, in interstate commerce, to dealers in neighboring states including Minnesota.

In upholding the Minnesota tax, the Court stated that "a net income
tax on revenues derived from interstate commerce does not offend constitutional limitations upon state interference with such commerce." [423]
Nor does it make any difference that the commerce engaged in in Minnesota
is purely interstate and that, in consequence, the tax was on income derived
exclusively from interstate commerce. The tax in question was part of a
general scheme of state taxation, reaching all individual and corporate net
income. The taxing statute was not sought to be applied to portions of the
net income of appellant because of the source of that income—interstate
commerce—but rather despite that source.[424] In the Court's view, it is not

an improper interference with interstate commerce to permit a state within whose borders a foreign corporation engages in activities in aid of that commerce to tax the net income derived therefrom on a properly apportioned basis.

The opinion in the *Northwestern States Cement* case is based upon ostensible rigid adherence to *stare decisis*. It repeatedly asserts that it is only adhering to principles laid down in prior decisions and disclaims any intent to break new constitutional ground. But, in actuality, the Court's holding is novel doctrine.[425] Though the cases already discussed sustain state taxes imposed upon companies engaged in commerce, in none of them was the tax exacted from a business whose revenue derived solely from interstate commerce.

This is not to say that there is not much to commend the high Court's recognition of such state power to tax even interstate commerce. The constitutional barrier against state taxation in this field was primarily intended to prevent interstate commerce being placed at a disadvantage. But this scarcely demands that interstate commerce be placed in a favored position. It, too, should share the burdens and costs of government and should not secure competitive advantage from tax immunity denied to local commerce. The Commerce Clause hardly requires that the tax burden be lower simply because state lines were crossed.

In the *Northwestern States Cement* case, equality is the result of the tax at issue. "The thrust of these statutes," said Justice Harlan, "is not hostile discrimination against interstate commerce, but rather a seeking of some compensation for facilities and benefits afforded by the taxing States to income-producing activities therein, whether those activities be altogether local or in furtherance of interstate commerce." [426] Income derived from sales in a state should not receive immunity from taxation simply because they are interstate, when such immunity is denied to income from similar local sales. Nor, according to the Court, is there any real danger of a multiple burden resulting from the exactions in question. "The apportioned tax," it stated, "is designed . . . 'to prevent the levying of such taxes as will discriminate against or prohibit the interstate activities or will place the interstate commerce at a disadvantage relative to local commerce.' " [427]

122
GROSS RECEIPTS
TAXES

As indicated in the discussion in the prior section of the *United States Glue* case,[428] the Supreme Court has drawn a distinction between a net income tax and one imposed upon gross receipts. The net income tax was said to affect interstate commerce only indirectly, since it does not arise unless a profit is shown. The gross receipts tax was held to impose a direct and immediate burden upon interstate commerce because it was levied irrespective of whether the business was profitable or not and could "so diminish the profit as to impede or discourage the conduct of the commerce." [429]

The distinction so drawn by the high bench has led it to treat the gross receipts tax differently from the net income tax in the cases on the subject. In the prior section, we saw that a state may tax the entire net income of a resident individual or domestic corporation. Where such resident is concerned, the state is not limited to the taxation only of that portion of the net income that is earned in the state.

The same is not true where a gross receipts tax is laid upon a resident or domestic corporation. This may be seen from *Adams Mfg. Co. v. Storen*,[430] where the highest Court had before it an Indiana tax on all the gross receipts of a domestic company, which sold 80 per cent of its products outside the state. This tax, it was held, was invalid insofar as it affected the company's interstate business. Such a tax reaches indiscriminately the gross compensation for both interstate commerce and intrastate activities and must fail in its entirety so far as applied to receipts from sales interstate.

In the Supreme Court's view, the chief vice of the tax at issue in the *Adams Mfg.* case was that it contained within itself the seeds of multiple taxation. If the state of domicile could impose such a tax, so could the states where the goods were sold. As Justice Stone put it, soon after the *Adams Mfg.* decision, in a case invalidating a similar Washington tax: "If Washington is free to exact such a tax, other states to which the commerce extends may, with equal right, lay a tax similarly measured for the privilege of conducting within their respective territorial limits the activities there which contribute to the service. The present tax, though nominally local, thus in its practical operation discriminates against interstate commerce, since it imposes upon it, merely because interstate commerce is being done, the risk of a multiple burden to which local commerce is not exposed." [431] The multiplication of state taxes measured by gross receipts from interstate transactions, Justice Stone has said in another case, would renew the barriers to interstate trade which it was the object of the Commerce Clause to remove.[432]

It should be pointed out that the danger of multiple taxation, which the high Court thus relied on in striking down a tax on all gross receipts imposed by the domiciliary state, exists to the same extent where net income taxes are concerned. With regard to such taxes, we saw,[433] the state may tax the entire net income, wherever earned, of its residents or domestic corporations. Yet, under the *Northwestern States Cement* case [434] discussed in the prior section, every other state in which the taxpayer does business is now also free to tax the income derived from activities within such state even though the business done there is wholly interstate. What was said in the gross-receipts-tax cases just discussed could consequently be said in the net-income-tax cases as well. It has not, however, been said by the Supreme Court and the law remains that the state may levy a tax upon the entire net income of a resident individual or domestic corporation engaged in interstate commerce, while it may not tax all the gross receipts earned by such person or company.

Our discussion thus far in this section has dealt with gross receipts taxes imposed on the total gross receipts of the taxpaper: both those earned from local commerce and from interstate commerce. All such taxes, we have seen, are invalid to the extent that they are levied upon receipts from business done outside the state, even where the taxing state is the domiciliary state. What happens when the state taxes gross receipts upon an allocated basis, under a formula which seeks to reach only that portion of the gross compensation attributable to the taxpayer's business activities within the taxing state?

The earlier cases on the subject held that all taxes levied on gross receipts were invalid to the extent that gross receipts from interstate commerce were included, even though such taxes were allocated so as to reach only the receipts from business activities in the taxing state.[435] The holdings to this effect were based directly upon the view, already stated, that the gross receipts tax constitutes a direct burden upon interstate commerce whose effect may be so to diminish the profits as to discourage the conduct of interstate business.[436] Said the Supreme Court, in a case invalidating a tax on the gross earnings of a New York City stevedoring company: "Although state laws do not discriminate against interstate commerce or in actuality or by possibility subject it to the cumulative burden of multiple levies, those laws may be unconstitutional because they burden or interfere with commerce." [437] A law imposing a gross receipts tax, the Court has held, is just such a law.

More recently, the high bench has modified its position with regard to allocated gross receipts taxes. In *Adams Mfg. Co. v. Storen,*[438] we saw, an Indiana tax measured by all the gross receipts of a company engaged in both interstate and local business was stricken down. On the other hand, when the Indiana gross receipts tax was applied only to the sales within the state of an interstate company, it was upheld.[439] The Supreme Court, in other words, now distinguishes between an apportioned gross receipts tax and a tax on all the gross receipts of an interstate business. Only the latter type of gross receipts tax is invalid. "The measurement of a tax by gross receipts," the Court has affirmed, "where it cannot result in a multiplication of the levies is upheld." [440] Where the gross receipts tax is apportioned to reach only income derived from activities within the taxing state, it should be unobjectionable.[441]

The one recent decision inconsistent with what has just been said is that rendered in the 1947 case of *Joseph v. Carter & Weekes Stevedoring Co.*,[442] already referred to, where a tax on the gross receipts of a New York City stevedoring concern was held improper, even though all the activities from which the receipts were earned occurred within the city. In this case, says one commentator, the high Court reaffirmed the ancient law that gross receipts from interstate transportation may not be made the direct subject of a state tax.[443]

One wonders, however, whether *Joseph v. Carter & Weekes Stevedoring Co.* does not stand alone today. Later cases seem clearly to settle state power to impose properly allocated gross receipts taxes on interstate businesses, including transportation companies. Thus, taxes on gross receipts have been held properly applicable to bus and railroad companies doing both interstate and intrastate business, where the taxes were allocated upon a mileage basis. In the words of Justice Douglas, in a 1951 case: "It is settled that a nondiscriminatory gross receipts tax on an interstate enterprise may be sustained if fairly apportioned to the business done within the taxing state. Where transportation is concerned, an apportionment according to the mileage within the state is an approved method." [444]

123

PROPERTY TAXES   We have already seen that a state may not tax articles engaged in interstate transit, simply because they happen to be within the state on tax day.[445] On the other hand, it is settled that property permanently located within a state is subject to property taxation there, even though such property is employed by a company engaged in interstate commerce. As the Supreme Court has stated it, "Property having its situs within the taxing state is not exempt from a nondiscriminatory property tax merely because the property is used in interstate commerce." [446] Hence, an interstate railroad is subject to local taxation on the value of its depots, terminals, roadbeds, repair shops, and other property located within the taxing state.[447]

Difficulties arise from the fact that much of the property used by companies engaged in interstate commerce has no permanent location, but is, on the contrary, migratory in nature, with no fixed situs in any state. The obvious example is the rolling stock of an interstate railroad. If such property can be fully taxed in every state through which it happens to pass during the year, it would be subject to a tax burden far in excess of that placed upon property permanently located within one of the states concerned. At the same time, if the opposite rule were adopted, with no state permitted to tax such migratory property, property employed in any business requiring continuous and constant movement from one state to another would escape taxation altogether.[448]

The result has been the adoption of a rule in between the two ex-
tremes just noted, which permits the states to tax migratory property upon
an apportioned basis. The way to this result was pointed in 1888 when
the highest Court stated specifically that the states were not barred from
imposing property taxes on railroad cars used in the state. "And such a
tax," it went on, "might be properly assessed and collected in cases like
the present, where the specific and individual items of property so used
and employed were not continuously the same, but were constantly changing, according to the exigencies of the business. In such cases the tax
might be fixed by an appraisement and valuation of the average amount
of the property thus habitually used." [449]

What was just quoted was, technically speaking, said only by way of
obiter. Yet, three years later, it became established Supreme-Court doctrine in the leading case of *Pullman's Palace Car Co. v. Pennsylvania*.[450]
The decision there permitted the state to tax such portion of the capital
stock of the Pullman Company as the number of miles over which it ran
cars in the state bore to the whole number of miles over which its cars
were run. According to the high Court: "This was a just and equitable
method of assessment; and, if it were adopted by all the States through
which these cars ran, the Company would be assessed upon the whole
value of its capital stock, and no more." [451]

The *Pullman* case laid down the basic rule, since followed in many
cases, permitting state taxation of migratory property employed in interstate commerce upon an apportioned basis. As Chief Justice Stone informs
us, "This Court has accordingly held invalid state taxation of vehicles
of interstate transportation unless the tax is equitably apportioned to the
use of the vehicles within the state compared to their use without, whether
the tax is laid by the state of the domicile or another." [452]

124

SAME: UNIT RULE Since the just-discussed *Pullman* case, the apportionment principle has been consistently applied in cases
involving state taxation of migratory property used in land transportation,
especially railroad rolling stock. From those cases there has emerged
the concept of the so-called "unit rule" in the field of property taxation.
Under it, all the assets of the company concerned could be treated as a
single unit for purposes of taxation; and the elements making up such unit
were not necessarily limited to the physical assets, but could also include
the entire going-concern value of the company.

The "unit rule" was first articulated in those terms in 1897 in *Adams
Express Co. v. Ohio*,[453] where the Supreme Court used it to justify the
state in taxing the property of an express company worth some $70,000

at a much higher figure, since the assessment did not exceed, in relation to the total capital value of the company, the proportion borne by the mileage which the company covered in the state to the total mileage covered by it. The property of companies engaged in interstate transportation, stated Chief Justice Fuller, "in the several states through which their lines or business extended, might be valued as a unit for the purposes of taxation, taking into consideration the uses to which it was put, and all the elements making up aggregate value, and . . . a proportion of the whole, fairly and properly ascertained, might be taxed by the particular state, without violating any federal restriction." [454]

The Commerce Clause permits a state to value the property used in interstate commerce within it if it uses a properly determined "unit property" and a proper allocation formula for apportioning to itself a part of the value of such unit. The value of the "unit property" may be ascertained by any reasonable method, including capitalizing net income at an assumed percentage rate, taking the total capitalization or the market value of the total capital securities, balance sheet values, or a combination of these values. [455]

Under the apportionment approach, the state must then assign to itself a fair share of the value of the "unit property." It may do so by any reasonable apportionment formula. We shall discuss in section 127 some of the problems presented by such formulas. Here, we need note only that the basic problem is to determine what portion of an interstate organism may appropriately be attributed to the various states in which it functions. [456] As we shall see, the high bench has tended to uphold practically all good-faith efforts by the states to resolve such problems in specific instances.

125

SAME: SHIPS AND AIRPLANES The apportionment approach to property taxes, laid down in the *Pullman* case discussed in section 123, has been consistently applied in cases involving land transportation. Different rules have, however, been applied in cases in which the migratory property involved was used in other modes of transportation.

Chief Justice Stone has stated the considerations which have led the Supreme Court to follow a different rule where vessels engaged in commerce have been concerned. According to him: "vessels ordinarily move on the high seas, outside the jurisdiction of any state, and merely touch briefly at ports within a state. Hence they acquire no tax situs in any of the states at which they touch port, and are taxable by the domicile or not at all." [457] The earlier cases had, it is true, held that vessels were taxable only at their home port, i.e., their port of registry. [458] Later cases, on the other hand, laid down the rule of taxability of ships solely at the domicile of their owners,[459] unless they had acquired a fixed situs elsewhere, as, for example, by being employed wholly within the waters of one state.[460]

In *Northwest Airlines v. Minnesota* (1944),[461] a bare majority of the high bench applied the ship rule of taxation by the state of domicile to the field of air transport. The decision upheld a property tax by Minnesota upon all the planes of an airline incorporated within the state and having there its principal place of business, which was listed as the home port registered with the Civil Aeronautics Authority. The tax was sustained, though it was levied on the entire property of the airline, and not apportioned as between Minnesota and the other states where the company's planes were flown. The rule of apportionment, said Justice Frankfurter, who delivered the judgment of the Court, grew out of, and has established itself, in regard to land transportation. The Court refused to carry it over to "the totally new problems" [462] presented by the very different mode of transportation by air. Instead, it followed the vessel rule of taxability by the state of domicile.

It can hardly be denied that there are important factual differences between transportation by land and that by water and air. "It stands to reason," Justice Frankfurter has asserted, "that the drastic differences between slow-moving trains and the bird-like flight of airplanes would be reflected in the law's response to the claims of the different States and the limitations of the Commerce Clause upon those claims." [463] One may wonder, nevertheless, whether the differences between the forms of transport alone justify the ship-aircraft rule of exclusive taxation by the state of domicile. Such a rule overlooks the fact that the property being taxed is migratory, and does receive benefits from the various states in which it is used. Only if those states are permitted to tax upon a properly apportioned basis can they exact a return for such benefits.

The Supreme Court itself has come to see the justice of the claims of nondomiciliary states in which migratory ships and airplanes are employed. In the 1949 case of *Ott v. Mississippi Barge Line Co.,*[464] it upheld a Louisiana property tax on barges doing interstate business on the Mississippi River, where the assessments were based on the ratio between the number of miles of the barge company's lines within the state and the total number of miles of the entire line. From a constitutional point of view, said the Court, "the only question is whether the tax in practical operation has relation to opportunities, benefits, or protection conferred or afforded by the taxing State." [465] That requirement was deemed satisfied where, as here, the tax was fairly apportioned to the commerce carried on within the state.

More recently, the high Court has applied the *Ott* holding to air transportation. In *Braniff Airways v. Nebraska Board,*[466] it ruled that there is now no bar to prevent states, other than the domiciliary state, from taxing planes in interstate commerce upon an apportionment basis, in accordance with their use in the taxing state. The *Northwest Airlines* decision was interpreted to permit states other than that of the owner's domicile to tax planes in interstate commerce upon the apportionment basis.

But where does this leave us, in view of the fact that the *Braniff* opinion expressly recognized the continued validity of the *Northwest Airlines* holding? If, under *Braniff,* other states can now tax upon an apportionment basis, the *Northwest Airlines* holding that the state of domicile is not limited by that basis means multiple taxation of the interstate enterprise. That result can be avoided only if the Supreme Court follows the rule applicable to land transportation and permits the domiciliary state, like other states, to tax upon an apportionment basis alone.

The considerations just advanced led to the decision in *Standard Oil Co. v. Peck,*[467] which denied to the domiciliary state the power to tax the vessels used in interstate river transportation on other than an apportioned basis. The *Ott* case,[468] according to the high Court, now precludes full taxation by the domiciliary state. "The rule," it said in *Standard Oil v. Peck,* "which permits taxation by two or more states on an apportionment basis precludes taxation of all of the property by the state of the domicile. Otherwise there would be multiple taxation." [469]

Standard Oil Co. v. Peck underscores the present anomalous position of the holding of *Northwest Airlines v. Minnesota.* At least so far as interstate commerce is concerned,[470] there is now no constitutional difference between vessels and railroad cars for purposes of property taxation. In either case, the domiciliary state, like all other states, may tax only on an apportionment basis. The same should be true for property taxation of aircraft. The high bench itself declared in the *Braniff* case: "We perceive no logical basis for distinguishing the constitutional power to impose a tax on such aircraft from the power to impose taxes on river boats." [471] If that is the case, there is now no logical reason for not fully applying the apportionment theory to interstate transportation by air just as it has been recently applied to such transportation by water.

126

PRIVILEGE TAXES   In the celebrated 1869 case of *Paul v. Virginia,*[472] the Supreme Court ruled that a corporation chartered by one state could do business in other states only with their consent, which "assent may be granted upon such terms and conditions as those States may think proper to impose." [473] Presumably, this would include a power in the state to require foreign corporations to pay a franchise tax as a condition to the privilege of doing business within the state. As it was stated by Justice Holmes: "as to foreign corporations seeking to do business wholly within a state, that state is the master, and may prohibit or tax such business at will." [474]

The Holmes statement just quoted was, however, made in dissent, at a time when the *Paul v. Virginia* doctrine had been substantially modified by the high Court. Such modification began two decades after *Paul v. Virginia* itself. At that time, the Court was presented with a flat annual license tax imposed upon a telegraph company doing both local and interstate business. Such a license fee, said the Court, in rejecting the *Paul v. Virginia* approach, must fall. "Can a state," it asked, "prohibit such a company from doing such a business within its jurisdiction, unless it will pay a tax and procure a license for the privilege? If it can, it can exclude such companies, and prohibit the transaction of such business altogether. We are not prepared to say that this can be done." [475]

That the *Paul v. Virginia* doctrine does not apply to a corporation engaged in interstate commerce is today clear. To carry on interstate commerce is not a mere privilege granted by any state; it is a right which every American is entitled to exercise under the Constitution.[476] As such, it is a right whose enjoyment may not be conditioned upon the grant of a franchise by any state in which the right is sought to be exercised.

What has just been said is settled in Supreme-Court jurisprudence where the business on which a franchise tax is sought to be levied is entirely interstate. This was reaffirmed in the 1951 case of *Spector Motor Service v. O'Connor,*[477] where a franchise tax imposed upon a foreign corporation for the privilege of doing a wholly interstate business within the state was held invalid, even though the tax was computed at a nondiscriminatory rate and apportioned to include only the business activities within the state. The constitutional infirmity of such a tax persists, said the high Court, no matter how fairly it is apportioned to business done within the state.

It had been urged in *Spector* that the immunity of a wholly interstate business from a privilege tax was out of line with more recent notions of state taxing power, particularly the cases already discussed [478] permitting the net income and gross receipts from interstate commerce to be reached upon a properly allocated basis. Though recognizing that interstate commerce could thus be taxed under those cases, the Court in *Spector* held that a franchise or privilege tax was quite another matter. "In this field," its opinion declared, "there is not only reason but long-established precedent for keeping the federal privilege of carrying on exclusively interstate commerce free from state taxation. To do so gives lateral support to one of the cornerstones of our constitutional law." [479]

It can scarcely be gainsaid that the distinction in this respect between franchise and other taxes is somewhat artificial, since it is the same interstate business that is burdened in both cases. Nevertheless, the *Spector* decision, which rests on the distinction, is still good law.[480] Thus, an allocated tax "on" the net income of a wholly interstate business is valid. But a franchise or other privilege tax, though measured by net income to the same extent, may still not be exacted upon a company doing an entirely interstate business.

The above is true where a franchise tax is levied upon a corporation engaged exclusively in interstate commerce. What happens where the company concerned comes into the taxing state to do both interstate and local business?

The more recent cases involving franchise taxes on foreign corporations doing a mixed business, with both interstate and intrastate elements, tend to allow such taxes, provided they are limited to levies imposed for the privilege of doing intrastate business. The Commerce Clause, the high Court has said, does not bar a state from imposing a tax based on the value of the privilege of doing an intrastate business merely because the taxpayer also does an interstate business.[481] This means that, where the business of the taxpayer is mixed, the tax must be apportioned so as to reach only the business done in the state. Provided that the apportionment basis used by the state is fair and reasonable, the tax will be upheld.

The present approach of the supreme bench in such cases is illustrated by *Ford Motor Co. v. Beauchamp*.[482] There a franchise tax measured by a charge upon such proportion of the outstanding stock, surplus, and undivided profits of the company as the gross receipts from its business in the state bore to its total gross receipts was upheld. Such tax, according to the Court, was "obviously" payment for the privilege of carrying on business in the state. The state has the power to make a charge against foreign corporations for the opportunity to transact such business. As the Court saw it, "When that charge, as here, is based upon the proportion of the capital employed in Texas, calculated by the percentage of sales which are within the state, no provision of the Federal Constitution is violated." [483]

On the other hand, where a nonallocated franchise tax is levied upon a company doing a mixed business, it must fall. The classic case here is *Western Union Telegraph Co. v. Kansas*.[484] In it, the Supreme Court condemned a so-called charter fee of a fixed percentage of the entire capitalization of a foreign corporation doing both interstate and local business, imposed as a condition of continuing to do local business in the state. A tax measured by the total capital stock is a tax upon values predominantly outside the state; it in effect taxes the company's entire business, interstate as well as local, and its property wherever located. Such a tax, said Justice Harlan, is "not simply a tax for the privilege of doing local business in the state, but a burden and tax on the company's interstate business and on its property located or used outside of the state." [485] A franchise tax based upon an unallocated assessment of extraterritorial assets cannot be laid as a condition to the doing of a mixed business in a state.[486]

127

APPORTIONMENT   According to one member of the highest Court: "The apportionment theory is a mongrel one, a cross between desire not to interfere with state taxation and desire at the same time not utterly to crush out interstate commerce. It is a rather illogical device to prevent duplication of tax burdens on vehicles in transit." [487]

It is, nevertheless, the theory of apportionment which serves as the basis for most of the Supreme-Court doctrine on state taxation of interstate commerce. As the prior sections have shown, where interstate business is concerned, apportionment is the key to valid imposition of taxes on net income, gross receipts, property, and the privilege of doing local business. Where the taxing state allocates to itself only its fair share of the interstate business, such taxes may properly be levied.

The theory of apportionment is, of course, grounded upon the need to avoid multiple taxation. If the taxes under discussion were permitted without any allocation, the interstate enterprise would be subject to far heavier tax burdens than its local competitors. The only alternative to a rule of complete exemption is one in terms of an apportionment between the taxing state and the other states in which the taxpayer carries on his commerce. The apportioned tax, the Supreme Court has said, "has no cumulative effect caused by the interstate character of the business. Hence there is no risk of multiple taxation." [488]

The apportionment principle itself was first developed in the cases on state taxation of migratory property used in land transportation, notably railroad rolling stock.[489] It was later applied, as we have seen, to other types of taxation, including taxes on net income, gross receipts, and privilege taxes. By now, the concept of the allocated tax has become the principal basis for upholding state power in the field of taxation of interstate business.

"Logically it is impossible," the Supreme Court has stated, "when the tax is fairly apportioned, to have the same income taxed twice." [490] In practice, however, whether such will, in fact, be the case will depend upon the apportionment formulas employed by the different states in which an interstate company does business.

What apportionment formula will be used will, to be sure, depend upon the type of tax that is involved. Where a state seeks to tax the property of an interstate carrier, a formula based on mileage is appropriate.[491] Thus, an interstate railroad could be assessed by taking such part of the value of the railroad's entire system as was represented by the ratio which the railroad's mileage within the state bore to its total mileage.[492]

Where income taxes are concerned, different apportionment formulas are normally used. Allocation of income to a state on the basis of the proportion of the taxpayer's property located within the state has been held proper.[493] Most commonly used has been a three-factor formula, which takes account of 1) property, 2) payroll, and 3) sales.[494] The employment of such a formula is illustrated by a case upholding a California tax measured by a formula which averaged the percentages which 1) value of real and tangible personal property, 2) wages, salaries, commissions, and other compensation of employees, and 3) gross sales, attributable to the California branch of the company taxed, bore to the corresponding items of all its branches. Such formula was calculated to allocate to the state that portion of the net income reasonably attributable to the business done in California.[495]

The same basic approach is followed where gross receipts and franchise taxes are involved. Where carriers are concerned, apportionment on a mileage basis is an approved method.[496] The same would be true of a three-factor formula like that used in the net-income cases. Likewise, the tax may be measured by such proportion of the company's sales or income as its capital invested in the taxing state bears to its total capital,[497] or by such proportion of its capital stock as the value of its property in the taxing state and the business done there bears to the total value of its property and business.[498]

It must be conceded that the apportionment theory itself, upon which state taxing power so often turns, is far from a perfect one. While, under the allocated tax, it is theoretically impossible to have interstate commerce subjected to multiple taxation, as the Supreme Court itself has put it: "In practical operation, . . . apportionment formulas being what they are, the possibility of the contrary is not foreclosed, especially by levies in domiciliary States." [499]

Any method of allocating to one state its fair share of an interstate unitary business must be, at the best, only a rough estimate. A court can hardly insist upon an ideal system of state taxation, if such a thing can, in truth, exist outside the mind of the doctrinaire.[500] All that can be required is a reasonable approximation to fair treatment of interstate commerce.

In the Supreme-Court decisions on the subject, there is a definite tendency to accept almost any bona fide state attempt to work out some allocation, mathematically inexact though the actual formula used may be. That apportionment may not result in mathematical exactitude, the high Court has declared, is not a constitutional defect. Rough approximation, rathar than precision, is all that is demanded.[501] In the Court's words, "Unless a palpably disproportionate result comes from an apportionment, a result which makes it patent that the tax is levied upon interstate commerce rather than upon an intrastate privilege, this Court has not been willing to nullify honest state efforts to make apportionments." [502] When the state has adopted a formula not intrinsically arbitrary, it will be sustained.[503]

128

DISCRIMINATORY   Basic in our discussion thus far has been the goal
TAXES   already emphasized of placing interstate commerce
               upon a plane of tax equality with local commerce.
Such goal is patently violated where a state tax clearly discriminates against interstate commerce. The Commerce Clause, without any doubt, absolutely prohibits the states from discriminating against interstate commerce, and a state tax which accomplishes that result must fall. *Brown v. Maryland* [504] itself, the very first case on state taxing power, involved a tax solely on those selling imported goods, which those selling domestic articles did not have to pay. As such, it was manifestly discriminatory; but Chief Justice Marshall did not base his condemnation upon that ground.

According to Justice Frankfurter,[505] Marshall's disregard of the element of discrimination in the statute at issue in *Brown v. Maryland* may well have stimulated resort to discriminatory state taxes and led state courts to sustain their use. It was not, indeed, until the 1876 case of *Welton v. Missouri* [506] that the Supreme Court specifically called a halt to taxes which patently discriminated against interstate commerce. The tax stricken down there was a license levy imposed on all peddlers dealing in goods which were not produced in the taxing state. Such tax, the Court held, plainly discriminated against interstate commerce because of its interstate character. The Commerce Clause protects goods, even after they have entered the state, from any burdens imposed by reason of their out-of-state origin. The states may, as we have seen,[507] tax articles brought from beyond their borders, even though they are still in their original packages, when once their interstate journey is terminated. But they cannot impose discriminatory taxes against such articles or those who deal in them, solely because of their extrastate past.

The holding of *Welton v. Missouri* has been repeated in many more recent cases. It was the basis of decision in *Best & Co. v. Maxwell,*[508] where a state law levied an annual tax of $250 on persons, not regular retail merchants in the state, who sold by samples displayed in hotel rooms. At the same time, regular retail merchants paid only a $1 annual tax. Such tax, the Supreme Court ruled, was invalid as a clear discrimination in favor of intrastate business: "A $250 investment in advance, required of out-of-state retailers but not of their real local competitors, can operate only to discourage and hinder the appearance of interstate commerce in the North Carolina retail market." [509]

What has been said about discriminatory state regulations in section 109 applies as well to discriminatory taxes. In fact, the entire law on the Commerce-Clause restrictions upon state power is but an application of the rule against discrimination. "The commerce clause," the high bench has declared, "forbids discrimination, whether forthright or ingenious." [510] The difficulty, of course, is that the states are rarely so ingenuous as to enact laws which are patently discriminatory on their face. Even in the *Best* case, for example, the statute at issue nominally taxed all who were not regular retail merchants in the state, regardless of whether they were residents or nonresidents. In actuality, all the same, those resident sellers competing with out-of-state sellers would normally be regular retail merchants. Hence, the tax favored local merchants and had to fall as a discrimination against the commerce of the nation.

129

CONGRESSIONAL   In sections 110 and 111, we saw that the Congress
POWER   possesses an overriding power both to permit state
regulatory action that might otherwise be barred by the Commerce Clause and to prohibit state regulatory action that might otherwise be permitted by the Commerce Clause. Is the same true where state taxation is concerned?

Before our own day, an answer to this question could hardly be given with assurance, for there were no cases involving Congressional attempts to relieve the states from the limitations on their taxing powers that had been judicially developed from the Commerce Clause. In its 1946 decision in *Prudential Insurance Co. v. Benjamin*,[511] however, the Supreme Court indicated that an affirmative answer to the question just raised is appropriate. In section 110, the *Prudential Insurance* case was discussed from the point of view of Congressional consent to state regulatory action. We saw there that, after the Supreme Court had ruled that insurance was commerce,[512] with the implication that it was subject (so far as it was interstate) only to federal regulatory power, the Congress enacted a statute expressly subjecting the insurance business to state laws. In section 110, we discussed that federal statute in its effect upon state regulatory authority. But the Congressional act was not limited to such authority. In addition, it subjected insurance to all state laws relating to the taxation of such business.

In the *Prudential Insurance* case, a 3 per cent state tax was laid upon the premiums received in the state by foreign insurance companies, without regard to whether the business done was interstate or local in character. No similar tax was imposed upon domestic companies. Such tax was clearly invalid under the cases already discussed [513] as a discriminatory exaction. The Supreme Court, nevertheless, upheld such tax because of the Congressional statute specifically subjecting insurance to state taxing power. Congress, in the Court's words, "clearly put the full weight of its power behind existing and future state legislation to sustain it from any attack under the commerce clause." [514]

The federal statute in *Prudential Insurance* was treated by the Court as "a determination by Congress that state taxes, which in its silence might be held invalid as discriminatory, do not place on interstate insurance business a burden which it is unable generally to bear or should not bear in the competition with local business." [515] In other words, under the *Prudential Insurance* decision, the Congress has an overriding power to permit the states to impose taxes which might otherwise be condemned under the Commerce Clause. This is true even of a state levy that patently discriminates against interstate commerce. Congressional authority over commerce is plenary and its power to permit state action is not restricted, except as the Constitution expressly provides, by any limitation which forbids it to discriminate against interstate commerce and in favor of local trade.

What is true of Congressional power to permit is also true of Congressional power to prohibit. The Congress can prohibit state taxation that would otherwise be valid under the Commerce Clause. Thus, after the decision in *Northwestern States Portland Cement Co. v. Minnesota*,[516] upholding state power to tax the net income of businesses engaged exclusively in interstate commerce, Congress enacted a statute limiting state power in the case of such businesses.[517] There are no cases specifically involving Congressional prohibitory power in the tax field. Yet there is no doubt that such power exists in that field to at least the same extent that it does in the field of regulation. In referring to the power of the Congress over commerce, the *Prudential Insurance* opinion declares: "Its plenary scope enables Congress not only to promote but also to prohibit interstate commerce, as it has done frequently and for a great variety of reasons." [518]

In section 110, we discussed the logical dilemma involved in permitting the Congress to override Commerce-Clause limitations upon state power. The same problem exists when we conclude that state lack of power can be cured by Congressional assent to the imposition of otherwise unconstitutional taxes. Yet, as we saw in section 110, the dilemma is more apparent than real. It is resolved by emphasizing the Commerce Clause as an affirmative grant to the national legislature. That grant is of the plenary power to prescribe the rule by which interstate commerce is to be governed. "That power," said the *Prudential Insurance* opinion, "does not run down a one-way street or one of narrowly fixed dimensions. Congress may keep the way open, confine it broadly or closely, or close it entirely." [519]

Congressional power includes the authority to prescribe that commerce shall be subject to relevant state taxes or be free from state exactions. What this means is that the negative aspect of the Commerce Clause is operative only until the Congress provides otherwise. The Supreme-Court jurisprudence discussed in this chapter is thus relevant only in the dormancy of Congressional power over commerce.

8

JUDICIAL POWER

130
JUDICIAL
DEPARTMENT

*E*VER since de Tocqueville, men have emphasized the primordial role of the judge in American society. For it has become almost a commonplace that the courts—and particularly the Supreme Court—are the fulcrum upon which our constitutional institutions turn. "Our courts," says Woodrow Wilson, "are the balance-wheel of our whole constitutional system; and ours is the only constitutional system so balanced and controlled." [1]

In no country, in truth, does the judge have a standing comparable with his place in the American polity. The respect in which the highest Court has generally been held has been surpassed only by the influence it has exerted upon the life of the nation. If it is excessive to say that American history could be written in terms of Supreme-Court decisions, it is not excessive to say that American history would be incomplete without a careful consideration of them. [2] "In the largest proportion of causes submitted to its judgment, every decision becomes a page of history." [3]

The Framers fully realized the significance of the judicial department. The want of a judiciary power, asserts Hamilton in *The Federalist,* crowned the defects of the Articles of Confederation. [4] National laws must remain a dead letter without national courts to expound and define their meaning and operation. As Chief Justice Marshall put it, "All governments which are not extremely defective in their organization, must possess, within themselves, the means of expounding, as well as enforcing, their own laws." [5] If we examine the Constitution, we find that its draftsmen kept this great principle in view.[6] Articles I and II establish the legislative and executive branches, while Article III provides for a coordinate judicial department. To it is granted "The judicial Power"—a delegation which enables it to receive jurisdiction to the full extent of the Constitution, laws, and treaties of the United States, when any question respecting them assumes such a form that judicial power is capable of acting on it.[7]

In drawing up Article III, the Framers were profoundly influenced by Montesquieu's famous remark, that "there is no liberty, if the judiciary power be not separated from the legislative and executive powers." More than that, they believed, with Hamilton, that, if there are such things as political axioms, the propriety of the judicial power of a government being coextensive with its legislative, may be ranked among them.[8] In Marshall's celebrated words, "the judicial power in every well-constituted government must be co-extensive with the legislative, and must be capable of deciding every judicial question which grows out of the constitution and laws." [9] Without an independent judicial department, clothed with the authority to ascertain and enforce the powers of the Union, the laws, the treaties, and even the Constitution of the United States would become sterile. The same scenes would be again acted over which began in the neglect, and ended in the ruin, of the Confederation.[10]

The Framers, then, were well aware of what they were doing in establishing, in Article III, a coordinate judicial department endowed with the judicial power of the Union. They gave to every person having a claim involving a federal question a right to submit his case to a court of the nation. However unimportant his claim might be, however little the community might seem to be interested in its resolution, the Framers deemed it essential to provide a national tribunal, as superior to sectional influence as possible, in which that claim might be decided.[11]

Yet, even the Framers, cognizant though they may have been of the importance of judicial power, were hardly so prescient as to foresee how exalted a role the courts would actually play in the polity which they were creating. "Let all men," it was said in the Tudor Star Chamber, "take heede how they complayne in wordes against any magistrate, for they are gods." [12] It has, however, remained for the American system to make of such Elizabethan figure of speech more than mere hyperbole.

The maintenance of a Constitution like that drawn up in 1787 depends upon the existence of a nonpolitical forum in which it can be impartially debated and enforced. That forum the courts supply. The constitutional system possesses complete poise and certainty of operation because it possesses the support and interpretation of authoritative, undisputable courts of law. It is in this sense, says Wilson in the passage already quoted, that the judiciary is the balance-wheel of the entire system:

"it is meant to maintain that nice adjustment between individual rights and governmental powers which constitutes political liberty." [13]

A judicial department which serves to maintain such adjustment must necessarily play more than a pure judicial role, in the traditional sense exemplified by the king's courts which developed at Westminster. This is particularly true of the tribunal which is the apex of the federal judicial system. Despite its name, the Supreme Court is not and has not been, since the time of John Marshall, only the usual type of law court. Public, not private, law is the stuff of Supreme-Court litigation. Elevation to the highest bench requires the judge to make the adjustment from preoccupation with the restricted, however novel, problems of private litigation to the most exacting demands of judicial statesmanship. "The Judges of the Supreme Court of the land," aptly declared Theodore Roosevelt in 1902, "must be not only great jurists, they must be great constructive statesmen." [14]

It is precisely the fact that the Supreme Court is more than the traditional law court that makes its work of vital significance to more than a relatively small number of legal scholars. It is the judge qua statesman who attracts public attention; the judge as jurist is relegated to the relative obscurity of professional journals.

The Supreme Court is not a common-law court which deals with the questions of private law that are the preoccupation and delectation of most lawyers. It is primarily a political institution in whose keeping lies the destiny of a mighty nation. Its decrees mark the boundaries between the great departments of Government; upon its action depend the proper functioning of federalism and the scope to be given to the rights of the individual.

A judge on such a tribunal has an opportunity to leave his imprint upon the life of the nation as no mere master of the common law possibly could. Only a handful of men in American history have made so manifest a mark on their own age and on ages still to come as did judges like John Marshall or Oliver Wendell Holmes. The same cannot be said of even the greatest of English judges.

To be a judge, endowed with all the omnipotence of justice, is certainly among life's noblest callings. But the mere common-law judge, even in a preeminently legal polity like that in Britain, cannot begin to compare in power and prestige with a Justice of the United States Supreme Court. A judge who is regent over what is done in the legislative and executive branches—the *deus ex machina* who has the final word in the constitutional system—has attained one of the ultimates of human authority.

131

DEPENDENCE   "No feature in the Government of the United States,"
reads an oft-cited passage by Bryce, "has awakened
so much curiosity in the European mind, caused so much discussion, received so much admiration, and been more frequently misunderstood,
than the duties assigned to the Supreme Court and the functions which it
discharges in guarding the ark of the Constitution." [15] To the European
jurist, whose conceptions of judicial power are much more limited than
those of his American confrere, the constitutional competence of the federal
courts seems most redoubtable. Looking at the power exercised by the
Supreme Court to invalidate statutes, indeed, he not unnaturally tends to
conclude that that tribunal is virtually a third chamber in the United
States.[16]

That the federal courts have attained their present preeminence is, at
first glance, somewhat paradoxical. "The judiciary," wrote Hamilton in
The Federalist, "is beyond comparison the weakest of the three departments." [17] The same view was expressed a century later by the highest
bench itself. The judicial department, said the Supreme Court at that
time, "is inherently the weakest" of the three branches: "Dependent as its
courts are for the enforcement of their judgments upon officers appointed
by the executive, and removable at his pleasure, with no patronage and no
control of purse or sword, their power and influence rest solely upon the
public sense of the necessity for the existence of a tribunal to which all
may appeal for the assertion and protection of rights guarantied by the
constitution and by the laws of the land, and on the confidence reposed
in the soundness of their decisions and the purity of their motives." [18]

The power of the judicial department is moral, not physical. It operates
by its influence, not by its power alone.[19] The courts themselves do not
directly command the force of the society. It is the executive which holds
the sword of the community. The judiciary must ultimately depend upon
the aid of the executive arm even for the efficacy of its judgments.[20] Andrew
Jackson is supposed to have reacted to an important Supreme-Court decision with the remark: "Well, John Marshall has made his decision; now
let him enforce it!" In the face of such executive refusals to enforce their
judgments, the courts themselves must remain helpless.

Yet, while such examples of direct executive disregard of judicial
authority have occurred, they have been relatively rare in the history of
American law. The weapons of the judiciary, though mainly moral, have
proved powerful ones, for they have been backed by public acceptance of
the necessity for judicial control as the balance-wheel of the constitutional
system. The universal sense of America has recognized that the basic
document itself depends upon respect for the courts and the law dispensed
by them.[21]

Despite occasional aberrations, acceptance of the judicial department and its authority in the constitutional sphere is as ingrained in the American consciousness as is the acceptance of the competence of the courts in matters of private law. The decisions of the Supreme Court, even those which may drastically restrict the scope of executive power, are regularly accepted without question by the Government—from the President down. Though the high bench does not, without executive concurrence, possess any means of enforcing its judgments, the necessary support is normally given without any difficulty.

The judicial department, we have just seen, is unable to function effectively without the backing of the executive. But it is, if anything, even more dependent upon the legislative branch. "I conceive," declared Justice Iredell, soon after the Constitution itself went into operation, "that all the courts of the United States must receive, not merely their organization as to the number of judges of which they are to consist; but all their authority, as to the manner of their proceeding, from the legislature only." [22]

The extent of judicial dependence upon the legislative department becomes clear if we look to the language of Article III itself. "The judicial Power of the United States," it provides, "shall be vested in one supreme Court, and in such inferior Courts as the Congress may from time to time ordain and establish. . . . The judicial Power shall extend to all Cases, in Law and Equity, arising under this Constitution, the Laws of the United States, and Treaties made, or which shall be made, under their Authority."

Under these provisions, only the Supreme Court itself is expressly provided for in the organic instrument. All other federal courts owe their existence, not to the Constitution, but to the legislature, for they are established by acts of Congress. And the same is basically true of the competence of the judicial department. Except for the original jurisdiction of the Supreme Court,[23] which is today of little practical importance, the basic document is silent with regard to the competence of the federal courts. The result is that the jurisdiction of the federal judiciary, with the exception of the original jurisdiction of the Supreme Court, is dependent upon the legislative department.

The judicial department is thus dependent upon the Congress with regard to both its organization and jurisdiction. The importance of such dependence makes it necessary to examine each of these in some detail.

132

ORGANIZATION: We have just noted that the organization of the
SUPREME COURT   judicial department is dependent upon the Congress.
                          What does this mean as a practical matter? Simply this: that the manner in which the federal judiciary is set up is within the discretion of the legislative branch.

Let us look, first of all, at the very existence of the federal bench. It is obvious, as a starting point, that Article III is not self-executing. It provides that "The judicial Power" shall be vested in the federal courts; but it does not itself provide for the establishment of such courts. It was not until the Congress, in the Judiciary Act of 1789, set up a system of federal courts that the bare outlines of Article III were turned into a working judicial system.

It is true that the Constitution does provide expressly for the existence of "one supreme Court." Hence, the highest bench is established directly by the organic document itself. It does not, all the same, exist as an operating tribunal only because of that fact. The action of Congress is necessary to create the particular body that is to constitute the Supreme Court, and that of the President and the Senate is required in order that it have the personnel which alone can make of it in fact a functioning organ of government.

The fact that the Supreme Court is provided for expressly in Article III does, without a doubt, impose upon the Congress the mandatory duty of setting up the high tribunal. "Could Congress have lawfully refused to create a supreme court . . . ?" asks Justice Story. "But one answer can be given . . . it must be in the negative." [24]

But the Constitution, though it does expressly provide for the Supreme Court, says nothing with regard to the composition of that tribunal. That is determined by the Congress, and the composition of the highest Court has been fixed by statute since the beginning of the Republic. The present membership of nine Justices (which is the number the Court has contained since 1869) has no constitutional basis; it is the number fixed by Congress in the Judicial Code. In actual fact, the membership of the high bench has varied from six (the number at the time of its creation) to five, to seven, to nine, then to ten, then seven again, and finally to the present membership of nine.[25]

The failure to fix the membership of the Supreme Court in the Constitution constitutes a dangerous lacuna in the basic document. In Bryce's phrase: "Here was a weak point, a joint in the court's armour through which a weapon might some day penetrate." [26] An unscrupulous President, whose party is dominant in Congress, but whose measures are declared unconstitutional by the high Court, has the way open to achieve his ends by securing legislation increasing the membership of the Court and then "packing" that tribunal with his own appointees. The new Justices then outvote the old ones; the Administration measures are held valid: "the security provided for the protection of the Constitution is gone like a morning mist." [27]

Under the organic document, as it is at present written, the legislative department may control, not only the composition of the Supreme Court, but also its internal organization and functioning. Congress has determined the time and place of sessions of the Court, going so far in 1801 as to change its terms so that for fourteen months, between December, 1801, and February, 1803, the high bench did not sit.[28] In addition, as we shall see in section 139, the Congressional authority in this respect extends even to the prescription of the procedural and other rules which govern the working of the Court.

It has sometimes been proposed that the Supreme Court be organized into sections or divisions, to enable it more effectively to dispose of its heavy case-load. Such proposals have at times been introduced in legislative form as bills by members of the Congress.[29] Chief Justice Hughes, writing in 1937 to the Senate Judiciary Committee, articulated doubts concerning the constitutionality of such device, declaring that "the Constitution does not appear to authorize two or more Supreme Courts functioning in effect as separate courts." [30] One wonders whether the doubts expressed are justified. To provide that a court is to function in sections is not to split up the court itself. Thus, the federal courts of appeals today generally sit in divisions, convening en banc only to hear the most important cases.[31] It is difficult to see why legislation could not provide essentially the same arrangement in the highest Court.

Even with what has been said about legislative control over the composition and functioning of the Supreme Court, the Congressional authority in this respect is limited by the constitutional basis of the high tribunal. The Supreme Court is provided for directly in Article III. This means that its existence must continue so long as the organic structure remains essentially unaltered. The Congress, it is true, had to turn the bare statement in Article III with regard to the Supreme Court into a living institution by the provisions setting up the Court in the Judiciary Act of 1789. Once established, however, the continued existence of the high tribunal became a matter beyond the power of the legislative department. From February 2, 1790 (the date of its first session) [32] to the present day, the Supreme Court has functioned as the only continuing governmental institution in the constitutional structure.[33]

133
SAME: The constitutional foundation upon which, we have
LOWER COURTS   just seen, the existence of the Supreme Court is
                      based is lacking when we turn to the other courts
in the federal judicial system. Article III provides expressly for the vesting of judicial power in "one supreme Court"; but it refers only in general terms to the existence of other tribunals in the judicial department, when

it states that judicial power shall also be vested "in such inferior Courts as the Congress may from time to time ordain and establish."

It has been urged that the existence of the lower federal courts, like that of the highest tribunal, may be derived from the Constitution itself. Under this view, just as a Supreme Court must be established under Article III, it is equally obligatory upon the Congress to establish the inferior courts referred to in that Article. In the words of a proponent of such view, "It would seem, therefore, to follow that Congress are bound to create some inferior courts, in which to vest all that jurisdiction which, under the constitution, is exclusively vested in the United States, and of which the Supreme Court cannot take original cognizance." [34]

Justice Story, whose high authority (both on [35] and off [36] the bench) may be adduced in support of the view just stated, has asserted that the absence of legislative discretion with regard to the creation of inferior courts is vital to the very existence of the judicial department: "If congress possess any discretion on this subject, it is obvious, that the judiciary, as a co-ordinate department of the government, may, at the will of congress, be annihilated." [37]

If the question were still an open one, much might be said in favor of the Story view. Law and practice have, all the same, combined to make that view only of academic interest at the present time. The law on the matter was well stated by the highest Court in 1943: "Article III left Congress free to establish inferior federal courts or not as it thought appropriate." [38]

The rule as so stated accords both with the intent of the Framers and the letter of the text drawn up by them. That Article III was intended to give the Congress complete discretion with regard to the creation of inferior federal courts is shown by the fact that the subject first taken up in the debate on the draft bill which became the Judiciary Act of 1789 was the question of whether there should be any inferior federal courts at all. It is not generally recalled that many of the strongest supporters of the Constitution expressed the belief that the function of executing federal laws should be left in the first instance with the state courts, subject to appeal to the Federal Supreme Court.[39] In the first Judiciary Act, the Congress opted in favor of establishing a set of inferior federal courts. But their debate on the matter shows that they were of the view that they were vested with the power to create or not to create such tribunals, in their discretion.

The organic language plainly supports the Congressional discretion in this respect. Article III vests judicial power in "such inferior Courts as the Congress *may* from time to time ordain and establish." [40] The use of the term "may" indicates that it is for the legislative department alone to determine what, if any, inferior courts to establish.[41] Consequently, only the existence of the Supreme Court itself is derived directly from the Constitution. Every other court created by the General Government derives its existence wholly from the authority of Congress.[42] And, in Justice Frankfurter's phrase: "Congress need not establish inferior courts." [43]

What is true of the Congressional power to create is also true of the power to abolish. The legislative authority in this respect was exercised as early as 1802, when the Judiciary Act of 1801 [44]—the so-called "midnight judges bill"—enacted at the end of the Adams Administration was repealed. The 1801 act created a new system of circuit courts and a number of new district courts, which were staffed by the outgoing President almost exclusively from his own party. After a sharp debate on the power of the Congress to do away with courts once they were created, the incoming Jeffersonians abolished the new courts soon after they took office, without any provision for the displaced judges.[45]

In the 1803 case of *Stuart v. Laird,*[46] a strong attack was made upon the constitutionality of the 1802 repealing Act. According to Charles Lee, arguing there, the Congress may modify the courts, but cannot destroy them, consistently with the organic regard paid to the independence of the judges.[47] This argument was rejected by the Supreme Court in a laconic opinion, which stated only that Congress had constitutional authority to establish, as they chose, such inferior tribunals as they deemed proper, and to transfer a cause from one such tribunal to another. "In this last particular," said the Court, "there are no words in the constitution to prohibit or restrain the exercise of legislative power." [48]

Since *Stuart v. Laird,* there has never been any legal doubt about the authority of the Congress to create and abolish inferior courts at will. During the present century, there have been two striking exercises of the Congressional power in this respect. In 1910, the United States Commerce Court was established to review orders of the Interstate Commerce Commission.[49] That court did not, however, work out as well as its sponsors had intended [50] and, in 1913, a statute was enacted legislating it out of existence.[51] Though the bill to abolish the Commerce Court gave rise to a Congressional debate on the organic power of the legislature to do away with courts, once enacted, the validity of the law abolishing the Commerce Court was accepted without question by all concerned.

More recently, in the Emergency Price Control Act of 1942,[52] the Congress created the Emergency Court of Appeals to review administrative decisions in the field of price and rent control. That tribunal continued in existence, with exclusive jurisdiction over price and rent control cases, during and after the war—until federal power in both areas was relinquished by Congress. The Supreme Court expressly upheld the Congressional authority to create the Emergency Court, with specialized jurisdiction in its particular field.[53] Nor has there been any substantial doubt about the legislative power to do away with the court when its very reason for existence terminated, with the practical disappearance of federal price and rent control cases.

It may thus be seen that the law has clearly come to recognize plenary power in the Congress over the existence of the inferior federal courts: the legislative department may create or abolish such tribunals in its discretion. That there are constitutional dangers in the Congressional power in this respect can scarcely be gainsaid. The argument of Charles Lee in *Stuart v. Laird*—that such power is inconsistent with true judicial independence [54]— has never really been answered. At the same time, it must be acknowledged that, as far as the law is concerned, the legislative authority in this respect is by now so firmly settled that any discussion of alternative possibilities is more or less academic.

134

SAME: "The judicial Power" under Article III extends to all
LEGISLATIVE COURTS federal cases which may arise, in law and equity.

Certainly, in creating inferior courts, the Congress may provide for the vesting in such tribunals of general jurisdiction in cases to which federal judicial power extends. Such, in fact, has been the case in the district-court system set up under Article III. But Congress is not restricted, in exercising its authority to establish tribunals under the highest Court, to setting up courts of general jurisdiction. It may create courts of specialized jurisdiction, such as the Commerce Court and the Emergency Court of Appeals discussed in the prior section. Such courts, established under Article III, are similar to other courts vested with "The judicial Power," except for the fact that their competence is confined to the specialized fields set forth in their enabling legislation.

Under the jurisprudence of the Supreme Court, at the same time, the power of the legislative department to set up judicial tribunals is not limited to the creation of Article III courts. As the high bench put it in a 1929 case: "it long has been settled that article 3 does not express the full authority of Congress to create courts, and that other articles invest Congress with powers in the exertion of which it may create inferior courts and clothe them with functions deemed essential or helpful in carrying those powers into execution." [55]

The Congressional authority to create other than Article III courts first received the imprimatur of the highest bench in 1828 in *American Insurance Co. v. Canter*.[56] In that case, the status of the courts which Congress had established in the Territory of Florida was drawn into question. The judges of those courts held office for terms of four years. It was argued that Congress could not, consistently with the provisions for life tenure in Article III, vest admiralty jurisdiction in such tribunals. According to Chief Justice Marshall, however, Article III did not control, since the territorial courts in question were not created under that Article.

The territorial courts, stated Marshall in the key portion of his opinion, "are not constitutional Courts, in which the judicial power conferred by the Constitution on the general government, can be deposited. They are incapable of receiving it. They are legislative Courts, created in virtue of the general right of sovereignty which exists in the government, or in virtue of that clause which enables Congress to make all needful rules and regulations, respecting the territory belonging to the United States. The jurisdiction with which they are invested, is not a part of that judicial power which is defined in the 3d article of the Constitution, but is conferred by Congress, in the execution of those general powers which that body possesses over the territories of the United States." [57]

The territorial courts in Florida, in other words, were created, not under the power of the Congress to establish inferior courts vested with "The judicial Power" under Article III, but under the power delegated in Article IV, section 3, to "make all needful Rules and Regulations respecting the Territory . . . belonging to the United States." Such courts are not "constitutional courts" set up under the Judiciary Article. They are "legislative courts," created by Congress in the exercise of other legislative powers, such as that to legislate for the territories. Their functions are directed to the execution of such powers, and are prescribed by Congress to deal with problems arising outside the normal context of Article III.[58]

What is true of courts in the territories is also true of courts in the District of Columbia. Those tribunals, too, the high bench has ruled, are created in virtue of a Congressional power other than that to create inferior courts granted by Article III—this time, the authority conferred by Article I, section 8, "To exercise exclusive Legislation" over the seat of government. In its capacity as the local legislature of the District of Columbia, Congress may create courts for the District.[59] Such courts also have been held to be legislative courts [60]—though as we shall see in section 137, such designation of the District of Columbia courts gives only part of the picture with regard to them.

In addition, the Supreme Court has said, legislative courts "may be created as special tribunals to examine and determine various matters, arising between the government and others which from their nature do not require judicial determination and yet are susceptible of it. The mode of determining matters of this class is completely within congressional control. Congress may reserve to itself the power to decide, may delegate that power to executive officers, or may commit it to judicial tribunals." [61]

Conspicuous among the matters referred to by the high Court are claims against the United States. Such claims may be vindicated legally only with the consent of the Congress, which may attach to its consent such conditions as it deems proper, including the requirement that suits be brought in a legislative court specially created to consider them.[62] The Court of Claims was established as such a court.[63] Similar legislative courts were set up to deal with claims arising from the disposal of public lands [64] and controverted claims to membership in certain Indian tribes.[65] More recently, the same has been the case with regard to matters arising out of the administration of the customs and revenue laws. The Customs Court, the Court of Customs and Patent Appeals,[66] and the Tax Court [67] were established as legislative courts to decide cases in those fields.[68]

The distinction between "constitutional" and "legislative" courts, first articulated by Marshall over a century ago, has been of great legal consequence. A constitutional court—i.e., one set up under Article III—may be vested only with "The judicial Power" conferred by that Article. The same is not true of a legislative court. Since such tribunal is not established under Article III, it may exercise whatever adjudicatory authority may be delegated to it by the Congress. Congress derives its authority to create constitutional courts from Article III and hence is bound by its limitations with regard to the jurisdiction which may be conferred upon such courts. Since, in setting up legislative courts, Congress need not act under Article III, it may delegate to such tribunals whatever adjudicatory authority it chooses without regard to the restrictions of Article III, which, we shall see in some detail,[69] control the competence of the ordinary federal courts.

What has just been said has been held applicable to all federal tribunals which do not have their sole source in Article III. Thus, in one case,[70] the authority conferred upon the courts in the District of Columbia to revise the valuations, rates, and regulations of the local Public Utilities Commission, and to make such orders as in their judgment the Commission should have made, was at issue. It was conceded that such revisory authority was plainly legislative in nature and consequently could not be conferred under Article III. Such a nonjudicial function could, nevertheless, the Supreme Court ruled, be vested in courts in the District of Columbia. As to the District, the Congress possesses the dual authority of a federal and local legislature. It may clothe the courts of the District, not only with the powers of federal courts, but also with such authority as a state may confer upon her courts. As the local legislature at the seat of government, Congress may, like a state legislature, confer upon courts of the District authority unconfined by the restrictions of Article III.[71]

The Court of Claims has also been vested with nonjudicial functions. From the outset Congress has required it to give merely advisory decisions on many matters. Under the statute creating it, all of its decisions were to be of that nature.[72] More recently, most of its decisions have taken effect as binding judgments, but some of them are still merely advisory.[73] A duty to give decisions which are advisory only, and so without force as judicial judgments, may be laid on a legislative court, but not on a constitutional court established solely under Article III.[74]

In addition, the Congress may revise the decisions of a legislative court —something it may not do consistently with Article III, so far as the constitutional courts are concerned.[75] In a 1944 case, the Court of Claims had rejected certain claims against the Government. Congress then passed a special act directing that court, "notwithstanding any prior determination" or "any statute of limitations," to rehear the claims in question and to give judgment under a different principle of liability and proof under which the calculation of the amount due would be more or less mechanical. The Court of Claims held such special act to be beyond the Congressional power even with regard to a legislative court. The Supreme Court reversed, ruling that there was no obstacle to Congress's imposing upon the Court of Claims (then considered solely a legislative court) the duty to pass upon a claim which that tribunal had previously rejected, in conformity to the particular rule of liability now prescribed by the Congress. The duty thus imposed upon the Court of Claims, said the high Court, is "such as it has traditionally exercised ever since its original organization as a mere agency of Congress to aid it in the performance of its constitutional duty to provide for payment of the debts of the Government." [76]

The rule that a legislative court may be vested with nonjudicial duties of a type that may not be imposed upon an Article III court gives rise, however, to certain difficulties. These have to do with the position of the legislative courts in the federal judicial system and their relationship to that august tribunal which stands at its apex. More specifically, since a legislative court may exercise nonjudicial functions, may its decisions be subjected to the appellate jurisdiction of the Supreme Court, when it is settled that that body may be vested only with "The judicial Power"?

The query just posed was answered in the negative in the 1865 case of *Gordon v. United States* [77] with regard to the Court of Claims. At the time *Gordon* was decided, that tribunal's decisions were purely advisory. Under section 14 of the Court of Claims Act of 1863: "no money shall be paid out of the Treasury for any claim passed on by the Court of Claims till after an appropriation therefor shall have been estimated for by the Secretary of the Treasury." According to Chief Justice Taney, this left it wholly up to the Secretary to determine whether to seek funds to pay a claim passed on by the Court of Claims and to the Congress to decide whether to vote the appropriation: "In this respect the authority of the Court of Claims is like to that of an Auditor or Comptroller." [78] That being the case, it is clear that the Court of Claims was not then a court at all, so that its decisions could be appealed from to the Supreme Court.

Soon after the *Gordon* case, the Congress amended the relevant statute by repealing section 14. Ever since, it has been held that the Supreme Court may entertain appeals from judgments of the Court of Claims. The high bench took jurisdiction for the first time from a final judgment of the Court of Claims in 1867 without even considering the question of whether such action violated Article III.[79] When, two decades later, the issue was raised, the Court ruled expressly "that, as the law now stands, appeals do lie to this court from the judgments of the Court of Claims in its general jurisdiction." [80]

The Court of Claims experience in this regard demonstrates that the fact that a court is considered a legislative court does not mean that its decisions may not be reviewed by the Supreme Court. The authority of the highest bench to exercise appellate jurisdiction over legislative courts turns, not upon the nature or status of such courts, but rather upon the nature of the proceeding before the particular court and the finality of its judgment. Where a legislative court decides a proceeding which is judicial in nature and admits of a final judgment, the Supreme Court may be vested with appellate jurisdiction.[81] It is only where a legislative court exercises nonjudicial power, as where it acts in exercise of its advisory functions,[82] that its action may not be subjected to review by the Supreme Court.[83]

We have seen in this section that the Congress has not been bound by the limitations upon "The judicial Power" contained in Article III in conferring competence upon legislative courts not created pursuant to that Article. Even more important perhaps is the corollary rule that, in establishing legislative courts, Congress has not been confined by the safeguards contained in Article III with regard to judicial tenure and compensation. The relevant restrictions of Article III—striking evidence of the regard which the Framers paid to the independence of the judicial department—have applied only to courts set up under the Judiciary Article. What this means as a practical matter will be discussed in some detail in section 137.

135

PERSONNEL   The outstanding feature of the American polity is
                  that it is a legal polity. Hence the courts necessarily
play a part in our system which they do not play elsewhere. In this country, the judge is a figure of the first magnitude. *Who's Who* contains sketches of the members of the important courts throughout the nation. In the equivalent books in other countries [84] one will hardly find the name of a single judge.[85]

The primordial role of the judge in American society has, not unnaturally, led to a focusing of attention upon the securing of proper personnel in the judicial department. It is almost a truism that the quality of
justice depends more upon the quality of the men who administer the law
than on the content of the law they administer.[86] Unless those appointed
to the bench are competent and upright and free to judge without fear or
favor, a judicial system, however sound its structure may be on paper, is
bound to function poorly in practice. That is why the problem of judicial
selection is the pivotal one in all discussions of the proper administration
of justice.

It should be noted that the approach to the problem of judicial selection
in the American system is different from that followed in most other countries. In European countries, for example, judgeship is a lifetime career.
Young judges, possessing prescribed professional qualifications, are re-
cruited for the lowest courts by means of competitive examinations. Successful appointees to the bench then gradually work their way up the
judicial ladder until they are appointed to one of the higher courts.

The Continental method of judicial selection, which appears more appropriate for the recruitment of civil servants than the staffing of the
bench, is, of course, wholly contrary to the Anglo-American conception
of judicial office. In the common-law world, promotion to the bench is
looked upon as a reward for service at the bar—the culmination of a distinguished professional career. Yet, even in Britain, certain professional
qualifications prescribed by law must be met by would-be appointees to
the bench. In the United States, on the other hand, the appointing authority
is left entirely at large with regard to the legal qualifications of those who
may be elevated to the bench.

The Constitution contains nothing on judicial qualifications, providing
only that the members of the federal bench are to be appointed by the
President, by and with the advice and consent of the Senate.[87] Nor has the
Congress, which has the undoubted power to fill in the organic gap by imposing statutory qualifications for appointment to the federal bench, really
added to the basic document in this respect. Aside from a requirement that
lower court judges reside in their respective districts and circuits,[88] the
statute book is silent on the professional or other qualifications which must
be met for selection as a member of the judicial department.

The silence of the written law—both constitutional and statutory—
means that, so far as the letter of the law is concerned, the President is not
restricted in any way in his choice of judicial selections. Legally speaking,
in fact, there is nothing to prevent the President from appointing someone
without any professional qualifications (who is actually not even a member of the bar) to even the highest Court. In practice, to be sure, none but

members of the legal profession have been chosen for federal judicial office. Yet, even so, the range of choice open to the President is far wider than that of the appointing authority in a country like Britain, where the judges must be chosen from among barristers of at least ten years' standing. The Presidential choice is not at all limited to that portion of the legal profession engaged only in the tasks of advocacy. The President is not, indeed, even required to select his judicial choices only from among those who are actually active at the bar. In recent years, a growing number of appointments to the federal bench has been made from among members of the bar not engaged in ordinary practice, such as members of the executive or legislative branches or law faculties.

It can scarcely be gainsaid that political considerations have, more than anything else, governed the selection of the vast majority of appointees to the federal judiciary. It is, in truth, difficult to see how the situation could be otherwise in view of the complete latitude which the law leaves to the President in the matter. The President is the leader of his political party. He will, not unnaturally, use his power of appointment—even to the bench—for partisan purposes. All too often, a seat on the highest Court itself is a reward, not for service to the law, but for service to the dominant political party.

Just as important as the emphasis upon political, rather than professional, qualifications, has been a tendency to elevate active members of the Administration in power to the federal bench. It is to be feared that men who have been part and parcel of the executive will be too favorable to its point of view. Though there may be no conscious effect, there is always the danger of bias in favor of the Government forming in the mind of such future judge. This is especially significant in view of the extent to which issues of public law now constitute the stuff of federal litigation.[89] A bench made up, in large part, of former members of the executive is bound to feel far more friendly toward government than its predecessors, drawn for the most part from the practicing bar.

Concern has long been expressed that members of the national bench are chosen more for political considerations than for judicial ability. Suggestions have from time to time been made that qualifications be prescribed for federal judicial appointees. These have been particularly urged with regard to those selected for the nation's highest Court. Thus, both President Eisenhower and his Attorney General stated the view that all those appointed to the Supreme Court should have had prior judicial experience. Bills have at times been introduced in the Congress to give effect to such view.

The proposal that prior judicial experience be required for elevation to the highest bench has been sharply criticized by Justice Frankfurter.

"One is entitled to say without qualification," he has declared in a strong public address on the subject, "that the correlation between prior judicial experience and fitness for the functions of the Supreme Court is zero." [90] Yet, even if we assume that this assertion is valid, it does not necessarily dispose of the proposed requirement, which is aimed, not so much at the fitness of future Justices, as at the minimization of political factors in the selection process. Where Supreme-Court appointees must be selected from those who have served at least a stated term on other courts, they are far less likely to be chosen to pay political debts. In addition, such appointees are less likely to feel as closely identified with the executive than they would if they were elevated directly from government service. This is a consideration of some importance in an era of ever-expanding governmental authority, when we look increasingly to the judicial department to hold the balance between the individual and the State.

From a constitutional point of view at least, it may not be doubted that the Congress has the authority to prescribe qualifications for members of the Supreme Court, whether they be prior judicial experience or other requirements. Nor will most students of the Court deny that the choice of Justices for reasons which have little to do with their legal ability should, so far as possible, be eliminated. The difficulty, of course is to combine the two: to exert the Congressional power in a manner that will do away with political and other factors that are irrelevant to judicial competence. A device that might well be fruitfully considered is that employed in some other countries—namely, that of giving the highest Court itself a veto over appointees. A mediocrity, chosen solely for political reasons, would hardly be likely to receive the endorsement of those already on the supreme bench.

136

TENURE AND COMPENSATION   The American colonies did not share in the blessing of an independent judiciary.[91] Their courts of justice did not consist of men conscientiously impartial between the king and the subject: some corrupt with hope of promotion, many more fearful of removal, almost all awe-struck by the frowns of power.[92] Those who built the American constitutional structure were well aware that judges of this type could not be counted on to perform the high functions imposed upon them by the organic instrument. Indeed, the subservience of the royal judges to George III was one of the grievances that helped bring on the Revolution. "He has made Judges dependent on his Will alone," reads the ninth specification of the Declaration of Independence, "for the tenure of their offices, and the amount and payment of their salaries."

The Founding Fathers were careful to ensure that such a complaint could not be articulated in the governmental system they were creating. "To that end," as Justice Frankfurter tells us, "they set apart a body of men, who were to be the depositories of law, who by their disciplined training and character and by withdrawal from the usual temptations of private interest may reasonably be expected to be 'as free, impartial, and independent as the lot of humanity will admit.' So strongly were the framers of the Constitution bent on securing a reign of law that they endowed the judicial office with extraordinary safeguards and prestige." [93]

To eliminate the possibility that American judges might emulate those who sat in the colonial courts, the Framers clearly and specifically provided the conditions for complete judicial independence. "The Judges," reads Article III of the basic document, "both of the supreme and inferior Courts, shall hold their Offices during good Behaviour, and shall, at stated Times, receive for their Services, a Compensation, which shall not be diminished during their Continuance in Office." Life tenure and a salary which could not be lowered by the political departments were intended to enable the judges, in the words of Chief Justice Taney, to uphold and maintain constitutional guarantees "free from every influence, direct or indirect, that might by possibility in times of political excitement warp their judgments." [94] The President might appoint the judges of the federal courts; but, once appointed, they could act without fear or favor, with what the highest Court has termed "that independence of action and judgment which is essential to the maintenance of the guaranties, limitations and pervading principles of the Constitution and to the administration of justice without respect to persons." [95]

The key to judicial independence is, without a doubt, the organic provision for security of tenure. "It is quite evident," the Supreme Court has affirmed, "that one who holds his office only during the pleasure of another cannot be depended upon to maintain an attitude of independence against the latter's will." [96] It was only when tenure during good behavior became the accepted practice that the independence of the Anglo-American judiciary was effectively secured; only since that time has the administration of common-law justice flowed on with an uninterrupted, pure, and unstained current. [97]

From the beginning, it has been clear that the organic guaranty of tenure during good behavior protects every judge sitting in a constitutional court established under Article III. It is true that the judges, like all other officers of the United States, can be removed from office by impeachment proceedings. Yet the organic provisions regarding impeachment do not really infringe upon judicial independence, since they do not permit the removal of a judge for political reasons or simply because the

Congress disapproves of his decisions. This has been settled since the failure in the early days of the Republic to secure the removal by impeachment of Supreme-Court Justice Chase for political ends. The danger of removal upon political grounds was dispelled with the miscarriage of this endeavor. In the words of a distinguished judge: "The Senate's verdict of 'Not Guilty' put an end to a theory of judicial tenure that would have meant the annihilation of an independent judiciary." [98]

Since the failure of the Chase impeachment, though impeachment proceedings have been brought against nine other federal judges,[99] in none of these cases was the effort to secure removal based upon political reasons. The "good Behaviour" required for judicial tenure under Article III may not, under the established practice, be considered through political spectacles.

Just as important as security of tenure as a *sine qua non* of judicial independence is provision for compensation of the judiciary to be free from control by the political departments. "In the general course of human nature," as Hamilton well puts it, "a power over a man's subsistence amounts to a power over his will." [100] The independence of the judicial department can never be realized in practice in a system which leaves it dependent for pecuniary resources on the occasional grants of the legislature.

The Framers were well aware of the relationship between judicial independence and control over judicial compensation. It is because of such awareness that they inserted in the basic document the express provision that the compensation received by the judges of the courts created under Article III "shall not be diminished during their Continuance in Office." The purpose of such provision has been stated by the highest Court as being, "like the clause in respect to tenure, to attract good and competent men to the bench and to promote that independence of action and judgment which is essential to the maintenance of the guaranties, limitations and pervading principles of the Constitution and to the administration of justice without respect to persons and with equal concern for the poor and the rich." [101]

What the prohibition against the diminution in tenure means in practice is shown by a comparison of the legal situation on both sides of the Atlantic when the British and American Governments sought to lower the salaries of the judges as part of the program of governmental economy adopted to meet the financial crisis of the early 1930's. In Britain, the reduction of judicial pay provided for in the National Economy Act, 1931, could not be challenged legally.[102] In the United States, on the other hand, it was held that a comparable provision in the Appropriations Act of 1932 reducing judicial salaries might not be constitutionally applied to the members of a court created under Article III.[103] The organic prohibition against diminution of judicial compensation means precisely what it says—that the salary of a federal judge may not be lowered while he continues in his judicial office—and that regardless of the ostensible public purpose that may induce such reduction. The public interest in judicial independence outweighs any possible motive, such as that of economy, which may be served by diminution.

In practice, the prohibition against reduction of judicial salaries has presented difficulty only in the field of income-tax legislation. In *Evans v. Gore*,[104] the Supreme Court ruled that the federal income tax could not be collected from a federal judge on the ground that the imposition of such tax would amount to an unconstitutional diminution in the judge's compensation. More recently, however, in *O'Malley v. Woodrough*,[105] this ruling was overruled and the salary of federal judges expressly held subject to the income tax. "To suggest," declared Justice Frankfurter in the Woodrough opinion, "that it makes inroads upon the independence of judges [because] Congress had thus charged them with the common duties of citizenship, by making them bear their aliquot share of the cost of maintaining the Government, is to trivialize the great historic experience on which the framers based the safeguards of Article III." [106]

Subjecting the judges to a general income-tax law has nothing whatever to do with the independence of the judicial department. To subject them to a general tax is only to recognize that judges are also citizens. To require a man to pay the taxes that all other men have to pay cannot possibly be made an instrument to attack his independence as a judge.[107]

137

SAME: LEGISLATIVE We have just seen how the safeguards of tenure and
       COURTS   compensation serve to protect the federal judges
                     from control by the political departments. The safeguards guaranteed by Article III have, at the same time, been applicable only to judges sitting on courts created under that Article. As noted at the end of section 134, the relevant restrictions of the Judiciary Article have not bound the Congress insofar as the legislative courts established under other organic provisions have been concerned.

What has just been said has been true even of the basic guaranty of security of tenure. In the already-discussed case of *American Insurance Co. v. Canter*,[108] the judges in the territorial courts in Florida held offices for terms of only four years. Such a limitation on judicial tenure, which would patently contravene Article III if it applied to a constitutional court, was held valid in the case of a legislative court established pursuant to the Congressional authority to make rules and regulations governing the territories of the United States.

Under *American Insurance Co. v. Canter,* legislative courts are not tribunals "in which the judicial power conferred by the constitution on the general government, can be deposited. They are incapable of receiving it." [109] It follows, as already pointed out,[110] that, in creating such courts, the legislative department is not bound by the tenure limitations which safeguard only the repositories of "The judicial Power" delegated by Article III. The Congress may, as in *American Insurance,* limit tenure in legislative courts to a term of years. It may even go further and provide that the members of such tribunals are not to be protected by any guaranty of tenure at all.

The extent of Congressional power in this respect is shown by *McAllister v. United States,*[111] where the removal from office by the President of a territorial judge was sustained, in view of a statute conferring discretionary removal power on the Chief Executive. "The whole subject of the organization of territorial courts," the high bench affirmed, "the tenure by which the judges of those courts shall hold their offices and the manner in which they may be removed or suspended from office, was left by the Constitution with Congress, under its plenary power over the territories of the United States." [112]

What is the case with regard to tenure is also true of compensation, so far as legislative courts are concerned. In *United States v. Fisher,*[113] the salary of the chief justice of the territory of Wyoming had been reduced by the Congress while that office was held by appellee. The Supreme Court held that such a reduction in the compensation of a territorial judge was within the Congressional organic authority.

The same result was reached in a 1933 case involving a legislative lowering of the pay received by a judge of the Court of Claims. In *Williams v. United States,*[114] the reduction in judicial salaries provided for in the Appropriations Act of 1932 (which, we saw in the prior section, could not be constitutionally applied to the members of a court created under Article III) was ruled properly applicable to the judges of a legislative court. In the *Williams* view, a tribunal like the Court of Claims "receives no authority and its judges no rights from the judicial article of the Constitution." [115] Instead, that court "derives its being and its powers and the judges their rights from the acts of Congress." [116] With regard to such a legislative tribunal, the Congress may provide what provision for compensation it sees fit, unhindered by the Article III prohibition against the diminution of judicial salaries.

In the already-discussed *McAllister* case, Justice Field delivered a vigorous dissent challenging the very concept of legislative courts—at least insofar as the nonapplicability to those tribunals of the Article III safeguard of security of tenure was concerned. According to him, the holding that a judge of a territorial court might be removed by the President at will overlooked the true character of such court. The territorial courts, said he, are clearly courts of the United States, designed to give that security and protection in the enforcement of the private rights of the inhabitants of the territories which the courts in the states are empowered to give to their citizens. In his view, "The same necessity for independence and freedom from apprehension of executive or legislative interference exists with reference to them as exists with reference to all judges appointed under the constitution." [117]

There is much to be said for the Field view in the matter. A dependent judiciary was listed by John Marshall as among the "greatest scourge[s] an angry Heaven ever inflicted upon an ungrateful and a sinning people." [118] The danger of judicial dependence is not lessened because the tribunals concerned are labeled legislative, rather than constitutional, courts. A legislative court, like the territorial court in *McAllister,* decides cases involving the rights and obligations of private individuals, just as do courts created under Article III. If, in Hamilton's oft-cited words, "The complete independence of the courts of justice is peculiarly essential in a limited Constitution," [119] that is true of all courts vested with what amounts to judicial power—whether or not such power be classified as that delegated by Article III. As Justice Field urged, "Whoever is here clothed with a judicial office, which empowers him to judge in any case affecting the life, liberty, or property of the citizen, cannot be restrained from the fearless exercise of its duties by any apprehension of removal or suspension, in case he should come athwart the will or pleasure of the appointing power." [120]

What has just been said has particular pertinence with regard to the courts established in the District of Columbia. As pointed out in section 134, the high bench has ruled that those courts are created, not directly under the Judiciary Article, but under the Congressional power to legislate for the seat of government. Yet, if the District of Columbia courts are treated wholly as legislative courts, it means, under the prior discussion in this section, that their members are not protected by the Article III safeguards of tenure and compensation. Such a result would be most unfortunate for the inhabitants of the District of Columbia, for, as far as they are concerned, the District courts dispense the combined judicial powers exercised by state and federal courts in other parts of the nation. It can hardly have been "intended that at the very seat of the national government the people should be less fortified by the guaranty of an independent judiciary than in other parts of the Union." [121]

The Supreme Court itself has come to realize the validity of the view just expressed. Through a long course of jurisprudence, the high tribunal had acted upon the principle that the District of Columbia courts were legislative courts, subject to Congressional control and presumably not protected by the tenure and compensation guarantees of Article III.[122] In the 1933 case of *O'Donoghue v. United States*,[123] on the other hand, the highest Court indicated that the designation of the District courts as "legislative" gave only part of the picture with regard to them.

The *O'Donoghue* case arose out of the already-referred-to provision of the Appropriations Act of 1932 reducing judicial salaries. The Comptroller General had applied such reduction to the judges of the Court of Appeals and the Supreme Court of the District of Columbia, on the ground that they were legislative, not constitutional courts whose judges were entitled to the protection of Article III. The highest Court held that the organic prohibition against the diminution of judicial salaries did protect the judges who sat in the courts of the District of Columbia. In so ruling, the high bench did not directly overrule the case-law on the status of the District courts as legislative courts created under the Article I power to legislate for the nation's capital. Instead, it declared that such courts were endowed with a hybrid heritage,[124] for they had been created both under Article I and Article III.

According to the *O'Donoghue* opinion, the Congress, in establishing courts for the District of Columbia, was acting in pursuance of two distinct organic powers—that to constitute courts inferior to the highest tribunal and that to legislate for the seat of government. The latter power enabled it to vest in the District of Columbia courts any powers which might be vested in purely legislative courts. "Congress," said *O'Donoghue*, "has as much power to vest courts of the District with a variety of jurisdiction and powers as a state Legislature has in conferring jurisdiction on its courts." [125] But the fact that the District courts were also created under Article III made the tenure and compensation provisions of that Article applicable to their judges.

If logic is to be the sole criterion, it is not easy to justify the *O'Donoghue* decision. It is difficult to see why the high Court's reasoning there is limited to the courts set up in the District of Columbia. It is true that, in *O'Donoghue*, a distinction is drawn between the District of Columbia courts and the territorial courts. The latter, it is emphasized, are parts of governments whose outstanding feature is their transitory character. In the Supreme Court's view: "it is not unreasonable to conclude that the makers of the Constitution could never have intended to give permanent tenure of office or irreducible compensation to a judge who was to serve during this limited and sometimes very brief period under a purely provisional government." [126] How different, contrasted the Court, are the characteristics of the District of Columbia! It was intended, not as an "ephemeral subdivision," but as "the capital—the very heart—of the Union itself, to be maintained as the 'permanent' abiding place of all its supreme departments." [127] Because Article III safeguards are inapplicable to the territories, it does not follow that they are also inapplicable to the District of Columbia, whose character is so different.

Even if we accept the distinction thus drawn between the territorial courts and the courts in the District of Columbia, it is hard to see why the *O'Donoghue* reasoning in this respect should be limited to the latter courts. Even if *O'Donoghue* validly differentiates the courts of the District from territorial courts, how does it differentiate them also from other non-territorial legislative courts?

From a logical point of view, indeed, it is difficult to see how a court can be both "constitutional" and "legislative" in character. A court may be created either under Article III, in which case it dispenses the judicial power outlined in that Article, or under some other organic provision, in which case it is a legislative court which does not exercise authority under Article III. Until *O'Donoghue*, it had always been assumed that there could be no intermixture or combination of the personnel, powers, or duties of constitutional and legislative courts.[128] If *O'Donoghue* does away with the prohibition against such merger, what is to prevent the Congress from cir-cumventing the limits of Article III by vesting the courts created under that Article also with jurisdiction springing from Article I? [129]

There is no completely satisfactory logical answer to this query. At the same time, the practical justification for *O'Donoghue* is clear. The District of Columbia courts, as seen in section 134, had been held not subject to the limitations upon Article III judicial power, insofar as the jurisdiction which might be conferred upon them was concerned. Yet, as already noted, the need for an independent judiciary is as great at the seat of government as in other parts of the nation. The high Court in *O'Donoghue* reconciled such need (which is at the base of the tenure and compensation guarantees of the Judiciary Article) with the cases permitting the District of Columbia courts to exercise nonjudicial functions by treating those tribunals as hybrid organs, created by the Congress in pursuance of two distinct powers.

More recently, a comparable result has been reached with regard to other legislative courts. In the 1962 case of *Glidden Co. v. Zdanok*,[130] the Court of Claims and Court of Customs and Patent Appeals were ruled courts created under Article III. Though both tribunals had under prior decisions been held solely legislative courts, the rulings to that effect were said to "stand uneasily next to *O'Donoghue*, much of whose reasoning in sustaining the Article III status of the District of Columbia superior courts seems applicable to the Court of Claims and the Court of Customs and Patent Appeals." [131] The same considerations which justify the holding that the District of Columbia courts should be protected by the tenure and compensation guarantees of Article III apply as well to other federal courts which dispense justice in this country—even though they had previously been considered solely as legislative courts.

It should, however, be noted that the *Glidden* opinion is not limited to mere application of the *O'Donoghue* reasoning to the courts concerned there. Instead, there is language implying that the whole concept of a legislative court is out of place outside the territories. More specifically, there are indications that, once a court is deemed a constitutional court under Article III, it may never exercise any nonjudicial duties, such as the advisory functions conferred by statute on the Court of Claims. Such indications should be treated with caution,[132] for they would require drastic revision of the previously settled law on the matter.

The *O'Donoghue* approach represents a workable compromise which should be applicable to other legislative courts as well—at least "When the peculiar reasons justifying investiture of judges with limited tenure have not been present." [133] Under *O'Donoghue,* a dual status [134] is, in effect, conferred upon such legislative courts: so far as their organization, and the tenure and compensation of their judges are concerned, they are constitutional courts, protected by Article III; with regard to their jurisdiction and powers, they are simultaneously legislative and constitutional courts, and as such can be vested with nonjudicial powers while sharing "The judicial Power" of the United States.[135]

138

EXTRAJUDICIAL   The men of 1787 voted down a number of proposals
FUNCTIONS   designed to confer nonjudicial functions upon the
judicial department. These ranged from Randolph's plan to associate the judges with the process of enacting laws to Morris's proposal to make the Chief Justice a member of a projected Council of State. The Framers' rejection of these proposals resulted in the delegation to the courts created under Article III of judicial power alone. This means, as we shall see in some detail in section 152, that the jurisdiction of the federal courts may be invoked only in circumstances deemed proper for the exercise of judicial power. Nonjudicial duties may not, consistently with the Judiciary Article, be imposed upon the constitutional courts.

In the present section, we are not concerned with application of the ban against nonjudicial duties to the functioning of the federal courts themselves. At this point, we shall discuss only what, if any, impact the organic limitation of "judicial Power" has upon the personnel of the judicial department. More specifically, does such limitation have any effect upon the assumption of extrajudicial duties by the judges?

From the founding of the Republic, individual members of the federal bench have undertaken extrajudicial assignments at the request of the Government. At the beginning, there was the famous example of Chief Justice Jay, who was appointed by President Washington in 1795 as Special Ambassador to England to negotiate a treaty of settlement of the controversies then pending. The President's choice of the head of the highest Court for such a mission was criticized in a Senate debate, but the appointment was finally confirmed. Jay himself had doubts about accepting the new task and did so primarily out of deference to the President's wishes.[136]

Jay's example in assuming extrajudicial duties has been followed by other members of the judicial department. An outstanding example was the participation by Supreme Court Justices in the Electoral Commission which resolved the disputed Presidential election of 1876.[137] In our own day, there was the Presidential appointment of Justice Jackson as chief counsel for the United States in the prosecution of the Nuremberg war-crime trials. There have been many other instances in recent years in which members of the federal bench have been called upon to perform extrajudicial tasks. According to Justice Roberts, indeed, it has gotten "to be a very common thing to call on federal judges, not only of the Supreme Court but from other federal courts, to take part in administrative work." [138] In the short period from 1942 to 1947, according to a Senate report,[139] there were no less than eleven instances in which members of the federal bench, two of them Supreme Court Justices,[140] were employed on special missions for the executive branch.

When Chief Justice Jay and his successor, Chief Justice Ellsworth,[141] were appointed to diplomatic assignments, the work of the Supreme Court was nominal and the concept of federal judicial office was not nearly as exalted as it has since become. Yet, even at that time, during the debate on the Jay nomination to be Special Ambassador, a resolution could be offered in the Senate that, "to permit Judges of the Supreme Court to hold at the same time any other office of employment emanating from and holden at the pleasure of the Executive is contrary to the spirit of the Constitution." [142] In 1800, proposed constitutional amendments and bills were introduced to bar judges from holding other appointments or offices.[143]

A century and a half later, we can see even more clearly that the assumption of extrajudicial duties by members of the federal bench is contrary to the very concept of judicial office provided for in the organic document. A judge, under the Constitution, is the human embodiment of the concept of justice. When the Framers set up the judicial department, they set it apart from the political branches, intending that, by withdrawal from the usual temptations of private interest, its members might reasonably be expected to be "as free, impartial, and independent as the lot of humanity will admit." [144] For the judges to accept nonjudicial offices is for them to compromise the organic intention in this respect. In Madison's words: "This was breaking in on a fundamental principle, that is, that you ought to insulate and cut off a Judge from all extraneous inducements and expectations." [145]

The policy of our system, with regard to extrajudicial duties, has been well stated by Justice Cardozo: "The policy," said he, "is to conserve the time of the judges for the performance of their work as judges, and to save them from the entanglements, at times the partisan suspicions, so often the result of other and conflicting duties." [146] A judge who undertakes official extrajudicial offices in another branch of the Government lays himself open to the charge that he is engaging in conflicting activities which may work a diminution in the prestige of the judiciary itself.[147]

Highly significant in this respect is the testimony of those members of the high bench who, in recent years, have actually embarked upon extrajudicial activities. They have expressed the opinion, after they had had the opportunity to reflect, that their assumption of nonjudicial duties was unfortunate. "I have every reason," declared Justice Roberts, "to regret that I ever did so. I do not think it was good for my position as a justice, nor do I think it was a good thing for the Court." [148]

It may be true that the assumption of extrajudicial duties does not violate the letter of the basic text. But the spirit of the organic document is quite another thing! As Justice Cardozo stated in declining the assumption of other official duties while he was chief of New York's highest court, his acceptance would lead many to "feel that there had been an offense against the spirit. I think I shall best maintain the dignity and fair fame of the great office that I hold if I avoid the occasion and the possibility of debate or misconstruction." [149]

It is hard for one fully cognizant of the concept of judicial office underlying Article III to disagree with Chief Justice Stone's conclusion that the performance of extrajudicial governmental duties is "incompatible with obligations which I assumed with the office of Chief Justice, and . . . likely to impair my usefulness in that office." [150] Since many members of the federal bench have not heeded the Stone view in the matter, it might be advisable to enact an express prohibition against the assumption by a federal judge of any other office or appointment while he remains on the bench. Such a prohibition is contained in the Constitution of the State of New York and it has been construed to bar judges from acting as delegates of the other departments for the performance of extrajudicial duties.[151] A similar interdiction, enacted under the Congressional power over the organization of the judicial department, would accomplish the same desirable end for the federal bench.

139

PROCEDURE RULES In a noted decision, the highest court of New Jersey has held that, under the constitution of that state, the judicial department was vested with inherent power to prescribe its own rules of practice and procedure—power which, in the opinion of the New Jersey court, was not subject to legislative control.[152] From a logical point of view, such a holding has much to commend it. If, as emphasized in section 34, the basic principle of internal autonomy must prevail insofar as the rules of procedure which govern the functioning of the legislative department are concerned, there is every reason why the same should be true of the procedural rules which govern the operation of the courts.

Despite what has just been said, it has been settled from the beginning that the Congress may control the procedural and other rules which govern the internal functioning of the federal judicial department. In the very first case on the subject, *Wayman v. Southard,*[153] the authority of the Congress in this respect was definitely established. The high Court there ruled that the process acts of 1789 and 1792 were valid exercises of the authority granted to the legislature under the Necessary-and-Proper Clause. The Congress, affirmed the opinion of Chief Justice Marshall, possesses the power to prescribe the rules which may govern the functioning of the federal courts.

Under *Wayman v. Southard,* it is for the legislative department to determine how its authority over judicial rules of practice and procedure is to be exercised. Hence, the Congress may itself prescribe the detailed rules which are to govern the working of the courts or it may delegate the power to prescribe such rules to the judges themselves.[154] In *Wayman v. Southard,* the delegation to the federal courts of power over process was attacked as an invalid delegation of legislative authority. Such contention was rejected by the Supreme Court, which stated specifically that Congress may delegate the power to prescribe rules of practice and procedure to the courts. Referring to the provision of the original Judiciary Act, which empowers the courts to regulate their practice, Chief Justice Marshall declared: "It certainly will not be contended that this might not be done by Congress." [155]

Acting in reliance on the principle just discussed, under which rule-making power may be delegated to the judges, the Congress has, since the judicial department was first established, vested it with broad powers to regulate its own practice and procedure, though subject to the supervisory authority of the legislative branch. From the first Judiciary Act [156] to our own day, the federal courts have been Congressionally endowed with the power to prescribe rules for the conduct of their own business.[157] Under the present Judicial Code, the Supreme Court is vested with the power to prescribe rules of practice and procedure for the district courts [158] and the rules of such courts themselves are valid insofar as they are consistent with the rules prescribed by the highest Court.[159]

It has been asserted that it is a misfortune that American courts ever gave up their control over their own procedure.[160] In this view, the New Jersey holding [161] that the judiciary is endowed with autonomy over its own internal functioning comparable to that acknowledged in the legislative department is preferable to the federal rule which recognizes Congressional primacy in the matter. Analytically, there is no more warrant for permitting the legislature to impose a strait jacket of statutory procedure upon the courts than there is for permitting the converse to happen.[162]

Be that as it may, it is too late by now to challenge the authority of the Congress in the premises. After over a century and a half of Congressional assertions of the power over judicial rules of practice and procedure, it is academic to assert that such legislative interference with the operation of a coordinate department is invalid. Hence we must concede that the Congress does possess the organic power to prescribe procedural rules for the federal courts—either directly through legislation or by delegation to the judges themselves. The Supreme Court has gone further, however, and stated that, in the absence of such delegation, the judicial department has no authority to promulgate rules governing its practice and procedure. Speaking of the various steps in judicial procedure, the high bench has stated: "The courts have no inherent authority to take any one of these steps, except as it may have been conferred by the legislative department; for they can exercise no jurisdiction, except as the law confers and limits it." [163]

To deny the judicial department any inherent power to promulgate procedural rules is to carry the concept of the courts as creatures of statute to an almost ridiculous extreme. The meanest assembly of persons is understood to possess the authority to prescribe its own procedures; shall we deny like authority to a coordinate department of government?

Over a century ago, the Supreme Court declared that: "There is inherent in every court a power to supervise the conduct of its officers, and the execution of its judgments and process. Without this power, courts would be wholly impotent and useless." [164] The same could well be said of the general power to prescribe rules governing practice and procedure. "In the very nature of things," the high bench has affirmed, "the courts of each jurisdiction must each be in a position to adopt and enforce their own self-preserving rules." [165] Otherwise, if the legislature failed to make any provision for rules to govern judicial practice and procedure, the administration of justice could hardly be carried on.

Under the approach suggested, the judicial department possesses inherent authority to govern practice and procedure before it, subject only to the overriding authority of the Congress to prescribe rules on the matter. Under the Judicial Code, as already seen, the federal courts are expressly empowered to promulgate practice and procedure rules. But, even in the absence of such statutory authorization, the courts would—simply because they are courts—possess the power to govern the conduct of their own business. Such power would include the authority which inheres in all common-law judicial tribunals to lay down procedural rules, admit and disbar attorneys from practice,[166] supervise the conduct of their officers, parties, witnesses, and jurors,[167] and to protect their authority through the contempt power.[168] These are powers which inhere in all courts; their existence is essential to proper execution of the judicial function. The moment the courts of the United States were called into existence and invested with jurisdiction over any subject, they became possessed of these powers.[169]

140

JURISDICTION   To determine the competence of the judicial department, says John Marshall, we must look to Article III—that pure fountain from which all the jurisdiction of the federal courts is derived.[170] Under the Judiciary Article, the judicial power of the United States extends to ten kinds of cases. The reasoning upon which the grant to the federal courts of competence over each of these cases is based was stated at the outset by Chief Justice Jay. According to him, in a passage which, because of its classic nature, still deserves to be quoted at length:

"The judicial power of the United States shall extend to ten descriptions of cases, viz.:

"1st. To all cases arising under this constitution; because the meaning, construction and operation of a compact ought always to be ascertained by all the parties, or by authority derived only from one of them.

"2d. To all cases arising under the laws of the United States; because as such laws, constitutionally made, are obligatory on each state, the measure of obligation and obedience ought not to be decided and fixed by the party from whom they are due, but by a tribunal deriving authority from both the parties.

"3d. To all cases arising under treaties made by their authority; because, as treaties are compacts made by, and obligatory on, the whole nation, their operation ought not to be affected or regulated by the local laws or courts of a part of the nation.

"4th. To all cases affecting ambassadors, or other public ministers and consuls; because, as these are officers of foreign nations, whom this nation are bound to protect and treat according to the laws of nations, cases affecting them ought only to be cognisable by national authority.

"5th. To all cases of admiralty and maritime jurisdiction; because, as the seas are the joint property of nations, whose right and privileges relative thereto, are regulated by the law of nations and treaties, such cases necessarily belong to national jurisdiction.

"6th. To controversies to which the United States shall be a party; because in cases in which the whole people are interested, it would not be equal or wise to let any one state decide and measure out the justice due to others.

"7th. To controversies between two or more states; because domestic tranquillity requires, that the contentions of states should be peaceably terminated by a common judicatory; and because, in a free country, justice ought not to depend on the will of either of the litigants.

"8th. To controversies between a state and citizens of another state; because, in case a state (that is, all the citizens of it) has demands against some citizens of another state, it is better that she should prosecute their demands in a national court, than in a court of the state to which those citizens belong; the danger of irritation and criminations arising from apprehensions and suspicions of partiality, being thereby obviated. Because, in cases where some citizens of one state have demands against all the citizens of another state, the cause of liberty and the rights of men forbid, that the latter should be the sole judges of the justice due to the latter; and true republican government requires, that free and equal citizens should have free, fair and equal justice.

"9th. To controversies between citizens of the same state, claiming lands under grants of different states; because, as the rights of the two states to grant the land, are drawn into question, neither of the two states ought to decide the controversy.

"10th. To controversies between a state, or the citizens thereof, and foreign states, citizens or subjects; because, as every nation is responsible for the conduct of its citizens towards other nations, all questions touching the justice due to foreign nations or people, ought to be ascertained by, and depend on national authority." [171]

At first glance, the establishment of a separate federal judicial department alongside the courts established in each of the states may seem like a needless duplication of judicial machinery and personnel. Yet, if we follow the reasoning of Chief Justice Jay, it becomes plain that the existence of the federal courts and the delegation to them of competence over the cases specified in Article III bear a direct relationship to the basic objects sought by the Framers. A federal judicature is needed in a system such as that set up in 1787 to interpret and apply the laws of the Union, and to compel obedience to them.[172] The laws of the whole would otherwise be in continual danger of being contravened by the laws of the parts. Without the competence of the federal bench, indeed, the laws and treaties, and even the Constitution of the United States might well become a dead letter.[173]

The alternative open to the Framers was to entrust the enforcement of federal law to the courts of the different states. But that would have been only to repeat the vital defect of the Confederation, when each state was obliged to acquiesce in the measure of justice which another state might yield to her or to her citizens,[174] and the nation itself was reduced to a servile dependence upon the state judiciaries. The lack of its own judicial department would, in Marshall's phrase, prostrate the Federal Government at the feet of every state.[175] Courts of justice are the means by which the law is enforced; and it is reasonable to expect that a government should repose on its own courts rather than upon others.[176]

The reasons which led to the establishment of a federal judicial department, wholly separate from the state judiciaries, also explain the jurisdiction conferred by Article III. Since the primary purpose of the federal bench is to ensure the proper interpretation and enforcement of the Constitution, laws, and treaties of the United States, their basic competence is in cases arising under them. In addition, in order to avoid the possibility of bias on the part of state courts where actions before them are between their citizens and those of another state, the federal judiciary is expressly rendered competent in cases involving such diversity of citizenship. These two classes of cases—those arising under federal law and those where there is diversity of citizenship—constitute the major areas of federal-court jurisdiction under the Constitution. Before dealing in some detail with these and the other cases to which federal judicial power extends under Article III, however, we must turn to the fundamental question of the extent to which the jurisdiction of the federal courts is subject to the control of the legislative department.

141

SAME:
LEGISLATIVE
CONTROL OF
LOWER COURTS

It is generally forgotten that the Articles of Confederation contained a limited grant of federal judicial power. In its ninth article, it empowered the Congress to establish courts to try piracies and felonies committed on the high seas and to determine appeals in cases of capture. In 1780, a Federal Court of Appeals in Cases of Capture (our first national court) was set up to act as an appellate tribunal from state admiralty courts in cases involving prizes captured by American vessels. In May, 1787, just before the Court of Appeals itself ceased to function, it decided that it was powerless to act in a case where the right of appeal had been taken away by the Congress. Where the legislature had limited the right to appeal to the federal court, such limitation had to be followed even though the decision below might have been illegal.[177]

The holding that the jurisdiction of the preconstitutional federal tribunal was wholly subject to the control of the Congress was, without a doubt, consistent with the principle of legislative primacy which dominated the government created under the Articles of Confederation. But is the same true under the organic document drawn up in 1787, in view of the Framers' devotion to the separation of powers and their establishment of the judicial department as a coordinate branch of the tripartite polity for which they provided?

A negative answer to this query is supported by the high authority of Justice Story. The Story view on the matter is a logical extension of his assertion, discussed in section 133, of the absence of legislative discretion with regard to the creation of the tribunals which constitute the federal judicial department. In *Martin v. Hunter's Lessee*,[178] Story stated his opinion on the mandatory nature of Article III in the strongest terms. In that case, he declared that, under the Judiciary Article, "the Congress are bound to create some inferior courts." [179] But he went further and asserted that, in such courts, there had to be vested "all that jurisdiction which, under the constitution, is exclusively vested in the United States, and of which the Supreme Court cannot take original cognizance." [180]

In the Story view, the organic duty of the Congress is to vest the whole judicial power in the federal courts which it creates. The judicial power, reads Article III, *shall* be vested (not may be vested) in the Supreme Court and such inferior courts as Congress may ordain and establish. "The language of the article throughout," Story asserts, "is manifestly designed to be mandatory upon the legislature. Its obligatory force is so imperative that Congress could not, without a violation of its duty, have refused to carry it into operation." [181] The Story position, in other words, derives the competence of the judicial department directly from the organic document. The jurisdiction of the federal courts is imperative and not subject to legislative limitation. Once established, the federal courts become endowed with all of the judicial power conferred by the Constitution and their competence necessarily extends, regardless of any Congressional provision in the matter, to all of the cases enumerated in Article III.

Justice Story's view on the mandatory jurisdiction of the federal courts was stated in *Martin v. Hunter's Lessee* by way of *obiter* only. In the *Martin* case itself, the Story dictum on the matter was criticized by Justice Johnson in a dissent. Both legislative and judicial construction have agreed with the Johnson opinion that Article III had nothing imperative in it, so far as the jurisdiction of the federal courts was concerned.[182]

From the very founding of the Republic, the legislative department has acted upon the assumption that it was endowed with complete discretion over the jurisdiction to be vested in the judicial department. The original Judiciary Act—that of 1789—which was a contemporaneous construction of the Constitution by the first Congress, rests on the assumption of the widest discretion on the part of Congress to create courts and to grant jurisdiction to or withhold it from them.[183] In section 133, we saw that this was true with regard to the creation of the inferior federal courts. If we now examine the competence conferred upon the newly created tribunals by the 1789 statute, we shall see that it was also the case with regard to the jurisdiction of the judicial department.

As Justice Frankfurter has pointed out, the content of jurisdiction conferred on the new judiciary by the first Judiciary Act was very limited in comparison with what it now exercises.[184] The bulk of the business of the lower federal courts under the 1789 statute concerned admiralty matters and the miscellaneous litigation depending upon the citizenship of litigants.[185] Although the protection of federally granted rights was a principal reason for the establishment of a system of federal courts, the first Congress withheld the vindication of federal claims from the jurisdiction of the new district and circuit courts.[186] The result was that original jurisdiction in cases arising under the Constitution, laws, and treaties of the United States was exercised by the state courts, subject to limited review by the Supreme Court under section 25 of the Judiciary Act.[187] It was not until 1875, indeed, that the Congress finally passed a law which authorized all cases arising under federal law to be brought in the federal courts, thus giving them concurrent jurisdiction with the state courts over cases involving federal questions.[188]

Justice Story himself declared, some two decades after the enactment of the 1789 Judiciary Act, that "it is somewhat singular, that the jurisdiction actually conferred on the courts of the United States should have stopped so far short of the constitutional extent." [189] The very first Judiciary Act plainly demonstrates the view of the Congress that it need not confer upon the judicial department all of the jurisdiction which it is capable of receiving under Article III. But Congress has also acted upon the premise that it may, in its discretion, limit the competence conferred upon the federal courts. The 1789 Judiciary Act limited the jurisdiction of the circuit courts over suits between citizens of different states to cases where the amount in controversy exceeded $500. Such jurisdictional-amount requirement (with the necessary amount raised at different times) [190] has consistently been imposed by successive Judicial Codes for most cases coming within the competence of the federal courts. Though it may be doubted whether it is necessarily sound policy to make access to the federal courts dependent upon the value of what the litigants are disputing about,[191] the organic power of the Congress to impose jurisdictional-amount require-ments has never seriously been doubted.

It may be argued that the language of the Constitution supports the view, already discussed, of Justice Story, rather than that upon which the Congress has acted with regard to its discretion over the jurisdiction of the federal courts. "The judicial Power," declares Article III, *shall* be vested in the federal courts and *shall* extend to the cases enumerated—language which certainly appears to support the Story assertion that it "is manifestly designed to be mandatory upon the legislature." [192] Despite the categorical manner in which the basic document is worded in this respect, however, the Supreme Court has consistently upheld the discretion asserted by the Congress over the competence of the judicial department.

The view of the highest tribunal on the matter was indicated soon after the Constitution itself went into effect. As early as 1793, Justice Iredell stated that all the federal courts "must receive all their authority . . . from the legislature only." [193] Six years later, the supreme bench had be-fore it the case of *Turner v. Bank of North America*.[194] It involved an action between citizens of different states to recover on a promissory note contrary to section 11 of the 1789 Judiciary Act, which forbade an action in the federal courts to recover on a promissory note or other chose in action, in favor of an assignee, unless such suit might have been prosecuted if no assignment had been made.[195] During the argument, counsel for the assignee contended that, since the case was between citizens of different states, the judicial power of the federal courts necessarily extended to it. In this contention, the grant of judicial power was a direct grant of juris-diction by Article III, which might not be limited by the legislative depart-ment.

The argument thus made led to questions by Chief Justice Ellsworth which indicated doubts with regard to its soundness,[196] as well as the fol-lowing comment by Justice Chase: "The notion has frequently been en-tertained, that the federal courts derive their judicial power immediately from the constitution; but the political truth is, that the disposal of the judicial power (except in a few specified instances) belongs to congress. If congress has given the power to this court, we possess it, not otherwise: and if congress has not given the power to us, or to any other court, it still remains at the legislative disposal. Besides, congress is not bound, and it would, perhaps, be inexpedient, to enlarge the jurisdiction of the federal courts, to every subject, in every form, which the constitution might war-rant." [197] In accord with the view so expressed, the high Court, in *Turner v. Bank of North America,* ruled that section 11 of the Judiciary Act gov-erned; hence the circuit court had no jurisdiction despite the diversity of citizenship between the parties.

It may consequently be seen that, at the very outset, the Supreme Court was of the view that the jurisdiction of the federal courts is subject to the discretionary control of the legislative department. Nor has the highest tribunal ever departed from such view—at least insofar as the lower federal courts are concerned. The holding of *Turner v. Bank of North America* was reaffirmed a half century later in the leading case of *Sheldon v. Sill*.[198] That case also involved the applicability of section 11 of the first Judiciary Act, which, there too, barred an action by an assignee of a chose in action against a citizen of another state. The assignee based his case upon the claim that section 11 was invalid because the right of a citizen of any state to sue citizens of another was conferred directly by Article III and hence Congress could not restrict that right. This reiteration of the argument in the *Turner* case was categorically rejected by the highest tribunal. The importance of *Sheldon v. Sill* is that, this time, the argument against legislative control of federal-court jurisdiction was directly answered in the opinion of the Court and not merely in a statement, during argument, by one of the Justices.

It must be admitted, concedes the *Sheldon v. Sill* opinion, that if the Constitution itself had established the inferior courts, and vested them with jurisdiction, such jurisdiction could not be restricted or divested by the Congress. "But," the opinion goes on, "as it has made no such distribution, one of two consequences must result,—either that each inferior court created by Congress must exercise all the judicial powers not given to the Supreme Court, or that Congress, having the power to establish the courts, must define their respective jurisdictions. The first of these inferences has never been asserted, and could not be defended, with any show of reason, and if not, the latter would seem to follow as a necessary consequence. And it would seem to follow, also, that, having a right to prescribe, Congress may withhold from any court of its creation jurisdiction of any of the enumerated controversies." [199]

Since *Sheldon v. Sill,* the power of the legislative department over the jurisdiction of the inferior federal courts has never seriously been doubted. *Sheldon v. Sill* has been cited, quoted, and reaffirmed many times.[200] The judicial power of the United States is thus (except in enumerated instances, applicable exclusively to the Supreme Court) dependent for its distribution, and for the modes of its exercise, entirely upon the action of Congress, which possesses the sole power of investing the federal courts with jurisdiction and of withholding competence from them to the extent which to Congress may seem proper for the public good.[201] Courts which are created by the Congress derive their jurisdiction solely from that body; [202] "Courts created by statute can have no jurisdiction but such as the statute confers." [203]

The same approach has been taken during the present century. The effect of Article III, affirmed the high bench in 1922, is not to vest jurisdiction in the inferior courts in the cases enumerated, but only to delimit the cases in respect of which Congress may confer competence. Every federal court other than the Supreme Court "derives its jurisdiction wholly from the authority of Congress," which may "give, withhold or restrict such jurisdiction at its discretion." [204]

What the Congressional discretion in this respect means as a practical matter is shown by two important statutory restrictions upon federal-court jurisdiction enacted in our own day. The first of these was the Norris–La Guardia Act,[205] which drastically restricted the jurisdiction of the federal courts to issue injunctions in cases involving labor disputes. At the time of its enactment, there were those who questioned its validity, in view of the provision of Article III that "The judicial Power shall extend to all Cases, in Law and Equity." According to opponents of the Norris–La Guardia Act, the "power to restrain by injunction is inherent in equity courts" and the legislature could not "so impinge upon their inherent equity powers . . . as to destroy altogether the power of the court to vindicate its existence and discharge its exalted functions." [206] Such argument was, however, of little avail, in view of the power recognized from the beginning in the Congress to control the jurisdiction of the inferior federal courts. The Supreme Court itself found little difficulty in sustaining the anti-injunction provisions of the Norris–La Guardia Act. When the question was presented to it, the high tribunal laconically stated, in reply to the constitutional objection: "There can be no question of the power of Congress thus to define and limit the jurisdiction of the inferior courts of the United States." [207]

In the Norris–La Guardia Act, the Congress had all but shorn federal courts of equity of their most essential power—that to issue injunctions in an important class of cases. One may, indeed, question whether an Anglo-American court can really be an equity court when it is deprived of the basic power that is characteristic of equitable jurisdiction. Yet, under the Congressional control over the jurisdiction of the judicial department, even such a drastic curtailment of equitable competence must be upheld.

An even more extreme restriction of federal-court jurisdiction was contained in the Emergency Price Control Act of 1942.[208] Under it, those aggrieved by price and rent control orders issued under the Act could challenge their validity only in a specially created Emergency Court of Appeals. All other courts were expressly declared ousted of jurisdiction to consider the validity of such orders and to enjoin them or set them aside. In *Lockerty v. Phillips,*[209] a suit was brought in a federal district court to enjoin the enforcement of a price order on the ground that it was contrary to the Constitution. It was argued that the federal courts could not validly be deprived of their basic authority to pass upon the constitutionality of statutes and regulations or orders issued under them. The Supreme Court gave short shrift to such argument, relying instead squarely upon the Congressional power to withdraw jurisdiction from the federal courts. "All federal courts," declared Chief Justice Stone, "other than the Supreme Court, derive their jurisdiction wholly from the exercise of the authority to 'ordain and establish' inferior courts, conferred on Congress by Article III." [210] The legislative power, in this respect, includes the authority to grant or withhold jurisdiction in the exact degrees and character which to Congress may seem proper. The Congress has power to divest the federal courts of the equity jurisdiction to restrain enforcement of a statute or of regulations and orders promulgated under it.

Under *Lockerty v. Phillips,* the Price Control Act—like the Norris–La Guardia Act—could restrict the equity jurisdiction of the federal courts by withdrawing from them their competence to issue injunctions in specified types of cases. But the Price Control Act did not limit itself to such taking away of the equity jurisdiction of the federal courts. It also drastically confined their criminal competence. The federal district courts were, it is true, made available for the enforcement of price and rent orders in criminal proceedings. The criminal courts were, however, barred from considering the validity of the price or rent orders upon which prosecutions before them were based. Under the Price Control Act, in fact, the issues were so cut down that little more than the fact of whether there had been a violation of the administrative order as written might be inquired into by the district courts. Thus, in criminal proceedings under the 1942 statute, a defendant could not set up the defense that he had committed no crime because the order he was charged with violating was itself invalid.

In *Yakus v. United States,*[211] the Supreme Court upheld the power of the Congress to restrict the criminal jurisdiction of the federal courts under the just-discussed provisions of the Price Control Act. According to the Court, these provisions presented "no novel constitutional issue." [212] The same considerations which had led to the decision in *Lockerty v. Phillips* were said to be equally applicable here. The Congressional authority over federal-court jurisdiction extends even to restriction of criminal competence such as that prescribed by the Price Control Act. Congress could give to the Emergency Court of Appeals exclusive jurisdiction to determine the validity of price and rent orders and withdraw from other federal courts jurisdiction to consider the validity of such orders, even as a defense to prosecutions for their violation.

The *Yakus* case graphically illustrates the extent to which the Congress has controlling authority over the jurisdiction of the inferior federal courts.

It is one thing for Congress to withhold jurisdiction. It is entirely another to confer competence and direct that it be exercised in a truncated manner. Yet, under *Yakus,* legislative control over federal-court jurisdiction extends even that far. One would have thought that whenever federal judicial power was called into play, it is responsible to the fundamental law and no other authority can intervene to require the judicial body to disregard it. Under *Yakus,* all the same, such intervention by another department is exactly what is permitted, for, according to the high bench's decision, the Congress can require the courts criminally to enforce even unconstitutional statutes and orders issued under them without regard for their validity.[213]

142

SAME:
OUTER LIMITS

During 1944–1946, the Supreme Court, in a series of decisions, ruled that the Fair Labor Standards Act required payment to mine employees for underground travel and other preliminary and incidental activities in connection with their work, which had not previously been regarded as compensable.[214] The same principle was then applied to similar "portal-to-portal" activities of employees in other fields.[215] However valid the Court's ruling may have been as a matter of statutory interpretation, it gave rise to serious practical difficulties. It rendered employers liable for tremendous amounts to their employees, when the work had been performed on the assumption that there was no such liability. In the half year after the high tribunal's "portal-to-portal" decisions, indeed, almost two thousand actions based on them were instituted in the federal courts, claiming over five billion dollars. The potential liability of the United States on War Department cost-plus contracts alone was estimated at almost a billion and a half.[216]

To deal with the situation so presented, the Congress enacted the Portal-to-Portal Act of 1947,[217] which sought to relieve employers from liability under the Supreme-Court decisions—at least so far as employment before those decisions was concerned. Under subdivisions (a) and (b) of section 2 of the 1947 Act, no employer was to be liable under the Fair Labor Standards Act for failure to pay wages or overtime for any activity prior to May 14, 1947, which was not compensable by an express provision of contract or by a specific custom or practice in effect at the time of the activity. This substantive bar against what was legislatively deemed the unfairly "retroactive" impacts of the Supreme-Court decisions was further implemented by subdivision (d) of the same section. Under it, no court "shall have jurisdiction of any action or proceeding" to enforce liability for an employer's failure to pay wages or overtime under the Fair Labor Standards Act, so far as such action or proceeding seeks to enforce any liability in respect to an activity not compensable under the already-given subsections (a) and (b).

Congress, in other words, dealt with the problem raised by the high-Court decisions by prescribing substantive immunity for employers against portal-to-portal suits based on liability incurred prior to 1947. In addition, it expressly withheld jurisdiction from the courts to entertain any such suits.

It was claimed, in a number of actions brought in the federal courts, that the Portal-to-Portal Act itself was unconstitutional, in that it retroactively deprived employees of their rights to compensation already earned. This claim was rejected on the merits by every court which considered it.[218] It should be emphasized that, despite the purported withdrawal of all court jurisdiction in such cases, most of the federal courts did not dismiss these cases on jurisdictional grounds, but instead considered them on their merits.[219]

Why was the jurisdictional bar contained in section 2 (d) of the Portal-to-Portal Act thus all but ignored by most of the federal judges?

A suggestive answer is given by the Court of Appeals for the Second Circuit in an important case.[220] The opinion of the court there starts by referring to the fact that a few district courts had sustained section 2 of the Portal-to-Portal Act on the ground that, since jurisdiction of the inferior federal courts is conferred by the Congress, it may at the will of Congress be taken away in whole or in part. These district-court decisions would, in effect, sustain subdivision (d) of section 2 of the Act, regardless of whether subdivisions (a) and (b) were valid. The instant court rejects such approach, asserting instead that, in such a case, the rule of complete Congressional control over judicial jurisdiction might have to give way.

"We think . . . ," declares the second-circuit court, in the key portion of its opinion, "that the exercise by Congress of its control over jurisdiction is subject to compliance with at least the requirements of the Fifth Amendment. That is to say, while Congress has the undoubted power to give, withhold, and restrict the jurisdiction of the courts other than the Supreme Court, it must not so exercise that power as to deprive any person of life, liberty, or property without due process of law or to take private property without just compensation. . . . Thus regardless of whether subdivision (d) of section 2 had an independent end in itself, if one of the effects would be to deprive the appellants of property without due process or just compensation, it would be invalid. Under this view, subdivision (d) on the one hand and subdivisions (a) and (b) on the other will stand or fall together." [221]

What the court is, in effect, saying here is that, if the right to compensation for portal-to-portal activities is a vested property right of which employees may not be deprived consistently with the Due-Process Clause, then the Congress may not completely eliminate the right to sue to vindicate such right to compensation. The implication is that Congressional power to withhold jurisdiction from the judicial department may not be pushed so far as to deprive individuals of all right to enforce their constitutional rights in a court. Where such rights are involved, all judicial competence may not be abolished.

The power vested in Congress over the jurisdiction of the judicial department may not, to put it another way, be employed so as to destroy rights guaranteed by the Constitution itself. The Congressional authority to prescribe the rules by which judicial competence is to be governed must be limited to such rules as do not completely eliminate the essential function of the courts in vindicating the rights guaranteed by the basic document. To hold otherwise would be to give the legislative department an all too easy way to circumvent the supreme law. It can scarcely be supposed that the Framers, concerned as they so clearly were with the danger of legislative dominance in the governmental structure they were creating,[222] intended to give Congress what amounts to the power to render organic rights unenforceable in its discretion. To push the Congressional power to withhold jurisdiction to the extreme of permitting constitutional rights to be made completely unenforceable would be to read the basic document as authorizing its own destruction.

What has just been said can be illustrated with reference to what is still the fundamental right of the person in our system—the right to habeas corpus. Let us suppose that the Congress enacts a law which purports to deprive all federal courts of their jurisdiction to issue the Great Writ. Would such an attempted ouster of jurisdiction mean that the judges of the United States are rendered utterly powerless to issue the writ that has been so basic to Anglo-American liberties?

An affirmative answer would place it within the power of the Congress to nullify, at will, the guaranty of the Habeas-Corpus Clause, under which the Great Writ "shall not be suspended, unless when in Cases of Rebellion or Invasion the public Safety may require it." In the words of one federal court: "It is established that a state court cannot inquire, upon petition for *habeas corpus,* into the validity of the confinement of a person held under the authority of the United States. Therefore, unless the federal jurisdiction statute be construed as coextensive with governmental action by United States officials, such action outside the specifications of the statute [223] would be wholly immune from judicial power; in other words, outside the necessity for compliance with the constitution. To state the proposition would seem to refute it." [224]

Any person deprived of his liberty under any purported authority of the

United States is entitled to petition for habeas corpus to determine whether his detention is illegal. Even though no statutory jurisdiction of such cases were given, the judicial department must be held to possess it as part of the judicial power of the United States in order to give effect to the constitutional right to the Great Writ.[225] It may be true that, as Chief Justice Marshall stated in the first case on habeas corpus: "the power to award the writ by any of the courts of the United States, must be given by written law." [226] In the case of the Great Writ, nevertheless, the necessary written law is to be found in the Habeas-Corpus Clause itself.

It will be contended that the discussion in this section, under which the Congressional power to withhold jurisdiction from the judicial department may not be used to divest individuals of all right to enforce their constitutional rights in a court, is contrary to the cases discussed in the prior section. How, it will be asked, can we assert that there are outer limits upon the legislative power over the jurisdiction of the federal courts in the light of statutes like the Norris–La Guardia and Emergency Price Control Acts and cases like *Lockerty v. Phillips* [227] and *Yakus v. United States?* [228]

Properly interpreted, nothing in the prior section is inconsistent with the present discussion. If we take a law like the Norris–La Guardia Act, under which, as we saw, the Congress all but eliminated the competence of the federal judges to issue labor injunctions, we must concede that it constituted a drastic limitation upon equity jurisdiction. But it did not affect the power of the federal courts to grant nonequitable relief in labor cases. And, even more important (since only the injunctive remedy really counts for anything as a practical matter in the labor field), the Norris–La Guardia Act did not in any way impair the equitable jurisdiction of the state courts.

There is nothing in the Constitution which requires Congress to afford suitors a remedy, in any particular case, in a federal court, in addition to those which they already possess in the state courts. Indeed, under Article III, Congress could have declined to create any inferior federal courts, leaving litigants to the remedies afforded by state courts.[229] When the Norris–La Guardia Act restricted federal-court jurisdiction to issue labor injunctions, it left unimpaired the power of the state judiciaries to issue such decrees.[230] Suitors, denied access to the federal judges for equitable relief in the labor field, could still petition the state judges for such relief. It may thus be seen that, in the Norris–La Guardia Act, Congress did not completely eliminate the right of litigants to obtain judicial relief in labor cases —but only restricted the jurisdiction of the federal courts to grant the injunctive remedy in such cases. That such restriction of judicial competence was upheld does not mean that the same would be true if all right of access to courts were barred in the labor field.

A law like the Norris–La Guardia Act, which affects only federal jurisdiction but leaves unimpaired the ability of litigants to resort to state courts for the vindication of their constitutional rights, comes within the outer limits of Congressional authority in this area and is not inconsistent with anything said in this section. But what of a statute like the Emergency Price Control Act? The jurisdictional bar contained in it was not limited in impact to the federal courts. Instead, under the relevant provision, "no court, Federal, State or Territorial, shall have jurisdiction or power" to consider the validity of price or rent-control orders or to enjoin them or set them aside. By this statute, said the high Court in *Lockerty v. Phillips,* Congress saw fit to confer exclusive jurisdiction to review price and rent orders on the Emergency Court of Appeals, and "At the same time it has withdrawn that jurisdiction from every other federal and state court." [231] Such withdrawal, we saw in the prior section, went so far as to preclude any court from considering the validity of price and rent orders even in enforcement proceedings (criminal or civil) brought against violators of such orders.

Under the cases discussed in the prior section, the Congressional attempt in the Price Control Act to limit state as well as federal-court jurisdiction was upheld. The legislative purpose was accomplished by exercise of the organic power to prescribe both the jurisdiction of inferior federal courts and the jurisdiction of all state courts to determine federal questions.[232] Yet, far-reaching though the Congressional ouster of judicial competence under the Price Control Act plainly was, it did not leave those affected remediless in the face of price or rent orders which deprived them of their constitutional rights. On the contrary, express jurisdiction to review price and rent orders was vested in the Emergency Court of Appeals—a court especially established for such purpose, which was given the status of a federal court of appeals.

In the Price Control Act, then, the Congress did not exercise its authority over judicial jurisdiction to bar those affected from all redress in the courts. Rather, it channeled all challenges to the validity of administrative action under the Act into a specially constituted court in which alone was vested the jurisdiction to entertain such challenges. In so doing, Congress sought to avoid or minimize the difficulties which the normal processes of judicial review might present to effective wartime price control by establishing a single procedure for review of price-control action.[233] Congress could plainly do this, where such procedure did give those affected an opportunity to have their constitutional rights protected by a court. And, where such opportunity was given—though in a single court—to challenge price-control action, the Congress could foreclose all further opportunity to question such action.

According to the high Court in its opinion in *Yakus v. United States,* the jurisdictional requirement of the Price Control Act was objectionable only if it would deny any adequate opportunity to be heard on the question of validity.[234] Since those affected had an opportunity to test price-control action in the Emergency Court, no organic objection might be raised. As the *Yakus* opinion puts it, "There is no constitutional requirement that that test be made in one tribunal rather than in another, so long as there is an opportunity . . . for judicial review which satisfies the demands of due process." [235]

The clear intimation in the statement just quoted is that, where no opportunity at all is given for review in a court, the constitutional limits have been passed. Yet this is essentially what we have been urging in this section—that Congressional authority to withhold judicial jurisdiction may not be exercised so as to foreclose all access to the judicial process for the vindication of constitutional rights. If the Price Control Act had simply purported to eliminate the jurisdiction of all courts to review the validity of administrative action taken thereunder, without providing any remedy in a court like the Emergency Court of Appeals, its jurisdictional bar could no more be given effect, consistently with the basic document, than a law (like that already discussed) which seeks to oust the courts of all jurisdiction to issue habeas corpus.

That a statute such as the Emergency Price Control Act could not validly preclude all access to the courts to challenge the legality of governmental action under it may be seen from an important opinion by Chief Justice Hughes.[236] In it, he denied that the Congress could vest in an administrative agency the authority conclusively to determine the facts in cases before it. The question posed by such Congressional action, he said, is that of whether Congress may substitute for constitutional courts, in which the judicial power of the nation is vested, an administrative agency for the final determination of the existence of the facts upon which the enforcement of the constitutional rights of the citizen depend. This question the Chief Justice answered in the negative. The power of the Congress to utilize the administrative process does not require the conclusion that it could oust the courts of all review authority over determinations of fact. "That," asserts the Hughes opinion, "would be to sap the judicial power as it exists under the Federal Constitution, and to establish a government of a bureaucratic character alien to our system, wherever fundamental rights depend, as not infrequently they do depend, upon the facts, and finality as to facts becomes in effect finality in law." [237]

If, under Chief Justice Hughes's opinion, the Congress may not cut off access to the courts on questions of fact in cases involving constitutional rights, it certainly follows that it may not bar all access to the judiciary in such cases. Yet this is precisely what has been urged throughout this section.

The prior section has shown the ample authority of the legislative department over the jurisdiction of the inferior federal courts. It may grant, withhold, or restrict the competence of those tribunals over any types of cases. Where constitutional rights are involved, however, the power over jurisdiction may not be employed to cut off the individuals concerned completely from the bar of justice. Constitutional rights may not be rendered bereft of all remedies.

To be sure, the Congress has never—even in the drastic cases discussed in the prior section—actually sought to push its authority over jurisdiction so far. The basic jurisdictional statutes actually enacted have allowed the judges to carry on their essential review functions with reasonable effectiveness. Though the avenues of review have been restricted in some areas, all access to the judiciary has never been barred where constitutional rights have been at stake. Organic limitations are not transgressed by such jurisdictional restrictions, so long as any court remains available for the enforcement of constitutional rights. But jurisdictional legislation which did preclude all courts from enforcing such rights would be beyond the limits of legislative authority. The organic power vested in the Congress over the competence of the judicial department does not enable it to act in a manner that would, in effect, negate all judicial authority to vindicate constitutional rights.

143

SUPREME COURT: The discussion in the two prior sections dealt with
ORIGINAL the jurisdiction of the inferior federal courts and the
JURISDICTION extent to which it may be controlled by the Congress.
We turn now to the situation with regard to that high tribunal which stands at the apex of the federal judicial department.

The inferior federal courts, we have emphasized, owe their very existence to the legislative department. Courts which are created by the Congress alone may not unnaturally be held to derive their jurisdiction solely from that body.[238] As it was succinctly put, in an already-quoted passage in *Sheldon v. Sill:* [239] "Courts created by statute can have no jurisdiction but such as the statute confers." [240]

The Supreme Court, unlike all other federal tribunals, is not a creature of statute. "The judicial Power of the United States," unequivocally declares Article III, "shall be vested in one supreme Court"—as well as in such other federal courts as may be established. It is thus directly by the Constitution that the highest bench is established and vested with judicial authority. The Congress may, it is true, as we saw in section 132, possess plenary power over the organization and composition of the Supreme Court. Yet that tribunal owes its existence, not to the legislative department, but to the organic instrument itself.

The Framers did not leave it to Congress to create the supreme bench by law. In order to secure its independence and enable it faithfully and firmly to perform its high organic duty, they engrafted it upon the Constitution itself.[241] This means that, once brought into being by the original Judiciary Act, the highest Court has had an independent existence, unaffected by the power of the other two departments. "So long, therefore," in Chief Justice Taney's famous words, "as this Constitution shall endure, this tribunal must exist with it, deciding in the peaceful forms of judicial proceedings the angry and irritating controversies . . . which in other countries have been determined by the arbitrament of force." [242]

If the inferior federal courts, owing their existence to the legislative department, are held to derive their jurisdiction as well from that body, does it not logically follow that the Supreme Court, which owes its existence to the Constitution, derives its jurisdiction from that same source? An affirmative answer would mean that the competence of the highest tribunal is not subject to any Congressional control or restriction. Despite the logical considerations in its favor, however, an unqualified affirmative answer may not be given—except with regard to the original jurisdiction of the Supreme Court.

Article III carefully distinguishes between the original and appellate jurisdiction of the highest Court. It provides that "In all Cases affecting Ambassadors, other public Ministers and Consuls, and those in which a State shall be Party, the supreme Court shall have original Jurisdiction. In all the other Cases before mentioned, the supreme Court shall have appellate Jurisdiction, both as to Law and Fact, with such Exceptions, and under such Regulations as the Congress shall make."

If we analyze this organic language on the competence of the Supreme Court, we must immediately note that that tribunal's original jurisdiction and its appellate jurisdiction stand upon different constitutional planes. The original jurisdiction is expressly specified in the Judiciary Article. From the beginning, the high bench has held that this means that its original jurisdiction flows directly from the Constitution and can therefore be exercised without additional enabling action by the Congress. This means further that such jurisdiction may not be controlled by the legislative department. The same is not true of the highest Court's appellate jurisdiction. Article III specifically contemplates legislative supervisory power over such jurisdiction, for it provides that it shall be subject to such exceptions and regulations as Congress may prescribe. In the next section, we shall examine in some detail the degree of control over the high tribunal's appellate jurisdiction which this provision vests in the Congress. In the remainder of the present section, let us look more closely at the Supreme Court's original jurisdiction.

Though the name of the highest Court suggests that it is solely an appellate tribunal, Article III does vest it with a limited original jurisdiction. Since such jurisdiction is spelled out specifically in the Judiciary Article, it is considered to be derived directly from the Constitution itself. As already noted, this has two principal doctrinal consequences. In the first place, since the high bench's original jurisdiction is self-executing, it may, as such, be exercised without any enabling legislation. So far as the Supreme Court is given original jurisdiction by Article III, Chief Justice Taney has said, it possesses authority "to exercise it without further act of Congress to regulate its powers or confer jurisdiction, and . . . the Court may regulate and mould the process it uses in such manner as in its judgment will best promote the purposes of justice." [243]

Even more important, as a consequence of the original jurisdiction of the highest Court being derived from the basic document itself, is the placing of such jurisdiction beyond Congressional control. This has been settled ever since *Marbury v. Madison*.[244] The statute held unconstitutional there was one which was construed as vesting the Supreme Court with the original jurisdiction to issue writs of mandamus. Chief Justice Marshall rejected the contention that, since the organic clause assigning original jurisdiction to the high bench contained no express negative or restrictive words, the power remained in the legislature to assign original jurisdiction in that Court in cases other than those specified. On the contrary, said Marshall, a negative or exclusive sense must be given to the cases of original jurisdiction spelled out in Article III.[245]

The grant of original jurisdiction to the Supreme Court over the cases specified is thus negative or exclusive of original jurisdiction in any other cases. As it was put by the high Court itself in a later case: "The rule of construction of the Constitution being, that affirmative words in the Constitution, declaring in what cases the Supreme Court shall have original jurisdiction, must be construed negatively as to all other cases." [246]

The statute at issue in *Marbury v. Madison* was ruled invalid because it sought to give the Supreme Court original jurisdiction in a case not specified by Article III. Under *Marbury v. Madison,* then, the Congress may not enlarge the original jurisdiction of the high bench. But the reasoning of that great case applies with equal force to legislative attempts to restrict the Supreme Court's original jurisdiction.[247] The constitutional definition of such jurisdiction deprives Congress of any power to define it. The legislative department may neither extend nor limit the terms of the organic grant.

Since the first Judiciary Act,[248] on the other hand, the Congress has assumed the power to vest concurrent jurisdiction in other courts over cases coming within the original jurisdiction of the Supreme Court. Thus, Congress has provided that the high bench shall have "original and exclusive" jurisdiction of all controversies between two or more states, while other cases in which a state is a party can be heard either by the Supreme Court or the inferior federal courts.[249] Similarly, the district courts are given jurisdiction "of all actions and proceedings against consuls or vice consuls of foreign states." [250]

As early as 1793, a circuit court sustained the Congressional assumption that the organic grant of original jurisdiction to the Supreme Court was not exclusive. The Constitution, said Justice Wilson in the case referred to, "does not preclude the legislature from exercising the power of vesting a concurrent jurisdiction, in such inferior courts, as might by law be established." [251] Almost a century later, the Supreme Court itself took a similar view. According to the Court then: "we are unable to say that it is not within the power of Congress to grant to the inferior courts of the United States jurisdiction in cases where the Supreme Court has been vested by the Constitution with original jurisdiction. It rests with the legislative department of the government to say to what extent such grants shall be made." [252]

More recently, in an action brought by the Federal Price Administrator against a state agency to enjoin sales by such agency in violation of the Emergency Price Control Act, the constitutional issue with regard to the exclusive or concurrent nature of the highest Court's original jurisdiction was raised again. It was contended that, since this was in effect a controversy between the United States and the state concerned, the Supreme Court had exclusive jurisdiction under Article III and the district court lacked power to try the case. This contention was rejected without difficulty by the high bench. In its words: "despite Article III, Congress can give the district courts jurisdiction to try cases between a state and the United States." [253]

If we apply the approach employed in *Marbury v. Madison* (under which the affirmative grant of original jurisdiction must be taken in a negative or exclusive sense, so far as Congressional power is concerned), we might well reach the result that Article III confers exclusive original jurisdiction upon the highest Court. That result, which may, at first glance, seem more consistent with Marshall's reasoning, has, nevertheless, been avoided because of the incongruity involved in requiring the august tribunal which heads the judicial department to assume original competence over every case—no matter how inconsequential—specified in Article III. As Chief Justice Taney once said, "It could hardly have been the intention of the statesmen who framed our Constitution to require that one of our citizens who had a petty claim of even less than five dollars against another citizen, who had been clothed by some foreign government with the consular office, should be compelled to go into the Supreme Court to have a jury summoned in order to enable him to recover it; nor could it have been intended, that the time of that court, with all its high duties to perform, should be taken up with the trial of every petty offense that might be committed by a consul in any part of the United States." [254]

If other courts may be vested by the legislative department with concurrent competence in cases coming within the original jurisdiction of the Supreme Court,[255] it should follow that, so far as the high tribunal itself is concerned, the original jurisdiction conferred by Article III is not compulsory. The Supreme Court has consistently held that the exercise of its original jurisdiction is not mandatory in every case specified. It has in its discretion withheld the exercise of its jurisdiction where there has been no want of another suitable forum to which the cause might be remitted in the interests of convenience, efficiency, and justice.[256] Its original jurisdiction, the high bench has affirmed, "is limited and manifestly to be sparingly exercised and should not be expanded by construction." [257] In particular, the Supreme Court's exercise of its original jurisdiction is subject to the restrictions which, as we shall see,[258] generally prevail upon the exercise of federal judicial power. Hence an original suit in the Supreme Court by a state must be dismissed where the state does not have the standing necessary to bring the action [259] or where there is no justiciable controversy presented.[260]

Despite what has been said, in one important type of case at least, the original jurisdiction of the Supreme Court has always been considered exclusive of that of other courts. The case referred to is that involving a suit between two or more states. The exclusive nature of the high tribunal's jurisdiction in such case has been recognized by the Congress itself—as in its nature it necessarily must be.[261] Under the relevant section of the Judicial Code, the Supreme Court shall have "original and exclusive" jurisdiction of all controversies between two or more states.[262]

According to the supreme bench, its original jurisdiction is one of the mighty instruments which the Framers provided so that adequate machinery might be available for the peaceful settlement of disputes between states: "The traditional methods available to a sovereign for the settlement of such disputes were diplomacy and war. Suit in this Court was provided as an alternative." [263]

That the highest Court was not exaggerating is shown by the actual history of disputes between the states. In at least four instances, we are told, armed conflicts between the militia or citizens of the contending states was a preliminary to the institution of the suits in the Supreme Court. In several of the other suits in the high bench as well, states of fact were presented which, if arising between independent nations, might well have been causes of war.[264]

When the Framers' Convention met, serious boundary disputes existed between most of the states.[265] It is hardly surprising therefore that, during the early part of our history, the first interstate controversies coming to the Supreme Court involved boundary disputes, nor that such disputes still give rise to the largest single number of suits between states. The power of the high bench to assume original jurisdiction over boundary disputes between states was settled in an elaborate opinion in the 1838 case of *Rhode Island v. Massachusetts*.[266] The words of Article III, said the Court there, apply to controversies between states. "It is not known," the Court stated, "that there were any such controversies then existing, other than those which relate to boundary, and it would be a most forced construction to hold that these were excluded from judicial cognizance." [267] Since the decision to this effect, it has, in the words of a later case, been the established doctrine of the Supreme Court "that it has jurisdiction of questions of boundary between two states of this Union, and that this jurisdiction is not defeated . . . because the decree which the court may render affects the territorial limits of the political jurisdiction and sovereignty of the states which are parties to the proceeding." [268]

In *Kansas v. Colorado*,[269] the Supreme Court was confronted with another type of original action by one state against another. The question there was whether defendant state had the right, by extensive irrigation works, to deplete the water supply of a river which flowed from defendant through plaintiff state. The highest Court held that such a suit, too, presented a justiciable controversy to be resolved by it in the exercise of its exclusive original jurisdiction. As Justice Holmes put it in an important case: "A river is more than an amenity, it is a treasure. It offers a necessity of life that must be rationed among those who have power over it." [270] Since *Kansas v. Colorado*, it has been the high bench that has determined the principles upon which interstate waters should be rationed and conflicting claims to water from interstate rivers have become the second most productive cause of Supreme-Court litigation between states.[271]

In *Kansas v. Colorado* itself, the Supreme Court indicated that its position in such a case between states was not that of the ordinary judicial tribunal deciding questions of private right according to principles of municipal law. Instead, it said, "Sitting, as it were, as an international, as well as a domestic, tribunal, we apply Federal law, state law, and international law, as the exigencies of the particular case may demand." [272] The determination, for example, of the relative rights of contending states in respect of the use of streams flowing through them does not depend upon the same considerations and is not governed by the same rules of law that are applied for the solution of similar questions of private right.[273] Instead, such cases involve the interests of "quasi sovereigns" [274] and are of the type which would be appropriate for an international tribunal if they arose between independent nations, rather than between members of a united federation. In Justice Brewer's words in *Kansas v. Colorado,* when that case was disposed of on the merits: "If the two states were absolutely independent nations it would be settled by treaty or by force. Neither of these ways being practicable, it must be settled by decision of the court." [275]

The cardinal rule which governs Supreme-Court decisions in controversies between states is the same as that which controls adjudications by international tribunals—namely, that of equality of right between the contending parties. The high Court, like an international tribunal, must settle the dispute in such a way as will recognize the equal rights of both parties and at the same time establish justice between them.[276] In resolving these disputes, Justice Brewer has declared: "this court is practically building up what may not improperly be called interstate common law." [277]

More accurate perhaps is the characterization of the high Court already intimated—namely, as more or less an international tribunal in its work in this area.[278] Disputes between states, the Supreme Court itself has affirmed, are to be considered in the untechnical spirit normally deemed proper for dealing with an international controversy.[279] Such a case, it has well stated, "is no ordinary commercial suit, but, as we have said, a quasi-international difference, referred to this court in reliance upon the honor and constitutional obligations of the states concerned." [280]

There is, to be sure, a fundamental difference between the Supreme Court exercising its original jurisdiction over controversies between states and an international tribunal seeking to resolve similar controversies between different countries. If the decision of an international tribunal is not complied with, there is no legal sanction to compel compliance. The same is not true of the Supreme Court's resolution of a "quasi-international controversy" [281] between states of the Union. Decisions of the high bench, in this as in other areas of its work, are enforceable by the normal processes available for the enforcement of judicial judgments and decrees.

It may well be that, in the acute phrase of Justice Holmes, "Great states have a temper superior to that of private litigants." [282] Yet, in only one case has a state ever failed readily to comply with the Supreme Court's resolution of its controversy with a sister state. In the case referred to, the Court had entered judgment against West Virginia for payment of a portion of the original debt of Virginia, under a compact between the two states, entered into when West Virginia became a state, binding it to pay its just proportion of the Virginia debt.[283] Two years later, Virginia filed suit to show cause why an order of the high Court should not be entered directing West Virginia to pay the judgment. The Court, in a strong opinion by Chief Justice White, categorically affirmed the enforceability of its judgment: "That judicial power essentially involves the right to enforce the results of its exertion is elementary. . . . And that this applies to the exertion of such power in controversies between states as the result of the exercise of original jurisdiction conferred upon this court by the Constitution is therefore certain." [284] The sanction that is lacking in international law to enforce the decisions of international tribunals thus exists under the Constitution so far as the "quasi-international law" dispensed by the Supreme Court, in the exercise of its original jurisdiction to decide controversies between two or more states, is concerned.

144

SAME: APPELLATE   In the prior section, we saw that the original jurisdic-
   JURISDICTION   tion of the Supreme Court, being expressly provided
                    for in the Judiciary Article, is not subject to control
by the legislative department. But cases involving exercise of its original jurisdiction today constitute but a minute part of the cases disposed of by the highest tribunal. Indeed, except for the resolution of controversies between two or more states, the original competence of the Supreme Court is now of almost no practical consequence. The essential work of the high bench (from both a qualitative and quantitative point of view) is, as its very name indicates, that of supreme appellate tribunal.

What is the constitutional situation with regard to the appellate jurisdiction of the Supreme Court?

Soon after the Constitution itself went into operation, the highest bench decided the case of *Wiscart v. D'Auchy*.[285] It involved the issue of whether an equity decree was reviewable in the Supreme Court by a writ of error or an appeal. In the course of the case, the high bench considered the nature of its appellate jurisdiction. Chief Justice Ellsworth, in an oft-cited passage, declared that the appellate jurisdiction of the highest Court depended entirely upon statute: "If Congress has provided no rule to regulate our proceedings, we cannot exercise an appellate jurisdiction; and if the rule is provided, we cannot depart from it." [286] The only question, therefore, said Ellsworth, in determining whether the Supreme Court has appellate jurisdiction in a given case is whether Congress has established a rule regulating its exercise in such case.[287]

The Ellsworth view on the matter was rejected by Justice Wilson, who urged, in a dissenting opinion, that the appellate jurisdiction of the highest bench was derived directly from the Constitution: "The appellate jurisdiction, therefore, flowed, as a consequence, from this source; nor had the legislature any occasion to do, what the constitution had already done." [288] Even in the absence of Congressional provision therefor, according to Wilson, the appellate jurisdiction of the Supreme Court may be exercised, resting as it does upon the strong ground of the Constitution itself.

Interestingly enough, both Ellsworth and Wilson had been prominent members of the Framers' Convention.[289] Yet, less than a decade after the basic document was drafted, they disagreed sharply on the organic nature of the appellate jurisdiction of the nation's highest tribunal. It has been customary to assume the correctness of Chief Justice Ellsworth's view. The constitutional provisions with regard to the appellate jurisdiction of the Supreme Court, categorically affirmed a federal court a century after *Wiscart v. D'Auchy,* are not self-executing. Consequently such jurisdiction can be exercised only pursuant to the acts and regulations of the Congress.[290]

The high Court itself has asserted a similar view. "By the constitution of the United States," it declared in 1847, "the Supreme Court possesses no appellate power in any case, unless conferred upon it by act of Congress." [291] Two decades later, the Court was, if anything, even more blunt, asserting that, "In order to create such appellate jurisdiction in any case, two things must concur: the Constitution must give the capacity to take it, and an act of Congress must supply the requisite authority." [292] The supreme bench's appellate jurisdiction is thus "wholly the creature of legislation." [293]

Despite the high authority of the cases just referred to, one wonders whether the holding that the Supreme Court's appellate jurisdiction is wholly the creature of statute results from a proper reading of Article III. "In all the other Cases before mentioned," [294] states that Article, "the supreme Court shall have appellate Jurisdiction, both as to Law and Fact, with such Exceptions, and under such Regulations, as the Congress shall make." The clear implication here is that the Supreme Court shall have appellate jurisdiction in every case to which the federal judicial power extends, subject to such limitations and regulations as Congress may enact. In the absence of any statutory provisions in the matter, the high Court's appellate competence is to reach every case specified in Article III. If that is true, the Court's appellate jurisdiction, no less than its original jurisdiction, flows directly from the Constitution, and does not require enabling legislation to be rendered operative. The appellate power of the highest tribunal extends to all cases within the federal judicial power, unless and until the power is confined within such limits as Congress sees fit to prescribe.[295]

The view just asserted was that taken by Chief Justice Marshall in two important cases. In *United States v. More,*[296] he conceded that, if the Congress had not, in the Judiciary Act, spelled out the jurisdiction of the Supreme Court, "The constitution would then have been the only standard by which its powers could be tested, since there would clearly be no exception on the subject." [297] Even more in point is the great Chief Justice's well known opinion in *Durousseau v. United States.*[298] Arguing there, Edward Livingston had asserted that the high bench, "has jurisdiction in consequence of its being the Supreme Court, and the other an inferior court." [299] The very name of the Court implied a general revisory power over the decisions of the inferior courts. Marshall acknowledged the force of this argument. He went on to state that, "Had the judicial act created the supreme court, without defining or limiting its jurisdiction, it must have been considered as possessing all the jurisdiction which the constitution assigns to it." [300] In such a case, the Congress, having failed to exercise the right of excepting from the high Court's constitutional appellate powers, necessarily left those powers undiminished.

From what has just been said, Marshall in *Durousseau* reached the same conclusion as that already asserted with regard to the nature of the Supreme Court's appellate jurisdiction: "The appellate powers of this court are not given by the judicial act. They are given by the constitution." [301]

Yet, though it is thus derived directly from the organic instrument, it is plain, from the very language of the Judiciary Article, that the appellate jurisdiction of the highest bench is subject to substantial control by the legislative department. For Article III, as already emphasized, provides that the Supreme Court is to have appellate jurisdiction in the cases therein specified, "with such Exceptions, and under such Regulations, as the Congress shall make." Under this provision, the high Court has said, while the appellate power of the Supreme Court extends to all cases within the judicial power of the United States, actual jurisdiction under the power is confined within such limits as Congress sees fit to prescribe.[302]

In his opinion in the already-discussed *Durousseau* case, Chief Justice Marshall stated that when the first Congress proceeded to carry the Judiciary Article into effect by enacting the Judiciary Act of 1789, they must be understood as intending to execute their organic power of making exceptions to the appellate jurisdiction of the Supreme Court: "They have not, indeed, made these exceptions in express terms. They have not declared, that the appellate power of the court shall not extend to certain cases; but they have described affirmatively its jurisdiction, and this affirmative description has been understood to imply a negative on the exercise of such appellate power as is not comprehended within it." [303] The affirmative grant of appellate jurisdiction in the first Judiciary Act, in other words, implied a denial of competence in those cases not mentioned.

The rule stated by Marshall, that an affirmative statutory bestowal of appellate jurisdiction implies the negation of all such jurisdiction not affirmed, has never since been questioned by the highest Court.[304] The Marshall rule may well be valid as applied to a statute such as the first Judiciary Act, whose comprehensive scope manifested a Congressional intent to except from the appellate competence of the Supreme Court those cases not affirmatively designated. As a general rule, however, that stated in *Durous-*

seau presents dangers. To infer an exception to all appellate jurisdiction not legislatively affirmed is, in practical effect, to make the competence of the Supreme Court turn solely upon the Congress, rather than the Constitution. If Congress, for example, were to amend the Judicial Code so as to confer upon the Supreme Court appellate jurisdiction only in antitrust cases, must we assume that this means the exclusion of all other exercises of the appellate power specified in Article III?

With a query such as this, we are brought directly to the seminal question of the extent of Congressional control over the appellate jurisdiction of the highest Court. The supreme bench's appellate power, under Article III, is subject to legislative exceptions and regulations. How far may the Congress go by virtue of its authority under the Exceptions-and-Regulations Clause? Could it enact a statute, analogous to that just referred to, excepting from the Supreme Court's appellate jurisdiction all cases other than antitrust cases?

It has been customary to assert that the Exceptions-and-Regulations Clause vests the legislative department with plenary power over the appellate jurisdiction of the Supreme Court. The high bench itself has at times used language supporting such assertion. What the appellate powers of the Supreme Court shall be, declares Chief Justice Waite (in what has been termed the Court's strongest pronouncement on the extent of Congressional control over its appellate jurisdiction),[305] "and to what extent they shall be exercised are, and always have been, proper subjects of legislative control. Authority to limit the jurisdiction necessarily carries with it authority to limit the use of the jurisdiction. Not only may whole classes of cases be kept out of the jurisdiction altogether, but particular classes of questions may be subjected to re-examination and review, while others are not." [306] Under this approach, it is for the Congress to determine how far appellate jurisdiction shall be given and, when conferred, it can be exercised only to the extent and in the manner prescribed by statute.[307] In Justice Frankfurter's words in a more recent case: "Congress need not give this Court any appellate power; it may withdraw appellate jurisdiction once conferred and it may do so even while a case is *sub judice*." [308]

In support of the statement just quoted, the learned judge cites *Ex parte McCardle*.[309] That case arose out of the arrest under the Reconstruction Acts of a Mississippi newspaper editor. Held for a trial by military commission, he petitioned for a writ of habeas corpus in the federal circuit court, challenging the validity of the Reconstruction Acts which authorized the military detention and trial of civilians. The writ was denied by the circuit court and an appeal was taken to the Supreme Court under an 1867 statute authorizing appeals from circuit-court decisions in all cases involving detentions in violation of the Constitution or federal laws.[310]

The high bench unanimously decided that it had jurisdiction to hear the appeal in the *McCardle* case under the 1867 statute just referred to.[311] The case was then thoroughly argued upon the merits and was taken under advisement by the Justices. The Court had two years earlier decided against the wartime trial of civilians by military commission in *Ex parte Milligan,*[312] and it was widely believed that it would seize the occasion presented by the *McCardle* appeal to invalidate the military governments authorized by the Reconstruction statutes. The Congress, to avoid the danger of such result, passed a bill repealing the already-mentioned 1867 statute, so far as it authorized an appeal to the Supreme Court from circuit-court judgments in habeas-corpus cases, and prohibiting the Court's exercise of any jurisdiction on appeals which had been or which might be taken. Though his impeachment trial had already begun, President Johnson did not hesitate to meet the Congressional attack on the high tribunal with a strongly worded veto. The bill was repassed over the Presidential negative.[313] The *McCardle* case was then reargued on the question of the authority of the Congress to withdraw jurisdiction from the Supreme Court over a case which had already been argued on the merits.

The high Court in its *McCardle* decision unanimously answered the question of Congressional power over its appellate jurisdiction in the affirmative even in such a case. "We are not at liberty," states the *McCardle* opinion, "to inquire into the motives of the legislature. We can only examine into its power under the Constitution; and the power to make exceptions to the appellate jurisdiction of this court is given by express words." [314] The effect of the repealing act, said the Court, upon the case before it was plain: namely, to withdraw jurisdiction over the appeal. "Without jurisdiction the court cannot proceed at all in any cause. Jurisdiction is power to declare the law, and when it ceases to exist, the only function remaining to the court is that of announcing the fact and dismissing the cause." [315] It is quite clear, therefore, the high bench concluded, "that this court cannot proceed to pronounce judgment in this case, for it has no longer jurisdiction of the appeal." [316]

It may not unjustly be said that *Ex parte McCardle* is a case more celebrated than understood. Commentators, both on and off the bench, have construed *McCardle* as the ultimate illustration of the unlimited power of the legislative department over the appellate jurisdiction of the Supreme Court. The result of *McCardle,* we are told,[317] is to vest an unrestrained discretion in Congress to curtail and even abolish the appellate jurisdiction of the highest tribunal. After referring to *McCardle,* Justice Roberts asks: "What is there to prevent Congress taking away, bit by bit, all the appellate jurisdiction of the Supreme Court?" [318]

One seeking to understand the *McCardle* case should certainly not seek unduly to minimize its impact. The repealing act there had as its aim the prevention of a decision by the highest Court on the constitutionality of the Reconstruction Acts. That was its sole purpose and end [319]—clearly understood as such by the Congress and the country, especially after President Johnson's veto message, which directly attacked such purpose as contrary to the spirit of the basic document. The law at issue in *McCardle* is, indeed, the only instance in American history in which Congress has rushed to withdraw the appellate jurisdiction of the Supreme Court for the purpose of preventing a particular decision on the constitutionality of a particular statute.[320] That law, in the pithy phrase of a contemporary press comment, "put a knife to the throat of the *McCardle Case*." [321]

The *McCardle* decision, upholding the Congressional authority, in effect, to prohibit the Supreme Court from deciding a pending case, has not unnaturally been interpreted as a vindication of the complete legislative power over the high tribunal's appellate jurisdiction. "Congress," wrote former Justice Curtis at the time of *McCardle,* "with the acquiescence of the country, has subdued the Supreme Court." [322]

It may appear rash, in the light of what has just been said, to assert that, far-reaching though the *McCardle* decision may be, it cannot be taken as a judicial confirmation of Congressional omnipotence with regard to the appellate jurisdiction of the highest Court. The organic position of the Supreme Court is specifically provided for in Article III and its appellate jurisdiction is also given directly by that Article. The appellate powers of the high bench flow, as a consequence, from the constitutional source.[323]

If we look to the organic role assigned by the Framers to judicial power in the polity which they were creating, it may be doubted whether they intended to vest in the legislative department authority which might be employed to nullify the practical exercise of such power. Nor can it be denied that the appellate jurisdiction of the Supreme Court (at least where questions arising under the Constitution, laws, and treaties of the United States are concerned) is essential to the operation of judicial review—by all odds the cardinal attribute of judicial power under the Constitution. In Marshall's famous words: "the necessity of uniformity, as well as correctness in expounding the constitution and laws of the United States, would itself suggest the propriety of vesting in some single tribunal, the power of deciding, in the last resort, all cases in which they are involved." [324]

It is essential to the very existence of the Constitution and the National Government established by it that a tribunal such as that referred to be set up—endowed with the power finally and conclusively to decide all cases arising under the Constitution, laws, and treaties of the United States. "It is manifest," Chief Justice Taney well states, "that this ultimate appellate power in a tribunal created by the Constitution itself was deemed essential to secure the independence and supremacy of the General Government in the sphere of action assigned to it; to make the Constitution and laws of the United States uniform, and the same in every State." [325] The appellate power of the Supreme Court is consequently as essential to the polity established by the Constitution as the powers vested in the other departments.[326] The alternative is a fifty-headed judicial hydra from which only contradictions and confusion can proceed.[327] As the high bench itself once put it, "The public mischiefs that would attend such a state of things would be truly deplorable; . . . and the appellate jurisdiction must continue to be the only adequate remedy for such evils." [328]

With the appellate powers of the Supreme Court of such consequence to the constitutional system which they were creating, can it have been intended by the Framers to confer upon the legislative department unlimited authority completely to abolish them at its pleasure? Such a result would enable the Congress at will to reduce a coordinate department to sterility and all but sweep away the judicial check upon unconstitutional governmental action.

The Framers themselves rejected a proposed amendment to Article III which would have expressly given the Congress unlimited power over the high bench's appellate competence.[329] Such rejection can hardly be construed as indicating an intent by the men of 1787 that the legislative department be vested with plenary control over such competence. The power given to Congress to prescribe exceptions and regulations with regard to the appellate jurisdiction of the Supreme Court cannot be taken to include the authority to do away with such jurisdiction. Instead, the purpose of the Exceptions-and-Regulations Clause was to authorize exceptions and regulations by Congress not incompatible with the essential organic function of the high tribunal as ultimate arbiter of the constitutional system.[330]

The Congressional power to prescribe exceptions to the Supreme Court's appellate jurisdiction may thus not be treated as authorizing exceptions which engulf the rule—even to the point of eliminating the appellate jurisdiction altogether.[331] The Supreme Court itself has affirmed that the Congressional authority in this respect is limited by the fundamental purposes of the Constitution: "What such exceptions and regulations should be it is for Congress, in its wisdom, to establish, having of course due regard to all the provisions of the Constitution." [332] The exceptions and regulations laid down by Congress must not be such as will destroy the basic role of the high bench in the constitutional scheme. Reasonably interpreted, the organic clause means: "With such exceptions and under such regulations as the Congress may prescribe, not inconsistent with the essential functions of the Supreme Court under the Constitution." [333]

Those who assert that there are no constitutional limits upon the power of the legislative department over the appellate jurisdiction of the Supreme

Court ignore the decision in *United States v. Klein*.[334] At issue there was a statute making proof of loyalty necessary to recover property abandoned and sold by the Government during the Civil War, notwithstanding any Presidential pardon or amnesty.[335] This law was ruled invalid as an attempt to impair the President's organic power to pardon.[336] What makes the Court's decision to that effect of moment to the present discussion is the fact that the statute in question was phrased in jurisdictional terms. It provided that, in the cases specified therein, neither the Court of Claims nor the Supreme Court was to have jurisdiction and directed that any cases involved should be dismissed forthwith for want of jurisdiction. Despite the Congressional authority to make exceptions and regulations, the high Court struck down the law at issue. "It seems to us," declared the opinion of Chief Justice Chase,[337] "that this is not an exercise of the acknowledged power of Congress to make exceptions and prescribe regulations to the appellate power." [338] Instead, the Congress had violated the separation of powers by dictating the effect in the courts of a Presidential pardon. "Can it," the Chief Justice asked, "prescribe a rule in conformity with which the court must deny to itself the jurisdiction thus conferred,[339] because and only because its decision, in accordance with settled law, must be adverse to the government and favorable to the suitor?" [340]

Under *United States v. Klein,* an unconstitutional attempt by the legislative department to dictate to the Supreme Court the result in a particular case is invalid even though the Congressional act is phrased in jurisdictional terms. Yet should not the same be true of any legislative attempt to abrogate the essential appellate function of the highest Court through the guise of a jurisdictional exception or regulation?

But is not what has been just said wholly contrary to *Ex parte McCardle,* where, as already seen, the Congress was sustained in ousting the high bench of competence over a case already *sub judice,* which was of such drastic import to the liberty of the individual concerned?

Those who would unqualifiedly assert that an affirmative response to this query is the only proper one overlook the real meaning of the *McCardle* case. Far reaching though its decision there doubtless was, the high Court in *McCardle* did not hold that the Congress could validly oust it of all appellate jurisdiction in habeas-corpus cases. The repealing act at issue there did not have such extreme result. In the words of the *McCardle* opinion: "Counsel seem to have supposed, if effect be given to the repealing Act in question, that the whole appellate power of the court, in cases of habeas corpus, is denied. But this is an error. The Act of 1868 does not except from that jurisdiction any cases but appeals from circuit courts under the Act of 1867. It does not affect the jurisdiction which was previously exercised." [341]

Prior to the *McCardle* statute, the Supreme Court could review denials of habeas corpus by lower courts either on appeals [342] or on petitions to it for habeas corpus.[343] The *McCardle* statute did no more than eliminate the first of these methods for obtaining high-bench review of decisions denying the Great Writ. But, as the Supreme Court itself held in *Ex parte Yerger*,[344] only a half year after its *McCardle* decision, it left unimpaired the other method of invoking the Court's appellate jurisdiction in habeas-corpus cases. The *McCardle* case consequently did not really present the question of the Congressional power to destroy the Supreme Court's appellate jurisdiction over denials of the Great Writ. The *McCardle* statute withdrawing jurisdiction, though successful to frustrate decision of the appeal in that case, left intact the power to review denials of the writ through the other procedure referred to. Indeed, under *Ex parte Yerger,* McCardle himself could presumably have petitioned the Supreme Court for a writ of habeas corpus to test the constitutionality of his military detention.

If the statute at issue in *McCardle* had attempted to oust the Supreme Court of all jurisdiction in habeas corpus cases, it may be doubted whether it would have been upheld. It is difficult to see how such a law would be any more consistent with the Habeas-Corpus Clause than that discussed in section 142, purporting completely to eliminate the jurisdiction of the inferior federal courts to issue the Great Writ.

In *Ex parte Yerger,* the same Court which decided the *McCardle* case strongly intimated that Congress lacked the power to deprive the high bench of all habeas-corpus jurisdiction. "It would have been, indeed, a remarkable anomaly," declares the *Yerger* opinion, "if this court, ordained by the Constitution for the exercise, in the United States, of the most important powers in civil cases of all the highest courts of England, had been denied, under a constitution which absolutely prohibits the suspension of the writ, except under extraordinary exigencies, that power in cases of alleged unlawful restraint, which the Habeas Corpus Act of Charles II expressly declares those courts to possess." [345]

The implication is that, by virtue of the Habeas-Corpus Clause, the jurisdiction of the Supreme Court to issue the Great Writ, once conferred, may not be withdrawn by the legislative department, except in cases of rebellion or invasion, despite its power to prescribe exceptions and regulations with regard to the high bench's appellate powers.[346] As the *Yerger* Court puts it: "it is too plain for argument that the denial to this court of appellate jurisdiction in this class of cases must greatly weaken the efficacy of the writ, deprive the citizen in many cases of its benefits, and seriously hinder the establishment of that uniformity in deciding upon questions of personal rights which can only be attained through appellate jurisdiction." [347] To permit the Congress to push its power over appellate jurisdiction to the extreme of abolishing the Supreme Court's competence in habeas-corpus cases is to empower it, at will, to abrogate the guaranty of the Habeas-Corpus Clause. For, in the language of the *Yerger* opinion, "it is evident that the imprisoned citizen, however unlawful his imprisonment may be in fact, is wholly without remedy unless it be found in the appellate jurisdiction of this court." [348]

All that has been said in this section indicates that the Exceptions-and-Regulations Clause of Article III does not vest the national legislature with unlimited power over the appellate jurisdiction of the Supreme Court. The organic clause does not permit the Congress to negate the essential functions of a coordinate department. The power to make exceptions may not be pushed so far that those prescribed eliminate the appellate jurisdiction altogether or leave only a trifling residuum of jurisdiction—as by an exclusion of everything but patent cases.[349] The authority to lay down regulations may not be construed to prohibit the entire sphere of judicial activity that is the subject of regulation. The power to regulate is not the power to destroy where the subject of regulation is so essential to the existence of the Constitution itself. The Congressional power is that to modify—not that to abolish.[350]

145

SAME: REVIEW OF STATE COURTS From a constitutional point of view, as significant as any jurisdiction vested in the Supreme Court is that to review decisions of the state courts. It is such review power which enables the high bench to maintain the supremacy of federal law when it conflicts with state law or is challenged by state authority. The importance of the Supreme Court's role in preserving national supremacy through exercise of such review power was underscored by Justice Holmes's oft-cited remark, already quoted in section 92, that the Union itself would be imperilled if the highest Court could not review the constitutionality of state laws and decisions: "For one in my place sees how often a local policy prevails with those who are not trained to national views and how often action is taken that embodies what the Commerce Clause was meant to end." [351]

From the very first Judiciary Act, the Congress has expressly preserved the Supreme Court's vital function of upholding national supremacy through its power to review state-court decisions. Section 25 of the 1789 Judiciary Act and its counterparts in later legislation [352] have empowered the high bench to review the decisions of state courts which (a) invalidate a statute or treaty of the United States or act of a federal official; (b) uphold a state statute or act of a state official against a claim that it is contrary to the Constitution, treaties, or laws of the United States; or (c) deny a "title, right, privilege or exemption specially set up or claimed by either party" under the Constitution, or any treaty or statute of, or commission held under, the United States.

"A vital chapter of American history," Justice Frankfurter informs us, "derives from the famous twenty-fifth section of the Judiciary Act of 1789. The story of its survival against legislative and judicial attacks is to no small degree a narrative of the conflict between national and state forces." [353] At almost the beginning of the Republic, such attacks gave rise to two of the landmark decisions in our constitutional jurisprudence: those rendered in *Martin v. Hunter's Lessee* (1816) [354] and *Cohens v. Virginia* (1821).[355]

Martin v. Hunter's Lessee arose out of the refusal of the highest court of Virginia to obey the mandate issued by the Supreme Court in an earlier case.[356] The Virginia decision there had been reversed on the ground that it was contrary to a treaty of the United States. The Supreme Court had then issued its mandate to the judges of the highest Virginia court "commanding" them to enter judgment in accordance with the Supreme-Court decision.[357]

"The question, whether this mandate should be obeyed," states the Reporter of the Virginia court, "excited all that attention from the bench and bar, which its great importance truly merited." [358] After lengthy argument and consideration, the Virginia court declined to obey the mandate, declaring that "The court is unanimously of opinion that the appellate power of the Supreme Court of the United States does not extend to this court, under a sound construction of the constitution of the United States;—that so much of the 25th section of the act of Congress . . . as extends the appellate jurisdiction of the Supreme Court to this court, is not in pursuance of the constitution of the United States." [359]

The Supreme Court, in a celebrated opinion by Justice Story which the historian of the high bench has characterized as "the keystone of the whole arch of Federal judicial power," [360] categorically rejected the holding that it could not be vested with appellate jurisdiction over state-court decisions. "The questions involved in this judgment," Story conceded at the outset, "are of great importance and delicacy. Perhaps it is not too much to affirm that, upon their right decision, rest some of the most solid principles which have hitherto been supposed to sustain and protect the constitution itself." [361] The Virginia court's refusal to comply with the high bench's mandate struck a blow at the very structure established by the Framers. The Virginia judges had denied that the federal courts, "belonging to one sovereignty," could be "appellate Courts in relation to the State Courts, which belong to a different sovereignty." [362] This notion of the states as separate sovereignties was vigorously rejected by the Supreme Court. The Constitution, Justice Story affirmed, "is crowded with provisions which restrain or annul the sovereignty of the states." [363] That being the case, "it is certainly difficult to support the argument that the appellate power over the decisions of state courts is contrary to the genius of our institutions." [364]

On the contrary, review by the federal courts of all state acts to ensure that they are not inconsistent with national supremacy is an essential feature of the system set up by the Framers. "The courts of the United States," said Story, "can, without question, revise the proceedings of the executive and legislative authorities of the states, and if they are found to be contrary to the constitution, may declare them to be of no legal validity. Surely the exercise of the same right over judicial tribunals is not a higher or more dangerous act of sovereign power." [365] If the state courts should misconstrue the Constitution or a law of the United States, there is no more reason for giving their judgments an absolute and irresistible force than for giving it to the acts of the other departments of the state governments.

The reasoning of the high Court in *Martin v. Hunter's Lessee* is basic to the very existence of an effective written constitution in a federation such as the American one. In the words of Justice Johnson, who delivered a concurring opinion: "the general government must cease to exist whenever it loses the power of protecting itself in the exercise of its constitutional powers." [366] If national supremacy itself is to be maintained, the highest Court of the nation must possess the power to override state action contrary to federal law. There must be a central revising authority to control the jarring and discordant judgments of the state judiciaries and harmonize them with the laws, the treaties, and the Constitution of the United States. If the situation were otherwise, the state decisions would, in effect, be paramount to the Constitution; the resulting conflict of jurisdictions would not only jeopardize private rights, but bring the public interest itself into imminent peril.[367]

Despite the unqualified nature of Justice Story's assertion of the constitutionality of the Supreme Court's review power over state-court decisions, the question decided in *Martin v. Hunter's Lessee* was presented again, in slightly different form, only five years later, in *Cohens v. Virginia*.[368] Defendants there had been convicted in a Virginia court of violating that state's law prohibiting the sale of lottery tickets. Defendants had claimed the protection of an act of Congress, since the lottery in question was sponsored by the District of Columbia, under a federal statute which authorized the District to conduct certain lotteries. After the conviction in the state court, the case was brought directly into the Supreme Court by a writ of error.[369] Defendants claimed there that, since the lottery tickets which they had sold were authorized by an act of Congress, any state law prohibiting their sale was in conflict with federal law and could not, consistently with the Constitution, be enforced. The state, in large part, repeated the arguments which had been made in *Martin v. Hunter's Lessee*.

Its objection to the appellate jurisdiction of the Supreme Court was "sustained chiefly by arguments drawn from the supposed total separation of the judiciary of a state from that of the Union, and their entire independence of each other." [370]

In *Martin v. Hunter's Lessee,* John Marshall had not been able to participate because of a personal interest in the case. In *Cohens v. Virginia,* there was no such bar and the great Chief Justice was able to lend the force of his reasoning and the prestige of his name to the opinion of the highest Court upholding its appellate jurisdiction over state courts. The Virginia argument against such jurisdiction, Marshall declared with typical force, is itself contrary to the Constitution. The states are not independent sovereignties; they are members of one great nation—a nation endowed by the basic document with a government competent to attain all national objects. "In a government so constituted," Marshall asked, "is it unreasonable that the judicial power should be competent to give efficacy to the constitutional laws of the legislature? . . . Is it unreasonable that it should also be empowered to decide on the judgment of a state tribunal enforcing [an] unconstitutional [state] law?" [371]

The questions thus posed must be answered in the negative. In a polity based upon the principle of national supremacy, it is consistent with sound reason to make all the departments of the nation supreme, so far as respects those objects of vital national interest and so far as is necessary to their attainment. As Marshall expressed it, "The exercise of the appellate power over those judgments of the state tribunals which may contravene the constitution or laws of the United States, is, we believe, essential to the attainment of those objects." [372] Let the nature and objects of the Union be considered; let the great principles on which the organic framework rests be examined; and the result must be that the Court of the nation must be given the power of revising the decisions of local tribunals on questions which affect the nation.[373]

According to Marshall's biographer, the opinion in *Cohens v. Virginia* is "one of the strongest and most enduring strands of that mighty cable woven by him to hold the American people together as a united and imperishable nation." [374] Certain it is that Marshall's magisterial opinion upholding the appellate jurisdiction of the Supreme Court [375] conclusively settled the legal question of the constitutionality of Article 25 of the first Judiciary Act and the competence of the high bench to review the decisions of state courts. Since *Martin v. Hunter's Lessee* and *Cohens v. Virginia,* state attempts to make themselves the final arbiters in cases involving the Constitution, laws, and treaties of the United States have been foredoomed to defeat before the bar of the highest tribunal.

Yet if the Supreme Court was thus able, early in the history of the Republic, to fix the law in favor of its appellate competence over the state courts, the same has not been true of the minds and passions of those who have never fully accepted the doctrine of national supremacy upon which such law is based. From Marshall's time to our own day, the power of the Supreme Court to review state-court decisions has been opposed as contrary to the true spirit of federalism. Prior to the Civil War, indeed, the courts of seven states denied the constitutional right of the highest bench to decide cases on writs of error to state courts. In the same period, the legislatures of eight states formally adopted resolutions or statutes against this power of the Supreme Court.[376] Bills have been introduced in Congress on at least twelve occasions to deprive the Court of its appellate jurisdiction over the state judiciaries.[377] Nor is the movement to curtail the high tribunal's review power over state courts of purely historical interest. As already pointed out in section 14, it has been revived in modern guise to support sectional opposition against Supreme-Court decisions enforcing the Equal-Protection Clause.

Thus far, all attempts to do away with the Supreme Court's review power over the state judiciaries—whether made in the legislative or judicial forum—have failed to achieve their purpose. In our own day, attacks on the high bench's appellate power over state laws and decisions have been rebuffed both by the Congress [378] and the Supreme Court itself.[379] From a constitutional point of view, it is difficult to see how there could be any other outcome. To repeal the modern counterpart of section 25 of the first Judiciary Act or otherwise to emasculate the Supreme Court's appellate jurisdiction over state-court decisions is to do away with an essential function of the national judiciary under the Constitution. In Chief Justice Taney's words: "no power is more clearly conferred by the Constitution and laws of the United States, than the power of this court to decide, ultimately and finally, all cases arising under such constitution and laws; and for that purpose to bring here for revision . . . the judgment of a state court, where such questions have arisen." [380]

The Federal Government is not so defective in its organization as not to contain within itself the means of securing the supremacy of its own laws proclaimed by the Constitution. Courts of justice are the means employed for such purpose; and it is reasonable to expect that the Government of the nation should repose on its own courts rather than on others.[381] National supremacy depends upon judicial power, equally clothed with authority, to carry it into execution. The supremacy so carefully provided by the Framers could not possibly be maintained peacefully, unless it was associated with such paramount judicial authority.[382] Whatever confidence may be reposed in the states, it must not go so far as to leave in them and their tribunals the power of resisting or defeating, in the form of law, the legitimate measures of the Union.[383]

146

JURISDICTION
BASED ON
CHARACTER OF
CASE: FEDERAL
QUESTIONS

In *Cohens v. Virginia*, Chief Justice Marshall stated, in terms that have become classic, the two bases upon which the jurisdiction of the federal courts is defined by Article III. "In one description of cases," said he, "the jurisdiction of the courts is founded entirely on the character of the parties; and the nature of the controversy is not contemplated by the constitution. The character of the parties is everything, the nature of the case nothing. In the other description of cases, the jurisdiction is founded entirely on the character of the case, and the parties are not contemplated by the constitution. In these, the nature of the case is everything, the character of the parties nothing." [384]

The Judiciary Article thus defines the jurisdiction of the federal courts on two different bases: character of the case and character of the parties involved. To deal fully with all the cases coming within the federal judicial power under this classification would be more appropriate to a treatise on the federal courts than to a commentary on the Constitution. The latter must, as a practical matter, deal with the two heads of federal competence only so far as is necessary to give a picture of the general competence vested in the judicial department by the organic instrument.

Under Article III, the federal courts may exercise jurisdiction over the following cases, in which their competence is based upon the character of the cause: (1) all cases in law and equity arising under the Constitution; (2) all cases in law and equity arising under the laws of the United States; (3) all cases in law and equity arising under treaties made under the authority of the nation; and (4) all cases of admiralty and maritime jurisdiction. The federal judicial power extends to any case falling within these four classifications, regardless of who the parties to the particular case may be.

The first three types of case just mentioned are essentially those which involve federal questions. The inclusion of cases of this character within the judicial power has enabled the national judicial department to make the ultimate decision on every issue of federal law.

"A case in law or equity . . ." says Chief Justice Marshall, "may truly be said to arise under the constitution or a law of the United States, whenever its correct decision depends on the construction of either." [385] A case arises under the Constitution whenever some constitutional right is denied, some right which the basic instrument gives, whether it be a right of the person or of property, so long as it be some right which can be traced to the Constitution. If such right be infringed, denied, or imperilled, it can be vindicated in the courts of the United States by virtue of Article III.[386] Cases arising under the Constitution within the meaning of Article III generally involve challenges of individuals against the enforcement of federal or state governmental action, whether an act of the legislature or executive action, which is asserted to be in violation of a provision of the Federal Constitution.

The clause extending the federal judicial power to cases arising under the Constitution is, of course, the direct organic source of the key power exercised by the judges in the American system, namely, that of judicial review. As such, it may well be characterized as the fountainhead of American constitutional law.[387] It is the textual source and origin of the judicial authority to pass upon the validity of legislative acts in cases before the courts and to strike down those which are deemed contrary to provisions of the basic document.

But the judicial power to decide federal questions is broader than that only to resolve those which involve the construction of the Constitution itself. As already indicated, the Judiciary Article also extends the competence of the federal judges to cases arising under the laws and treaties of the United States. Such cases are those whose decision depends upon the construction of a federal law or treaty.[388] Whenever an individual has a claim or right under a statute of the United States which he seeks to enforce, this can be done in one of the different organs in the judicial department of the nation.[389] "Cases arising under the laws of the United States," the Supreme Court has said, "are such as grow out of the legislation of Congress, whether they constitute the right or privilege, or claim or protection, or defense of the party, in whole or in part, by whom they are asserted." [390] The same is true of a case arising under a treaty, since, as we shall see at some length,[391] a treaty entered into by the United States has the same domestic effect as a federal law.

The language of Article III is drafted in terms sufficiently broad to include every case in which a federal question is presented. The judicial power, it reads, "shall extend to all Cases, in Law and Equity" arising under the Constitution, laws, or treaties of the United States. The terms used are advisedly wide enough to cover all types of litigation in which federal questions may arise.[392] The organic clause, in the words of a famous statement by Marshall, enables the judicial department to receive jurisdiction whenever any federal question assumes such a form that the judicial power is capable of acting on it.[393]

The constitutional language embraces alike civil and criminal cases arising under the Constitution and federal laws. Both are equally within the domain of the judicial power of the United States and there is nothing in Article III to justify an assertion that whatever power may be exerted over a civil case may not be exerted as fully over a criminal one.[394]

Early in the history of the Republic, it was contended that the term "Laws of the United States," in the clause of the Judiciary Article under discussion, covered federal common law as well as statutes enacted by the national legislature. In this view, the common law, according to the jurisprudence of England, which our ancestors brought with them upon their emigration, was part of the federal law to which the judicial power of the nation extended. "Here, then, at least," declares an adherent of this view, "the constitution of the United States appeals to, and adopts, the common law." [395]

To read Article III in the manner just stated would, however, push the federal judicial power too far, for it would extend, regardless of the nature of the parties, to every case cognizable at common law, even though no federal question is presented. The Supreme Court itself has rejected the notion that federal judicial power includes cases merely because they arise under the common law. "Courts which originate in the common law," it has affirmed, "possess a jurisdiction which must be regulated by the common law . . . but courts which are created by written law, and whose jurisdiction is defined by written law, cannot transcend that jurisdiction." [396] The federal courts, being creatures of the written law,[397] cannot exercise jurisdiction over a case solely because it involves a question arising under the common law. Only when a case arises under a statute passed by the Congress does it arise under the "Laws of the United States" within the meaning of Article III, so that the character of the case is one to which the federal judicial power extends, whoever may be the parties in such case.

Whether a case involves a federal question so as to give a federal court jurisdiction under the Judiciary Article is to be determined by the allegations of the complaint, and not upon the facts as they may turn out, or by a decision of the merits.[398] To bring the case within the national judicial power, a right or immunity created by the Constitution, laws, or treaties of the United States must be an essential element of the plaintiff's cause of action. The right or immunity must be such that it will be supported if the Constitution, laws, or treaties of the United States are given one construction or effect, and defeated if they receive another.[399] The federal nature of the controversy must appear from the face of the complaint, unaided by the answer.[400] Nor is federal jurisdiction present if the federal claim set forth in the pleading is plainly insubstantial,[401] either because obviously without merit or because its unsoundness so clearly results from previous decisions of the highest Court as to foreclose the subject and leave no room for the inference that the question sought to be raised can be the subject of controversy.[402]

It is not essential for a case to fall within the federal judicial power on the basis under discussion that every issue involved in it concern the Constitution, laws, or treaties of the United States. It is not, the Supreme Court has said, "any objection that questions are involved that are not at all of a Federal character. If one of the latter exist, if there be a single such ingredient in the mass, it is sufficient." [403] The leading case so holding is *Osborn v. Bank of the United States*.[404] The action there had been brought in a federal court by the Bank of the United States, which had been incorporated under an act of Congress which gave it the capacity to sue in the courts of the United States. It was contended that the suit of the Bank was not one arising under a law of the United States within the meaning of Article III because several questions might arise in it, which depended on the general principles of the law, not on any act of Congress. "If this were sufficient to withdraw a case from the jurisdiction of the federal courts," declared Chief Justice Marshall, in rejecting such contention, "almost every case, although involving the construction of a law, would be withdrawn. . . . There is scarcely any case every part of which depends on the constitution, laws or treaties of the United States." [405]

In *Osborn v. Bank,* the federal jurisdiction was upheld in an action brought by a corporation organized under a federal statute. For jurisdictional purposes, such action was one arising under a law of the United States, even though the substantive issues involved in the case depended upon local, rather than federal, law. Such a holding presents no difficulty in a case like *Osborn,* where the corporation bringing the action is, in effect, an agency of the Federal Government,[406] which should, as such, have unimpeded access to its courts.[407] But the Supreme Court did not confine the *Osborn* holding to such corporate instrumentalities of the Government. Instead, in a later case, it extended it to suits by or against any corporation deriving its charter from an act of Congress.[408] Private corporations chartered under federal law, particularly railroads, could consequently bring into the federal courts solely on the basis of federal incorporation cases involving no real federal question. The Congress itself has indicated its disapproval of such extension of *Osborn v. Bank.* Statutes have abolished federal incorporation as a ground of federal jurisdiction except where the United States holds more than one-half the stock.[409]

The statutes just referred to well illustrate the overriding authority of the legislative department in this field. In this, as in other aspects of federal jurisdiction, it is for the Congress (subject only to the limitations discussed in sections 142 and 144) to determine the specific cases over which the national judiciary possesses jurisdiction. The cases specified in Article III, in other words (such as those based on the character of the case discussed in this section), are those over which the federal judicial power is capable of extending. But Congress must so provide by statute before the jurisdiction of the federal courts attaches over any of the cases specified.[410]

It is also within the Congressional authority to determine whether the jurisdiction vested in the federal courts over any of the cases designated in the Judiciary Article is to be exclusive in them or concurrent with similar jurisdiction in the state courts. In the absence of Congressional provision to the contrary, it has been settled from the beginning that the jurisdiction of the federal courts over cases arising under the Constitution, laws, and treaties of the United States has not been exclusive. The mere inclusion of such cases within the federal judicial power by Article III and the different Judiciary Acts does not of itself deprive the state courts of power to take jurisdiction of such cases. In those cases where, prior to the Constitution, state tribunals possessed jurisdiction independent of national authority, they may now exercise a concurrent jurisdiction.[411] In such cases, their concurrent competence is not ousted by the fact that federal questions may be presented. The Framers plainly contemplated that such cases, though within the judicial cognizance of the nation, might also be decided in the state courts. It is for that reason that the Supremacy Clause of Article VI is specifically directed to the state judges, who are enjoined to follow the Constitution, laws, and treaties of the United States as supreme law—anything in the constitution or laws of their own states to the contrary notwithstanding.[412]

Yet if, in the absence of Congressional provision to the contrary, the state courts may retain concurrent jurisdiction in cases where they possessed preconstitutional competence independent of national authority, it is no less clear that, even in such cases, the Congress may confer exclusive jurisdiction upon the federal courts. From the first Judiciary Act, Congress has legislated upon the supposition that, in all the cases to which the judicial powers of the United States extended, it might rightfully vest exclusive jurisdiction in its own courts.[413] The Congressional authority in this respect received the early imprimatur of the highest Court. "It is manifest," Justice Story declared in *Martin v. Hunter's Lessee,*[414] "that the judicial power of the United States is unavoidably, in some cases, exclusive of all state authority,[415] and in all others, may be made so at the election of Congress." [416]

A recent illustration of the Congressional power to withdraw from the state courts the concurrent jurisdiction which they would otherwise possess over cases coming within the federal judicial power is contained in the Emergency Price Control Act of 1942. Under its provisions, as we have already seen,[417] the constitutionality of the Act and the legality of administrative action under it could be challenged only in a specially constituted federal court—the Emergency Court of Appeals. All other courts, federal and state, were expressly deprived of jurisdiction to consider such challenges. In *Bowles v. Willingham,*[418] it was argued that Congress could not constitutionally withhold from the courts of the states jurisdiction to entertain suits attacking the Price Control Act on constitutional grounds. This argument was speedily rejected by the Supreme Court. Such a case, it said, was one arising within the Constitution and laws of the United States and therefore within the federal judicial power as defined in Article III. "Hence," it concluded, "Congress could determine whether the federal courts which it established should have exclusive jurisdiction of such cases or whether they should exercise that jurisdiction concurrently with the courts of the States." [419]

The authority of the Congress to withhold all jurisdiction over cases coming within the federal judicial power from the state courts includes the power to restrict the occasions when that jurisdiction may be invoked.[420] It also includes the authority to provide for removal from the state to the federal courts of any such cases. Since the Judiciary Act of 1789, Congress has provided for such removal—the present statute providing for removal on petition of defendants of all cases over which the federal courts possess original jurisdiction.[421]

In *Martin v. Hunter's Lessee*,[422] counsel conceded the authority of the Congress to provide for a removal before final judgment of a case within the scope of the federal judicial power.[423] The Supreme Court itself expressly confirmed the Congressional power in this respect in several cases decided soon after the Civil War.[424] According to the Court in one of these cases, the jurisdiction given to the federal courts under removal statutes "involves the same principle, and rests upon the same foundation with that conferred by the 25th section of the judiciary act of 1789." [425] Like the latter, it is designed to give effect to the right of the nation to have its Constitution and laws interpreted and applied by its own judicial tribunals.[426]

Another aspect of the Congressional removal power concerns cases involving state prosecutions of federal officials. The Congress has frequently provided for the removal of state actions or prosecutions against federal officials for acts committed under the color of federal authority. The first permanent statute of this type was the so-called Force Act of 1833,[427] enacted in response to South Carolina's threats of nullification. It provided for the removal from state courts of all suits or prosecutions against officers of the United States on account of any act done under the revenue laws.[428] A similar law enacted during the Civil War authorized the removal of cases brought against federal officials for acts committed during the war and justified under the authority of the President or Congress.[429] In 1948, the Judicial Code was amended to extend removal to any action or prosecution against any officer of the United States "for any act under color of such office." [430]

The Congressional power to protect its officers in the performance of their functions through the removal power was challenged in *Tennessee v. Davis*,[431] which arose out of an attempted state prosecution of a deputy collector of internal revenue for killing a man while engaged in enforcing the revenue laws. The Supreme Court, in strong language, upheld the authority of the nation to use the removal power in such a case. The General Government, it declared, must cease to exist whenever it loses the power of protecting itself in the exercise of its constitutional powers. If, when acting within their authority, federal officers can be arrested and brought to trial in a state court, and the Federal Government is powerless to interfere, the operations of the General Government may at any time be arrested at the will of one of its members.[432] Nor may it be doubted that the necessary protection of federal officers may be effected by the removal power. The constitutional right of Congress to authorize the removal of civil cases has, as already seen, been accepted from the beginning. Yet, as pointed out earlier in this section,[433] the jurisdictional clause of Article III makes no distinction between civil and criminal cases. Hence, the Congressional authority to authorize removal from state courts is as great in the one type of case as in the other. The power to authorize the removal of criminal cases, in which federal questions are presented, is as ample as the power to authorize the removal of a civil case.[434]

147

SAME: ADMIRALTY   The Judiciary Article, in specifying those cases com-
        CASES   ing within the federal judicial power because of the
                     character of the cause, regardless of who the parties may be, provides essentially that such cases are those involving federal questions (discussed in the prior section) and "all Cases of admiralty and maritime Jurisdiction."

The provision for federal competence in admiralty and maritime causes accorded with the general sentiment of those who drew up the basic document, as well as that of their contemporaries. "The most bigoted idolizers of state authority," asserted Hamilton in *The Federalist*, "have not thus far shown a disposition to deny the National Judiciary the cognizance of maritime causes." [435] The reason the admiralty power was given to the federal judiciary, Justice Miller informs us, was that it was considered to be in the nature of an international relation.[436] Cases falling within the power, it was pointed out in an early case, necessarily belong to national competence, since the seas are joint property of nations, whose rights and privileges relative thereto are regulated by the law of nations and treaties.[437]

Even more important perhaps is the fact that, before the Revolution, maritime law had been a separate corpus administered by British vice-admiralty courts, rather than in the colonial courts, which were the predecessors of the state judiciaries. It is true that state admiralty courts were set up after independence, though, even under the Articles of Confederation, federal concern was shown by provision for appeals from their decisions to a Federal Court of Appeals. Since most of the commerce of the period was maritime, it was natural for the Framers, in pursuance of their basic goal of promoting commerce and removing state obstacles to it, to provide for admiralty and maritime jurisdiction in the national judiciary.

Since the first Judiciary Act, the Congress has vested general admiralty competence in the federal courts of general jurisdiction—i.e., the district courts. Yet, despite the fact that the federal admiralty power appears to be derived directly from that of the British High Court of Admiralty, from the beginning, Congress has assumed that the Constitution provides for a much broader conception of admiralty and maritime jurisdiction than was the case under the British practice. In Britain, at the time the Constitution was drafted, "maritime" referred to cases arising on the high seas; while "admiralty" meant primarily causes of a local nature, such as police measures regulating shipping, harbors, fishing, and the like.[438] In the 1789 Judiciary Act, wider admiralty and maritime jurisdiction was conferred on the district courts. They were given competence "of all civil causes of admiralty and maritime jurisdiction, including all seizures under the laws of imposts, navigation or trade of the United States, where the seizures are made on waters which are navigable from the sea by vessels of ten or more tons burthen, within their respective districts, as well as upon the high seas." [439]

Under this provision, according to the case-law, the federal jurisdiction was not limited to the relatively narrow scope of the British practice. The extent of the admiralty and maritime jurisdiction of the United States, said Justice Washington on circuit in an 1829 case, is not to be determined by that of the British admiralty court.[440] This view received the support of the highest bench itself in 1848 in *New Jersey Steam Navigation Co. v. Merchants' Bank.*[441] Referring to the provision of the 1789 Judiciary Act, quoted at the end of the prior paragraph, the Court there pointed out that it involved a wide departure from the English limit of admiralty jurisdiction, since the High Court of Admiralty never had original jurisdiction of causes arising under the revenue laws, or laws concerning the navigation and trade of the kingdom. Whatever doubt there might have been originally as to the true construction of the organic grant, whether it had reference to the jurisdiction in England or to a more enlarged one, the question had become settled in favor of the latter interpretation.[442] In accord with this view, the high tribunal held that the federal courts sitting in admiralty had *in personam* jurisdiction over controversies arising out of contracts of affreightment between New York and Providence.

Perhaps the basic step in enlarging admiralty jurisdiction under Article

III, as compared with the more restricted British practice, was taken in the 1852 case of *The Genesee Chief*.[443] In an earlier case, the Supreme Court had confined the territorial extent of the federal jurisdiction substantially to that followed under English doctrine, namely, to the high seas and upon rivers only as far as the ebb and flow of the tide extended.[444] In a small island like Britain, where practically all streams are tidal, such a limitation might be adequate. But it hardly proved such in a country of continental extent. "It would," in Chief Justice Taney's words, "be contrary to the first principles on which the Union was formed to confine these [admiralty] rights to the States bordering on the Atlantic, and to the tide water rivers connected with it, and to deny them to the citizens who border on the lakes, and the great navigable streams which flow through the western States." [445] In 1845, the Congress enacted a statute vesting in the district courts admiralty jurisdiction over the Great Lakes and connecting navigable waters.[446] The constitutionality of this law was upheld in *The Genesee Chief*.

The opinion of Chief Justice Taney in *The Genesee Chief* well illustrates the manner in which the law changes to meet changed external conditions. When the basic document went into operation, the English "tidal-flow" test of admiralty jurisdiction may well have sufficed. In the original thirteen states, as in England, almost all navigable waters were tidewaters. With the movement of the nation to the west, and the consequent growth of commerce on the inland waterways, the English test became inadequate. "It is evident," says the Taney opinion, "that a definition that would at this day limit public rivers in this country to tide water rivers is utterly inadmissible. We have thousands of miles of public navigable waters, including lakes and rivers in which there is no tide. And certainly there can be no reason for admiralty power over a public tide water, which does not apply with equal force to any other public water used for commercial purposes." [447]

With the decision in *The Genesee Chief,* the way was opened to an extension of the federal admiralty jurisdiction to all the navigable waters within the United States.[448] Under the cases since *The Genesee Chief,* the entire navigable waters of the country are covered by the federal jurisdiction,[449] even those which are wholly within a single state,[450] regardless of whether they be natural, or only artificial, waterways.[451] The admiralty and maritime jurisdiction of the federal courts, summed up Justice Bradley in an 1889 case, "extends wherever public navigation extends,—on the sea and the great inland lakes, and the navigable waters connecting therewith." [452]

As intimated in our discussion of *New Jersey Steam Navigation Co. v. Merchants' Bank,*[453] the federal admiralty and maritime jurisdiction is broader than its British predecessor not only with regard to the rule governing its territorial extent. Under the cases interpreting the grant of competence in Article III and the different judiciary statutes, the admiralty and maritime jurisdiction is sweeping enough to cover two great classes of case: the one dependent upon locality, the other upon the nature of the contract or other transaction involved in the case. The first respects acts done upon the high seas or other navigable waters; the other relates to contracts and other transactions connected with shipping and other maritime services on the seas and navigable waters.[454]

The first category just mentioned includes prize and seizure cases, as well as torts, injuries, and crimes committed on the high seas or navigable waters. Locality is the determining jurisdictional criterion in this class of case.[455] Federal jurisdiction depends entirely upon the commission of the wrongful act on the seas or other navigable waters.[456] The principal subjects of admiralty jurisdiction in the cases under this category are maritime torts.[457]

The second category referred to includes contracts, claims, and services maritime in nature, and touching rights and duties appertaining to commerce and navigation.[458] Jurisdiction in this class of case depends upon the nature of the contract or other transaction involved in the case.[459] Contracts constitute the principal subjects involved in the cases falling within this category. All contracts relating to commerce and navigation, wherever made, to be performed on the high seas or other navigable waters, are maritime contracts for the purposes of admiralty jurisdiction.[460] Speaking of this heading of federal competence, the Supreme Court has stated: "it may now be said, without fear of contradiction, that it extends to all contracts, claims and services essentially maritime." [461]

In *Martin v. Hunter's Lessee,*[462] Justice Story, in referring to those cases in which the judicial power of the United States is unavoidably exclusive of all state authority, stated his opinion that the admiralty and maritime jurisdiction was of such necessary exclusive cognizance.[463] In accordance with this view, admiralty and maritime causes were placed, from the commencement, exclusively within the competence of the federal courts.[464] In the very first Judiciary Act, the Congress proceeded in conformity with this view by providing that the district courts "shall have exclusive original competence of all civil causes of admiralty and maritime jurisdiction." [465] This provision was intended to make the federal admiralty jurisdiction exclusive of state-court jurisdiction.[466] "It has been made exclusive by Congress," the Supreme Court has affirmed, "and that is sufficient, even if we should admit that in the absence of its legislation the state courts might have taken cognizance of these causes." [467]

The Judiciary Act of 1789 did, however, preserve to suitors "the right of a common law remedy, where the common law is competent to give it." [468] The facts constituting a maritime tort or contract may give rise to a right of action at common law. Under the saving clause of the Judiciary Act, suitors may, if they choose, still resort to such common-law remedy in the appropriate state courts.[469] There is no constitutional obstacle to the Congressional grant of permission to resort to such common-law remedies in state courts,[470] since the effect of the saving clause is, not to permit state courts to exercise admiralty jurisdiction, but to give suitors the option of pursuing any common-law remedies they might otherwise have.[471] In addition, the states may still continue to exercise whatever police powers they may possess over their navigable waters [472] and may even create rights by their laws which are enforceable in federal admiralty courts.[473] What they may not do is to entertain suits in the nature of an admiralty proceeding— i.e., to enforce rights arising under maritime law by a proceeding *in rem* against a vessel.[474]

According to Chief Justice Taney, the determination of the boundaries of admiralty jurisdiction is a judicial function [475] and this is true as well, as a general proposition, with regard to the substantive rules of maritime law. In the main, such rules are to be derived from the decisions of the federal courts in admiralty cases.[476] But here, as in other areas of judicial jurisdiction, the legislative department possesses a general overriding authority. Thus, as we saw, it was the Congress which first extended the territorial scope of admiralty jurisdiction beyond the English "tidal-flow" test—an extension which was upheld in *The Genesee Chief*.[477]

Similarly, it has been ruled that the substantive corpus of maritime law is subject to alteration by Congress. "It cannot be supposed," said the high bench in the leading case upholding Congressional authority in this respect, "that the Framers of the Constitution contemplated that the law should forever remain unalterable. Congress undoubtedly has authority under the commercial power,[478] if no other, to introduce such changes as are likely to be needed." [479] More recently, the Supreme Court has affirmed that, "it must now be accepted as settled doctrine that . . . Congress has paramount power to fix and determine the maritime law which shall prevail throughout the country." [480] The Congressional power in this respect includes the authority to create new substantive rights to be enforced through the admiralty jurisdiction.[481]

The Congressional authority over maritime law is, like all other legislative power in our system, not unlimited. Any Congressional action must operate within an area deemed appropriately within the admiralty and maritime jurisdiction. In Chief Justice Hughes's words: "in amending and revising the maritime law, the Congress necessarily acts within a sphere restricted by the concept of the admiralty and maritime jurisdiction." [482] In addition, the high bench has held, Congress is bound by the basic purpose of the Admiralty Clause of Article III—to ensure a body of maritime law that should, so far as its essential features are concerned, be uniform throughout the country.[483] In *Southern Pacific Co. v. Jensen*,[484] the Supreme Court ruled that this basic purpose of uniformity barred a state from applying its workmen's compensation law to employees engaged in maritime work. The Congress then enacted a statute saving to persons injured in the course of maritime employment their rights and remedies under state workmen's compensation laws.[485] But this statute was invalidated on the ground that Congress itself could not modify the uniform character of the general maritime law by allowing the rules followed in the different states to control.[486]

The decisions just discussed have been subjected to much criticism.[487] In particular, there appears to be little justification for the judicial restriction of Congressional authority by the implicit purpose of the Framers to obtain a uniform maritime law. The power of the legislature to make exceptions to admiralty jurisdiction was exercised without question at the beginning in the already-discussed saving clause of the admiralty provision of the first Judiciary Act.[488] As a practical matter, the gap in employee protection left by the Supreme-Court decisions was filled in by the enactment by Congress of federal workmen's compensation laws for those workers injured in maritime employment, who could not validly be compensated under state statutes.[489] Its constitutional authority to pass such statutes, under the admiralty power, has never really been questioned.[490]

148
JURISDICTION BASED ON CHARACTER OF PARTIES

In section 146, we saw that Article III divides the cases subject to the federal judicial power into two broad categories: those based upon the character of the case, whoever may be the parties; and those based upon the character of the parties, whatever may be the nature of the case. In the last two sections, we dealt with the first of these categories—the character of the case. We turn now to the second head of federal competence—that based upon the character of the parties.

The cases based upon the character of the parties to which the judicial power under Article III extends are (1) cases affecting ambassadors and other foreign envoys; (2) controversies to which the United States is a party; (3) those between two or more states; (4) between a state and citizens of another state; (5) between citizens of different states; (6) between citizens of the same state claiming land under grants of different states; and (7) controversies between a state, or the citizens thereof, and foreign nations, citizens, or subjects.

Four of these heads of federal jurisdiction based upon the character of the parties can be disposed of briefly in this section. Cases between two or more states, we have already seen, fall within the original competence of the Supreme Court and, as such, have been discussed in section 143. Controversies between citizens of the same state claiming land under grants of different states are today of no practical importance. The motivation for extending federal judicial power to such cases was the existence of boundary disputes affecting ten states at the time the Constitution was drafted. With the settlement of such disputes and the passing of state land grants, this clause has become obsolete.[491]

The jurisdiction conferred by the clause concerning controversies between a state or its citizens and foreign nations, citizens, or subjects was intended to enable justice to be done in cases which concerned other countries and their citizens. "We well know, sir," declared Madison, "that foreigners cannot get justice done them in these courts, and this has prevented many wealthy gentlemen from trading or residing among us." [492] If the clause in question is read literally, it seems to authorize suits in the federal courts against foreign nations by American states or their citizens, as well as suits against states of the Union by other countries and their citizens. The Supreme Court has, however, held that such suits may not be entertained. Under international law, no nation may be sued in the courts of another without its consent, and such sovereign immunity extends to actions brought in the federal courts by a state of the Union or its citizens.[493] Similarly, the Eleventh Amendment, barring suits against any state of the Union by citizens of another state or of any foreign nation, has been construed to bar actions by a foreign nation against a state of the Union.[494]

The view which has prevailed in this respect is that once expressed by Madison. "I do not conceive," he said, "that any controversy can ever be decided, in these courts, between an American State and a foreign state, without the consent of the parties." [495] Hence, the competence conferred by the organic clause under discussion comprehends only suits brought by a state against aliens,[496] by foreign nations against American citizens,[497] and those between aliens and American citizens.[498]

The extension of federal judicial power to cases "affecting Ambassadors, other public Ministers and Consuls" is based upon considerations similar to those involved in cases involving foreign nations and their citizens. All such cases, which may bear intimately upon foreign relations, are to be submitted to the judicature of the nation.[499] The provision relating to foreign envoys was intended as a protection to the representatives of other powers in this country; consequently, it applies only to diplomatic personnel accredited to the United States by other countries, not to those representing the United States abroad.[500] It should be noted that, since foreign ambassadors and ministers accredited to the United States are immune from suit in American courts under the law of nations,[501] the practical effect of the organic provision for federal jurisdiction over cases involving such diplomats is to permit them to sue in the federal courts. Whether an individual is an ambassador or public minister within the provision in question is a matter on which the courts will be bound by the appropriate executive determination, normally in the form of a certificate by the Department of State.[502]

Under Article III, the Supreme Court is vested with original jurisdiction over cases involving foreign diplomatic representatives. As already seen,[503] it is up to the Congress to determine whether such original competence of the highest bench is to be exclusive or concurrent. In line with this principle, Congress may vest jurisdiction over cases involving consuls in the district courts.[504] There is little doubt also that Congress may make the federal jurisdiction exclusive of all state competence over cases involving foreign representatives, though it has been held that Article III does not by itself exclude state jurisdiction in every case in which a diplomatic or consular agent of a foreign nation is a party.[505]

It should be emphasized that, in all of the cases discussed in this and the next three sections, which are based upon the character of the parties, the subject matter involved in particular cases is irrelevant so far as the amenability of such cases to federal jurisdiction is concerned. Where the parties are among the seven categories specified in the Judiciary Article, the federal judicial power is competent, regardless of what the case in question is about. As Marshall put it in *Cohens v. Virginia:* [506] "If these be the parties, it is entirely unimportant what may be the subject of controversy. Be it what it may, these parties have a constitutional right to come into the courts of the Union." [507]

149

SAME: STATES   The federal judicial power under Article III is ex-
AS PARTIES   pressly stated to extend "to Controversies . . . be-
                  tween a State and Citizens of another State." Soon
after the Constitution itself went into effect, the highest Court, in *Chisholm v. Georgia,*[508] ruled that, under this provision, a state was liable to suit in a federal court by a citizen of another state. This holding—that the constitutional category of cases in which a state was a party included equally those where a state was a party defendant—appears justified by the literal sweep of the relevant language of the Judiciary Article.[509] Nevertheless, the Supreme Court itself informs us, the *Chisholm* decision created such a shock of surprise that the Eleventh Amendment was at once proposed and adopted.[510] It provides that the federal judicial power "shall not be construed to extend to any suit in law or equity, commenced or prosecuted against one of the United States by Citizens of another State, or by Citizens or Subjects of any Foreign State."

The Eleventh Amendment, by its own terms, does not do away with federal competence over all cases in which a state may be a party. Its provisions are aimed solely at actions brought *against* a state; it does not affect the right of the states to resort to the federal forum as parties plaintiff. Likewise, in *Cohens v. Virginia,*[511] the Supreme Court held that the prosecution of a writ of error to review a state judgment in an action instituted by a state did not commence or prosecute a suit against the state in violation of the Eleventh Amendment, but only continued that begun by the state.[512] Thus, the Eleventh Amendment does not eliminate the competence of the federal courts over suits instituted by the states as plaintiffs or over appeals from judgments in favor of states in such cases.

At the same time, it is plain that, to suits against a state, without her consent, brought by citizens of another state or by citizens of a foreign nation, the Eleventh Amendment erected an absolute bar.[513] In addition, it is clear that the states, in the absence of consent, are immune from suits brought against them by their own citizens,[514] although such suits are not within the explicit prohibition of the Eleventh Amendment.[515] The same is true of actions against the states by corporations created under federal statutes [516] or (as we saw in the prior section) by foreign nations.[517] In all such cases involving actions against states, the Eleventh Amendment constitutes a categorical prohibition against the assumption of competence by the federal courts.

The Eleventh Amendment does not, however, tell us when a particular suit is one against a state within the meaning of its bar to federal jurisdiction. In the 1824 case of *Osborn v. Bank of the United States,*[518] the Supreme Court, speaking through Chief Justice Marshall, laid down a purely formal test to determine whether the prohibition of the Eleventh Amendment was violated. According to Marshall in *Osborn,* the determining criterion was the party formally named in the record of the case: "It may, we think be laid down as a rule which admits of no exception, that, in all cases where jurisdiction depends on the party, it is the party named in the record." [519] Under this approach, the operation of the Eleventh Amendment is limited to those suits in which a state is a party defendant on the record.

The test laid down in *Osborn* was departed from only four years later in *Governor of Georgia v. Madrazo.*[520] The action there was brought against the governor of a state for the recovery of moneys in the treasury of the state and slaves in its possession. In such a case, said Marshall, speaking again for the high bench, the state itself may be considered as the real party in interest; it was actually though not formally the defendant in the suit. This was, of course, a departure from what had been said in *Osborn* —a departure which has always since been followed. The governing rule has thus become that stated by Justice Lamar in a later case: "It is the settled doctrine of this court that the question whether a suit is within the prohibition of the Eleventh Amendment is not always determined by reference to the nominal parties on the record, as the court will look behind and through the nominal parties on the record to ascertain who are the real parties to the suit." [521]

According to Justice Frankfurter, a formal test such as that laid down in *Osborn* could not long survive experience.[522] The abandonment of the *Osborn* test was, it must be conceded, necessary if the Eleventh Amendment was not to be deprived of all practical efficacy. If the *Osborn* test had prevailed, it would be easy for private litigants to frame all actions against states in the form of complaints naming some state officials as formal parties defendant—with the result being the complete abrogation of state immunity despite the Eleventh Amendment.

At the same time, to clothe an officer with the state's immunity every time he acts in an official capacity is, in effect, to remove state action from subjection to the rule of law. How is the Constitution itself to be maintained as the supreme law of the land if state officials acting contrary to its provisions may take shelter behind the Eleventh Amendment whenever those aggrieved by their unconstitutional action seek judicial redress?

In *Osborn v. Bank,* defendants were state officers who had seized moneys belonging to the Bank of the United States under a state law imposing a prohibitive yearly tax on each branch of the Bank. The Bank sued in the federal circuit court for an order directing the return of the money. Defendants claimed that such an action was, in reality, one against the state and, as such, barred by the Eleventh Amendment. As already seen, Marshall, in his *Osborn* opinion, ruled that the Eleventh Amendment was inapplicable where the state was not formally named as party defendant in the record—a ruling which, we noted, is no longer adhered to. But Marshall in *Osborn* did not base the decision that the suit there could be maintained solely on the formal test already discussed. He relied also on the fact that the action of defendants at issue constituted an unconstitutional interference with the functioning of a federal instrumentality. The state statute under which defendants acted was clearly invalid under *McCulloch v. Maryland*.[523] In such a case, defendants could derive neither authority nor protection from the law which they executed: "a void act can[not] afford any protection to the officers who execute it." [524] It was, Marshall concluded, proper to sue defendants if the state statute was repugnant to the Constitution or a federal law so as to furnish no authority to those who took the money for which the suit was instituted.[525]

Under the part of the *Osborn* opinion just discussed, a state official may be said to possess no official capacity when acting illegally and hence can derive no protection from an unconstitutional state statute.[526] If that is true, a suit to prevent an officer from enforcing an invalid state law is not one against the state within the prohibition of the Eleventh Amendment. Rather, the officer concerned may be deemed to be acting only in his private capacity, since the invalidity of the statute deprives him of his official character.

The *Osborn* holding on the effect of unconstitutionality of a state statute upon the official character of action taken thereunder was the foundation upon which the Supreme Court constructed its landmark 1908 decision in *Ex parte Young*.[527] In that case, a federal circuit court had issued a preliminary injunction against a state attorney general restraining him from enforcing a state statute which was found to violate the Federal Constitution. After determining that the statute in question did, indeed, violate the Fourteenth Amendment, the high tribunal turned to what it termed "the most material and important objection made to the jurisdiction of the Circuit Court,—the objection being that the suit is, in effect, one against the State." [528] Such objection was rejected. Instead, said the *Young* opinion, the governing principle is "that individuals who, as officers of the State, are clothed with some duty in regard to the enforcement of the laws of the State, and who threaten and are about to commence proceedings, either of a civil or criminal nature, to enforce against parties affected an unconstitutional act, violating the Federal Constitution, may be enjoined by a Federal court of equity from such action." [529] Jurisdiction of this character, declared the high bench, has been exercised by federal courts ever since *Osborn v. Bank*.

The reasons given for allowing the suit against the state officer in *Ex parte Young* are essentially similar to those stated by Marshall in the second part of his *Osborn* opinion. The state statute whose enforcement is at issue, the *Young* opinion emphasized, was itself unconstitutional. "If it be so," the opinion went on, "the use of the name of the State to enforce an unconstitutional act to the injury of complainants is a proceeding without the authority of and one which does not affect the State in its sovereign or governmental capacity. It is simply an illegal act upon the part of a state official in attempting by the use of the name of the State to enforce a legislative enactment which is void because unconstitutional. If the act which the state Attorney General seeks to enforce be a violation of the Federal Constitution, the officer in proceeding under such enactment comes into conflict with the superior authority of that Constitution, and he is in that case stripped of his official or representative character and is subjected in his person to the consequences of his individual conduct." [530]

It can hardly be denied that the *Young* Court, like Marshall in *Osborn* before it, was indulging in a fiction when it said that an officer who acts under an unconstitutional statute is stripped of his official character. Of course, he is still an officer when he is obeying what the state legislature has officially enacted.[531] But the *Osborn-Young* approach—founded on fiction though it may be—is essential if the Eleventh Amendment is not to immunize state action contrary to the Constitution from judicial scrutiny. The Eleventh Amendment, the Supreme Court informs us, may have been intended to leave the state "free to carry out its functions without judicial interference directed at the sovereign or its agents, but this immunity from federal jurisdiction does not extend to individuals who act as officers without constitutional authority." [532] Only by such an approach can the status of the Constitution as supreme law of the land be maintained with regard to state action by the federal courts.

The matter boils down to this: the federal judges are not barred from adjudicating a claim against a state officer who invokes statutory authority for his action if the constitutional power to give him such a claim of immunity is itself challenged.[533] In our system, certain rights are protected by the organic document itself against governmental action and, if such rights are infringed by the actions of state officials, it is proper that the federal courts have the power to grant relief against those actions.[534]

What is true of unconstitutional action is also true of official action in excess of statutory authority. The *Young* principle has been applied to sustain suits against a state official where, though he acts under a valid statute, he exceeded the authority with which the state had invested him.[535] On a theory basically similar to that already discussed, where the state officer's powers are limited by statute, his actions beyond those limits are considered individual, not state, actions. The officer is not doing the business which the state has empowered him to do or he is doing it in a way which the state has forbidden.[536] Suit against an *ultra vires* act, like that against an unconstitutional act, furnishes no occasion for invocation of the Eleventh Amendment's bar.[537]

150

SAME: UNITED STATES AS PARTY   The Judiciary Article includes among the cases to which the federal judicial power extends those "to which the United States shall be a party." This provision gives no difficulty when the United States comes into a federal court as party plaintiff. Indeed, no constitutional provision is necessary to enable the United States to bring such a suit, since, in Justice Story's words, "It would be a perfect novelty in the history of national jurisprudence, as well as of public law, that a sovereign had no authority to sue in his own courts." [538] From the first Judiciary Act, the district courts have been vested with jurisdiction to hear all suits of a civil nature brought by the United States,[539] though the Supreme Court early held that the nation could sue in its own name even without benefit of any statutory authorization.[540]

The Eleventh Amendment has been held to have no effect in suits brought in the federal courts by the United States. The jurisdiction of the federal courts in actions brought by the United States against a state has been said by the highest Court to be inherent in the very constitutional plan itself.[541] The Framers, according to it, "could not have overlooked the possibility that controversies capable of judicial solution might arise between the United States and some of the states and that the permanence of the Union might be endangered if to some tribunal was not intrusted the power to determine them according to the recognized principles of law." [542] It might be argued that the Eleventh Amendment, coming as it did almost a decade after the Constitution went into effect, supersedes the original organic plan in this respect. Yet the Amendment nowhere refers to actions brought by the United States, but only to those instituted by private parties. Its restriction on the right to sue has consequently been ruled inapplicable to suits brought against states by the nation itself. Controversies to which the United States is a party, within the Jurisdiction Clause of Article III, in other words, include actions brought by the Federal Government against one or more states.

But the converse of what has just been said is not also true. "It does not follow," the Supreme Court has stated, "that because a State may be sued by the United States without its consent, therefore the United States may be sued by a State without its consent. Public policy forbids that conclusion." [543]

There is, to be sure, no constitutional provision like the Eleventh Amendment which justifies any immunity for the United States from suit—whether by a state or any other litigant. The Supreme Court has nevertheless developed a general principle of such immunity which is construed to bar all actions against the Federal Government without its consent. The doctrine of sovereign immunity so derived has been wholly judge-made; it has had its foundation neither in the basic document nor in any act of the legislative department.

As early as *Chisholm v. Georgia*,[544] Chief Justice Jay expressed doubt whether the United States might be subjected to suit. The first recognition by the high bench as a whole of the sovereign immunity of the nation came in *Cohens v. Virginia*,[545] where Chief Justice Marshall, speaking for the Court, declared that "The universally received opinion is, that no suit can be commenced or prosecuted against the United States." [546] Since the *Cohens* case, the doctrine of the exemption of the United States from suit without its consent has been followed in many cases.[547] Some sixty years after the Marshall statement in *Cohens,* Justice Miller could affirm that the sovereign immunity of the nation "has always been treated as an established doctrine." [548]

The Judiciary Article, as already seen, extends the federal judicial power to cases to which the United States is a party. As far as its language is concerned, no distinction is made between cases in which the United States appears as plaintiff and those in which it is sued as defendant. "Now, it may be said," as the Supreme Court has acknowledged, "that if the word, party, comprehends both plaintiff and defendant, it follows, that the United States may be sued by any citizen, between whom and them there may be a controversy." [549] The doctrine of sovereign immunity, however, prevents this result from being realized in practice.

Though, literally, Article III includes cases to which the United States is a party, whether it be plaintiff or defendant, the Supreme Court has asserted that, "in the light of the rule, then well settled and understood, that the sovereign power is immune from suit, the conclusion is inadmissible that the framers of the Constitution intended to include suits or actions brought against the United States." [550] The relevant language of Article III must consequently be read as extending the federal judicial power only to "controversies to which the United States shall be a party plaintiff or petitioner." [551] The jurisdiction of the federal courts does not include actions brought against the United States as a party defendant. The doctrine of sovereign immunity constitutes an absolute prohibition against all suits against the United States without its consent. [552]

If the United States is sued directly as a formal party defendant, the case is, of course, plainly within the bar of the sovereign's immunity from suit. The difficulty arises (as in the cases discussed in the prior section on the exemption from suit vested in the states by the Eleventh Amendment) when an officer of the United States, rather than the Federal Government itself, is named as the formal defendant in a case. Of course, if such officer is sued as a private citizen, for action taken as an individual and not as an official, a suit directed against such action is not a suit against the sovereign. [553] What happens, all the same, when such officer is sued because of action taken by him in his capacity as a functionary of the Government?

The basic principle in cases against federal officers is similar to that discussed in the prior section with regard to the analogous problem of when an action against a state officer violates the state's immunity from suit granted by the Eleventh Amendment. Here, too, the governing rule is that a suit against the officer is not a suit against the sovereign when the official acts upon which it is based were in violation of the Constitution or in excess of statutory authority. The principle of Ex parte Young [554] is thus as applicable to cases involving actions against federal officials as it is to those involving suits against state officials. In Justice Hughes's words in an important case: "The principle has frequently been applied with respect to state officers seeking to enforce unconstitutional enactments. . . . And it is equally applicable to a Federal officer acting in excess of his authority or under an authority not validly conferred." [555] In the cases of federal, as in those of state, official action, the theory upon which judicial relief is granted is that the action concerned is beyond the officer's powers either because it is *ultra vires* or because, though the power has been conferred in form, the grant is lacking in substance because of its constitutional invalidity. In either case, the conduct against which relief is sought is not treated as the conduct of the sovereign.[556]

Of course, the theory just set out is founded on fiction as much when it is used to sustain a suit against a federal officer as it is when employed for a similar purpose to avoid the prohibition of the Eleventh Amendment. In either case, the officer concerned is actually acting as a governmental representative, not as a private citizen, regardless of whether he acts within constitutional and statutory limits. Yet treating an officer acting beyond such limits as stripped of his representative character is the means which the high bench has developed to enable actions to be brought directly to challenge the legality of federal official action. Without such approach, any such legal challenges would be met with the insurmountable bar of sovereign immunity. In this sense, the *Ex parte Young* [557] approach, particularly in its application to federal officers, bears an intimate relationship to the rule of law itself.

The relationship referred to is nowhere better seen than in the classic 1882 case of *United States v. Lee*.[558] The Arlington estate of General Robert E. Lee had been taken over by the United States under a title acquired by sale for nonpayment of taxes. In actuality, payment of the taxes had been tendered and refused by the relevant officials which, in the high Court's view, rendered the tax sale invalid. The plaintiff, the heir of Robert E. Lee, brought suit in ejectment against the federal officers in charge of the property to recover possession. The United States intervened, through the Attorney General, and set up the claim that, since it was in possession of the property involved, the suit should be dismissed as in effect a suit against itself.

The Government's contention in the *Lee* case was far-reaching. If, as the Supreme Court held, the United States had derived no valid title through the tax sale, it followed that plaintiff had title. That being the case, the property "is and was the property of the plaintiff, and was taken without any process of law and without compensation." [559] In other words, the official action at issue deprived plaintiff of his property in violation of the Fifth Amendment and was therefore an unconstitutional action.[560] "In such cases," declares the *Lee* Court, "there is no safety for the citizen, except in the protection of the judicial tribunals, for rights which have been invaded by the officers of the government, professing to act in its name." [561] Yet, under the Government's argument, even in such a case, the immunity of the sovereign was an absolute bar to any legal remedy.

The *Lee* decision categorically rejected the Government's claim that the suit infringed upon its sovereign immunity. There is no immunity from suit where the action is against officials who had no lawful authority to act as they did. In the words of the *Lee* opinion, "Not only no such power is given, but it is absolutely prohibited, both to the executive and the legislative, to deprive any one of life, liberty, or property without due process of law, or to take private property without just compensation." [562] In such a case, where the official conduct complained of was unlawful, the courts must be available to give redress. "Courts of justice," declares Justice Miller, in a pregnant portion of the *Lee* opinion, "are established, not only to decide upon controverted rights of the citizens as against each other, but also upon rights in controversy between them and the government." [563]

The *Lee* opinion rebounds in language which emphasizes the rule of law itself as the underlying basis for rejecting the claim of immunity from suit. Shall it be said, asks Justice Miller, that the courts cannot give a remedy when the citizen has been deprived of his property without any lawful authority, without any process of law, and without compensation, simply because this has been done by the action of Government officials? If such be the law, it sanctions a "tyranny" in this country contrary to "well-regulated liberty and the protection of personal rights." [564] Then, in the most famous passage of his opinion, Justice Miller declares, in language whose eloquence has not been dimmed by constant judicial repetition: "No man in this country is so high that he is above the law. No officer of the law may set that law at defiance with impunity. All the officers of the government, from the highest to the lowest, are creatures of the law and are bound to obey it." [565]

With *United States v. Lee*'s insistence upon the relationship of the right to challenge the unlawful action of federal officials in the courts to the rule of law should be compared the more recent decision in *Larson v. Domestic & Foreign Commerce Corp.*[566] The War Assets Administration, a federal agency, had sold some surplus coal to plaintiff, a private company. The plaintiff arranged for resale of the coal to another, but the W.A.A. unilaterally informed plaintiff that the contract was canceled and contracted to sell it to another concern. Plaintiff, alleging ownership in the coal under its contract, then sued in the federal district court to restrain the War Assets Administrator from transferring the coal to anyone other than plaintiff. The Supreme Court held that the suit had to be dismissed as one which contravened the sovereign immunity of the United States.

The *Larson* decision stands in striking contrast to that rendered in *United States v. Lee*. In both cases, plaintiffs were deprived of their property —in the one case coal, in the other realty—by the unlawful action of federal officials. In *Lee,* the high bench asserted that the right to legal redress in such a case was an essential element of the rule that no man, from the highest officer to the humblest citizen, is above the law. In *Larson,* the

Court ruled that, even if the coal was in law the plaintiff's property, there could be no redress because the suit, though nominally only one against the officer, was, in substance, a suit against the Government over which the federal courts have no jurisdiction. In *Larson,* the wrongdoer could, in effect, say successfully to the Court, "Stop, here; I act by order of the United States, and the progress of justice must be stayed." [567]

How are we to explain the difference in result in the *Lee* and *Larson* cases? It is all too easy simply to say, as the high tribunal does in its *Larson* opinion: "There are a great number of such cases and, as this Court has itself remarked, it is not 'an easy matter to reconcile all the decisions of the Court in this class of cases.' " [568] Of course, the subject of sovereign immunity is not free from casuistry.[569] But it is hardly enough, in commenting on the subject, merely to point out the seeming disharmony of Supreme-Court decisions and let it go at that.

The *Larson* opinion itself concedes that a suit against a federal officer will not be dismissed as a suit against the sovereign where he acts beyond his statutory powers or his action transcends constitutional limitations. "These two types," asserts the high bench, "have frequently been recognized by this Court as the only ones in which a restraint may be obtained against the conduct of Government officials." [570] In *Larson,* says the Court, neither type is present: "There is no allegation of any statutory limitation on his powers as a sales agent. . . . There is no claim that his action constituted an unconstitutional taking." [571] The case alleged is rather only that of wrongful action by a federal official in violation of plaintiff's property rights. That is ruled not enough to require the doctrine of sovereign immunity to give way. "We hold," *Larson* concludes, "that if the actions of an officer do not conflict with the terms of his valid statutory authority, then they are the actions of the sovereign, whether or not they are tortious under general law, if they would be regarded as the actions of a private principal under the normal rules of agency." [572]

It may be argued that, in thus attempting to justify the result reached in *Larson,* the high Court was overexalting form over substance. In effect, the plaintiff company was barred from the judicial forum because it failed to allege that no statute had authorized the Administrator to commit a tort and that the taking of plaintiff's coal without compensation was a violation of its constitutional rights.[573]

But the *Larson* decision is subject to an even more fundamental defect. The ruling there refuses to follow *United States v. Lee* in the case of a federal official committing a tortious act, such as the wrongful taking of private property. It may be doubted whether such a limitation of *Lee* is justified. When a public officer commits a tort, how can it be said that he acted within his delegated powers? As it was well put by Chief Justice Taft, speaking for the Court in *Goltra v. Weeks,*[574] a case basically similar on its facts to *Larson:* "If it was a trespass, then the officers of the Government should be restrained whether they professed to be acting for the Government or not. . . . By reason of their illegality, their acts or threatened acts are personal and derive no official justification from their doing them in asserted agency for the Government." [575]

The *Larson* opinion recognized that the Taft approach in the *Goltra* case was contrary to its own decision, but it refused to follow *Goltra.* Instead, it ruled that the mere fact that a tort is committed by a federal official is no ground for allowing suit to be brought against him. In other words, sovereign immunity is a bar in such a case even though government officials have wrongfully seized a citizen's property and the sole issue presented is one of property law.[576] The very elevation of official action above the law which *United States v. Lee* endeavored to avoid is the inevitable consequence.

The doctrine of sovereign immunity itself, it should not be forgotten, is one that has come into increasing disfavor.[577] The Government's exemption from suit is an anachronistic survival of monarchical privilege and, as such, runs counter to modern democratic notions of the moral responsibility of the State.[578] For the Supreme Court to treat the immunity of the United States from suit as a principle of justice which must be safeguarded at all costs is for it to ignore that such immunity is without moral validity.[579] The doctrine of sovereign immunity is one "which—whatever its historical basis —is hardly . . . based upon moral considerations." [580] A state judge has, indeed, gone so far as to assert that "the reasoning which supports the doctrine of sovereign immunity in cases of this character is so fallacious and unsound that it should shock the intelligence, as well as the sense of justice, of those who believe in the American way of life." [581]

The way out of the injustice caused by the sovereign-immunity doctrine is by the fiction, already discussed, under which the officer who acts illegally is "stripped of his official or representative character." [582] There is as much reason to follow that fiction in a case where an official commits a tortious act, as in the *Larson* case, as there is in cases like *United States v. Lee* [583] and *Ex parte Young.*[584] If the basis of sovereign immunity is the English rule that the king can do no wrong, it should also be accompanied by the corollary thesis that, if the king's agent does wrong, that action cannot be the action of the king. When a Government official acts tortiously, just as when he acts beyond his constitutional or statutory powers, his action should be treated as personal, for purposes of the sovereign-immunity doctrine. In Justice Douglas's words, referring to a case where public officials become tort-feasors by unlawfully seizing or holding a citizen's property: "The dominant interest of the sovereign is then on the side of the victim who may bring his possessory action to reclaim that which is wrongfully withheld." [585]

151

SAME: CITIZENS   The most prolific source of federal-court jurisdiction
OF DIFFERENT   is that provision of Article III which extends the
STATES AS PARTIES judicial power of the United States to "Controversies
            . . . between Citizens of different States." From the
first Judiciary Act, the Congress has specifically empowered the federal
judges to exercise the diversity jurisdiction organically authorized.[586] Provided that the requisite jurisdictional amount be present in the case, the
federal forum has been open where there has been diversity of citizenship
—regardless of the nature of the case or whether it involved questions of
federal, or only local, law. As the Supreme Court has stated, "The Constitution imposes no limitation upon the class of cases involving controversies between citizens of different States to which the judicial power of
the United States may be extended; and Congress may, therefore, lawfully
provide for bringing, at the option of either of the parties, all such controversies within the jurisdiction of the Federal judiciary." [587]

Since, in diversity cases, the federal competence does not at all depend
upon the subject matter of the case, the only jurisdictional problem [588] is to
determine when the requisite diversity of citizenship exists. As far as natural persons are concerned, citizenship, for purposes of diversity jurisdiction, turns upon domicile.[589] Under the early decision in *Strawbridge v.
Curtiss,*[590] if there are multiple parties in a diversity suit, all the persons on
one side of the case must be citizens of different states from all persons on
the other side.

The *Strawbridge* rule gave rise to a serious problem in diversity suits
involving corporations. When the citizenship of corporations, for diversity
purposes, first came before the highest bench, it was ruled that they might
sue where all of their stockholders were citizens of a state other than that
of defendant's citizenship.[591] Such a rule, coupled with that in the *Strawbridge* case, might have all but closed the federal courts in diversity cases
to large corporations with stockholders in every state. The Supreme Court,
to avoid this result, held that there was a presumption that the members of
a corporation were all citizens of the state of its incorporation.[592] In the
course of time, this presumption became an irrebuttable one.[593] It may well
be that the right to resort to the federal forum thus opened to corporate
entities has at times been abused by them.[594] At the same time, it is difficult to see how the Supreme Court could change the present rule on the
subject, without unduly barring corporate entities from the bar of federal
justice, under the *Strawbridge* case.

For purposes of diversity jurisdiction, the Judiciary Article has been deemed to require that the party alleging his diversity of citizenship be a citizen of the United States and of a state different from that in which the other party maintains his domicile. It is, however, possible to be a citizen of the United States without being a citizen of any state. That is the case, for example, where a citizen of the United States is domiciled in the District of Columbia or one of the territories. In *Hepburn v. Ellzey*,[595] the high Court, speaking through Chief Justice Marshall, held that, so far as diversity jurisdiction was concerned, a citizen of the District of Columbia did not have the standing of a citizen of one of the states of the Union. A similar result was later reached with regard to a citizen of a territory of the United States.[596]

If a citizen of the District of Columbia or a territory is not a citizen of a state within the Diversity Clause of Article III, it can be argued that the federal judicial power itself may not be extended to include a diversity case involving such a citizen. In *Hepburn v. Ellzey*, nevertheless, Marshall indicated that such an extension of federal jurisdiction was within the legislative competence.[597] In 1940, the Congress for the first time acted on the Marshall assumption in this respect and provided that the diversity jurisdiction of the district courts should include actions "between citizens of different States, or citizens of the District of Columbia, the Territory of Hawaii, or Alaska, and any state or Territory." [598] This provision was upheld in *National Mutual Insurance Co. v. Tidewater Transfer Co.*[599] Under that case, though *Hepburn v. Ellzey* states the rule under the Diversity Clause in the absence of statute, the Congress may provide otherwise and vest diversity competence in the federal courts based upon citizenship in the District of Columbia or a territory.

The question that has given rise to the most difficulty in connection with diversity jurisdiction has been that of what law the federal courts should apply in cases before them arising from controversies between citizens of different states. Until a generation ago, this question appeared to be one solely of statutory interpretation, involving construction of a statutory provision which the very first Congress enacted to deal with the matter. More recently, the Supreme Court has indicated that the basic issue involved is one of constitutional law—at least so far as the question concerned had until then been answered by the federal judges.

Section 34 of the Judiciary Act of 1789 directed that "The *laws* of the several states . . . shall be regarded as rules of decision in trials at common law in the courts of the United States in cases where they apply." [600] This was a simple rule to apply if there chanced to be an applicable state statute.[601] But what happened if there was no such statute relevant to the case? Did the Congressional command require the federal courts to apply the decisional law of the state courts as well as the statutory laws of the several states?

In its celebrated 1842 decision in *Swift v. Tyson*,[602] the Supreme Court answered this query in the negative, holding that the federal courts were not bound by state-court decisions, at least insofar as those in the field of commercial law were concerned. Commercial transactions, its opinion asserted, should not be governed by the decisions of purely local tribunals; instead, there was a general commercial law, applied throughout the common-law world, which should control in the federal courts. In matters of "general law," such as those governing commercial transactions, the decisions of the state courts were not binding on the federal courts sitting in the state; the federal courts were free to follow the rules of the common law in accordance with their judgment of what those rules were. Quoting Cicero's famous statement that the law is not one thing in Rome and another in Athens, the high bench concluded that the same must be true of New York and Boston.[603] The word "laws" in section 34 of the Judiciary Act applied only to statutes and matters of purely local concern (such as the rights and title to real property), not to court decisions on matters of "general law," such as the law controlling ordinary commercial transactions. As to such matters, the federal courts were allowed to apply rules of their own, different though they might be from those which would be applied if the case were tried in a state court.

It can hardly be gainsaid that the doctrine of *Swift v. Tyson* was, in practice, attended by serious inconveniences. Under *Swift v. Tyson,* the federal courts fashioned their own "federal common law" which they would apply in matters of "general law." This concept of a "federal common law" which *Swift v. Tyson* had held should govern in commercial transactions, was extended by later Courts so as to cover most nonstatutory aspects of the law. But, since the state courts continued to follow their own rules of decision, even when they were contrary to the "federal common law," the result in many instances was the existence of two conflicting rules of law in the same state, with the outcome of suits dependent upon whether they were brought in the state or federal courts. *Swift v. Tyson* made the rights enjoyed under the general common law vary according to whether enforcement was sought in the state or federal courts. "This dual system," to quote from a discussion by Justice Jackson, "for application of state laws was bound to produce conflicts, for if a litigant could get his case into a federal court, it might be decided by a more favorable rule than that of the state court. There was much shopping for favorable forums, and no doubt there were serious abuses." [604]

If these abuses were all that *Swift v. Tyson* had produced, its doctrine would scarcely have lasted almost a century. There is actually no easy answer to the problem at issue in *Swift v. Tyson;* the mere overruling of that case has, we shall see, by no means settled that problem. Section 34 of the Judiciary Act of 1789 placed before the Supreme Court a dilemma and it has since shifted from horn to horn, finding either position very uncomfortable.[605] For the federal courts to apply their own rules would lead to the difficulties, already mentioned, arising from conflicting rules in the state and federal courts. On the other hand, for the Supreme Court to be bound by the decisions of the state courts would be for it to declare one rule of law one day and another the next, depending on the state whose laws were applicable. This would wholly defeat the dream of a uniform system of common law—a dream which has moved men ever since the days of the Roman republic.

No matter which view the highest tribunal might adopt, it could not escape from the quandary inherent in section 34 of the Judiciary Act: if the federal courts were to be uniform among themselves, they must be at variance with some of the states; if they were to try to be uniform with the states in which they sat, they would be at variance among themselves.

With no sure way out of the dilemma, one would have thought the balance was in favor of adhering to the hundred-year-old precedent, despite the difficulties arising from it. Nevertheless, in the 1938 case of *Erie Railroad Co. v. Tompkins*,[606] the doctrine of *Swift v. Tyson* was categorically overruled. In that case, the high bench conceded that, "If only a question of statutory construction were involved, we should not be prepared to abandon a doctrine so widely applied throughout nearly a century." [607] According to the Court, however, more than mere interpretation of the Judiciary Act was involved. In its view, the Constitution itself had been misconstrued in *Swift v. Tyson*. For the 1842 Court to interpret the Judiciary Act as it had was for it to invade rights reserved to the states. According to the *Erie Railroad* opinion: "Except in matters governed by the Federal Constitution or by Acts of Congress, the law to be applied in any case is the law of the State. . . . There is no federal general common law. Congress has no power to declare substantive rules of common law applicable in a State whether they be local in their nature or 'general,' be they commercial law or a part of the law of torts. And no clause in the Constitution purports to confer such a power upon the federal courts." [608]

The Supreme Court's decision in *Erie Railroad Co. v. Tompkins* overruling *Swift v. Tyson* is remarkable in a number of ways.[609] It reversed a century-old precedent, which counsel before it had not even questioned. The Erie Railroad declared expressly: "We do not question the finality of the holding of this Court in *Swift v. Tyson*." [610] Despite this, the high bench's opinion opens with the statement that "The question for decision is whether the oft-challenged doctrine of *Swift v. Tyson* shall now be disapproved." [611] The *Erie* decision is truly, as Justice Jackson termed it, a volunteered confession of a century of error.[612]

Even more striking, perhaps, is the fact that the *Erie Railroad* opinion, for the first and only time in our constitutional history, held action of the Supreme Court itself to have been unconstitutional. In doing so, the Court in effect declared Justice Story (the author of the *Swift v. Tyson* opinion) and his colleagues and successors in the federal courts for ninety-six years to be guilty of a usurpation of power unwarranted by the basic document. This is a most startling conclusion, especially when one recalls that the *Swift v. Tyson* Court was only interpreting a Congressional law which prescribed rules of decision for the federal courts, as the federal legislature appears to have the perfect right to do.

What was it that led the *Erie Railroad* Court to its decision? Two main reasons are given in the Court's opinion. In the first place, an article which had then recently been published had convinced the high bench that *Swift v. Tyson* had misinterpreted section 34 of the 1789 Judiciary Act, at least insofar as the intent of its draftsmen was concerned.[613] That may well be true; but the Judiciary Act in 1938 is not necessarily only what its words meant to its Framers in 1789. The gloss of a century of interpretation is not to be disregarded because of a scholarly suggestion that it was probably erroneous. By 1938, *Swift v. Tyson* was at least as much a part of the Judiciary Act as the words of which that statute was originally composed.

Even more important was the belief of the 1938 high Court that the doctrine of *Swift v. Tyson* had revealed "defects, political and social" [614] so great as to call for its repudiation. These defects have already been mentioned. To the *Erie Railroad* Court, it was, in Chief Justice Hughes's language, "inadmissible that there should be one rule of law for litigants in the state courts and another rule for litigants who bring the same question before the federal courts owing to the circumstance of diversity of citizenship." [615]

If it was the defects which experience had revealed in *Swift v. Tyson* that led to its overruling, one may logically ask whether the situation in this respect has actually been improved under *Erie Railroad Co. v. Tompkins.* Just before his death, Justice Jackson asserted that *Erie Railroad* "did not end the confusion, the conflict or the shopping for forums." [616] If anything, the confusion and conflict are even more inevitable today when the Supreme Court has pushed the *Erie Railroad* decision to its logical extreme. *Erie Railroad,* we saw, repudiated the *Swift v. Tyson* view that the federal courts could apply their own rules of law; instead, the high Court held, they must henceforth follow the rules laid down by the courts of the state in which they sit, unless only a question of federal law is involved in the particular case. This does not, it is true, present too much difficulty in a case like *Erie Railroad* itself, where the applicable rule on the question of tort law there at issue had been laid down authoritatively in a line of decisions by the highest court of the state. All too often, however, the application of the *Erie Railroad* doctrine is not so obvious.

As the Supreme Court has interpreted the *Erie Railroad* doctrine, the federal courts must frequently decide cases on the basis of a theoretical "state law" which really does not exist because there is no state decision in point.[617] The Supreme Court has held that, if there is no decision of the highest court of the particular state, the federal courts in that state must follow the relevant decisions of the lower courts of the state. As the Court has put it: "a federal court is not free to reject the state rule merely because it has not received the sanction of the highest state court, even though it thinks the rule is unsound in principle or that another is preferable." [618] In another case, the Supreme Court went even further and held that a federal court had to follow the decisions of a state court of original jurisdiction.[619] It is true that, in one case, the high bench drew the line and refused to rule that a federal court in South Carolina was bound by an isolated decision by a trial court of that state, whose decisions were not reported and not considered as precedents under state law.[620] But this refusal to reduce *Erie Railroad* to absurdity does not really answer for the federal courts the question of what is the binding state rule where the point has never been passed on by the highest state court.

The difficulties for lower courts under the *Erie Railroad* case have been well stated by a member of the highest Court. Where the federal judge, in his words, "has to divine what the state law is, he often has to proceed on fragmentary data. The court of last resort in the State may not have spoken. There are rulings of intermediate tribunals that squint one way and rulings of lower courts that squint another. What is the main current of the state law? What would the highest court of the State decide if the question were put to it?" [621]

Under the Supreme Court's doctrine, lower state-court decisions often control the final result of litigation in the federal courts, even though such decisions might be reversed if they reached the highest state court. This, in substance, is to subordinate the federal to the state courts and to make their judgments subject to changes in policy or personnel of the latter. And what happens if there are no decisions by courts of the particular state or they are hopelessly in conflict? According to the Supreme Court, the difficulty of determining state law does not excuse a federal court from following the *Erie Railroad* case.[622] It must, as best it can, determine what the state law would be if there were an authoritative decision on the point. Even if the state law is not clear, the federal judge may not exercise his own judgment of what the proper rule should be and do justice according to his best lights; he must instead try to place himself in the shoes of a member of the state's highest court and make his own determination of what that court would probably rule in a similar case.

This is, in effect, to make federal law merely a prophecy of what the state courts are likely to do in fact.[623] That may be all very well as a definition of law from the point of view of Justice Holmes's celebrated "bad man"; [624] it is, to say the least, disconcerting when it is the concept of law upon which federal courts must decide questions on which important interests both of property and person may turn.

One who has read this far will find it hard to disagree with the judgment on the effect of *Erie Railroad* rendered off the bench by Justice Jackson: "The problem of which court has jurisdiction and which state law is applicable and whether it has been applied exactly as a state court would have done, is perplexing to the point of frustration to any person who tries to solve the question in a particular case without the consolation of a retainer. A vast and utterly unjustifiable part of federal litigation concerns only the question of jurisdiction, on which great time and labor and expense are expended before the merits of a question are ever reached." [625]

The diversity jurisdiction of the federal courts, we are told, was the most tenuously founded and most unwillingly granted of all the heads of federal jurisdiction which Congress was empowered by Article III to confer.[626] What *Erie Railroad v. Tompkins* and its progeny do is to give immediacy to the question of whether the diversity jurisdiction has continued contemporary utility. *Erie Railroad* may not have ended the difficulties of the federal judges with regard to what law they should apply in diversity cases. But it does end the justification for continuing our system of dual jurisdictions based on diversity of citizenship.[627]

The diversity competence of the federal courts is not founded in logical considerations. On the contrary, ours is the only federation that has set up a dual system of state and federal courts, with the latter authorized not only to protect federal rights but also to enforce state law in cases between citizens of different states. The diversity jurisdiction given to the federal courts in the Constitution was based solely on the desire of the Framers to assure out-of-state litigants courts free from local bias. The experience after the Revolution led to the fear that parochial prejudice by the citizens of one state toward those of another would lead to unjust treatment of citizens of other states in the state courts: "Such was the reason for enabling a citizen of one State to press a claim or stand on a defense, wholly state-created, against a citizen of another in a federal court of the latter's State." [628]

The fear of the Founders may have been a valid reason for diversity jurisdiction in the fledgling Republic, still dominated by the excessive sectionalism that had rendered the Articles of Confederation unworkable. Over a century and a half later, these reasons are much less compelling. The permeation of national feeling and the mobility of modern life have destroyed most of the prejudice that formerly existed against the out-of-stater. And, even if some sectionalism still persists, it hardly affects the ability of the now-mature state-court systems to do justice to all who come before them. Justice Frankfurter has pointed out how Madison believed that Congress would return to the state courts judicial power vested in the federal courts "when they find the tribunals of the states established on a good footing." [629] Can one fairly deny that the state courts are now established on a sufficiently "good footing" so as to be trusted to mete out justice to citizens and noncitizens alike?

It is plain that, under the present system, a flood of state litigation is being diverted into the federal courts. And it is this flood that is, more than anything, responsible for the swamping of the federal courts by litigants in recent years. Over half of the civil cases in the federal courts are diversity of citizenship cases; most of them involve no question of federal law. An act for the elimination of diversity jurisdiction could fairly be called an act for the relief of the federal judges.[630]

But such a statute would have an even more important beneficial effect. It is essential to a vital federal system that the state governments should not be deprived of powers rightly theirs. An effective state-court system to dispense state law is a fundamental element in state government. But how can the state courts be truly effective when they are deprived of so large a proportion of the cases that should rightfully be theirs? Under *Erie Railroad v. Tompkins,* according to a Supreme Court statement, the federal court enforcing state law in a diversity case is in substance "only another court of the State." [631] Yet, if that be true, what justification is there any longer for diversity jurisdiction? "The whole purpose of diversity jurisdiction," Justice Jackson well states, "is to give one of the parties a better break in federal court than he would expect in state court. Take that away, use the same jurors, make the federal judge rule as a state judge would rule, and the purpose sought in diversity jurisdiction is gone." [632]

It may be objected that the caliber of most state courts is still below that of the federal courts. That alone is not, all the same, a justification for diversity jurisdiction. On the contrary, the best way to improve state tribunals is to make litigants realize that they have only those tribunals to resort to on state issues. In Justice Frankfurter's query, "Is it sound public policy to withdraw from the incentives and energies for reforming state tribunals, where such reform is needed, the interests of influential groups who through diversity litigation are now enabled to avoid state courts?" [633] In addition, the elimination of the present emasculation of their jurisdiction may be expected to have a correcting influence within the state courts themselves. We should not forget the wisdom contained in Justice Brandeis's dictum [634] that responsibility is the great developer of men.

152

JUDICIAL   Almost a century ago, an English judge used strong
SELF-LIMITATION   language in categorically denying any judicial power
                              to review the validity of statutes enacted by the Par-
liament. "Are we," he asked, "to act as regents over what is done by
parliament with the consent of Queen, lords and commons? I deny that any
such authority exists. . . . The proceedings here are judicial, not autocratic, which they would be if we could make laws instead of administering
them." [635]

In the United States, of course, the courts have rejected the English
doctrine of complete judicial abnegation in the constitutional sphere. The
most striking aspect of the American system, indeed, has been the power
of the Supreme Court to invalidate acts of the duly elected representatives
of the people. To outside observers, the power thus exercised by American
judges smacks more of political, than judicial, power. To them, the Supreme Court has appeared virtually to exercise the functions of what an
English writer termed "a third chamber in the United States" [636]—and, if
anything, a chamber superior to the two Houses of Congress, for it possesses an absolute veto over the laws enacted by them. Shortly after the
Supreme Court upheld, by a bare majority only, the authority of the Congress to devalue the dollar in the already-discussed *Gold-Clause Case*,[637]
Justice Jackson (then not yet a member of the high bench) was asked by
Swedish lawyers and bankers how we could allow within one of a majority
of our Court to hold that the nation lacked power to change its monetary
policy: "Why, anyway, should lawyer-judges be supreme over the national
parliament, the President, the Treasury, and the whole government in a
matter so vital to economic life?" [638]

Those who conceive of the American judges in this manner not unnaturally look upon them as exercising precisely the power (so absolutely disclaimed by the English judge in the case quoted from at the beginning of
this section) to act as regents over what is done by the other departments.
Their awesome power to strike down laws and other governmental acts is
seen to make their proceedings autocratic, not judicial—encompassing the
authority to make law instead of merely administering it. Significantly, the
leading French study of review of the constitutionality of laws by the United
States Supreme Court is entitled *Government by Judiciary*.[639]

To Americans, such foreign characterization of the role of the judge in
the United States is greatly overdrawn. Most Americans would agree with
the declaration made in 1952 by the highest Court itself that "we do not sit
as a super-legislature." [640] On the contrary, under American conceptions,
the power of the courts to rule on the constitutionality of laws is of the very
essence of the judicial function. It is, in Marshall's famous phrase, emphat-

ically the province and duty of the judicial department to interpret the law.[641] The power to interpret the law, in our theory, necessarily involves the power to determine whether a law is conformable to the Constitution.[642] In any case involving two conflicting laws, the judge must decide which is to govern. "So if a law be in opposition to the constitution; if both the law and the constitution apply to a particular case, so that the court must either decide that case conformably to the law, disregarding the constitution; or conformably to the constitution, disregarding the law; the court must determine which of these conflicting rules governs the case. This is of the very essence of judicial duty." [643]

The basic theory, which was first expressly articulated by Marshall in *Marbury v. Madison* and has been followed by the highest tribunal ever since, turns upon the proposition that the judges, in ruling upon the constitutionality of laws, exercise only true judicial power. The Supreme Court, in this view, is not sitting as a court of appeal from the legislative department when it decides on the validity of an act of Congress. It is only applying the law to the facts of an actual case before it, brought by adverse parties who have resorted to the forum provided by the law of the land for the resolution of justiciable controversies.

"Judicial power," says Justice Miller, "is the power of a court to decide and pronounce a judgment and carry it into effect between persons and parties who bring a case before it for decision." [644] It is precisely such power which American courts exercise when they dispose of cases whose decision turns upon application of a provision of the organic instrument. As the highest Court has expressed it, "The right to declare a law unconstitutional arises because an act of Congress relied upon by one or the other of such parties in determining their rights is in conflict with the fundamental law. The exercise of this, the most important and delicate duty of this court, is not given to it as a body with revisory power over the action of Congress, but because the rights of the litigants in justiciable controversies require the court to choose between the fundamental law and a law purporting to be enacted within constitutional authority, but in fact beyond the power delegated to the legislative branch of the government." [645]

The high bench merely does, in its higher position as the Court of last resort, what every other judge in the land has to do, in applying relevant constitutional and statutory provisions to dispose of cases arising in the progress of ordinary litigation.[646] Its power lies in its duty to decide, in conformity with the Constitution, the particular controversies which come to it; it does not arise from some generalized power of supervision over national and state governments.[647]

It is essential, if the theory just spelled out is to be adhered to, that the Supreme Court confine its exercise of the power to pass on constitutionality to cases calling for a true exercise of the judicial function. The Founding Fathers deliberately withheld from the high bench power that was purely political in form, such as a forthright power to veto or revise legislation. Instead, they delegated to the Court "The judicial Power" alone—a power which, by the express language of the Judiciary Article, extends only to the resolution of "Cases" and "Controversies." The Supreme Court, august though its role may be in the constitutional sphere, must act only as a law court in resolving actual cases brought before its bar by adverse parties. However far-reaching may be the result of its decisions, they do not go one step beyond the administration of justice to individual litigants.[648]

It may well be, in the words of Lord Birkenhead, that the notion that the Supreme Court, even in constitutional cases, is only a law court dispensing justice between citizens is "a little subtle," for when a case brought by an individual raises the question whether a law is constitutional or not, the decision of the high bench authoritatively disposes of that question and, if the decision is against the legislative power, the law is deemed stripped of its attempted authority.[649] At the same time, the insistence of the high Court that its power to pass upon constitutional issues be limited to such issues as assume such a form that the judicial power is capable of acting on them [650] has been of the utmost significance. It has enabled the Justices to eschew the appearance of sitting as the constitutional superiors of the other departments. For the highest tribunal to act in other than actual cases brought before it would be for it to assert authority that would bring it into open conflict with the governmental organs whose action it was reviewing. It would then directly be part and parcel of political controversies, and, lacking the sword of the executive, the purse of the legislature, and the authority of both which comes from their direct election by the people, it would soon be in an untenable position.

It should not be forgotten that the basic support of the federal judiciary is not in its constitutional position, which, as already seen, is, in many ways, inherently a weak one in comparison with that of the political departments, but in the acceptance by public opinion of its position as guardian of the Constitution. The Supreme Court has been able to maintain its role as the ultimate expounder of constitutional law only because it has, in the main, received the support of the nation for its continued performance. "The Court's authority," states Justice Frankfurter, "possessed neither of the purse nor the sword—ultimately rests on sustained public confidence in its moral sanction." [651]

The Supreme Court itself has recognized the inherent weakness of its position unless it is supported by public sentiment.[652] The high bench, reads a celebrated passage by Bryce, "feels the touch of public opinion. Opinion is stronger in America than anywhere else in the world, and judges are only men. To yield a little may be prudent, for the tree that cannot bend to the blast may be broken." [653] Realizing this, the Supreme Court has, so far as possible, tried to minimize the possibility of conflicts between it and the other departments and the loss of public confidence that might result. It has done this by evolving a number of self-imposed limitations on judicial review of issues of constitutionality. These self-limitations have been intended to keep the high bench out of active participation in the political processes.[654]

The limitations referred to have essentially been derived by the highest Court from the fact that it is a judicial tribunal—restricted to the decision of actual cases upon which judicial power is capable of acting—that has been vested with the role of constitutional censor in our system. They have, to be sure, not altered the political impact which the work of the Supreme Court has in a polity such as ours. In substance, in fact, it may be said that any decision which confirms, allocates, or shifts power as between different branches of government, or between the State and the individual, is essentially political—no matter whether the decision be reached by a legislative or a judicial process.[655] But even, if in this sense, most of the important issues decided by the Supreme Court are really political in nature, still they will not be faced by the Court itself unless they are presented to it in legal form appropriate for a judicial tribunal.

153

CASES AND   During the Framers' Convention, a motion was made
CONTROVERSIES   by Dr. Johnson to extend the federal judicial power
                     to cases arising under the Constitution of the United
States, as well as under its laws and treaties. Mr. Madison then "doubted whether it was not going too far to extend the jurisdiction of the Court generally to cases arising under the Constitution, and whether it ought not to be limited to cases of a Judiciary Nature. The right of expounding the Constitution in cases not of this nature ought not to be given to that Department." Despite the Madison animadversion, we are told: "The motion of Docr. Johnson was agreed to *nem: con:* it being generally supposed that the jurisdiction given was constructively limited to cases of a Judiciary nature." [656]

The supposition of the Framers, just referred to, is one that has consistently been given effect in the jurisprudence of the highest Court. "In endowing this Court with 'judicial power,' " Justice Frankfurter has stated, "the Constitution presupposed an historic content for that phrase and relied on assumption by the judiciary of authority only over issues which are appropriate for disposition by judges." [657] In the view of the Supreme Court: "courts are not charged with general guardianship against all potential

mischief in the complicated tasks of government." [658] The judicial function
is a more limited one. Judicial power, however large, has an orbit more or
less strictly defined.[659] It "could come into play only in matters that were
the traditional concern of the courts at Westminster and only if they arose in
ways that to the expert feel of lawyers constituted 'Cases' or 'Controversies.'
. . . Even as to the kinds of questions which were the staple of judicial
business, it was not for courts to pass upon them as abstract, intellectual
problems but only if a concrete, living contest between adversaries called
for the arbitrament of law." [660]

The Judiciary Article, as was emphasized in the prior section, extends
the federal judicial power only to the resolution of "Cases" and "Controversies." In the words of the high bench: "by the express terms of the
Constitution, the exercise of the judicial power is limited to 'cases' and
'controversies.' Beyond this it does not extend, and unless it is asserted in a
case or controversy within the meaning of the Constitution, the power to
exercise it is nowhere conferred." [661] The result of the constitutional restriction is that the federal bench's sole power is to decide lawsuits between opposing litigants with real interests at stake, and its only method of proceeding is by the conventional judicial process. Judicial power is the right only
"to determine actual controversies arising between adverse litigants, duly
instituted in courts of proper jurisdiction." [662] The judges will not decide a
question unless it is presented in a form and under conditions "appropriate
for judicial determination." [663] The nature of the action challenged, the
kind of injury inflicted, and the relationship between the parties must be
such that judicial determination is consonant with traditional exercise of
the judicial function.[664]

As a practical matter, the "Case" or "Controversy" requirement, as it
has been construed by the highest bench, has resulted in government by
lawsuit [665] as the outstanding characteristic of the American constitutional
system. Fundamental constitutional issues are ultimately determined through
the technical forms of the lawsuit. "By cases and controversies," Justice
Field tells us, "are intended the claims of litigants brought before the courts
for determination by such regular proceedings as are established by law or
custom for the protection or enforcement of rights, or the prevention, redress, or punishment of wrongs." [666] It is only when a constitutional issue
is presented to it in the form of an action at law or in equity between two
adverse parties that a federal court may attempt to dispose of it. No matter
how important the issue may be, or how pressing its resolution may be for
the nation, its decision by the courts—and ultimately the highest Court—
must await the presentation to them of an actual suit for settlement.

154

SAME: ADVISORY   In the conversation already referred to [667] between
OPINIONS   Justice Jackson and Swedish lawyers and bankers on
                  the *Gold-Clause Case*,[668] he was asked: "How could
American business intelligently function while such basic questions were
pending in the Court? Why could you not learn the answer earlier?" [669]

Of course, in a system like the American one, where judicial interpretations of the Constitution may have such significant political consequences,
there might be great advantages in knowing at once the legal powers of the
Government.[670] It would certainly be convenient for the parties and the
public to know promptly whether a particular statute is valid. The desire
to secure these advantages led to strong efforts at the Constitutional Convention to associate the Supreme Court as a Council of Revision in the
legislative process. The efforts failed, as Justice Frankfurter puts it, because
the disadvantages of such a rule by the judiciary were deemed greater than
the advantages.[671] Instead, the judges were limited to the decision of actual
cases presented in a form appropriate for resolution by judicial power.

From the beginning, the Supreme Court has construed the "Case" or
"Controversy" requirement of Article III as precluding the federal courts
from acting as advisers to the other departments. The very first Court felt
constrained to withhold even from the Father of his Country an advisory
opinion on questions regarding which Washington was most anxious to
have illumination from the highest tribunal.[672] In 1793, the President, acting
through Secretary of State Jefferson, had sent to the Supreme Court a letter
asking the advice of the Justices with regard to a list of questions relating to
international law, which had become of importance since the outbreak of
the international conflict which had grown out of the French Revolution.
After the members of the high tribunal had considered the matter, Chief
Justice Jay replied directly to the President in a letter which, though with
due deference, firmly denied the advice sought as beyond the Court's competence to give.[673] "Our being judges of a court in the last resort," Jay
wrote, "are considerations which afford strong arguments against the propriety of our extra-judicially deciding the questions alluded to." [674]

It is true that there were instances in the early history of the Republic
in which individual members of the supreme bench expressed extrajudicial
legal opinions to the Chief Executive.[675] Yet, as Chief Justice Hughes has
stated, with reference to one such instance: "This, of course was extra-
official, but it is safe to say that nothing of the sort could happen today." [676]
As a practical matter, the refusal of the high Court as a whole to answer
Washington's international-law questions has definitely settled the inability
of courts vested with "The judicial Power" under Article III to render mere
advice—either at the instance of the Government or private citizens.

There are, to be sure, a number of states in which the judicial department is required by express organic provision to issue advisory opinions on constitutional questions at the request of the other departments. In acting under such provisions, the judges in the states concerned act directly as constitutional advisers of the other departments.[677] It is, however, settled that in the absence of such express constitutional provisions permitting them, the rendering of advisory opinions is beyond the power of the American judiciary.[678] This has been particularly clear in the case of the federal courts. The governing principle, Chief Justice Taft has stated, "is that the jurisdiction of this court and of the inferior courts of the United States ordained and established by Congress under and by virtue of the third article of the Constitution is limited to cases and controversies in such form that the judicial power is capable of acting on them and does not extend to an issue of constitutional law framed . . . for the purpose of invoking the advice of this court." [679]

With the highest tribunal's refusal to render advisory opinions, it is believed, few informed observers will disagree. The great weakness of decision without a true case is that, being rendered *in vacuo,* it is divorced from the real life of actual facts. Advisory opinions are consequently bound to move in an unreal atmosphere and to be based upon sterilized and mutilated issues.[680] A body which functions in the form of a law court cannot, by an omnibus answer to an omnibus question, adjudge in advance the rights of all. That is not the way in which a system of case-law properly develops. A court deals with the particular instance; and it waits till it arises.[681] It is only with the light afforded by a real contest that opinions on questions of the highest importance can safely be rendered.[682]

The judicial refusal to allow the federal bench to act in an advisory capacity stems directly from the feeling already adverted to that it would be unwise for courts, whose constitutional authority has such significant impact upon the work of the political departments, to exercise such authority except when it is absolutely imperative for the decision of an actual case. For the judges to act as advisers to the other departments would be for them to descend from Olympus directly into the political arena. If the system set up by the Framers requires the courts to resolve issues which have political implications, it brings them into contact with such issues independently of their own will. The judge judges the law because he is obliged to judge a case; the political issue which he may be called on to resolve is connected with the interest of the parties and he cannot refuse to decide it without abdicating the duties of his office.[683] However much his action may bear upon the activity of the political departments, he may still be said to be exercising purely judicial power.

155

SAME: GOVERNMENTAL REVISION

Closely connected with the refusal of the federal courts to act as advisers to the other departments is their insistence upon finality of judgment as an essential attribute of federal judicial power. Unless the decision of a court is binding upon the parties and subject to direct enforcement by execution or process directed against the person, it is not really a judicial judgment, but only in the nature of advice to those to whom it is directed. It has, the Supreme Court declared in 1948, "been the firm and unvarying practice of the Constitutional Courts to render no judgments not binding and conclusive on the parties and none that are subject to later review or alteration by administrative action." [684]

The judicial landmark which established the principle of finality of judgment at the very outset was *Hayburn's Case*.[685] It involved the validity of a 1792 statute which authorized the federal circuit courts to determine the pension claims of invalid veterans of the Revolution and certify their opinions to the Secretary of War, who might then grant or deny the pensions as he saw fit.[686] *Hayburn's Case* was argued in the Supreme Court, but that tribunal never rendered decision, for Congress intervened by providing another procedure for the relief of the pensioners.[687] But the statute at issue was considered in the different circuit courts and their opinions are given in a note to *Hayburn's Case* by the reporter.

All of the circuit courts concurred in the holding that they could not validly execute the statute as courts set up under Article III.[688] In their view (expressed in opinions concurred in by the members of the highest bench, who then sat in the different circuit courts),[689] the duty imposed, when the decision was subject to the revision of an executive official, could not be executed by a court vested with judicial power. Since, under the statute, "the decision of the court is not made final, but may be at least suspended in its operation by the secretary of war . . . ; this subjects the decision of the court to a mode of revision which we consider to be unwarranted by the constitution." [690] By the organic document, neither the Secretary, nor any other executive officer, nor even the legislature, is authorized to sit as a court of errors on the judicial acts of a constitutional court.[691]

According to Chief Justice Taney, though there was no decision by the Supreme Court in *Hayburn's Case,* the opinions expressed by the members of that tribunal on circuit clearly established that the power proposed to be conferred upon the federal courts by the 1792 statute "was not judicial power within the meaning of the Constitution, and was, therefore, unconstitutional, and could not lawfully be exercised by the courts." [692] Since *Hayburn's Case,* it has been settled that the federal judges may not act in cases where their judgments are subject to revision by the executive or legislative departments. Thus, where a statute authorized the district judge for the northern district of Florida to decide claims for losses for which the United States was responsible under the treaty by which Spain ceded Florida, but where his decisions in favor of claimants were to be reported to the Secretary of the Treasury, who was to pay the claims only if he thought them just and equitable, it was ruled that an award by the district judge was not a judgment of a court and did not afford a basis for appeal to the Supreme Court.[693] The crucial element in such a case was the fact that the claim became a debt of the United States upon the decision of the Secretary—not upon that of the judge.[694]

The same principle applies where the decision of a court is subject to legislative, rather than executive, revision. Such a situation was presented when the Court of Claims was first set up. As already seen in section 134, the applicable statute then provided that no money should be paid on any Court of Claims judgment "till after an appropriation therefor shall have been estimated by the Secretary of the Treasury." In *Gordon v. United States*,[695] it was held that this statute denied to the Court of Claims the judicial power, from the exercise of which alone appeals could be taken to the Supreme Court. Under the statutory scheme, said Chief Justice Taney, the Court of Claims was subjected to both executive and legislative review. After the Secretary passed on the matter, the claim, as Taney stated, "will be opened to debate, and whether the appropriation will be made or not will depend upon the majority of each House. The real and ultimate judicial power will, therefore, be exercised by the Legislative Department, and not by that department to which the Constitution has confided it." [696]

Under the cases discussed, judgments, within the powers vested in the courts by the Judiciary Article, may not lawfully be revised, overturned, or refused faith and credit by another department. If the executive or legislative branches may disregard the judgment of a constitutional court, such judgment is one the court may not validly be authorized to render. When the decision of a court is not binding upon the other departments, it is in substance only advice to them, which they may or may not follow, in their discretion. To render a judgment which has only the force of a recommendation is to render what the Supreme Court has termed an advisory opinion in its most obnoxious form.[697]

156

SAME:
FEIGNED AND
HYPOTHETICAL
CASES

The "Case" or "Controversy" requirement of the Judiciary Article derives from the recognition that the adjudicatory process is most securely founded when it is exercised under the impact of an actual conflict between antagonistic demands, actively pressed, which make resolution of the controverted issue a practical necessity.[698] If that be true, it is obvious that, to be susceptible of decision by the judicial department, a case must grow out of a real clash of conflicting interests. A friendly suit, collusively arranged between parties without adverse interests in the matter, to obtain the judicial settlement of some constitutional issue, is one which may not be brought in courts created under Article III.[699] "It never was the thought," the Supreme Court has asserted, "that, by means of a friendly suit, a party beaten in the legislature could transfer to the courts an inquiry as to the constitutionality of the legislative act." [700]

That Article III does not permit the federal judges to entertain feigned suits between parties whose interests are not antagonistic has been settled since *Lord v. Veazie*.[701] The action there was arranged between plaintiff and defendant, between whom there was no real dispute. The Supreme Court ruled that, in such a case, the federal courts were without jurisdiction. According to Chief Justice Taney: "any attempt, by a mere colorable dispute, to obtain the opinion of the court upon a question of law which a party desires to know for his own interest or his own purposes, when there is no real and substantial controversy between those who appear as adverse parties to the suit, is an abuse which courts of justice have always reprehended." [702]

The type of abuse involved in the collusive suit is well shown by a more recent case.[703] It involved an action by a tenant against a landlord to recover treble damages under the Emergency Price Control Act.[704] The defense asserted the unconstitutionality of the Act. The district court ruled on the constitutional question on the merits, but, in the Supreme Court, the Government, which had intervened, submitted an affidavit which showed that the action was collusive. In fact, the proceeding was brought by plaintiff in a fictitious name; it was instituted as a "friendly suit" at defendant's request; plaintiff did not employ, pay, or even meet, the attorney who appeared of record in his behalf; he was assured by defendant that he would incur no expense in bringing the suit; and he had no knowledge of the amount of the judgment prayed until he read of it in a local newspaper. In these circumstances, it is obvious that defendant was the real party in interest on both sides of the case and that he instituted the action in the hope, that being thus in control of the presentation by both parties, he might be better able to secure from the courts the judgment on constitutionality which he desired. "Such a suit," declared the Supreme Court, in holding that the cause must be dismissed, "is collusive because it is not in any real sense adversary. It does not assume the 'honest and actual antagonistic assertion of rights' to be adjudicated—a safeguard essential to the integrity of the judicial process, and one which we have held to be indispensable to adjudication of constitutional questions by this Court." [705]

The problem of the collusive suit has presented most difficulty in cases involving suits by stockholders to restrain corporations from complying with allegedly unconstitutional statutes. Some of the most important decisions of the highest Court have arisen out of just such suits. This was true, for example of the decisions rendered in *Pollock v. Farmer's Loan & Trust Co.*[706] and *Carter v. Carter Coal Co.*[707]—to take two already-discussed *causes célèbres* in American constitutional law. The *Carter* case was particularly striking in this respect. There, the president of the company concerned brought suit, in his capacity as stockholder, against the company and its officials (among whom was his father, the vice-president of the company).[708]

In a case like *Carter,* there is a very real danger that both formal parties to the action are actually interested in obtaining a decision striking down the statute concerned. The stockholders' suit may, in such a situation, become a device for securing a desired judgment in a collusive action. It was the possibility of this which led Justice Brandeis to urge, in a noted opinion in *Ashwander v. Tennessee Valley Authority,*[709] that the high bench should refuse to allow constitutional issues to be raised in such stockholders' suits. The majority of the Justices, however, declined to follow the Brandeis view, holding instead that stockholders have a right to seek equitable relief whenever the managers of their corporation have refused to resist the enforcement of a statute alleged to be unconstitutional.[710] This has been the general rule in Supreme-Court jurisprudence; the possible abuses involved in such actions have not been enough to deny to stockholders an opportunity to contest the validity of governmental requirements to which their corporation was submitting.[711]

The danger involved in the stockholders' suits such as those discussed is the absence in such suits of a party genuinely interested in supporting the constitutionality of the challenged legislation. This danger is avoided where the Government intervenes to present the case in favor of the legislation. Under a 1937 amendment to the Judicial Code,[712] the Government must be notified by the court of any private action "wherein the constitutionality of any Act of Congress . . . is drawn in question." The Government has the absolute right to intervene in any such action, with all the rights of a party. This, at least, ensures that the case in support of any federal law that may be challenged in a suit between private citizens will be presented to the court, even though neither formal party may really be interested in having the law upheld.

What is true of the feigned or collusive case is also true of the abstract or hypothetical case.[713] It has, in Chief Justice Stone's phrase, always been the Supreme Court's "considered practice not to decide abstract, hypothetical or contingent questions." [714] Such questions may present intellectually interesting and solid problems. But the high bench does not sit to satisfy a scholarly interest in such issues.[715] A party cannot, in other words, bring an action for what Justice Holmes once called "a mere declaration in the air." [716] On the contrary: "A case or controversy in the sense of a litigation ripe and right for constitutional adjudication by this Court implies a real contest—an active clash of views, based upon an adequate formulation of issues, so as to bring a challenge to that which Congress has enacted inescapably before the Court." [717]

The leading case illustrating the refusal of the federal courts to determine a constitutional issue in the abstract, in the absence of an actual case between adverse litigants, is *Muskrat v. United States*.[718] The action there was instituted under an act of Congress authorizing certain named Indians to bring suits against the United States in order to test the validity of statutes restricting the alienation of certain Indian lands and increasing the number of persons entitled to share in the final distribution of such lands. The plaintiffs sued under this statute, without indicating that they were affected, in their individual capacities, by the laws which they were attacking nor that there was a real danger that such laws would be enforced in such a manner as to deprive them of any rights. Rather, they relied solely on the statute empowering them to challenge the statutes regardless of whether their suit arose out of an actual controversy between them and the United States.

The Congressional attempt in *Muskrat* to secure a judicial determination on constitutionality in the abstract was ruled invalid by the high tribunal. "Is such a determination within the judicial power conferred by the Constitution," asks Justice Day, "as the same has been interpreted and defined in the authoritative decisions to which we have referred? We think it is not." [719] This was not a true "Case" or "Controversy," for the United States as defendant had no interest adverse to the claimants. The object was not to assert any property right as against the Government, or to demand compensation for alleged wrongs because of action upon its part. Instead, this was a suit arranged by the United States and the plaintiffs, whose whole purpose was to determine the constitutional validity of a certain class of legislation—not in a suit arising between parties concerning a property or personal right necessarily involved in the decision in question, but in a proceeding whose only object was to obtain a judgment settling the doubtful character of the legislation.[120] For the courts to entertain such a suit on the constitutionality of a law, in the absence of a concrete case, is for them, in effect, to act in an advisory capacity to the parties concerned. In the words of the *Muskrat* opinion: "If such actions as are here attempted . . . are sustained, the result will be that this court . . . will be required to give opinions in the nature of advice concerning legislative action." [721]

157

SAME:
DECLARATORY
JUDGMENTS

The emphasis by the Supreme Court on the need for an actual "Case" or "Controversy" and its consequent refusal to permit judges endowed with "The judicial Power" to render advisory opinions gave rise to difficulty with the development during the present century of the declaratory-judgment procedure. When the matter first came before the highest Court, there were responsible expressions of doubt that constitutional limitations on federal judicial power would permit any federal declaratory judgments.[722] In one case, the Court ruled squarely that a declaratory judgment authorized by statute could not be rendered by a court established under Article III.[723] In another, Justice Brandeis categorically stated that a declaratory-judgment proceeding was not a "Case" or "Controversy" within the meaning of the Judiciary Article: "What the plaintiff seeks is simply a declaratory judgment. To grant that relief is beyond the power conferred upon the federal judiciary." [724]

The Supreme Court, in indicating that the declaratory-judgment technique was inconsistent with Article III, was inaccurately equating the declaratory judgment with the advisory opinion. An advisory opinion is one rendered by a court at the request of some governmental organ in response to a constitutional issue framed by such organ. It is a judicial response to such issue, posed in the abstract, in advance of any actual case in which it may be presented. A declaratory judgment is one in which the court declares the rights of the parties before it. It may resemble the advisory opinion in that it is not capable of execution by coercive order. But there the similarity ceases. A declaratory judgment is issued only in an actual case between adverse parties and it settles the rights between them by the judicial declaration which is issued. "Herein," a state judge informs us, "lies the distinction between declaratory judgments and . . . advisory opinions. The declaratory judgment is a final one, forever binding on the parties on the issues presented. . . . an advisory opinion is but an expression of the law as applied to certain facts not necessarily in dispute and can have no binding effect on any future litigation between interested parties." [725]

The Supreme Court itself soon came to see that the declaratory judgment was not necessarily subject to the defects inherent in the advisory opinion. In *Nashville, C. & St. L.R. v. Wallace*,[726] the high bench reviewed a declaratory judgment rendered by a state court and held that a controversy which would be justiciable in an Article III court if presented in a suit for an injunction was not the less so because the relief sought was declaratory.[727] Nor was the fact that declaratory relief could not be executed determinative. While the ordinary course of judicial procedure results in a judgment which may be carried into effect by execution, such relief is not an indispensable adjunct to the exercise of the judicial function.[728]

Encouraged by the *Nashville* decision, and guided by the fact that some three-quarters of the states had already enacted such laws, the Congress, in 1934, voted into law the Federal Declaratory Judgment Act.[729] It provides that "in cases of actual controversy," the federal courts may "declare the rights and other legal relations" of any party "whether or not further relief is or could be sought."

The Declaratory Judgment Act was adjudged constitutional only by interpreting it to confine the declaratory remedy within conventional "Case" or "Controversy" limits.[730] The Act was upheld in *Aetna Life Insurance Co. v. Haworth*.[731] There, as the highest Court has more recently put it,[732] Chief Justice Hughes used the whole catalogue of familiar phrases to define and delimit the new remedy within the "Case" and "Controversy" bounds laid down by Article III. The operation of the 1934 statute is consequently procedural only: it provides a new remedial device; yet it restricts its use to controversies which are such in the constitutional sense.[733]

The Declaratory Judgment Act is thus not a grant to the federal judges of the power to render an advisory opinion upon a hypothetical basis, but only of that to issue a declaration of present right upon established facts.[734] When a conflict of interests between adverse parties has ripened to the point where there is a controversy of the type required for the grant of a traditional remedy in law or equity, then the 1934 statute gives to the parties the alternative of seeking relief in declaratory form. However, the act does not attempt to change the essential requisites for the exercise of judicial power.[735] The relief provided for is available only for a "concrete case admitting of an immediate and definite determination of the legal rights of the parties." [736] It does not permit litigants to obtain constitutional rulings in advance of the necessity presented by an actual case.[737]

The decisions under the Declaratory Judgment Act are not inconsistent with the "Case" or "Controversy" requirement of Article III. That law, we just saw, is valid only because its operation has been limited to the judicial declaration of rights in actual cases alone. To attempts to obtain a declaration of rights upon a hypothetical state of facts, the federal forum must still remain closed.[738] Where a plaintiff seeks to have his rights declared in the air, the judges must still, in Justice Jackson's earthy query, naturally ask, so what? [739]

158

RIPENESS OF CONSTITUTIONAL ISSUES

Closely related to what has been discussed in the prior section is the requirement of what may be termed "ripeness" [740] of constitutional issues presented to the judicial department for decision. Briefly stated, such requirement bars the courts from considering constitutional issues prematurely. Constitutional rights are protected by the courts solely against actual or imminent invasion. A constitutional question is ripe for judicial review only when the governmental act being challenged has direct adverse effect upon the individual making the challenge. Until such stage of actual adverse effect, there is no real "Case" or "Controversy," since the challenge is one to the hypothetical operation of a governmental act, which has not yet had actual impact on private rights and obligations.

The judges will not, in other words, anticipate a question of constitutional law in advance of the necessity of deciding it.[741] Such necessity exists only when the statute or other official act whose validity is attacked has had actual (not hypothetical) consequences upon legal interests. The courts must be alert to avoid imposition upon their jurisdiction through obtaining premature interventions.[742] The impact of the challenged law or other action must not be nebulous or contingent, but must have ripened to actuality. In the 1952 phrase of the high bench, the "conflicts of interest must be 'ripe for determination' as controversies over legal rights." [743]

When is a governmental act ripe for constitutional challenge in the sense above indicated?

In answering the query just posed, one must distinguish between statutes and other acts [744] that are self-executing and those that are not. If a statute is self-executing, it is ripe for challenge as soon as it is enacted. With regard to such a statute, it is not necessary, for the statute to be subject to judicial review, that it be applied by an administrator, a prosecutor, or some other enforcement officer, in a concrete case.[745]

In the sense in which the term is here used, a law is self-executing if its mere existence on the statute book in fact has adverse effect upon private rights and obligations.[746] Such is the case when a statute requires those subject to its prescriptions to do or to refrain from doing specified acts and subjects them to specified legal consequences in the event of their noncompliance. When such a statute is at issue it is ripe for challenge even in advance of specific official action to execute its provisions. The touchstone to justiciability is adverse effect upon a legally protected right.[747] When such effect occurs upon the mere enactment of a statute, its constitutionality presents a justiciable question.

Many cases illustrate the proposition that a self-executing law, which involves immediate consequences for those coming within its provisions, is subject to judicial review even before a direct attempt at its enforcement occurs. Two usually cited in this connection are *Euclid v. Ambler Realty Co.*[748] and *Pierce v. Society of Sisters.*[749] In the *Euclid* case, the Supreme Court entertained a suit to enjoin execution of a municipal zoning ordinance which restricted the use of plaintiff's property to residential purposes. It was objected that the action was premature, since there had been no threat of actual enforcement of the restriction against plaintiff.[750] According to the Supreme Court, however, the very existence of the ordinance imposed a serious economic burden upon plaintiff: "The ordinance of its own force operates greatly to reduce the value of appellee's lands, and destroy their marketability for industrial, commercial . . . uses." [751] That being the case, the Court concluded, "the existence and maintenance of the ordinance in effect constitutes a present invasion of appellee's property rights and a threat to continue it. Under these circumstances, the equitable jurisdiction is clear." [752]

The *Pierce* case was basically similar. It involved an action by operators of private schools to enjoin enforcement of a state statute which required parents to send their children to public schools. The injunction was granted even though the statute itself was not to become effective until more than seventeen months after the case was argued in the Supreme Court.[753] The mere passage of such a statute, said the high bench, posed a present threat to the private schools in the state. Its practical result, if left unchallenged, would be destructive of such schools. Parents, coerced by the criminal sanctions of the law,[754] would hardly assume the risk that noncompliance would entail. Nor would they wait until the statute's effective date before removing their children from the private schools. Parents who know that such schools are likely soon to have no pupils are not to be expected to delay until the last moment before making arrangements consistent with the statutory scheme. The injury was thus, as the *Pierce* opinion stated, "present and very real, not a mere possibility in the remote future. If no relief had been possible prior to the effective date of the act, the injury would have become irreparable." [755]

In the *Pierce* case, there was present the added factor of a criminal penalty, since, under the challenged statute, parents who did not comply with the law's requirements were to be guilty of a misdemeanor. When a statute provides a penal sanction to ensure compliance with its prescriptions, its self-executing nature, so far as those subject to its provisions are concerned, appears obvious. In the case of such a statute, those affected are placed under threat of criminal prosecutions as soon as the law is enacted. Unless an affected individual may seek immediate judicial review, he must either comply with the statute, in which case he will be deemed to have lost his right of challenge,[756] or violate the law and set up the invalidity of the law as a defense in the criminal prosecution to which such violation will subject him. But the latter road to judicial review is open only at the risk of incurring the criminal penalty provided in the statute, if its constitutionality should be upheld.

That a federal court may entertain a challenge to the validity of a statute which is enforceable through criminal sanctions even in advance of the institution of prosecutions for violation has been settled ever since the already-discussed case of *Ex parte Young*.[757] The high tribunal there permitted an injunction suit to be brought against enforcement of a state statute containing criminal penalties. Where such a statute is at issue, the Court said, those affected need not wait for criminal enforcement before being able to obtain judicial review. In its words, "To await proceedings against the company in a state court, grounded upon a disobedience of the act, and then, if necessary, obtain a review in this court by writ of error to the highest state court, would place the company in peril of large loss and its agents in great risk of fines and imprisonment if it should be finally determined that the act was valid. This risk the company ought not to be required to take." [758]

The *Young* ruling in this respect has been followed in many cases.[759] In 1961, indeed, Justice Harlan was able to state that "it should by now be abundantly clear that the fact that only Constitutional claims are presented in proceedings seeking *anticipatory* relief against . . . criminal statutes does not for that reason alone make the claims premature." [760] The mere fact that a criminal statute has not been enforced to the stage of actual prosecution is not alone sufficient to make a case instituted by those subject to prosecution too remote, not "ripe" enough for adjudication, at the stage at which anticipatory relief is sought.[761]

In several cases, it is true, the highest bench has refused to permit the federal courts to entertain first-instance review proceedings challenging the constitutionality of state statutes containing criminal penalties. At times, in such cases, language has been used seeming to deny the ripeness of such statutes for challenge in advance of prosecutions instituted under them.[762] Yet, in these cases, all that the Supreme Court was really doing was to lay down a rule that the federal courts should not consider the constitutionality of a state statute in the absence of a controlling interpretation of its meaning and effect by the courts of the state itself.[763]

The premise of the cases just referred to was that first-instance relief should be obtained, if possible—with ultimate review on the constitutional issues in the highest tribunal—in a state court, which could then authoritatively construe a new state statute.[764] Looked at in this way, these cases turn upon a principle that is a logical corollary of the federal system. The Congress itself, it has been noted, may limit the availability of the federal forum for suits against state governmental action.[765] Congress has, in several statutes, adopted the policy of leaving generally to the state courts the trial of cases involving state criminal statutes, subject to review by the Supreme Court of any federal questions involved.[766] In the cases discussed, the high Court itself has sought to conform to such policy. But those cases have nothing to do with the ripeness for constitutional challenge of the criminal statutes involved in them. They hold, not that such statutes may not be challenged in advance of criminal prosecutions, but only that such challenges to state legislation should normally be brought in the first instance in the state courts themselves.

It is only when a statute is not self-executing and does not confront the private citizen with the dilemma of either complying and thus giving up the chance to challenge or risking criminal penalties that it should be considered not ripe for immediate challenge.[767] Only in the case of such a statute should an action for anticipatory relief raising the constitutional issue be deemed premature and hence not presenting a "Case" or "Controversy" cognizable by the federal judicial power.

Nor, in applying the rule of "ripeness" to self-executing statutes containing penalties for noncompliance, is it proper to assume that it is only the statute backed by criminal sanctions that is ripe for immediate review. As the previous discussion of cases like *Euclid v. Ambler Realty Co.*[768] and *Pierce v. Society of Sisters* [769] indicates, a law may be considered self-executing, for purposes of ripeness for challenge, if it has immediate consequences upon private rights and obligations. The statute containing a criminal penalty is but an extreme example of such a statute. The right of immediate challenge should exist whenever the mere enactment of a law subjects those affected to adverse consequences—whether they be criminal or civil in character.

The law of ripeness in this area is based upon the view that it is unjust to require those affected in their rights and obligations by a law to assume the burden of violating such law and suffering the consequences therein provided before they can obtain a judicial decision on the validity of such law. The Supreme Court itself has at times not acted upon this view. A significant case illustrating this is *United Public Workers v. Mitch-*

ell,[770] where federal employees sued to restrain enforcement of the
Hatch Act [771] on the ground of its unconstitutionality.[772] The challenged
law forbade federal employees from taking an active part in political management or in political campaigns. The plaintiffs claimed that such statute
violated their constitutional right to engage in political activities, but the
Supreme Court ruled that, since none of them had as yet committed any
acts in violation of the Act, their suit was premature.[773]

According to the high Court in the *Mitchell* case, the challenged statute
was not ripe for review in the circumstances presented because, in advance of any violation, only a "hypothetical threat" [774] to the rights of
plaintiffs was presented: "No threat of interference . . . with rights of
appellants appears beyond that implied by the existence of the law." [775]
In a case like *Mitchell,* however, the mere existence of the challenged
statute did restrict the right of all federal employees to engage in political
activities, which they otherwise had the clear right to do, and did so subject to the penalty of dismissal for violations. Under the Court's ruling,
the only way in which the law would become ripe for challenge would be
upon its being violated—with the consequent risk of loss of employment
that such violation would entail. In the words of a dissent in *Mitchell,* "to
require these employees first to suffer the hardship of a discharge is not
only to make them incur a penalty; it makes inadequate, if not wholly illusory, any legal remedy which they may have." [776]

That the Supreme Court itself has come to see that, in a situation like
that presented in *Mitchell,*[777] the challenged statute has self-executing
impact which should make it sufficiently ripe for review is shown by its
more recent decision in *Adler v. Board of Education.*[778] At issue there was
a state statute which provided for the removal of schoolteachers who had
engaged in specified activities deemed "subversive." [779] The action attacking the constitutionality of such statute was brought by, among others,
teachers in the state who, so far as the complaint showed, had not engaged in any of the proscribed activities. Justice Frankfurter, who dissented, urged that the case was on all fours with *Mitchell* which consequently had "controlling relevance." [780] The majority of the Justices, on
the contrary, held that the *Adler* suit could be maintained. In fact, since
the majority opinion did not even refer to the matter of ripeness, it must
be assumed that the *Adler* Court considered its jurisdiction too clear to
merit discussion.

Though it was doubtless incongruous for the high bench to decline
even to mention the ripeness issue in a case presenting it so squarely, only
five years after its contrary ruling in the *Mitchell* case, the *Adler* holding
on the matter seems clearly sound in the light of the prior discussion. A
statute which bars the teacher from engaging in certain activities, upon

pain of dismissal, is as ripe for challenge as any other law which confronts those affected with the dilemma of complying with its prescriptions or incurring the risk of substantial penalties—be they civil or criminal in nature.

In a 1961 decision on the subject, a sharply divided Supreme Court ruled that "the mere existence of a state penal statute would constitute insufficient grounds to support a federal court's adjudication of its constitutionality in proceedings brought against the State's prosecuting officials if real threat of enforcement is wanting." [781] The decision referred to—that in *Poe v. Ullman* [782]—was rendered in an action brought for a declaratory judgment that a state statute prohibiting the use of contraceptives was unconstitutional. The statute in question contained a criminal penalty for violations of its prohibition. The action had been instituted in a state court and the highest bench of the state had decided in favor of the statute on the merits. The Supreme Court affirmed without reaching the merits—ruling instead that the statute under attack was not ripe for review in an action for declaratory relief in the circumstances presented.

How could the high tribunal reach such a decision on the ripeness of a statute proscribing private conduct, backed by substantial criminal sanctions? The Court justified its holding by the fact that, though the challenged law had been on the books for more than three quarters of a century, only one prosecution (and that a "test case") had been initiated under its provisions. This was true despite the fact, admitted by counsel, that contraceptive devices were commonly and notoriously sold in the state. This, it was said, made the case too remote, too contingent, too hypothetical for adjudication.[783] As the Court saw it, "the fact that Connecticut has not chosen to press the enforcement of this statute deprives these controversies of the immediacy which is an indispensable condition of constitutional adjudication." [784]

One wonders whether the *Poe v. Ullman* decision was correct in characterizing the criminal statute at issue there as a harmless, empty shadow.[785] Desuetude does not deprive a statute of its legal effect; a criminal law may be enforced at any time by prosecution so long as it remains on the statute book, regardless of whether any prosecutions had ever previously been brought. In these circumstances, the criminal penalty remains a Damocles's sword over all who come within the statute's proscription—subject to descent at any moment should a prosecutor decide to exercise his absolute discretion to enforce the law according to its terms. In such a case, where all that stands between the citizen and jail is the unfettered whim of the prosecutor,[786] it is unreal to treat the statute as one raising only a hypothetical threat to those subject to its provisions. "It would," in the striking language of an English judge, "be a blot on our system of law and procedure if there is no way by which a decision on the true limit of [governmental] power . . . can be obtained by any member of the public aggrieved, without putting himself in the invidious position of being sued for a penalty." [787] This is true of any criminal statute, while it remains capable of enforcement. The prosecutor's discretion can hardly be considered as in any way analogous to those other contingencies which make remote a controversy presenting constitutional claims.[788]

159

STANDING   Judicial power under Article III, we have seen, extends only to the resolution of concrete controversies between adverse litigants. Under the settled jurisprudence of the Supreme Court, there can be no actual "Case" or "Controversy" if the individual bringing the particular action does not have a real personal interest in having the governmental act which he challenges ruled unconstitutional. Unless he is adversely affected personally, as an individual, he is seeking only a judgment in the abstract upon the validity of such act. Such a proceeding, as has been emphasized, is not enough to call for the exercise of federal judicial power. Its exercise is "legitimate only in the last resort, and as a necessity in the determination of real, earnest, and vital controversy between individuals." [789]

The action seeking to review the constitutionality of a law in the federal courts is thus clearly not the *actio popularis* of the Roman law: litigants cannot bring it simply in the interest of the community as a whole to see that the rule of law is respected by the legislative and executive departments.[790] Unless the action is brought by one who has a direct personal interest, he does not have the "standing" required to bring the suit.

"A petitioner does not have standing to sue," Justice Frankfurter informs us, "unless he is 'interested in and affected adversely by the decision' of which he seeks review. His 'interest must be of a personal and not of an official nature.' " [791] As the Supreme Court stated in 1962, the key question is: "Have the appellants alleged such a personal stake in the outcome of the controversy as to assure that concrete adverseness which sharpens the presentation of issues upon which the court so largely depends for illumination of difficult constitutional questions?" [792] In other words, the controversy must be one which is in truth and fact the litigant's own; the party who invokes judicial power must be able to show not only that a challenged law is invalid, but that he has sustained or is in danger of sustaining some direct injury as the result of its enforcement.[793]

In the ordinary case, the question of whether an individual has the necessary standing to raise a constitutional issue is not a difficult one. A statute normally affects the rights and obligations of those who are subject to its provisions. Such persons are generally directed by the law to do, or to refrain from doing, specified things, or their property or personal rights are restricted by the statutory prescriptions. Of course, any person, whose rights and obligations are thus directly affected by the provisions of a statute, has standing to challenge their validity. From a constitutional point of view, such persons, who come within the class of those against whom a law is specifically directed, may be designated the *obvious parties plaintiff*, insofar as the standing to challenge such law is concerned.

Examples of "obvious parties plaintiff" come readily to mind under different statutory schemes. They include, to refer to cases already discussed: landowners whose use of their property is restricted by a zoning law; [794] parents required by a statute to send their children to public schools; [795] a railroad company whose rates are fixed by a statute; [796] schoolteachers whose freedom of advocacy and association is limited by a law proscribing specified activities on their part; [797] and a husband and wife whose right to use contraceptive devices to prevent pregnancies dangerous to the health of the wife is taken away by a statute prohibiting the use of such devices. [798]

All of the persons just referred to were the "obvious parties plaintiff," so far as their standing to challenge the statutes involved in their cases was concerned, since they were members of the classes against whom such statutes were specifically directed. The statutes directly affected (and were passed for that purpose) their right to use their property as they saw fit, or their personal right to engage in such activities as they chose. Clearly, if any persons have a personal interest in challenging the statutes, it is those who come squarely within their prescriptions—who are, in this sense, the subjects or, more accurately, the objects of the statutory provisions. There can be little doubt that such persons, whose rights and obligations are plainly affected, have a real and concrete interest in vindicating the claim that the statutory restrictions are invalid. [799]

When an individual is an "obvious party plaintiff" in the sense in which that term has been used—i.e., he is a member of the class at which the statutory prescriptions are aimed—his standing presents little problem. Modern society, however, is characterized by the interconnections in its parts and the interdependence of its members, particularly in the economic sphere: "A society such as ours is an elastic medium which transmits all tremors throughout its territory." [800] That being the case, a statute or other governmental act may have impact beyond those at whom it is directed. The radius of effect may, indeed, be much wider than those who are the immediate subjects or objects of the law.

Thus a statute may—like that at issue in *Ex parte Young* [801]—fix railroad rates. Of course, as already stated, the railroads, whose right to charge what they choose for their services is restricted, possess the standing needed to challenge such law. But it is erroneous to assume that, in the case of such a statute, only those whose rate of return is directly regulated have an interest in the constitutionality of the regulatory law. What about a competitor of the railroads, such as a motor carrier, whose ability to compete may be drastically affected by the rates which the railroads are permitted to charge? Plainly such competitor has a personal interest in the statute—but is such interest enough to give it standing? And what of a shipper or member of the public, who uses the services furnished by the railroads? Does the fact that the rates which they pay for such services are increased by the statute give them standing?

It may be argued that the competitor and the consumer have financial interests comparable in kind (if not in degree) to those of the companies directly regulated by the law themselves. But there may be an even wider class which, in a system such as ours, may have an interest in challenging the constitutionality of a statute like that in question. For example, there is the taxpayer who has an interest in ensuring that state funds are not spent in execution of invalid laws. Should such interest give the taxpayer standing? And, in a polity dominated by a written Constitution, is there not an even broader interest in any member of the community to vindicate the interest of the society as a whole in preventing the political departments from acting contrary to the basic document?

In the succeeding sections, we shall discuss the standing of persons other than "obvious parties plaintiff" to challenge the constitutionality of governmental action—dealing first with those like the competitor and the consumer, who have an economic interest similar in kind to that of those directly subject to statutory provisions, and then with those like the taxpayer and the citizen, whose interest is entirely different (though perhaps nonetheless real), so far as the raising of the constitutional issue is concerned.

160
SAME: The interest of a competitor in avoiding increased
COMPETITORS   competition or reducing existing competition should
                     be enough to give him standing to challenge the constitutionality of a statute which directly affects his competitive position, even though the statutory provisions are not in terms aimed at him and do not order him to do, or refrain from doing, anything.

The competitor's standing should be clear if we look to the very basis of the standing requirement itself. That requirement stems from the recognition that, within the framework of our adversary system, the adjudicatory process is most securely founded when it is exercised under the impact of a real conflict between antagonistic demands.[802] Hence, it follows that the case must be one which is, in actual fact, the litigant's own, so that it will be pressed by him to the extent needed to sharpen and illuminate the constitutional issues.[803] If we look to the financial interest of a businessman, whose competitive position is directly affected by a statute aiding his competitor, it is surely unreal to find that such businessman does not have the personal interest required to permit him to seek to have such statute ruled invalid. When he himself is financially harmed by the statute concerned, it is hardly to be feared that he will do less than his utmost in pressing his challenge to the law.

The Supreme Court itself upheld the standing of a competitor in *Frost v. Corporation Commission*.[804] A state statute required a license to engage in the business of cotton ginning, which could be secured only upon a showing of public necessity. Appellant, having made such a showing, had obtained a license. The statute was then amended to permit cooperatives to obtain a license without any showing of public necessity. Appellant, alleging that the amendment contravened due process and the Equal-Protection Clause, brought suit to enjoin the issuing of a license to respondent cooperative, which proposed to enter into the cotton-ginning business in the same locality as appellant, in competition with him. The high bench, on these facts, ruled that appellant had standing to raise the constitutional issue.

More recently, however, the supreme tribunal has decided the other way on the standing of a competitor in cases which appear analogous. In *Tennessee Power Co. v. Tennessee Valley Authority*,[805] the Court held that private power companies had no standing to challenge the constitutionality of the distribution of electricity by the Government-owned T.V.A., even though such electricity was sold in competition with the companies concerned in areas served by them. According to the high bench's opinion, an interest in freedom from competition is not such a legally protected right as will justify a suit raising the constitutional issue. As its doctrine was stated by Justice Frankfurter in a later case, a determination whether the Government is within its powers in distributing electric power may have great financial impact upon a private power company, but it has no standing to raise the issue.[806]

It may well be true, as Justice Frankfurter states, that "The common law does not recognize an interest in freedom from honest competition." [807] Yet this does not, despite his apparent view to the contrary, conclude the issue of standing involved in the *Tennessee Power* case. Perhaps no one has a right to be free from competition; but does that apply to Government competition that is illegal? Justice Frankfurter assumes that the competition against which the power companies complained was "honest," when that was the very question presented to the Supreme Court and the question which it was precluded from resolving by its decision on the standing issue.

The *Tennessee Power* decision on the standing of a competitor is directly contrary to that rendered in *Frost v. Corporation Commission.* Yet, in a case basically similar to *Tennessee Power,* where standing was denied to a private power company to challenge the competing sale of power by municipalities, the high Court stated that such a case presented an altogether different situation from that in *Frost:* "The difference between the Frost Case and this is fundamental; for the competition contemplated there was unlawful while that of the municipalities contemplated here is entirely lawful." [808] Such reasoning is subject to the same defect as that of Justice Frankfurter referred to in the previous paragraph, for it confuses the issue of standing with the merits of the constitutional issue itself. The plaintiffs in *Tennessee Power* were claiming that the competition which they were challenging was unlawful, and the Supreme Court was denying them any opportunity to demonstrate the unlawfulness. The question was not whether the companies had standing to challenge lawful competition, but whether they had standing to challenge competition the very lawfulness of which was at issue.[809]

The Supreme Court itself has come to see the validity of what has just been said. In the 1958 case of *Chicago v. Atchison, T. & S.F. Ry. Co.,* [810] it was argued that a competitor had no standing since the competition complained of was lawful. In reliance on the *Tennessee Power* case, it was contended that a party had no right to complain about lawful competition. This time, however, the high bench rejected the contention, stating: "It seems to us that [the] argument confuses the merits of the controversy with the standing . . . to litigate them." [811] As Justice Black aptly put it, appellant's standing can hardly depend on whether or not it is eventually held that its competitor is operating lawfully.[812]

In *Chicago v. Atchison, T. & S.F. Ry. Co.,* Parmelee Transportation Company, a transfer company which had had an arrangement with the railroads to carry rail passengers between the different Chicago terminals, was held to have standing to raise a constitutional issue with regard to a city ordinance requiring a license for Railroad Transfer Service, another transfer company whom the railroads had agreed to use instead of Parmelee.[813] The high bench's answer to the question of whether Parmelee's competitive interest was sufficient to give it standing was disarmingly simple: "It is enough, for purposes of standing, that we have an actual controversy before us in which Parmelee has a direct and substantial personal interest in the outcome. Undoubtedly it is affected adversely by Transfer's operation." [814]

The approach just stated appears to be the correct one in determining the standing of a competitor. Of course, recognition of such standing does not mean that an individual must always be held to have a cause of action merely because he competes with those who are directly affected by a statute or other governmental act.[815] The effect on the competitive interest may be too remote to make his interest come within the standing requirement.[816] But, to determine the question of standing, all that need be done, in this type of case, is to determine whether the competitor has a direct and substantial interest in the outcome of the case. The interest of a competitor, in other words, is sufficient to make for standing if the governmental act being challenged is one that does substantially affect his competitive interest. Despite cases like the *Tennessee Power* case, such an approach is supported both by the already-discussed *Frost* case and the high bench's most recent decision on the matter—i.e., *Chicago v. Atchison, T. & S.F. Ry. Co.*[817]

The approach of the *Frost* and *Atchison* cases is, as already indicated, preferable to that taken in a case like *Tennessee Power*. The standing requirement, Justice Harlan has warned, should not become a catchall for an unarticulated discretion on the part of the judge to decline to adjudicate constitutional issues.[818] In a system such as ours, based upon judicial enforcement of a written Constitution, it is of the utmost importance that the courts not employ a jurisdictional restriction like that requiring standing in such a manner as to place governmental acts in a position of practical immunity from constitutional attack. Yet that is what the decision in a case like *Tennessee Power* really did, since the competing power companies there were the only parties with sufficient interest to bring suit. It may be highly doubtful on the merits, to say the least, that, under the cases discussed in section 81, the Supreme Court would hold that a statute authorizing the governmental generation and sale of electric energy is beyond the power of the Congress. All the same, under the Court's *Tennessee Power* decision, the constitutional question is one which must remain unanswered, since, without anyone's possessing the requisite standing, the Congressional exercise of authority is placed beyond practical constitutional inquiry.

161

SAME: CONSUMERS What is true of the standing of a competitor should also be true of that of a consumer. If the price he has to pay each time he purchases a product or service is increased by some governmental act, he has a direct financial interest, analogous to that of the competitor, which supports his right to challenge the validity of such act. The same should be the case where the nature or quality of the product or service received by the consumer is adversely affected by a governmental act. There, too, the consumer has a direct personal interest which should give him standing.

That a consumer does have the standing necessary to raise a constitutional issue is shown by *Henderson v. United States*.[819] Appellant there was a Negro who brought suit to set aside an Interstate Commerce Commission order approving segregation in interstate railroad dining facilities on the ground that it unduly subjected Negroes to discrimination. The Supreme Court rejected the argument that there was no standing, stating, on the contrary, that "It is clear that appellant has standing to bring these proceedings. He is an aggrieved party." [820] One who uses the railroads is, in other words, sufficiently aggrieved by governmental action which permits the furnishing to him of inferior rail service to give him the personal interest required to challenge the validity of such action. Other cases, too, uphold the standing of consumers to seek review of governmental acts which adversely affect the quality of the product or service which they purchase.[821]

If the consumer's standing is recognized with regard to statutes or other governmental acts which impair the quality of the product or service which he receives, the same should be true where the impact is upon the price which has to be paid. Somewhat incongruously, nevertheless, the Supreme Court has held that the price-fixing case does not stand upon the same footing, so far as the standing of a consumer is concerned. In *Atlanta v. Ickes*,[822] the high bench ruled squarely that a coal consumer had no standing to challenge the validity of a governmental act fixing minimum prices for coal. The *per curiam* opinion on the matter was confined to one laconic sentence: "The judgment is affirmed on the ground that the appellant has no standing to maintain this suit." [823]

Atlanta v. Ickes, Justice Frankfurter informs us, stands for the proposition that "a consumer has no standing to challenge a minimum price order." [824] This is so even though the order clearly requires him to pay an increased price for the product he uses. The *Atlanta* opinion itself, as already noted, does not explain why there is no standing in such a case. The reasoning behind the *Atlanta* holding has, however, been explained by the high bench in other cases. As explained *Atlanta* rests upon two considerations. In the first place, the Supreme Court has intimated, the economic interest of the consumer is too remote to permit him to challenge price-fixing action.[825] In such a view, the action challenged does not affect the consumer with sufficient "directness." [826] In addition, where price-fixing action is involved, consumers may normally resort to an administrative agency charged with their protection.[827] In such a situation, the Court has said, in cases seeking judicial review of such action, there are only two necessary parties: the administrative agency and the company whose prices or rates are being regulated; the agency must be relied on to protect the consuming public.[828]

The justifications thus given by the high bench for its *Atlanta* holding do not really support it. If the financial interest of a competitor is sufficient to give him standing, why is the same not true of a consumer? If a governmental act makes him reach that much deeper into his pocket each time he purchases the product or service, is it not dealing in abstract legal learning rather than the realities of the case [829] to hold that he does not have a direct personal interest in challenging the validity of such act?

As in the *Tennessee Power* case [830] discussed in the prior section, the Supreme Court's decision in *Atlanta v. Ickes* overlooks the need to ensure that *someone* will possess the necessary standing to see that invalid governmental action will not be left untouched. When prices are increased by governmental order, only the consumer has a real interest in challenging the validity of such order. The proposition that the relevant administrative agency adequately represents the consuming public is often, at the best, a pious fiction. If the consumer may not challenge price-fixing action, such action is, in practice if not in theory, placed in a position of immunity from legal attack.

Despite *Atlanta v. Ickes,* a number of more recent cases in the lower federal courts uphold the standing of consumers to challenge the validity of price-fixing governmental action. The most important of them is a well reasoned decision of the Court of Appeals for the Second Circuit which, after thoroughly analyzing the subject, ruled that an association of coal consumers possessed standing to challenge a governmental order increasing the minimum prices of coal. In its view: "It would seem clear, . . . that a consumer threatened with financial loss by a Commission's order, which fixes prices and prevents competition among those from whom the consumer purchases, is also a 'person aggrieved.' " [831]

The Supreme Court itself has not had occasion since *Atlanta v. Ickes* directly to reconsider the standing of a consumer to challenge the validity of governmental price-fixing action. Yet it has, in the more recent *Henderson* case,[832] as already seen, recognized that a consumer may have standing in certain circumstances to challenge governmental acts adversely affecting the quality of the service purchased by him. It has also, in another case since *Atlanta,* upheld the standing of the patrons of a street railway company to attack on constitutional grounds a governmental order permitting the broadcast of radio programs in the railway's passenger vehicles.[833]

Even more directly in point is the high bench's 1953 holding in *United States ex rel. Chapman v. Federal Power Commission.*[834] In it, an order of the Commission granted a license to a private utility to construct a dam. The validity of such order was challenged [835] by an association of rural electric cooperatives which claimed that, under the law, such dam could be constructed only by a federal agency, not a private company. It based its standing on the fact that, under the law, as an organization of consumers, it was entitled to a preference in the sale of power developed by public authorities. This was to assert an interest grounded essentially on the higher power prices the association would have to pay under the F.P.C. order. Reversing the lower court in this respect, the Supreme Court upheld the standing of the consumer association.[836] It is hard to see how such a decision could be rendered consistently with the *Atlanta v. Ickes* rationale.

162

SAME: CITIZENS   In the prior three sections, we have dealt with cases where those seeking judicial review of the validity of a statute or other governmental act had a direct personal interest in raising the constitutional issue. The person against whom a statute is directed (i.e., the "obvious party plaintiff," as we have designated him), the competitor, the consumer—all of these normally have a financial interest in challenging the governmental act concerned. And, if all except the "obvious party plaintiff" may be said to suffer only a consequential detriment, still the impact on their legal interests is "direct" enough to give them the required standing.[837]

In a system such as ours, at the same time, the direct financial interest of people like those discussed, affected immediately or consequentially by some governmental action, are not the only interests concerned with the raising of constitutional issues. It may be argued that the society as a whole has a plain interest in ensuring compliance with the organic document. If that is true, should not any member of the community be able to vindicate such interest by an action challenging the constitutionality of a statute or other governmental act?

The federal courts have answered this question with a categorical negative. The Supreme Court, in an action brought by a citizen challenging the validity of the Nineteenth Amendment, held that the interest of a citizen was not enough to confer standing. As Justice Brandeis put it: "Plaintiff has only the right, possessed by every citizen, to require that the government be administered according to law and that the public moneys be not wasted. Obviously this general right does not entitle a private citizen to institute in the federal courts a suit to secure by indirection a determination whether a statute, if passed, or a constitutional amendment, about to be adopted, will be valid." [838] The consistent jurisprudence of the lower federal courts is to the same effect.[839] It is, indeed, difficult to see how the result could be otherwise, if the requirement of standing under Article III is to retain any practical effect.[840]

163

SAME:
FROTHINGHAM V.
MELLON

Governmental action normally involves expenditure of public funds. If such action is invalid, public funds may be spent illegally. If that is the case, does a taxpayer have standing to challenge the constitutionality of a statute or other governmental act?

The question of the taxpayer's standing was answered in the negative by the Supreme Court in *Frothingham v. Mellon*.[841] It arose out of an action brought by plaintiff as a taxpayer of the United States to enjoin on constitutional grounds a federal statute which provided for appropriations of money to be apportioned among the states for the purpose of reducing maternal and infant mortality. Plaintiff's asserted standing was based on the contention that the effect of the appropriations would be to increase the burden of future taxation and thereby to take the taxpayer's property illegally. The Supreme Court dismissed the action, holding that plaintiff did not have standing. Under its decision, a federal taxpayer has no standing qua taxpayer to challenge the validity of a Congressional enactment.

The *Frothingham* opinion gave two principal reasons to justify the denial of standing there: (1) the federal taxpayer's interest is too remote; (2) the federal taxpayer has no personal interest in the statute which he challenges. Let us examine these reasons more closely.

The first of the reasons just referred to was the high bench's view that the interest of the federal taxpayer "in the moneys of the treasury—partly realized from taxation and partly from other sources—is shared with millions of others, is comparatively minute and indeterminable, and the effect upon future taxation, of any payment out of the funds, so remote, fluctuating and uncertain, that no basis is afforded for an appeal to the preventive powers of a court of equity." [842]

It may be doubted whether the asserted small size of the taxpayer's interest in a federal expenditure should really bear upon his standing to challenge the constitutionality of such expenditure. In the first place, the *Frothingham* assertion of comparative minuteness of the federal taxpayer's interest may well be inconsistent with the facts. In fiscal 1958, for example, with federal expenditures at roughly $72 billion, the American Telephone and Telegraph Company paid some $915 million in federal income taxes.[843] Such a taxpayer can scarcely be said to have only a "minute" interest—speaking comparatively or absolutely—in any federal expenditure of substance.

More important is the question of whether the size of the tax bill alone should be the determinative factor. The requirement of standing is intended to ensure that constitutional issues will be raised only by those having an actual interest in bringing them before the courts. If the interest of the plaintiff is a real one, its size should be irrelevant. If size is the criterion, we should allow the giant corporation to challenge a federal expenditure, but deny the standing of a competitor whose total business is worth only a minute fraction of the corporation's annual tax bill.

The second reason given in the *Frothingham* opinion is based, not upon size of impact, but upon the lack of personal impact. In the language of the high Court: "The administration of any statute, likely to produce additional taxation to be imposed upon a vast number of taxpayers, the extent of whose several liability is indefinite and constantly changing, is essentially a matter of public and not of individual concern." [844] Whatever the impact of a tax statute, in other words, it does not distinguish the individual from the whole body of taxpayers. He sues, not to vindicate any rights which he possesses individually, but only those which he shares with an indeterminate number of his fellows.[845] One wonders, however, whether the size of the class affected by a governmental act should be decisive. If it is, the consumer and many competitors as well would have to be denied standing. If there is adverse financial effect upon an individual or his class, his is not the sort of claim which is too remote ever to be pressed by anyone, because no one is ever sufficiently involved.[846]

According to *Frothingham v. Mellon,* nevertheless: "If one taxpayer may champion and litigate such a cause, then every other taxpayer may do the same, not only in respect of the statute here under review, but also in respect of every other appropriation act and statute whose administration requires the outlay of public money, and whose validity may be questioned. The bare suggestion of such a result, with its attendant inconveniences, goes far to sustain the conclusion which we have reached, that a suit of this character cannot be maintained." [847]

To permit constitutional issues to be raised by anyone, to state it another way, regardless of whether he has a personal interest unique in himself or only an interest common to a large group, such as the taxpaying public, might, the Supreme Court has feared, be to open the floodgates of constitutional-law litigation. Justice Frankfurter has aptly expressed this risk in a case involving a governmental act affecting a large industry: "So much by way of limitation seems necessary to prevent . . . mass appeals by the industry at large, with resulting hopeless clogging of the [governmental] process by judicial review." [848]

One wonders whether the fear articulated, which underlies *Frothingham v. Mellon* and other restrictive standing decisions, is not more theoretical than real. Of course, nobody outside Bedlam supposes that the reason why the courts possess the review power is that the Framers believed happiness to consist in the greatest possible amount of constitutional-law litigation.[849] But to assume that the courts will be flooded with countless cases if judicial review is made widely available is unwarranted. Widespread access to the courts does not inevitably produce a plethora of cases. A constitutional case is expensive and time-consuming; it is rarely resorted to for its own sake or merely to subject the Government to needless harassment by people who have no real interest in the governmental action whose validity they are seeking to have reviewed.

164

SAME: OTHER   Though, as the discussion in the prior section in-
TAXPAYER CASES   dicates, the reasoning behind *Frothingham v. Mel-
                    lon* [850] is subject to criticism, the decision of the
Supreme Court there with regard to taxpayer standing has never since been
departed from.[851] It is, therefore, of great importance to determine the
exact reach of the ban declared by the high bench on taxpayers' suits.

In the first place, it should be emphasized that *Frothingham v. Mellon*
does not mean that a taxpayer may never raise a constitutional issue. On
the contrary, the taxpayer, like anyone else in our system, may contest the
validity of governmental action directed against his property rights. Hence,
there is no doubt that a taxpayer may resist the imposition of a tax upon
him on the ground that it is unconstitutional.[852] In such a case, he would
have the standing to challenge such tax, either in defense to an action
seeking collection by the Government or in an action brought by him to
recover any taxes paid. Such standing of a taxpayer to resist invalid tax
exactions is not affected by *Frothingham v. Mellon*. What that case does is
to bar the taxpayer from challenging any other type of governmental action.
Under it, the taxpayer has no standing qua taxpayer to attack the execution of a federal statute on the ground that it is invalid and will consequently result in taxation for illegal purposes.[853]

In addition, it is basic that the *Frothingham v. Mellon* holding is limited
to the standing of a federal taxpayer to challenge the validity of a Congressional enactment. The *Frothingham* Court itself recognized this. Referring
to a case in which the right of a taxpayer of the District of Columbia to attack the legality of action by the District government was upheld,[854] the
Frothingham opinion states that it illustrates the rule "that resident taxpayers may sue to enjoin an illegal use of the moneys of a municipal
corporation." [855] That rule, declares the high bench, "is upheld by a large
number of state cases and is the rule of this court." [856]

The *Frothingham* Court's statement with regard to the standing of a
municipal taxpayer in state courts is supported by the fact that the vast
majority of the state courts which have ruled on the matter have sustained
such standing. At the present time, virtually all the states permit *local*
governmental action—i.e., that at the municipal level—to be challenged

by taxpayers.[857] The states have, it is true, been slower to allow suits by state taxpayers challenging *state* governmental action. It can, nevertheless, be stated that such challenges by state taxpayers are now allowed in some three-fourths of the states.[858] Interestingly enough, the federal courts themselves have tended to reach a similar result in analogous cases. While the *Frothingham* case rejects the standing of the federal taxpayer, other federal cases have entertained suits by territorial [859] and District of Columbia [860] taxpayers.

The state decisions upholding the standing of municipal and state taxpayers are, without a doubt, based upon rejection of the already-discussed *Frothingham v. Mellon* reasoning. In *Frothingham,* we saw, the interest of the taxpayer in the federal statute which was challenged was deemed too inconsequential. In the state cases, on the other hand, the nominal nature of the individual taxpayer's interest is held not to rule out his standing.[861] In the phrase of one state court, the "de minimis" nature of the taxpayer's interest does not alone defeat his right to attack the constitutionality of a law or other governmental act.[862]

More basic is the rejection by the state courts of the fear of flooding the judicial calendar with constitutional-law litigation which was the prime motivating factor behind the *Frothingham* decision. To the state judges, of greater importance has been the need to ensure that invalid public action will not be rendered immune from organic attack. In the state view, the taxpayer, both as such and as a member of a society grounded upon the rule of law, is intimately concerned with the validity of action taken by the government which his tax dollars support.[863] To the claim that, to recognize such concern as a basis for standing is to open the door to hopeless clogging of the processes of government by countless constitutional cases, the state judges have answered that the fear of such a result has no foundation in fact: "The general indifference of private individuals to public omissions and encroachments, the fear of expense in unsuccessful and even in successful litigation, and the discretion of the court, have been, and doubtless will continue to be, a sufficient guard to these public officials against too numerous and unreasonable attacks." [864]

The state cases, influenced by the approach just outlined, have not confined the taxpayer's standing to cases of so-called "pocketbook actions" [865]—i.e., where the challenged governmental action involves the expenditure of public funds which, if invalid, may result in an illegal increase, however minute, in the taxes which the plaintiff may have to pay. Instead, the states tend to uphold the standing of taxpayers, even when the issue raised is nonfiscal and has nothing to do with the amount of public expenditures or with the amount of taxes to be paid.[866] Thus, to take a recent state case which will shortly be discussed more fully, a New Jersey taxpayer was held by the highest court of that state to have standing to challenge a statute requiring Bible reading in the public schools.[867] This was true although such requirement had no effect on the costs of the school system or on the taxes raised to pay such costs. In such nonpocketbook cases, the state courts have come close to allowing the taxpayer to sue as a citizen generally demanding enforcement of the rule of law.[868]

The states may, without a doubt, in a federal system such as ours, fashion their own rules concerning standing. They are not bound to curtail access to their courts, in cases like those involving taxpayers, as strictly as the Supreme Court has restricted access to the federal courts in analogous cases. The highest bench's interpretation of the limits upon the exercise of "The judicial Power" under Article III is not controlling upon the state judges in their construction of the judiciary articles of the different state constitutions.

What happens, however, when a state decision involving a federal question is appealed to the Supreme Court? In such a case, if the plaintiff, whose standing had been upheld by the state courts, lacks standing under the relevant federal cases, what should the high bench do?

Until 1952, the Supreme Court tended to follow the state law on the issue of standing in cases which came up to it from the state courts. In accord with this approach, the high tribunal had accepted cases from the state courts instituted by state taxpayers and others who had no standing under the rules governing the right to sue in the federal courts.[869] An oft-cited case illustrating the highest Court's deference to the states on the standing issue in actions brought to it from the state courts is *Heim v. McCall*.[870] There the New York courts had entertained an action by "a property owner and taxpayer" challenging a state statute providing that only citizens might be employed in the construction of public works—and giving a preference to citizens of the state. The Supreme Court accepted the New York Court of Appeals' recognition of standing, although the plaintiff "is not one of the contractors nor a laborer of the excluded nationality or citizenship" [871] and hence would not have had standing in a comparable case instituted in the federal courts.

Under cases like *Heim v. McCall,* the Supreme Court had, in effect, upheld the right of the states to liberalize their own standing requirements. The 1952 case of *Doremus v. Board of Education,*[872] on the other hand, adopts a more restrictive attitude. *Doremus* involved an attack upon a New Jersey statute which provided for the reading of certain Old-Testament verses at the beginning of each public-school day. Plaintiffs claimed that this law violated the Federal Constitution, alleging the interests of citizens and taxpayers. The state itself had waived the possible defense of lack of standing [873] and the highest New Jersey court had upheld the plaintiffs' capacity to sue, though it ruled in favor of the challenged statute on the merits.[874] Despite this, the Supreme Court decided that the appeal to it must be dismissed because of lack of standing. According to it, though the state courts may render decisions on federal questions even under circumstances which do not constitute a true "Case" or "Controversy," as in a case where there is a want of standing, the Supreme Court, bound as it is by the restrictions of Article III, may not accept any such state decision as the basis for review.

Though the contrary has been asserted, the *Doremus* decision does not mean the complete abandonment by the high bench of its prior deference to the states on the standing question in cases instituted in state courts. That this is true is shown by the reference in the *Doremus* opinion to *Everson v. Board of Education,*[875] where the Supreme Court had reviewed [876] the decision of the highest New Jersey court in a suit brought by a local taxpayer to enjoin the reimbursement of transportation costs to parents who sent their children to Catholic parochial schools.[877] *Doremus* did not presume to overrule a case like *Everson.* Instead, it distinguished it on the ground that "a justiciable controversy" had been found there.[878] If that was true in *Everson,* where a taxpayer sued to restrain state action on the ground that it infringed the separation between church and state imposed by the First and Fourteenth Amendments, why was it not also true in *Doremus,* where a taxpayer challenged state action on similar grounds?

The *Doremus* opinion's answer was that "Everson showed a measurable appropriation or disbursement of school-district funds occasioned solely by the activities complained of. This complaint does not." [879] *Doremus,* in other words, was not a pocketbook action, since it was not shown that the Bible reading at issue there added any cost to school expenses. Hence, said the Court in *Doremus:* "It is apparent that the grievance which it is sought to litigate here is not a direct dollars-and-cents injury but is a religious difference." [880]

The *Doremus* limitation on taxpayers' standing consequently applies only to taxpayers' suits which are not pocketbook actions, since the statute or other act challenged does not have any impact upon the cost of government. In such a case, the Supreme Court will not entertain the case on review from the relevant state court even though the latter's rules on standing permit such suits. Where, on the contrary, a taxpayer, in a state which allows taxpayers' suits, challenges a governmental act which does involve an expenditure from funds to which his taxes contribute,[881] the Supreme Court will still be able to hear his case on appeal.[882] Such a case, like *Everson,* meets the test of a justiciable controversy. As it was put in the *Doremus* opinion: "The taxpayer's action can meet this test, but only when it is a good-faith pocketbook action." [883] Since governmental action does normally involve some expenditure of public funds—however slight —the *Doremus* case may not prove as restrictive in practice as many have feared.

Even as just explained, it may be questioned whether the *Doremus* decision is justified. It is one thing for the high bench to apply its own rigid approach to taxpayer standing in cases in the federal courts. At the same time, why should not a state like New Jersey be free to fashion her own rules governing the institution of suits in her own courts? If she wants to give all taxpayers standing to sue, it is hard to find anything in the Constitution to prevent it.[884]

The difficulty presented where the *Doremus* limitation applies is that, in such cases, since the Supreme Court, under *Doremus,* may not entertain the case on appeal from the decision of the highest state court, that decision is left standing as the final resolution of the constitutional issue involved in it. This seems utterly inconsistent with the basic purpose behind the Supremacy Clause of Article VI—the desire of the Framers to have only the one national tribunal as the supreme expounder of the Constitution, laws, and treaties of the United States. Under *Doremus,* the highest court of New Jersey may decide the claim of violation of the First and Fourteenth Amendments one way, while other state courts, in similar actions, may decide differently. Since *Doremus* requires the supreme bench in Washington to refuse to intervene in such cases, the basic policy of uniformity in constitutional interpretation is frustrated.

165
SAME: GOVERNMENTAL STANDING

Massachusetts v. Mellon [885] was a companion case to the already-discussed case of *Frothingham v. Mellon.*[886] The *Massachusetts* case arose out of an original action in the Supreme Court by Massachusetts challenging the constitutionality of the same statute that was at issue in the *Frothingham* case. That law, it will be recalled, provided for federal appropriations to be allocated among the states for the purpose of reducing maternal and infant mortality. The allotment to each state (in accordance with the formula of federal grants-in-aid that has been developed during the present century) [887] was made conditional upon acceptance by the state of the terms of the statute, and the states were also to contribute financially. Massachusetts claimed that the challenged statute was unconstitutional as a usurpation of power reserved to the states by the Tenth Amendment. It argued that, even though it had not accepted the law, its constitutional rights were infringed by the option imposed either to yield part of its reserved rights to the Federal Government or to lose its share of the appropriation.

The Supreme Court ruled that Massachusetts did not possess the standing needed to challenge the statute at issue. As far as the state's suit in its own right was concerned, no direct interest of Massachusetts was involved, since the statute did not require it to do or yield anything, and no burden was imposed upon it. "In that aspect of the case," said the high bench, "we are called upon to adjudicate, not rights of person or property, not rights of dominion over physical domain, not quasi sovereign rights actually invaded or threatened, but abstract questions of political power, of sovereignty, of government. No rights of the state falling within the scope of the judicial power have been brought within the actual or threatened operation of the statute." [888]

Massachusetts v. Mellon lays down the general rule that a state does not have standing, simply because it is a state, to challenge the constitutionality of a federal statute. The state may not bring an action against the nation to have an act of the latter ruled invalid on the ground that such act violates the state's political rights under the Constitution. Nor, under *Massachusetts v. Mellon,* may a state maintain a suit attacking a federal law as the representative of its citizens. Its citizens are also citizens of the nation. "It cannot," the high bench asserted, "be conceded that a state, as parens patriae, may institute judicial proceedings to protect citizens of the United States from the operation of the statutes thereof." [889] While the state may, in some circumstances, sue in such capacity for the protection of its citizens,[890] it is no part of its duty to enforce their rights as against the Federal Government.

Is what is true of the states, however, necessarily true of the nation itself?

In our discussion in sections 149–50 of the immunity from suit of the states and the United States we saw that the determining principle is not that of equality as between states and nation. While the Federal Government is immune from suits by the states, the same is not the case with regard to suits against the states by the nation. The jurisdiction of the federal courts over actions brought by the United States has, it was noted in section 150, been held by the highest bench to inhere in the very nature of the constitutional scheme.

The same considerations which justify a difference in result so far as the immunity of states and nation from suit by each other is concerned should apply in the standing field as well. *Massachusetts v. Mellon* may bar a state from challenging the constitutionality of a federal government act. But that does not mean that the nation should not have standing to assert the inconsistency of a state statute or other governmental act with the Federal Constitution.

Recognition of the standing of the United States in such a situation can be based upon a logical extension of the already-discussed *Debs* case.[891]

In it, the standing of the Federal Government to secure an injunction against a railroad strike, which impeded interstate commerce and the carriage of the mails was upheld. In *Debs,* it was argued that the Government had no such direct interest in the subject-matter of the case as would enable it to appear as party plaintiff. The Supreme Court rejected such argument, saying that every government, entrusted by the very terms of its being with promotion of the general welfare, has the right to apply to its own courts for such purpose, though it may have no pecuniary interest in the matter. In the Court's words, "The obligations which it is under to promote the interest of all and to prevent the wrong-doing of one resulting in injury to the general welfare is often of itself sufficient to give it a standing in court." [892]

The *Debs* reasoning may be used to support the standing of the United States, when confronted with a statute not of its own making, to assert its inconsistency with the fundamental law of the land—the Constitution.[893] The obligations which the nation is under to promote the interest of all and prevent acts contrary to the general welfare vest it with a direct interest in ensuring compliance with the basic document under which it is chartered. Thus, the United States has what a court has termed "an obvious interest in securing for all citizens the enjoyment of constitutional rights." [894] Where a state statute or other governmental act violates such rights, the nation, no less than the individuals concerned, should possess standing to assert its constitutional invalidity.

The standing of the nation in such a case may, indeed, be a necessary condition for effective implementation of the Supremacy Clause. We cannot overlook the fact that particular state infringements upon the provisions of the basic document may not, for practical reasons, be subjected to judicial challenge by private citizens. In such a situation, the Supremacy Clause itself would give way if the nation were not entrusted with the right to challenge the state action according to recognized principles of law. To whom, in truth, could so momentous a trust be more appropriately committed than to the Government which the people themselves constituted with authority to speak for all the people? [895]

166

SAME: RIGHTS   It is basic to the law of standing that parties must
OF OTHERS   rely only on constitutional rights which are personal
to themselves.[896] "Ordinarily," the high tribunal has said, "one may not claim standing in this Court to vindicate the constitutional rights of some third party." [897] A person cannot challenge the constitutionality of a governmental act unless he shows that he himself is injured by its operation.[898]

The case generally cited to show that standing may not be based upon

assertion of the rights of others is *Tileston v. Ullman*.[899] It arose out of an
action by a physician for a declaratory judgment that a state statute prohibiting the use of drugs or instruments to prevent conception, and the
giving of assistance or counsel in their use, was unconstitutional. The
physician alleged that the statute would prevent his giving professional
advice concerning the use of contraceptives to three patients whose health
was such that their lives would be endangered by childbearing. The Supreme
Court, holding that the physician did not possess standing, declared that
the rights asserted were those of the patient—not those of the physician
himself: "His patients are not parties to this proceeding and there is no
basis on which we can say that he has standing to secure an adjudication
of his patients' constitutional right to life, which they do not assert in their
own behalf." [900]

The rule that one does not have standing to vindicate the rights of
another is one that has been followed consistently.[901] Nor, despite the fact
that some lower-court decisions apply the rule too rigorously,[902] is it easy
to see how the governing principle could be otherwise, so long as the
standing requirement retains any validity. It is true that there are three
types of case which, at first glance, may appear to do violence to the
Tileston v. Ullman rule. On closer examination, however, they are seen to
be not inconsistent with it.

The first type of case referred to is illustrated by *National Association
for the Advancement of Colored People v. Alabama*.[903] In it, plaintiff association was held to have standing to assert the rights of its members in
challenging the constitutionality of a state order requiring it to produce its
members' names and addresses. According to the high Court: "If petitioner's rank-and-file members are constitutionally entitled to withhold
their connection with the Association despite the production order, it is
manifest that this right is properly assertable by the Association." [904]

A case like *N.A.A.C.P. v. Alabama* is not at all inconsistent with the
rule forbidding parties to assert the rights of others. This is true because,
for legal purposes, an association may be considered as the authorized
representative of its members. As Justice Jackson once expressed it: "The
only practical judicial policy when people pool their capital, their interests,
or their activities under a name and form that will identify collective interests, often is to permit the association or corporation in a single case to
vindicate the interests of all." [905] For purposes of standing, to put it another way, the association and its members are, in every practical sense,
identical.[906] When the association sues to vindicate rights belonging to its
members, it is really suing on behalf of its own rights as the collective
personification of the membership.

A second type of case which may appear contrary to the rule that one may not have standing to vindicate the constitutional rights of some third party is exemplified by *Barrows v. Jackson*.[907] The plaintiffs there sued for damages for breach of a restrictive covenant prohibiting the sale of realty to non-Causasians, which the parties had entered into as owners of residential real estate in the same neighborhood. The defense was that the awarding of damages by a state court would amount to a violation of the Fourteenth Amendment. Such action by a state court would, in effect, sanction the restrictive covenant and would, as such, constitute state action discriminating against non-Caucasians contrary to the Equal-Protection Clause.[908] The difficulty, from the standing point of view, was that defendant, in so arguing, was asserting a violation of the rights of non-Caucasians, whose constitutional rights alone were infringed by enforcement of the covenant. The Supreme Court recognized this difficulty, but held nevertheless that the defense based on violation of the rights of non-Caucasians not before the Court could be raised.[909]

The *Barrows v. Jackson* opinion justified the holding permitting defendant to raise the constitutional defense by stating that this was a case where the normal standing restriction should not be applied: "in the instant case, we are faced with a unique situation in which . . . it would be difficult if not impossible for the persons whose rights are asserted to present their grievance before any court. Under the peculiar circumstances of this case, we believe the reasons which underlie our rule denying standing to raise another's rights, which is only a rule of practice, are outweighed by the need to protect the fundamental rights which would be denied by permitting the damages action to be maintained." [910]

One wonders whether the fact that those whose constitutional rights are being asserted are themselves unable to vindicate such rights before a court is of itself enough to cause the standing requirement to be disregarded. If there is no "Case" or "Controversy" unless the constitutional issue is raised by one who has a direct personal interest, it is hard to see how this is changed only because it is difficult, if not impossible, for such person to present his grievance before any court.

According to a more recent opinion, in a case like *Barrows v. Jackson,* the rule requiring that parties rely only on constitutional rights personal to themselves "is not disrespected where constitutional rights of persons who are not immediately before the Court could not be effectively vindicated except through an appropriate representative before the Court." [911] To treat the defendant in *Barrows* as the authorized representative of non-Caucasians in general is, however, unwarranted. There is no nexus between defendant and such non-Caucasians sufficient to permit him to act as their representative, comparable to that which exists between an association and its members.[912]

Barrows v. Jackson really turns upon the difference between initiating a proceeding to challenge the constitutionality of governmental action and setting up the constitutional issue as a defense in an action brought against the party setting up such issue. A defendant always has standing to call to the court's attention the fact that a decision against him will violate some provision of the organic document.[913] From this point of view, permitting the defense of unconstitutionality in *Barrows v. Jackson* was not actually inconsistent with the standing requirement. Defendant there was asserting his own right not to be proceeded against by a state court with a judgment contrary to the Constitution.

Looking at *Barrows v. Jackson* as we have just done brings us to the third type of case which may seem inconsistent with the rule that one does not have standing to raise constitutional issues that only affect the rights of others. This type may be seen in cases like *Truax v. Raich*[914] and *Pierce v. Society of Sisters.*[915] In *Truax,* an alien employee was allowed to challenge a state law requiring employers to discharge all but a specified proportion of their alien employees and, in *Pierce,* a private school was permitted to attack a statute requiring parents to send their children to public schools.[916] In both cases, the statutes challenged prescribed criminal penalties, but they were to be imposed only on the employers and parents, not the plaintiffs in the two cases. It was contended that the employees could not complain for their employers, nor the schools for the parents— since it was only the employers and the parents whose rights were infringed.

It is erroneous to assume that, in permitting suit in the *Truax* and *Pierce* cases, the Supreme Court was allowing the employees to assert the rights of the employers and the schools those of the parents. It is true that the statutes in both cases were held invalid, at least in part, because the one violated the right of employers to choose their own employees while the other deprived parents of their liberty in bringing up their children. But this hardly means that the plaintiffs in the two cases were not personally affected by the statutes which they were challenging. On the contrary, they were directly aggrieved by laws which required others to terminate advantageous relationships which they had with them. It is such adverse effect which gave them standing. As Justice Frankfurter has said, referring to the *Truax* and *Pierce* cases: "The fact that an advantageous relationship is terminable at will does not prevent a litigant from asserting that improper interference with it gives him 'standing' to assert a right of action."[917]

Those who state that cases like *Truax* and *Pierce* are inconsistent with the bar against assertion of the rights of others are really confusing the standing to raise a constitutional issue with the substance of the issue raised. To have standing to challenge a governmental act, one must show that he personally is adversely affected in his person or property by such act; it is not enough to show such effect upon some third person. In a case like *Pierce v. Society of Sisters,* the private schools were clearly able to make such showing, since the law which they were challenging posed a plain present threat to their continued operation.[918] Once standing was made out, the Supreme Court could take jurisdiction under Article III. It made no difference, then, so far as such jurisdiction was concerned, that plaintiffs, on the merits, urged that the law was invalid because it violated the rights of parents to direct the education of their children. Once a valid "Case" or "Controversy" was presented, it became the judicial duty to resolve it on the merits with regard to the constitutionality of any statute directly applicable to such case.

167

SAME: STATUTORY   In *Massachusetts v. Mellon,*[919] we saw, a state was
    STANDING   held without standing to challenge the validity of a
federal statute appropriating moneys to be paid to the states for maternity benefits. In the more recent case of *Oklahoma v. Civil Service Commission,*[920] on the other hand, a state was ruled to possess standing to attack the constitutionality of a federal law providing for the withholding of federal grants from states which refused to remove state officers who took an active part in political management or political campaigns. The relevant federal agency had found that a member of the Oklahoma Highway Commission had engaged in the proscribed political activities and issued an order directing his removal. This order foreshadowed, if he were not removed, a further order that federal highway grants be withheld from Oklahoma in an amount equal to two years' compensation of the state officer concerned.

Oklahoma brought an action in the federal courts seeking review of the order which had been issued, asserting the unconstitutionality of the statute under which it had been made. Interestingly enough, the constitutional claim was essentially similar to that urged in *Massachusetts v. Mellon*—namely, that the federal statute, so far as it attempted to regulate the internal affairs of a state, was an invasion of the rights reserved to the states under the Constitution. Yet, as already stated, Oklahoma, unlike Massachusetts in the earlier case, was held to have standing to raise this constitutional issue.[921]

The sharp difference in result as between *Massachusetts v. Mellon* and *Oklahoma v. Civil Service Commission* may be explained by the fact that the federal statute in the latter case contained an express provision authorizing judicial review of any order issued under it by "any party aggrieved." The Supreme Court ruled that a state like Oklahoma was such a party within the Congressional intent, and that, under the statutory review provision, it could attack the constitutionality of the statute. As the Court put it, "By providing for judicial review of the orders of the Civil Service Commission, Congress made Oklahoma's right to receive funds a matter of judicial cognizance. Oklahoma's right became legally enforceable. Interference with the payment of the full allotment of federal highway funds to Oklahoma made the statutory proceeding to set aside the order a case or controversy between Oklahoma and the Commission whose order Oklahoma was authorized to challenge." [922]

If the standing of the party initiating a constitutional action is essential to the existence of a "Case" or "Controversy" under Article III, how can a statutory provision confer standing where, under *Massachusetts v. Mellon,* none would otherwise exist? And how can the Supreme Court say that the statutory proceeding makes for a "Case" or "Controversy" over which the judicial department has jurisdiction, when no such jurisdiction could constitutionally be exercised in the absence of the statutory standing provision?

In a suggestive opinion, Justice Douglas has implied that a statutory standing provision may not go so far as to make for a "Case" or "Controversy," where none would otherwise exist. According to him, unless one seeking to challenge a governmental act "can show that his individual interest has been unlawfully invaded, there is merely *damnum absque injuria* and no cause of action on the merits. . . . On that assumption I fail to see how an appeal statute constitutionally could authorize a person who shows no case or controversy to call on the courts to review an order of the Commission." [923]

From the point of view of strict logic, it is difficult to rebut the Douglas position on the Congressional power to confer standing where none would otherwise exist. The only answer which the Supreme Court has given to such position was expressed in the majority opinion in *Scripps-Howard Radio v. Federal Communications Commission* [924]—the case in which the Douglas opinion quoted from was delivered in dissent. Referring there to the standing conferred by the Communications Act of 1934 [925] to seek review of governmental action taken under that statute, the *Scripps-Howard* opinion states that the Act "did not create new private rights. The purpose of the Act was to protect the public interest in communications." [926] That being the case, those private litigants whom the Communications Act permitted to bring review actions "have standing only as representatives of the public interest." [927]

What the high bench is saying in *Scripps-Howard* is that, in an action brought to challenge the validity of governmental action, "the rights to be vindicated are those of the public and not of the private litigants." [928] That is the case even though, in our system, the public interest in maintenance of the rule of law is normally vindicated in an ordinary lawsuit instituted by private litigants. "That a court is called upon to enforce public rights and not the interests of private property," said the Court, "does not diminish its power to protect such rights." [929]

If, under *Scripps-Howard,* the action to secure judicial review of the validity of a governmental act vindicates the public interest, it should follow that the legislative department, as the representative of the public, can delegate the task of vindicating such public interest as it chooses. If it sees fit, it can confer such task upon some public official, such as the Attorney General, or even upon some private litigant, who might not otherwise possess standing.

The approach just expressed has been best articulated judicially in a remarkable opinion on the subject by Judge Jerome Frank. As he puts it: "While Congress can constitutionally authorize no one, in the absence of an actual justiciable controversy, to bring a suit for the judicial determination either of the constitutionality of a statute or the scope of powers conferred by a statute upon government officers, it can constitutionally authorize one of its own officials, such as the Attorney General, to bring a proceeding to prevent another official from acting in violation of his statutory powers; for then an actual controversy exists, and the Attorney General can properly be vested with authority, in such a controversy, to vindicate the interest of the public or the government. Instead of designating the Attorney General, or some other public officer, to bring such proceedings, Congress can constitutionally enact a statute conferring on any non-official person, or on a designated group of non-official persons, authority to bring a suit to prevent action by an officer in violation of his statutory powers; for then, in like manner, there is an actual controversy, and there is nothing constitutionally prohibiting Congress from empowering any person, official or not, to institute a proceeding involving such a controversy, even if the sole purpose is to vindicate the public interest. Such persons, so authorized, are, so to speak, private Attorney Generals." [930]

As seen in section 165, the United States has a direct interest in ensuring compliance with the organic instrument. That being the case, an action seeking to ensure such compliance, brought by a federal official, such as the Attorney General, who is duly authorized by the Congress to institute such action, presents a justiciable controversy. Following the Frank view, Congress may, instead of designating the Attorney General, or some other public officer, to bring such action, enact a statute conferring upon some private citizen authority to bring suit. When such a suit is brought, such "private Attorney General" is vindicating, not his own personal interest (which may not be affected at all by the governmental act which is challenged), but that of the public, asserted in accordance with the governing provision enacted by the people's representatives. If that is true, there is still an actual controversy whenever the public interest is asserted by a duly authorized Congressional delegate.

If the Frank approach just outlined is followed, it makes for a different result in a case like *Muskrat v. United States*,[931] discussed in section 156. There the Supreme Court ruled that it was beyond the judicial power to entertain what was essentially a test case framed by the Congress.[932] The legislative department was held without authority to create a "Case" or "Controversy" by statute merely by stating a constitutional issue and designating parties who might raise it. Under the Frank approach just discussed, such a Congressional statute could be sustained on the theory that those designated possess the standing of "private Attorney Generals" vindicating the Congressional interest in ensuring compliance with the basic document.[933]

168

POLITICAL QUESTIONS

In 1460, the Duke of York brought suit to have himself declared the rightful heir to the throne. The judges, however, decided that they "durst not enter into eny communication thereof, for it perteyned to the Lordes of the Kyngs blode and th' apparage of this his lond, to have communication and medle in such maters." [934] Ever since, Anglo-American courts have refused to exercise jurisdiction in cases in which the exercise of judicial power was felt to be inappropriate. These cases have involved what the American courts have come to term "political questions."

The "Case" or "Controversy" limitation of Article III discussed in the prior sections—barring consideration of constitutional issues unless they arise in the course of actual litigation between interested adverse parties—is thus but one of the limitations developed by the judges upon the exercise of their authority. Even in true cases presented to it for decision, not all constitutional issues will be determined by the judicial department. For political questions have, by their very nature, been considered unsuitable for decision by courts. Such questions, the highest bench has said, "are wholly confided . . . to the political departments of the government." [935] The judges have kept their hands off them because they have feared the consequences of interfering in matters deemed primarily political. As Justice Frankfurter has put it: "Courts ought not to enter this political thicket." [936]

The doctrine of political questions, like so much else that is basic in American constitutional law, was first articulated by Chief Justice Mar-

shall. In the course of his classic opinion in *Marbury v. Madison,* he declared categorically that "Questions in their nature political . . . can
never be made in this court." [937] In the *Marbury* opinion itself, Marshall
went on to draw a distinction between cases in which the President and
those acting as his agents exercise purely political powers and those
in which they exercise specific duties assigned by the law, upon
which duties the rights of individuals depend. It is only in the latter
case that the officer concerned is amenable to the laws for his conduct. Where, on the contrary, "the President is invested with certain important political powers, in the exercise of which he is to use his own
discretion, [he] is accountable only to his country in his political character
and to his own conscience." [938]

But though the great Chief Justice clearly stated the rule that the decision of political questions was not within the competence of the judicial
department, he did not indicate what made a question political in nature
within the meaning of the rule. His failure in this respect has not been
remedied in subsequent cases. One court has, indeed, been candid enough
to concede that it is easier to state the doctrine that political questions are not within the province of the judiciary, than to define the phrase
"political question" or to determine what matters fall within its scope.[939]

"What are these political questions?" asks one observer. "To what matters does the term apply? It applies to all those matters of which the court,
at a given time, will be of the opinion that it is impolitic or inexpedient to
take jurisdiction." [940] In the language of Chief Justice Hughes in an important case, "In determining whether a question falls within that category, the appropriateness under our system of government of attributing
finality to the action of the political departments" is a dominant consideration.[941] As the Supreme Court has more recently put it, it is the relationship
between the judiciary and the coordinate branches of the Federal Government which gives rise to the political question.[942] In this view, "The non-
justiciability of a political question is primarily a function of the separation
of powers." [943]

But this does not really tell us what political questions are; it only
indicates that the judges will not decide such questions because they feel
that it is more appropriate to have them determined by the political departments.

In an important 1962 case, the high bench expanded upon this consideration. According to its opinion there, "Prominent on the surface of
any case held to involve a political question is found a textually demon-
strable constitutional commitment of the issue to a coordinate political
department; or a lack of judicially discoverable and manageable standards
for resolving it; or the impossibility of deciding without an initial policy

determination of a kind clearly for nonjudicial discretion; or the impossibility of a court's undertaking independent resolution without expressing lack of the respect due coordinate branches of government; or an unusual need for unquestioning adherence to a political decision already made; or the potentiality of embarrassment from multifarious pronouncements by various departments on one question." [944]

Yet these formulations, too, do not define the political-question concept; they merely tell us some of the factors which have been present in the cases governed by that concept. More fruitful than attempt at definition is the drawing up of a list of the matters recognized by the judges as coming within the term and, as such, not within judicial cognizance. Such a list of the matters which the courts have considered to be political questions would include both matters relating to foreign affairs and those relating to internal affairs.

From the beginning, it has never been gainsaid that the doctrine of political questions must have its greatest scope in the area of external relations.[945] In many ways, in fact, the very purpose of the doctrine is to emphasize the autonomy of the political departments in the field of foreign affairs. The doctrine of political questions, without a doubt, has—ever since its first application there in 1796[946]—been most widely used in that field, because of the feeling that the exercise of judicial power is peculiarly inappropriate with regard to it. The conduct of foreign relations, declared the Supreme Court at the outset of its history, involves "considerations of policy, considerations of extreme magnitude, and certainly entirely incompetent to the examination and decision of a Court of Justice." [947]

In section 210 (part of our general discussion of foreign relations), we shall examine the principal matters relating to external affairs on which the courts defer to the decisions of the political departments. Questions relating to them, we shall see, are dealt with as political questions beyond the sphere of judicial competence. The following are the matters we shall refer to in section 210 which are so treated because of their relationship to the external affairs of the nation:

1. Questions involving the recognition of foreign nations and governments; [948]

2. Questions relating to sovereignty over a given area; [949]

3. Questions involving the conduct of diplomatic relations; [950]

4. Questions with regard to the existence of a state of war or belligerency[951] and the relation of the United States to any conflict; [952]

5. Questions relating to treaties.[953]

In addition, there are other matters closely connected with the field of foreign affairs, which involve the force of the nation, directed outside our borders. Questions in that area, to be discussed in Chapters 10 and 11, which are treated by the courts as political questions, include:

1. Questions involving the employment of the armed forces abroad; [954]

2. Questions relating to the commencement and duration of a war in which the United States is engaged.[955]

It is not difficult to comprehend why the political-question doctrine is so closely adhered to in the foreign-affairs field. The conduct of external relations is completely confided by the Constitution to the political departments.[956] The courts have neither the ability nor the responsibility to make decisions for the nation relating to foreign policy. In the field of foreign affairs, in truth, it would be intolerable to have the Government speak with more than one voice [957]—to have, for example, a government, recognized as such by the courts, but not the executive, able to recover property in this country, which might directly contravene the President's foreign policy in relation to the country concerned.[958]

The courts have not, however, confined the doctrine of political questions to the field of foreign affairs. On the contrary, a list of the matters which the judges have treated as political questions must include a number relating to the government of internal affairs. Such list would include the following matters, already touched upon in earlier portions of this volume:

1. Questions relating to the constitutional guaranty of a republican form of government; [959]

2. Questions involving the constitutional guaranty against domestic violence; [960]

3. Questions concerning the membership, organization, and procedure of the legislative department; [961]

4. Questions relating to whether laws have been validly enacted.[962]

169

SAME: If we look at the matters just listed, which relate to
INTERNAL AFFAIRS   internal affairs, which the highest Court has held to
                   come within the political-question doctrine, we may
note that they fall into two main classes:

1. Those relating to the domestic use of the armed forces to effectuate the guarantees of Article IV;

2. Those involving the internal autonomy of the legislative department.

It is not hard to see why these matters should be treated as outside judicial cognizance. The Article IV guarantees of republican government and against domestic violence are, in practice, given effect through employment of the force of the nation.[963] The same considerations which, we shall see,[964] induce the courts to abstain from decision of questions involving the employment by the President of armed forces abroad justify similar abnegation when the President acts to effectuate the guarantees of Article IV.[965] One can likewise easily explain the judicial refusal to decide questions concerning legislative organization and procedure or the enactment of a legislative act. These matters involve the internal functioning of a coordinate department, and regard for the separation of powers, if nothing else, should lead the judges to respect the internal autonomy of the legislature.

Prior to 1962, the Supreme Court had included a third class of matters relating to domestic affairs within the political-question doctrine, namely, that concerning apportionments of voting power. The high bench itself had indicated that allocations of electoral power are so intimately a part of the political process that courts should not become involved in it. In its view, "due regard for the effective working of our Government revealed this issue to be of a peculiarly political nature and therefore not meet for the judicial process." [966]

The statement just quoted was made in the 1946 case of *Colegrove v. Green*.[967] It involved an action by voters seeking to invalidate a state's law governing the apportionment of its seats in the Federal House of Representatives. The law at issue gave voters in some districts a vote disproportionate to that given voters in other districts; in fact, the population of the election districts in the state (each of which elected one Representative) ranged, at the time of the case, from 112,000 to over 900,000. Petitioners—voters in three of the districts which had the largest populations —claimed that the apportionment law denied them the equal protection of the laws guaranteed by the Federal Constitution. Even though their claim in this respect touched upon such an essential attribute of citizenship as the right to vote, the majority of the Supreme Court dismissed the action on the ground that it involved a political question beyond judicial competence. The remedy for unfairness in districting, said Justice Frankfurter, is in the legislature, not the courts. Nor did it matter that, under petitioners' allegations, the constitutional command of equality was violated: "The Constitution has many commands that are not enforceable by courts because they clearly fall outside the conditions and purposes that circumscribe judicial action." [968]

The *Colegrove v. Green* approach, under which the validity of apportionment laws constituted a political question beyond judicial cognizance, was, however, repudiated by the 1962 decision in *Baker v. Carr*.[969] There, too, an action was brought by voters challenging a state apportionment statute as contrary to the Equal-Protection Clause. The law at issue was a 1901 statute apportioning the seats in the state legislature. In the more than half a century since that law was enacted, there had been no new apportionment, though the population make-up of the state had become completely altered. It was alleged that a vote from the most populous county had only a fraction of the weight of one from the least populous county. The disproportion here was, indeed, so great that the population ratio for the most and least populous districts was more than nineteen to one. Despite this, the lower court had dismissed the complaint, relying upon *Colegrove v. Green.* The Supreme Court reversed, holding that a justiciable controversy was presented.

If one thing is clear from the decision in *Baker v. Carr,* it is that cases involving apportionments of voting power can no longer be considered as involving political questions and, as such, beyond the competence of the courts. "There is no doubt," as Justice Douglas states, in concurring in the *Baker* case, "that the federal courts have jurisdiction of controversies concerning voting rights." [970] From this point of view, *Baker v. Carr* is a logical continuation of all the cases in which the high Court has intervened to protect the right to vote against claims of constitutional violation, such as those where such right is infringed on racial grounds contrary to the Fifteenth Amendment.[971] It is true that the Court had previously, under cases like *Colegrove v. Green,* considered challenges to apportionment laws to present only political questions. Yet there is no more valid reason for so holding with regard to them than with regard to other governmental acts involving the right to vote. "Of course," in the language of *Baker v. Carr,* "the mere fact that the suit seeks protection of a political right does not mean it presents a political question. Such an objection 'is little more than a play upon words.' " [972] When an apportionment law makes for an inequality in voting so great as to be a violation of the equality guaranteed by the Equal-Protection Clause, the constitutional violation should be amenable to judicial correction.

But what about the fear expressed in the pre-*Baker* cases of the high bench's becoming unseemly embroiled in politics? "It is hostile to a democratic system," declares Justice Frankfurter's *Colegrove* opinion, "to involve the judiciary in the politics of the people. And it is not less pernicious if such judicial intervention in an essentially political contest be dressed up in the abstract phrases of the law." [973]

One may wonder whether such language is justified from a member of a tribunal that has, from the very nature of its constitutional function, been making political decisions from the beginning of its history. Many cases, as already noted, protect the right to vote as a basic constitutional right, particularly where it is impaired in violation of the Fifteenth Amendment. To be sure, all such cases are, in one sense, "political"; voting is, of course, a part of elections and elections are preeminently political in nature. Yet, as the *Baker* opinion aptly points out, "The doctrine of which we treat is one of 'political questions,' not one of 'political cases.' The courts cannot reject as 'no law suit' a bona fide controversy as to whether some action denominated 'political' exceeds constitutional authority." [974] The individual voters in these cases are seeking to enforce personal rights guaranteed them by the basic document. It is difficult to see why, in a system like the American one, the courts should be required to refuse even to hear the claim that so important a constitutional right has been violated. "It is ludicrous to preclude judicial relief when a mainspring of representative government is impaired." [975]

170

SAME: In *Marbury v. Madison,* where, as noted near the
PRIVATE RIGHTS   beginning of section 168, it was first indicated that
political questions were not within the judicial competence, Chief Justice Marshall drew a distinction between governmental acts involving such questions and those directed at the rights of private individuals. When an official exercises purely political powers, said Marshall, he is accountable only in his political character. When, on the other hand, his action has a direct impact upon private rights, the situation is otherwise. In Marshall's words, "when the rights of individuals are dependent on the performance of those acts; he is so far the officer of the law; is amenable to the laws for his conduct; and cannot, at his discretion, sport away the vested rights of others." [976]

The distinction thus drawn by the great Chief Justice is of basic importance to proper application of the political-question doctrine. That doctrine should render a governmental act immune from judicial scrutiny only when it is based upon a policy decision which is not aimed directly at individual activities—when, in Marshall's phrase: "The subjects are political: they respect the nation, not individual rights." [977] When, on the contrary, a governmental act is intended to and does directly affect the person or the property of private individuals in this country, such individuals who consider themselves injured should have a right to resort to the law for a remedy.[978] Governmental acts which are directed against private rights should not be immunized by the political-question doctrine.

How the distinction just referred to has been applied in practice may be seen in the 1961 case of *Gomillion v. Lightfoot.*[979] At the time it was decided, as we saw in the last section, the Supreme Court refused to entertain actions to invalidate legislative apportionments on the ground that they involved political questions beyond judicial cognizance. *Gomillion v. Lightfoot* also involved an action challenging the validity of a state apportionment statute, this time one redefining the boundaries of the City of Tuskegee, Alabama. The complaint alleged that the law in question, which transformed the city from a square into an irregular twenty-eight-sided figure, was intended to and did effect the removal from the city of all but four or five of its Negro voters while not removing a single white voter

or resident. The result, it was claimed, was to deny Negroes their right
to vote, in defiance of the Fifteenth Amendment.

At the end of the prior section, we saw how the highest bench in 1962
overruled the inclusion within the political-question doctrine of matters
relating to the apportionment of political units. At the time *Gomillion v.
Lightfoot* was decided, however, such matters were treated as political
questions. The *Gomillion* complaint was nevertheless held to state a justiciable cause of action, though the Court there was careful not to repudiate
the rule that apportionment cases were generally beyond judicial cognizance.

The *Gomillion* opinion itself explains the result just stated by relying,
in essence, upon the distinction already referred to between governmental
acts not directed at private rights and those so directed. The normal apportionment law is not intended to deprive specific individuals of their full
right to vote. If any such deprivation does occur, it is as a result of population shifts that take place after such law has been enacted. In *Gomillion v.
Lightfoot,* what petitioners complained of was an affirmative legislative
act which singled Negroes out for special discriminatory treatment. While
in form, the law at issue was merely one redefining political boundaries,
its whole purpose was to despoil colored citizens, and colored citizens only,
of their theretofore enjoyed voting rights.[980] As explained more recently by
Justice Frankfurter, *Gomillion* was "a case in which a state has, through a
device however oblique and sophisticated, denied Negroes . . . a vote, or
given them only a third or a sixth of a vote." [981] A statute accomplishing
such result, aimed directly at the deprivation of private rights, is not immune to attack simply because the mechanism employed is a redefinition
of municipal boundaries. "Apart from all else," declares the *Gomillion*
opinion, "these considerations lift this controversy out of the so-called
'political' arena and into the conventional sphere of constitutional litigation." [982]

The distinction between governmental acts not directed at private rights
and those so directed is one that is relevant even in the field of foreign
relations, where, as noted in section 168, the doctrine of political questions has had its broadest scope. Governmental acts in that field are normally based upon foreign-policy decisions which are not directed at the
person or property of private citizens. Such decisions are concerned with
the external affairs of the nation, not individual rights,[983] and may properly
be rendered immune from judicial scrutiny under the political-question
doctrine. But where a governmental determination is directed against private rights, the same result of immunity should not apply, even though the
determination in question may have some repercussions upon foreign affairs.

In section 211, we shall see that the courts have been coming to rec-ognize the distinction just referred to. In the present judicial view, where governmental authority is turned outward against the outside world for the security of the society, there may be every reason to render it con-clusive—at least insofar as control by the courts is concerned. But the same should not be the case where such authority is directed inward at the rights of private citizens.[984] In the latter situation, the individuals involved should have a right to resort to the law to challenge the legality of any adverse impact upon their person or property. Otherwise, the public of-ficials concerned could, in Marshall's phrase, at their discretion, "sport away the vested rights of others." [985]

In dealing with the political-question doctrine, it should not be for-gotten that it itself is an anomaly in a system in which governmental acts may ordinarily be weighed in the judicial balance and, if necessary, found constitutionally wanting. That is what led Justice Douglas, concurring in the already-discussed case of *Baker v. Carr,* to imply that the whole po-litical-question doctrine is one that should be applied most narrowly, if at all. "I feel strongly," he declares, "that many of the cases . . . involv-ing so-called 'political' questions were wrongly decided"—and he goes on to state that "the category of the 'political' question is in my view narrower than the decided cases indicate." [986]

There is much to be said for the Douglas view in the matter. A good case can be made for restricting the political-question doctrine so that it has no application outside the field of foreign affairs. It is one thing, as already emphasized, to hold that there must be judicial self-limitation in cases bearing directly on the transaction of external relations—at least where the governmental acts concerned are not directed at private rights. It is quite another to use the political-question doctrine as a formula to avoid decision in cases involving only internal affairs. If there is one prin-ciple that is the keystone of the organic arch, it is that of having the ju-diciary as the ultimate arbiter on all domestic constitutional questions. That, indeed, is what Americans normally mean by the rule of law.

From this point of view, the political-question doctrine itself is an exception to the very rule of law, since its effect is utterly to preclude any legal test of those matters deemed within the doctrine. Therein, of course, lies its great danger. If you make just one exception to the rule of law, you cannot tell where it will lead you. To make such exception is to take the fatal first step toward totalitarian doctrine and say that "The State itself is above every particular rule of law." [987]